South Asia's Modern History

This comprehensive history of modern South Asia explores the historical development of the subcontinent from the beginning of the eighteenth century to the present day from local and regional, as opposed to European, perspectives. Michael Mann charts the role of emerging states within the Mughal Empire, the gradual British colonial expansion in the political setting of the subcontinent and shows how the modern state formation usually associated with Western Europe can be seen in some regions of India, linking Europe and South Asia together as part of a shared world history. This book looks beyond the subcontinent's post-colonial history to consider the political, economic, social and cultural development of Pakistan and Bangladesh as well as Sri Lanka and Nepal, and to examine how these developments impacted the region's citizens.

South Asia's Modern History begins with a general introduction which provides a geographical, environmental and historiographical overview. This is followed by thematic chapters which discuss state formation and empire building; patriotisms and nationalisms in the nineteenth and twentieth centuries; agriculture and agro-economy; silviculture and scientific forestry; migration, circulation and diaspora; urbanisation and industrialisation; and knowledge, science, technology and power, demonstrating common themes across the decades and centuries.

This book will be perfect for all students of South Asian history.

Michael Mann is the head of South Asia Studies at Humboldt-Universität zu Berlin. His previous publications include *British Rule on Indian Soil: North India in the First Half of the Nineteenth Century* (1999, second edition 2002); together with Carey A. Watt (eds): *Civilizing Mission in Colonial and Postcolonial South Asia: From Improvement to Development* (2011) and *Sahibs, Sklaven und Soldaten: Geschichte des Menschenhandels rund um den Indischen Ozean* (2012).

South Asia's Modern History
Thematic Perspectives

Michael Mann

LONDON AND NEW YORK

First published 2015
by Routledge
2 Park Square, Milton Park, Abingdon, Oxon OX14 4RN

and by Routledge
711 Third Avenue, New York, NY 10017

Routledge is an imprint of the Taylor & Francis Group, an informa business

© 2015 Michael Mann

Translated by Ian Mills

The right of Michael Mann to be identified as author of this work has been asserted by him in accordance with sections 77 and 78 of the Copyright, Designs and Patents Act 1988.

All rights reserved. No part of this book may be reprinted or reproduced or utilised in any form or by any electronic, mechanical, or other means, now known or hereafter invented, including photocopying and recording, or in any information storage or retrieval system, without permission in writing from the publishers.

Trademark notice: Product or corporate names may be trademarks or registered trademarks, and are used only for identification and explanation without intent to infringe.

Publisher's note: Every effort has been made to contact copyright-holders. Please advise the publisher of any errors or omissions, and these will be corrected in subsequent editions.

British Library Cataloguing in Publication Data
A catalogue record for this book is available from the British Library

Library of Congress Cataloging in Publication Data
Mann, Michael, 1959-
South Asia's modern history : thematic perspectives / Michael Mann.
pages cm
Includes bibliographical references and index.
1. South Asia--History. 2. South Asia--Politics and government. 3. South Asia--Economic conditions. I. Title.
DS340.M35 2014
954--dc23
2014012842

ISBN: 978-0-415-62865-5 (hbk)
ISBN: 978-0-415-62866-2 (pbk)
ISBN: 978-1-315-75455-0 (ebk)

Typeset in Times New Roman
by Taylor & Francis Books

Contents

List of illustrations		viii
Foreword		x

South Asia: a geographical, environmental and
historiographical introduction 1
Geographical and political South Asia 1
Historiography of modern South Asia since the 1980s 8
The concept of this book 15
Notes 19

1 State formation and empire building in South Asia
c. 1660–1800 20
Forms and models 20
State formation in the eighteenth and nineteenth centuries 28
Notes 51

2 Patriotisms and nationalisms in the nineteenth and
twentieth centuries 54
The Great Rebellion (1857–9) 55
National movements (1860–1947) 63
Notes 85

3 State formation and empire building in South Asia (1858–1998) 89
The British Raj in India (1858–1947) 90
Indian monarchies and principalities 97
India, Pakistan and Bangladesh 105
Gorkha-Nepal and Ceylon-Sri Lanka 120
Notes 133

4 Agriculture and agro-economy 137
Themes and subjects 137
South Asia's agriculture in the eighteenth century 138

vi Contents

    Continuities, changes and breaks under colonial rule *142*
    Characteristics and consequences of colonial
       agrarian policy *172*
    The Green Revolution and the Gene Revolution
       (1960–2010) *174*
    Notes *180*

5 Silviculture and scientific forestry   184
    Nature, culture and time *184*
    Forest management in South Asia until 1860 *187*
    The impact of scientific forestry *(1860–1920)* *192*
    Increasing exploitation and growing resistance 1920–90 *197*
    The new millennium *207*
    Notes *209*

6 Migration, circulation and diaspora   212
    Theories and thoughts *212*
    Early South Asian migration and diaspora communities *216*
    South Asians on the new subcontinental and global
       labour markets *219*
    Recruitment of indentured labourers *225*
    Migration and settlement *231*
    South Asian communities overseas *234*
    Migrants, twice migrants, guest workers *246*
    A global Indian diaspora? *257*
    Notes *259*

7 Urbanisation and industrialisation   264
    General observations on urban history and urban development *264*
    Overall trends in crafts and industries *268*
    Industrialisation and de-industrialisation *272*
    Indian-owned industries *276*
    The labour market and labourers' organisations *283*
    Urbanisation *290*
    Municipality and urban planning *295*
    Urban development after 1947: metropolises, megacities,
       middle towns *304*
    Notes *310*

8 Knowledge, science, technology and power   315
    Themes, theories and subjects *315*
    Education: schools, colleges, universities *316*
    History and historiography *320*
    Natural sciences: botany, geography and geology *325*
    From medical knowledge to scientific medicine *332*

Irrigation systems and hydraulic constructions   338
Railway construction and railway networks   346
Telecommunication systems and networks   352
Notes   359

Afterthought and prospect   364
Notes   366

Bibliography   367
Index   420

List of illustrations

Tables

7.1	Development of the cotton industry in India, 1875–6 to 1918–19	275
7.2	Development of the jute industry in India, 1854–5 to 1938–9	275

Figures

1.1	Undivided, hierarchical-pyramidal organisation and divided, multi-lateral shared sovereignty of the "little kings" in South Asia from the 1720s	27
1.2	Portrait of Tipu Sultan	41
1.3	Safdar Jang's Tomb in Delhi	50
1.4	Chota Imambara in Lakhnau	50
3.1	"Imperial Darbar" in Delhi, 1911–12	91
3.2	The Bangladeshi National Flag, 1971	119

Maps

0.1	A map showing the overlapping definitions of the term "South Asia"	2
0.2	A map showing the topography and natural borders of the South Asian region	3
0.3	Monsoon and precipitation in South Asia	6
0.4	The historical regions	9
1.1	Provinces (subas) of the Mughal Empire c. 1700	21
1.2	Zones of rule and resistance in Bengal	36
1.3	Territorial expansion of Awadh between 1720 and 1775	48
2.1	The expansion of the Great Rebellion in British India 1857–9	60
2.2	Partition of British India	82
3.1	Land rights and revenues of the *nizam* and his nobility	101
3.2	Ceylon in the mid-eighteenth century	125
4.1	Resistance and rebellion in Bengal 1780–3	148

4.2	Forests and agricultural infrastructure of the Central Doab (Ganga-Yamuna) c. 1800	154
4.3	Forests and agricultural infrastructure of the Central Doab (Ganga-Yamuna) c.1850	155
4.4	Spatial reorganisation of economic and migration routes under the colonial rule	175
5.1	Forest coverage in South Asia c. 1650	188
5.2	The Tarai	191
5.3	Forest cover in British India, c. 1900	200
5.4	Forest cover in the Republic of India, c. 2010	201
6.1	Trading zones of the Indian Ocean in the mid-eighteenth century	218
6.2	Spaces of circulation	222
7.1	South Asia's fertile crescent	266
7.2	New Delhi–Old Delhi: English landscape gardening in India	300
7.3	Industrial and Business Park of Bangalore, c. 2005	308
8.1	Sub-continental canal system as envisaged by Sir Arthur Cotton	340
8.2	Indian River Inter-Link Project	346
8.3	Telephone network 1923–24 and 1932–33	357

Foreword

Numerous history books about South Asia have been published in recent years, and this trend has been especially pronounced in the field of Anglo-American historiography. The spectrum that these publications cover is truly diverse, ranging from slender textbooks to voluminous, ambitious accounts. Thus, to place one's own work – and in doing so to remain innovative – in the face of such competition is certainly a challenge. I willingly accepted the task as the Schöningh-Verlag approached me to become an author for the new UTB series of non-European history. Then, five years following the publication of the German edition (*Geschichte Indiens. Vom 18. bis zum 21. Jahrhundert*, 2005), the challenge became even greater as Routledge offered to release an English translation of the book. Of course, this translated copy is not merely a reworking of previous scholarly undertakings into a second language, but rather should, naturally, take into consideration the research results of the interim years; a process I, of course, consider to be necessary.

Moreover, the present title *South Asia's Modern History: Thematic Perspectives* is not only the result of concentrated literary review and analysis of the past decade, but it also draws on my experiences, work, research and teachings of South Asian history spanning a quarter of a century. During this time the research into South Asia has undergone a significant paradigm shift leading to the necessity that parts of the history of the subcontinent have had to be completely rewritten. It can therefore be assumed that this development is fluid, evidence of which can be seen in the research trends of recent years. It is against this background that the present title, *South Asia's Modern History: Thematic Perspectives*, aims to deliver the reader not only an appraisal of the current field of study, but also simultaneously a presentation, both in content and form, of South Asian history. This book, however, could not have been written without the constructive criticism and support of numerous colleagues, and friends from within the field of South Asian Studies. To them I offer my heartfelt thanks. Last but not least, I would also like to extend my thanks to Ian Mills for the wonderful, faithful translation of my work.

Michael Mann
Leipzig and Berlin, March 2014

South Asia
A geographical, environmental and historiographical introduction

Geographical and political South Asia

As the subtitle of the book indicates, the narrative of this work does not place national states, their historical legitimation and their history in the foreground, but rather aims instead to accentuate the trans-regional and trans-local historical aspects of South Asia. This approach has been favoured as state and national borders are, after all, drawn somewhat arbitrarily and are fleeting. The first emergence of the term "South Asia" as well as "Southeast Asia" dates from a German school atlas of the late nineteenth century.[1] Following the Second World War the geographical label of South Asia gradually became vernacular within the sciences after which US military strategists defined the zone of operations east of British India as Southeast Asia. In this way political correctness has inhibited the identification of independent India embodied in the newly formed Indian Union and with that the whole geographical area.[2]

Meanwhile, within the academic community the synonym "South Asian subcontinent" is commonly used alongside "South Asia".[3] The term "Indo-Pakistan subcontinent",[4] championed in Pakistani national historiography, has, however, not been able to assert itself internationally. Thus, South Asia is able to take its place in the contemporary nomenclature of terms denoting the different major regions of the Asian continent alongside that of East Asia, Central Asia and Southeast Asia. That said, however, defining what comprises South Asia as a major region is contentious as, according to the United Nations' geographical region classification, it comprises the countries Afghanistan, Bangladesh, Bhutan, India, Iran, Maldives, Nepal, Pakistan and Sri Lanka,[5] whereas other definitions and interpretations also sometimes include Burma and Tibet, but omit Iran. For the purposes of this book, however, South Asia will be taken to include only those territorial states marked as dark grey in Map 0.1.

Geographically, South Asia marks the southern reach of the Eurasian subcontinent which can be distinguished by its distinctive triangular form surrounded by the Indian Ocean. The west coast of the peninsular is defined by the Arabian Sea, and to the east the Gulf of Bengal in which the Maldives and Sri Lanka, both independent states, as well as the Laccadive and Andaman archipelagos are located. Politically, these island groups belong to the Indian

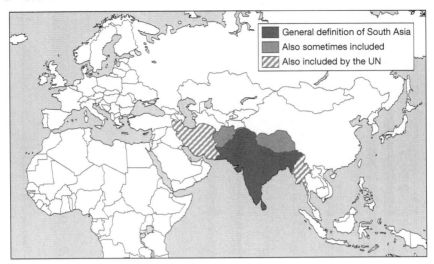

Map 0.1 A map showing the overlapping definitions of the term "South Asia"

Union; although the location of the Andaman Islands, at least, would rather assign it to Southeast Asia. The Arakan Mountains and the Brahmaputra River in the northeast, the Himalayan mountain range in the north and the Indus Valley in the west with the Sulaiman and the Kirthar mountains form the "natural boundaries" of the region (see Map 0.2).

Since ancient Greece, India from a European perspective has been denoted as the land of the Indus. This is reflected in the Arabic-Persian culture which names India as the "land beyond the (S)Indus" and the inhabitants of which are understood to be called Hindus.[6] In the course of the history of South Asia, four empires have ruled over the entirety, or at least a large part, of the subcontinent. Of these four, the Maurya Empire commanded by Emperor Ashoka (c. 274–236 BCE) succeeded in bringing all but the islands and the southernmost tip of the entire subcontinent under his control. At its height, the Gupta Empire (CE 320–500) spanned the whole of north India and parts of the Dekhan Plateau. During the eighteenth century and the reign of Aurangzeb (1658–1707), the Mughal Empire encompassed virtually the whole subcontinent. This expansion of control was then emulated in the middle of the nineteenth century with the creation of the British-Indian Empire or, as contemporary Britons called it, the British *Raj*.[7] It is clear that the emergence of the empires was something of an exception in the long history of South Asia and that regional realms and states were the organisational rule of societies and polities.

Agriculturally, the Indian subcontinent can be roughly divided into three distinct regions; namely the Himalayan mountain range, the north Indian lowlands of the Indus, Ganga (Ganges) and the Brahmaputra Rivers, and finally the Indian peninsula known as the Dekhan Plateau.[8] The Himalayan

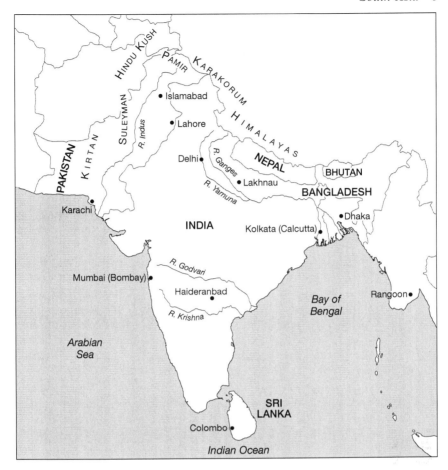

Map 0.2 A map showing the topography and natural borders of the South Asian region

mountain range can be divided into five regions. First, the high mountains of the Tibetan Himalayas followed, second, by the almost entirely snow-capped range with its ten summits all over 8,000m. Third, the lesser Himalaya range which gains in width and height as it stretches from east to west forming the Kathmandu and Kashmir Valleys. Despite access difficulties, this narrow mountain chain, or more specifically its valleys, are an old and significant settlement area which has been used to different agricultural ends.

In front of this ridge lies the fourth sub-region, the Sivalik Hills, a range of mountains rising to 1,200m covering a strip of land 1,700km in length and between 10 and 80km in width. Occasionally the inhabitants of the river valleys in the Sivalik region migrated into new areas bringing with them intensive farming and forestry techniques. Such areas are known as Duns. South of the Sivalik Hills lies the Terai, a 25 to 50km wide humid marshy forest area, which, on account of its high infection rate of malaria and the barren soil, has long been sparsely inhabited compared to the nearby Gangetic Plain.[9] Even today the area has a low population density. The fifth agricultural sub-region that can be identified is the highly fertile Ganges-Brahmaputra valley running between the Himalayan Mountains and the Dekhan Plateau which profits from layers up to 2000m thick of rich sediment topped with alluvial deposit.

The Ganges valley itself can also be divided into different sub-regions. The western part is composed of a number of Doabs (lit.: *do ab*: two waters), the most well-known and the longest of which is the Ganga-Yamuna Doab. The Gandak and the Son are major tributary rivers feeding the Ganges east of Allahabad (confluence of the Ganga and the Yamuna) on the Awadh plain. The eastern part of the Ganges Valley forms the delta region of the Brahmaputra and the Ganga with their numerous tributaries, which over time have produced the Sundarbans, an ecologically unique area of mangrove forest. To the west of the Ganges Valley, separated from Delhi only by the Aravalli Range, lies the Panjab (lit.: *panch ab*: five waters/rivers: the Satlej, the Beas, the Ravi, the Chenab and the Jhelum), the upper part of the Indus River system. The fertile floodplains defined by the curve of the river from its mouth to the Ganga-Yamuna Doab played host to the Harrappa civilisation, South Asia's earliest advanced urban civilisation. Moreover, the greater area of Delhi is recognised as the oldest permanently populated region of South Asia.

The Dekhan Plateau, the third largest biosphere of subcontinent, is found in southern India. The plateau differs succinctly in its geological makeup and regional characteristics to also be divided into sub-regions. The easterly sloping large inland plateau is the first of such characteristic features. Other than the Narmada and the Tapti rivers, all of the other major rivers flow eastwards. Although the southern part of the plateau experiences copious precipitation, the run-off is too fast on account of the geological composition of the area for the water to be used agriculturally. This has given rise to a culture of irrigation distinguished by the building and maintenance of a number of dams. The northern area of the Dekhan Plateau is characterised by a number of rifts and trenches such as Narmada Valley and mountain massifs such as the Satpura and Vindha Ranges. The mostly wide river valleys provide for surface irrigation of agricultural land.

The highlands of Chota-Nagpur (covering parts of the present-day federal states of Jharkhand and Chhattisgarh) mark the natural boundary of the Ganges Valley in the east. The hilltops of this area were the chosen territory of the Munda people as they retreated from the advancing invaders from the west. Today, the area continues to be something of a retreat, though admittedly now it is from the invasion of the large mining industries attracted by the wealth of the natural minerals in the surrounding area. The so-called Adivasi (lit.: original inhabitants) live in this area of the subcontinent that is known as the Tribal Belt; a relatively dense forest strip that stretches from Gujarat in the west to Assam in the east.

The mountain ranges of the Western and Eastern Ghats define the limits of the plateau. Whilst the Western Ghats, known for their dense forest and biodiversity, rise to a height of 2600m, the Eastern Ghats reach less lofty heights of 1600m. The plateau is lined by a narrow, flat coastline constituting a second physical region characterised by the large deltas of the Mahanadi, Godaveri, Krishna and Kaveri Rivers along the Coromandel Coast. The area with its highly fertile alluvial soils continues to earn the region the title of the "rice bowl" of South India. Despite the mere 20 to 50km wide strip of rugged coastline that comprises the Malabar and Konkan Coast, intensive agriculture is made possible through the interception of the abundant monsoon rains.

Ultimately, it is the monsoon rains (Arabic: *mausim*: season) that determines the climate and the agro-economic cycle of South Asia. As approximately 70 per cent of the current agricultural industry is dependent on the amount of natural precipitation, the timing and the length of the monsoon rains are determinant factors for crop yield and harvest success as well as water supply for the population. Generally speaking the monsoon is divided into the southwest summer monsoon occurring in late June until September, fading between October and December and the northeast monsoon from December to February followed by a hot spell from April to May. By virtue of the monsoon being a relatively shallow air stream, precipitation can vary considerably from season to season. Weather conditions, humidity, wind speeds and temperature all have a deciding influence in the onset of the monsoon, its advance and its precipitation levels.

As the warm monsoon winds that gather over the Arabian Sea are forced up over the Western Ghats the air is cooled, producing sudden cloud bursts of torrential rain and giving rise to the oft cited "burst of the monsoons". Once over the Western Ghats the monsoon front advances fairly rapidly over the rest of the subcontinent whereupon the westerly winds over Bengal force the monsoon along the southern flank of the Himalayas as the monsoon proceeds in a northwesterly direction. As a result the highest annual precipitation levels of up to 2,500mm fall in the Western Ghats and the southern slopes of the Himalayas in east India. The lee side of the Western Ghats experiences relatively little annual precipitation of 400 to 600mm whilst levels in Rajasthan and Pakistan, to the west of the subcontinent, record levels under 400mm and often less than 150mm.[10]

The unpredictability in levels of precipitation has, and continues to represent a serious problem for South Asia's agriculturists. Fluctuations in rainfall affect the drier regions of the subcontinent most dramatically, particularly when lack of rainfall leads to drought conditions and the loss of the harvest. On the other hand, rain-laden regions, especially those areas around the Himalayan foothills as well as the Ganga-Brahmaputra delta, are equally prone to harvests being destroyed by flash flooding. The monsoon's rainfall is so fundamental for agriculture that farmers distinguish between the harvests that follow each monsoon: with the *kharif* crop following the summer monsoon and the *rabi* crop following the winter monsoon. In Tamil Nadu and in the northeast of Sri Lanka the rice harvest following the main wet season

6 South Asia

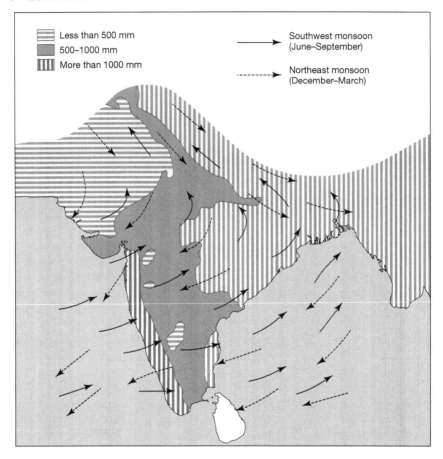

Map 0.3 Monsoon and precipitation in South Asia. Adapted from Hermann Kulke and Dietmar Rothermund, *A History of India*, 5th Edition (Routledge: 2010), p. 3

from October to January is known as *samba* and *maha*, respectively. Temperature is another important element affecting the harvest. Temperatures rise in the summer months along the latitudinal lines, developing distinct continental conditions. In north India, for example, temperatures can occasionally exceed 50°C whilst annual averages for the area are between 27–29°C. Temperature fluctuations are lowest along the humid Malabar Coast and in Sri Lanka.[11]

One noticeable element concerning the climate of the subcontinent is the contrast between the seasonal wet regions and the year-round rather dry zones, both environments deeply influencing the way of people's lives. Alongside the differing methods of cultivation and staple crops such as wheat and rice which are grown in the areas of heavy rainfall, the thinning forests and light groves are the natural, vegetative border to the Arid Corridor which extends from the Thar Desert through the Dekhan Plateau on the Coromandel Coast to the so-called Dry Zone in northern Sri Lanka. Not only did this corridor influence the migratory movements of the semi-nomadic and nomadic populations of the area, but also military lines of approach. In stark contrast to this arid area, those regions that experience high levels of precipitation covered with dense forests, such as the Tribal Belt in the east of the subcontinent, have been influenced little by migratory peoples. It was first with the discovery of rich minerals during the nineteenth century and then the development of deforestation methods that opened up this area, allowing the settlement of outsiders who brought with them the lucrative undertaking of agriculture.[12]

Whilst the area of the South Asian subcontinent is considerably larger when compared to that of Western Europe, a number of historically important regions have been formed on account of the subcontinent's natural landscape, climatic, geological and ecological conditions. Furthermore, these conditions have had a formative effect on the regional and local cultures of the people. Such a historical region, so often marked by some geological or climatic communality, was often settled with familial groups, clans and societies who were aware of their own pasts, histories and specific culture by virtue of the numerous forms of traditions. Whilst such a region can be denoted by specific linguistic regions, this is rather the exception than the rule in the South Asian subcontinent. It is rather the case that a historic region is characterised by common symbols, myths, history, clothing habits, rituals, celebrations and customs. Noteworthy examples of such historic regions include Tamil Nadu, Bengal, Orissa and Gujarat, smaller historical regions include the Ganga-Yamuna-Doab, Bundelkhand, Chhattisgarh and Khandesh, among others.[13]

The South Asian subcontinent can be roughly divided into three main regions wherein the process of state and empire building was a constant characteristic, which, at its core, was based on historical regions. The first such region is that of the north Indian floodplains of the Indus and the Ganga, the second being the east coast of the continent with its main focus of the Coromandel Coast, and third, the highlands of the Dekhan which is separated by the central Indian vegetation belt from the north Indian floodplains. An integral moment in the formation and stabilisation of rule over this area was the extent of military range featured under pre-modern organisation and logistic conditions which featured a 300km radius around the centre of power and the ability to intervene militarily within 900km of the centre.[14] Even the modern Mughal Empire was based upon such conditions giving rise to provinces of appropriate military operational size. Likewise the state-building process on the provincial level of the Mughal Empire was also based on this organisational pattern during the eighteenth century.

Furthermore, the area of the Ganges Valley encompasses the Delhi-Agra (Doab) region, followed by the Awadh region with the cities of Allahabad, Kanpur, Lakhnau and Varanasi (Banaras), as well as the Bihar and Bengal regions with the urban centres of Patna, Dhaka and Kolkata. The area of the Tribal Belt also felt the effects of state formation such as in the east on the fertile levels of Chhattisgarh (lit.: 36 castles), in the area of the central Indian city of Nagpur, further west on the Malwa Plateau with its cities Ujjain and Indore as well as Rajputana in the west with Udaipur and Jaipur. These regions were by no means isolated power or cultural centres, as in every direction trade relations and cultural contact could be found. Also the Arid Corridor offered possibilities of migration and military action and it was via this corridor that the Mughals were able to advance south at the end of the seventeenth century and then to the Maratha to the north in the eighteenth century.

The macro-geographical region of the Coromandel Coast can be subdivided into four historical areas in which the year-round abundant water supply from the river deltas is not only advantageous for rice cultivation, but also makes textile production of the colourful printed fabrics, so iconic of the region, possible. This is particularly true for the Krishna-Godaveri-Delta, the Kanchipuram region, the Kaveri-Delta and finally the Madurai area. In turn, the central highlands of the Dekhan Plateau can also be differentiated into four historical core areas: first the fertile area around Aurangabad and the region of Maharashtra in the north, second the area of Haiderabad/Golkonda in the southeast located roughly in the provincial region of Andhra, third Chota Nagpur-Orissa in the east and last the area of Maisur-Bangaluru/Bangalore in the south. Malabar, far in the south on the west coast of the subcontinent, is also a separate historical region.

As can be seen in Map 0.4 the thick lines of division between the different regions indicate the relative isolation of those regions they encompass. Of particular note are the regions of Kashmir, Nepal and Assam with their relative impermeable borders. Whilst the Tribal Belt forms one barrier region between the lowlands of the north and the mountains of the south, a second barrier region can be distinguished along the Eastern Ghats from Orissa to the Godaveri made notable by its paltry soil, moderate agriculture and low population density. A further barrier region can be found to the south of Krishna. The varied landscapes and natural areas found on the Indian subcontinent have consequently led to relatively stable agricultural relations and thus, in the course of history, also to the establishment of stable political governance. Such areas found themselves in intense political, economic and cultural exchanges with one another. However, marginal regions also existed, which remained relatively isolated due mainly to their geographical location.

Historiography of modern South Asia since the 1980s

Until the last quarter of the twentieth century, the historiography of modern Indian history had been divided between that of the British "imperialist history" (which focused heavily on the long-term benefits of colonial rule), and that of the "nationalist history" originating from Indian scholars. One branch of this national(istic) history writing broached the subject of the exploitative character of colonial rule whilst a second branch, somewhat radically,

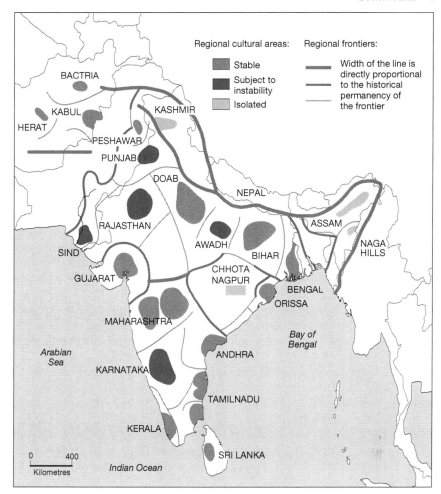

Map 0.4 The historical regions. Adapted from © miljoshi/CC Licensed

postulated a prior superiority of the Indian civilisation compared to that found in Europe in ancient times. This approach, on the one hand, aimed to reject the British claim of enacting a civilising mission in India, whilst on the other hand, stressed the necessity that Indians need remember only their own values in order to accomplish the establishment of a new nation. Despite the different approaches Indian, Pakistani and Bangladeshi historians were occupied until well into the 1980s with the question as to why their respective states had not yet been able to secure the national basis on which the nation-state could be established and to ask why the nation-building process was not yet complete.[15]

Meanwhile, however, questions have been raised of the continuities of Indian socio-economic structures as well as the longevity and transformative ability of institutions before, during and since British colonial rule – a topic that has inspired some fascinating debates. At the beginning of the 1980s, Christopher Bayly laid the foundations for a paradigm shift.[16] Yet it can be observed that with the growing nationalisation in Indian politics at the end of the twentieth century a partial renaissance of the nationalistic-Indian historiography (re)emerged. As a variant of the well-known constructs this re-emergence attempts to idealise the pre-colonial conditions of the subcontinent whilst describing the role of the British as brutal "colonial-imperialist destroyers of culture", something, which in such a sweeping nature, is unacceptable.[17] Of course, it cannot be denied that in the course of British colonial rule fundamental socio-economic transformations in South Asia were enacted; however, these were by no means uniformly applied across the subcontinent and moreover differed in their intensity over a period of 150 years.

Aside from the emphasis on the long-term developments of the subcontinent, since the end of the twentieth century a growing number of historians have come to understand, and interpret, the Indian Ocean in line with the literature conceptualising the Mediterranean Sea as a world region. The Indian Ocean's neighbouring areas are seen in a larger context whilst the ocean, despite the many dividing elements, is regarded as a means of connection. In the meantime original research has been undertaken into trade history, migration movements and cultural exchange in which trans-locality and inter-continental exchange comes to the fore. Above all, following this change in research perspective, the historiographical paradigm was reopened for assessment; this starting with the European "discovery" of a maritime route to South Asia in 1498 which initiated the economic development and the intensive trade between the coastal regions of the Indian Ocean. The paradigm shift has made the realisation all the clearer that, contrary to first thought, the Europeans, initially at least, merely participated and hardly instigated this trade in the Indian Ocean, whilst "Indians" were considerably more economically and socially mobile than was believed.[18]

A number of notable books concerning Indian history have been published since the paradigm shift in the historiography of South Asia. Among them is Stanley Wolpert's *A New History of India*.[19] In what can be termed a "classic" manner, Wolpert's 1977 work comprises a history of the subcontinent dating from its ancient times to the current day. Whilst the 20 chapters in the eight editions since its original publication can only be seen as a partial success, the book triumphs in its chapter covering the political development of South Asia since the implementation of Emergency Rule (1975–77) under Indira Gandhi. The major shortcoming of the book is that Wolpert seems to hold an ever-present teleological belief in the unity of South Asia as the significance of its history which is exemplified in the numerous chapter titles that include the idea of "unification". Despite this the period following the independency of British India in 1947 is almost entirely dealt with from the perspective of the development of India whilst Pakistan is portrayed, at best, as an opponent, and at worst as a secessionary state.

Herrmann Kulke and Dietmar Rothermund's book, *A History of India*, is similar to that of Wolpert's in more than merely its title. First published in German in 1982 and then republished in an English translation in 1986, the book has reached its fifth edition following a change of publishers.[20] This fluently written text is, above all, a political history of the subcontinent spanning the Indus civilisation to the present day. The book's shortcoming however, is, likewise, its presentation of the period following the independence of British India in 1947 as it restricts itself to the Indian Union whilst Pakistan and Bangladesh are only referred to in connection to the Indian state. The book's major merit is the clearly noticeable shift to the South Asian perspective in which the presentation of South Asia's realms and states as well as the "Indian freedom fight" is duly highlighted. Without doubt, Sumit Sarkar's *Modern India, 1885–1947* is among the best grand narratives of the new history of South Asia, which, since its first publication in 1983, has been re-edited a number of times, most recently in 2003. Whilst the book is organised around traditional topics, a conventional emphasis of theses and periodisation, the book manages to deliver, for the first time, what can be regarded as a modern social history of South Asia. Its only limitation is that of the narrow period the author has chosen to cover.[21]

Judith M. Brown's *Modern India* has also developed into an important resource for the history of South Asia, albeit if occasionally rather too detailed for an introductory text. In the context of the forming of political will and that of the Indian states, Brown is able to emphasise continuity of the Indian institutions. Led by its idiosyncratic observation that the Indian Union is, reportedly, the only decolonised Asian state to have been able to establish a stabile democratic political system, the premise of the work focuses on the democratisation process of British India.[22] Such an approach is, however, problematic in as far as Western democracies are taken as a point of reference. Such a criticism can also be applied to many of the grand narrations of the history of South Asia mentioned thus far in which Western values such as human rights, freedom, democracy, development, to name but a few, are either explicitly or implicitly dominant in the presentations and relegate the states of the South Asian subcontinent to positions behind that of the West.

It is widely acknowledged that Crispin Bates' *Subalterns and the Raj* ranks among the best general overviews of South Asian history since the turn of the millennium.[23] Bates begins his account of South Asian history in 1600 and thereby is able to mark the modern developments in the history of the subcontinent, which is a gratifying innovation. That said, however, the first four chapters present something of a prolegomena to the actual account of the book which concentrates on the British *Raj* post-1858. Where the aforementioned titles fall short, Bates excels as he is able to consolidate not only Pakistan, but also Sri Lanka, in the accounts of historical-political developments following decolonisation. Admittedly, however, Bates' book is not free from critique as the all too often presented Western values are, once again, included; this is especially the case with regard to the political development of the region. For example, the South Asian postcolonial states are portrayed as a poor copy of the colonial power. In this way the contemporary states of the subcontinent are dealt the double burden of, first, accepting the colonial heritage in which many of its faults are ignored, and second, faced with the necessity of creating the postcolonial state according to Western parameters.

The book's merit, however, is in Bates' innovative use of research trends since the paradigm shift of the historiography of South Asia of the 1980s, including the findings of the Subaltern Studies group. Not only are the South Asian actors elevated to the focal point of historical events, but also Bates is able to add increased attention to the resistance movements, a field that had hitherto been underrepresented in the history writing of South Asia. Having said this, however, Bates could have gone further in his exploration of subaltern agency within resistance itself which remains somewhat restricted when compared to the focus paid to the formation of social movements. In some instances the historical narrative of the colonial power is perpetuated, as in the case of the political development, for example. The narrative consists of a strongly actor-orientated history in which, on the face of it, political leaders single-handedly crafted the fortunes of a state regardless of whether this refers to the state-building in India, Pakistan, Bangladesh or Sri Lanka.

The approach taken by the French South Asian scholar Claude Markovits, is a successful attempt at presenting a modern history of the subcontinent in a number of separate chapters covering the period from 1480 to 1950. Markovits succeeds in handling a comprehensive period from a procedural, as well as a method-orientated approach. Such an analytical method also provides the chance to settle a number of recent research findings and interpretations. Admittedly, however, the text is not free from conventional presentation norms, notably as exemplified in the repeated standardised phases of periodisation. Despite this, history seems only to take place in British India whilst sections pertaining to the princely and monarchic India that comprised some 40 per cent of the land area of the continent and approximately 25 per cent of the population is awarded a single sub-section of 25 pages. The same 25-page treatment is given to the account of the French exploits in India in a book totalling some 600 pages.[24]

Peter Robb's handling of the history of India is similar in that it focuses strongly on the actor-orientated influence of Indian history at certain key dates. Whilst most of the South Asian historians have recently focused on the cultural, political and economic variances of the subcontinent, and, above all, its history, Robb adopts the opposite position in his postulation over the entity of "India" in stark comparison to the disunity exemplified in Europe. Apart from this, the many subtitles portray something of a general account. According to Robb, the modernisation process began in the West with the spread of British colonial rule. From the second half of the eighteenth century British rule is presented as virtually the single dynamic force within the subcontinent in which Indians appear, if at all, simply as the governed. Clear diagrams to such end are included in the cartographic material that accompanies the publication in which the growing territorial extent of British colonial occupation is depicted as a shaded area of land whilst the rest of India is simply shown as blank space.[25]

In the same year (2002) David Ludden's *India and South Asia: A Short History* was also published.[26] As with many of the overviews of South Asian history, Ludden also begins with the pre-history of the subcontinent by introducing the Harappa civilisation which is followed by an account of the "Classical-Vedic-Age". This is followed by a violent "Muslim Middle Age" including the Mughal Empire. Ludden's modern period of South Asia's history begins with the British colonial rule over the subcontinent. The history of the successor states in British India is handled in a rather curious way as the newly formed nation-states are portrayed as poorer versions of the colonial regime. An area of contention within the book surrounds Ludden's concept of "ethnic identity", which, according to the author, emerged during the Middle Ages. However, it is not always clear to the reader what is meant by this. As a result a variety of ethnic groups are introduced, intermixed and used almost interchangeably between the titles of "ethnic groups", "religious communities", "castes" and finally as "colonial elites". In general, the overriding impression of the text is that it was the elites that were the catalyst driving the history of South Asia. It is therefore by no means surprising that here, too, the modern history of South Asia once more appears to be the history of the British in India.

It is in this point that Barbara and Thomas Metcalf's compact presentation of Indian history differs. In just over 300 pages, the authors are able to present a wide spectrum of topics which are well-conceived and handled in a balanced fashion. Although this narrative and descriptive approach is successful, the book lacks analytical sharpness. Despite this drawback, however, the book impresses and should be recommended as a short but solid introductory overview of the field.[27]

Conceived explicitly for use as a textbook, Sugata Bose and Ayesha Jalal have succeeded in delivering a very course-orientated introduction into the history of South Asia by incorporating fitting debates and research results of late. In compact chapters of around ten pages each, the authors are able to guide the reader chronologically from the early twentieth century through a number of notable points in South Asian history, often portrayed in an authoritative manner, to the present day. The goal of writing South Asian history is fulfilled in as far as the history of the successor states of British India are equally treated and also in the fact that Sri Lanka too is mentioned occasionally.[28]

Burton Stein offers a highly innovative view of the history of India.[29] As a self-confessed opponent to teleological, development-orientated historiography, Stein is able to animate past events within contemporary occurrences as history is not merely a succession of incidences taking place as time unfolds, but should rather be understood as a collection within which the individual entries are variable and can therefore always be repositioned or reordered. Speaking also for this approach is not only the fact that numerous new findings are able to be discovered in comparison to conventional historiography, but that a new methodology and a re-evaluation of existing evidence as well as the consideration of facts hitherto not considered as historical evidence affords the possibility to construct a genuine Indian history of intrinsic value.

The attempt of opposing the perspective of the Indian Union, and the Hindu perspective accordingly, in the conventional presentation of South Asian history by a Muslim-accented history of British India has been only partly successful. S. M. Burke and Salim Al-Din Quraishi's voluminous historiographical work entitled *The British Raj in India: An Historical Review* seems to be an ideologically prefabricated text which establishes the necessity in henceforth creating a Muslim state within the subcontinent from a historical perspective – which is, in fact, ahistorical. This, however, is also true for many of the "pro-Indian" overview histories mentioned above since they too often pay tribute to the founding fathers of the Indian Union and most prominently to Jawaharlal Nehru and Mahatma Gandhi. Neither is Burke and Quraishi's work void of such political tribute to the fathers of Pakistan.[30]

In contrast, Christophe Jaffrelot's edited edition of competent authors offers insights into individual aspects of Pakistan's history and is thereby a critical introduction into the history of the country. The authors attempt to distance themselves from the previous stereotypes and to allow the country and the state its own history without falling into nationalistic trappings.[31] Ian Talbot provides a further offering of Pakistan's history in a work which effectively offers easy access to a still difficult historiographical field.[32] Meanwhile, a useful overall view of Bengal history can be found in the form of Sirajul Islam's guide-like history of Bangladesh which covers the history of this region from 1704 to the formation of the Bengali state.[33] Recently Willem van Schendel succeeded in offering a highly innovative and superb presentation of Bengal's and Bangladesh's history. Entitled *A History of Bangladesh,* the work takes on a long-term examination of the historic region of Bengal starting with the geographical, ecological, geological and climatic characteristics before moving on to focus on the Mughal period and then further on to the present-day history of the country and its people, including the young nation-state after 1971.[34]

Despite its age, the best introductory text to Sri Lankan history remains Kingsley M. De Silva's *A History of Sri Lanka* published in 1981, and subsequently re-edited for its reprint in 2007, which places the political history of the island along with its socio-political and economic history at the forefront of the book's aims. Admittedly the book does exhibit a strong concentration on the developing constitutional process of the twentieth century; this, however, is not detrimental but, on the contrary, helps develop a good and knowledgeable overview of the island.[35] A more updated history and historiographical account of the island state that does not slip into the trappings of a national narrative is imperative for the academic field. In contrast, John Whelpton's *A History of Nepal* couples conventional political history with the concepts of culture, environment and society in his account of Nepal.[36]

This recent publication updates and replaces Rishikesh Shaha's two-volume *Modern Nepal*.[37]

The representations of the history of South Asia, and specifically of individual nation-states of the subcontinent since the turn of the millennium, are increasingly considered in the context of the paradigm shift of the 1980s. However, the "classical" historical representations continue to find their own place and succeed in providing re-editions for the readership.[38] The danger hereby, however, is that old narratives, obsolete views and national parameters continue to be handed down to future generations of South Asian (history) scholars. The more recent grand overviews that exhibit a tendency of over-playing a Hindu-national bias do not serve to offer a timely historiographical account of South Asia. This is especially true of D.R. SarDesai's book which is based on the historiographical concepts of the 1950s and 1960s, presenting history as a chronological sequence of Indian rulers (Mughal, Maratha) and prime ministers of the Indian Union. The aim of presenting a new form of historical enquiry into the history of India which makes use of a new periodisation and focuses on the lower classes has, unfortunately, not been delivered.[39]

In clear distinction to the above-mentioned works, the aim of this present account is to attempt to not present the history of South Asia along national narratives paying strict adherence to chronological depictions, but rather to approach South Asian history from a thematic perspective. Themes such as migration, environment, work, urbanisation, transformations in agricultural techniques and agricultural economics, colonial-capitalistic asymmetry, social change and the formation of political will form the focus of this work. The approach of dealing with Indian history and South Asian societies from a thematic perspective is advantageous in that such organisation will allow for a break from the conventional historiographies, as well as providing the foundations to introduce a new form of history writing of the subcontinent in which a multitude of actors form the centre of the historical analysis and interpretation.

The concept of this book

This books aims to considerably distance itself from the previous master narratives indicated above with their noted failings; this will largely be achieved in the organisation and conception of the book along thematic rather than chronological lines. Such a reorganisation contrary to conventional practice has been deemed necessary on account that the sheer size of the area of study with its variety of regions, landscapes, inhabitants and cultures make a uniform sequential narration (and narrative) impossible. Only when approached from a plurality of perspectives can an adequate history of the subcontinent become achievable. Under the guiding headings of "State formation and empire building in South Asia c. 1660–1800"; "Patriotisms and nationalisms in the nineteenth and twentieth centuries"; "State formation and empire building in South Asia 1858–1998"; "Agriculture and agro-economy"; "Silviculture and scientific forestry"; "Migration, circulation and diaspora"; "Urbanisation and industrialisation"; and "Knowledge, science, technology and power", this book will attempt to map a social history of the South Asian subcontinent. It goes without saying that it is not the aim herein to pass final judgement on the difficult historiography of the area, but rather to comment on and synthesise contemporary historical research.

In order to facilitate the introduction to each topic area, each chapter is fronted with a general, theoretical outline. Furthermore, the numerous cartographic materials and pictures serve not merely as illustrations, but should rather be seen as supplementary material aimed at expanding the knowledge expressed in the text. Historiographical debates as well as the most recent research results will also be introduced and built upon. Such additions aim to show that history is not a static given, but is rather a dynamic process that evolves through constant discussion, interpretation and reinterpretation not only to illustrate contemporary societies' conditionality, but also to give them meaning. This meaning does not lie in the nation-state itself as the bastion of history as if history would no longer exist if that state were to cease in its existence. Instead the attempt will be undertaken to offer and develop other avenues to historical understanding and realisation along a thematic field of historical study.

Following the paradigm shift in the 1980s a new research focus has developed in the area of historical sciences in South Asia which has influenced the selection of thematic blocks explored in this publication. The emergence of modern states, and specifically the process of state and empire-building, is still of great academic interest. This, among other things, has contributed to the necessary revision of the stereotypical image of South Asia being politically static. Under such changed paradigms, even the eighteenth century – so often characterised as "anarchic" and "chaotic" – becomes dynamic as it depicts the Mughal Empire not as simply collapsing, but of undergoing a process of state-building initiated from below, as well as from within, forcing organisation and reorganisation. A comparison with the "Empire" – as the British labelled the Holy Roman Empire until the middle of the eighteenth century before it was replaced with Britain's own "Empire" – could well be helpful for our purposes herein. Furthermore, the South Asian wars of dynastic succession of the eighteenth century, so similar to those occurring in Europe at the same time, will not be viewed as bringing about the collapse of the Mughal Empire, but instead rather viewed as serving the necessary method in bringing in what is known in history as the early modern period during which early modern states were formed on the foundations of historical regions out of the centrally controlled Mughal Empire into a more federally transformed structure.

The South Asian agricultural practices have always, and still continue to, attract the interests of the historians, anthropologists and ethnologists. According to accounts originating from such sources, peasants formed the backbone of all the regimes in South Asia. In recent years interest in agricultural history with regards to technology and maximisation of production has now become a subject of social history. Following changes in land division, taxation systems and yield maximisation, an increased social mobility of landed individuals is noticeable and forms the forefront of such social studies. The question of where and when levels of society and even classes of the new wealthy peasants and conversely the impoverishment of the landless peasants began to develop is of importance here. This broad question encompasses others, such as the extent to which peasants had access to land and their abilities to secure it. Here too, it is necessary to investigate in what way the British colonial state influenced this development, where it may have accelerated this crystallisation of social levels and, similarly, where it may have successfully attempted to halt it.

Just as in the field of agricultural development the issues of mobilisation and immobilisation are of importance when examining industrialisation and the control of the emerging workforce. Even before industrialisation in British India began in the middle of the nineteenth century – rather limited and hesitant in a number of regional cities at first – British plantation owners were already looking to recruit labourers in South Asia for the British colonies in the Indian Ocean and the Caribbean in order to compensate for the chronic labour shortage following the abolition of slavery and the slave trade in the British Empire in the first half of the nineteenth century. Issues pertaining to labour and migratory organisation played an integral role for the British colonial state in the whole of South Asia, which, from the middle of the nineteenth century, was visible in the factories in the industrial centres of Bombay, Ahmedabad and Calcutta, as well as on the tea plantations in Assam and on the sugarcane fields of Mauritius to the Caribbean islands, Malaysia and Fiji. This plantation industry became characterised by the division of labour organisation and agro-industrialisation.

This initial transoceanic migration, which enabled the high mobility of the South Asian population, laid the foundation for what would become known as the "Indian Diaspora". This mobility has, in recent years, been characterised by Indian nationalists at the turn of the millennium who see the millions of Indians at work overseas not as exploitation and in line with the former terminology of a "brain drain", but instead as a profitable contemporary global "brain bank". Furthermore, it must be recognised that the Indian diaspora plays a growing role in the societies in which they find themselves. Often many will become first truly aware of their Indian origin, despite the many differences in the Indian society, whilst away. However, the Indian diaspora is much more multifaceted when compared to other diaspora groupings around the world; for example, the religious importance as paid to the Jewish diaspora is but a single feature, if at all, among many characterising the Indian diaspora. Far more influential and telling is the global networking of the Indian diaspora via the internet, mobile telecommunications and international travel, which in turn reiterates the mobility of south Asian migrants.

Industrialisation and urbanisation are two phenomena of modern history that cannot be separated or viewed in isolation. Once again the issue of migration (i.e. mobilisation) of the labour force and their settling (i.e. immobilisation) comes to the fore. On the one hand this implies identity as well as class formation of the labour force in their new urban surroundings, whilst on the other hand it also makes the issue of work organisation in the context of factory production relevant. If the influx of job seekers was particularly noticeable in the industrial areas in which the population density was already extreme, so too was the rapid population growth recorded in the other cities in British India. Soon many suffered in South Asian towns, and still continue to suffer, from housing shortages, lack of water supply, inadequate waste, refuse and sewage disposal and poor medical care. Whilst in Europe urbanisation was attempted to be managed through town planning, the British colonial power in South Asia failed to address these problems adequately, the effects of which continue to be seen, and felt, today.

The question of whether India was modernised during British colonial domination is a highly contested arena of research within which a number of ideological skirmishes are fought. For example, steam-generated power supply, and its implied social mobilisation, continues to be the yardstick against which many historians measure modernisation. As a testament to this modernisation process such commentators enthuse in the ability to catalogue impressive lists of figures pertaining to the progressive nature of development whilst the long-term use and harm caused by many of the gigantic canal and railway construction projects, pursued with vigour by the successor states of British India, especially in the Indian Union, have only been analysed since the 1970s from a rather naïve positivist belief in progress. In the meanwhile such interpretations have been reassessed.

It is clear that the conventional, well-known topic areas have acquired a new relevance through a new approach of enquiry. Simultaneously, new topic areas have become the subject of historical interest in the research on South Asia. The main trends of this shift are presented in this book whilst further important areas are also addressed. The thematic organisation of this book will allow for, on the one hand, the historicisation of the nation-state and thereby also pave the way for a social history of the subcontinent that is free from the nation-state as a point of reference. On the other hand, such organisation will also permit long-term developments in trans-national and trans-local perspectives to be highlighted whilst also firmly placing various actors, not states, at the centre of historical events.

The research results from the 1980s have, for the most part, shed light on some magnificent findings in relation to the history and society of South Asia, permitted the development of theoretical models and delivered a basis for the new historiography of this world region. Curiously, however, such impetus has seldom found its way into the master narratives of the area. The goal of this book, therefore, is to fill this historiographical gap whilst remaining a readable and useful account of the modern history of South Asia. Given the sheer wealth of material discovered in undertaking this work it became obvious that not all aspects of this history would be able to receive the same attention. Furthermore, some thematic holes had to remain unfilled. Completeness, however, was also, understandably, never envisaged from the outset, yet despite any shortcomings I hope that this book remains enlightening and entertaining.

Notes

1. Debes, Kirchhoff and Kropatschek 1905: 49. Edition first awarded at the International Geographical Congress in Bern, 1891. Map no. 33: "South Asia", map no. 36: "Southeast Asia".
2. Bose and Jalal 2004: 3.
3. Pye and Pye 1985: 133.
4. Juergensmeyer 2006: 465.
5. Cf. United Nations Statistics Division 2012.
6. Wink 1990: 1–3.
7. Cf. Kulke and Rothermund 2010: see maps pp. 69, 90, 201, 256.
8. Bronger 1996: 52–5.
9. Bohle 1995: 19–28. The following sections also refer to this work.
10. National Atlas & Thematic Mapping Organisation 2007; Bohle 1995: 31–3. Bronger 1996: 60–9; Stang 2002: 13–26.
11. Bohle 1995: 33–34; Farmer 1993: 7–8.
12. Farmer 1993: 8.
13. Cohn 1987a: 100–35.
14. The following paragraphs are based on Kulke and Rothermund 2010: 9–12.
15. Cf. the Subaltern School volumes published after 1982 address the question of why India so far has failed to become a nation. The Subaltern School will be dealt with below.
16. Bayly 1983.
17. Two such works include: Chaudhuri S. 1995, Parthasarathi 2001.
18. Chaudhuri K.N. 1990; McPherson 1998; Pearson M.N. 2003; Bose S. 2006.
19. Wolpert 2009.
20. Kulke and Rothermund 2010. Original title: *Geschichte Indiens*, 1982.
21. Sarkar 2003.
22. Brown 1985.
23. Bates 2010.
24. Markovits 2002. Original title: *Histoire de L'Inde Moderne*, 1994.
25. Robb 2002.
26. Ludden 2002.
27. Metcalf and Metcalf 2002.
28. Bose and Jalal 2004.
29. Stein 1998.
30. Burke and Quraishi 1995.
31. Jaffrelot 2004.
32. Talbot 2005.
33. Islam S. 1992.
34. Schendel 2009.
35. De Silva 1981.
36. Whelpton 2008.
37. Shaha 1996.
38. Embree and Wilhelm 2000.
39. SarDesai 2007.

1 State formation and empire building in South Asia c. 1660–1800

Forms and models

Large realms were the exception rather than the rule in South Asia. The Maurya Empire, under the rule of Ashoka (r. 268–233 BCE), was one such exception encompassing virtually the entire Indian subcontinent. Similarly, the Gupta Empire, between 320 and 500 CE, stretched across the whole of north India. The Mughal Empire, formed in 1525 by Babur (1483–1530), successfully conquered Delhi from Afghanistan and established the Timurid dynasty there. Its descendants built upon Babur's foundation on which Akbar (r. 1556–1605) led the empire to its cultural flowering whilst Aurangzeb (r. 1658–1707) brought the empire to its maximum territorial expansion. However, this expansion, both militarily and administratively, surpassed the organisational infrastructures of the central(ised) government. As a result, in the 1720s a number of provinces of the empire began to form new states. Some of these newly formed states, such as Awadh and Haiderabad, covered an area as large as the contemporary states of France or Spain, whilst others held proportions rather more similar to the size and importance of German principalities. Meanwhile, in Rohilkhand in the north and in Bhopal in central India, immigrant Afghan clans began to establish new dynasties whilst the Marathas were able to stretch their sphere of influence over large parts of central India.[1]

Much has been written concerning the causes of "decline of the Mughal Empire". The bulk of this previous research can be summarised as follows:[2] taking the death of Aurangzeb Alamgir as the starting point in 1707, a number of party struggles within the nobility of the Mughal court in Delhi were ignited, which, in the long term, questioned the central political power of the Timurid dynasty. Amid the power struggles between Turani and Sayyids and between the Rajputs and the Iranians, Aurangzeb, and his successors in particular, were unable to continue a balanced mediation between the different factions. A further reason for the disintegration of the Mughal Empire can be found in territorial expansion, which, in a large part, was led by Aurangzeb and which resulted in the impossibility to govern the empire and its provinces with the same intensity. Crises in the personnel and institutional system are also noted as reasons for the escalating de-territorialisation. The consequence of this

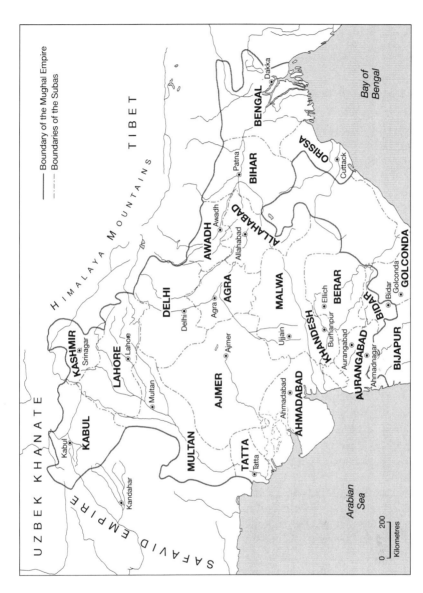

Map 1.1 Provinces (subas) of the Mughal Empire c. 1700

disintegration within the administrative structure of the empire was an overproportional growth of the empire's nobility relative to territorial expansion. Their basic economic revenue, originating mainly from land revenue, no longer sufficed to fulfil the nobility's obligations towards the maintenance of the Mughal cavalry units.

Coupled with these internal structural issues, the Mughal Empire was also under threat both externally (militarily) and internally (insurgent groups). Thus, the Afghan invasions of 1739, 1752–3 and 1759–61 – including the looting of Delhi and the expansion of the Marathas of Satara and Pune to Rajasthan – contributed to the long-lasting decline of central power in the Mughal Empire. Nowhere can this be seen more clearly than in the famous battle of Panipat in 1761 between the Marathas and the Afghans as both expansionist military forces were tested to breaking point. Meanwhile, this development allowed the Sikh-*rajas* in the Panjab to declare independence from the Mughals whilst the East India Company (EIC) in Bengal and Bihar obtained administrative and political power after 1765. The empire's political capacity at the end of the eighteenth century was but a shadow of its former glory. However, the capital city's function as seat of legitimisation and the Mughal's position as overlord were never doubted since none of the newly established dynasties declared independence from the Mughal Empire.[3]

A characteristic element of the transformation processes which the Mughal Empire underwent during the eighteenth century is not one of external collapse, but rather of internal crystallisation during the process of centralisation within the provinces. It is at this administrative level that the ideal type of a centralised state apparatus of the Mughals could be implemented as in the Subas Bengal and Awadh and the Maratha region, for example. State formation followed the cultural groundings of historical regions as in the case of Haiderabad, Awadh and Bengal. At the same time, the Mughal ruler and the Mughal's residence became all the more important as they were increasingly regarded as being the source and origin of honour and dignity of the polity and of political legitimacy. Gradually, during the eighteenth century, a Mughal myth came into existence which became politically more binding than the Mughal's former military and political dominance had been able to achieve. The British, as new provincial rulers, also lined up, if somewhat reluctantly, against the background of the sovereignty of the Mughals. Their empire ended *de jure* in 1858 with the British defeat of the Great Rebellion. Shared sovereignty which had prevailed and had strengthened throughout the eighteenth century was replaced by the European concepts of undivided sovereignty. As a result, the British finally halted the ongoing processes of state formation, and it was only the independence movement of the 1920s and 1930s that saw the emergence of a new Indian political will.[4]

The middle of the eighteenth century seems to mark a caesura in the political, as well as in the economic and social development of the Indian subcontinent. This is, for example, exemplified in the Battle of Panipat in 1761, which was fought between the invading Afghan forces under Ahmad Shah Abdali and an alliance of Maratha rulers as they each attempted to extend their own influence in the Panjab. This battle not only tested the military limits of the two expanding powers, but the Singhs, a Sikh noble family, also drove the *faujdar* (military governor) Ahmad Shah Abdali from Amritsar, uniting the territory between the Satlej and the Indus rivers under Sikh control. After the failed invasion by Afghan and Maratha forces, the Singhs declared independence from the Mughal Empire as well as from the Afghans in 1765. They expressed this point by acting as a sovereign ruler and henceforth began to mint their own coins.[5] The new state obviously emerged out of the Mughal Empire and was therefore able to reform its administrative and military structures and to finally consolidate its territory of state.[6]

A year following the Battle of Baskar in 1764, fought between an alliance of Mughal and Awadhi forces on the one side and the joined forces of the EIC and the *nawab* of Bengal on the other, the EIC obtained the *diwani* of the Mughal provinces of Bengal, Bihar and Orissa from Mughal Shah Alam II (r. 1759–1806). Shah Alamm II appointed the EIC the right to administer revenues and have jurisdiction over civil rights in the provinces and to forward a fixed part of the tax and revenue collections to the Mughals, since he regarded the EIC as a powerful and reliable contractor for the revenue collection in the east of his empire. The British henceforth began to construct and develop their idea of territorial rule in India, ushering in the beginnings of a "Modern India".[7] Expression of this still insecure and "fragile" position of the British in India was, at least until the 1790s, the debate about the continuity with the "ancient constitution" of the Mughal Empire, and the establishment in Bengal, in order to fit their own authority in the framework of legitimacy.[8]

This construction has been challenged by a critical historiography over the past decades, which can be observed in the critique towards the notion on the "decline of the Mughal Empire" and the emergence of the so-called "successor states". None of the emerging states saw themselves as the succession in the wake of a sinking empire. Recent research has begun accentuating the long-term developments in order to present a more balanced overview of the state formation process. Such undertakings seek not only to make a link and find continuities with the Mughal Empire, but also to widen their lens of investigation further and take into account states such as the Vijayanagara Empire (1350–1668). Simultaneously, such a construct of continuity does not come without its own inherent downfalls as the omnipresent danger of transcending once again into the trappings of creating a historiography in which unchangeability, and therefore an implied static state of South Asian history and society is given. Internal differences in the individual state formation process also need to be addressed and given just as much consideration as external developments.[9]

This revisionist approach generally accents a concentration of economic activities on the local level, which often went along with the intensification of the land–city relationship through the growing exchange of goods and labour. This "re-urbanisation" of the eighteenth century was made possible through the commercialisation of agricultural activities as observed in Bihar and Bengal, as well as in parts of Gujarat and in Maharashtra. At the same time, a centralisation of revenue collection following a number of administrative and fiscal reforms were introduced and enacted in the aforementioned regions. The increase in revenue resulted primarily from changes in the calculation of the assessment base for land revenue, the emergence of bureaucratisation and the progressive monetisation of the economy. Such an increase in revenue intensified pressure on agricultural and artisan products to levels previously unknown. Although centralisation processes in terms of taxation took place, a gradual decentralisation can also be identified as the intensification of revenue collection rights were awarded to individuals who received land as *watan* (hereditary ownership of land) or as *inam*, or respectively as *mu'afi* (revenue-free land). This provided the space for semi-autonomous domains trying to establish local territorial power that were hardly controlled by the centre.[10]

Since the 1980s, historians of South Asia have attempted to present different models of the state formation processes to explain the phenomenon of divided sovereignty. A first attempt was made by Burton Stein, whose model of the "segmentary state" differed from that of the European concept of the centralised state in which sovereignty lies within a clearly defined territory of control, and is coupled with the idea of centralised administration based on an efficiently operating bureaucracy and the monopoly of state power. Contrary to this European concept, Stein presents the segmentary state as a conglomerate of small domains sharing a centralised king, but which were autonomous political units with a divided sovereignty. The common bond between these various domains was the ritualistic sovereignty of a "superior" overlord who presided over princes or lower rulers and was thus able to hold together the various parts of the realm's territories.[11]

Nicholas Dirks expanded upon Stein's segmentary model with his concept of "little kings". Dirk's innovation of the segmentary model was the division of "political" and "ritual sovereignty" of a given ruler and thereby readdressed the relation between power and ritual. As a result, Dirk discovered that it was power that served the ritual, not vice versa as ceremony was not form, but rather content. A central part of many of the rituals was the royal proffering of gifts, be that in symbolic form through the presentation, the adornment of articles of clothing, or materially in the form of land grants and revenue exemptions as constitutive elements of the state. Segmentary states occupied different political centres in which governance and power (*rajadharma*) were carried out by a number of different actors. Thereby the little kings commanded a certain degree of independency on account of the number of varied rituals they oversaw, whilst the highest level of sovereignty was reserved for the generally accepted king (*raja, maharaja*).[12] Dirk's model is however criticised for being guilty of dismissing religious ritual in a Machiavellian manner as mere tools employed to aid the political power within the system.[13]

Hermann Kulke adds a considerable spatial and temporal dimension to both Stein's, as well as Dirk's, respective monocentric segmentary state and little king models by appending his own evolutionary model of *samantacakra*, the polycentric process of empire formation on both micro and macro levels.

In their ideal form, such empires rise in the following three distinct stages: first, the inclusion of the tribal population on the peripheries of the small domains through the development of legitimising rituals for the governing powers; second, provided the extent to which the agricultural economic base can allow an excess in production, nearby domains could also be incorporated into the sphere of influence of the economically and politically potent little kingdoms; and third, a pyramidal organisational structure gradually begins to develop from which larger realms arise. André Wink, in his book entitled *Land and Sovereignty in India: Agrarian Society and Politics under the Eighteenth-Century Maratha swarajya*, attempts to explain the constantly altering alliances and separation of these domains (*fitna*) as well as the rivalries between the little kings, which he observed in his research regarding state formation in the Maratha *swarajya* of the eighteenth century. Wink's model is also based on shared sovereignty and overlapping areas of influence and authority over the subordinate power holders.[14]

Little kingdoms can best be described as being highly dynamic, relativistic and procedural forms of governance which function best as a network of relations between kings of different hierarchical rankings. A little king therefore is one that is found in an ever-changing, conflictive relationship with another king that can be seen as their superior; superior on account of the political and ritualistic resources the king can take advantage of in the redistribution and division of land, offices, titles and honours which symbolises his monarchical authority. With these powers he is able to bring numerous little kings of various lower ranks into his universalistic orbit of control and either hold them there or dismiss them as and when he sees fit. Thus, power in India, at least from the assessment of the little king model, appears to have been negotiable. This of course does not mean that the physical display of power was absent from Indian history, yet the use of power in conflict was rarely used to completely defeat the opponents, but rather to apply enough pressure to break their alliances.[15]

Burton Stein further expands on the concept of the little kings as rulers applying the concept of the European military-fiscal state to India during the eighteenth century. No regime that attempted to increase territorial expansion and consolidate control in India was able to succeed in these measures without the little kings acting as a central "agency" for the introduction of revenue collection (a large part of which had hitherto consisted of varying tributes) and the transfer of these revenues to the treasury (*khalsa*). This was in stark contrast to Europe where set rates of taxation (*fiscus*) had been gradually implemented. Increased revenue originating from the commercialisation of agriculture and industry could be further intensified through centralised revenue administration. The taxes and revenues gathered allowed for the development of a standing army equipped with new munitions and artillery units under European command, whilst the infantry were often trained by European drill sergeants. In the last decades of the eighteenth century the state of Maisur came to embody the textbook case of such a military-fiscal state.[16]

The European trading communities, which had been expanding their influence in the labour market as well as in the production processes in the hinterland of their coastal factories in addition to their influence in the Indian courts since the 1720s, participated in the "localisation" of governance and in the overall economic process. This involvement was further accelerated in the 1740s in both Bengal and on the Coromandel Coast as French-British commercial-cum-political competition intensified. With the onset of territorial governance in the 1760s, the British carried forward the politics of their predecessor states. This was especially the case in Karnataka, Bengal and Awadh where the EIC not only increased the annual revenue by raising revenue rates and abolishing fiscal privileges, but also invested a growing percentage of the revenue in their military apparatus.[17]

Apart from this Indian income, the British commanded additional financial and armed resources that were raised on the European capital and military markets and then transported to South Asia. As an incorporated trading company, which also administered a number of public functions, the EIC introduced new forms of decision making, which were reflected in an increasingly bureaucratised administration. However, within a few decades the effect of the extraction and export of Indian revenue as trade capital meant that an acute shortage of money began to be felt at the beginning of the nineteenth century; this was especially the case in Bengal as well as in Maharashtra. Due to this monetary shortage, it is feasible to assume that intermediate social, cultural and economic foundations of entire regions were disturbed as credit became almost impossible to secure. In some cases, as evidenced in Awadh and in Gurjarat, the EIC's economic penetration of neighbouring states as well as the permanent state of political conflict and military campaigns destabilised the polity of large regions on the subcontinent.[18]

The state formation processes of the eighteenth century could thus be summarised using the following descriptive model:[19]

1. The governor (*subadar*), as well as the sub-provincial Mughal military personnel (*faujdar*) obtained the facility to appoint and deploy revenue collectors.
2. The governor is able to control his own succession. During the 1720s and 1730s this was only possible with the explicit confirmation from the Mughal; thereafter succession control was afforded by means of formal confirmation from the Mughal.
3. Revenues and taxes originally payable to the Mughals were withheld at provincial and sub-provincial levels. The few remaining payments that were made took on the guise of a formal ritual "donation" (*peshkash*) and awarded to *subadars, faujdars, kiladars* (commander of a fortress), etc.
4. The *subadars* (*nawabs*), in particular, began to operate their own independent foreign policy and to wage war.
5. New dynasties founded new residence cities and with this established their own style of governance along with new architectural styles, as well as literary and cultural activities, giving the state its own unique image.

6 As a symbol of the state's autonomy, revenue calculation was undertaken in the name of the ruler and no longer in the name of the Mughals. This was similarly the case in the allocation of revenue-free land holdings (*inam, mu'afi*) and revenue exemptions.
7 In a further step towards the autonomy of the state, many rulers minted their own coins, thus replacing the common single currency of the silver rupee (*sikka rupia*). The introduction of a calendar was an additional sign of autonomy.
8 The final step in the formal expression of autonomy is observed in the reading of the Friday prayers (*khutba*) among the Muslim monarchs – not in the name of the Mughals, but rather in the name of the different rulers of a given area.

In order for the new rulers to be legitimised, the would-be ruler was required to exhibit the necessary skills and fulfil a number of requirements (*rajadharma*). These included:

1 Proving himself as the protector of the people, both from external threats and from internal unrest.
2 Being a capable military leader, who conducted himself in a courtly manner.
3 Ideally being the eldest son and heir succeeding the previous ruler.
4 Being the holder of a *farman* or *sanad* of a superior ruler who would in turn legitimise his own rule over his domain.[20]

Against this background, an undivided, hierarchical-pyramidal organisation of sovereignty on the one hand and the divided, multi-lateral shared sovereignty based on little kings on the other hand can be depicted as the following:

The Mughal rulers stressed the need for an undivided sovereignty at its centre; however, through the centralisation of the state and the administration

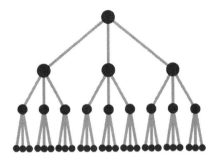
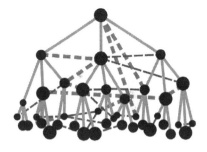

Figure 1.1 Undivided, hierarchical-pyramidal organisation (left) and divided, multi-lateral shared sovereignty (right) of the "little kings" in South Asia from the 1720s

in the provinces, they were simultaneously confronted with divided sovereignty in many parts of the empire. In turn, this seems to have been an important catalyst in the state formation processes of the eighteenth century which reified the strength of regional and local networks of both kingship and ritual, thereby placing both firmly as the central focus of state legitimisation. The British colonial state also operated within this model of governance. When their territorial hold and political dominance grew on the subcontinent, they gradually implemented the concept of "paramountcy". The British never explained exactly, never mind defined, this doctrine, which implicitly allowed for British hegemony even over the formally independent states of the subcontinent. British legitimacy and undivided sovereignty was finally secured on account of their superior weaponry during the Great Rebellion of 1857–59, followed by the proclamation in 1876 of the English monarch as the "Emperor/Empress of India" (*kaisar-i-hind*) and remained so until 1947.[21]

Following such a systematic analysis of divided or shared sovereignty, it now becomes necessary to look at a number of specific cases in which the aforementioned aspects of state and empire formation will be illustrated. There still exists a lack of detailed studies on the various historical regions and the emerging states between the seventeenth and nineteenth centuries, so that it has been necessary here to select cases in line with conclusive and current research.

State formation in the eighteenth and nineteenth centuries

Maratha swarajya (1674–1818)

The ruler (*chhatrapati*) of the Marathas, Shivaji Bhonsle (1630–80), originated from a small *deshmukh* family in Bijapur in today's Karnataka state. As a 16-year-old he was recruited by the mounted militia who were based in the mountainous forests surrounding his homeland. Shivaji Bhonsle not only witnessed the subordination of the neighbouring *deshmukhs,* but also observed local traditions and learnt how to employ them for his own means, which, together with his young age, ultimately won him the attention of the successful Maratha military leaders.[22] In spite of his charisma and obvious military strengths, it was only possible for Shivaji to ascend through the hierarchy of the military as far as the rank of military leader since the Sultan of Bijapur held the position of supreme commander over the Maratha troops. After 1650 Shivaji's ascendance to territorial and political power in the *desh*, the area between Sartara and Pune, began. In the mid-1660s, he succeeded in defeating the advancing army of Mughal Aurangzeb led by General Jai Singh. By 1673, the military successes of Shivaji against the Sultan of Bijapur eventually earned him political autonomy. At that time Aurangzeb's attention had been focused on the insurrections occurring in north India. In this politically favourable situation Shivaji seized the chance to establish a separate kingdom.[23]

However, Shivaji, the "self-made ruler", was stigmatised as belonging to the social group of the *shudra* (peasants), the lowest *varna* (lit.: colour, i.e. ritual colour of distinction or colour of the skin, often wrongly conceptualised by Europeans as "caste"). As a result, in order for Shivaji to legitimise his kingship he had to assert his power both internally over the heads of other Maratha families as well as the rival *deshmukhs,* whilst also expressing his power externally in the context of the Mughal Empire and specifically in opposition to the Sultanates of both Bijapur and Ahmednagar. In the context of this political melee, Shivaji relied on recognised concepts of legitimacy to support his mandate to rule, namely that the ruler had to be the heir to a heroic tradition, which in the Hindu context meant the inclusion in the ideal of the heroic warrior, the *kshatriya* (the second *varna*), whilst social and political status qualified and committed him to the maintenance of the secular order and norms (*rajadharma*).[24] Shivaji succeeded in combining the *Rajput* traditions together with religious legitimation by a *brahman* (highest *varna*) in Banaras who not only supplied Shivaji with a *kshatriya* past, but also discovered (or created) a coronation ritual based on Vedic texts taken from the Rajput tradition and staged them accordingly.[25] Shivaji had met the prerequisites of achieving the status of a heroic warrior on account of his successful military campaigns, thereby confirming his martial kingship (*chhatrapati*).[26]

A deciding factor in the generation of legitimacy was, however, the *darbar,* the final assembly, during which gifts were received and *dakshina* (opulent royal gestures in the form of money or other goods) were divided among the *brahmans* as well as the newly elected and, above all, the old nobilities. As an expression of his sovereignty, Shivaji awarded *inam-* and *watan-* or *jagir* land to his serving officers. Such endowments and gifts had a long-lasting effect as they proved to be highly integrative, so much so that they were documented by Shivaji's successors well into the 1770s. Shivaji achieved accession to the throne on the merits of a "created" Hindu ritual and was able to establish a kingdom along with a new era that lasted until the beginning of the nineteenth century.[27] Furthermore, it should be noted that the Maratha *chhatrapati* never declared independence from the Mughal Empire, not even after the Marathas had occupied Delhi/Sahjahanabad in 1784.

After Shivaji's death, an inner circle of 15 families determined Maratha policies. Among the most important families were the Bhonsle, Gaikwad, Holkar and Sindhia families, who were able to form their own domains of control on account of the continuing process of territorial expansion during the eighteenth century. At the same time, the *brahmans* influenced the political dealings of the time and soon came to occupy seats in the most important offices in the Council of Eight. The highest office was that of the *peshwa*, the first minister. Of note is Balaji Vishvanath who held this post from 1713 to 1720. During this time Vishvanath was able to obtain a *farman* from the Mughal in 1719 in which the Maratha realm was conceded *swarajya* (self-rule) as well as the right to collect the *chauth* (one-quarter of the harvest) and the *sardeshmukhi* (the king's share of revenue) in their territory. In addition, the *raja* (*chhatrapati*) of Satara sent a *wakil* as a permanent representative to the Mughal court. From this point onwards the position of the *peshwa* as the political leader of Maratha families remained virtually unchallenged.[28] However, the Maratha political system was not a confederation, as for this the *peshwa's* political alignment was too obvious, nor was it a centrally administered empire which had developed a single currency and a specific domain culture. Rather, it was a network of alliances in accordance with ethnic charisma that best characterised the Maratha political system which could be best described as a union.

During the following decades, territorial expansion to the areas of Malwa, Gujarat, Rajasthan, Hindustan, Bengal and Orissa intensified under the military leadership of the *peshwa* which was paralleled by the consolidation of the Maratha's governance.[29] The *peshwa* was ultimately able to enforce his claim to political leadership by summoning all of the heads of the Maratha families to a meeting amid the escalating threat of constitutional crisis following the death of *raja* Shahus (r. 1719–49). *Peshwa* Balaji Baji Rao, better known under that charismatic name of Nana Saheb (in office 1740–61) removed the Maratha administration from its seat in Satara to Pune where it remained until 1818. With this relocation all governmental power would henceforth first go through the *peshwa* whilst the *chhatrapati* simply became the ruler of the Maratha in title alone whilst holding no real authority. The Marathas proceeded with their territorial expansion; the only serious challenge to the Maratha Union and to the *peshwa* coming in 1761 in the aforementioned Battle of Panipat between the Maratha and the Afghans in northern India which demonstrated the momentary standoff of both expansionist forces.[30] However, Nana Saheb's successor, Madhav Rao (r. 1761–72) was quickly able to return to the expansive politics of the Maratha Union in the late 1760s.[31]

Starting at the end of the 1770s, a centrifugal movement within the Maratha Union began to gradually build following the open opposition to the *peshwa* led by Sindhia and Holkar, but was unsuccessful in binding the Maratha families together in a common cause. The Treaty of Salbai, signed in 1782 between the Maratha Union and the EIC, allowed British colonial power to enter into the conflict between Maratha and the southern Indian states of Haiderabad and Maisur for the first time. The British allied themselves with the *nizam* of Haiderabad and the most prominent Maratha family, the Sindhia, against Haider Ali of Maisur. The successfully led campaign brought notable territorial gains for the alliance during the following decades. In 1795, *peshwa* Ragunath Rao died without leaving an heir; the ensuing instability highlighted the self-serving interests of each of the Maratha families. The subsequent five-year civil war ultimately deeply weakened the Maratha Union. This was compounded by the deaths of a number of principal members of prominent Maratha families at the end of the eighteenth century, which, in turn, created an unstable military and political situation. It was a situation of disorientation that Richard Wellesley (1760–1842), Governor General of the EIC (in office 1798–1805), was able to use to the EIC's advantage. Wellesley had long been of the opinion that the British needed to strive for paramountcy over the

Indian states in order to secure their own hegemonic position in the subcontinent. Thus, with targeted individual, negotiated agreements, the British played the Maratha houses off against each other, thereby neutralising their powers.

Once Wellesley had raised the necessary capital by redirecting commercial investment from England totalling £2.5 million for military purposes, he was able to change his strategy from diplomacy among the Maratha Union to the aggressive politics of expansion.[32] In the first years of the nineteenth century, the British conquered both Sindhia and Bhonsle in a series of successful military campaigns, forcing both into large cessions of territory. The success on the part of the British lay not in military supremacy, but rather in their superior funding and their advanced sourcing of information.[33] A second war in 1817–18 allowed the British to dispose of the *peshwa* and annex his entire territory, thereby signalling the definitive end to the Maratha Union. In its place the British had risen to become the dominant power in the subcontinent and had succeeded in making their colonial-political ideal of paramountcy a reality.[34] The somewhat peaceful outer picture of their rule is, however, something of a misnomer as in many regions the British encountered immense difficulties impeding their execution of effective rule. Such difficulties are exemplified in the case of the Bhils in Khandesh and in Dang where the British were confronted with prolonged opposition during their entire colonial rule.[35]

Bengal (1713–1793)

The provinces of Bengal, Bihar and Orissa were among the first parts of the Mughal Empire to acquire autonomous status. At first, this autonomy was highly instable as Murshid Quli Khan, founder of the *nawab* dynasty in Bengal, was not able to permanently legitimise his rule. M.Q. Khan had been instated as *subadar* of Bengal by the Mughals in 1716 and appointed the administrative offices of the *nazim* and the *diwan* through which he became responsible for defence, criminal and civil justice as well as revenue collection. He succeeded in holding both the *nazim* and the *diwan* offices in personal union until his death in 1727. His successor, Shuja Khan (r. 1727–39) was able to institutionalise this personal union of offices and thereby introduced the territorialisation of Bengal. Despite this however, succession, and thus legitimacy of the ruler, continued to be subject to approval by the Mughals in Delhi. Invariably, the succession of the *nawab* was contested and Alivardi Khan (r. 1740–56) was forced to recruit his own army from Bihar to seize his rightful place on the throne in Bengal. His position was, however, only approved on the payment of an opulent *peshkash* to the Mughal. Admittedly, although such homages were paid, it did not prevent the Mughals then supporting other affluent pretenders to the throne.[36]

At first the *nawabs* of Bengal took over the administrative order of the Mughal Empire and appointed their own representatives (*naibs*) to the district level (*sarkar*). Similarly, they increasingly assigned their own military leaders (*faujdars*). The role of revenue administration was held by the so-called *mutaseddi* who held his office partly on a hereditary basis. The chancellor of revenue administration, the *rairayan*, monitored the receipts of the central revenue collection office (*khalsa*). Already by the middle of the eighteenth century, little of the Mughal's administrative structure remained in Bengal, Bihar and Orissa. In order to finance a new army composed of Pathan units from north India, the *nawabs* confiscated the Mughal's *jagirs* in Bengal and transferred them to the less lucrative peripheral areas in Bihar and Orissa. In doing so the *nawabs* managed to bring the productive Bengal *jagirs* to their disposal.[37]

Additionally, the *nawabs* reduced the regular transfer of revenue to the Mughals from that of ₹10 million during Murshid Quli Khan's reign to ₹4 million during Alivardi Khan's reign. The collection of revenue was also centralised by raising the dues of the *zamindars* (revenue contractors and holders of various titles with respect to land and people) to the basic levels of the new revenue appraisals in individual villages. In 1722, total revenue, consisting of land revenue, excises and extra duties (*abwabs* and *sair*) was calculated to amount to ₹33 million, by 1751 this had increased to ₹45 million, and in 1763, two years before the takeover of Bengal's *diwani* by the EIC, revenue was reported to be ₹63 million, equalling roughly £2.7 million. These set rates of revenue demand (*jama*) did not, however, correspond to the actual paid revenue (*hasil*) as loss of revenue was an omnipresent occurrence resulting from reluctance to pay, poor harvests, peasant migration, unrest and the effects of war.[38]

The rights to revenue collection were first auctioned to the highest bidding *zamindars* during the rule of Murshid Quli Khan. The *zamindars* were then responsible for the collection of revenues. Mir Qasim (r. 1760–63) intensified the whole system of revenue farming. After 1765, the British adopted this practice of revenue farming and continued to intensify it with the help of *naib* Muhammad Reza Khan (1717?-91), the finance minister of the still ruling, at least in title, *nawabs* until the enactment of the so-called Permanent Settlement in 1793. This finally ended the 70 year ongoing process of revenue centralisation. Whilst in 1728 six of the largest *zamindars* contributed one-third of the total revenue, in 1793 twelve paid some 55 per cent of the total. A small number of revenue contractors were welcome which significantly reduced the administrative expenditures as well as disputes regarding the payment or delay of revenues. The *zamindars* were simultaneously part of the newly promoted classes and were thereby aligned with Bengal's leading elites which also included merchants and trading families, among them the widely known Jagath Seths of Calcutta.[39]

It would have been impossible to have increased the revenues to such levels without an evaluation of the agricultural and commercial sectors. The evaluation allowed both areas of cultivation as well as agricultural productivity to be expanded; this was especially true for the fringes of the eastern delta where internal colonisation was encouraged.[40] From as early as the end of the seventeenth century, excesses in the production of rice had been exported to Pegu, Malaka and Lanka[41] and a closer look at the expansion of the textile industry not only effectively shows the importance of the Bengal export market highlighted in the increasing number of European trading companies active there, but also confirms the case for considerable economic growth. During the first half of the eighteenth century the number of spinners, dyers and weavers active in the textile industry grew from one million to five million in a total population of an estimated 20 million inhabitants.[42] A rise in prices for agricultural products as well as an increasing division of labour allowed for the commercialisation of the agricultural sector to continue to develop during the second half of the eighteenth century. A serious setback to these economic and social transformations came between 1769 and 1770 in the form of widespread droughts and an ensuing famine. In many districts in the west of Bengal up to one-third of the population died of malnutrition and its associated diseases. The inherent consequences of this humanitarian and economic catastrophe could still be felt in the first decade of the nineteenth century.[43]

After the EIC had exerted its economic influence among Bengal's wholesalers, bankers and the *rajas* of Bardwan, Midnapur, Nadia and Dinajpur, they were able to use this influence in the following decades to increase their political domination in Bengal. Unaccommodating *nawabs* dropped the British when convenient and allowed themselves to be awarded with new revenue collection rights and numerous tributes following the coronation of respective successors. After 1760, *nawab* Mir Qasim attempted to simultaneously eliminate the British influence from the northern part of Bengal and Bihar by withdrawing from the southern districts of Bardwan, Chittagong, Midnapur and the so-called 24 *Parganas* which had hitherto been signed over to the British, and also by relocating the seat of power from Murshidabad to Monghir in the northern interior. In order to ensure financial independency, Mir Qasim ordered an audit into the revenue administration in his remaining land and also instructed a recalculation of the land revenue assessment to be carried out which together resulted in a ₹3 million increase in revenue.[44]

At the same time Mir Qasim also led a comprehensive reform of the army including the appointment of the Armenian Gurgin Khan, a highly decorated and proven military tactician. In this new role Gurgin Khan disbanded almost 90,000 soldiers as the new army's organisation was to be rather supported by the capacity and abilities of the mounted units which numbered some 15,000 men, a 25,000-strong infantry and a newly formed artillery regiment. Furthermore, Khan used the newest European training methods to drill these newly recruited troops as well as arming them with weapons produced in Bengal.[45] Such a policy and attention to military detail soon yielded results as within just a few months the *zamindars* that had defected in the eastern and northern provinces had almost all been subdued, resulting in the relative rapid formation of a group of *zamindars* and *rajas* loyal to the *nawab*. Monghir soon developed into a fortified city and a number of troops began to be stationed in the border regions which allowed Mir Qasim to occupy a significant sphere of influence. This development worried the British who regarded the advanced armaments and the modernisation of the military's organisation as a serious threat to their, still unstable, position in the country.

This latent British suspicion came to a head in open aggression in 1763 among growing hostility between British and Bengal soldiers in Patna. Finally, the British overpowered Mir Qasim's still inexperienced soldiers who fled with Mir Qasim to neighbouring Awadh where he succeeded in forging an alliance against the EIC with the *nawab* of Awadh and Mughal Shah Alam II, yet the combined armies were defeated by the British in the aforementioned Battle of Baksar in 1764. However, Shah Alam II, once again and for the third time after 1758, offered the EIC the *diwani* for Bengal, Bihar and Orissa. Supposedly the Mughals hoped to receive regular revenue payment from a seemingly reliable trading company rather than from unreliable *nawabs* pursuing personal and dynastical ends. The headquarters of the EIC in Calcutta and London were still hesitant to react and shied away from such an administrative burden, only to accept the offer in 1765.[46]

British India (1757–1856)

From 1757, the British were able to intensify their colonial penetration of Bengal as the EIC successively signed over numerous revenue districts and eventually granted the *diwani* of Bengal, Bihar and Orissa in 1765. In the following years, poor commercial transactions, corruption and greed from their own employees – as well as the costly burden of stationing troops in Bengal and Madras – caused the leading EIC employees in India to pursue unauthorised action which aimed at further territorial expansion to increase the revenue income of the infant colonial state. Fears over security policies (both real and imagined), as in the cases of Maisur and the Maratha, led to armament and ultimately warfare. Among the military officers – the so-called "men on the spot" – career motivations were clearly exhibited in the readiness to become warmongers, whilst EIC administrative employees pursued their own economic interests, ultimately leading to the annexation of economically prosperous areas bordering British areas of control. Without doubt the EIC and its leading personnel initially had no "master plan" to act upon; however, as British power expanded, the idea of paramountcy eventually moulded military-political thinking and planning into this overarching concept from the 1790s onwards.[47]

Following a number of hair-raising financial and political machinations on the part of the EIC – particularly in India yet also in London – that almost brought it to the point of insolvency in 1771, the English parliament appointed various committees of enquiry. This measure resulted in the parliamentary control of the EIC which was implemented in 1772 with the appointment of a Governor-General along with his council as well as a supreme judge. In 1784, after another series of manipulations, alongside the Board of Directors of the EIC in London, a parliamentary controlling committee, the Board of Control, was formed, the chair of which was given to Henry Dundas (Viscount Melville 1742–1811) by the then Prime Minister William Pitt the Younger (1759–1806). From this point on Dundas was charged with determining the political interests of the EIC. The public control of the EIC was ensured in 1789 with the

"India Budget" and Dundas was responsible for annually introducing the colony's financial budget in the English Parliament. Such steps ultimately led to the integration of British-held Indian territories into the British Empire.[48]

Yet centralisation was not only a matter of parliamentary regulations. The EIC named their administrative "Presidencies" (Bombay, Madras and Calcutta) which worked independently of one another under the control of the supervisory board in London. By the end of the eighteenth century the Presidency in Bengal succeeded in bringing those in Madras and Bombay under its control. Further to the annexing of land, the EIC embedded itself into the Presidencies and created a level of provinces with a Lieutenant-Governor at the top of the hierarchy whilst also having vast effects on the district level. A Revenue Collector, as well as a District Magistrate in a number of cases, presided over each district. Both were powerful administrative officials who were often entrusted to make decisions based on their own discretion, this setting the basis of a paternalistic colonial regime which remained intact and unchanged until British governance came to an end in India in 1947. However, in order to distinguish the colonial regime until the Great Rebellion of 1857 and the dissolution of the EIC in 1858 from the Crown Colony or the British *Raj*, recent historical science terms the EIC rule in India between 1765 and 1858 as the "Company State".[49]

On account of the EIC's regulation of the *diwani* the British were able to exercise control over civil jurisdiction whilst the first Governor-General, Warren Hastings (in office 1773–85) also pushed for control over criminal jurisdiction. However, it was not until Hastings' successor Governor-General Charles Lord Cornwallis came to office (1786–93) that criminal justice and the death penalty were able to be integrated into the British-controlled judiciary. This change in policy followed wide-sweeping reforms in the area of justice, many of which had been initiated by Hastings himself. Additionally Cornwallis circulated regulations for pleadings, proceedings and filing of trials.[50] From the perspective of revenue policies, Cornwallis was able to implement the Permanent Settlement Act in 1793, thereby establishing permanently fixed land revenues in Bengal. The widespread legislative policies that Cornwallis implemented whilst in office have become known as the Cornwallis Code. The very fact that such, and so many, reforms were able to be successfully campaigned for and introduced lay, on the one hand, on Cornwallis' personal resolve, and on the other on the parliamentary backing he received from the President of the Board of Control, Henry Dundas, and Prime Minister William Pitt.[51]

Just as the *nawabs* had been confronted with numerous violent uprisings and protests against the fiscal and judicial alterations in Bengal, so too were the British in British India similarly challenged. The tension that this produced was felt especially on the periphery of the British territories where it became hardly possible to suppress the multitude of risings. Just as the *rajas* in Ghatsila, Bardwan and Mayurbhanj in western Bengal and their neighbours, the *zamindars*, the little kings also initiated embittered attempts to fend off the efforts of the colonial state to demarcate borders and settle revenues.[52] Between 1781 and 1783 a widespread rebellion broke out in Banaras *raj*, an area that the British had annexed from neighbouring Adwah in 1775, following the mobilisation of a number of little kings, *zamindars* and peasants alongside the *raja* against the British. Once the British lines of communication and transport links had been overthrown the British were forced to use brute force to overthrow the uproar.[53]

A simultaneous revolt also broke out in Awadh. In Gorakhpur district, with the backing of Warren Hastings' appointed British Colonel Alexander Hannay, revenues had been exacted following a regime of terror enacted by the British Indian soldiers. British communication links collapsed within just a few days of the start of the uprising, almost paralysing British activities. In contrast to the revolt in Banaras, the uprising in Gorakhpur was a success as Hannay was personally called by the Governor-General to withdraw from the conflict. Whilst the success of the Gorakhpur rebellion momentarily hindered further informal British territorial expansion into Awadh, both rebellions in Gorakhpur and Banaras showed how violently charged the open border between Awadh and Bengal had become on account of the destabilising British colonial policies. All too often this colonial policy was decided upon by the private interests of the "men on the spot" without regard for the wider political interests of the colonial regime, or the economic implications for the

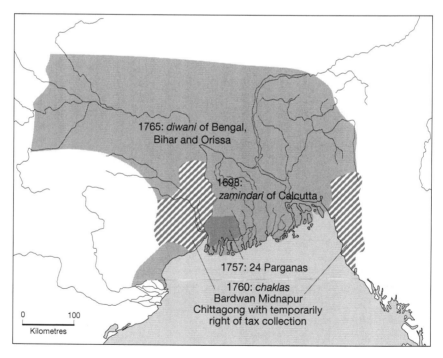

Map 1.2 Zones of rule and resistance in Bengal. Adapted from Michael Mann, *Bengalen im Umbruch: Die Herausbildung des britischen Kolonialstaates 1754–1793* (Franz Steiner Verlag: 2000), p. 82

EIC.[54] The potential for further revolt occupied British minds until the end of colonial rule. Meanwhile, however, effective British rule was barely felt beyond the Calcutta-Murshidabad region until the mid-nineteenth century.[55]

Resistance movements at that time, however, were not explicitly anti-colonial since apart from the rigid fiscal policies coupled with their accompanying jurisdiction and the increased commercialisation of the textile industry, the influences of colonial rule were not to be felt on a wide scale. Taken together, however, such effects undoubtedly led and contributed to the intensification of both the economic and social situation of the country and tension within its society. Resistance continued to resemble that of the peasants' rebellions of the seventeenth and eighteenth centuries led by the local *zamindars* in opposition to the Mughal *subadars* and the Bengal *nawabs*. The demands of these rebellions overwhelmingly called for a reinstatement of vested rights, the reduction in taxation and governmental support in times of need. Anti-colonial sentiment and resistance movements were first recognised during the rebellions and revolts starting in the mid-nineteenth century.[56]

Just as in Bengal and Banaras, so too were the same effects true of other regions of India where the British had annexed territory between 1765 and 1856 as uprisings and rebellions became an omnipresent accompaniment to British colonial rule. An example of such is the annexing of the little kingdom of Kerala on the Malabar Coast by the British at the end of the eighteenth century. The differing conceptions of sovereignty between the British and the Indians soon violently clashed, resulting in many years of fierce skirmishes. Basically the British were unable to integrate the Mappilla – in many cases converted Muslims, and in many instances descendants of Arabian immigrants – on the Malabar Coast into their system of control. During the entire nineteenth century the British were constantly challenged by socially and economically motivated uprisings, the most severe of which could only be suppressed with great effort on the part of the British in 1921.[57] The British were always wary of rebellions of discontented peasants or "tribal savages". Even the establishment of British paramountcy after 1818 did not obstruct the fact that on local levels at least, British rule was rarely noticeable, much less assured.

Despite the highly present and powerful colonial regime that the British managed to install on the subcontinent, it would be a serious oversight to omit that alongside the advancing territorial expansion and the formation of a centralised political system, the establishment of interior peace and effective governance of the country was only partially achieved. Pax Britannica, the blueprint for lasting peace suggested at the end of the Napoleonic wars in 1815 not only for India, but for the entire British Empire, was merely a political façade behind which liberal economic interests lay. On no account did British colonial practices become more peaceful following Pax Britannica's implementation; on the contrary, imperial goals were more aggressively sought than ever before. This was especially the case in India where the colonial regime was continually willing to resort to violence to quell both exterior and interior threats.[58] On account of interior resistance to the colonial regime a somewhat weak state prevailed which exerted and maintained power with its bayonet points rather than relying on the consensus of its citizens.[59]

Nevertheless the British succeeded in conquering large parts of the subcontinent during the last two decades of the eighteenth century. This success, in part, should be attributed to the changing alliances of the major powers found on the subcontinent as well as the increasing numbers of European and Indian troops which were accompanied by a growing civil administrative apparatus.[60] In 1816 the areas of Kumaon and Garwahl were annexed after a bloody two-year war with the Gorkhas followed by the ultimate defeat of the Maratha Union in 1818. Further annexations came after the war against Burma in 1826, leading to the annexing of Arakan and the coastal region of Tenasserium followed by Pegu ("Lower Burma") after the 1850–52 war. Moreover, Sind on the lower reaches of the Indus River was conquered and annexed in 1842, whilst after two successive wars (1845–6; 1848–9) against the Sikh Kingdom, the Panjab was finally seized in 1849.[61] This essentially completed the "western expansion" of the British in India, except for their disastrous continuing attempts of overpowering Afghanistan.[62]

British priorities changed to "internal expansion" once military external expansion at the fringes of their empire had reached its limits. One tool in implementing this change in policy was the use of a concept known as the Doctrine of Lapse, which limited the right of Hindu rulers to determine dynastic successors. This was especially used in the case of overriding Hindu laws concerning the succession of adoptive sons, with the result that numerous dynasties were deposed of, allowing their territory to be annexed by the British. A further tool utilised by the British in their goal of expansion was that of "mismanagement", whereby governments or monarchies adjudged by the EIC as corrupt could be sporadically or even definitively disbanded. By employing this method the British were able to achieve a row of annexations with that of Awadh in 1856 as the pinnacle. The ensuing uprising in 1857 is seen as a direct response to this kingdom's annexation and shows how brusquely the British had disregarded the still existing constitutional framework of the Mughal Empire.

Maisur (1760–1799)

The Wodeyar Kartars were able to establish their own dynasty in south India after 1610, acknowledging the still prevalent ritual power of the *rajas* of Vijayanagara which the latter still performed despite the loss of their political-cum-military power. Through marriages to the Kalale family, who obtained the office of the supreme military commander, the Kartars soon lost influence to the Kalales so that from the mid-eighteenth century the Kartars had become mere puppets of the Kalale family.[63] In 1760 a *coup d'état* failed due to the loyalty of the military commander Haider Ali (1722–82). He had gained strong influence as an army general during the south Indian war of succession in the 1740s and 1750s. Haider Ali exiled the Kalale family and put the Wodeyar Kartars under trusteeship. Eventually, the mid-eighteenth century saw a period that ushered in a new political military constellation of the subcontinent during which the French and British trading companies were able to directly influence the political skills of the princely houses.

For the first time in the history of the subcontinent, soldiers from both the French and British trading companies were hired out in large numbers on the request of the respective rulers and pretenders to the throne in Arcot and Haiderabad. On account of this action the governments of the two rival European powers succeeded in not only instrumentalising their respective trading companies in South Asia against their professed goals,[64] but also succeeded in broadening their political influence in the region. The Battle of Bobbili (Orissa) saw the defeat of the local ruler at the hands of the French in 1757. Local historiography documenting the event describes the battle to have been a "war of extermination" on account of the massive use of artillery by the French.[65] Following the Battle of Wandiwash in 1760, in which the French proved to be weaker tactically than the British and their allies, the French played no further military role in South Asia, an action that was sealed in the Peace of Paris in 1763 terminating the Seven Years' War in Europe.[66]

The Battle in Panipat in North India in 1761, which momentarily paralysed the Maratha's military forces in the south of the subcontinent, provided Haidar Ali with the opportunity to consolidate his hitherto unstable rule and to bring a number of *palayakarar*s and *nayak*s (little kings) under his control. The following year, Haider Ali achieved conclusive military victories over the powerful alliance of the *naizam* in Haiderabad, the *peshwa* in Pune and the British in Madras, allowing him to dictate the conditions of peace. It was under Haider Ali that Maisur recorded its first successful war of expansion.[67] Haider Ali died during the second Anglo-Maisur war (1780–84) and was succeeded by his son Tipu Sultan (1749/50–99), whose official titles were Fatih Ali Khan Tipu Sultan Bahadur, or Sultan Fateh Ali Khan Shahab, and who took over control of the army and the rule of Maisur in 1783. Tipu successfully ended the war against the *peshwa* and the British alliance by overpowering them in 1784.[68] As a result of this victory, the territory of Tipu Sultan comprised land nearing that of the former empire of Vijayanagara.

Alongside the military actions initiated by Haider Ali, reforms in revenue administration were continued by his successor, Tipu Sultan. This was reflected in the detailed rules for individual administrative units (*taluq*). Such reforms comprised land surveying and productivity reports. Concurrent to this exercise of surveying and reporting, the reforms also met the provisions of (re)settlement of disbanded soldiers as colonists and provided for the rudimentary social care for widows of servicemen, their orphans and handicapped veterans.[69] Furthermore, systematic financial support for sugar plantations was provided whilst general data concerning trade and industry were also collected to plan and aid future development.[70] The military-fiscal state, as it was seen in many parts of contemporary Europe at the time, found a clear counterpart in Tipu Sultan's state where all effort was made to modernise the country. For example, Tipu distinguished between the private coffers of the monarch and the public treasury. The same was true in the distinction made between civil and military administration. All of these measures served not only to increase the general wealth of the state, but also to finance future military actions.[71]

The most significant reforms, however, took place in the fields of commerce and trade. From 1786, Tipu Sultan maintained foreign trade exchanges with Maskat and a number of Armenian merchants, offering them attractive trading conditions such as low tariffs and low customs, the free movement of goods, the opportunity to form trading subsidiaries and the raising of credit. Between five and six ships began to annually circulate between Mangalore, Maskat and the Île de France (Mauritius) trading wheat, spices and arms.[72] Even the development of direct trade links and relations with China were pursued.[73] Such economic policies allowed Tipu Sultan to build the most modern army in India, characterised by a strict hierarchy of officers, a central authority, a regime of training, modern armaments and regular pay from the treasury.[74] Despite these huge advancements in the organisation of the military, Tipu Sultan lost the war against the newly formed alliance of *nizam*, *peshwa* and the British in 1792. It was a defeat that saw the annexation of almost half of his territory.

In no way dispirited by the defeat and its consequences, Tipu Sultan increased land revenue by 30 per cent and he also initiated an economic programme in 1793 and 1794 that established state monopolies. State subventions of approximately £130,000 served as investment support for foreign trade. In addition to this, 16 trade offices were established in India and one in Maskat, whereas Madras (EIC), Haiderabad and Arcot were explicitly excluded from these measures. In total, Tipu Sultan established 30 depots at different places from which *gomashtas* (trading agents) were able to organise trade and commerce. A general monopoly on pepper and sandalwood was enjoyed along the Malabar Coast whilst public manufacturers in Seringapatnam, Chitaldurg, Bengaluru and Bednur – which employed European, Indian and Chinese workers – produced, among other items, shears, knives, paper, textiles, sugar, arms and cannons. This industry increased general economic development as well as state revenue. In order to implement his mercantilist economic policies, Tipu Sultan established a trade council headed by nine officials whose role was to oversee both production and trade about which they would submit annual reports.[75]

Military conflicts, above all with the *nizam* of Haiderabad, were primarily based on Haider Ali's, and later Tipu Sultan's, dismissal of the *nizam*'s nominal sovereignty. After unsuccessful attempts to obtain a *farman* from Mughal Shah Alam II in Delhi for his autonomous rule, Tipu Sultan sent envoys to the Muslim rulers of Afghanistan, Iran and the Ottoman Empire in 1786. The mission to Sultan Abdul Hamid I (1725–89) in Istanbul was especially designed to secure an independent and separate legitimacy for his rule. The Sultan obviously complied with this appeal as from 1787 Tipu Sultan carried the official title of "Shadow of the highest merciful God, Tipu Sultan Padash

State formation and empire building, c. 1660–1800   41

Figure 1.2 Portrait of Tipu Sultan. © De Agostini Picture Library/The Bridgeman Art Library

Ghazi". Alongside the currency minted in his own style, which had been in circulation for a number of years from 1784, a new calendar was also created in which the reading of the Friday prayers (*khutba*) was carried out in Tipu Sultan's name.[76]

In a country in which the majority of the population was of Hindu faith or Muslim belief, a ruler like Tipu Sultan had to respect and equally support all religious groups to be explicitly legitimised as *padshah*, the supreme Muslim ruler. This, of course, did not rule out the fact that Tipu Sultan did not favour Muslim individuals and institutions. During official ceremonies and court receptions (*darbars*), Tipu Sultan appeared as the sovereign ruler, which, on the one hand, maintained traditional ritual; whilst on the other such court receptions were a clear demonstration that his style of rule was a clear break from that of the predecessor's regime. To this end he created his own symbol of rule using the well-known icons of the sun and the tiger. To these he added the *babri* stripes along with an abstract flame which further symbolised the sun and which became Tipu Sultan's signet adorning many buildings and textiles. Aside from this, Tipu Sultan often embarked on regular journeys across the country in the attempt to increase acceptance of the new dynasty. Tipu Sultan saw himself as a ruler who embodied the idea of universal authority whilst simultaneously uniting regional customs and practices of his monarchy to create a new form of governance.[77]

Tipu Sultan realised, like no other contemporary Indian ruler, the danger for India posed by the British, which led him to relentlessly attempt to forge alliances against the EIC. He also realised that without free access to the sea, it would be impossible to expand the important foreign trade links that were vital for the economy of his state. This perception led to protracted wars of expansion against both Malabar and Tranvancore. The armament and warfare involved in these conflicts not only weakened Maisur, but also the whole of the Karnataka region leading to catastrophic consequences for both the economy and the population of these regions by the mid-eighteenth century. The economic devastation forced entire regions of the country into poverty as the population was weakened by looting, the destruction of the infrastructure, failed harvests, famine and epidemics. Many of those affected attempted to flee the hardships by escaping to the coast, whilst those from the coastal areas fled in the opposite direction in the hope of finding food in the interior.

The lasting result of this protracted warfare was enormous demographic shifts and distortions. Some regions during the war of 1780–84 saw some 400,000 people emigrate, this equating to almost 40 per cent of the total population. The wars also caused targeted displacement and forced relocation; for example, Tipu Sultan allowed specific textile workers to be deported from the coastal areas into the highlands around Maisur. Peasants, many of whom were tenants, were relatively easy to resettle on the promise of entitlement to agricultural land holdings should they move.[78] Under the pretext of Tipu Sultan's raid on the neutral territory of Travancore, Governor-General Richard Wellesley instigated a campaign of destruction against Masiur in 1799, during the course of which Tipu Sultan's residential fortress in Seringapatnam was stormed and he was ultimately killed in this final battle. Subsequently, the British reinstated the Wodeyar dynasty which henceforth served as a puppet in British politics in South India.

Kota-Rajasthan (1707–1838)

From the end of the seventeenth century to the beginning of the nineteenth century, the little kingdom of Kota in Rajasthan with its shifting alliances and attempts of secession (*fitna*) of individual local potentates in "power plays" with their neighbouring states of Amber (Jaipur) and Rampura can be regarded as an example of the polycentric model of state formation in South Asia. At the same time, the example of Kota demonstrates the gradual transition and integration of a little kingdom into the British colonial state. However, this was no linear process in which the colonial regime can be seen as the sole agency. To the contrary, until well into the nineteenth century the actors in Kota were firmly in control of the country's trade and they also enjoyed a striking degree of autonomy following the integration of the state into the "formal empire" of the British. The *raja*, especially, profited from this new political constellation who had hitherto not known such a plenitude of power.[79]

The political landscape was shaped by *raja* Maharao Umed Singh (r. 1771–1819) and especially by his influential First Minister, *rajrama* Zalim Singh (1739–1824). Similar to the *peshwas* in the Maratha Union, the First Minister in Kota decreed the guiding principles of policies in administrative and military issues. Consequently, Zalim Singh, son of a long-established and influential Rajput family, gracefully took to his office without however infringing on the symbols of authority held by the *raja*. Nevertheless, shortly after taking office in 1770, Zalim Singh insisted that his own private living quarters be built within the premises of the royal palace which dominated the palace itself as well as the city. Even Zalim Singh's personal guards outnumbered that of Maharao Umed Singh's with 631 soldiers compared to 156 men for the *raja*. In the grand style of a little king, Zalim Singh began sponsoring the arts and distributing alms to priests and holy men and charitable institutions with the aim of raising his own reputation.[80]

Far-reaching land reforms, to which numerous *jagirs* fell victim, as well as the centralisation of the *khasla,* allowed Zalim Singh to develop his army to number a further 16,000 soldiers whilst the troops of the remaining *jagirdars* comprised some 7,000 men. Although the *jagirdars* were mostly composed of cavalry units and thereby among the most mobile military units available, the royal troops controlled the artillery, strategically the most important technology of war. Like many of his contemporary counterparts, Zalim Singh engaged the services of deserted European drill sergeants or recruited them directly from the European armies based in India, and even from other Indian princes. Favoured above all others were the European artillery officers who were skilled in this fairly new art of warfare. Soldiers from Pathans and Marathas also found their place within this newly organised army and belonged to the numerous roaming mercenary brigades whose commander had recruited them from the soldier markets of north India.[81]

Yet this army was by no means a "professional army" as it still lacked a clear structure of command among the composition of the various units and within the hierarchical ranks of the army. Nor did a systematic recruiting programme exist, with most of the soldiers being recruited directly through their troop commanders who often built their units up from within their own ethnic groups in order to be able to profit from the effects of personal contact and relation to the soldiers. A consequence of this was that often the soldiers showed more commitment and a stronger bond to their commanders than to the commander-in-chief. The appointment of French military officers from the mid-eighteenth century onwards introduced a hierarchical structure to the military organisation as they rearranged units and subunits into approximate equal sizes. The European officers also ensured that soldiers' uniforms were produced by centralised manufacturing workshops and that they were distinguishable according to the function of the given unit that wore them. Regular pay, as well as a state disability allowance and life insurance, made the occupation of military service an attractive prospect for many.[82]

With this newly created military body, Zalim Singh was able to lead constant wars of expansion into the region of Mewar in southeast Rajasthan in 1774, 1776, 1778, as well as almost annually between 1782 and 1791 and again between 1799 and 1805.[83] This new military strength exemplified in the successful expansion of territory could not however change the fact that Kota continued to be subject to the payment of tributes to the Maratha *peshwa* that had been in place since the 1730s. Within the Maratha Union, Kota had a privileged position on account of its economic strength so that during campaigns of expansion into north India the Maratha army enjoyed unrestricted food supplies, especially of grain. Such an agreement in turn caused Zalim Singh to levy systematic tolls and taxes through which he was able to increase state revenue five-fold between 1780 and 1804. Simultaneously, Zalim Singh began the internal colonisation of Kota. The settlement and cultivation of land, despite severe labour shortages, was achieved by offering potential peasants reduced revenue rates and other privileges.

By the end of the nineteenth century, British observers noted that virtually the entire area of arable land had been turned over to agriculture. Meanwhile a countrywide development programme had been initiated by Zalim Singh in order to further advance the agrarian economy. Small-scale irrigation systems based on both canals and water tanks became the backbone of the agricultural programme. Additionally successful experimentation with different crops and changes in ploughing techniques further promoted agriculture. Innovative cultivation techniques as well as the concentrated rearing of oxen for ploughing purposes were also promoted. Finally, agricultural exhibitions ensured the diffusion of knowledge and experience gained through this process of development which ultimately resulted in an agricultural boom and guaranteed the success of Kota's agriculture.[84]

As in other regions in India, so too in Rajasthan and especially in Kota the commercialisation of the economy can be read from the growing number of *qasbas* (local markets-cum-administrative centres).[85] According to contemporary observers, the inhabitants of such *qasbas* could well have amounted to one-fifth of the entire population. Towns became centres of trade and production, especially in the field of textile production and distribution. High-quality cotton textiles from Kota were renowned across the whole of South Asia and were even found to have been traded as far afield as Persia. Similarly, Kota's trade in grain, as mentioned before, was among the most important in the region. The *raja* of Kota belonged to the largest landowners whose land produced up to half of the grain surplus of the country, thus he became one of the main providers of grain to the *qasbas* and the small town markets (*ganjs* and *mandis*) as well as the small weekly village markets (*hats*).[86]

Raja Maharao Bhim Singh had called for the first land survey of the region in 1717. Zalim Singh ordered a new, systematic survey in 1792 in which every field, every village and every lot of land that had yet to be tilled or was not agriculturally useful was registered. Revenue rates were then calculated according to crops and other stipulations, and, as far as was possible, revenue rates were fixed in monetary units. Another administrative reform followed this survey in 1805, thereby further optimising revenues for the state. Zalim Singh abolished the established, hierarchical system of the Mughal administration and replaced it with a direct system for the payment of revenue rates in which a single village mayor (*patel*) was the sole person responsible for the collection and transfer of the revenue amount. With this structure in place and with the survey results of 1792 recorded, Zalim Singh ordered a further survey to be carried out in 1807 with the goal of standardising the revenue evaluation, resulting in a 12 per cent increase in revenue income. Aside from the fiscal successes of these administrative reforms, they also triggered social mobility and the formation of a new social strata composed of rich peasants and wealthy local businessmen.[87]

The position that Kota held as the most important grain market in Rajasthan was decisive in Zalim Singh's handlings with both the Maratha and the British as he was able to keep his almost 22,000-strong army neutral in the third British-Maratha war, 1817–18. As a "reward" for this neutrality, following the defeat of the Maratha the British allowed Kota to retain its autonomy despite being integrated into their "formal empire". Conflicts of succession and disputes surrounding the succession of Zalim Singh and *raja* Maharao gave the British the opportunity to smoothly and gradually involve themselves in the domestic concerns of Kota. Ultimately in 1838 Kota's territory was divided into two domains between the *raja* and the *rajrana*. Thanks to British regulation, *raja* Ram Singh (r. 1827–1866) exercised such extensive control over his *jagirdars* that his predecessors of the eighteenth century could only have dreamed of. On account of its principles of indirect control the colonial regime appeared to be more conservative than the regimes of either the Maratha or that of Kota.[88]

Awadh (1722–1856)

The land between Yamuna, Son and the Himalayas is the historical region of the Indian subcontinent that is richest in literal tradition. Awadh, derived from Ayodhya, the mythical birthplace of Rama and capital of the former Kosala Empire, became the focal point of the Ramayana epic. Ayodhya was also of historical significance for Indian Muslims, as it was here that according to the Quran Job and Seth are thought to be buried. In 1722, Mughal Muhammad Shah (r. 1719–48) appointed Saadat Khan (1680–1739) as *subadar* and *nawab* of the Provinz Awadh. Saadat Khan was an Iranian immigrant and like many of his fellow countrymen had enjoyed a rapid career through the services of the Mughal administration. In 1721, he had been appointed as *subadar* to the province of Agra, but was then transferred to that of Adwah.[89]

As early as 1723, Saadat Khan had obtained the Mughal's approval that his nephew, Safdar Jang, would succeed him as *nawab-wazir* of Awadh. Safdar Jang's marriage was emphatically supported by the Mughals, which contributed further to the legitimation of the new dynasty. Aside from this, in the following years Saadat Khan succeeded in extending Awadh's eastern border through the annexations of the *sarkars* of Banaras, Jaunpur, Ghazipur and Chumagarh. In 1736, Saadat Khan also annexed the *suba* of Allahabad to the southwest of Awadh. However, confederations with the *nizam* of Haiderbad and a spectacular military defeat at the hands of the Maratha prevented any further expansion to the north. Following this defeat, Awadh and Maratha entered into a bilateral agreement in which both sides would forego territorial and financial claims to one another's states which turned the hitherto open southern flank of Awadh into a stable border.[90]

In comparison to most of the newly formed states of the eighteenth century, the *nawabs* of Awadh largely continued the administrative systems of the Mughals, keeping it virtually untouched. Furthermore, the *nawabs* even continued to recruit personnel for the administrative system from the families of the Mughal elite whilst simultaneously also tethering the long-established elites to their person, providing them with additional rights for revenue collection. Saadat Khan later also gave important offices to members of his family, and in doing so was able to detract them from the influence exerted by the Mughals. A new self-image was formed among the members of this administrative elite, characterised by an intense loyalty to the ruler. Numerous visits paid by the prominent families of the state to the ruler, who often resided in the *qasbas*, further intensified the relationship between the administrative elite and the new dynasty. The strength and development of this identification with the dynasty was exemplified in the mid-eighteenth century as the Awadhi administrative elites refrained from taking office outside of Awadh. Indeed, at this time one can speak of a patriotic feeling among the Awadhi nobility and notables orientated towards the dynasty.[91]

Shuja ud Daulah (r. 1754–75) pursued the policies of expansion started by his predecessor Safdar Jang (1737–53). Thus, during Shuja ud Daulah's reign, Awadh not only obtained its largest territorial expansion, but also possessed the highest degree of autonomy in north India. Following the escape of Mir Qasim from Bengal in 1763, the *nawab* of Awadh was able to easily build impressive alliances with Mughal Shah Alam II, *raja* Balwant Singh of Banaras and numerous *zamindars* of the north Indian Ruhelas. These alliances collapsed, however, following the Battle of Baskar in 1764. In the Treaty of Allahabad concluded in 1765, Shuja ud Daulah had to accept payments to the EIC that strained his fiscal resources to such an extent that he was forced to seek further sources of finance. Such a source was offered in August 1773 as the *peshwa* was assassinated in Pune. Shuja ud Daulah at once seized the moment of current weakness in political leadership of the Marathas and annexed the central part of the Ganga-Yamuna Doab.[92]

In order to increase his military power and to ensure the success of his army, Shuja ud Daulah requested military help from the British for his territorial expansion into the northern areas of Rohikhand. The military reforms, including the replenishment of troops, as well as armament with modern artillery, came at a price, for which reason the lucrative revenue area of Rohikhand was first targeted in order to repay the debt of military development. Governor-General Warren Hastings, who himself was battling with immense financial issues with the EIC at this time, willingly took up Shuja ud Daulah's invitation of assistance. In the Treaty of Banaras concluded in 1773, Shuja ud Daulah agreed to station a brigade of some 8,000 British and Indian soldiers (*sipahi*, Engl. corruption: sepoy), along with extensive artillery, in his country. The maintenance of this military force amounted to approximately ₹210,000 per month, which was to be carried by the *nawab-wazir*. The same sum would also apply to every further brigade that was to be stationed.

The results of this agreement, from a British perspective, was, on the one hand, an easing of the maintenance costs of troops that had to be met by the EIC and, on the other, the intensification of British military influence in Awadh. In return, Shuja ud Daulah benefited from additional, well-trained units with which he was able to successfully occupy Rohikhand by 1774. The financial pressure that this subsidiary agreement placed on Awadh was, however, unforeseeable prior to its implementation. The British may well have overestimated the revenue potential of Awadh, yet they certainly wanted to extract as much money as possible to meet their own financial demands caused by constant warfare and economic strains.[93]

The Treaty of Allahabad also ensured free duty on trade for merchants of the EIC and its agents (*gomashtas*) in Awadh. This was a rather one-sided agreement which established asymmetrical economic relations. Soon, the *gomashtas* acted in Awadh as if they were eligible to separate (ex-territorial) legislation. Meanwhile, private British traders joined forces with French officers, who were in the service of the *nawab-wazir*, in order to build an independent market in Awadh. In order to prevent further economic strain, the supervisory board of the EIC in London deposed of duty-free trade in 1768, only to reinstate it three years later, this time without the *nawab-wazir's* involvement. Ultimately, uncontrolled transactions paralysed the labour market on account of the bottlenecks that it caused in the huge recruitment drive for labour in the expanding EIC factories, leaving labourers for the harvest in 1773 in scarce supply. Warren Hastings finally brought the rather uneconomic situation to an end by revoking the privileges enjoyed by British merchants as neither the EIC nor the *nawab-wazirs* were interested in such free transactions continuing as they were obviously damaging the economic climate.[94]

After Asaf ud Daula's death (r. 1775–98), the *masnad* (throne) of Awadh was succeeded by Shuja ud Daulah's widow, Sadr un-nisa Begam, who took over control of the government. She commanded sizeable personal financial assets which she had been able to amass over a ten-year period on account of the signing over of revenues on her husband's part and which she was able to now use to significantly influence political affairs in Awadh. Yet she was unable to prevent Asaf's newly appointed and overly ambitious ministers from dismissing and alienating large proportions of Awadh's nobility, sparking an exodus of leading military and administrative personnel just a few months following his accession to the throne. In order to eliminate his family's influence, especially that of his mother, Asaf relocated his residence from Faizabad to Lakhnau in 1775. This move did not, however, aid Asaf in stabilising the political situation in the country.[95] Such weaknesses in leadership gave the British the opportunity to urge the *nawab-wazir*, along with his First Minister, into the cession of the Banaras *raj* as well as the additional stationing of further *sipahi* units in Awadh.

Under pressure, Asaf agreed to these suggestions, with the deployment of EIC troops being the only option in safeguarding the northern borders of Awadh

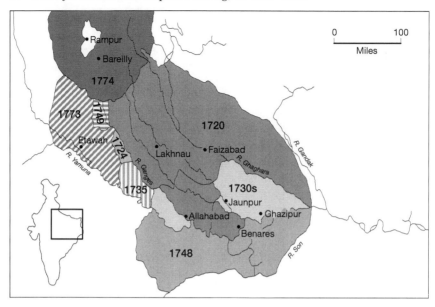

Map 1.3 Territorial expansion of Awadh between 1720 and 1775. Adapted from R. B. Barnett, *North India Between Empires* (University of California Press: 1980), p. 24

following the emigration of many of his own military officers. Territorial loss was compounded by the resulting reduction in revenue in the reduced territories, a situation that was to be exacerbated further by administrative incompetency on the part of the new and inexperienced personnel. On account of further subsidiary agreements, by the beginning of the nineteenth century Awadh's fiscal and political system became significantly undermined. In 1800, *nawab-wazir* Saadat Ali Khan (r. 1798–1814) was forced into additional subsidiary payments for the maintenance of the EIC troops in his service. Governor-General Wellesley took Saadat's statement that he was no longer able to honour his subsidiary agreements as cause to annex the lower districts of the Ganga-Yamuna Doab, all of Rohilkhand and the *sarkar*s of Gorakhpur and Basti in 1801. Allegedly measured in revenue yield, these districts were actually chosen for their economic and strategic use.[96]

The institution of the British Resident also contributed greatly to the political destabilisation of Awadh. Following the permanent representation (*vakil*) of an Indian ruler at the court of other friendly rulers and the establishment, for the first time, of official relations with the EIC by the *nawab* of Bengal in 1757, the British were able to develop the "residency system" into the perfect instrument of "indirect rule". In the Treaty of Allahabad the British explicitly demanded a Resident provided with special economic and political rights. Empowered in such a way, the Residents were able to quickly found a parallel jurisdiction within the country, and soon the Awadhis also profiteered from the economic connections with the EIC. The deposits alone made by the Awadh nobility to the EIC amounted to some ₹30 million in 1849, whilst annual salaries and pensions of the Awadhis employed in the services of the EIC added a further ₹5 million to the EIC coffers.[97]

The Residents' holding of court in Lakhnau with all its pomp, which was as a demonstration of their power, also had an effect on the urban population. In 1798, for the first time in Awadhi history, the British Resident took part in the election of Asaf ud Daulah's successor and helped ensure that Saadat Ali Khan, the favoured candidate of the EIC, was installed on the *masnad*. Finally, the British Resident allowed the royal ground to be bombarded by British artillery stationed in Lakhnau in 1837 until one of the EIC-sympathetic successors, Mohammad Ali Shah (1837–42), was enthroned.[98]

However, the British failed in their attempt to allow the *nawab-wazir* to be crowned as the sovereign ruler in India, thus replacing the Mughal in Delhi. Shortly before Ghazi al Din acceded to power in Awadh in 1814, the British openly summoned the most prominent Indian rulers of the Mughal Empire to disassociate themselves with their supreme sovereign. None of those approached enacted this request, except the *nizam* of Haiderabad who brusquely rejected the slanderous action. Three years later the British forced the *nawab-wazir* to declare his independence. However, Indian rulers never addressed the ruler of Awadh as "King of Awadh".[99] Despite, or rather because of the lack of legitimacy, Ghazi al Din also began minting his own coins after 1819, thus demonstrating his independent rule, although the process and production remained close to that of the Mughal tradition which demonstrates that the ruler of Awadh still viewed himself as bound to the Mughal. The remaining rulers continued to regard Ghazi al Din simply as the *nawab-wazir* of Awadh and with this the British intention of destabilising Mughal sovereignty had come to nothing.[100]

Despite rather narrow room for manoeuvre with regards to political and economic policies, Awadh was able to secure a leading role as a cultural centre on the Indian subcontinent at the end of the eighteenth century. As ruler in Faizabad, Safdar Jang did not embark on any major building projects there, preferring instead to concentrate his architectural activities on Delhi; his mausoleum there ranks among the most impressive examples of late Mughal architecture. In contrast, Asaf ud Daulah systematically built Lakhnau, a city already with large palatial grounds, into a cultural metropolis and seat of princely power. The Bara Imambara, which was begun in 1784, competed against the extensive store arcades of Charbagh and ushered in a new architectural style which became typical for the dynasty. Asaf's successor continued with these substantial building activities and completed a number of majestic projects such as the Jama Masjid, the Chota Imambara and Qaisarbagh until the mid-nineteenth century.[101]

Apart from these extensive building activities the *nawab-wazirs* also systematically sponsored the country's courtly literary scene. Of particular note is the development of poetry after Asaf's death in 1797. Within just a few decades

Figure 1.3 Safdar Jang's Tomb in Delhi. © Anders Blomqvist/Lonely Planet Images/Getty Images

Figure 1.4 Chota Imambara in Lakhnau. © Idris Ahmed/Alamy

the poets in Lakhnau departed from the established Indo-Persian style of the Mughal court in Delhi and developed their own style, making the literary language of Persianised Urdu an acceptable language in princely courts throughout North India as well as the Muslim court of Haiderabad. Added to that was the emerging art of storytelling, which remains a distinctive genre of Urdu literature today. In order to further the country's literary scene, the *nawab-wazirs* employed the most famous poets from the Mughal court, thereby underlining Lakhnau's importance at the centre of cultural development. The same development can also be witnessed in the support and funding of the scientific and academic institutions of the city. As was to be expected by such ambitious cultural projects, Awadh's state coffers were stretched considerably.[102]

From the beginning of the nineteenth century, the British had continuously complained of the ever-worsening fiscal and judicial administration in Awadh. When Governor-General James Dalhousie came to office in 1848 (where he remained until 1856), the somewhat conciliatory politics that had hitherto been employed began to change. With the EIC's budget in British India in an alarming deficit, Dalhousie was forced into action as he introduced a policy that led to the annexation of numerous states, the gained revenue of which was envisaged to consolidate the colonial state's budget. As seen above, such action was based on the British judgement of what they regarded as mismanagement in Awadh (as well as other Indian states), coupled with the assumed moral obligation to free the Indian population and subjects of such incapable rulers from the malaise of corrupt and ineffective administration. As alluded to throughout this chapter, the alleged mismanagement allowed the British to finally annex the rest of Awadh in 1856.[103]

Notes

1 Marshall 2003: 1–6; Husain I. 1994.
2 Alam and Subrahmanyam 1998: 1–71.
3 Cheema 2005.
4 Rothermund 1965.
5 Grewal J.S. 1990: 88–95; Gupta H.R. 1999: 64–7.
6 Banga 1997: 84–111.
7 Cf. Marshall 1987a: 76–95; Mann 2000a: 57–93.
8 Travers 2007.
9 Perlin 1985: 420–5; Bayly 1988: 7–44; Singh U. 2011.
10 Perlin 1985: 463, 475–6; Perlin 2003: 54–5; Washbrook 1988: 62–72.
11 Stein 1989a.
12 Cohn 1962: 312–20; Cohn 1987b: 483–99; Richard G. Fox in: Fox 1971; Dirks 1987; Gordon 2003.
13 Berkemer and Schnepel 2003: 17.
14 Wink 1986.
15 Berkemer and Schnepel 2003: 18–19; Richards J.F. 1998.
16 Doornbos and Kaviraj 1997; Stein 1985: 389–92; Washbrook 1988: 73–4.
17 Stein 1985: 392–408; Stein 1994: 6322–54
18 Perlin 1985: 477–79; Perlin 1983: 81–4 and Perlin 2003: 53–61, especially 55–6; Washbrook 1988: 76–95; Marshall 2003: 53–61.

19 Deyell and Frykenberg 1982: 1–25; Wink 1986: 237–8; Barnett 1987: 21–2.
20 Gordon 1998: 341.
21 Price 1996.
22 Wink 1986: 162–83.
23 Gordon 1993: 41–52, 59–65, 84–6; Guha S. 1999: 85–8.
24 Bayly S. 1999: 52–7; Dirks 1987: 37–8; Wink 1986: 36.
25 Gordon 1993: 87–9; Heesterman 1998: 13–40.
26 Heesterman 1998: 17.
27 Wink 1986: 238–50.
28 Ibid.: 47–51, 71
29 Gordon 1993: 128–29, 139–44; Gordon 1994: 23–63.
30 Gommans 1999: 54–66.
31 Wink 1986: 75–8, 85–152; Gordon 1993: 114–23, 146–8, 156–8.
32 Förster 1992: 119–256.
33 Cooper 2004.
34 Gordon 1993: 154–77.
35 Guha S. 1999: 108–21, 130–45; Hardiman 1994: 89–147; Skaria 1999: 153–297.
36 Marshall 1987a: 48–9.
37 Ibid.: 50–1.
38 Mann 2000a: 178.
39 McLane 1993: 37–42; Marshall 1987a: 55–60; Mann 2000a: 79–81, 358–74; Calkins 1970: 799–806; Little 1920: 111–200; Little 1921: 1–119.
40 Eaton 1993: 194–227.
41 Arasaratnam 1988: 531–49.
42 McLane 1993: 29–30; Chaudhuri K.N. 1978.
43 Datta R. 2000; Chaudhuri S. 1995; Chowdhury-Zilly 1982.
44 Marshall 1987a: 86.
45 Mann 2000a: 57–65, 72–3; Seth 1992: 383–416.
46 Ibid.: 73–4.
47 Förster 1992; Watson 1980; Alavi 2002.
48 Mann 2000a: 326–35; Marshall 2005: 207–28; Stern 2011.
49 Sikka 1984.
50 Derrett 1999: 225–91; Singha1998: 1–35; Mann 2000a: 201–12.
51 Travers 2007: 235–6; Singha 1998: 80–120; Mann 2000a: 341–50; Fisch 1983.
52 Sivaramakrishnan 1999: 34–120.
53 Mann 2000a: 226–59; Bryant 1986: 3–19; Kaviraj 1972.
54 Barnett 1987: 184–5, 200–3.
55 Yang 1989: 55–111.
56 Mann 2012b: 121–49.
57 Frenz 2000; Dale 1980.
58 Chamberlain 1988; Bayly 1989.
59 Guha R. 1997.
60 Europeans serving in "India": c. 1750: 3,000 soldiers and 500 civilians; c. 1830: 40,000 soldiers and 10,000 civilians; c. 1914: 80,000 soldiers and 100,000 civilians. Proportion of British and "Indian" troops 1794: 16,000–82,000; 1808: 24,500–154,000; 1857: 45,522–232,224, Omissi 1998: 133.
61 Heathcote 1995; Alavi 1995.
62 Blackburn 2008; Moreman 1998.
63 Satyanarayana 1996.
64 Mann 2010a: 99–126.
65 Narayana Rao, Shulman and Subrahmanyam 2001: 24–79.
66 Manning 1996: 195–220.
67 Sheik Ali 1963.
68 Sheik Ali 1982: 41–90; Sen, A. 1977: 71–4.

69 Kulkarni 2006a: 68–78.
70 Sheik Ali 2002: 3–22.
71 Bayly 2002: 66–83, esp. 74–6.
72 Risso 1986: 102–4, 147.
73 Sen, A. 1977: 81–3.
74 Gordon 2002: 171–2.
75 Sen, A. 1977: 83–92, 95–9.
76 Brittlebank 1997: 65–81; Qureshi 1999: 69–78; Kulkarni 2006a: 75.
77 Ibid.: 58–61, 97–9, 131–3.
78 Ahuja 1999: 130–45.
79 Peabody 2003.
80 Ibid.: 112–20, 132, 141.
81 Kolff 1990.
82 Peabody 2003: 136–9.
83 Ibid.: 120–5.
84 Ibid.: 131–2.
85 Bayly 1983: 189–93, 346–68.
86 Peabody 2003: 96–100.
87 Ibid.: 132–3.
88 Ibid.: 167.
89 Fisher 1987: 26–7; Mohan 1997: 32–4; Anwar 2001: 18–39; Athar Ali 1997: 14–37.
90 Alam 1986: 255–60, 270–7; Barnett 1987: 23–36.
91 Ibid.: 224–36; Fisher 1987: 31–2, 49–59; Bayly 1998: 1–35, esp. 20–6.
92 Barnett 1987: 42–66; Husain I. 1994: 160.
93 Barnett 1987: 90–5; Husain I. 1994: 148–67.
94 Barnett: 1987: 83–90; Marshall 1975: 465–82; Nightingale 1970.
95 Barnett 1987: 98–107.
96 Ibid.: 142–63, 223–38; Fisher 1987: 90–9; Jafri S.Z. 1998: 147–55.
97 Fisher 1987: 186.
98 Fisher 1981: 69–82; Fisher 1984: 393–482; Llewellyn-Jones 2001: 88–114; Mukhopadhyay 1990.
99 Fisher 1987: 117–59.
100 Ibid.: 133–5, illustrations 6 and 6a.
101 Llewellyn-Jones 2001: 167–96; Mohan 1997: 75–7. Sharar 2001: 79, 94–8.
102 Mohan 1997: 79–4; Fisher 1987: 41–3, 71–76; Sharar 2001: 76–102.
103 Fisher 1987: 234–38.

2 Patriotisms and nationalisms in the nineteenth and twentieth centuries

The middle of the nineteenth century represents a caesura in the history of the South Asian subcontinent. Following the Great Rebellion (1857–9), persistent military operations and an aggressive policy of annexation allowed the Company State to expand into further areas of the subcontinent; this was especially the case in present-day Myanmar (former Burma) and in northwestern India, the Panjab and Afghanistan. Political changes also accompanied the acquisition of the Company State by the British Crown as it then evolved into the British Raj. This ultimately brought with it a "traditionalisation" of society. Seen from a social perspective, such changes sparked a number of far-reaching social dislocations, as on the one hand the *brahmans*, recognised as scriptural elite, enjoyed a restoration of their former social-political influence under the colonial regime, whilst on the other peasants experienced the effects of increasing poverty and deprivation. The ruptured social edifice mirrored the dramatic transformations that were also underway in the economic sector, which had had varying degrees of influence in the different regions of the subcontinent.

The first half of the nineteenth century was marked by increasingly tense relations resulting from mixed economic and political developments, which the Company State was unable to solve, or rather did not take seriously enough to deem necessary of solving. Attempts at "modernising" society, the economy and the polity were undertaken according to European notions without regard for the actual situation found in South Asia. The Company State noticeably distanced itself from the political and constitutional framework of the Mughal Empire as it no longer observed the required ritual form of the established ceremonies (*darbar*), thereby compromising the sovereign, the Mughal, of the state. The Indian rulers, as well as the intelligentsia in the courts and in the seats of royal power, viewed this with both suspicion and disapproval. At the same time, the Indian subjects of the EIC became more suspicious of the British whilst, simultaneously, the EIC also increasingly alienated itself from the political fabric of the Mughal Empire. This led to a rebellion against foreign rule in 1857 which, at the same time, was also seen as a war of liberation targeted against the external regime and displayed glimpses of a developing local patriotism.

The political and economic caesura of the mid-nineteenth century is, however, not unique to South Asia. Europe, North America and East Asia all experienced significant political changes too, including revolutions and restoration producing what can be seen as substantial political transformations of the time. From a global perspective, the mid-nineteenth century was a turning-point in the economic as well as the political development of various world regions. Whilst until this time particular regions in Eastern China and Western Europe, for example, were indeed comparable in terms of their industrial development, the so-called "deep divide" between the industrialising "West" and other parts of the world began widening from the mid-nineteenth century.[1] In the first half of the twentieth century many regions of the world fell under European, American and Japanese colonial rule or hegemonic control. The colonies and dependent countries increasingly experienced economic exploitation with regard to raw materials exported and as a sales market for industrially manufactured goods that were imported. This asymmetric relationship was also decisive in Great Britain's relations with British India and Ceylon.

The Great Rebellion of 1857–9 and the end of the Mughal Empire did not mean, however, that there was no continuity between the Company State and the British Raj. On the contrary, many of the political and economic structures that were already in place in the Company State, including the Mughal Empire's revenue systems, were adopted and intensified during the British Raj. It was this systemic intensification of and, at the same time, political break with the Mughal regime that had far-reaching consequences which became decisive, not only for the British Raj, but also for its later successor states; namely India and Pakistan after 1947 and until 1977 when both states embarked on major political transformations. This *longue dureé* approach marks a clear departure from the established periodisation of South Asian history which may help in overcoming the conventional concept of the pre-colonial, colonial and post-colonial periods. Instead it stresses that long-term developments in political, economic, social and cultural fields also need to be taken into account.

The Great Rebellion (1857–9)

Without doubt, the Great Rebellion marks one of the most important caesuras in modern South Asian history. The British commentators of the time denoted the war as a "mutiny", more specially the mutiny of the *sipahi*, thus coining it the "Sepoy Mutiny". However, in doing so historiography reduces the war to a single aspect and thereby serves as justification for the brutal suppression of the uprising by the British. This label of "mutiny" can still be found in modern British historiography. In contrast, some Indian historians interpret the uprising of soldiers, traders and peasants as the first war of independence against the British imperial power. It was Vinayak Damodar Savarkar at the first anniversary of the rebellion in 1907 who demanded that Indian history be written by Indians, thereby turning historiography into a constructive duty for building the Indian Nation.² As a result, the Great Rebellion – as the uprising has meanwhile been termed by the majority of historians – is occasionally interpreted as the departure point for the freedom struggle of the Indian people and nation against the colonial regime, without considering the fact that at this point in history an Indian people, let alone an Indian nation, did not exist.³

However, it is possible to speak of a patriotic uprising against the foreign regime of the British which began to assume the characteristics of a war of liberation, similar to that in central and Eastern Europe from 1812–14 against Napoleon's regime of occupation. This war of liberation (*Befreiungskriege*) saw a revolt of large numbers of people from Austria, Prussia and numerous German states forming a patriotic movement, which German historians later took as the starting-point of the national movement in Germany. A similar process can also be observed in India.⁴ Patriotism, defined as pronounced love of the country, its culture and traditions as well as dynasties can be observed in many regions of the South Asian subcontinent from as early as the eighteenth century as exemplified in Awadh, Rajputana and especially in Maratha Desh. As shown in the previous chapter, the establishment of the *chhatrapati* kingship eventually led to an identification of the population with the ruling dynasty as well as the country. The effect of this was that it seemed to close the gap between the country and the ruler, producing something akin to a "fatherland": the *patria*.⁵

Patriotic identification seems to have been the case with the Timurid dynasty in 1857. The British were somewhat surprised at the outbreak of the revolt as they believed that their rule, which according to colonial rhetoric was based on "equality, liberty and good governance", was widely met with acceptance among the Indian population. They assumed that their politic of "material and moral improvement" was generally well regarded by the population.⁶ However, most "Hindustanis" interpreted this British politic more as a cultural, material and institutional penetration. Following the annexation of further parts of north India, including the British occupation of Delhi in the first years of the nineteenth century, the Mughal's territory had been reduced to the palace-fortress Lal Qila (Red Fort) in Delhi. On account of their increasing territorial expansions, the British came to find themselves in the then unrewarding situation of controlling the Mughal, but not possessing any sovereign power. The achievement of this was the stated aim of the British, which had led them to openly compromise the Mughal since the 1820s, thus challenging the dignity of his dynasty and, in the long run, the existence of the Mughal Empire.

In this threatening situation, it seemed that assistance would be offered by the Persian Shah. It was only the short war against Persia in 1856 and the then pro-British attitude of Afghanistan that hindered preventative action and the liberation of Delhi through Persian-Afghan forces. The annexation of Awadh that followed shortly thereafter through the British Indian army fused the simmering potential for discontent. Alongside the social-economic order, the political-cultural existence of the Mughal Empire, along with its traditions, seemed to be under serious threat. In 1857, "Hindustanis" from Delhi to Patna and beyond to Nagpur gathered to defend their supreme ruler. The *sipahis* opposed the British who, according to their understanding, were rebellious, to safeguard the political and moral order (*dharma* and *deen*) and to expel the "interferers".[7] It was in this historical moment that the *nawab-wazir* of Awadh waived all entitlements of a *padshah* (official title of the Mughal) in an act of patriotic loyalty to the Mughal.[8]

The outbreak of the Great Rebellion marked the culmination of a long line of local revolts which had become endemic in British India in the first half of the nineteenth century. Until well into the 1820s, *zamindars* and little kings of the Ganges Valley had been able to be pacified only after numerous British military expeditions. However, there were repeated riots in the towns and cities as grievances began to be voiced surrounding the introduction of new taxes and the lack of government price regulation and measures against the hoarding of grain in times of need which led to considerable social pressure and unrest.[9] Large uprisings such as the Santal Hul in Bihar in 1855–6 did not lead the British to reflect on the reasons for the unrest and link this to the probable defects of colonial rule, but rather led them to term the Santals a "criminal tribe", thereby justifying British actions as "counterinsurgency". It was this latter view of counterinsurgency that was presented in both the London and colonial press in Calcutta, determining the discourse on colonial rule in India and at home.[10]

The Santals were portrayed in a way similar to that of the "dacoits" of the 1770s and the "thags" of the 1820s. The "dacoits" had been seen as an organised gang that threatened an already tense social landscape following a famine in Bengal between 1769 and 1770, whilst the "thags" were identified as organised highway men that were becoming increasingly numerous in North India. Among the local population however, the "thags" had some backing and often operated in cooperation with the *zamindars* in the region around Agra. However, among the colonial administration, as in the Gothic literature that was soon to appear in Victorian England, the "thags" were simply reduced to groups of religious-ritualistic murderers and marauding bandits.[11] Taken together, both discursive constructions represent the successful attempt on the part of the colonial state to form an unofficial category which the colonial state's extraordinary power was then able to control. As these groups had been defined as enemies of the state, the British effectively implemented their new legal construct in pursuit of alleged subcontinental (i. e. international) operating criminal groups only to expand their control in the mid-nineteenth century, including "criminal tribes" elsewhere in the subcontinent and beyond.[12]

All three examples of such discursively invented and constructed criminal groups indicate that these constructions were largely based on misinterpretations and misunderstanding. Furthermore, the British also underestimated the growing potential of unease in the towns and the countryside during the 1850s as even serious warnings in the form of critical reports in local newspapers were not heeded.[13] The few, but intensive, points of contact between the representatives of the British power and the local population were in the areas of the administration of revenue and justice, which proved to be additional areas of friction and sparked growing unrest. This was further exacerbated by the colonial administration shortly before the outbreak of the Great Rebellion as huge cuts were made to the pay and pension entitlements of the Indian soldiers. This resulted in many *sipahi*s feeling threatened by a relegation of their social standing.

Much has been written about the background, causes and the reasons for the Great Rebellion. The leading narratives of this event have been the contemporary publications by Charles Ball, *The History of the Indian Mutiny* (1858); J.W. Kaye, *A History of the Sepoy War in India* (1864–76); and G.B. Malleson, who complemented Kaye's volumes of the subject in volumes 4–6 (1878–89). These works lay the foundations for an interpretation of the uprising as a "mutiny" and as a "conspiracy". The then colonial reporters also added to this one-sided, reductionist view of the "mutiny" in their journalistic presentation of events in British India in the British press. The "Kandy Rebellion" of 1848 and the aforementioned Santal Hal served as the harbinger of a style of reporting which reduced opposition in the colonies to criminal acts.[14] The same can also be seen in the years after 1857 as the media and literary presentation, in word and image, deeply implanted the "mutiny" as an abominable criminal act in the minds of the British in India and at home.[15]

The almost exclusive interpretation of the war as a mutiny of soldiers is based on a single incident in the barracks in Mirat (Meerut) where *sipahis* refused to follow the order to load their rifles. Resistance stemmed from a new design of ammunition that was introduced at the beginning of 1857. This new ammunition was stored in greased cartridges that had to be bitten open before the bullet could be loaded into the barrel. The soldier's refusal to load their weapons came from the cultural and religious notions of the Hindus and Muslims to avoid contact with any animal fat (Hindus) and especially pig fat (Muslims), which both assumed was contained in the greased packaging. In order to prove the innocuousness of the cartridges, the British planned to make an example of the cartridges in the Mirat barracks on 9 May 1857. According to the established "Mutiny" narrative, the selected regiment refused to obey the order to attend. The *sipahis* were then disarmed and arrested; a humiliating act for the proud Indian soldiers of the British Indian army. In the days following, the barracks in Mirat were set alight and the cantonment of the town was plundered by its shopkeepers, traders and the soldiers and all the British in the town were killed.

The interpretation of the Great Rebellion as a conspiracy was based on the assumption that the revolt in the barracks of Hindustan had been planned and coordinated; otherwise the area which it covered within such a short time would not have been explainable. Further fuel for the conspiracy thesis was to be found in the *chapatti,* pita breads, which had been discovered since the beginning of the year in villages in North India, which had been quickly distributed and were allegedly found to have contained secret symbols pertaining to the beginning of the rebellion. Furthermore, the Muslim elite was suspected of conspiring against British rule in order to restore the Mughal regime and thereby regain its past influence. The mounting "Mussulmanophobia" of 1857 allowed space for these sentiments of mistrust to develop. However, more than half of the contemporary British civilians in India did not perceive a conspiracy to be directed towards them. This sentiment of conspiracy was however dispersed and intensified by the British military, particularly its officers, who ensured that this interpretation of the situation became a constituent element of the British master narrative of British India's and British history.[16] Neither of the interpretations of the "cartridges" or the "conspiracy" truly describe and encompass the whole situation. Rather it seems to be a mixture of both fear and rumour that was finally able to determine the British perception of the precarious situation they had found themselves in.[17]

*Chapatti*s actually had been circulating since the beginning of 1857 in North India as they began to spread from central India following the outbreak of cholera which infected large parts of the country. In order to spread awareness of the virulent nature of the disease, *chapatti*s were distributed along many routes throughout central and northern India. This, however, had no link with the outbreak of the rebellion. The conspiracy thesis, therefore, cannot be upheld as it is rather speculative whether the outbreak of the rebellion in so many barracks in North India had been planned over a period of time. Furthermore, on closer examination, it is obvious that a certain lag time existed between the rebellion in one barrack and the uprising in the next. Instead of a conspiracy, it can be assumed that due to the increasing rumours, the British became more and more nervous and, ultimately, their fear of something mysterious going on became unbearable which in turn became the background for the conspiracy thesis.[18]

The reason for labelling the uprising as a "mutiny" can clearly be seen in the dispersion of the cartridges. However, in no way did all of the *sipahis* refuse to use them, as the case of the aforementioned regiment in Mirat demonstrates where, when the new cartridges were distributed, 85 of the 90 soldiers present refused to use the new munitions. The refusal to follow orders was less of an issue of religious belief, but rather that it was simply a single regiment of all of the troops stationed in Mirat that had been ordered to use the new ammunition. The *sipahis* felt as if they had been abused and vilified by this public demonstration. Added to this was the fear and the rumour that supposedly 2,000 fetters had been produced and were on their way to Mirat to put the *sipahis* in chains. This, coupled with the rumour that the 85 mutineers would be blown from the guns and that European troops were approaching Mirat, helped the violently charged environment escalate. The fear of death was barely containable and it induced the *sipahis* to set the barracks alight and to kill both British officers and civilians in the city and then to loot the bazaar.[19]

The revolts then quickly spread to the surrounding villages of Mirat as the peasants of the area joined the rebellion. On 11 May 1857 the rebels reached Delhi where chaos quickly broke out and which could only be ended after much difficulty in the course of the following weeks.[20] In Hindustan, the rebels, mostly peasants, systematically destroyed the revenue records kept in the district headquarters. Similarly, the rebels also systematically stormed the houses of the *bania* and *mahajan*, local traders and money-lenders, and destroyed the documents related to credits. In both the cities as well as in the countryside, the uprising brought with it numerous cases of looting after the British were forced to leave.[21] The printing houses were also the main targets for destruction as they, among others, produced the Christian missionary literature.[22] Within just a few weeks the whole of Hindustan was in a state of rebellion and British rule was no longer discernable.[23] The destruction and interruption of the communication lines also aided the rebels' cause as the British were unable to quickly consolidate their communication links, parts of which were dependent on the telegraph, whilst the rebels, in contrast, were able to mobilise their highly efficient *harkara* (runner) system, which over time allowed them to secure an edge in information dispersion.[24]

In many towns and cities in Hindustan councils soon formed in the days and weeks following the outbreak of the uprising which included the old legal experts and administrative elites as well as committees of the *mohallas*.[25] In

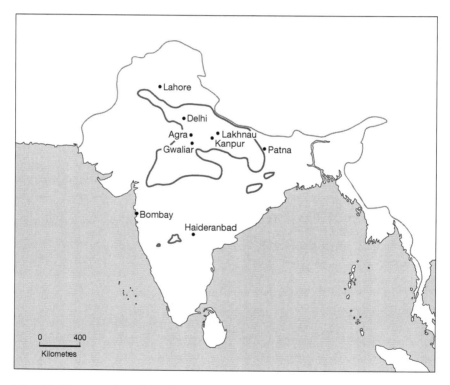

Map 2.1 The expansion of the Great Rebellion in British India 1857–9. Adapted from Gordon Johnson, *Cultural Atlas of India: India, Pakistan, Nepal, Bhutan, Bangladesh and Sri Lanka* (Andromeda Books: 1996)

Delhi too, a government was formed under Mughal Bahadur Shah II (r. 1837–58).[26] On 25 August 1857, the government in Bahadur Shah II's name issued a proclamation in which the grievances of all the social strata were henceforth to be addressed, including the *zamindars*, the traders, the craftsmen and the intelligentsia as well as the civilians and military personnel employed in the service of the British.[27] This proclamation goes some way in explaining how the rebellion soon flowed over into a war that affected all levels of society.[28] Across the entire society new alliances were forged and old ones reactivated as in some instances Adivasi societies, peasants and *rajas* joined and acted against the British.[29] In Lakhnau, the war was not only supported by many of the dignitaries and merchants, but entire city quarters rose up in support of the rebellion. Of particular note was the resistance of the socially highly esteemed courtesans (*tawa'if*) in Qaisarbagh who offered financial support to the rebels.[30] The high degree of solidarity among sections of the population had traits of a patriotic movement and allowed the rebellion to truly adopt the guise of a liberation movement, if only for a short time and in a very few places.

It took months for the British to bring the situation in Hindustan under control again. On the one hand the British succeeded in this by bringing supplementary troops to the Asian subcontinent by the end of the year, following the conclusion of the Crimean War (1853–6) which freed these troops and allowed the British to develop their tactics from a defensive stance to one of counterinsurgency. On the other hand, the British were able to take advantage of the heterogenic nature of the rebellion. It lacked any homogeneous policy of central leadership which meant that the provision and replenishment of munitions and financial capital was insufficient to outlast the defence shown by the British. This lack of central strategy often made it easy for the British to overpower individual "peasant gangs", "batches of soldiers" as well as rebel armies. Additionally, the Sikhs in the Panjab remained loyal to the British and their integration into the British Indian army following the annexation of the Sikh kingdom in 1849 proved to be an invaluable advantage in suppressing the rebellion. The Sikhs, as highly motivated soldiers, helped in storming Delhi in September 1857 and thereby helped usher in the turning-point in the war.[31]

The suppression of the rebellion was followed by brutal revenge enacted by the British which soon escalated into a spiral of violence.[32] The violence often took the form of summary executions of the men of entire villages as they were found guilty (either proven or alleged) of having supported the rebellion, or they were simply in the wrong place at the wrong time. Villages on the road between Kanpur and Allahabad were systematically burnt and almost the entire male population was either hanged or shot. In Lakhnau and Delhi, entire quarters of the city were demolished, allegedly to create safety cordons, but actually to decimate the houses and the number of inhabitants and to reorganise the city.[33] Plans existed for Delhi that once the looting of the city had been halted, the city would be razed to the ground and historical-cultural sites such as the Jama Masjid would be replaced by a cathedral. However, on account of the huge costs and efforts involved in such a project, this plan was soon sidelined.[34]

The brutal violence and the merciless atrocities of the British in the aftermath of the rebellion paralleled the suppression of the slave uprising in the Caribbean in the first decades of the nineteenth century, where pardons were also absent. Indeed, the Afro-Jamaican uprising of 1865–6, initiated by the fear of a new wave of enslavement, was also suppressed in a shockingly brutal manner.[35] A British contemporary wrote in his diary in 1858 that for Kanpur the situation was, at its most simple, about the uprising in India of "black men who had dared shed the blood of their masters".[36] It seems to be likely that this commentator had been influenced by the circumstances and conditions of the slave masters in the Caribbean that had reigned until only recently. In a final act of retaliation, a British officer shot Bahadur Shah II's sons in cold blood. Following this, the British mounted the world's first trial of treason against a head of state after which the last Mughal in Burmese Yangon (Rangoon), which had been a British colony since 1852, was deported.[37]

Whilst the rebellion was not only intensely reported in the Indian and British press,[38] in the continental European press it became a journalistic debate in which the justness or unjustness of the British rule in India was called into question. Furthermore, "1857" also became a literary subject.[39] The atrocities of the British handling of events after the suppression of the rebellion shocked readers in Great Britain. Rather than being a just retribution of treacherous and heinous Indian soldiers betraying their loving masters, it was the sheer brutality of a revenge which cast doubts on Victorian values in contemporary British public opinion. Soon society was torn between retributive justice and what was regarded as modern (British-European) civic values of the time. Likewise, for a brief period the "Mutiny" questioned Muslim fanaticism contrasting it with Evangelical fanaticism which let Satan loose during the rebellion. Cruelties on the Indian side and mercilessness on the British side pushed the war beyond humanity, leaving behind, at least for some time, a traumatised British public.[40] After the Crimean War, the Great Rebellion was the second war of the nineteenth century to have been detailed so heavily and keenly debated in the press. Within just a few years the British press was opening the eyes of the British public to the cruelty of the wars. The aforementioned brutal suppression of the Afro-Jamaican uprising of 1865–6 caused huge political and public waves which brought into question the legitimacy of colonial rule.[41]

The Great Rebellion was, without doubt, a restorative uprising against the British colonial regime. It succeeded in being simultaneously motivated by patriotism whilst also, if only partly and for a short time, unifying the different social strata and various circles into a common cause for the continuation of the Mughal Empire. Admittedly, one of the main causes in the collapse of the rebellion was the lack of a concept and vision of how this reinstated Mughal Empire should have been composed. A re-erection of the Empire to the times of Akbar and Shah Jahan at the end of the sixteenth century to the mid-seventeenth century was no longer realistic, whilst a confederated realm, as had evolved in 1720, could have been achievable. For the British, the Great

Rebellion with the "Cawnpore Massacre", in which all the European inhabitants of the city were killed contrary to the promise of being spared by the rebels, as well as the military suppression of the "Mutiny" established a culture of remembrance (and historiography) that continues to determine British national consciousness.

In many regions, such as in Bundelkhand, colonial-political order still had not been reinstalled until well into the 1860s.[42] The British attempted to establish an effective jurisdiction which would document their just and, most importantly, legitimate rule. To this end, the trial of high treason against the Mughal was used to demonstrate their ambitious aims. Furthermore, judicial reforms, as they had been considered since the 1830s, were prepared, enacted and implemented. The new forms of the penal system should also be seen in this context. A penal colony was established on the Andaman Islands to create a regime of colonial discipline; its first prisoners were convicts of the "Mutiny" trials.[43] More than ever before, surveillance, monitoring, policing and punishment served to legitimise British rule in India and became an integral part of the colonial regime during the following decades as the civilising mission became ever more differentiated and the sole justification and legitimisation for colonial rule.[44]

National movements (1860–1947)

Early debates on political and social reforms

Following the brutal suppression of the Great Rebellion, it seemed that the social and religious movements calling for reform had, for the time being at least, been halted. One such movement had occurred at the beginning of the nineteenth century and had been initiated by Ram Mohan Roy (1772–1833), and was eventually formed into the Brahmo Samaj in 1828.[45] However, calls for reform never fell completely silent, even if these calls were only ever actually heard in the circles of the elite and that their socio-political relevance was, at first, slight.[46] Indeed, in educated Muslim circles (*ulama*), the debates calling for reform experienced a setback after many of them had been dismissed from their privileged positions in the EIC's colonial administration after 1857. However, their debates did not completely come to a halt. In fact reform circles continued to operate and develop. Among the old and newly established groups, a huge network of organisations and people came into being that attempted to introduce social reforms and a cultural renewal. Throughout the following decades, these movements became more nationalistic in their aim.[47]

From the mid-nineteenth century, the members of the emerging Hindu elite were engaged in debates concerning the future of the "Indian" territorial state. Externally, this was defined by the existing borders of British India as the colonial space offered the foundations for the re-territorialisation of the Mughal Empire as a Hindu state. The land (*desh*) increasingly came to be understood as a static unity and less as a geographical mass. The north Indian-Brahminic concept of *bharat* (see Introduction) simultaneously led to the transformation of the entire cultural space of the Hindus. The same was also true of Hindustan which, until then, was only referred to as northern India, from which this Hindu cultural space suddenly spread to the rest of the subcontinent, thereby demarcating the colonial space as a Hindu space. A prolonged discourse during the 1860s and 1870s bore the idea of an Indian national state prefixed by "Hindu" whose origin could be traced back to ancient *bharat* and its people, the *Arya*. Thus, the future of the Hindu-Indian national state needed merely to evoke memories of these ancestral roots in order to justify the merits of an allegedly already existing nation. Such a discourse increasingly ostracised Muslims as well as the British as foreigners in the country.[48]

From this national movement, which it became in the 1880s, the Hindu-nationalistic approach became just as hard to ignore as the religious-social reform currents stemming from it. Indeed, one can also speak of institutional, as well as personnel, continuity despite the socio-political reforms around the caesura of 1857. Nevertheless, the first sign of real political will leading towards the all-India national movement can be first observed in the 1870s. This development can be divided into four phases: first, the embryonic formative stage between 1870 and 1919 which focused mostly on political participation; second, the radicalisation stage between 1920 and 1930 as widespread population strata were conceived; third, the phase between 1930 and 1946 which was marked by debates surrounding the form of British India's future constitution, political representation and the transformation of the Indian political landscape dominated by the Indian National Congress (INC) and the Muslim League in 1945; and fourth, the period between 1945 and 1947 which saw both the existing British Raj and the imagined Indian Nation collapse.

First phase: organising national movements

The fundamental characteristic of the political movement in the 1870s was the partially new personnel, which had been trained in the British educational institutions and now, fed by Western liberal ideology, wanted to be involved in the development of public policy in British India. A significant point in these early political movements was that few organisations specifically pursued an all-India concept. The question of what and who would constitute the "Indian Nation" surfaced first in the 1890s. This, of course, does not exclude the fact that options were already being debated as to how to ensure that organised Hinduism could operate not only within the social framework of the reforms, but also on the political stage. Therefore it was necessary to form an appropriate Hindu organisation. Like the colonial space the colonial form of organisation served as a template from which a number of political organisations originated in the 1870s, which were perceived by the colonial power as a representative body.[49]

As early as 1849 Prarthana Samaj in Bombay had been founded by Ram Balkrishna Jaykar as a West Indian counterpart to the Bengal Brahmo Samaj.

The Maratha judge Mahadev Govind Ranade (1842–1901) founded the Poona Sarvajanik Sabha in 1870 whilst Dayanand Saraswati (1824–83) founded the Arya Samaj in 1875 in Bombay which was followed in 1876 by the foundation of the Calcutta Indian Association by Surendranath Banerji (1848–1925). What was striking, however, was the regionally confined focus of these political organisations which rather favoured a Maratha or Bengal nationalist stance or the prescription of social-religious reforms than following an "all-India" cause.[50] A further striking factor was that many of the reform movements took on the form of one or another of the set of criteria extolled by the British with regard to the alleged social defects of Hinduism specifically, and of the Indian society more generally. This was mainly the case in the abandonment of caste, abolition of untouchability, widow remarriage, female education and the abolition of child marriage.[51]

Under these newly formed organisations, the Sarvajanik Sabha soon attracted attention on account of its distinctive method of representation. In order to become a member each candidate was required to hold a letter of representation signed by 50 men from Pune and the surrounding districts, who had appointed the candidate as their spokesman in the dealings with the Sarvajanik Sabha. This criterion meant that the political organisation had a tangible representative basis, albeit with a rather limited social and geographical context. By 1871 the Sarvajanik Sabha represented some 17,000 citizens of Pune. The British government in Bombay observed this form of direct representation in political organisation with some mistrust. According to the sentiments published in the Indian-English newspaper *The Englishman*, the colonial government was not prepared, and therefore not willing to give room for such a kind of popular representation in which the representative body would exercise a power incompatible with the existing system of administration. Subsequently the danger that emanated from the principles of representation was of a kind of "premature democracy" which fundamentally questioned the autocratic British Indian regime.[52]

Despite this premature representative development, or rather because of it, the political climate in British India began to change for the worse during the tenure of Governor-General Lord Lytton (1876–80). Lytton fostered a growing sentiment of dissatisfaction among a growing number of Indians on account of the war he had led against Afghanistan (1878–80) and the high price this had in Indian soldiers' lives. He raised further fury with his Vernacular Press Act in 1878 which placed the Indian press in British India under tightened censorship in order to supress further seditious statements against the regime, whilst the British press was free from such censorship constraints. The successful agitation of indignant Britons against the so-called Ilbert Bill (1883–4), which would have subjected them to the sentences of Indian judges, ultimately provided the decisive thrust for a campaign demanding an India for Indians.[53] One year later, in 1885, the INC was founded in Bombay.

However, the Indian Association, the Calcutta-sponsored organisation that represented the educated middle-class community of Bengal and which held its second national conference in Calcutta in the same year, soon became more popular than the INC, i.e. Congress.[54] The cause for Congress's growing acceptance was the educational background of its founding members and its leaders who almost entirely belonged to the British acculturated Indian intelligentsia and with this to an urban elite that was naturally orientated to British India as a whole.[55] This widespread support is the reason why Congress met annually in different cities and in doing so was able to spatially cover all of British India and represent the British Indian society, at least its elite, both personally and politically. However, it must be noted that on account of the mushrooming of numerous political organisations, Congress, according to contemporary Indian politicians' opinion, did not represent a so-called political India.[56] The construction of such a political India, let alone an Indian nation, was still to be forged.

By contrast, the British saw in Congress something of an all-India organisation that served as a particularly liberal-bourgeoisie assembly of notabilities until Congress's radicalisation following the First World War. Indeed, Congress was primarily interested in responsible cooperation rather than revolutionary change. This stance can be clearly seen in the resolutions of questions of administration, education and economics. In this first phase, Congress had an almost in-system stabilising function which questioned neither the power, nor presence of the colonial state.[57] Although the resulting Indian nationalism was formed in line with European ideologies, Indian politicians did not adapt or simply imitate the concepts of nationalism which had evolved in the course of the nineteenth century in the European states. Rather, Indian politicians repeated a proto-nationalism that was regionally orientated.[58]

An illustrative example of this is that of Maharashtra and the extent to which the population identified with their country. In a speech made by the aforementioned M.G. Ranade in Marathi at the beginning of the 1870s, which was directed at the people of the region who had been severely affected by drought, famine and emaciation, Ranade offended not only the British, but also many of the educated Indians who regarded English as the sole language of political communication. In addition, religious festivals taking place at the turn of the century were transformed into political demonstrations and generated an intensified Hindu-Indian awareness in the rural regions of Maharashtra and beyond. At the same time, Hindu-Maharashtrian history writing transformed regional heroes, such as Shivaji, into Indian national heroes by placing them at the core of a future Indian nation.[59] The consequence of old patriotic and pseudo-religious traditions increased the acceptance and the speed of the spread of a national ideology and constituted a specific Indian variant of nationalism.[60]

The process of nationalisation can be explained using the case of political radicalisation of Arya Samaj between 1880 and 1925.[61] The organisation targeted the anxious Hindu middle-class intelligentsia and promoted the restoration of the self-image as well as the integrity of the Hindus. To this end, Hinduism was to be fundamentally reformed, one may also claim formed in the first place, and it was to be constructed in sharp distinction to missionary Protestantism.[62] On the scriptural basis of the Veda, the *dharma* of the ancient Aryan civilisation was to be restored and all later additions and elements of corruption were to be eliminated. However, these elements were more or less identical with what Christian missionaries and British administrators regarded as "evils of Hinduism". The Arya Samaj harshly criticised the arbitrariness of the *pandits* and the Brahmanic concept of the *avatar* (reincarnation) as well as *varna vyavastha* (the alleged "caste system" of the Vedic society). In order to disseminate their message the Samajis copied British methods of fundraising alongside the traditional instruments such as disputation and devotional songs. Furthermore, they also built a network of sub-organisations, *mandirs* ("temples"), educational institutions supported by well-trained teachers as well as newspapers in the Hindi-speaking region of North India.[63]

Consequently, the aim of the reform was a concise and purified "Hinduism". Outspoken opponents were the Christian missionaries, whilst the demarcation of the Muslims was initially of secondary importance. This changed in the 1880s as *brahman* "counter reformatory" organisations were formed and the Arya Samaj declared itself as a qualified "watchdog" of a true Hinduism in parts of India, now seeking open and public confrontation with the Muslims. The situation ultimately escalated as a prominent Arya Samaj preacher was murdered by a Muslim in 1897. This "martyrdom" bestowed much sympathy on the Arya Samaj and also meant that from that point on an anti-Islamic sentiment was a constant feature of the Arya Samaj policy. With this in mind, the *shuddhi*-campaign was introduced which was concerned with the reintegration of former Hindus into the Hindu community. Originally conceived as a purifying ceremony for *brahmans*, it soon changed to a movement against Christians and their conversion of untouchables and *dalits* as well as being openly against Muslims in British India after 1899 who were now seen as converted Hindus.[64]

The ideologues of the Arya Samaj constructed a so-called inferiority complex of the majority, meaning that the majority of the population – in this case the "Hindus" – were threatened by a steadily growing number of "Muslims". Sooner or later the "Muslims" would, therefore, turn the "Hindus" into a minority in what they regarded as their own country. This inferiority complex became one of the striking features of political Hinduism in the twentieth century.[65] The more the Hindu ideology of the Arya Samaj found support, especially among the "Hindu" middle class, the more it alienated the Muslims. Admittedly, just as in the cow protection movement which had been restricted to a number of north Indian cities and principalities and had been a rather more vertically orientated elite-Brahmanism concern than a horizontal, egalitarian movement, the *shuddhi* campaign failed to prove itself as a suitable instrument to strengthen the reportedly threatened Hindu community over a longer period of time.[66] In contrast to the religiously motivated civilising mission of the Arya Samaj, the Hindu Mahasabha (founded 1915) and the Rashtriya Swayamsevak Sangh (RSS, founded 1925) were purely political organisations of the developing and viable cultural Hindu nationalism.[67]

This Hindu nationalism increasingly came to define itself along the ideology of an imagined or constructed constituency and less as a homogeneous community of Hindus that represented a nation. This was based on an assumed shared culture, a culture which was configured by a particular notion of Hinduism. It was an ideology that was largely developed by middle-class, urban-based Indians. Against this backdrop of an emerging "national orientation", political positions began to radicalise in British India at the beginning of the twentieth century. The racist, confrontational politics of Viceroy Nathaniel Curzon (in office 1899–1905) significantly contributed to this polarisation. His political legacy was that of the division of Bengal in 1905, which was carried out on alleged administrative grounds.[68] However, the demarcation of borders was based on the respective majorities of Hindus as well as Muslims. The result of this was that in the new province of West Bengal and Bihar the Bengalis became a minority to the Biharis and Orias, whilst in the new province of East Bengal and Assam the Hindu Bengalis became a minority to the Muslims. Ultimately the division manifested itself in demonstrations, political agitation (such as the *swadeshi* movement which called for a Bengal-wide boycott on foreign textiles and increased local production) and an increasing number of terror attacks against representatives of the colonial state.[69] Solidarity campaigns outside of Bengal and intensive media coverage in Bengal and other Indian press organs contributed to the first sentiments of an imaginable Indian nation.[70]

This open support by the colonial state in favour of the Muslims, at least in the eyes of the north Indian, urban Hindu middle class, which came with the division of Bengal, triggered the Hindus' demand for further action. This manifested itself in 1906 in the foundation of numerous organisations and *sabhas* (assemblies) in the course of the so-called *sangathan* movement. It was the aim of the *sabhas* to protect the interests of the Hindus whereby the sentiments of self-respect and self-worth were first to be strengthened whilst mutual cooperation was also to be facilitated. However, the aggressive campaigns of Arya Samaj in the Panjab in 1907 contributed to turning the existing communal fissures into widening social gaps. For their part, the Muslims felt increasingly threatened, which led to the sentiment of a threatened community, thereby forcing them to band closer and tighter together. Communalism is a kind of discursive framework that streamlines the social, cultural, economic and political interests of the imagined and constructed community against other religious communities and in particular the Muslims in India.[71]

At the same time, Muslims too began to organise themselves politically. The Muslim League, founded in 1906 in Dhaka, was envisaged to play a prominent role in the political organisation of the Muslims. Muslims no longer found themselves to be satisfactorily represented in Congress as the number of their delegates had declined dramatically in the previous years; which on the one hand had an obvious negative effect on the possibilities of representation, and on the other hand showed a growing malaise among the community.[72] The foundation of the Muslim League is also seen as the result of an increasingly strengthening and persistent debate surrounding the self-conception of Muslims in British India that had been on their political and cultural agenda since the 1860s. Over the course of half a century, members of the *ulema* (scholars) and *ashraf* (political elites) succeeded in building a cultural identity with regards to rights, custom and community whereby, first and foremost, the political and legal category of "Muslims" emerged as a response to British allegations of deficits with regard to their loyalty.[73]

Almost simultaneously, the *sangathan* movement won so much popularity and support that in 1915 the All-India Hindu *shabha* was founded, which became known as the Hindu Mahasabha in the 1920s.[74] It distinguished itself through its Hindu nationalism that had its roots and connotations explicitly in the concept of a nation being a "cultural nation" (similar to that of the German nation). Personnel overlaps between Arya Samaj, Hindu Mahasabha[75] and Congress ensured that the Hindu Mahasabha was represented and, above all, was able to act as a pressure group within Congress.[76] Alongside these political organisations was also the Home Rule League, conceived between 1916 and 1917 by Bal Gangadhar Tilak (1856–1920) and Annie Besant (1847–1933), following the Irish model which in contrast to the alignment of the communities and constituencies sought to establish indigenous administration within the British Empire as the overall objective of the national movement.[77] In the course of the protest campaign by Congress following the First World War, especially the Non-Cooperation campaign of M.K. Gandhi in 1920–1, the organised network of the Home Rule League succeeded in securing additional legitimation for Congress in their claim of representing an Indian nation.[78]

The radicalisation of the politics also manifested itself in the factional struggles within Congress. Alongside the moderate politicians, with whom the British sought to cooperate, were also an increasing number of radical representatives who favoured sweeping changes of the political system. They were also willing to use violence in the pursuit of this goal, such as the assassinations in Bengal. Soon the different sentiments became incompatible with one another and Congress finally split in 1908 into the Moderates and the Extremists, the latter of which however termed themselves "Nationalists". Centrists such as Pherozshah Mehta (1845–1915) and Gopal Krishna Gokhale (1866–1915) were politically sidelined. Those that replaced them and came to the fore were the radicals under the leadership of B.G. Tilak ("Lokamanya"), who had already become prominent for his political Shivaji stagings in Pune and the Maratha Desh, Lala Lajpat Rai (1865–1928) from the Panjab who was active in the Hindu Mahasabha, and Bipin Chandra Pal (1858–1932) from Bengal. This trio was active under the Bal-Lal-Pal name along with Aurobindo Ghose (1872–1930), also from Bengal.[79]

The First World War greatly contributed to the radicalisation of the political landscape in British India. The British Indian army added considerable support to the war that was played out on the world stage as, in order to fight on the fronts of Western Europe, on the maritime borders of the Ottoman Empire, and in the Mediterranean and Persian Gulf, the British had to increase the British Indian army from some 315,000 soldiers to 1.2 million during the course of the war. From the Panjab alone an extra 355,000 men were recruited. Approximately 600,000 British Indian army soldiers fought in Mesopotamia, some 110,000 in France, whilst 50,000 fought in the Persian Gulf and in the Gulf of Aden.[80] In these theatres of war, these soldiers were eyewitnesses to the barbarity with which the "civilised" European powers slaughtered each other and, in many cases, were also captured and experienced life as prisoners of war.[81] On top of this immense human resource supplied by British India, economic resources were also given. Huge quantities of grain were exported from British India to Mesopotamia for horse feed, whilst, at the same time across many regions of British India, vast numbers of the population were suffering from the effects of severe food shortages. Besides this, the economic burden of the war increased to a figure approaching 300 per cent of the pre-war level which resulted in huge price hikes between 1914 and 1920.[82]

In Mesopotamia, the war ended catastrophically as a campaign to seize Basra and secure the oil deposits failed. Whilst the British Indian troops made swift inroads and good initial progress, materials and logistical power did not suffice which saw them pushed back at Ctesiphon in November 1915. The casualties in this defeat were extremely high. A contributing factor to the defeat had been a decision made for cost-cutting reasons resulting in the systematic neglect of wounded soldiers who ultimately died a pitiful and arguably preventable death.[83] In March 1917, Baghdad was finally seized.[84] The background to this offensive was the plan to occupy Iraq and to transform the south of the country into a settlement colony for demobilised Indian soldiers. The army conscripted many thousands of workers from British India who were then deported to Mesopotamia to work on projects such as the construction of a harbour in Basra as well as a network of roads. Only after the settlement plan had been shelved following the end of the First World War were these workers allowed to return home. Similar plans soon surfaced with the occupation of German East Africa, but which were similarly unachievable on account of the huge opposition initiated by British settlers in neighbouring Kenya.[85]

Second phase: radicalisation of nationalism

The end of the First World War refocused the violence back on British India which became manifest in the massacre of Amritsar and the subsequent bombing of cities in the Panjab in 1919. These events and the countrywide campaign of Non-Cooperation that had been organised by M.K. Gandhi in the same year introduced the second phase of the Indian national movement which was gradually seen as the fight for freedom.[86] At first, Gandhi was aligned with the moderate politicians of Congress. He believed in collaboration with the British and simultaneously wanted to clarify to the British that they were, above all, dependent on cooperation with the Indians. Indeed, not only was the domestic political arena intensified following the First World War, but the international arena too became somewhat radicalised. On the one hand this was the result of the US president's (Woodrow Wilson: "Wilsonian Moment") publicised right to self-determination which gave the peoples of British India ample material to open debates on the status of the inhabitants of the country as well as the nation. On the other hand, this was also the result of the deposition of the Sultan of Istanbul and the possible abolition of the caliphate which produced a considerable amount of insecurity among South Asian Muslims. The Khilafat Movement, which was transgressive in the fight for the preservation of the Ottoman caliphate, offered Gandhi and the Congress the possibility of a targeted cooperative agreement with this new Muslim organisation against the British colonial state and for a pan-Indian cause.[87]

In agitation, Gandhi reverted to the tested South African strategy of *satyagraha*. Between 1893 and 1915 he had lived in South Africa and had been active as a counsellor for the Indian minority of kuli migrants and had initiated protest action against unjust legal sanctions. Now he applied *satyagraha* to the "Indian majority" in British India. In contrast to the relative homogeneous kuli migrants in South Africa, who had acquired their Indian identity when registered at the time of immigration, such a common identity had first to be created in British India. This entailed considerable strategic and conceptual changes that had to be made to *satyagraha*.[88] *Satyagraha*, taken literally as a concept, means "to insist on the truth", which also included the search for truth. A central means in this concept is non-violence (*āhimsa*). Seen generally, *satyagraha* is a hybrid ideal of norms which unites elements of Christianity, theosophism, Jainism and Vishnaya Hinduism. *Satyagraha* was not meant to provide the foundations for political action, but rather to help determine the foundations for all spheres of life.[89]

Furthermore, Gandhi integrated the *swadeshi* movement into his agitation concept and in doing so chose the spinning-wheel (*charkha*) as the symbol of the locally hand-spun and hand-woven cotton textiles (*khadi*). Also Gandhi used *hartal*, the suspension of public life through the closing of businesses, to increase the pressure on the colonial regime following the boycott of the British Indian educational institutions. Ultimately he wanted the representatives of the colonial regime to realise the necessity of constitutional reforms. With this political demand, namely *swadeshi*, or "Home Rule" (based in the model of contemporary Ireland),[90] within just one year Gandhi succeeded in attracting both workers and peasants, two societal groups that had hitherto been unattainable for Congress. When agitation escalated into violence with the murders of police officials in February 1922, Gandhi promptly halted the Non-Cooperation campaign. Despite this, Gandhi was held responsible by the British and was sentenced to six years' imprisonment.[91]

Gandhi also reorganised the structures of the Congress, taking advantage of the boon of mass mobilisation of 1919 and prepared Congress for the emerging harsh conflict with the colonial regime. He grouped the organisation's entities along linguistic lines rather than according to the provinces of British India. Furthermore, he established a permanent working committee and ensured a larger representation of the rural population.[92] Hereby, Gandhi was able to address and mobilise the wider population on any issue from religious, economic and social restraints to help avoid further crisis. With the end of the Non-Cooperation campaign the political agitation of Congress began to ebb. When Gandhi was released from prison ahead of his six-year sentence in 1924 he was confronted with a politically inactive "India". However, in lieu of non-violent political activity was the increasing number of conflictual disputes between Hindus and Muslims which both sides claimed to be "freedom struggles". A homogeneous national movement was far from recognisable.

The disappointment of the failed Khilafat–Non-Cooperation movement seems to have been echoed in the increasing number of assaults committed between followers of both of the large religious communities who used violence as a pressure valve for the situation.[93] It was first in the 1920s in which the word "communalism" obtained its pejorative meaning.[94] It was also in this same decade in which a marked vulgarisation of political relationships began to be recognisable, manifest in rude defamation of political opponents.[95] Furthermore, it was in the 1920s in which yet another series of organisations was formed. To these belong a number of non-parliamentary organisations such as the aforementioned Rashtriya Swayamsevak Sangh as well as parties such as the Communist Party of India (CPI), the Hindustan Republican Association and the Nationalist Muslim Party.

The CPI was founded by the leading ideologist, M.N. Roy in 1920 in central Asian-Russian Tashkent.[96] Soon afterwards the CPI began to build a party organisation inside India. Small communist groups were formed in Bengal, Bombay, Madras, the United Provinces and the Panjab. However, during the 1920s and the beginning of the 1930s the CPI was badly organised, as several communist groups worked with only limited coordination. Since the British colonial authorities had banned all communist activity, the task of building a united party had become very difficult. Additionally, between 1921 and 1924 there were four conspiracy trials against the communist movement. The last one, the Cawnpore Bolshevik Conspiracy case, had a particular political impact. Several members were charged for seeking to deprive the King-Emperor of his sovereignty of British India by complete separation of India from imperial Britain by a violent revolution. Newspapers reported daily on sensational communist plans and, for the first time and certainly contrary to the intention of the colonial state, people learned about communism. A further conspiracy case in 1929 brought the activities of the CPI to a halt. It was only following the end of the Second World War that the CPI was able to organise itself throughout India as well as in a number of other states such as Kerala and Bengal where it entered into government.[97]

Kashav B. Hedgewar (1889–1940) formed the Rashtriya Swayamsevak Sangh (RSS) in 1925 in Nagpur. Translated literally, the RSS is the "Voluntary Corps of the Realm" and the recruits of this non-parliamentary organisation were found especially among the youth and young men. Alongside strict discipline and tough physical training, politically controversial topics were also debated. Above all, these meetings of political debate served in the preparation of the future reinstatement of cultural and political nationalism, in short:

the nation of India. A New India was the aspired aim. Within just a few years the RSS had expanded over wide expanses of India and had organised demonstrations or had taken part in the festivities of the political Shivaji cults as security personnel. After Hedgewar's death, the leadership of the RSS passed into the hands of Madhav S. Golwalkar (1906–73). Golwalkar solidified the RSS and finally succeeded in reaching the higher *jati*s of the middle classes in the urban areas who had increasingly become involved in paramilitary and cultural activities.[98] As the movement was wholly focused on the future of India, it rarely participated in the daily politics of the agitation during the 1930s and 1940s. Meanwhile, their explicit Hindu nationalistic orientation became ever more overtly displayed.[99]

The Hindustan Republican Association had been founded in Lahore in 1924 and became the Hindustan Socialist Republican Association (HSRA) in 1926. Its aim was to establish a Federal Republic of the United States of India by an organised and armed revolution. In the same year Bhagat Singh (1907–31), one of the HSRA's spokesmen, founded the Naujawan Bharat Sabha as the propaganda wing of the revolutionary movement, the goals of which attracted the revolutionary youth. The major sphere of influence remained, however, to be located in the Panjab and the western United Provinces of Agra and Oudh. The movement pursued a double revolution which saw, on the one hand, the aim of securing political independence and, on the other, the ushering in of a social revolution. Simultaneously, the revolutionaries demonstrated against the religiously motivated *shuddhi* movement of the Arya Samaj as well as against the orthodox Islamic awakening and missionary movement of Tablighi Jamaat founded in 1926.[100]

In preparation for the revolution, the qualities of plain living, physical fitness and a sense of brotherhood were sought along with the significance of the Indian civilisation and a spirit of patriotism for the establishment of a united Indian nation. Ideologically, and with regard to the methods employed by the HSRA, the HSRA was certainly removed from the RSS and Arya Samaj, but not necessarily so far removed in as far as virtues were concerned as they all sought to create a free and new India. Insofar as organisation and membership numbers are concerned, the HSRA and Naujawan Bharat Sabha lagged somewhat behind the RSS, yet they were considerably more prepared to employ the use of violence in the pursuit of their goals. The numerous bombings between 1928 and 1930 in the course of the Simon Commission and the Civil Disobedience campaign of Congress, which, taken together, introduced a politically strategic change of course, served to increase the public awareness of the revolutionaries.[101]

The Simon Commission caused a storm of outrage as it was entirely made up of British representatives who suggested a number of constitutional reforms for India in 1928. Subhas Chandra Bose (1897–1945) introduced a radical resolution at the annual meeting of Congress in 1928 which demanded immediate Indian independence from the British. Only after Gandhi's considerable intervention could the resolution be halted because he feared uncontrollable radical mass actions. In the following year, Gandhi accepted the draft resolution of Jawaharlal Nehru (1889–1964) which promoted *purna swaraj*, complete independence, as it became clear that the British were not prepared to grant India the Dominion Status within the British Empire as they would with the white settlement colonies of New Zealand, Australia and Canada in the near future. In order to show the seriousness of the current political situation, Gandhi organised a countrywide campaign for which he was given a free hand by Congress. The entire situation escalated after Lala Lajpat Rai was attacked at a silent, non-violent anti-Simon Commission demonstration in Lahore on 30 October 1928 with a *lathi* club (long baton) and later died from his injuries.[102]

Although Lajpat Rai was certainly no supporter of the HSRA or Naujawan Bharat Sabha (he held Bhagat Singh for a disdainful Russian agent), followers of these groups came together after his death to take revenge against a leading British police official. The assassination was led by Bhagat Singh, Rajguru and Chandrashekar on 27 December 1928. At the beginning of April 1929 the revolutionaries close to Bhagat Singh were arrested after the bombing of the Central Legislative Assembly in New Delhi. Finally, on 23 December 1929, an attempt on the Governor-General's life only narrowly missed its target. With these events Gandhi realised that his aim to organise peaceful protests of the Indian masses was in danger. He publically denounced the revolutionaries as "deluded patriots" who were "past reason" and were a "waste of energy".[103] Bhagwati Vohra of the HSRA disagreed with Gandhi and he claimed that independence would not be achievable by solely relying on *satyagraha* as the sole force of the movement, but rather that "physical force" was also necessary. A further debate on this disagreement, however, never transpired as in the meantime the majority of the HSRA revolutionaries had been charged with high treason and were either in prison or had gone to ground.[104]

At the same time, Gandhi was able to unite all of the other political parties and organisations for his civil disobedience campaign. Gandhi chose the salt monopoly of the colonial state as his object of the campaign. It was a law that could easily be broken by the vast majority of Indians and would thereby cause the British the most problems. All strata of the Indian population were equally concerned and affected by the salt law as salt is a basic need for humans and their water balance. This is especially the case in hot climatic regions on account of the effects of perspiration. The previously informed international press reported on the "Salt March" of selected *satyagrahi*s, who travelled along the west coast of India in 1930 and ended on the beach of Dandi where they collected salt. Particularly in the coastal regions, salt was reclaimed from salt water and the country's prisons began to rapidly fill with thousands of law breakers which threatened to be crippling for the justice system. Gandhi's Eleven Point Programme complemented the campaign with further concrete political demands which, in substance, meant *purna swaraj*. All in all, the salt campaign contributed decisively to Gandhi's myth as a political leader of the non-violent campaigns and the worldwide image of Indians as a peaceful people.[105]

However, the civil disobedience campaign would have petered out, had the effects of the Great Depression not hit India so severely.[106] In many regions of British India, the extent of impoverishment among the rural population became so extreme at the turn of the 1920s that they remained considerably poor until well into the second half of the twentieth century. Furthermore, the pressures exerted by the crisis increased the possibility of local violence by uncontrollable local campaigns and actions such as the refusal of peasants and tribal societies to pay revenues. For the bourgeois Congress leadership it was imperative that it gained and remained in control of all resistance movements and to coordinate them as "nationwide" campaigns.[107] The salt campaign continued to be a success in just a handful of coastal regions despite it being a package of coordinated and uncoordinated protest actions such as the excise campaign in Bihar which ultimately led Governor-General Lord Irvin (in office 1926–31) to meet with Mahatma Gandhi, as he was now called, as representative of Congress, to settle the conflict. On 5 March 1931 an agreement was made between Gandhi and Irwin, the content of which made hardly any political concessions for the Indians, but for the first time it was agreed that an Indian was an equal negotiation partner with a representative of the British crown.[108]

Not everyone saw the Gandhi–Irwin Pact as a success; critics of the pact mostly comprised communists and revolutionaries and could even be found within Congress itself. The negotiations ending the civil disobedience campaign also secured the amnesty of those imprisoned revolutionary activists who had acted peacefully. The revolutionaries loyal to Bhagat Singh who were part of the failed assassination attempt against the Governor-General were, along with Bhagat Sing, hanged on 31 March 1931.[109] The execution literally decapitated the political leadership of the revolutionaries and their violent fight against the colonial state which, at the same time, provided Gandhi with the opportunity to impress a non-violent line in the freedom fight and follow his specifications as a *satyagraha* movement. As a result, the idea of a double revolution with regard to independence from the colonial state as well as a fundamental social revolution, were excluded from the future mainstream freedom movement, with far-reaching consequences. The successor states of British India – India, Pakistan and Bangladesh – continued, and continue, to suffer on account of the deficit that the struggle for independence did not include comprehensive social reforms.

Phase three: high noon of nationalisms

The 1930s were marked with rather more constitutional and organisational problems than by concrete demands for independence as echoed in the 1935 Indian Act and the subsequent elections in 1937 which resulted in an overwhelming success for Congress.[110] It was the Second World War which re-energised the Indian freedom fight. Although British India's contributions to the war were only half that of the First World War, the troops that were sent were once again stationed in all of the major theatres of conflict: in Europe, Africa and Asia. In stark contrast to the First World War, however, India's industrial production was vastly adjusted to the war effort and wartime economy and included its own five-year plan.[111] With the entrance of Japan to the war and its capture of Singapore in 1942, the situation of British India was sharpened to dramatic levels. The advancing Japanese were supported by the Indian National Army (*Azad Hind Fauj*) which had been recruited by the aforementioned Subhas Chandra Bose appealing to Indian kuli labourers as well as to former prisoners of war in Southeast Asia. As a result, Panjabis, Bengalis and Tamils soon found themselves serving in a national liberation army consisting of 40,000 men who Bose, together with the Japanese units, led against British India in 1943.[112]

Bose's battle cry of *Chalo Dilli* ("To Delhi!") and the greeting of *Jai Hind* ("Long live India") succeeded in creating further national enthusiasm for the cause. The Japanese-Indian invasion ultimately succumbed in 1944 near Imphal in eastern Bengal. Sometime afterwards Bose died in a mysterious plane crash.[113] This unexplained incident ultimately resulted in the creation of legends and transformed Suhbas Chandra Bose into a national hero, a notion which precipitated even into scientific literature.[114] On account of his position as commander of the first independent Indian army in a century and his "heroic" death, "Netaji" Bose became to be seen as the true freedom fighter and that not only by Hindu nationalists. By conscious distinction from the pacifist Gandhi, who stood for the rather more "weak Indian" as a variation of the "effeminate Indian" and thereby without doubt adherence to the European-oriental stereotype, Subhas Chandra Bose represented a genuine "Indian" ideal of the war-like Rajput pride and a (now newly formed) national devotedness.

At the time of the Japanese-Indian advance into British India in 1942, the Cripps Mission triggered the last phase of the Indian freedom fight. Winston Churchill was forced to acknowledge the Indians as loyal partners in war following the fall of Singapore at the hands of the Japanese, the pressure exerted by the United States and from at home emanating from the Labour Party. Stafford Cripps's offer to the Indian politicians contained *inter alia* that in case of a federal constitution, individual provinces of British India would not be compelled to join an Indian Union. First, however, Congress ministers resigned from all government offices in the provinces in 1939 following the unilateral declaration of war by Governor-General Linlithgow (in office 1936–43). Cripps urged Congress members to enter into a responsible national government whilst the Governor-General would take on the role of a constitutional guardian. In response, Congress demanded the immediate transfer of the defence portfolios, which Cripps was not authorised to give, whilst Linlithgow was not seen to be in the position to take over the proposed role of a guardian. The Cripps Mission therefore suffered a resounding failure.[115]

In response to this debacle, Congress passed the Quit India Resolution on 8 August 1942 which called for the immediate British withdrawal from India.

Under the slogan "Do or Die", which Gandhi had implemented, millions of Indians were mobilised for national protest actions and demonstrations. Led by students and workers in the cities, the "August Revolution" soon spread to the rest of the country where peasants systematically attacked revenue offices, police stations, post offices, train lines and telegraph lines as well as hoisted the tricolour flag of Congress – which became the national flag of the Indian Union after independence – on government buildings. In some districts in the United Provinces of Agra and Oudh as well as in the Bombay Presidency and in Bihar and Orissa, administration collapsed completely. Similar to the Great Rebellion, this rebellion transcended both class and social strata, but this time it certainly had a countrywide cause so that a national uprising can be spoken of. Only with the use of immense military force were the British able to restore some sort of order.[116]

Few Muslims took part in these actions. Thus far, most Muslims had not developed any political ideas, let alone consciousness, of an independent British India either as a centralised political union or federal state. Meanwhile however, Mohammad A. Jinnah had announced his infamous "two-nation theory" at the annual assembly of the Muslim league at Lahore in 1940. In later political phraseology and historiography it would be known as the Pakistan Resolution, in which Jinnah claimed that Hindus and Muslims belonged to two culturally different nations which had led to the absence of any commonalities between the two groups on the South Asian subcontinent. Yet at no point did Jinnah mention an independent national territory, and much less of a Pakistan, which would have instantly raised a debate on the definition and demarcation of a future border. At the same time, the Muslim League's claim to sole representation for all Muslims in British India was not generally accepted. Parallel to Jinnah's vision, diverse Muslim ideas of a future Muslim state on the South Asian subcontinent began to develop.

Among the visionaries was Rahmad Ali (1895–1951), who founded the Pakistan Movement in 1933 in England and coined the term "Pakistan". He did not attach this ideal to a certain territory, although he did envisage it to be located in the northwestern regions of the British Raj. The philosopher Mohammad Iqbal (1877–1938) presented the idea of a Muslim "homestead" as a separate state, which would also be located in the northwest of British India. This notion of a "homestead" probably took up the wording of the Balfour Declaration of 2 November 1917 in which Great Britain had already proposed the creation of a "national homestead" for the Jewish people migrating to Palestine after the end of the First World War. Simultaneously, Iqbal advocated a federal state which comprised all regions and provinces of British India regardless of religious or ethnic groups.[117] Neither in the Muslim League nor in the other Muslim organisations, at least until the division of British India, was a debate held about the setting of possible borders for a Muslim state, the criteria of which were far too complicated to be settled unanimously.

Essentially Jinnah's "theory" represented a final point in the development of India which the British had initiated following the defeat of the Great

Rebellion as they reduced the land and the people of India to a place of two religions, two peoples and, as a result, two nations thus dividing the subcontinent and its inhabitants.[118] After Jinnah had completely withdrawn from political activity at the beginning of the 1930s, he returned again to India's political stage in 1936 from where he acted, especially during the war years. Only now did he succeed in offering himself as a reliable partner of the colonial state and thereby gradually established the Muslim League as the exclusive stakeholder of Indian Muslims. The confident Jinnah was courted by the British who established him as a skilled negotiator opposing the prominent leaders of the Congress, consequently continuing their politic of *divide et impera*. Ultimately Gandhi was forced into long debates with Jinnah in 1944, after which Gandhi had to realise that an autonomous Muslim state was no longer avoidable.[119]

The end of the war resulted in a last countrywide protest which showed the public's position against the British and the division in Indian society. The treason trial against three Azad Hind Fauj soldiers in the Red Fort in Delhi at the turn of 1945 was used by the British as a show trial which united the different interests of Congress, the Muslim League and other political groups for the last time.[120] The British selected representatives of the three major religious communities, Hindu, Muslim and Sikh, of having waged war against their monarch. Despite enormous public mobilisation and prominent defenders, among them Jawaharlal Nehru, the military tribunal sentenced the three defendants to lifelong deportation, which in comparison to the possible sentence of the death penalty must be seen as a mild judgment. In order to preserve public peace, which the Commander-in-Chief could see would be threatened, he decided to release the three accused from jail.

The trial not only sparked numerous protests, but also a number of mutinies from within the British Indian military units representing a new dimension as well as a new quality of national opposition. Of these uprisings, that of the Indian Royal Navy in Bombay is particularly noteworthy.[121] Furthermore, during the demonstrations the green flag of the Muslim League, the red of the communists and tricolour of Congress could often be seen flying together. It became obvious that under these circumstances henceforth the British no longer had either the coercive power or a sufficient number of collaborators to suppress escalating events of this magnitude. Additionally, Governor-General Archibald Wavell (in office 1943–7) received little support from the government in London. This was furthered in March 1946 with the so-called Cabinet Mission to India which was to elicit the possibilities and modalities of independence. The governments in London and New Delhi feared that the elections scheduled for March could further complicate the situation.[122]

In their own way the elections ensured "clarity" as they placed the Muslim League as a new political force in the Legislative Council, and since the smaller parties were almost all eliminated, the elections effectively established a two-party system in the Muslim-majority provinces of Panjab and Bengal which, at the same time, fatally reflected the two-nation theory. In the Panjab, it was the Muslim League that managed to outstrip the hitherto dominant Unionist Party, representative of the conservative landlords and elite colonial administration. Meanwhile, the local organisations of the Muslim League surpassed the Unionist Party and for the first time were able to nominate candidates for all deputy positions from their own party rather than have to enter a coalition. Even the *ulema* now showed sympathy for the Muslim League's cause. When the economic manifesto of the Unionist Party failed to match the expectations of its own electorate, the agitators of the Muslim League claimed that the economic difficulties of the peasants had been created by the Unionist Party's politics and that the solution to these problems was to be found in Pakistan. With this the elections in the Panjab were turned into a plebiscite for an independent Pakistan.[123]

The Muslim League had enjoyed great popularity and support in the urban areas of Bengal since 1944. In order to win the support of the Muslim peasants, however, in 1946 the Muslim League promised the confiscation of the *zamindari* estates without compensation which had been permanently fixed with the Permanent Settlement of 1793. Thus, peasants were once again to become landowners. In Bengal the success of the Muslim League lay with the failure of the opposing parties, since here Congress had been poorly organised, the Communist Party failed to offer an alternative and the Bengal Kisan Sabha was not fully representative.[124] The results of the 1946 polls showed that the majority of votes depended to a considerable degree on the parties' organisation. In the context of the separate electorates that had been introduced in 1909 to British India, in 1946 the Muslim League had been able to secure and unite 76 per cent of all Muslim votes, whilst this figure had been a mere 4.8 per cent in the elections of 1937. The national cause of the Muslims had achieved a decisive breakthrough in both the understanding of the Muslim League as well as a large majority of voters. Nevertheless, despite having the strongest faction in the Panjab, the Muslim League was unable to form a government as Congress succeeded in forming an anti-League coalition. Such an outcome sowed the seeds of discord and provided the catalyst and willingness to revert to violent opposition.[125]

The Cabinet Mission was thus faced with the two winning parties: Congress and the Muslim League, both of whose willingness to compromise in the face of electoral success was decreased significantly, leading to something of a stalemate situation. The constitutional draft of the Cabinet Mission envisaged a tripartite federation, the highest level of which (the central government) would control defence and foreign affairs. The Mission's aim was to ensure the unity of British India. The plan was, however, far too complex as it did not offer sufficient room for interpretation. Despite having many reservations, both Congress and the Muslim League agreed to the Mission's plan, thanks mainly to its vagueness. After much deliberation and debate, Wavell was finally able to form an interim government, thereby putting Indian issues in Indian hands. However, on 10 July 1946 Nehru was quoted by the press as saying "we are not bound by a single thing except that we have decided to go into the Constituent Assembly", thus blowing the question of the unity of India and indeed the political future of the subcontinent completely open.[126]

Duped in such a way, Jinnah retracted the Muslim League's approval of the Cabinet Mission's plan on 17 July and called for a "Direct Action Day" on 16 August. In order not to hinder the initiated constitutional process, Wavell assigned the posts of the interim government to members of Congress alone. Jinnah, however, had not defined what he meant by direct action. A *hartal*, the suspension of public life, was deemed the best method. However, the Muslim League Chief Minister of Bengal, Husseyn Suhrawardy (1892–1963) had his own interpretation and launched a wave of violence in Calcutta, where within 72 hours more than 4,000 people were killed and over 100,000 were left homeless.[127] Whether the Calcutta riots were a product of political naivety or a calculated pogrom is still a subject of debate. This action was particularly shocking for the urban population for whom this level of violence was entirely new in a metropolis, which had a strong tradition of regional (Bengal) patriotism and collaborative governance where powerful trade unions and anti-imperial organisations cut across religious lines. Riots followed in Noakhali District in northern Bengal in October 1946 which surpassed even the violence and atrocities of the Calcutta riots.[128]

Phase four: independence and partition – the failed Indian nation

The growing situation of violence was exacerbated by the British government which lacked clear political will, let alone the ability to give an official government statement on the future political organisation of India. On 20 February 1947, Prime Minister Attlee announced that British India was to be given independence by June 1948. Once again no government policy statement was given to back this surprising and short-term step. Attlee's announcement and the resignation of Governor-General Wavell alienated many people in India and in particular in the Panjab which led to a dramatic increase in violence in the province. From early March 1947, cases of robberies, stabbings and arson became commonplace in the cities as the RSS and the Muslim League National Guard mobilised their troops in the area.[129] Together with the immense political pressure originating from the British government in London – which was applied in a haphazard manner and was devoid of any accompanying measures as well as the escalating violence in the country – the partition of British India seemed to be the likely outcome.

At the end of March 1947, Lord Louis Mountbatten was sent by the British government to New Delhi as the last Governor-General of British India. After observing the political situation on the ground he announced in a statement made on 3 June 1947 that, first, British India should be divided without further ado and, second, that the target date for independence should be brought forward by one year to August 1947.[130] In calling for such matters to be resolved in relevant haste, Mountbatten was undoubtedly attempting to force the deadlock into motion and make the Indian politicians act.[131]

The Working Committee, Congress's core decision-making group, had already debated partition on 8 March which lead to Congress and the Muslim League both accepting Mountbatten's plan. Despite the fact that politicians and supporters of all parties involved had very mixed feelings about partition, the Hindu Mahasabha spoke out openly against the partition plan. Many people, especially in the Panjab, were horrified by it yet partition had now become the watchword and solution for the conflict. At the same time, a handful of British and Indian politicians created the illusion that partition would only be a temporary solution.[132]

In order to substantiate the partition plan Mountbatten appointed Sir Cyril Radcliffe, an administrative officer, to determine the details of partition.[133] Neither the British nor the Indians seemed to be concerned that Radcliffe had never been to India and thus had no first-hand experience of the country. At Radcliffe's side stood the Boundary Commission, which was charged with defining the modalities of partition in the provinces of both the Panjab and Bengal, the foundations of which were based on the Muslim and non-Muslim majority districts as had been recorded in the 1941 Census. However, "other factors" also played a role in determining which district, or part of a district (*tehsils*), could be added to one or the other successor state to meet the criterion of "contiguous majority areas". Although Mountbatten was aware of the fact that in such plans of partition the Sikh community would be considered the least, if at all, he did not see a solution to such a concern.[134] As for the issue of the 500-plus Indian monarchies and principalities, a plan for their future role did not even exist, so many rulers therefore speculated on having their full sovereignty reinstated following independence.[135]

As long as the Boundary Commission worked on the partition, Indian parties concerned could provide input and critique. After reviewing the arguments, even Radcliffe concluded that the positions between the Muslim League, Congress and Sikhs were so different that they could not be mutually agreed upon. Ultimately the Radcliffe Award took geostrategic, political, economic and security concerns into account in the allocation of individual districts and *tehsils*. Since Congress was granted the right to appoint the members of the Boundary Commission from Mountbatten, it is hardly surprising that the ideas of Congress were implemented almost completely with respect to the boundary in Bengal and to a lesser degree in the Panjab. What became obvious is that commercial and security interests were of a higher importance in the drawing of boundaries than demographic, social, ethnic or "communal" criteria.[136]

The consequences for the Panjab were dramatic, since although many members of the Sikh community had called for partition, it lost in terms of land, industrial regions, institutions and mainly cultural and religious sites. The alliance of Congress and Sikh representatives was unable to enforce its demands on the Muslim League concerning this issue. Generally politicians in each of the independent states were suspected of having exerted influence on the Boundary Commission to draw the boundaries for the benefit of the respective successor state. The Ferozpur case poisoned the political atmosphere in

82 *Patriotisms and nationalisms*

India and Pakistan for years to come. Ferozpur was a district in the Panjab that was controversially included into India despite a clear Muslim majority, allegedly following personal intervention by Nehru with Mountbatten, because one of the most important British military establishments in India was situated in this district.[137] Apart from this local political factionalism, as an overall result of partition the Panjab lost its Panjabi identity, because it was replaced by Muslim, Hindu, Sikh, Indian and Pakistani identities in two separate countries.[138]

The Radcliffe Award was first announced on 17 August 1947, two days after independence had been granted, despite the fact that the award had been finalised on 12 August. In spite of repeated warnings from senior British officials that this delay could be interpreted as a deliberate cover-up and give rise to

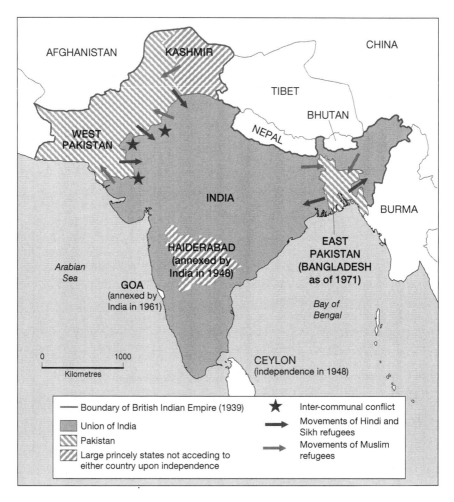

Map 2.2 Partition of British India. © themightyquill/CC Licensed

unrest, Mountbatten decided to wait until after the independence of the two successor states to make the award public. In fact, independence and the uncertainty about the future, especially in the territorially affected districts, had the effect of raising tension in the population to unbearable levels. With the announcement on 17 August, a concurrent migration began on the subcontinent as Hindus and Sikhs moved from the new state of Pakistan to the new state of India and Muslims fled to Pakistan from India.[139] In the violence that ensued, some 12 million people were displaced and up to a million people are reported to have died, whilst systematic looting and killings as well as the collective public rape of women and their subsequent burning alive were among the cruellest events surrounding the displacement.[140]

In the collective memory of both successor states, partition has been reflected as a traumatic experience. On the one hand attempts were made to capture the events in literature and fictional works, somewhat comparable to the literary scene in Germany following the Second World War, in which the incomprehensible events were vocalised and the expression of shame was explored. In these attempts the loss of "home" is a subject that is frequently revisited with the juxtaposition of loss and lack of replacement being accentuated along with the feeling of being lost in a strange land. An entire population had become embittered by the loss they had endured and desperate never to return to those places where such unimaginable violence had taken place for which they could never have been prepared.[141] At the same time there is also a certain glorification of the "home" in literature, which sometimes borders on nostalgia. This exploration of "home" sometimes left aside that for all of the commonalities and communities in both the towns and villages in India and Pakistan, tensions also existed between different religious groups; this was not merely confined to conflicts between Hindus, Sikhs and Muslims, but also influenced relations between Shia and Sunnis.[142]

Initially the literature of partition reflected rather more the fate of the middle class and the elite than the general population, whilst the fate of the lower classes and women has only recently been an addition to the literature.[143] Such a "phenomenon" can also be seen in scientific literature concerning partition. Furthermore, these stories were invariably told by men of the upper middle class, who used this chance to bring their role as family heroes to the fore. An example of such is the Panjabis in Delhi where men rescued their families and brought them to safety and prosperity. Their stories, condensed, invented and reduced to personal moments of commemoration, determined the Indian national narrative of partition to be a history of everyday life before partition, the "last journey" and life after partition.

A different picture emerges, however, when the immediate causes of violence, the extent of killings, the spatial location of violence and the involvement of women are considered.[144] Women remember partition quite differently as politically motivated murders of husbands, fathers and sons had occurred years before partition, thus the remembrance of this and partition together became part of the same breath.[145] Whilst research undertaken in the first half century following independence and partition focused on the history of the victims in their own or in the other country, recently comparative research has led to a new level of understanding into the fate of people, families, communities, villages and towns during the course of, and after, the displacement in direct relation to one another. Eviction and emigration went on until the end of the 1950s, which forced another four million people to leave their home country.[146]

Both the Pakistani and Indian governments were caught virtually unprepared for the extent of the flight and the displacement that was caused by partition; the British did not expect such an exodus and had therefore not installed the necessary measures to deal with it. As such neither state was prepared for an exchange of population that would create a number of remaining minorities. Nehru was "not in favour of the wholesale migration of population. It was not in the interest of the majority of people to be uprooted from the soil. The lives and interests had to be protected by both the governments who were responsible for the minority well-being." Not until mid-October was a joint Evacuation Movement plan formulated to investigate the possibilities of transportation.[147] However, the mass evacuation targeted the lower strata of the population rather than the elites since a large part of the Hindu and Sikh elite in the cities of the Panjab, especially in Lahore and Rawalpindi, had previously fled to secure areas as well as sold properties and transferred bank accounts. With this inequality a so-called "zero hour" at which the same opportunities were available to all cannot be identified.[148]

Cities such as Delhi, Lahore, Karachi and Lakhnau were particularly hard hit as they were subjected to an enormous population exchange. Numerous Muslims from Lakhnau moved to Karachi in the hope of finding a similarly cosmopolitan environment there. However, they were seen as unwelcome refugees which, with their Urdu, gave the Sindhi-speaking city a completely new character. Soon the foreign Laknavis were decreed as *mohajirs* (migrants) in Karachi. Settled in separate colonies, the Laknavis became more conscious of their own identity and soon called for separate political representation in Karachi, Sind and Pakistan.[149] In India, Delhi has become the mirror of British India's partition.[150] From the Indian national perspective, the term partition (in the literature always spelled with a capital P) reflects rather the national narrative of the events whilst the "secession" of Pakistan is often associated in the sense of a renegade state. In comparison, in Pakistan the term "creation" dominates discourse which, of course, ushered the new state of Pakistan into being.

In any case, the "Indian nation", which was the political target of the freedom movement, did not come true. Ultimately only partition according to the "two-nation theory" seemed to be a viable solution, which of course made contradictions, tensions and desperation all the more visible. According to the understanding of a majority in independent India, Jinnah and the Muslim League were responsible for partition and the failed nation. Yet Hindu nationalists also remained dissatisfied. Mahatma Gandhi became the most prominent victim of that dissatisfaction when he voted for a proportional division of the military treasury between the two successor states. Gandhi's sense of justice ended in a deadly hatred led by Hindu nationalist Nathuram Godse, former private secretary to Vinayak Savarkar and a member of the RSS, who assassinated Gandhi in Delhi on 30 January 1948.

Contemporary historiographical assessment confirms how differently the disaster of partition has been dealt with. On the one hand is the Muslim League and its agitation, especially that of Muhammad Jinnah who is blamed as an ambitious dogmatist for demanding an independent Pakistan. On the other hand, the growing Hindu nationalism, manifested in the Hindu Mahasabha and the RSS, is seen as a major cause for the gradual exclusion of Muslims from the Indian nation. Recently, Congress's policy has also been accused of not only working towards the goals of extreme Hindu nationalists, but also being visibly engaged in the course preferred by the British government. Congress lost sight of its original and supreme goal, namely the unity of the Indian nation and population regardless of creed, class, descent, ethnicity and community, whilst trying to secure its own political dominance in an independent India. The British have been similarly criticised for their inability to secure an ordinary "transfer of power" despite the ongoing political unrest in the years 1946–7 and their leaving India in such a hurry. Moreover, the British Indian government has been seen as not exhausting all possibilities in attempting to maintain the (national) unity of India.[151]

In the most recent literature in the field of partition, comparisons of displacement and death tolls have even been drawn with "holocaust" and "genocide".[152] However, a terminological comparison with Hitler's extermination of European Jews between 1933 and 1945 cannot be claimed, as "holocaust" (rather: *shoah*) may only refer to the unique, systematic, bureaucratically and industrially organised extermination of Europe's Jews by the Nazis during the Third Reich. Likewise, the killings of Muslims, Hindus and Sikhs cannot be seen as genocidal in that, first, it lacked the appropriate organisation and logistics and, second, in contrast to the situation of the Jews of Europe, none of the religious communities' and ethnic societies' physical existence had ever been threatened. Aside from such inappropriate names for the interpretation of partition it is obvious that the causes and background to the tragic events surrounding the partition of the subcontinent will continue to fuel historiographical debate for many years to come.

Notes

1 Pomeranz 2000; Pomeranz and Topik 2006; Bayly 2009; Sachsenmaier 2011: 1–37.
2 Mann 2009: 67–8.
3 Joshi 1957; Pati 2008: xiii–xli; Pati 2010: 1–15; Roy T. 1994: 1–20.
4 Ray 2003: 353.
5 Bayly 1998: 1–35.
6 Sen S. 1992.
7 Ray 2003: 356–60.

8 Buckler 1985: 43–74.
9 Heitler 1972: 239–57; Pandey 1990: 23–65; Mann 2005a: 5–34.
10 Rycroft 2006: 205–71.
11 Wagner 2007, 2009.
12 Lloyd 2008: 201–37.
13 Taban 2008: 11–17; Moosvi 2008: 18–27.
14 Rycroft 2006: 167–204, 272–87.
15 Herbert 2008: 273–88.
16 Powell A.A. 2010: 175–8.
17 Ray 2003: 395–98; Wagner 2010.
18 Wagner 2010: 61–77.
19 Ibid.: 131–68.
20 Husain I. 2008: 28–38.
21 Roy T. 1994: 222–7.
22 Llewellyn-Jones 2007: 37–50.
23 Stokes 1986; Khaldun 1957: 1–70.
24 Guha R. 1983: 117–19, 228–40.
25 Ray 2003: 417–30.
26 Ibid.: 431–64.
27 Azamgarh Proclamation, issued in the name of Bahadur Shah, 25 August 1857, in: Ball 1859: 630–2, reprinted also in: Bates 2010: 68–70.
28 Roy T. 1994.
29 Sinha S.S. 2010: 16–31; Das Gupta S. 2010: 32–45; Pati 2010: 63–81.
30 Oldenburg 1984: 151–3, 183–91; Oldenburg 1991: 23–61, esp. 26–7.
31 Domin 1977; Major 1996.
32 Llewellyn-Jones 2007: 154–79.
33 Oldenburg 1984: 22, 32.
34 Llewellyn-Jones 2007: 132–7, 171–2.
35 Kostal 2005: 1–18.
36 Russell W.H. 1860: 29.
37 Husain S.M. 2006; Dalrymple 2006: 431–45.
38 Rahman T. 2009: 212–29.
39 Mazumdar S. 2011.
40 Herbert 2008.
41 Kostal 2005: 23–68.
42 Roy T. 1994: 241–4.
43 Sen S. 2000.
44 Fischer-Tiné and Mann 2004; Watt and Mann 2011.
45 Kopf 1988.
46 Bayly 2010: 26–43, 104–31.
47 Veer 2000: 25–33.
48 Goswami M. 2004: 165–208; Bayly 2010: 214–44.
49 Zavos 2000: 24–31.
50 Masselos 1986: 55–77.
51 Zavos 2000: 38–57; Fischer-Tiné 2000: 107–28, esp. 108.
52 Zavos 2000: 69.
53 Barns 1940; Kolsky 2010: 97–103.
54 McLane 1977: 43–4.
55 Ibid.: 50–85.
56 Bayly 1975: 4.
57 Bandhu 2003: 19–38.
58 Bayly 1998: 98–132.
59 Kulkarni 2006b.
60 Cashman 1975; Samarth 1975; Kaur R. 2003: 1–69.

Patriotisms and nationalisms 87

61 Zavos 2000: 45–50.
62 Oddie 2003: 155–82.
63 Fischer-Tiné 2000: 108–9.
64 Ibid.: 110–14.
65 Jaffrelot 1996: 19–25.
66 Zavos 2000: 81–92.
67 Fischer-Tiné 2000: 118–20.
68 Ludden 2012: 483–525.
69 Heehs 2004; Gossman 1999: 34–48; Chakrabarti H. 1992; Ghosg 2005.
70 Mann 2011a: 71–99.
71 Zavos 2000: 5–6, 99–125.
72 Burke and Quraishi 1995: 114, 128–135, 142–165. At the Congress's annual meeting in 1889, among the 1,502 delegates were 254 Muslims; in 1904 among 1,010 only 30; and in 1905 just 20 Muslims among 757 delegates. Cf. Bandhu 2003: 57–71.
73 Jalal 2007: 139–65.
74 Zavos 2000: 112–21.
75 Rai L.L. 1915.
76 Jaffrelot 1996: 17–25.
77 Besant 1925.
78 Zavos 2000: 112–13.
79 Sarkar 2003: 65–137.
80 Voigt 1987: 8–9.
81 Roy F., Liebau and Ahuja 2011.
82 Metcalf, T.R. 2007: 89–101.
83 Sehrawat 2009: 151–72.
84 Busch 1971.
85 Metcalf, T.R. 2007: 166–87.
86 Pouchepadass 1999.
87 Minault 1999.
88 Huttenback 1971.
89 Blume 1987: 59–12; pt II, 173–303.
90 Silvestri 2007; Foley and O'Connor 2007: 225–90.
91 Sarkar 2003: 195–227.
92 Bandhu 2003: 83–9.
93 Minault 1999: 192–8.
94 Veer 2000, *passim*. Pandey 1990: 233–61.
95 Mann 2009: 155–8.
96 Roy S. 1998.
97 Koteswara Rao 2003: 88–112.
98 Andersen and Damle 1987: 31; Sarkar 1992: 163; Six 2006: 22–43.
99 Kanungo 2003: 35–67; Jaffrelot 1996: 33–79; Andersen and Damle 1987: 30–8.
100 Reetz 2006: 96–7, 151–3.
101 Habib I.S. 2007: 22–5; 41–3; 58–69; 105–31.
102 Saran 2008; Sharma S.R. 2005. A less panegyric and more critical – let alone scientifically sound – biography of Lala Lajpat Rai is still an academic desideratum.
103 Gandhi M.K. 1930: 4–5.
104 Habib I.S. 2007: 33–7, 205–17.
105 Weber 1994: 192–214 (vol. 1).
106 Rothermund 1992.
107 Chaturvedi 2007: 132–50. This aspect will be dealt with in the subsequent chapter.
108 Sarkar 2000: 101–32.
109 Noorami 2005.
110 Menon V. 2003.

111 Voigt 1987: 72–81.
112 Lebra-Chapman 2008; Fay 1993.
113 Bose S. 2011.
114 Bose S.C. 2005.
115 Moore 1988: 86–105.
116 Sarkar 2003: 388–405.
117 Sayeed 2007: 102–9.
118 Moore 1988: 105–35; Hardy 1972: 72.
119 Burke and Quraishi 1995: 403–9.
120 Singh H. 2003.
121 Gourgey 1996.
122 Bose and Jalal 2004: 161–4.
123 Singh A. 1987: 125–36.
124 Hashmi 2005: 6–40.
125 Singh A. 1987: 136–41.
126 Khan Y. 2007: 55–61; Talbot and Singh 2009: 39; Sengupta N.K. 2007: 115–6.
127 Sengupta D. 2006: 288–95.
128 Khan Y. 2007: 63–70.
129 Nair N. 2011: 179–218; Hansen 2002: 109–13.
130 Wolpert 2010: 7–9.
131 Hasan M. 2003; *The Partition Omnibus* 2002, with an Introduction by Mushirul Hasan and consisting of: David Page, *Prelude to Partition: The Indian Muslims and the Imperial System of Control 1920–1932* (1982); Anita Inder Singh, *The Origins of the Partition of India 1936–1947* (1987); Penderel Moon, *Divide and Quit* (1961) and G.D. Khosla, *Stern Reckoning: A Survey of the Events Leading up to and Following the Partition of India* (1989).
132 Khan Y. 2007: 85–97.
133 Godbole 2006: 24–92.
134 Ahmed I. 2005: 116–67.
135 Khan Y. 2007: 97–100.
136 Chatterjee J. 2005: 168–202.
137 Wolpert 2010: 16.
138 Nair N. 2011: 94–8, Ahmed I. 2005: 161–4.
139 Godbole 2006: 109–214.
140 Kaur R. 2007: 30.
141 Zaman 1999: 19–58.
142 Bhalla 2006: 7–45; Husain I. 2002.
143 Ravikant and Saint 2001; Kaur R. 2007: 24.
144 Kaur R. 2007: 11–19, *passim*.
145 Datta N. 2009.
146 Talbot and Thandi 2004; Talbot 2006.
147 Kaur R. 2007: 71–80, quote 71.
148 Ibid.: 66–9.
149 Ansari 2005.
150 Pandey 2001.
151 Mahajan 2000: 17–35, 143–202.
152 Hansen 2002; Godbole 2006.

3 State formation and empire building in South Asia (1858–1998)

The indicated period in the chapter's title from the mid-nineteenth to the end of the twentieth century is unusual in the historiography of South Asia. In general the period is divided between the era of the British Raj from 1858 to 1947 whilst the states of India, Pakistan and Ceylon that followed the subcontinent's independence are commonly denoted as the "post-colonial" narrative. The year 1858 undoubtedly stands as a dramatic watershed in modern Indian history as the territorial possessions of the EIC were declared to be a British crown colony. This watershed also included the brutal suppression of the Great Rebellion and dismissal of the Timurid dynasty, events that produced a profound rupture in the self-understanding and awareness of many "Indians". However, independence of British India in 1947 was no less of a dramatic caesura. Indeed, the increasing distance between the tragic humanitarian events and the serious political changes that the division of British India brought with it made the structural continuities of the colonial state in the successor states of Pakistan and India all the more conspicuous and, for decades following independence, the post-colonial states remained cognate to their former colonisers.

It seems that it was the "emergency" (1975–7) of Prime Minister Indira Gandhi, daughter of Jawaharlal Nehru, which triggered a political development of India ultimately overcoming the "post-colonial state". Political change included a multi-party parliamentary system hitherto unthinkable since Congress had held the majority of votes and seats for decades. Gradual liberalisation of the Indian economy through the deregulation of several industrial sectors, which had so far been dependent on government licences, did not commence abruptly and unexpectedly in 1991, but was rather part of the economic transformation which had taken place since the beginning of the 1980s. Furthermore, since the "emergency" it is the "religious moment" which came to play an ever increasing role in Indian politics. Moreover, in Pakistan the politics of "Islamisation" began in 1977. However, political, societal and economic changes also occurred in Sri Lanka from 1984 onwards, as well as in Nepal. It seems historiographically reasonable to set 1998 as a major caesura of South Asian history since transformation processes seem to have, *inter alia*, culminated in the ignition of an atomic bomb in both Pakistan and in India and it is during this year that the assassinations of Sri Lankan politicians reached unprecedented numbers.

In this book, the histories of Nepal and (Sri) Lanka since the eighteenth century are dealt with in separate sections as both current states were not part of British India. During the eighteenth century, large parts of Ceylon (as per colonial terminology) were free from colonial rule, only coming under British rule in 1818. When Ceylon gained independence in 1948, it retained its Dominion status within the British Commonwealth, similar to Canada and Australia, until 1972. In many ways continuities with the colonial system, especially in Ceylon, are to be observed far beyond the formal independence of the country. Whilst Nepal never belonged to the British Empire, a residency was established in Kathmandu, yet its functions were limited. An essential part in its formal independence was the fact that Nepal's foreign policy had been crafted independently, unlike the monarchies and principalities in British India.

The British Raj in India (1858–1947)

Even before the Great Rebellion had finally been crushed, the British Government in London had withdrawn EIC rule over India and British India was declared a Crown Colony in 1858, commonly known as the British Raj. With the status of Crown Colony the dual power structure as had been established in the India Act of 1784 came to an end. The parliamentary Board of Control of the EIC was converted into a separate ministry (the India Office) and from then on the Governor-General led under the unofficial title of "Viceroy". He was appointed an advisory council of eight members selected by the Crown and a further seven elected members who had been elected by the Council itself. In 1861, a bill was passed endowing the Council with the power to pass legislation itself. Simultaneously, the portfolio system was introduced which allowed the Governor-General to transfer separate tasks to the members of the Council. Furthermore, the Governor-General also received the right to issue decrees that were valid for a period of up to six months without having to first consult with the Council. On the whole, the law deprived the Council's legislative authority over the executive, and thus resembled the autocratic system of the EIC.

The system of British paramountcy remained unquestioned and still undefined, which allowed the British to exert their indirect control over the formally independent kingdoms and principalities. Ultimately, the success of the British rule in India was due to this intentional blur of uncertainty and the flexibility it afforded them. On the one hand, the British considered Indian princes as oriental despots. Against this backdrop the British felt justified in their actions between 1878 and 1886 to acquire the postal and telegraph networks of all of the Indian states; to close all of the minting services; and finally, at the end of the nineteenth century, to enforce a salt monopoly on all but the production for local needs. Despite the territorial and dynastic guarantee of existence in Queen Victoria's proclamation in 1858, the British retained the administration of Maisur that had been acquired in 1831, and were thus able to continue with their system of direct rule until 1881 when power was finally returned to the *maharaja*.¹ Such rigid policy towards individual monarchs did not prevent the British, on the other hand, from recognising Indian princes as the natural leaders of their people and integrating them as a conservative constitutional element of the British Raj.²

In order to give international status to the growing importance of the territory and the empire, Queen Victoria was proclaimed "Empress of India" (*kaisar-i-hind*) in 1876. To this end a specially designed, pompous ceremony of proclamation was held in Delhi in 1877 to demonstrate the British succession to the Mughal throne. The colonial rediscovery and invention of Indian authorities (monarchs and princes) and their simultaneous integration in a feudal-hierarchical power structure initiated the preservation of social and political power structures in India, the aim of which was to stabilise the colonial political regime.³ A contemporary and historiographically persistent image of a traditional "true" India, an India of "Princely States" was constructed which was portrayed as backward and was placed in direct comparison to the modern, advanced British India thereby standing as justification of British colonial rule. The clearest expression of the sense of traditionalism was embodied in the "Delhi Darbars" (Royal-Imperial Assemblage) which became a representation of power and thereby were supposed to increase the legitimacy of the British rule in 1902–3 and 1911–12. This was only partly successful and often inhabitants of Delhi spoke not of a *darbar*, but rather of, and tellingly, a *mela* (fun fair).⁴

Figure 3.1 "Imperial Darbar" in Delhi, 1911–12. © Mary Evans/Grenville Collins Postcard Collection

Conversely, the ruling class of the British showed little respect for most of the Indian nobility. The contempt for the allegedly incompetent Indian monarchy was no more clearly stated than by Viceroy Lord Curzon (in office 1899–1905) who, after Governors-General Richard Wellesley and Lord Dalhousie, was the highest-ranking representative of British India with the most distinctive imperial sense of mission and impressive colonial-monarchical habit. In the style of an absolute (European) monarch, Lord Curzon incorporated himself into the Delhi Darbar of 1903 as a "white" Mughal. In his position as a self-understood "sovereign Indian ruler", at times he dictated to "his princes" their "proper place" more than any European monarch could ever do. He was able to enforce this by insisting on first having to approve any of the princes' foreign travel plans. He deposed, either temporarily or permanently, as many as 15 monarchs whom he reproached for mismanagement and poor administration. Despite Queen Victoria's guarantees, paramountcy had nevertheless been extended and enacted to previously unknown dimensions which the colonial administration finally attempted to calm with the reforms of 1909.[5]

Without calling paramountcy fundamentally into question, a liberalisation process gathered momentum on different constitutional levels following the First World War, which, among other things, was reflected in the establishment of the Chamber of Princes. However, this chamber held only a consultancy function as the Governor-General maintained the power to convene meetings, held the presidency and dictated the agenda. Meanwhile, the "princes" merely held the right to propose items for the agenda and were given the opportunity to suggest special sessions. As a result the Indian monarchs lacked a representative body within the constitution capable of representing their own interests. Distaste at this kind of exclusion was manifest in non-participation in meetings to which only a third of the states sent their delegates to preside at. Since the monarchs did not have to pay for the maintenance of an army to defend their country, they, due to the unaltered revenue assessments, disposed of fiscal means which contributed to the (European) image of the marvellously rich Indian *maharaja*.[6] This was certainly not applied to all monarchs as for many princes, and especially little kings, such an assessment was not applicable.[7] However, it must also be noted that, in some cases of the little kings, some of them obtained amazing power.[8]

On the face of it, the administrative structures of the British Raj remained virtually unchanged when compared to those of the Company State. However, an increased bureaucratisation came to be established, the most visible expression of which was the creation of new administrative departments and the configuration of an administrative corps in the form of the Indian Civil Service (ICS). The nearly 1,000 posts that this bureaucracy created were filled exclusively by the British, and even when Indians were awarded access to positions within the ICS they first had to pass exams based on European educational content, thereby denying entrance to most applicants in the majority of cases. This changed following the First World War, more as a result of the waning British interest in India rather than a structured approach aimed at helping Indians develop careers within the ICS themselves.[9]

Conversely, legal reform policies changed little. After almost 30 years of work, the Civil Procedure Code, the Penal Code, Contract Act and the Evidence Act were adopted in the 1860s, which saw British India submit to a single jurisdiction and standardised legal procedures.[10] However, despite this standardisation, the legal system was by no means fair and equal, but rather paradoxically in context of its codification, extremely unjust as violence against Indians by Europeans was dealt with extremely mildly, even in the case of murder. However, in the opposite circumstance of cases of Indian violence against Europeans, the law was quick to show no mercy and exert its full force.[11] The legal system became more rigid in the 1920s and 1930s when political agitation by Congress and extremist organisations such as the HSRA, as well as public unrest, increased. Collective punishments and the amount of punitive measures such as, for instance, the Goonda Act of 1932 provided the pursuance, imprisonment and sentencing of so-called "bad elements" and "hooligans", which also increased.[12]

The nineteenth century saw very little change in terms of constitutional structure in the provinces of British India. Although the government established provincial councils in Bengal and in the Madras and Bombay presidencies in 1861, few appointed and non-official Indians in the various councils were consulted in legislative matters. In any case, Indians were not afforded the right to a say in such matters. The liberalisation of the 1880s changed little, although Indians in both urban and local bodies were granted more participation. However, this occurred against the background of general municipal financial distress, as institutions had to henceforth be financed from their own taxes (*octroi*). In turn this freed the British Indian Government from the burden of having to raise new, and thereby unpopular, taxes. In 1892 the proportion of Indian members in municipal bodies was again increased; however, this was not accompanied by an extension of their powers whilst the participatory appearance was merely produced in the form of a so-called representative government.[13]

Since the early nineteenth century, Indian intellectuals had been participating in the debates about the legality and the need for constitutional reform of what, until 1858, still constituted *de jure* the Mughal Empire and only later British India. These debates were led by liberal ideas which also arose simultaneously in Europe and America. This was, however, not a simple copy of such concepts furthered by Indian liberals who instead attempted to initiate social reform debates that were also directed against the British and their rule in India. The Bengal intellectual, Ram Mohan Roy (1772–1833) paved the way for this Indian liberalism just as the economist Romesh Chandra Dutt (1848–1909) did for Gandhi, Nehru and Jinnah. Conversely the practised liberalism of Ram Mohan Roy had a lasting influence on contemporary discussions about religion and the politics of Britain.[14] In various countries of the world around the turn of the twentieth century, a liberal public sphere became noticeable from within which reforms to society, government and politics were debated.[15]

Such liberal discourse did not influence the Morley-Minto reforms of 1909 which instead merely applied a *laissez-faire* cladding to the democratic façade of the authoritarian-paternalistic colonial regime. That said, however, initial steps towards the decentralisation of power and its institutions began to manifest themselves. In some cases among the various councils the number of Indians more than doubled, thus increasing representation. Following an elaborate system, representatives were elected according to the participatory nature of the reforms that were to be implemented. At the insistence of the Muslims the British introduced the principle of separate constituencies whereby not only the Muslims, but also Hindus were counted. The total number of the latter was, however, significantly decimated by the separate registration of the so-called untouchables (those not actually belonging to the "caste system", but nonetheless still part of it) and low caste groups in election lists. Whilst the British certified solid community and constituency for the Muslims, the Hindu constituency came into question on account of the apparent curtailment of the community as "high caste" Hindus. Consequently, the latter saw their political influence to be in danger.[16]

Although the reforms in the provinces of British India provided, for the first time, a clear majority for the appointed non-official Indian members, the central government led by the British continued to exercise exclusivity of power. The idea of a "responsible government" in which the accountability of finances would lie with the representative body was at no point considered.[17] The Montague-Chelmsford reforms of 1919 introduced the Dyarchy which saw the "soft" ministries such as health and education transferred to Indian ministers whilst the "hard" ministries such as finance, justice and police would remain in British hands. In this way the impression was created that democratic principles had begun to work their way into the political landscape of British India, whilst, in reality, the British continued to hold the power in the subcontinent without restraint. Thus the dramatic increase in the proportion of elected members in the Legislative Assembly was rather more of a cosmetic move than a true development of democratic principles. Though the right to vote was also extended to women, the electorate of 1926 comprised a mere 2.8 per cent of the entire population.[18]

There was no transfer of power within the central government as the Governor-General continued to be responsible to the English Parliament ahead of the Secretary of State for India. In British India the Governor-General held a general veto power, was able to make regulations without having to hold consultation sessions and had the power to block legislative action. British India's legislature was based on a two-chamber system, consisting of the Legislative Assembly and the Council of State. However, the deputies of these councils were forbidden from discussing the budget of the colonial state. The process of drafting reforms continued to be conducted without the aid of the Indian ministers, although occasionally a leading Indian politician was consulted. The introduction and successful codification of the religious community as a basis for political constituency was crucial for the political development in

British India. In 1909 and 1919, the British responded to the various political interest groups and organisations that were forming along (religious) communal lines with the concept of *divide et impera*.[19]

The unsatisfactory constitutional reforms ultimately culminated in 1919 after the adoption of the Rowlatt Act in that same year. Government feared the escalation of violent protests following the demobilisation of Indian troops after the end of the First World War. The Rowlatt Act, named after the judge responsible for its design, provided for emergency regulations of sorts which were intended to maintain (martial) law and order. The emergency regulations were justified by the threat towards colonial rule that was posed by terrorism and revolutionary Bolshevism as well as the threat to public peace. Any constitutional reforms that had been resolved and implemented thus far were therefore a farce.[20] After the Rowlatt Act was published in the Panjab, the general disappointment following the lack of political reforms that the Act offered in "reward" for their war efforts led to a number of open demonstrations that the British were quick to ban.

In Jallianwala Bagh, a walled courtyard in Amritsar, British General Rex Dyer decided to make an example of the demonstrators and shot into a crowd of people who had peacefully gathered in protest of the Rowlatt Act. According to differing reports, up to as many as 600 men, women and children are said to have been killed and many hundreds more were injured. The uprisings that ensued were only quelled following the British bombing of the major cities in the Panjab and the use of machine-gun fire into the groups of protesters. The measures taken in the repression of these uprisings are reported to have resulted in the deaths of 1,200 people and the injury of another 3,600. In the subsequent trials British judges summarily adjudged the protesters as guilty of inciting public unrest and sentenced them to public flogging. At the same time, the entire population was subjected to months of continued harassment.[21] The massacre at Amritsar lost the British colonial government crucial legitimacy. The soldiers from the Panjab were not only eyewitnesses of inhumane warfare that had taken place in Flanders, but also of the inhuman behaviour of the British in India after the First World War as part of constitutional reforms and their suppression in the Panjab, which culminated in the massacre of Amritsar and revealed the fragile concept of the "civilising mission" as a justification for colonial rule.[22]

The reforms of 1919 proved so inadequate that subsequent constitutional reforms needed to be planned and debated in the early 1920s. The internal political situation was partly characterised by a growing political will as well as by serious socio-economic and religious tensions which culminated in increasingly violent outbursts. The consequences of the global economic crisis and Mohandas K. Gandhi's civil disobedience campaign (salt-*satyagraha*) forced the viceroy and his government to eventually make concessions at the beginning of the 1930s. Meanwhile the British were working on an all-India, federal solution that would integrate the Indian states in a future constitution. Ultimately the British aimed to stabilise the colonial regime in the long term with the aid of the conservative monarchs' autocratic systems yet without conceding particular constitutional rights to them. At the same time the British tried to keep debates concerning a "responsible government", let alone independence, away from the political agenda.

For most monarchs of the time, the highest priority on their political agenda was the recovery of their full sovereignty. Between November 1930 and December 1932 Indian monarchs sent their representatives to the three Round Table Conferences that were held in London to clarify the future status of India in the British Empire. A federal Indian solution was discussed at these conferences for the first time. However, the smaller and medium-sized states were not party to this suggestion that would see a "Great India" encompass the entire subcontinent in which they feared they would be dominated by a confederation of the larger states.[23] Conservative "diehards" in London as well as the *maharaja* of Patiala, who was confident of having the support of almost half of all Indian monarchs, were only able to hinder rather than prevent the federation following the creation of a dedicated governmental commission that succeeded in bringing the most important states back to the colonial line.[24]

Henceforth, all further reforms were characterised under the term of an Indian Federation despite the fact that none of the parties involved, the British, the monarchs or the Indian politicians, ever worked with great determination to make this model succeed. Moreover, in both London and in New Delhi the British seemed to have fallen for the illusion that they would be able to keep a contented India within the Empire. However, in order to ensure such a politically contented India, whether in the form of Indian states or in the British Indian provinces, far-reaching concessions regarding the Dominion status had to be agreed. However, this would have led to the removal of British India from the Empire.[25] Consequently, British politicians from all parties were not willing to make firm commitments on the future status of the Indian colony and limited reforms to parliamentary powers which were ultimately implemented in the Government of India Act in 1935. In reality this law was again merely a freshly painted façade of the same authoritarian buildings of the colonial state in which the extensive rights of the Governor-General in terms of finance, foreign affairs and defence as well as his right to veto were reconfirmed.[26]

On the central level, a federal system based on the two-chamber system of the British model was to be set up whereby in the upper chamber (Council of States) 40 per cent of the seats were to be reserved for Indian states whilst the rest would be divided between the remaining provinces of British India. The lower chamber (House of Assembly) would have 33 per cent of its members taken from the Indian States, despite the fact that these areas represented just 25 per cent of the population, and the rest was made up from British India. An integral part of the elective legislature system was the Governor-General who held the role of its leader and who was able to convene, to dismiss, or to dissolve the House of Assembly at his discretion. The Governor-General was even able to suspended or prohibit the debate of certain issues within the assembly. One striking aspect of the law is that the right to vote was not even mentioned despite the fact that it only found 14 per cent of the population eligible to exercise this participatory right. Furthermore, the proposed Indian Federation lacked a legally binding basis as indifferent monarchs were left to ratify the federal parts of the India Act, an action they never took.[27] As such, the law was passed in the imperial interests of the British in India rather than for Indians themselves whilst simultaneously contributing considerably to the temporary consolidation of the late colonial rule.[28]

On the provincial level the Dyarchy was abolished in 1919 leaving all ministries as well as the legislative system in Indian hands (Burma withdrew as a province, becoming a separate colony in 1936; in the same year Orissa, like Sind, became a separate province). The number of representatives increased from 1,021, as was established in 1919, to 1,982.[29] The head of the executive, the governor of each province, was the sole representative with the power to appoint the Indian ministers, most of whom came from the ranks of the veteran ICS officers and selected on account of the majorities held in the provincial legislatures. On account of his position as the chief executive, the governor maintained almost unlimited power. In a position similar to that of the Governor-General, the governor of a province was able to exercise, at will, power over meetings, discussion topics and debates. Furthermore, should the danger exist that such affairs were not in accordance with constitutional law the governor also had the right to suspend government and manage the province through autocratic control.[30]

The British Raj was anything but a homogeneous political entity; the aforementioned observations suggest rather the opposite conclusion: that of a disparate political landscape. Internally, British India was divided into three presidencies, each structured and organised differently, which in turn were subdivided and managed in different provinces. For example, the province of Bengal was governed in accordance with the Cornwallis Code and was therefore marked as a regulated province, whilst the Panjab, also a part of the Bengal Presidency, was a non-regulated province in which the British administration employed a seldom-monitored paternalistic style of governance. Moreover, and as will be shown in the following subsections, a number of very different power relations existed between monarchs and princes. Contrary to the contemporary and historiographical self-representation the British were forced to acknowledge the fact that their empire in India, as the Mughal Empire before them, "resembled a 'patchwork quilt' rather than a 'wall-to-wall carpet'".[31]

Indian monarchies and principalities

Alongside the large states such as Haiderabad, Maisur, Travancore and Kashmir as well as the historically significant principalities of Rajputana or the Maratha rulers of Baroda and Gwaliar, three-fifths of the approximately 600 states that the British denoted as being "princely" were located in the present-day Indian federal state of Gujarat.[32] Obviously, this circumstance has made a lasting impression on the perception and the historiographical narrative of the Indian principalities as they were referred to in the then British history writing, and still today in the historiography on South Asia, simply as principalities rather than monarchies and states. In fact, many of these miniature principalities only came into being following colonial policy in the first half of the nineteenth century. Their own and contemporary understanding of the considered "Indian Princes" was not of a prince *per se*, but rather, in many cases, as a monarch, as was the case in the European concept of monarchy. Simply put, a South Asian *maharaja*, *raja* or *sultan* was the equivalent of a European king and not sorted into the subordinate categories of duke, count or baron.

Of note is the fact that the British were not the first to create these Indian monarchs and princes, many of whom had existed long before the colonial era. However, during the late eighteenth and nineteenth centuries the sovereignty of these positions was transformed and reduced following a series of contracts or, much in the style of the Mughals, unilaterally issued *sanads* in which the Timurids expressed their firm protection.[33] The separation and assimilation of rulers at a lower level was particularly evident in Rajputana where the British sorted the originally combined local magnates found in *bhayat*s into semi-independent territorial princes and merged them together under a newly established princely overlord. He was put under the control of a Political Agent who was comparable to the British Resident in other Indian states. The Political Agent represented all of the magnates and princes merged in the then established Western India States Agency.[34]

However, this transformation did not prevent the fact that following the dissolution of the Mughal Empire, and despite the banishment of the Timurids, many of the monarchs and princes were in favour, and were guarantors, of administrative, cultural and ritual continuity. Domestically, the monarchs and princes continued to be bound to their duties after the *annus horribilis* of 1857 maintaining the social order (*rajadharma*) and acting self-consciously as promoters, founders and patrons in all social and cultural areas. For this reason the monarchs continued to be venerated by their subjects and in no way did the people see them as merely cruel "oriental despots" that harassed and oppressed the population. In many cases, these sentiments were instead held for the British. Since the Indian rulers remained formally autonomous, they were able to retain substantial authority over their subjects and power over their states until 1947, partly on account of the fact that the British did not, in many cases, interfere in the internal affairs of these states as long as they did not deem this necessary.[35]

Indian monarchs exhibited, or rather retained, a great deal of decision-making competence and responsibility. They were, for example, able to block the flow of information to the British Resident and thereby, at times, isolate him almost completely. That is not to say that the Resident was without influence, but rather that the extent to which he could exert his power in the different states could vary greatly and not necessarily have immediate effect. Many of the monarchs were in contact with one another and exchanged secret diplomatic information despite the fact that such "independent" communication was prohibited by the Resident. The British found it increasingly difficult to control this contact the more they attempted to extend and intensify their rule in India. Consequently, the Indian rulers were by no means mere puppets in the theatre of British colonial rule, but rather semi-autonomous actors; some even purposefully pursued their own interests, sometimes with considerable success, as exemplified in the changing coalitions they would make with all political forces, both British and Indian.[36]

Other than this ability to manoeuvre themselves politically, the monarchs also had their own understanding of the various origins and the values of their dynasties in an Indian context. Thus the *kshatriya*-Rajputs of Rajasthan looked down on the *shudra*-Marathas of the Sindhias from Gwaliar just as they looked down on the Jat and Sikh "upstarts". However, the British reduction of the Indian monarch to that of a territorial hierarchical leader is an example of the blatant disregard that the British paid to the Indian order of honours and dignity. The result of this disregard was to place the *nizam* of Haiderabad at the top of the diplomatic ranking, officially recognised as His Exalted Highness and Faithful Ally, and then, perhaps in accordance with the Mughal former position of deputy (*nizam-wazir*), followed by the monarchs of Maisur and Kashmir. This ornamentalisation of the nobility and the implementation of orders, such as the Star of India together with the light blue cloaks that had to be worn on formal occasions, was rejected by many monarchs throughout the nineteenth century. Succumbing to a colonial *realpolitik* in the twentieth century this princely resistance weakened gradually.[37]

However, it would be a fallacy to regard the Indian monarchs and princes as a homogeneous aristocratic class, tied one end to the British Crown, as this interpretation would ignore both the divergent interests of the Indian rulers and flexible policies of the British in this regard.[38] Ultimately, the individual interests of the monarchs and princes predominated. This was supported by the British policy to isolate them and thus prevent their mutual cooperation. More than ever before the monarchs and many of the lesser princes were aware of their autonomy which had been defined in the proclamation of Queen Victoria in 1858. This did not hinder the monarchs from appointing an increasing number of Britons as ministers into their services in the 1930s and 1940s.[39] In general, the British cherished the illusion of counterbalancing the violent "nationalistic turns" which had taken over in the provinces of British India with the help of satisfied Indian monarchs and princes thus slowing down the reform process in its own territory.[40]

As can be seen in the example of Kotah (see Chapter 2), the British promoted the creation of autocratic structures through the settling of protection treaties. Just as some of the rulers in these "princely enclosures" sometimes formed a despotic reign, a handful of princes and monarchs introduced participatory institutions in their respective countries, institutions which, among others, included parliamentary accountability. Occasionally the systematic expansion of the infrastructure, including the construction of new ports, was undertaken by these regimes. In areas such as in Baroda in Western India and Maisur in Southern India, the rulers introduced an educational policy that was clearly demarcated from that of the British Indian system whilst at the same time using the university system and curricula already in place as a vehicle to implement their own reforms. The result, to the dismay of the British, was that in the two states an elite came into existence which, although it had been schooled to Western educational standards, had not been examined by the colonial institutions and was thus uncontrolled.[41]

The most decisive attempt to evade British influence was made by the rulers of Haiderabad. After the cession of the Northern Sirkars in 1766, the despatch of a Resident and the stationing of British troops in 1788 followed by the subsidiary treaty of 1798 which implied political and fiscal constraints, the economically important cotton region of Berar was signed over to the British as a result of the large debts that had been incurred by Haiderabad in 1853. Without doubt, this series of asymmetrical treaties weakened the economic development of Haiderabad, especially as further contracts on mineral exploration and railway construction were imposed.[42] Despite these drawbacks, the deployment of British troops and the establishment of the largest residency in India, the maintenance of which was the responsibility of the *nizam*, the latter was nevertheless able to restrict the Resident's influence. In the twentieth century the Resident was almost completely isolated and political and economic contacts with him were prohibited. In contrast to most of the other Indian states the British extra-territoriality remained confined to the Cantonment in Sikanderabad near Haiderabad. The *nizams* refused to accept Western-European categorisation in the administration of the state and also initiated the adoption of Urdu as the language of instruction in the Osmania University in Haiderabad city.[43]

Furthermore, the limits of British autonomy were made clear as *nizam* Osman Ali Khan (r. 1911–48) dismissed his entire British administrative staff from their offices without explanation. Following this, the British viceroy made it unequivocally clear that such action would be considered as an act of disloyalty prompting the *nizam* to immediately revoke all the dismissals he had made. Although Mir Osman had shown his solidarity and loyalty to the British cause at the beginning of the First World War by donating a substantial amount of money to the British Indian exchequer, this did not prevent the British, once having won the war, from criticising the *nizam* and openly accusing his administration of mismanagement. This was a clear indication that the patrimonial regime of Haiderabad, which relied heavily on personal ties between the monarch and his ministers as well as the administrative staff forming a kind of extended household, was still the preferred method of rule as opposed to an independent government and administrative staff bound by the law.[44]

In Haiderabad, the political system rested on the nobility who, alongside the *nizam*, controlled approximately 15 per cent of the income from the *jagirs* from a total of 27 per cent of the overall area of land. The *jagirs* were originally established to support Haiderabad's military establishment; however, when the defence of the state was taken over by the British it was the Paigah family that gained most benefit from the new political (and defence) situation as they were no longer accountable for the application of their revenue income. This fiscal uncertainty could also be seen at the head of state where the private funds of the monarch and the public exchequer were only rarely distinguishable. In 1926 the British finally forced a governmental reform, which, on the one hand, granted them a number of key ministerial posts, whilst on the other implemented a bureaucratisation of the administrative system. What, from the outside, appeared to be a mere reshuffle of the cabinet system, devoid of constitutional political consequences would, in the long term, change the relationship between Mir Osman and the British as well as the fundamental foundation of his cabinet and would lead to future conflict.[45]

As in many other Indian states in the first decades of the twentieth century, a number of political organisations came to be formed in Haiderabad, and among these were Ittehad ul Muslimin and the Haiderabad Political Conference. Both parties gained ground and became stronger in the following years as they came to be the respective representatives of the Muslim and Hindu groups in the state. Gradually, as in the rest of India, the political scene in Haiderabad was radicalised. This radicalisation became clear in the 1930s in the change from harmless petitions to open demonstrations as well as the organisation, even mobilisation, of large sections of the population. Hitherto, Haiderabad had not

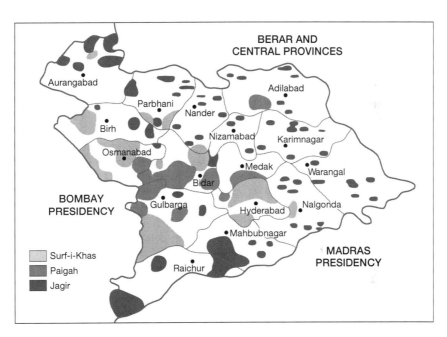

Map 3.1 Land rights and revenues of the *nizam* and his nobility. Adapted from Y. Vaikuntham, *State, Economy and Social Transformation: Haiderabad State (1724–1948)* (Manohar Publishers and Distributors: 2010), p. 27

been seen as an "Islamic" state. Similarly, however, a regional cultural nationalism was also not an argument for a separatist state whereby the simple fact of the sheer number of subjects was justification of a particular rule. For this reason the Osmania dynasty did not consider cultural nationalism a Mughal legacy.

However, in the Marathi areas of the country, a linguistic nationalism developed based primarily around the Marathi language and, not least, orientated around the popular *chhatrapati* ruler Shivaji. According to the Census of India of 1901, by far the largest language group was Telugu with 46 per cent of residents in Haiderabad State, followed by 26 per cent Marathi speakers, 15 per cent Kannada and less than 10 per cent Urdu speaker groups.[46] Among the issues that arose with language policy were also problems such as freedom of the press and freedom of assembly as well as the further expansion of participatory institutions. The cultural and religious polarisation ultimately threatened to divide the country and this danger was intensified further by a number of foreign-controlled campaigns (originating from British India) which increasingly destabilised the Haiderabad State.

A further factor in the fragmentation of Haiderabad State and the British Raj was the communist trans-regional Telangana movement which was able to attract considerable support from the local population in the eastern part of the country. The campaign of "Dakhani-nationalism", a movement based on an assumed south Indian identity, was insufficient in stopping the process of internal fragmentation. Whilst the foundation of the Osmania University failed in initiating an intended Haiderabad-typical cultural synthesis, a Telugu language led nationalism was successfully triggered by the local Muslim elite which ultimately led to the founding of the Indian Union state of Andhra Pradesh in 1956.[47] On a regional level, cultural and linguistic identity building surfaced again after the turn of the millennium. In October 2013 the Union Cabinet approved the creation of a new state of Telangana by separating the region from the existing state of Andhra Pradesh. However, the resolution has still to be approved by the Government of India.

Since 1927, the All-India States People's Conference (AISPC) attempted to coordinate the activities of various local political groups in a trans-state programme. From the outset its political programme was aimed at the constitutional-monarchical order. However, on account of the strong influence exerted by the Bombay workforce, the AISPC was at no point a generally accepted representative for all of the political groups combined. Similarly, the British also refused to recognise the AISPC as a representative institution. Likewise, the vast majority of the Indian rulers refused, often for reasons of self-perception, to allow the public to be represented by the organisation. Nevertheless the rulers of the Mewar and Sindhia both allowed the AISPC to hold its annual meeting in their residential towns of Udaipur and Gwaliar in 1945 and 1946, respectively. Moreover, many smaller princes on the Kathiawar peninsula seemed to be in favour of the developing "paramount power" of the Congress as it ensured their existence in a federal India. Few monarchs openly opposed the Indian independence movement, although various liberal newspapers and the participation in political meetings that had an "all-India-nation" agenda were banned.[48]

Despite the fact that Congress had previously been able to contain political activity and even agitation in the Indian states, some states in the Western India States Agency now saw their population take part in campaigns of civil disobedience against British colonial rule. This only changed with the India Act in 1935 when the political movement in Maisur demanded the right to self-determination in the context of responsible government. The movement became increasingly radical until 1937 when the civil unrest spread to some small neighbouring West Indian states. Following lengthy internal debates Congress resolved to abandon its policy of non-interference and, in 1939, decided henceforth to respond to the calls for help from the people in the Indian states. This action marks the start of a period of close cooperation between Congress and the AISPC which is most clearly exhibited in the choice of Jawaharlal Nehru as the AISPC's president in the same year. Despite the developing political will, as well as the political agitation that was continuing to spread, the majority of the population in the Indian states remained loyal subjects of their rulers until just after independence.[49]

The Labour Party victory in the parliamentary elections in Great Britain in July 1945 and the announcement by the new government to grant British India independence by 1948 raised Mir Osman Ali Khan from his political lethargy in Haiderabad as he quickly had to mobilise all the political and economic resources of the country in order to secure his dynastic survival after the withdrawal of the colonial power. However, firm plans as to future reforms or constitutional organisation were not formulated by either Osman Ali or his ministers. It was expected that the prospect of the restoration of sovereignty would be upheld. The *nizam* continued to show disinterest in an Indian federation, but rather favoured a close alliance with the British Crown which would, in a democratic political environment, legitimise his monarchical rights. Despite Jawaharlal Nehru's assertion that any state that did not send a delegate to the Constituent Assembly would henceforth be considered as a hostile state and would have to bear the consequences of this, Mir Osman sent no representative. He was however strengthened in his position by the statement made by Mohammed Ali Jinnah that all Indian states could, if they wished, become independent.[50]

The last attempt to recognise Haiderabad as a state failed on account of the unyielding position of Ittehad ul Muslim and the *nizam*. After 1946 the Ittehad benefited from an increasing number of paramilitary activists, the Razakars, who filled its ranks and followed their leader Qasim Rizvi. They pursued a strategy that demanded a fully sovereign Muslim state. Their cause found partially open support from the *nizam* which resulted in intensified communal tensions in the country. After the adamant refusal of joining the Indian Union following the independence of British India in 1947, the Haiderabad State Congress began a *satyagraha* campaign along the lines of Gandhi's strategy. Students were encouraged to leave their educational institutions and lawyers and judges to boycott courts. Within just one year the education and justice systems had reached breaking point. On the other hand Ittehad launched a number of violent attacks resulting in the death of more than 2,000 people. Finally in May 1948 the *nizam* entered into a tactical alliance with the communists against the declared common enemy of the new "bourgeois" India and the Congress.[51]

In effect Mir Osman aimed to restore his full sovereign rights without having to share them or his power with any other organisation or institution. However, Mir Osman could only claim such a position as his country had key economic foundations. For the vast majority of Indian states, especially those which were grouped in the so-called agencies, only two options were available: join one of the new successor states of British India, or enter into a union with a number of independent Indian states. For this, the British had developed the Instrument of Accession, which offered the Indian rulers the opportunity to join one of the two successor states, India or Pakistan. Furthermore, in spring 1947 the British Government in London made it clear that it would not recognise the independence of individual Indian "princely states". This made the chance of international diplomatic recognition unlikely, a fact that was made even more implausible in August of the same year as the United States adopted the same position.[52]

In Haiderabad, the Indian chief representative regarded himself the successor of the former British Resident, demanding that the former system of paramountcy prevail through the use of force if needed. The patience of the Indian Government was at breaking point as Mir Osman declined the Standstill Agreement that he had previously ratified, but was yet to sign, and then, supported by the Minister of Police who was a member of the Ittehad, took the Indian delegation into custody. Just a few days later Liaq Ali, a significant supporter and benefactor of the Ittehad, was appointed First Minister. The Ittehad and the *nazim* gambled that this *coup d'état* in late 1947 would likewise lead to an amicable solution with India. The situation escalated in the first half of 1948, when the regime of Razakars became so violent against the Hindu population that they fled in droves to neighbouring India. All negotiations for an amicable solution for the future of the Haiderabad State were thus doomed to failure.

The Indian Government occupied Haiderabad State by the end of 1948. In the wake of the invasion, a pogrom-like programme of violence against the Muslims was initiated to which up to 20 per cent of the male population fell victim.[53] The violent resolution of the conflict showed not only the inability of political leaders in Haiderabad to face political realities, but also the weakness of the young Indian state. Furthermore, the lack of resolutions to problems in Haiderabad exemplified the limitations of the police, military and bureaucracy which had been inherited from the colonial state. Thus, in good colonial tradition, prisons were considered more as places of detention than as disciplinary, let alone socially rehabilitative, institutions, whilst the Indian police force often acted quickly and brutally in true colonial style. However, the Congress-Nehru regime quickly learned to provide for the welfare of the

Haiderabad peasants following the integration of the communist-led Telegana rebellion (Vetti Chakiri Udyamam, 1946–51) against the feudal landowners and the *nizam*.[54]

When the British gave up India it left the Indian monarchs and princes politically isolated as they had to deal with the new Congress Government in New Delhi in order to manage their affairs. Following the "secession" of Pakistan, the Government of India under Jawaharlal Nehru took a pragmatic course, namely to imagine the new nation-state as territorially non-vulnerable.[55] After Haiderabad, with its Muslim dynasty, was annexed by India, the first military conflict between India and Pakistan occurred when the Hindu-*maharaja* of Kashmir decided to join India in 1948 after Pakistani paramilitary actions threatened to occupy the kingdom. Originally he wanted to stay independent since his state would have bordered China, India, Pakistan and Afghanistan. Unlike Haiderabad, where a Muslim dynasty ruled over a majority Hindu population, the Muslims in Kashmir represented by far the largest share of the population. The colonial "communal seed" eventually germinated with the independence of British India into the formation of the two successor states, and since has developed into ongoing conflicts and violent eruptions, the last of which was the so-called mini-war in Kargil in 1999. In colonial and post-colonial readings, the tensions in Kashmir continue to be seen as communal riots.[56]

India, Pakistan and Bangladesh

The history of the two, or rather three, successor states of the British Raj is paradigmatic of the independence of the so-called "coloured" colonies in their quest for self-determination and the establishment of parliamentary institutions. From the outset the successor states oriented themselves constitutionally with that of the old colonial power and its heritage. This fact helps explain why so many of the existing political and social problems in both India and Pakistan are expressions of structural continuities. Constitutionally, both India and Pakistan began independence with a provisional arrangement in the updated Constitutional Assembly of 1946, the adapted version of which originated from the 1935 Government of India Act. Alongside the now secured Dominion status, both Pakistan and India were orientated along new federal, as well as old centralist lines. In a successful balancing act of the interests between the centre (central government) and the periphery (federal states or provinces) the political stability of the republics of India and Pakistan has endured to the present.

Union of India/Republic of India

The Constitution of 1950 saw the change of the Dominion of India to the Republic of India with its own head of state and a parliamentary system constructed in accordance to the Westminster model. At its core was the two-chamber system with an upper house (Rashtriya Sabha), a lower house (Lok Sabha) and a majority voting system. The constitution was based largely on the India Act of 1935, from which some centralised elements of the colonial regime were transferred. Moves to eliminate these elements failed in many cases. For example, the office of the former governor was initially removed from the constitution only to be later reinstated. The governor was appointed by the central government as the highest state representative of a federal state and held the same traditional power as the British governor of a province of British India had. Other centralist elements that were retained included the so-called President's Rule in which, based on the recommendation of the governor, the president was empowered with the ability to declare a state of emergency in a given federal state, allowing the immediate takeover of the federal government by the central government.[57] This measure was based on the veto of the former Governor-General.

The last line in ensuring the balance and stability of the political system in the early years of the Republic was ultimately Jawaharlal Nehru and what became unofficially known as the "Nehruvian Consensus". It comprised the idea of non-alignment, self-sustainability and secularism. However, the secular state model was not based on the French design in which all signs and forms of religion were banished from public life, but rather a balanced policy towards all religious groups. Economically, the Indian state relied on import substitution in order, first, to be independent, especially from the former colonial power, and second, to promote its own production in line with *swadeshi* (see Chapter 2). In foreign policy and confronted with the Cold War, it was concluded that India join the non-alignment states and thereby gain recognition as a major power in the long term. The "Nehruvian Consensus" was never explicitly formulated; however, its maxims were unquestioningly valid until well into the 1970s.[58]

The first signs of change in the political landscape of India came in the early 1970s and pointed to a growing instability of the political system. Increasingly Governor or President's Rule became the instrument employed by the central government against unwanted and/or opposition governments in the federal states. This was especially evident in the Panjab which had been under the tutelage of the Congress-led central government from 1987 to 1992. Conversely, the governor of Gujarat failed to declare a state of emergency in the growing violent riots between Hindus and Muslims in 2002. At this time the ruling Hindu nationalist Bharatiya Janata Party (BJP) endorsed the violent excesses by their tacit attitude at both the central as well as at the federal levels.[59] What started out as an exception soon degenerated into a means of unscrupulously disciplining governments and populations of the federal states. Instead of being an instrument of management at the time of emergency it soon came to escalate violence further, if not triggering it in the first place.[60]

Additional problems for India originated from continued adherence to the province borders drawn more or less arbitrarily by the British colonial government. In the former Madras Presidency these political boundaries, alongside overlapping linguistic and cultural identities, culminated in protests in 1952. However, it was only after the death of activist Potti Sriramalu following a campaign of fasting that the need for action was acknowledged by Prime

Minister Nehru. Within a few weeks of Sriramalu's death, Andhra Pradesh and Tamil Nadu were founded as new federal states. In 1956, the State Reorganisation Act then created a further 14 federal states based on linguistic regions, organised as administrative units of the Congress, as had been laid out in Gandhi's reforms in the early 1920s. In addition, six Union Territories were formed under the direct administration of New Delhi; among these were former Portuguese colonies Goa, Daman and Diu,[61] which were occupied by India in 1961, and the former French settlements of Pondicherry and Mahé.[62]

New problems began to surface in Madhya Pradesh (1960) and in the Panjab (1966). The latter was divided into the federal states of Haryana and Panjab with the aim of creating a federal state where the Sikh community was in the majority and was therefore able to develop its own identity.[63] Linguistic and cultural arguments mingled with political and ethical issues in Assam, which was eventually split into seven federal states in the 1980s.[64] In order to expand its regional power base, the coalition government, under the leadership of the BJP, promoted further federal division and created three new federal states in the year 2000 (Uttaranchal, Chhattisgarh and Jharkhand) bringing the total number of federal states to 28.[65] This process of "regionalisation" is far from a *fait accompli* and, against all odds, has not contributed to a decentralisation and fragmentation as expected, thus weakening the Union, but has succeeded in being a stabilising and strengthening factor.[66]

The process of participation in the early years of the Republic had, largely, been designed by Congress, which had been unchallenged in the governments of the federal states as well as the central government itself until the elections of 1967. Its share of votes lay consistently between 42 and 48 per cent, which, on account of the majority voting system, gave Congress a share of between 65 and 75 per cent of seats.[67] Congress succeeded in implementing a secular political system, mobilising millions of people on account of the allocation quotas for the so-called untouchables and integrating the federal states into the Union whilst simultaneously promoting "regionalisation". Unlike the British colonial regime, the independent Indian state in the 1960s and 1970s was able to promote its technical, administrative and social infrastructure in many parts of society. The political system was further opened up with the general elections of 1971 which had been held early in order to decouple them from the federal elections and which in the long term strengthened the power of federal states in relation to the central government.[68]

The decline of the Congress system in the 1970s can be accounted for in the critical manipulation of the party by Indira Gandhi during her time as Prime Minister between 1966 and 1977 and again between 1980 and 1984. On the one hand these terms split Congress to eliminate inconvenient party competitors and, on the other, they inhibited democratic decisions in favour of authoritarian decisions that were supported by a partisan clique. From 1974 the domestic political situation deteriorated and led to high inflation and strikes so that even the successful ignition of an atomic bomb could not save Indira Gandhi's reputation. She was accused of fraud in the following year in the general elections of 1971 and ultimately found guilty, thereby losing her parliamentary seat in the Lok Sabha. Only by being able to transform this personal state of emergency into a constructed national emergency and encouraging the president to proclaim "Emergency Rule" did she escape dismissal as Prime Minister. She was then able to introduce a ban on strikes, take drastic fiscal measures and implement the radical sterilisation programme for population control all under the motto of "nation building".[69]

Despite some successes, but in disregard of the actual political situation, Indira Gandhi called for general elections in 1977 which she lost in a landslide victory for the opposition. For the first time the Indian-wide opposition parties joined forces under the banner of the Janata Party. This was a loose conglomeration of left and right regional parties that shared the common cause in their opposition to Indira Gandhi and a common objective in wanting to subject her to a bitter electoral defeat. However, within just a few years the common motivation of the cause was overshadowed by specific and regional interests of the various groups, allowing Indira Gandhi to be re-elected as Prime Minister in the elections of 1980. With even greater commitment she then continued to prevent the sectionalism in what she continued to propagate as "nation building". Indira Gandhi's intensified centralist policies seem to be the result of the serious problems in Assam, the Panjab and Kashmir. Sikh extremists in the Panjab, and from even as far afield as Canada, demanded the independent state of Khalistan.[70] Regional and state terror culminated in June 1984 with the storming of the Golden Temple in Amritsar by the Indian Army which was then followed by the assassination of Indira Gandhi by her Sikh bodyguard in October and the resulting anti-Sikh pogroms launched by Congress in Delhi and beyond in November of the same year.[71]

In the 1980s secular nationalism lost its attraction, not least because in order to stabilise her "nation building" programme Indira Gandhi had introduced religious elements in the policy. This paved the way for parties to build their programmes on the exploitation of religious symbolism and rituals. In the end, the Hindutva-family was formed out of the BJP, the RSS and the VHP (Vishwa Hindu Parishad: World Hindu Council). Hindutva, helped by many other Hindu nationalist groups under the umbrella organisation Sangh Pariwar (Family of Associations), was able to radicalise politics, both domestically and externally, in what was now increasingly (pseudo) religious terms.[72] The Hindutva ideology, as developed in the 1920s by V.D. Savarkar, helped provide the foundations for Hindu nationalist groups as Savarkar had defined a Hindu to be anyone whose sacred places lay in India; India being the land lying between the Indus and the Bengal Sea. It was impossible for Muslims, Christians and Jews to be Hindus or even convert to Hinduism as they had no Indian blood. Thus Savarkar succeeded in giving a concise and simple Hindu state ideology using the concepts of *rashtra* (common holy realm), *jati* (common descent) and *sanskriti* (common culture).[73]

At the time of its publication in 1923 the book had no great effect, although the Hindutva ideology reached unexpected popularity in the 1980s which was, in part, aided by the agitation of the RSS. With the BJP – founded in 1980 and successor to the Bharatiya Jana Sangh founded in 1951, with many refugees from Pakistan among its early members – the RSS, also strengthened by the refugees from Pakistan, now had a parliamentary wing which gave the entire movement added impetus.[74] However, the country could not rid itself of the ghosts that Indira Gandhi and her son Rajiv had called into being as Prime Ministers of India as Indira Gandhi made visits to *mandir*s whilst Rajiv accepted public blessings by Hindu gurus. What had initially emerged as sporadic communal riots in colonial India expanded after the 1920s, and in particular after the partition of British India in 1947, into an increasingly employed instrument of political and social controversy. This also explains why voters more and more opted for the "original" in the form of the Hindu nationalist BJP rather than for the bad copy that Congress offered.[75]

In 1984, the VHP announced for the first time that it aimed to free the Ram-Mandir in Ayodhya which had supposedly stood on the site of the present Babri Masjid (mosque) until the sixteenth century. The VHP and its allied organisations maintained that Ram, the hero of the well-known Ramayana epos, had been born at this site. The Rāmjanmabhūmi movement culminated initially in the Rath Yatra Ram[76] action led by Lal Krishna Advani (b. 1927 and BJP president from 1986) who knowingly merged elements of the Hindu pilgrimage and procession into political demonstrations thereby mobilising the Hindu masses.[77] On 6 December 1992, the RSS eventually ignited its political beacon with the destruction of the Babri Masjid. It took just a few hours for the almost 300,000 fanatical RSS *kar sevaks* ("volunteers") to destroy the Masjid which was followed by pogrom-like riots against Muslims and resulted in the deaths of over 1,700 people and the injury of a further 5,500 by January 1993.[78]

This excessive use of violence caused shame even among members of the BJP, which has in turn led to their now more conciliatory policy aimed at de-escalation. Many of the political parties continue to feel committed to secular principles, even if they take these principles as having different meanings.[79] However, neither secularism nor shame prevented violence between religious groups from breaking out in line with party political and power motivations or the exploitation of social tensions for political ends. This was most explicitly played out in Gujarat in 2002 as, under the eyes and tolerance of the police, if not the active participation of the Shiv Sena-led government, more than 1,000 people were killed and a further 70,000 were displaced, almost all of them Muslims.[80] This renewed use of excessive violence – together with the motto of "India Shining" employed by the BJP in the 2004 electoral campaign – ultimately led to the defeat of the BJP and the National Democratic Alliance (NDA) government lead by A.B. Vajpayee from 1998. Clearly India was not a shining country for all of its inhabitants. Despite Congress knowing how to mobilise its old supporters among the impoverished peasants, it only managed to return to power under Manmohan Singh with the coalition help of the United Progressive Alliance (UPA), a coalition that has continued to hold strong even after the general elections of 2009.[81]

Islamic Republic of Pakistan

From the beginning of its existence, Pakistan's inner conflict was mirrored in the two parts of the country (the East and West wing) as well as the particular, separatist interests found in West Pakistan. It is wrongly assumed that present-day Pakistan has no historical roots, since, as already shown, the historical region of the Indus Valley comprises present-day Sind and the Panjab. Moreover, Pakistan is located at the historic interface of western South Asia, eastern West Asia, and southern Central Asia; as a result it is culturally influenced by each of these regions and is economically intertwined with them. The Harappan civilisation is not the only testimony of the unique geographical position, but also the Greco-Bactrian kingdom of Gandhara from between the second century BCE and the first century CE and the millennia-long importance of Karakoram, Pamir and Hindukush as points of trade, migration and state formation which was re-emphasised following the collapse of the Soviet Union in 1992.[82]

It would therefore be wrong to characterise, *a priori*, Pakistan as a purely artificial construct as, without exception, each nation-state is a historical-political construct. However, in the case of Pakistan, plurality, diversity and particularity are obvious; at the same time, the political-military establishment of Pakistan is more dominant in comparison to other nation-states in creating uniformity and hegemony. With this background it is necessary to ask what the conundrum of "consensus" constitutes in Pakistan, as Pakistan meant, and means, different things to different people and these multiple meanings have, in the long run, to some extent frustrated the cohesion of the national community and the imagined national identity. The question is also whether it is the Muslim-Islamic identity alone, which within Pakistan is also far from homogeneous and uniform, that holds the national territory of Pakistan together. However, the nation-state perspective alone, or rather a claimed national Muslim identity, is no longer sufficient in addressing these issues. Rather these questions must be taken up in the analysis of local levels and multiple identities found in Pakistan.[83]

Contemporary narratives inadequately emphasise this diversity and plurality, and in some cases fail to acknowledge it altogether; Western media are particularly guilty of this. Here, as in the general historiography of Pakistan, the narrative has been established that the Pakistani state is essentially the culmination of a religious movement which began sometime in the nineteenth century. Thus, this narrative also implies that Pakistan's current problems stem almost exclusively from religious extremism. According to literature, Pakistani nationalism is based on a Muslim identity alone, and accordingly on an Islamic identity, which is assumed to tend towards radicalisation *per se*. This analysis overlooks the fact that, first, nationalism is based on a construction of identities and, second, nationalism is, by definition, a discourse of power and is as such highly competitive, within which religion may play a role. It is therefore advisable to look at those social forces that were, and are, involved in the discourse and have been hitherto ignored in the historiography because they did not fit into the national self-image.[84]

A large proportion of problems that reach into present-day Pakistan can be derived from the colonial period.[85] As a result of the division of British India, Pakistan lacked a functional administrative infrastructure as well as economic and political organisation. This first became apparent during the military conflict with India over Kashmir between 1947 and 1949 during which both the military and administration found strength in the hour of "national threat". The increase in taxes to finance the war gave Pakistan's bureaucratised administration the possibility to purchase military equipment, giving the bureaucracy unprecedented influence on the state apparatus. In this way the military and the administration attempted to dominate the Eastern Wing of the country in pursuit of political-military objectives as well as economic and fiscal exploitation. The growing resentment in the provinces of Sind and Baluchistan at the rising and almost overwhelming presence of Panjabis in the military and administration, which increasingly influenced the country's economy, had little integrative effect, either in the West Wing or in binding the two wings.[86]

After Muhammad Ali Jinnah died in 1948 and Liaquat Ali Khan, the first prime minister, was assassinated in 1951, the drafting of the constitution and the first general elections were postponed. Meanwhile, on account of the lack of support from the population, the "imported" Muslim League failed to set a unifying national agenda in the face of the strong regional traditions that continued. Despite the constitution which was finally approved in 1956, the Islamic Republic of Pakistan seemed to remain divided between the two parts of the country and their increasingly vested interests, making the constitution little more than a temporary arrangement. The growing political dilemma was compensated for in the provincial periphery by a growing level of centralisation. During the military rule of Ayub Khan from 1958 to 1971, the second constitution was drawn up in 1962 which significantly strengthened central executive powers. In 1965, Ayub Khan was elected as president from a pre-selected electorate of just 80,000 voters.[87]

Tensions between the provinces and the central government, however, escalated and came to a head in 1968 in a general uprising against Ayub Khan's regime. During the uprising he was hardly able to enact his governmental power without resorting to the use of the Emergency Law in the constitution. In 1969 Kahn was virtually powerless and thereby transferred power to the military. The conciliatory attitude that the military commander, General Yahya Khan, took during this national crisis of 1970 paved the way for the first general election. During the election the electorate punished the undemocratic, non-solidarity behaviour of the previous regime by electing the regional leading party in each half of the country. In the West Wing this meant the election of the Pakistan People's Party, led by Zulfikar Ali Bhutto, whilst in the East Wing the Awami League led by Mujibur Rahman was brought to power, also gaining him the majority of votes in both parts of the country.[88]

In a complete misunderstanding of the political situation in the East Wing, Yahya Khan believed he was able to refuse the post of prime minister to the election winner Mujibur Rahman. This resulted in huge waves of protest in the East Wing and especially in Dhaka which were further exacerbated by the General's resolution to bring the rebellious Dhaka under control through military force. Yahya Khan seemed unaware that he had provoked the collapse of the state as a whole. The brutal repression by the Pakistan Army that was flown in from the Panjab to quell the uprising in and around Dhaka, and especially on the campus of Dhaka University, resulted in an unexpected solidarity among the people of the East Wing. On 25 March 1971, Mujibur Rahman finally called for a War of Liberation, which, following nine months of an orgy of violence against the civilian population, led to the independence of the country named Bangladesh; the land of the Bengalis. A significant event influencing the outcome of the war was the intervention of the Indian Army in favour of the "rebels" which General Khan, in disregard of the international situation, had obviously not expected.[89] On account of the huge casualties caused by the war in Bangladesh, the account of this war has become the central part of the national historical narrative, whilst in Pakistan the cruelties and consequences of the war have become almost completely forgotten as they have been reduced to the history of an Indo-Pakistani war that failed to address the loss of land it resulted in.[90]

What could have been seen as a massive political crisis for the West Wing led, however, to the consolidation of the country, not least on account of Bhutto's charismatic leadership. His first *succès d'estime* came in the bilateral negotiations with Indira Gandhi at the Simla Summit in 1972 in which he was able to secure the repatriation of 90,000 Pakistani prisoners of war. To the displeasure of the military, which saw its opportunity for political influence curtailed, "bilateralism" was to become Bhutto's concept of foreign policy.[91] Bhutto also drafted a new constitution for Pakistan which was adopted as the country's third constitution in 1973. It significantly restricted the president's power, leaving the position only with the right to appoint and dismiss the prime minister and to dissolve parliament. These powers were often used by the following presidents which led, above all in the 1990s, to the destabilisation of the elected parliaments and their prime ministers.

In order to, at least partially, limit the political influence of the military, Bhutto founded the Federal Security Force, thereby depriving the army of its privileged position as the sole defensive force. Furthermore, Bhutto initiated a nuclear programme which was aimed at underlining Pakistan's new self-understanding in the South Asian region as well as entering the stage as an international power. In an effort to offer an alternative to the muddled foreign policy situation that was determined by the image of the arch enemy India and the United States which was regarded as indifferent and unreliable, Bhutto successfully agreed bilateral contacts with the People's Republic of China. This move had far-reaching consequences for the geopolitical landscape of South and Central Asia. Furthermore, the skilful foreign policy move of declaring

Pakistan as a non-aligned power allowed Pakistan to challenge India's leadership in the group of non-aligned powers.[92]

Domestically, Bhutto pursued a policy of "Islamic-Socialism" for which he received great support, not least from a very active Left which had found a common cause in the 1970s with Bhutto's line of the nationalisation of businesses. Despite this support, Bhutto was successful in suppressing the cultural and political Left. However, he suffered a failure at the hands of the ingenuity of the landowners who divided their property among a variety of relatives so as to avoid loss of land on account of the proposed reforms. Bhutto's programme of the nationalisation of industries had the effect of rallying the country's businesses against his plans as he became increasingly alienated from the establishment, military and country's elite. This ultimately made him into a tragic figure in Pakistan's history as he was unaware of the negative effect his autocratic style of rule was having on the country.[93] Yet Bhutto's term in government seems to have been the only period in Pakistan's history in which there was noticeable political and social optimism, both of which were characterised by "socialism" and "anti-imperialism".[94]

Whilst the 1977 general elections were a resounding victory for Bhutto, the defeated opposition parties called for open protests against his rule. The ensuing violent protests could only be quelled with the aid of the military under the leadership of General Zia ul Haq. He staged a coup against the government, arrested and tried Bhutto and finally took him to the gallows in 1979.[95] Zia ul Haq remained in power under martial law until 1988 during which time the attempt to Islamise Pakistan's society came to characterise his rule. Until this point, Pakistan's presidents and prime ministers generally did not concede legislative powers to religious people or institutions, such as the Islamic Advisory Council, founded in 1962 and renamed the Council of Islamic Ideology (CII) in 1973, in order to maintain the claim of secularism.[96] Obviously the Islamisation of the country was not to be taken in terms of fundamentalism which would see a return to the Quran and Sharia, but rather should usher in a contemporary socio-political interpretation of this.[97] To institutionalise Islamic modernism in Pakistan had however been part and parcel of policy since the early days of the state.[98]

That said, during Zia ul Haq's rule this moderate attitude was changed somewhat as he set the timeframe of nine years to Islamise Pakistan. In 1977, the CII was occupied with more clergy than ever before, who launched a campaign of Islamisation, calling for the introduction of Arabic as an official language and the mandatory undertaking of study of the Quran. However, the CII proposals were only partially implemented by the government, resulting in fierce criticism from the *ulama* which did not impress politicians and parliamentarians. At the same time the desired degree of Islamisation was hardly feasible on account of the prevailing different legal interpretations and different cultural traditions found in the country. Despite this Zia ul Haq utilised the policy of Islamisation politically and hurriedly employed this rhetoric in the referendum of 1984 and again in his policies leading to the 1985 elections where he was confirmed as president for a further five years.[99] In 1988, Zia ul Haq was killed in a plane crash alongside many of his generals and two US journalists in circumstances that were never fully explained.[100]

Despite the fact that Pakistan continued to be struggling regime, a decade of democratic participation followed during which time a two-party system developed. On the one side was the Pakistan People's Party (PPP) which had been founded by Zulfikhar Ali Bhutto as a centre-left party and which was the only true people's party in Pakistan.[101] In the 1990s Bhutto's daughter Benazir, who benefited from the charisma of her late father and also profited from her own charm, twice held the position of prime minister (Dec. 1988 to Aug. 1990; Oct. 1993 to Nov. 1996). On the other side, the second party was the resurrected conservative Pakistan Muslim League[102] (PML) led by Nawaz Sharif and who also twice held the post as prime minister (Nov. 1990 to July 1993; Feb. 1997 to Oct. 1999).[103] With these two parties, the political spectrum at the national level was exhausted, at least with regards to their political influence and importance. However, on the regional levels various political parties flourished. The Muttahida Qaumi Mahaz (MQM) was one such party that had considerable influence in Sind and more specifically in Karachi. Clearly regional parties were able to represent the particular problems and interests of their individual provinces far more adequately than the nationally aligned parties.[104]

Both prime ministers, Benazir Bhutto and Nawaz Sharif, were mainstream leaders. Neither challenged the consensus which had grown around the idea of Pakistan as a Muslim and Islamic state and neither included this on the agenda of their politics. Occasional gestures to an Islamic unity should be understood more demonstratively than programmatically. With the army onside, albeit in the background, the government simultaneously attempted to rearrange its organisation and expand its political power. However, political room for manoeuvre was too limited to allow for the social, political and, above all, economic reforms to be addressed, for which massive international support would have been necessary. After the events of 1989 in Europe and the collapse of the Soviet Union in 1992, the US interests on Pakistan waned, similarly for the entire South Asia region, as it concentrated its foreign policy on maintaining the *status quo* as the only remaining superpower. As a result, Pakistan therefore intensified its eastern contacts with China so as to be able to actively participate in a West Asian order.[105]

Growing corruption and dissatisfaction within the military together with growing support for the Taliban in Afghanistan and the disastrous economic performance, as well as the fourth dissolution of parliament by the president, destabilised the already fragile polity of Pakistan. Nawaz Sharif's war in Kargil (Kashmir) in 1999 and the suspicion that Sharif wanted to overthrow, and even assassinate, General Pervez Musharraf prompted the latter to go on the offensive. In a *coup d'état* in the same year, Musharraf overthrew Nawaz Sharif and placed himself in the position of the "chief executive" and in doing so suspended all parliamentary and constitutional instruments. Musharraf's tenure was marked by dramatic changes in the political landscape both in and around Pakistan, whereby the events of 11 September 2001 are of significant influence. In order not to be sidelined internationally, Musharraf felt obliged to cooperate with the United States in its "war on terror" and allow US military into the country. The announcement in 2002 to transform Pakistan into a moderate Muslim state and introduce a new era for both the land and its people was almost revolutionary in its aims.[106]

Nevertheless, Musharraf had no strategy as to how he would implement his political and social ideas. Musharraf suffered a first massive loss of international faith as he was accused of not providing adequate protection for Benazir Bhutto who had been murdered on 27 December 2007. Furthermore, his cooperation with the United States in its war against Afghanistan also significantly damaged his national public image. Musharraf's downfall has been attributed to a chain of events that can be traced back to his attempt to dismiss the Chief of Justice, Iftikhar Chaudhary Muhamman, from office in March 2007, which, when Chaudhary refused to resign, saw Musharraf suspend him from his office. The Supreme Court hearing in July of the same year reinstated Chaudhary as Chief of Justice, who soon afterwards reflected on Musharraf's eligibility as a legitimate candidate in the upcoming elections. Musharraf reacted in November 2007 by declaring a state of emergency, suspending both the country's constitution as well as the Supreme Court judges. This was met by an unprecedented wave of protests, supported by the community of lawyers, civil society organisations (both liberal and Islamist), and large parts of the population, almost entirely isolating Musharraf. In the first half of the following year the wave of protests continued to swell as backing for civil unrest, anti-government protests and mass support for the lawyers' movement increased.[107]

The PPP won a landslide victory in the postponed general elections which were finally held on 18 February 2008. Benazir Bhutto's widower, Asif Ali Zardari, co-chairman of the PPP, and the leader of the PML, Nawaz Sharif, formed a coalition government, which immediately started impeachment proceedings against Musharraf. Musharraf finally stood down on 18 August 2008 and since the end of that year Zardari has been in office as Pakistan's President after having successfully united the PPP and MQM votes in the election. The MQM represents the Mohajirs from India who migrated to Pakistan after 1947 and settled there, especially in Karachi and Haiderabad in the Sind province. Soon the party was able to develop the economy and the administration dominated by an urban middle class. Originally named Mohajir Qaum Mahaz, it changed its name in 1997 to Muttahida QM (United People's Movement) in an attempt to develop its national focus. Whilst still a provincial party with an urban focus, it has achieved national success and wields national influence as evidenced in the successes of the presidential elections in 2009.[108]

Since the 1980s the MQM has proved to be an effective and progressive party in Sind which has clearly taken on the problems and concerns of the province, in particular Karachi, that has seen rapid growth from a population of about 2 million in 1960 to an estimated 21 million inhabitants in 2012.[109]

Despite all the violence that repeatedly flares up in the cities and the heavy death toll that results, the numbers, compared internationally, are not exceptionally higher than in New York City or Mexico City. Under MQM municipal administration communications and public services have been improved greatly and, according to businessmen in the city, the corruption has been almost entirely stopped within MQM, which is in stark contrast to the other parties such as the PPP and the PML. Thanks to the MQM's administration and against all predictions, Karachi has not sunk into shambolic misery. It is in fact not merely the best-run city in Pakistan, but one of the best-run cities in South Asia, without the mass poverty that characterises so many Indian and Bangladeshi cities.[110]

In 2009, partly under pressure from the army, Zardari restored the power of the Supreme Court which has since then begun to approach international standards. In the same year Zardari also reformed the financial structures of Pakistan, which are now increasingly based on fiscal decentralisation in favour of the provinces. The Eighteenth Amendment to the constitution limited the power of the president in that he was henceforth no longer permitted to dissolve parliament or suspend the constitution whilst also removing the two-term limit on prime ministers. Furthermore, it also removed all formal executive control over judicial appointments.[111] This in no way means that everything has changed for the best in Pakistan; however, it is testament to the fact that Pakistan's politicians and the military are quite capable of implementing reforms and stabilising both the society and the country. It is rather the United States' imposed "war on terrorism" against the Tehrik-e-Taliban Pakistan (TTP Pakistan Taliban, in contrast to the Afghanistan Taliban) that could escalate into civil war which would in turn threaten the existence of Pakistan rather than any pressures derived internally.[112]

Bangladesh

The foundation of the state of Bangladesh was unforeseeable until 1970. Only after the military coup in West Pakistan in March 1970, which annulled the results of the previous general elections, did unrest break out. The effects of the conflict were intensified by the devastating cyclone in the East Wing of Pakistan which killed an estimated 500,000 people and to which the aid offered by the central government in Islamabad was, first, late and, second, grossly insufficient. These facts confirmed the eastern Pakistani-Bengali population's impression of being a mere annex of the West Wing. As the West Pakistan military was flown in to suppress the violent riots in the east, Mujibur Rahman called for the independence of East Pakistan and the State of Bangladesh. The War of Liberation ensued leading to the deaths of up to three million people in the course of the nine-month campaign that was only finally brought to an end with the massive intervention from Indian troops.[113] Besides this huge death toll, the famine of 1943 which claimed the lives of an estimated 3.5 million people, as well as the partition of Bengal in the wake of the partition of British

India in 1947, should be seen as essential components in the writing of Bangladesh's national history.[114]

The war of 1971 released the tension that had been created by the centralist regime of Islamabad since the state had been founded in 1947. Furthermore, it also revealed the lack of support for a Pakistan-wide national identity. From the state's beginnings, the political, military and economic elite of West Pakistan had succeeded in keeping Bengalis from taking governmental and business positions. The linguistic conflict that followed was but a cultural expression of this exclusion. Within the whole of Pakistan the figure of those that spoke the official language of Urdu was estimated to be less than 3 per cent, whilst in comparison Bengali was spoken by almost everyone, albeit if only in East Pakistan. Seen economically, the West Wing exploited the East Wing by using the income from agricultural exports of the eastern region to finance the industrialisation of the Panjab. In the early 1960s the per capita income of Bengal was one-quarter lower than that of the West Pakistanis. It is therefore easy to understand why East Pakistan pushed for partial autonomy, and appropriate representation as a minimum. It is against the background of these structural continuities that the national history of Bangladesh and its domination by West Pakistan (1947–71) is often written as a continuation of foreign rule by the Mughals (1576–1757) and the British (1757–1947).[115]

Mujibur Rahman was unable to provide the young Bangladesh nation with a new social foundation which would have required extensive reforms, including a land reform, whilst a carbon-copy of the Indian model in which a single party dominated parliamentary democracy was similarly not the goal. Essentially, the State of Bangladesh instead continued Pakistan's system. This eventually included the takeover of government by the military, which had, until the assassination of Mujibur Rahman in 1975, played little role in the political and social landscape of Bangladesh.[116] For the next 15 years the army would now determine the political fate of the country, and even after the popular uprising in opposition to the military regime in 1990 the army never really withdrew to the barracks. Whilst in office between 1975 and 1981, General Ziaur Rahman established a parliamentary system, which, together with the support of the nationalist Bangladesh National Party (BNP), pushed through radical economic reforms in which nationalised companies were re-privatised and an export-oriented, state-subsidised agricultural sector was promoted. This process of partial liberalisation of the economy has continued to the present day.[117]

Following the assassination of Ziaur in 1981, General Ershad took up the office of president until 1990 and ruled from 1986 under the legislation of a permanent emergency. However, in autumn 1990 opposition against the Ershad regime finally broke out and was soon joined by nationwide demonstrations. The protest was largely organised by the students of Dhaka University. The military action that was employed to suppress the demonstrations on the university campus created a general wave of solidarity and inadvertently helped coordinate the protest movement further. In his distress Ershad asked for the political

118   *State formation and empire building, 1858–1998*

backing of the military, which he was refused, thereby effectively signalling the end of the Ershad regime. The general elections of 1991 and 1996 returned Bangladesh to a parliamentary-representative regime.[118] From the various parties at this time, the BNP continued under the leadership of Ziaur's widow, Khaleda Zia, whilst the old Awami League, led by Mujibur Rahman's daughter Sheikh Hasina, each registered electoral percentages well over 30 per cent, making them truly people's parties. As in India, and partly also visible in Pakistan, the forming of a dynasty in the mainstream parties in Bangladesh can also be observed.[119]

The emerging two-party system experienced a setback ahead of the scheduled general elections in 2006 caused by nationwide riots that were spearheaded by the Awami League. As a result, in January 2007 an interim government supported by the military came into office. Among others issues, the interim government fought the notorious corruption with help from the military and police, which resulted in the arrest of many notable politicians and officials, among them Khaleda Zia und Sheikh Hasina, along with large numbers of lesser officials and party members, on corruption charges. In total several hundred thousand men were arrested and interrogated, yet most of them were released after a short time whilst the general election was postponed until the end of 2008. However, attempts made by both the military and the interim government to oust the "two begums" (women) from politics failed. The Awami League's Sheikh Hasina won a landslide victory in the elections and she was sworn in as prime minister on 6 January 2009.[120] It seemed as if the parliamentary system had become an integral part of the political culture of the country, despite military interference.

Since Bangladesh's independence, its society has undergone significant political and cultural changes. The Bengali identity, based on common language, literature and culture has made space for a Bangladeshi identity following independence in 1971 which has been based on a growing Muslim identity. The partition of Bengal in 1905 made many Bengalis aware that they could also have a Muslim identity and they were able to choose between this Bengali and Muslim identity. In independent Bangladesh, following the seizure of power by the military, the "Bengaliness" of the country has been surpassed by a "Bangladeshiness". Ziaur Rahman found additional legitimacy in Islamic symbolism (less in religious content). In a clear sign of his intent he eliminated secularism from the constitution of the country and instead replaced it with Islam. General Ershad continued in this vein during his tenure so that since then the propagated national identity has been increasingly based on an Islamic-Muslim identity. To be Bangladeshi today is increasingly to be Muslim.[121]

The boundaries of the new state were seen for the first time, and only briefly, in the national flag during the War of Liberation as a yellow area in a red circle against a green background. The new nation had been given an area with visible boundaries and was thus no longer the neglected accessory of Pakistan. However, unlike the border between India and Pakistan which since the 1980s has become increasingly opaque, a specific borderland regime became reality in the periphery areas of Bangladesh. On the one hand this is the result of the governments of India, Bangladesh and Burma attempting to implement cross-border regulations, whilst on the other hand it has been the effect of uncontrollable central government developments in the borderland. Neither the partition of British India in 1947 nor the metal fences, which have been under construction since 2006, have hindered the cross- and trans-border connections such as family networks, religious groups and trade routes that transect the area; to the contrary, some connections seem to have intensified. Following the independence of Bangladesh in 1971 the number of transnational, inter-regional connections grew on account of the number of migrants, smugglers and dealers including Islamist networks.[122]

The vast majority of Bangladesh's borders remain volatile, a fact that is not uncommon across many border crossings between the states of the South Asian subcontinent. The attempt by the young country of Bangladesh to militarily suppress the Chittagong Hill Tracts between 1975 to 1997, and to prevent autonomy, shows how the new state demanded national integrity that was based on physical territoriality and undivided sovereignty.[123] As a minority culture, the hill people of Chittagong insisted on partial self-determination, which had already been politically constituted as early as 1972 by the Jono Shonghoti Shomiti (JSS: United Peoples Party). In 1975 open insurgency began, supported by India not least to prevent it from spreading to its own territory, where autonomous movements in the state of Assam were also generating unrest in border areas. Only once India ended its military support in 1996 was a peace agreement possible. However, with an office of three chiefs, or *rajas*, a local system of taxation and land rights as well as special forms of representation, the peace regulations that followed are reminiscent of the system of indirect rule of the British colonial state.[124]

Figure 3.2 The Bangladeshi National Flag, 1971

Despite the tremendous growth in both population and poverty, the state has thus far managed to avoid countrywide famine, which, to a large extent, can be attributed to the development of the country's infrastructure (streets, schools and sanitation) during the 1980s. Furthermore, in recent decades, governments have been working to internationalise its economy despite the poor starting conditions it had to deal with in 1971. Exports for the textile industry as well as remittances of migrant workers from the Gulf States significantly contribute to the country's GNP. Nevertheless, one weakness of the state has remained in its inability to truly serve its people and parties which in turn has led to the development of a strong civil society, supported by the world's densest network of NGOs.

Gorkha-Nepal and Ceylon-Sri Lanka

Gorkha-Nepal: from Kingdom to Republic

The writers of Nepal's national historiography are in the fortuitous position of being able to rely on an early founding father of the present-day national state. From his accession in 1743 until his death in 1775 Prithvi Narayan Shah of Gorkha aimed to control the entire Kathmandu Valley and from there to extend the dominion of the Gorkhas east to Sikkim. After the reigning Newar-king of Kathmandu called on the assistance of British-Bengali troops to help him defend himself and the Kathmandu Valley from Prithvi's expansionist ambitions, Prithvi finally defeated the British force in 1767. During the following year he conquered the rest of Kathmandu Valley. Still today this "national union" of the Malla kingdom in Kathmandu Valley and the Chaubis with its 24 principalities by *maharajadhiraj* Prithvi Narayan Shah in 1768 is an unchallenged and "unifying" theme of the history as well as the national identity of Nepal.[125] Until the Anglo-Gorkha War of 1814–16, the ruler of Gorhka controlled a territory that spanned today's Indian federal state of Uttaranchal (formerly Garhwal and Kumaon), the current Nepalese state as well as its bordering areas to the east.

In 1771 Pirthvi was given the title of *bahadur shamsher jang* by Mughal Shah Alam II; however, this nominal recognition of Mughal sovereignty had no effect on the political independence of the Gorkha kingdom. Despite this, and as already shown in the examples in the first chapter, this move certainly strengthened the legitimacy of Prithvi's rule. The western extension of the kingdom as well as an aggressive policy toward Tibet which provoked military intervention by China was carried out under Prithvi's successor Bahadur Shah between 1785 and 1794. Following the successful Chinese military invasion of 1792, Gorkha rulers were compelled to acknowledge China's over-lordship in five annual tribute missions to Beijing.[126] As in the case of Mughal Delhi, this recognition was a mere formality, especially as the last battle of the short war was won in favour of the Gorkhas. The consolidation of the Gorkha state seemed to provide a buffer between the two major continental powers to the north and south.[127]

The expansive British Company State, which had shared a common boundary with Gorkha/Nepal since the beginning of the nineteenth century, wanted a clear and unambiguous border; the fluid and overlapping systems of control at this open frontier, that characterised the Tarai (as it did the political landscape of eighteenth-century South Asia), did not suit their understanding of revenue administration dependent on regular fiscal income from fixed territorial units. The continuing tensions, which related primarily to trade concessions and access to Tibet, eventually led to the aforementioned Anglo-Gorkha War of 1814–16 and the Gorkha's defeat which was followed by the Treaty of Sagauli and set the still lasting boundaries of Nepal. Moreover the king was also forced to accredit a British Resident in Kathmandu who tried, as in the other monarchies of South Asia, to exert massive influence in the policies of the Gorkha kings. This only changed in 1840 as the then Governor-General of British India, Lord Auckland, ordered a disengagement of the residency from involvement in Nepal's internal affairs.[128]

Various conspiracies and plots at the court after 1847 led to the gradual establishment of the Rana system that would exist unchallenged from 1885 to 1951. During the confusion, King Rajendra Bikram Shah (r. 1816–47) fled to Banaras in 1846. In the following year Prime Minister Jang Bahadur Kunwar (1816–77) informed the troops of the exiled king's treasonous activities, announced his dethronement, and elevated Rajendra's son to the throne as Surendra Bikram Shah (r. 1847–81). King Rajendra Bikram was captured later that year in the Tarai and he was placed under house arrest for the rest of his life. By 1850 Jang Bahadur Kunwar had eliminated all of his major rivals, installed his own candidate on the throne, appointed his brothers and cronies to all the important posts, and ensured that major administrative decisions were made by him in his position as prime minister. The system of government was much like that of the *peshwa* of the former Maratha Union (*swarajya*). Jang Bahadur travelled to Britain and France in 1850–1. The main result of the tour was a great increase in goodwill between the British and Nepal. Recognising the power of industrialised Europe, Jang Bahadur Kunwar became convinced that close cooperation with the British was the best way to guarantee Gorkha's independence.

In 1856 a royal decree was issued conferring the title of Maharaja of Kaski and Lamjung to Jung Bahadur Kunwar. The document gave him full authority within his new domains and broad supervisory powers over the king. Evidently, Jang's intention was that the rank of *maharaja* and its prerogatives should be inherited by his own family whilst the premiership would be passed on by agnate succession among his brothers, sons and grandsons. In addition, *maharajadhiraj* Surendra of Gorkha bestowed upon Jang Bahadur Kunwar the honorific title of Rana in 1858, an old title denoting martial glory used by Rajput princes in northern India. In the long term, Jang Bahadur Rana wanted to replace the ruling Shah dynasty; however, such ambitions frustrated the neighbouring British. Further political unrest in 1885 finally secured the Rana family permanent political power in Gorkha. A strong identification of the Gorkha's political interests now also took place with the British Raj, in which of course the Ranas were not willing to give up any their sovereign rights or land.[129]

A "brahmanisation" and "Sanskritisation" of the different communities of the Gorkha kingdom began under the leadership of Jang Bahadur Rana. Concurrently, *brahmans* who were involved in military service were reimbursed with *birta*-lands (revenue-free land). Religious practitioners were also patronised because, in the first place, they provided the ruling Ranas with the kind of legitimate aura they obviously lacked and, second, *brahmans* supplied the state with an organisational framework in regions where the state was rather weak. Elaborate land surveys were undertaken in 1854 and 1868 as well as the 1870s, published, *inter alia*, in the Muluki Ain that put the rent and revenue system on a new basis which ultimately led to the development of a land market. Over the following decades, the Rana regime ensured consistently growing revenue income, which rose from ₹1.4 million in 1850 to about ₹12 million in 1900. The newly reclaimed land in the Tarai, which had been farmed by peasants from British India who had fled there from the harsh landlord–tenant system, contributed particularly to the development of this strip of land and the increase in revenues. A relatively efficient administration of law and order, as well as what appeared to be a fair control of revenue collection, gradually stabilised and legitimised the Rana regime.[130]

The Rana family increasingly presented themselves as Hindu rulers in order to continue the unifying process of the state. In doing so they overshadowed the fact that the far more important legitimation of the Hindu ruler was, in fact, found within the royal family, the head of which was regarded as an incarnation of Vishnu. Thus, Prithvi Narayan Shah saw his kingdom as a land of Hindus contrasting with *Mughlana* and the Company State. Furthermore, as the territory expanded, the Hindu *dharma* also expanded to the peripheries of the kingdom. Against this backdrop, territorial boundaries were fixed as per the Treaty of Sagauli from 1816 which was a new and additional function for Gorkha as these boundaries levelled the difference between *desa* (realm) and *maluk* (possession). Within the defined territory shared memories developed a new and binding meaning which was expressed in royal festivals and rituals, as in the celebration of the royal Dasain festival. At the same time the lower caste Khasas in the western regions of the country invited *brahmans* to perform various religious rites and ceremonies in order to increase their status as Chetris. This process has become known as "Sanskritisation".[131]

According to the current narrative, the Nepalese national historiography is closely entwined with the historical merit of Prithvi Narayan Shah in the face of an external threat to the internal "Hindu lifestyle" of the Kathmandu Valley and, in the long run, provided the basis for a national unity to develop. This Hindu culture is based on the tradition that immigrant Rajputs and *brahmans*, who had fled from the new Muslim regimes in South Asia in the thirteenth century, established themselves in the Kathmandu Valley.[132] What is obvious from the historiography, and indeed stressed by it, is the fact that despite the programmes of Hinduisation and Sanskritisation, the country and its people are still determined by their ethnic, linguistic, cultural and religious differences. It is not then without reason that contemporary historians of Nepal still see the nation-building process as continuing and speak of "national reconstruction". Obviously, the almost century-long Rana regime did not contribute to the development of a national unity.[133]

The Rana regime remained conservative to the end and was rarely willing to introduce social or political reforms. Dev Shamsher Rana, who reigned in 1901 for only 144 days, did however show some liberal leanings when he presented a plan for vernacular schools and sought to abolish the slavery of women, at least in the Kathmandu Valley. This period also saw the founding of the first newspaper of Gorkha, the *Gorkhapatra* (The Rising Nepal). However, aside from the newspaper, which has since degenerated into a government gazette, nothing remains of Dev's reform initiatives. It was Chandra Shamsher Rana (r. 1901–29) who finally abolished slavery in Nepal in 1925. This was rather more the result of external pressure than domestic policy as the Rana sought to procure Gorkha a place within the League of Nations following the First World War, which in turn would give the Rana the international recognition he desired.[134]

Political Gorkha, which since the 1930s called itself Nepal, was formed in the mid-1940s. In 1947, the All India Nepali National Congress and the Calutta-based Gorkha Congress united to form the Nepali National Congress (NNC), which has since been one of the leading organisations and political parties in Nepal. As a result of the NNC-targeted agitation alongside the actions of Jawaharlal Nehru and the Congress Government of India, the Rana regime finally collapsed in 1951. With the aid of the Indian Government, King Tribhuvan (1906–55), who had fled to India during the political crisis of 1950, could now turn crisis into triumph and return to Kathmandu. In one of his first official acts on returning to Nepal, Tribhuvan revoked the privileges that were given to the Ranas in 1846–57. With the latter disempowered, the monarchy of the kingdom was re-established and empowered. Consequently, parliamentary representation providing the NNC and its leader, B.P. Koirala, with some scope of political design was not as successful.[135]

Domestically, the *coup d'état* led by King Mahendra (r. 1955–72) on 15 December 1960 and the subsequent establishment of an autocratic regime to further preserve the already decrepit structures contributed to the growing discontent among the population. The *panchayat* system, a type of basic village parliamentarianism, did not lead to an increase in general participation, but rather strengthened the hierarchical structures of the kingdom, the sole beneficiary of which was the monarch. Externally Nepal floundered in the growing tensions in various conflicts between the People's Republic of China and the Indian Republic. The more Nepal was torn between the fronts of the two rival Asian hegemonic powers, the greater were topics such as Nepal's geopolitical positioning and the country's adequate role in foreign policy discussed in scientific literature as opposed to domestic issues.[136]

Movement eventually came in the domestic political landscape of Nepal in 1990 as the NNC, alongside communist factions that had merged into the United Left Front, formed a powerful opposition against King Birendra (r. 1972–2001), forcing the monarch to submit to a constitutional regime within two months. However, additional constitutional, let alone social, reforms did not follow resulting in the growing discontent of the population. Numerous political parties now tried to influence the political formation of the country and in 1995 the Communist Party of Nepal (Maoist) (CPN-M) was founded. By using brutal police force, the government tried to prevent local branches of CPN-M from forming in the districts of the country. In response, the Maoists presented government with a 40-point programme to which the government did not respond. Thus in January 1996 the CPN-M announced and began a "People's War" which was fought over the course of a ten-year period, the latter half of which alone claimed the lives of 13,500 people.[137]

King Birendra fell victim to a massacre of the royal family in 2001 that had been initiated by his son and apparent heir, so that Birendra's brother Gyanendra ascended to the throne. Gyanendra pursued similar restorative and autocratic politics as Mahendra before him by successfully interpreting reputed gaps in the constitution to favour his monarchical position. On 1 February 2005, and with the help of the army, Gyanendra successfully completed his *coup d'état* and took over numerous government offices. By calling a national emergency, Gyanendra was able to rule as a dictator for a period of three years. The ensuing wave of incarceration and imprisonment, as well as the general harassment of the population, soon woke society's civic courage. In late April 2005 Gyanendra was forced to reinstate the parliament and elections were scheduled for early May 2008 which resulted in a victory for a constituent assembly. However, previous to this the CPN-M had managed to abolish the monarchy and enforce its own leading role.[138] Nepal became a republic on 28 May 2008 with its constitution still pending due to the factionalism of the country's multifarious ethnic groups who seek sufficient representation within a parliamentary system.

Ceylon–Sri Lanka

In the eighteenth century, the rule of the island was divided between the kings of Kandy in the southern highlands, and the Dutch East India Company (VOC) on the plains to the west, north and east of the island. Despite this, however, the kings of Kandy claimed sovereignty over the entire island. In Kandy in 1739 an almost unnoticed dynastic change took place as Nāyakkar Shri Vijaya Rajasimha (r. until 1747) ascended to the throne on account of his maternal links to the previous dynasty. The Nāyakkar were originally a Telugu-speaking dynasty of princes from the Madurai region in southern India. Thus the accession to the throne in Kandy represented a substantial increase in status for this house of hitherto little political relevance. The fact that Nāyakkar's accession did not spark any disputes is partly due to the position that Vijaya Rajasimha displayed as the guardian of Buddhism. This fact made him well accepted by the population and also ensured the continuity of political, administrative, social and religious structures. The observance of custom, tradition and convention as well as being an example of a "good prince" also enhanced the reputation and the legitimacy of the new dynasty.[139] A sort of Kandy-Sinhalē patriotism developed between the ruler of the country and its people that endured into the nineteenth century and which the British were confronted with in the course of their invasions of Kandy.[140]

Since the middle of the seventeenth century, the VOC had made every effort to have its territorial rights confirmed by the kings of Kandy; territory it had gained through the conquest of the Portuguese settlements and the transfer of the kingdom of Kotte from the Portuguese to the VOC. However, the kings constantly refused to do so. In turn, the VOC caused the Kandy rulers financial difficulties after having managed to secure control of the coasts of Ceylon in the first half of the eighteenth century, establishing a trade monopoly. In retaliation, the Kandy kings responded by stopping deliveries of goods to the VOC. After a brief war, the treaty of 1766 transferred sovereignty to the Dutch of areas up to 40 miles inland spreading from the coastal regions and closed many ports for external trade to Kandy. In further demonstrations of their power over the island, the Kandy kings occasionally undertook military campaigns in the lowlands up to the borders of the Dutch settlements. The kings of Kandy ruled over the greater part of the island, albeit with varying degrees of intensity, and were, however, the only ones who were regarded as legitimate rulers.[141]

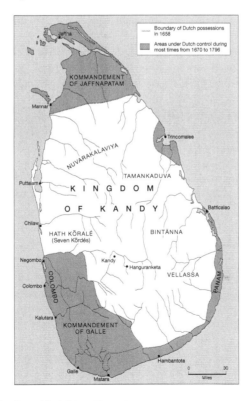

Map 3.2 Ceylon in the mid-eighteenth century

Once the Batavian Republic (The Netherlands, 1795–1806) had entered into a defensive alliance with France in 1795 during the Revolutionary Wars in Europe, the EIC occupied the VOC's bases in Galle, Colombo, Jaffna, Trincomalee and Batticaloa in 1796. After Ceylon became a British Crown Colony following the signing of the Treaty of Amiens (1802), the king of Kandy attempted to revise the treaty of 1766, but failed. Instead he now had to cope with the fact that his neighbouring colonial power had changed from that of a weak power to the strongest European colonial power. In its new colony, the British took over the administrative structures from the Dutch just as the Dutch had taken over the existing organisational power structures from the Portuguese before them. These structures were based on local institutions, law and custom as well as the local personnel. As in any example of colonial rule, these continuities contributed significantly to the stabilisation of foreign rule.[142]

The death of King Rājādhi Rajasimha (r. 1782–98) was followed by a period of disputes and uncertainty, allowing the British to take advantage of the situation by attempting to impose upon the potential successors a subsidiary treaty as characterised by the indirect rule of Governor-General Richard Wellesley in British India at that time. Once a *casus belli* had been found, British-Ceylonese troops marched on Kandy in 1803. However, once they arrived they found that Kandy's troops had left the city and that the population was hostile to their presence. Within a short time the British-Ceylonese troops suffered from food shortages and the outbreak of diseases. Most soldiers died in the expedition or were wiped out during their retreat along the Mahanadi River and almost all prisoners of war were executed. Despite this victory King Shri Virkrama Rajasimha (r. 1798–1815) was unable to permanently stabilise his rule. This in part was due to him successfully making enemies of the region's nobility and alienating prominent *bhikkhu* (ordained Buddhist monks). Furthermore, he also exacted *rājakaria* (king's or temple's labour duty) from the population without due regard to the conventions and practices governing such labour in constructing the Kandy Lake and improving his palace, which resulted in the alienation of the common people too.

Under the pretext of freeing the oppressed population of Kandy, British troops once again marched on Kandy in 1814, this time successfully. The captured king was exiled to Vellore in British India. On 2 March 1815 the Kandy Convention was passed which saw the seizure of the Kingdom of Kandy by the British. However, they had not anticipated that the population of Kandy would identify so strongly with their Nāyakkar dynasty. When a former *bhikkhu* claimed to be a descendant of the Nāyakkar and called for resistance against the foreign rulers in 1817, the British were soon met by uprisings and opposition in many parts of the island, the outbreak of which took them by surprise. The rebellion took a patriotic course as all levels and many sectors of society showed their support for the rebels, making their guerrilla tactics all the more effective. Only once the British had brought in extra troops from India did they succeed in overthrowing the rebellion, which, like the Great Rebellion in British India, can be described as an attempt at liberation from foreign rule.[143]

After the rebellion had been quelled the British set about implementing far-reaching reforms on the island, which, according to the utilitarian *zeitgeist*, meant stringent economic liberalisation including restrained regulatory policy and an administrative hierarchy. In order to introduce such radical reforms to Ceylon, the extent of which had not been seen in India or let alone in Great Britain, the Colonial Office sent a Royal Commission led by W.M.G. Colebrooke and C.H. Cameron to the island in 1829. The aim of the Royal Commission was to organise space and society according to the aforementioned criteria and homogenise the island. The radical proposals of the Colebrooke-Cameron Commission of 1831 came very close to their target of the complete unification of the country and people. After having been first examined, these proposals were implemented almost in their entirety in 1833. Hardly any other country in the world had experienced such far-reaching social, administrative, economic and political reforms in such a short amount of time.

In a first step, the island was stripped of all its local historical traditions and boundaries of the five new administrative units (Provinces) were redefined, mainly at the expense of the former Kingdom of Kandy and along the coastal regions, which were then given simple names according to cardinal points. On the economic front, all state and trade monopolies on spices were abolished. Similarly, the *rājakaria* system was also abolished in order to promote private enterprise, whilst, in a reduction of stamp duties, the courts were made equally accessible to all classes of people. Furthermore, judges and administrators were to come from all social groups and were to be promoted not by birth, but by merit. In summary, the legal and administrative processes were designed to be consistent and easily accessible, simply and hierarchically organised in order to as closely as possible resemble the ideal of a single chain of command. Executive and legislative councils controlled the power of the governor, whose influence, however, was not reduced.[144]

The reforms laid the foundations for the British administration to implement a form of colonialism so characteristic of asymmetric economic relations. Of particular interest in this regard was the plantation economy that came to dominate the island as various cash crops, including coffee, coconut and sugar, had been experimented with from the 1820s. The Crown Land Encroachment Ordinance of 1840 allowed the government to declare anything as a "wasteland" (jungle, forests, uncultivated and periodically uncultivated land), to confiscate it and then sell it as plantation land. In this way the entire highlands of the island were approved to be transformed into coffee plantations. However, the plantation landscape only came into existence at the end of the nineteenth century in the form of tea plantations after large areas of the primary forests had been cleared to make way for "Tea Gardens". A first recession of the plantation economy began in 1846, which deteriorated a year later to a severe depression that affected the coffee and cinnamon trade most acutely. At this untimeliness the colonial administration decided to implement a revenue reform which would revert to a model of land revenue similar to that which had been introduced in British India.

Particular resentment was caused by the Road Ordinance which evoked memories of *rājakaria* in the Kandy region, but was now used in the form of forced labour to build roads for the plantation owners. Finally, in 1848 unrest broke out in Colombo and some districts in the Kandy Province. The colonial laws of the 1840s had led to a worsening economic situation in the country and as a result had produced a landless peasantry which had been further aggravated by the restriction of communal rights such as grazing cattle in the forests and on the wastelands at the periphery of villages. The increase in crime was the precursor to riots and peasants were often criminalised when they tried to exercise their old rights.[145] The magnitude of the "Kandy Rebellion" never reached the dimensions of the liberation war in 1818 as the rebellion was quickly suppressed by the British. However, the reporting of the "Kandy Rebellion" in the British press reduced, for the first time, the resistance in colonies to a criminal act which required sharp repression with consequences in the public perception of the "Great Rebellion" of 1857 in British India.[146]

The outcome of the "Kandy Rebellion" was to lay bare the fact that the old elites, aristocrats and *bhikkhus* were hardly able to represent society. Thus, over the next century, new forms of representation came into being that copied European-British institutions and organisations. This process involved the search for, and the definition of, new identities as well as an emerging nationalism. The aggressive Christian missionary societies sparked a religious revival, which, in the Ceylonese case, saw a revival of Buddhism. Sinhala nationalism was first vocalised by Anagarika Dharmapala (1864–1933), an eloquent advocate of the revival movement. Dharmapala openly demanded Buddhist-Sinhalese dominance in Ceylon. The Sinhalese were constructed as the "Lion Race"; mythologically derived from a distant past and contemporarily depicted as excessively romantic and martial. The religious and cultural renewal was positively defined by the (European) Temperance Movement which fought against the use of alcohol, whilst Dharmapala used negative comparisons to (alcohol-drinking) Christians and (corrupt-trafficking) Muslims to help root the renewal.[147] As has been reflected in historiography, the virulence of the early Sinhala nationalism was found in this peculiar combination of puritan morality and alleged racial superiority.[148]

Increasing polarisation mainly between the Sinhalese and the Tamils in Colombo in 1915 led to the first outbreaks of violent clashes between the two communities. The violence was directed towards the "Indian Moors" and the "Coast Moors" specifically, Muslim traders and labourers who had emigrated from the South Indian Malabar Coast. An economic conflict existed between the immigrant Indian retail traders who were in direct competition with the Low Country Sinhalese and were accused of giving dubious loans.[149] Further unrest had been quelled for a time. Nevertheless, an obvious yet gradual polarisation of the political landscape soon began to develop. This was expressed in the Ceylon Reform League which launched the nationwide mobilisation and politicisation of the peasants in the supra-regional Sinhāla Mahājana Sabhā and the local Mahājana Sabhās in 1918.

On the one hand this increased tensions between Tamils and Sinhalese, whereas on the other hand tensions with Christians also increased after Buddhist representatives of the Sabhās were proved unwilling to accept Christian candidates after 1923.[150] In 1921, the Tamils were once again aggrieved by their under-representation resulting in their organisation into the Tamil Mahājana Sabhāi and Ceylon Tamil Mahājana Sabhāi political bodies.[151] As in British India, the establishment of these new identities in the form of associations and organisations was promoted by the national censuses. The census of 1901 was the first to differentiate between the Low Country from the Sinhalese Kandiyan, whilst the census of 1911 included a further distinction between the Ceylon Tamils and the Indian Tamils (immigrant tea-pickers from South India). Finally, the 1921 census made a distinction between ten principal races, three pairs being subdivisions of larger groups. These pairs were the Low Country and Kandyan Sinhalese, the Ceylon and Indian Tamils, and the Ceylon and Indian Moors (Muslims). The four specified races were the Burghers (of Dutch male descent), Eurasians (the "rest"), Malays and the Veddas ("aborigines").[152]

Unlike in British India, the category "caste" remained of secondary importance in Ceylon. However, the British considered what they perceived as the "high castes" of Kandy as the true guardians of the Buddhist tradition and Ceylonese culture. Thus religion, as recognised in the categories of "races", also played a significant role. This certainly contributed to the Buddhist revival and sharpened the category of "religion" within the censuses. The origins of the form of communal/racial representation can be traced back to the establishment of the Legislative Council of 1833 in which Ceylonese representatives were selected by religion and ethnicity.[153] This distinction, as can be seen in the censuses of 1901, 1911 and 1921 laid the foundations on which to build new identities that had hitherto little meaning in the social order and history of the country. Founded in 1919, the Ceylon National Congress (CNC) was unable to close the growing gap between the new political and social identities. The latent tensions to ensure adequate representation and personal profiling allowed the CNC to become the exclusive representative of the Sinhalese and led, as seen, to the establishment of the Tamil Mahājana Sabhāi in 1921.[154]

The polarisation of the political landscape continued unabated during the 1920s as the colonial government shifted political representation in favour of the Tamils in 1923 following constitutional reforms.[155] At the same time, regionalism became ever more noticeable as exemplified in the case of the Kandy Sinhalese in comparison to the Low Country Sinhalese. In the course of the nineteenth century the British had consolidated their rule over the Tamils and the Sinhalese of the Low Country whilst often excluding the Kandyan Sinhalese from political participation. Apart from that, the Low Country Sinhalese established themselves as traders, labourers and shopkeepers and filled the gaps in supply that had developed on account of the monoculture of the plantations found in the highlands.[156] Both actions resulted in the social, economic and political discrimination of the Kandy Sinhalese.[157] In response to this perceived and/or real alienation, the Kandy National Association made the British colonial government a suggestion relating to the federal structure of the island in 1924. Accordingly, Ceylon was to be divided in three states: one consisting of the five Kandyan provinces, one of the two Tamil provinces and one of the two Low Country provinces. Internal matters were to be regulated by legislative councils in each state whilst central matters would be dealt with by a federal government.[158]

From a British perspective, such constitutional reforms in the given form were not feasible; yet constitutional reforms were urgently needed. To this end the British Government set up the Donoughmore Commission in 1927 to draft a new constitution, the aim of which was to develop reform proposals after consultation with Ceylonese stakeholders. After much debate, the proposals were finally accepted by a narrow majority in Colombo and implemented in 1931. The reforms were indeed radical as for the first time in a colony general elections with adult universal suffrage (age 21) was introduced. A second major change was the introduction of the principle of territorial election which no longer took into account the role of minorities. Thus, the island was divided into 50 approximately equal-sized constituencies. In order to grant the Tamils and Muslims some protection, the governor was empowered with the role of appointing eight additional members to the State Council. In the event, the small minority groups lost proportionately less than the Tamils who regarded themselves as the losers of reforms.[159]

Whilst the freedom struggle in British India turned confrontational after 1919, in Ceylon it remained "constitutionalist". More than any other, it was D.S. Senanayake (1884–1952) who sought a path for cooperation in Ceylon having been a member of the State Council since 1931. He founded the United National Party (UNP) in 1946 and was the first prime minister of an independent Ceylon from 1948 until his death in 1952. Senanayake began to formulate a draft constitution following the conditions laid down by the Colonial Secretary of State in 1943. He began to develop a "Ceylonese" vision for the independent state based on the cooperation of all ethnic and religious groups. In the following year the Soulbury Commission arrived in Ceylon for final consultations. The new constitution introduced the two-chamber system as per the Westminster model, retained the existing voting rights and marginally restricted the governor's discretionary powers. However, Senanayake failed in his desire to obtain the Dominion status within the British Empire for Ceylon. The rapid independence of British India after the Second World War accelerated negotiations on the independence of Ceylon, which was finally granted in 1948 when Ceylon became a Dominion in the British Commonwealth, whilst maintaining the constitution and the British plantation estates.[160]

Continuities with the colonial state were so obvious and lasting that the Soviet Union refused to recognise Ceylon as a member of the United Nations until the mid-1950s. During the first 50 years of an independent Ceylon, the political landscape became dominated by just two families from which the prime ministers and presidents originated and their two respective parties that dominated coalitions and saw each come to the government through elections. The UNP ruled from 1947–56, 1965–70, 1977–94 and 2001–04 whilst the Sri Lanka Freedom Party (SLFP), which had been founded in 1951 by S.W.R.D. Bandaranaike, led coalition governments in 1956–65, 1970–7 and 1995–2000. Since 2004, it has once again entered government and since 2005 also holds the presidency in Mahinda Rajapaks. Initially the Senanayake-Wijewardena family dominated the UNP and politics whilst it took the Bandaranaike family the course of a decade to manage to build a family dynasty in the SLFP. Meanwhile, the ideological differences that originally dominated and divided the two parties have virtually all but disappeared. During the first two decades of independence the UNP distinguished itself with liberalist, pro-Americanist and anti-Communist policies. Since the late 1970s the UNP has taken up a more popular, multicultural and modernist image due mainly to the initiative of Ramasinghe Premadasa (prime minister and later president) and J.R. Jayewardene (president). Despite this, the link to Buddhism has remained a constant feature of the UNP's rhetoric.[161]

Comparatively, the SLFP profited from the protection of Buddhism and Sinhala culture in that the SLFP is a faction of the UNP. In his role as prime minster from 1956 to 1959, S.W.R.D. Bandaranaike was responsible for radical linguistic and cultural policies which, among other things, established Sinhala as the sole official language of the country. These policies stirred up memories of the past to which he became a victim and was murdered in 1959 by a *bhikkhu*. Bandaranaike was succeeded by his widow Sirimavo Bandaranaike who during her second term (1970–7) introduced a republican constitution in 1972, abolished Dominion status, nationalised the tea and rubber plantations and renamed Ceylon, Sri Lanka. A year earlier saw the uprising of the Janatha Vimukthi Peramuna (JVP: People's Liberation Front). The party had been founded in 1965 as a revolutionary organisation which differed from other left-wing parties such as the Lanka Sama Samaja Party (LSSP) and the Communist Party and mostly attracted the young. The JVP accused the previous government of doing nothing against economic conditions dating from the colonial era and the persistent problem of poverty in the country. Whilst the uprising was brutally suppressed it did help usher in the reforms of 1972.[162]

The systematic marginalisation of Tamils by Sirimavo Bandaranaike's government led to the establishment of the Tamil United Liberation Front (TULF) and other Tamil organisations in the 1970s. From this background the Liberation Tigers of Tamil Eelam (LTTE) was founded in 1976 with its demand for a separate state in the north and east of the island.[163] This demand was not based on any historical construct or commonality, but rather made use of a certain "Tamilness" that was defined as being linguistically and culturally unique. In addition to the government's language policy, it was primarily the settlement policies in the north of the island which had led to an increasing alienation of the Tamils by the government, and, as a result, prompted an influx to the LTTE. To achieve its political objectives, the LTTE was willing to use acts of terrorist violence. After LTTE activists had killed 13 government soldiers in 1983, civil war broke out in July of the same year. Within just a few months some 3,000 people had been killed and 200,000 were on the run.[164]

With the eruption of violence the government turned LTTE activists into terrorists and, at the same time, provoked solidarity among the Tamil separatists making it possible for the LTTE to enforce its hegemonic claim within the secessionist movement. The spiral of violence escalated so dramatically in the following years that the Indian Government under Prime Minister Rajiv Gandhi urged J.R. Jayawardene to sign the Indo-Lanka Accord in 1987. With this India underpinned its already cherished claim to hegemony in South Asia rather than having to mediate between the conflicting Sri Lankan parties. The Accord defined Sri Lanka as a multi-ethnic and multicultural country in which the Northern and Eastern Provinces were acknowledged as areas of historical habitation of the Tamil-speaking people. The Indian Government sent the Indian Peace-Keeping Force (IPKF) into Sri Lanka partly to disarm the militant groups, but also to ensure the protection of the Sri Lankan Tamils. Within months the IPKF had swelled to an occupying army of 100,000 men and in 1987 the LTTE declared war on the IPKF.[165]

For the JVP the stationing of IPKF soldiers was reason enough for a second campaign of insurgency which lasted from 1987 to 1989. The insurrection brought the government almost to its knees through the terrorist actions, which cost thousands of civilians their lives, and the *hartals* it called. Government forces captured and killed the JVP leader Rohana Wijeweera (b. 1943) and his deputy in November 1989 in Colombo. By early 1990 government forces had killed or imprisoned the remaining JVP politburo and detained an estimated 7,000 JVP members. Although the government won a decisive military victory, there were credible accusations of brutality and extrajudicial methods. On both sides violence knew no bounds and the result was sheer terror.[166] Although President Ranasinghe Premadasa had won a victory against the JVP and delivered on his campaign pledge to make the Indian Government withdraw its troops completely from Sri Lanka in 1990, the LTTE broke the already fragile ceasefire in the same year.[167] In 1991 Rajiv Gandhi was murdered by a suicide bomber at an election rally in Tamil Nadu and Premadasa was assassinated by an LTTE activist just three years later.[168]

Thereafter, the 1990s were characterised by ongoing military confrontations between LTTE and government forces, as well as numerous ceasefires and attempts to negotiate peace. By the beginning of the millennium the LTTE had managed to occupy about three-quarters of the north and east of Sri Lanka and to establish Killinocchi as the headquarters of an autonomously managed area. A ceasefire was brokered by Norway that lasted between 2002 and 2006.[169] The breakdown of peace talks in Geneva in 2006 led the new president, Mahinda Rajapaksa, who had been in office since 2005, to once again seek a military solution to the conflict and in 2007 the government launched its offensive against the LTTE. Government forces finally succeeded in taking Killinochi following a large-scale military operation in 2009, which resulted in the LTTE conceding defeat in May of the same year. The conflict that resulted from the unresolved problems of the colonial and post-colonial regimes is far from over and it is uncertain that these problems may ever be resolved.[170] Meanwhile the current government's programme of soft authoritarianism is designed not to solve the conflict, but rather to control it.[171]

Notes

1. Copland 1999: 15–21; Fisher 1991: 411–13.
2. Ramusack 2004.
3. Metcalf T.R. 1990.
4. Cohn 1987c: 632–82; Mann 2005b: 215–48.
5. Goradia 1993: 133–60; Ramusack 2004: 107–11.
6. Ashton 1982: 65–103.
7. The opposite opinion is found in the research of Dirks 1987.
8. Moran 2007: 147–77.
9. Potter 1996: 83–101.
10. Jain M.P. 1966: 660–96.
11. Kolsky 2010.
12. Sherman 2009.
13. Rothermund 1965: 47–9.
14. Zastoupil 2010.
15. Bayly 2010.
16. Zavos 2000: 76–7.
17. Robb 1992: 184–203.
18. Bhatterjee 1978: 1–36.
19. Meeto 2007: 1–22.
20. Sarkar 2003: 187–95.
21. Ram 1969; Draper 1981; Bose A. 1994: 152–7; Datta V.N. and Settar 2000.
22. Mann 2004: 1–26.
23. McLeod 1999: 115–65.
24. Copland 1999: 91–112.
25. Leue 1981.
26. Bhatterjee 1978: 126–78, esp. 128–36.
27. Copland 1999: 138–40.
28. Bridge 1986.
29. Reetz 2006: 41.
30. Bhatterjee 1978: 137–44.
31. Alam and S. Subrahmanyam 1998: 57.
32. Burke and Quraishi 1995: 563; Copland 1987: 1–2.
33. Ramusack 2004: 51–2, 85, 137–64, 174–9.
34. McLeod 1999: 25–7.
35. Ikegame 2013.
36. Fisher 1991: 269–315, 432–58.
37. Copland 1999: 9–12; Gordon 2003.
38. The fallacy succumbed: Cannadine 2001.
39. Ramusack 2004: 118–9.
40. Copland 1999: 32–48.
41. Bhagavan 2003; Ikegame 2013.
42. Schwerin 1980.
43. Fisher 1991: 386–402; Burke and Quraishi 1995; Pernau-Reifeld 2000: 93–114.
44. Pernau-Reifeld 2000: 114–32; Bawa 1992.

45 Vaikuntham 2002: 56–67; Pernau-Reifeld 2000: 161–90; Aleem 1985.
46 Ramusack 2004: 210, 221–3.
47 Pernau-Reifeld 2000: 229–94, 322–44; Sherman 2007: 489–516.
48 Copland 1999: 29–32.
49 McLeod 1999: 47–8; Copland 1999: 125–7; Ashton 1982: 175–84.
50 Burke and Quraishi 1995: 568–9.
51 Sherman 2007: 491–4.
52 Ibid.: 547.
53 Copland 1993: 361–95; Pernau-Reifeld 2000: 295–344.
54 Sherman 2007: 496–503.
55 Raghavan 2010.
56 Burke and Quraishi 1995: 563–608; Menon V.P. 1999; Rai M. 2004, 2003.
57 Reddy and Joseph 2004.
58 Menon N. and Nigam 2007: 2–4; Nayar and Paul 2004: 115–58.
59 Reddy and Joseph 2004: ch. 8.
60 Singh I.K. 2009.
61 Ramani 2008.
62 Rai A. 2008.
63 Kinger 2005; Punia 2009.
64 Baruah 1999.
65 Singh A. 2009.
66 Berthet and Girish 2011.
67 Rösel and Jürgenmeyer 2002: 67–96.
68 Mitra 2011.
69 Dhar 2000: 223–68; Tarlo 2003.
70 Singh J. 2011; Shani 2008; Basran and Bolaria 2003: 56–76.
71 Grewal J. 2007.
72 Ghosh P.S. 1999.
73 Savarkar 1923.
74 Ghosh, P.S. 1999.
75 Brass P.R. 2003.
76 Actually *yātra*: pilgrimage with a *rātha*: coach, car, wheel.
77 Kanungo 2003: 192–5, 199–206.
78 Ibid.: 208–9.
79 Bajpayi: 198–218.
80 Ghassen-Fachandi 2012.
81 Adeney and Sáez 2005; Sáez and Singh G. 2012.
82 Jaffrelot 2004: 2–5.
83 Shaik 2007; Ayres 2009.
84 Toor 2011: 3–4.
85 Talbot 2005.
86 Jalal 1990; Siddiqa-Agha 2007.
87 Khan H. 2001: 166–94.
88 Conrad 1999: 204–5.
89 Yunus 2011.
90 Saikia Y. 2010: 177–209.
91 Cohen S.P. 2004: 79, 142.
92 Ibid.: 77–80, 138–45.
93 Hasan M. 2002.
94 Toor 2011: 117–49.
95 Ahmad 2008.
96 Iqtidar and Gilmartin 2011: 491–9.
97 Malik J. 1989: 42–66.
98 Qasmi 2010.

99 Burki and Baxter 1991; Cohen S.P. 2004: 81–3.
100 Hanif 2009 is a novel yet the only comprehensive piece of literature dealing with the crash.
101 Kumar R. 2008.
102 Rahman S. 2002a: 103–10.
103 Cohen S.P. 2004: 133–7.
104 Jafri A.B.S. 2002.
105 Ibid.: 86–90.
106 Ibid.: 92, 153–8.
107 Cohen S.P. 2011: 1–69, esp. 3–5.
108 Rahman S. 2002b: 59–65.
109 Thenews 2012; Khan A.S. 2012.
110 Lieven 2011: 249–53.
111 Cohen S.P. 2011: 8–9.
112 Lieven 2011: 410–23.
113 Rose and Sisson 1990; Biswas S. 2005; Biswas S. 2007.
114 Umar 2003; Umar 2006.
115 Schendel 2009: 159–91.
116 Karim 2005.
117 Schendel 2009: 193–7.
118 Jahan 2000: 3–41.
119 Sobhan 1993: 12–75.
120 Ali S. 2010: 251–66.
121 Schendel 2009: 202–7.
122 Schendel 2004: 332–63.
123 Schendel 2000: 65–105.
124 Schendel 2009: 211–4.
125 Vaidya 1993.
126 Bajracharya 1992.
127 Whelpton 2008: 35–9.
128 Ibid.: 42–4.
129 Ibid.: 46–50.
130 Ibid.: 54–5.
131 Ibid.: 56–7.
132 Adhikari 1998: 17–20, quote 20.
133 Ibid.: 1.
134 Mann 2012c: 206–10; Whyte 1998: 311–39.
135 Whelpton 2008: 68–72.
136 Uprety 1980, 1984; Ramakant 1968; Mojumdar 1973; Upadhya 2012.
137 Lawoti 2010.
138 Ogura 2008.
139 Dewaraja 1988: 79–93, 150–207.
140 Roberts 2004.
141 De Silva 2005: 209–13, 217–36.
142 Ibid.: 237–64, 275–86.
143 Pieris 1950; Powell G. 1988; Wickremesekera 2004.
144 Mendis 1956: xxxi–lxiv.
145 De Silva 2005: 354–9.
146 Rycroft 2006: 167–204, 272–87.
147 De Silva 1981: 373–426; Wickramasinghe 1995: 34–6.
148 Pieris 1920; Senaveratna 1924; Senaveratne 1930.
149 Kannangara 1984: 130–65; Kearney 1970: 219–66.
150 De Silva 1967: 70–102, cf. 98.
151 Wickremeratne 1975: 49–67, cf. 54, fn.15.

152 Wickramasinghe 2006: 47, 54, 123; Wickramasinghe 1995: 10.
153 Wickramasinghe 1995: 28.
154 Ariyaratne 1977: 57–82; De Silva 1967.
155 Wickramasinghe 1995: 46.
156 Ibid.: 41–2.
157 Wickremeratne 1975: 49–67.
158 De Silva 1981: 421, fn 6.
159 Wickramasinghe 1995: 56–98; Russell J. 1982.
160 Wickramasinghe 2006: 163–210.
161 Prinz 1990.
162 Gunaratna 1990; Wickramasinghe 1995: 232, fn. 78.
163 Wickramasinghe 2006: 282–3.
164 DeVotta 2004.
165 Hellmann-Rajanayagam 1994.
166 Chandraprema 1991.
167 Destradi 2012: 62–95.
168 Wickramasinghe 2006: 252–98.
169 Gunaratna 2005; Keethaponcalan 2008.
170 Uyangoda 2011: 16–38; Uyangoda 1999: 92–118.
171 DeVotta 2011.

4 Agriculture and agro-economy

Themes and subjects

On account of the climatic, geographic, geological and ecological diversity of the Asian subcontinent, it makes little sense, and it is virtually impossible anyway, to look at South Asia as a single agricultural area. Thus, general findings related to agriculture possess only limited value in the analysis of the region; this is all the more poignant when regional, or even local, conditions are extrapolated to give subcontinental dimensions. Such was the grave deficit of the early British, and later Indian, historiographical undertakings on South Asia.[1] Since then, new insights have developed. The weight of these new investigations has been borne in research into the peasant–landlord relationship,[2] commercialisation, capitalisation and control of agricultural structures[3] as well as economic and social structures.[4] Meanwhile, the resistance of peasants against the British colonial regime and independent India has also received significant attention in a number of books.[5] Finally, the weight of research has shifted to highlight the environmental and ecological consequences of the colonial and post-colonial agricultural economy.[6]

As is so often the case in scientific investigations into South Asia, the regional focus of such research has invariably centred on the North Indian region, whilst only a handful of publications exist that explore agriculture in southern India.[7] Despite this clear "skew" in focus, at the end of the twentieth century it was possible, for the first time, to synthesise the new findings for agriculture.[8] Since then, the interest in agricultural history has declined, a trend reflected in the global historical sciences. Aside from a few exceptions, it seems that the representation of peasants as a driving force in society has been almost entirely ignored.[9] However, questions still remain as to the extent of access that they had to the land and how it was used, leaving scope for further investigation. Furthermore, questions concerning the social and economic stratification of peasants are, to a large extent, still a fallow field. This fact reflects an ongoing colonial discourse that places more weight on agricultural productivity, which formed the basis for revenue collection, than on the availability and access to land for peasants.

Despite the clear regional differences in terms of the characteristics of the South Asian climate, as alluded to above, one similarity does exist that must be regarded as the foundation of agriculture on the subcontinent: the dependence on the monsoon and the resulting alignment of subsequent harvests: *kharif* (September–October) and *rabi* in the cold season (January–February). However, regional variations with regard to rainfall, environmental, climatic and geological conditions, predominate South Asia's agriculture. As such, rice production in southern India can only partially be compared to wheat cultivation in northern India. In order to compensate for the varying agricultural output on account of the variances in annual rainfall from the monsoon and to intensify agricultural output, the construction, expansion and maintenance of irrigation systems is of fundamental importance.

The controlled use of water in agriculture has been an omnipresent factor with which harvests could be ensured and yields maximised since the early settlement history of the subcontinent. Simple but highly efficient water distribution systems in the fields of the Indus floodplains were a characteristic of civilisation there that can be dated to as early as the third millennium BCE.[10] In fact all south Asian regions can be seen to be based, and are dependent, on such "hydraulic agriculture".[11] The same is also true of Sri Lanka where the kings of Anuradhapura implemented irrigation systems during the CE 200 to 500 period in the semi-arid parts of the country allowing for continuous agricultural production.[12]

Each form of irrigation, whether simple wells and tank irrigation systems or the large-scale canalisation projects, led to the intensification of agriculture through the productive use of the ground as well as the expansion of cultivated areas. It has often been observed that instead of the locally controlled, labour-intensive yet water-saving well irrigation system, centralised powers have favoured, initiated and financed wide-scale and costly hydraulic systems.[13] Even today, no alternative to agro-hydraulic agriculture exists that will help to secure the food supply for the still growing population of the subcontinent.[14] The question remains, however, as to what types of irrigation are economically, environmentally and ecologically appropriate. This is without doubt one of the main continuities of South Asia's agricultural history from time immemorial. More information on canal construction, irrigation schemes and their consequences is provided in Chapter 8.

South Asia's agriculture in the eighteenth century

A noticeable intensification of agricultural production from the beginning of the eighteenth century onwards took place in South Asia. This, as well as the increase in revenue income, was part of the state formation as explained in the first chapter. It was thanks to this process and the increasing revenues from agriculture that the British were able to build their colonial regime. A characteristic of the colonial agricultural economy, as it was operated in British India from the nineteenth century, was the gradual transformation of its structure from a subsistence economy to a market capitalist form of agricultural economics.[15] However, a subsistence economy should not be understood as a poor form of production merely for individual consumption and not for the livelihood of a local or regional market. On the contrary, it was from this agrarian subsistence economy that notable surpluses were produced, thereby forming the early European image of India as a region rich in food and with a wealth of skilled manual labourers. Likewise, it would also be wrong to ascribe the agriculture and industry in South Asia to have no tendencies towards commercialisation before the advent of Europeans.[16]

Agriculture in South Asia can be divided into four categories. First, the geological–geographic determinant characterised by peasant access to land and water. Second, the environmental determinant that essentially implies the use and nature of the physical environment such as soil qualities which, aside from climatic conditions and the use of human and animal labour, decisively influence the productivity of agriculture. Third, the institutional determinant which takes into account the different forms of social hierarchies that form South Asian societies. Within this category the *panchayat*, the village council composed of the dominant status groups, plays a key role in the regulation of the common affairs of the village including the distribution of land. The smallest social unit constitutes the family group with the landowning families being the main formative element of the structural composition of the hierarchy. Fourth, the economic determinant focusing on the increasing cultivation of arable land from the beginning of the eighteenth century and the associated monetisation of agriculture as the economy developed.[17]

In the eighteenth century an ecologically adapted and intensive system of agriculture was implemented in almost all regions of India. The cultivation of rice was especially dependent on the sufficient supply of water and the provision of enough nutrients for its production. These additional nutrients, along with both the regular maintenance of irrigation facilities and the quality of the water helped increase rice yield. Furthermore, fallow periods and crop rotation were an integral part of the agricultural economy. Depending on the fertility of the soil, the appropriate process of crop rotation meant that some areas were able to dispense entirely of the need to allow for fallow periods for the ground to recover, a practice that had been established in Bengal and Bihar long before it became common practice in Europe. Less fertile soils benefited from natural fertilisation methods such as the incorporation of manure and the mixture of "good soil" in the ploughing process. Financial loans, but more often loans in the form of seed, resulted in a consistently productive agricultural sector. In effect, it was only the erratic monsoon that was an incalculable risk factor which had the potential to destroy any plans that had been laid.[18]

Revenue income came almost exclusively from agriculture. The basic assessment of these revenue rates had been assessed by the administrators of Mughal Akbar (r. 1556–1605) and continued well into the eighteenth century. Occasionally local recalculations were made; these were, however, mostly undertaken in the areas nearest to the centre of power as can be seen in the cases of Jat Raj in the Agra-Delhi-Rohtak region, in Awadh, Kotah, and in Maisur as well as in Bengal. More often than not, one-third, and occasionally even up to half of the gross harvest turnover was collected as revenue. This was often paid in kind, but with an increasing tendency towards pecuniary payment. The most direct form of revenue calculation was *zabt* which was calculated annually by accounting for the land, soil fertility and current crop. In stark contrast to this was *nasaq*, a simple revenue estimate based on local customs or established revenue rates lacking fundamental calculations.[19] These systems and structures of revenue assessment and settlement remained the basis for the British colonial state's revenue administration.

Depending on the region, revenue estimates were made either before or immediately after the harvest. As a result the actual revenue collection (*hasil*) could, and often did, differ from the revenue estimate (*jama*). The respective intensities of rule across the subcontinent can be seen in the variances between revenue estimation and actual revenue collection. In the heartland of the Mughal Empire peasants were usually directly assessed whilst in the more distant provinces, such as Bengal and Haiderabad, *zamindars, taluqdars, chaudhuris, maliks* or *palayakarars* were empowered as revenue collectors. As remuneration (*nankar*) they usually received 10 per cent of the collected revenue amount. The *zamindar* deserves special attention on account of the fact that alongside his position as a landowner he was also an administrative official who had held office even before the Mughals, the position of which had merely been incorporated in the central Mughal administration.[20]

Compared to the rural population, these local, mostly rural leaders were obliged to protect the local population in times of armed conflict or in the case of poor harvests that could lead to food shortages and famine. Loans in the form of seeds for the next harvest, known as *taqavi* bonds, were used to help ensure the survival of the population whilst the distribution of food aid was used for the relief of the neediest. Moreover, the *zamindars* and *palayakarars* also invested heavily in the country's infrastructure such as in the construction of wells and irrigation systems, the building of roads and paths, the construction and maintenance of *sarais* (resting and sleeping stations along the highways at a distance of a day's march from one another) and donated revenue-free land (*mu'afi, lakhiraj, inam*) in religious pilgrim centres. A balanced system of endowments was in place which saw Muslim rulers donate equally to Hindu mandirs or Hindu monasteries just as Hindu rulers donated to Muslim religious orders. In this way they were able to promote agricultural development and more intensive agriculture in the form of "internal colonisation".[21]

In no way should one be under the impression that this created an idyllic rural environment as it was, in fact, an arena that suffered under harsh economic and social conditions. This was due to the lack of government salaried officials, which caused rural elites to try to squeeze the maximum fees and rents possible from the peasants. As land was abundant whilst labour was in short supply, the oppressed peasants gained some room for negotiation regarding revenue assessment and revenue collection. Common forms of resistance to these revenue requirements were the hiding of crop yields or the misreporting of the harvest size. In extreme cases peasants of a village emigrated to neighbouring regions where they cleared forests or grassland, thus establishing their rights over the newly appropriated land. On the other hand, the *zamindars* in northern India often held back revenues which exposed the military pressure of Mughal rule (*sarkar*). Since the beginning of the eighteenth century, frequent rebellions over fiscal resources emerged against the background of the regional state formation as peasants and/or local magnates protested against either the military provincial governors (*subadar*) or the civil administration (*nawab*), the resistance of which pitted local *zamindars* against their regional counterparts.[22]

During the eighteenth century the integration of rural and urban markets became visible at the provincial level (weekly markets: *hāt*; market-sites at fords: *ganj*; annual fairs: *mēla*). This process was not only the result of the provincial governor's consolidation of power in his endeavour to secure autonomy, but rather the fact that this was even made politically possible on account of economic integration. Simultaneously, the increasing cultivation of cash crops such as cotton, indigo and sugarcane led to a growing commercialisation of agriculture and a gradual integration into the world markets. This is particularly evident in the growing volume of trade with the European East India Companies. The EIC alone saw its exports of Indian textiles and raw materials to European, American and African markets multiply from the second half of the century. The territorial expansion of the EIC on the Indian subcontinent accelerated this process, as not only were the agricultural production areas and artisanal production centres penetrated, but loans for agricultural or handicraft products such as cotton and cotton textiles initiated the monetisation of the economy which consequently made it possible for the British to collect almost half of the land revenue in cash from the territories they controlled by the end of the eighteenth century.[23]

More often than not, the British took over the dominant revenue system and modified it to suit their own needs. In doing so two key changes took place: first, they introduced the concept of property according to contemporary European legal ideas, and in this context the enforcement of contract law was essential and allowed the British to make Indian landlords and revenue contractors legally liable for their property; and second, the British created an artificial land market. According to their understanding, land was a marketable good and thus had a corresponding value. However, this idea was based on theoretical concepts and the practical reality of contemporary England, where land was scarce whilst agricultural labour was abundant; consequently these two determinants regulated the price of land. Such conditions, however, did not exist in India. Instead, the value of the land could not be measured in any monetary value in the sense of a product as land was sold at different times for varying amounts.[24]

In addition to the landowning and revenue-paying classes and the peasants, the landless peasants and peasant labourers have begun to occupy a larger space in the research into the agricultural history of India. Originally British historiography perpetuated the image of a complacent and self-regulating, timeless "village community", a community in which the land-poor and landless agricultural labourers were not considered.[25] At the beginning of the twentieth century peasant labourers became a rubric in the Census of India. Yet the quantitative scale and qualitative definition of peasants is still largely unexplored. Without doubt, considerable interaction existed between landowning peasants whose harvests provided self-sustainability, and the poor landowning peasants who had to work on the rich peasants' and landlords' fields to secure their income, as well as the landless peasants who were forced to work on neighbouring rich peasants' fields and sometimes even to migrate over great distances to other regions in order to secure their livelihood.[26]

During the previous centuries, various forms of slavery, bonded labour, dependent employment and wage labour came into existence in Indian societies and were controlled by the landowning classes.[27] Landless peasants, especially, were bought as slaves, labourers, casual labourers and seasonal labourers to work temporary or seasonal foreign fields on which they were forced to undertake almost all earthwork duties or were employed as herdsmen, the latter of which entailed the collection and spreading of manure as fertiliser; work that was physically demanding and socially despised by the superior social groups.[28] The British colonial government adopted, transformed and integrated the various labour regimes, which had the effect of not only stabilising their own political regime, but also preserved the economic, and ultimately the social, system in British India in the long term and even after colonial rule.[29]

Continuities, changes and breaks under colonial rule

With the expansion of British rule on the Indian subcontinent economic, political, environmental and social changes slowly began to be introduced which had differing effects in the various regions of British India. These varying effects of British colonial rule, just as in the case of the varying continuities between pre-colonial, colonial and post-colonial states, should also be viewed away from the conventional manner. Despite not being an institutionally or an organisationally homogeneous state, the emerging colonial state nevertheless attempted to force its new territory into a corset of uniformity. Rhetoric-laden reports sent to London and a corresponding "court history" of the EIC, as well as the integration of Indian history into that of the British, began to describe a new centralised state in the tradition of the Indian empires, as it had last been during the Mughal Empire. However, as shown above, the British Raj was anything but a unitary central state, a fact that was clearly reflected in the agricultural sector. This contrasts with the contemporary commentators and their historiographical representation of the Raj that originated in the District Gazetteers and continued through the use of the Census of India into the publications on uniform land revenue.[30]

Until recently, and despite all the differences, Indian agriculture has always appeared to be one "national economy". Numerical comparisons of production volumes, export and import data, revenues and surpluses as well as labourer numbers suggest a uniformity that is misleading.[31] The following section of this chapter, therefore, describes the individual historical agricultural regions which are discussed first by the practice of the revenue assessment and the reorganisation of Indian states according to colonial revenue administration. This is followed by land use in the region, irrigation facilities, the impact of the expanding agricultural land and its social implications. Due to lack of detailed studies of all regions, however, such analysis cannot be of equal weight in all areas.

Bengal, Bihar and Assam

When the EIC accepted the *diwani* of Bengal in 1765, the fiscal income of the Bengal land revenue and taxes were envisaged as commercial capital, thereby making the Company's London-based board of directors independent of the annual borrowing in the European capital markets. From a military perspective, the trading company and growing colonial power in Bengal was regulated to provide safe annual revenues with which the British could finance their wars of expansion as well as their trade. In Bengal, the British had observed the ongoing fiscal centralisation process under the *nawabs*. After the acceptance of the *diwani* the main interest for the British revolved around ascertaining the "real owner of the soil" with whom they then sought to negotiate contracts. In fact, the local revenue assessments and settlements remained largely incomprehensible or irredeemable for the British. Over a period of almost a quarter of a century, the British experimented with revenue settlements, making sure that each report referred to the alleged modernity of the form of settlement, which was based on the individual rather than collective use of property rights.[32]

In order to put an end to the experimentation, in 1789 the British colonial government in Bengal resolved the so-called Zamindari Settlement, thereby agreeing on a ten-year revenue rate. However, this settlement was turned into the "Permanent Settlement" in 1793 which indeed remained valid until the end of British rule in India. With this single stroke of the pen, all legal titles of peasants regarding land were cancelled and they were turned into mere tenants, whilst the *zamindars* – as "landowners" yet not proprietors – were henceforth made solely responsible for the payment of revenues. Within a few years, land was forcibly auctioned following the late payment of revenues, ultimately prompting a transfer of ownership. This transfer had occurred less as a result of the strict implementation of the British revenue legislation and more on account of the tight credit market that forced the *zamindars* into the predicament of not being able to pay their revenue. An artificial land market developed based not on the value of the land, but rather on the total of revenue that it represented. Whilst in the decades before the Permanent Settlement almost half of the land changed ownership, after 1820 this figure still remained at 45 per cent, of which a large proportion of the agricultural land changed hands within half a century. Only in the mid-nineteenth century did the land market stabilise.[33]

Peasants (*raiyats*) were ultimately indifferent to the new legal relationship, as for them whether they paid rent or revenue was indeed of no difference.

Problems only arose with the increasing scarcity of land as owners increased rents. The British knowingly omitted this matter from the Permanent Settlement; however, by the mid-nineteenth century they were forced to address the issue. In doing so, the British operated on two levels: on the one hand they wanted to encourage agricultural expansion by developing a class of smallholders, whilst on the other strengthening the consumption power of these peasants, thereby turning them into prospective buyers of manufactured products. The famous Act X of 1859 (Rent Act) guaranteed the *raiyats* a permanent and fixed lease on land they had cultivated uninterruptedly for the previous 20 years. The same was also true for peasants who had cultivated fields at different rent rates continuously for between 12 and 20 years. All other tenants were, however, left empty-handed by the law.[34]

In 1851 the landlords of Bengal founded the British Indian Association, whilst it took the tenants considerably longer to form their own Indian Association. This pan-Indian organisation represented the medium and small peasants and aimed to protect them from British legislative activities. After the formation of opinions in both Britain and British India into the future role of the tenants, the British-Indian Government set up a Rent Law Commission at the beginning of the 1880s, which led to the Bengal Tenancy Act in 1885. For the first time a land title was applied to the payment of rent. However, the British were not willing to regulate the rent according to a set of rules resulting in settlement officers sometimes arbitrarily fixing the amount of rent. The land poor and landless *raiyats* were also excluded from this legislation. With this policy, the British objective was to stabilise their rule through supporting a small but legally strengthened medium and conservative landowning class.[35]

During the following decades, this policy did gradually undermine the rights of the *zamindars* which had been awarded in 1793. A Country Revenue Commission, assembled in 1940, recommended the abolition of the existing title deeds and the payment of compensation to those adversely affected by this act. The Second World War delayed the implementation of this law. Only after the independence of British India did the Indian states of West Bengal (1951) and East Pakistan (1953) see the abolition of the Permanent Settlement and the associated titles of tenure. Until this abolition, the brunt of the reforms was invariably felt by peasants with hardly any land and the landless peasants.[36] These individuals suffered overwhelmingly by having to take credit from the urban *banias* and *mahajans* and the rural *zamindars* and *taluqdars*. Thus, legal relations had emerged from the previously common-law structures of dependence. Soon credit agreements and the colonial juridical system supporting creditors superseded status in favour of contracts. No sooner had the colonial state halfway freed the peasants from their status and related labour duties, than they found themselves once again in contractual labour services, legally protected by that same state.[37]

The dramatic change in the figures relating to the agricultural sector illustrates the increases in leases and the expansion of the agricultural area in the nineteenth century. Whilst leases increased several times from 1840 to 1880, the agricultural area increased by just 20 per cent. Similarly, the expansion of arable land and its use reflects the agricultural economic disparity. By the end of the eighteenth century about 46 per cent of the agricultural land was devoted to rice cultivation and approximately 20 per cent to cash crops. By 1927 this relationship had been reversed as now 56 per cent of arable land was used for cash crops and only 36 per cent was reserved for rice. At the same time, the total agricultural land of the country had been expanded from about one-third to almost 80 per cent. Although this allowed yields to increase, the population increase between 1895 and 1920 of 11 per cent resulted in an absolute decline in food supply.[38]

These changing proportions were also reflected regionally within Bengal where, since the beginning of the nineteenth century, agriculture had gradually shifted from the western to the eastern districts. This change came against the background of the water-intensive cash crop economy. The small-scale irrigation tank, dam and canal projects proved to be too cost intensive in the west and north of the country whilst, in contrast, the expansive river delta in the east offered almost ideal conditions for cash crop cultivation. Deforestation to obtain revenue-free agricultural land and the water-intensive agriculture had the effect of bringing the existing ecological balance out of kilter. Due to the lack of soil protection, the effects of surface erosion soon set in, leading to the waterlogging and siltation of rivers and making effective irrigation in the affected areas almost impossible. This was compounded by irregular and lower average rainfalls from the beginning of the nineteenth century.[39]

These man-made interventions in the agricultural environment became noticeable in the first decades of the twentieth century. The development of the railway embankment in particular had severe ecological consequences. The construction of the railway lines started in the 1870s. Due to the geological conditions almost all railway lines were built on artificially erected high embankments with many lines stretching from East to West and thereby crossing the natural river system running from North to South. As the embankments had too few ducts and bridges, they caused severe ecological problems such as flooding and waterlogging which consequently led to decreased agricultural outputs on the one hand and to a substantial increase in diseases and the development of malaria in otherwise malaria-free regions on the other. Critique, in particular from the local population, was dismissed by the British who regarded peasants as being unable to understand and appreciate the benefits of modernisation. By the 1930s, railway construction had caused a substantial change in the environment, agriculture and human health of the Bengal delta.[40]

The ecosystem of Bengal further deteriorated on account of the spread of the water-hyacinth. The origin of the water-hyacinth remains obscure, yet it seems very likely that it was imported at the end of the nineteenth century because of its beautiful flower. Around 1900 the plant started to spread. Within less than four decades the weed affected a total area of 35,000 square miles which is equivalent to one-ninth of the delta's plain. Measures to stop the infestation concentrated on experiments for the economic utilisation of the plant rather than its eradication. Fodder, fuel and fertiliser were the options for the future use of the plant. Experiments, however, prolonged effective measures to prevent the spreading of the water-hyacinth. Still, the legislation of 1936 included the possibility of the weed's economic utilisation despite the fact that the weed was indeed choking the economy and ecology of the country. By the 1940s the weed caused severe problems in regard to navigation on which the peasant and trading economy depended.[41]

The development of both commercialisation and capitalisation of agriculture ultimately came at the expense of the natural fertility of the land. This "modern" economy can be divided into three categories: first, the commercialisation of small *raiyat* subsistence economies, which were now forced into a mixed cultivation of cash crops and food crops such as rice and jute; second, an increasing dependence on the cash crop economy from external (British) investors, particularly evident in the demand for indigo and opium; and third, the labour and capital intensive cultivation of tea in the form of the plantation economy in Assam. Loans were essential instruments in the transformation of the agricultural sector, and were organised by the Calcutta-based British agency houses and later more professionally by the managing agencies that had emerged. Without this pre-financing the cultivation of cash crops would have been unthinkable as it was only through the high investment costs that mass cultivation and, as a result, high profit could be guaranteed.[42] However, many small peasants, as in Saharanpur (Bihar), succeeded in defending themselves against becoming dependent on the money-lenders by refusing to grow cash crops such as sugarcane.[43]

The vulnerability of this form of externally controlled agriculture is evident in the various bankruptcies of domestic cash crop markets. The collapse of the indigo market in London, for example – where the price of indigo fell by half between 1825 and 1831 – triggered the bankruptcy of the agency houses in Bengal. Yet British planters received legal aid from the colonial state which placed the Indian peasant, as was the case with contemporary English industrial workers, in a contractual relationship to his employer. Now legally obliged to perform work, they could be prosecuted for non-compliance. Despite rigid regulations, proposed deliveries remained unachievable. As the British-dominated Bengal Union Bank found itself bankrupt, the managing agencies were faced with the same problems as their predecessors had been since the late 1840s. In order to stabilise the economic situation, British planters and Bengal landowners forced their peasants to grow additional indigo crops. However, the peasants' patience had run out. In the indigo districts of Bihar the peasants refused to grow additional indigo and instead planted rice during the so-called Blue Mutiny of 1859–60. However, this revolt was not simply directed at the oppressive landlords; the peasants' resistance also took the form of organised workers' strikes. Using British legal institutions, the striking peasants also fought their cases in court.[44]

Just as indigo had penetrated broad areas of the agricultural landscape, so too did jute. In the 1930s nearly half of the rural population worked in the jute cultivation areas in eastern Bengal on farms of less than 4,000 square meters of arable land. The cultivation of rice and jute was now inextricably linked through the rapid transformation of the subsistence economy. This enabled the peasants to respond to the possible annual fluctuations in demand for jute and instead planted rice. Both were export goods, which during the Great Depression from 1929 to 1939 had a dramatic impact. When the price of rice and jute fell by half within the first months of the Great Depression, the Bengal peasants tried desperately to expand the area for the additional cultivation of cash crops. In the long term, however, this inter-changeability resulted in the shortage of rice. This led to tragic consequences during the Second World War as between 1943–44 famine saw nearly three million people die from the effects of man-made food shortages.[45] To make matters worse, the British-Indian Government showed little interest in alleviating the plight due to the tense military situation in Asia.[46]

The causes of the famine did, however, not only have a military-political and economic background. The environmental changes caused a general pauperisation of peasants who became landless labourers. This transformation accelerated from the beginning of the twentieth century, when many of the peasants were already living below the poverty line and thus were the first ones struck by the food scarcity in 1943. Due to the waterlogged land, plants were increasingly attacked by various crop diseases. This was particularly true of *urfa* and *hispa*, both of them ravaging the rice fields of eastern Bengal. Various other diseases also contaminated the paddy fields and destroyed many of the crops. One plant disease severely struck the rice fields in 1942, thus additionally contributing to the food scarcity of the following year. Diseases affecting humans such as cholera, malaria and smallpox also spread in the eastern delta and infected the already weakened population during the famine. No wonder that Bengal, known for the worst public health in British India and the latter known for the worst public health in Asia, was struck so catastrophically in 1943.[47]

An entirely new sector of agriculture originated with the tea plantations of Darjeeling and Assam. The first plantations were operated purely through European capital on land that British owners had purchased cheaply from the colonial government. However, during the second half of the nineteenth century, Indian investors then became involved in the development of Indian tea plantations so that by 1892 Europeans managed 13.4 million square meters whilst Indians had succeeded in cultivating 22.4 million square meters of tea crops. In the following decades, this ratio shifted further in favour of the Indians.[48] In contrast to the overseas sugar and cotton plantations and the domestic industries, the tea plantations were dominated by female kulis (coolies).[49] Despite the constant lack of kulis to meet the growing tea cultivation demands, their wages amounted to only about half of the income of agricultural labourers in the immediate surroundings. Both Indian and British plantation owners and managers seemed to be toeing the same line in the India Tea Association which enabled them to maintain wages between 1920 and the independence of British India on the same level. In 1946 a government commission noted that the numerous attempts to ensure fair wages and to regulate working conditions within the tea plantations in the 1930s had all failed.[50]

The massive transformation of Bengal agriculture meant that peasants repeatedly turned against the sometimes unbearable revenue burdens. From the late eighteenth century peasants joined forces and gathered together in all parts of the Bengal Province when revenues became too overwhelming or the revenue collection was too rigorous. With the beginning of their territorial domination in Bengal the troops of the EIC were deployed almost annually to quell local peasant rebellions. To prevent the spread of the riots, the British stifled the unrest by destroying seed, burning villages and expelling the population, *ad terrorem* for the general population as was repeatedly reported in the contemporary British reports. A conflagration of unrest threatened following the peasants' resistance of the 1780s during which villages were burnt in the northern and southwestern and eastern boundaries of the province where riots erupted. Only the lack of consistent leadership on the part of the insurgents and the massive employment of troops by the British during the uprisings prevented an early end to British rule in Bengal.[51]

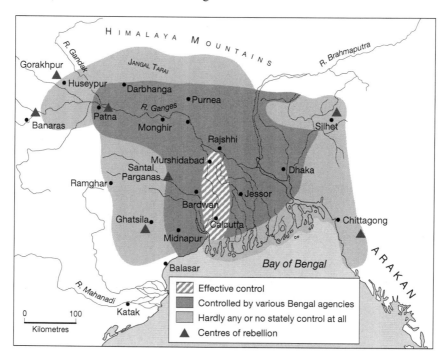

Map 4.1 Resistance and rebellion in Bengal 1780–3. Adapted from Michael Mann, *Bengalen im Umbruch Die Herausbildung des britischen Kolonialstaates 1754–1793* (Franz Steiner Verlag: 2000), p. 244

The most illustrative example of such regional peasant resistance is the rebellion led by Titu Mir in southwestern Bengal in the late 1820s. After his pilgrimage to Mecca, where he stayed from 1822 to 1827, Titu Mir (1782–1831) attempted to further a strong Muslim identity among the Muslim peasants of his native region by prohibiting gravestones, and *pir*-worship as well as to prescribe dress codes, and the wearing of a beard – steps that were obviously inspired by the ideology of the Wahhabi branch of Islam. To prevent the cultural-religious identity and assumed new and therefore dangerous peasant solidarity from gaining support, *zamindar* (and landlord) Krishna Dev Ray – on whose estate Titu Mir and some of his followers lived – began to extract special duties, among which was the so-called "beard tax". The first resistance to attempts made to collect these special duties resulted in uprisings led by Titu Mir against the *zamindar*'s revenue collectors. Within a few months, Titu Mir had, according to different sources, gathered a force of up to 8,000 peasants with whom he waged a guerrilla war against the *zamindars* of the region.[52]

The hitherto local conflict spread through the region after the British magistrate refused a court case concerning the legality of the special duties. The resistance movement attracted large numbers of supporters in the wake of the aforementioned indigo crisis as British indigo planters forced peasants into the uneconomic cultivation of cash crops. The situation ultimately reached its peak in 1831. The British regarded the growing turmoil in the country with suspicion and through various police actions tried to keep the situation under control. Meanwhile Titu Mir had brought three districts under his control, declared the end of British rule, declared himself *badshah* (actually the official title of the Mughal) and now openly led a war against the British. Yet, in November 1831 Titu Mir and his 600 fighters were finally defeated by the British Indian troops and Mir was killed in battle. With this the localised confrontation between a movement based on socio-religious identities and the local elite that was supported by the state (*sarkar*), came to an end without developing into an explicit anti-colonial struggle.[53]

In the 1830s, the Faraizi Movement, which is usually depicted as a religious movement, gained momentum. In fact it started as a Muslim reform movement addressing socially deprived weavers, mostly Muslims, which was soon transformed into a peasant movement covering large parts of eastern Bengal. According to different sources, between 80,000 and 300,000 were involved in the resistance movement of the 1840s and 1850s. It was hierarchically organised and originated at the grass-roots level, which decisively contributed to the strength of the movement. In contrast to Titu Mir's war against the state which had ended in disaster, the Faraizi Movement never acted openly against the colonial state. Instead it successfully broadened its social base, building horizontal coalitions between peasants of different beliefs and social backgrounds against any perceived threat from the landed elite. During the 1860s and 1880s the movement was omnipresent in eastern Bengal. Yet, after the death of its leader Noa Miyan the movement lost much of its strength and consequently its political influence.[54]

150 *Agriculture and agro-economy*

In today's Indian state of Jharkhand a massive Santal rebellion broke out in 1855–6 in resistance to the progressive deprivation of rights by the local *zamindars* on the one hand and by the colonial regime on the other, which, as seen in the case of Titu Mir's rebellion, supported the local elite(s). The tribal societies that lived in the region retreated into the Rajmahal District in an attempt to avoid the advancing revenue settlement of the *zamindars* and the *sarkar*. However, the *zamindars* attempted again to enforce their alleged rights. Additionally, the corrupt practices of money-lenders resulted in the permanent debt of the tribal societies, ultimately driving them into debt slavery. On 30 June 1855 the Santals, under the leadership of Sidhu and Kanhu Murmu, rebelled against the *zamindars* and money-lenders, killing many of them. The British colonial government responded with full force and retaliated brutally. This counter-insurgency action, for the first time, shaped the British image of the uncivilised and savage Indian, who could only be controlled with the utmost rigour and necessary use of violence.[55]

Hindustan

In the mid-eighteenth century, the *nawab-wazirs* of Awadh began to centrally collect the revenues of the Mughal province in order to finance the territorial expansion of the country and to consolidate their rule. In order to achieve this, new revenue districts, *taluqas*, were established, old or new local elites, *taluqdars*, were installed and were directly linked to the government in Lakhnau. As in Bengal, the rights to revenue collection in Awadh were auctioned to the highest bidder (*ijara*-system). Following the annexation of the western districts of Awadh by the EIC (the "ceded" of the British Ceded and Conquered Provinces; the "conquered" were annexed from the Sindhia-Maratha) at the beginning of the nineteenth century, revenue collection was further intensified in the remaining territory as now every village was assessed separately. Additionally the *ijara*-system was successfully reinforced and implemented as the revenue contractors felt compelled to invest their income in the infrastructure of their country. The following figures illustrate this process of centralisation: in the Ceded and Conquered Provinces at the time of 1803–5 assessment, only 20 per cent of the revenue contracts were in the hands of *taluqdars*; however, by 1856 this had increased to about two-thirds of the revenue contracts in the central area of Awadh.[56]

The territory of the Ceded and Conquered Provinces was one of the oldest, most fertile and most heavily used agricultural areas in northern India which had been prized for its productivity by the Marathas, Jats, Ruhelas, Sikhs and the Mughals in the eighteenth century. However, the *nawabs*' central revenue settlement system was limited in its function in the Ganga-Yamuna Doab before the annexation. A century of intense domination and a relatively dense population led to complex modes of settlement. Alongside the *zamindari* rights, individual and village (*pattidari*) settlements existed with peasants, some even with groups of peasants. However, this did not rule out the fact that even within a single village (*mahal*) there could be several revenue settlements. In the first decades of their rule, the British experimented with the existing revenue partners, leading to a gradual increase in revenues without a substantial reorganisation of the revenue system (Mahalwari system).[57]

In order to increase revenues further, the British confiscated most of the revenue-exempt *lakhiraj* or *mu'afi* land until 1840, which, when taken together, represented the largest area of arable land in the districts of the Ceded and Conquered Provinces/North-Western Provinces (NWP). Between 1833 and 1865 approximately 40 per cent of land is likely to have changed hands through confiscations, auctions and enforced sales. Often auctions resulted in no buyers which meant the British colonial administration was forced to sell the land either at knockdown prices or grant a suspension of any debt owed from the land to the former owners. In many cases, the land remained in state hands. In contrast to Bengal, the revenue assessment in the NWP led to an extensive social restructuring to which the established elites fell victim whilst the winners were often the *banias* and *mahajans* who, as urban entrepreneurs, began to have an increasing influence on the agricultural production of the area.[58]

The British systematically transformed the Ceded and Conquered Provinces/NWP in an area of cash crop production in the first decades after the annexation. Targeted government lending-*taqavi*-bonds for irrigation were given only in combination with the cultivation of cash crops; the urban *banias* and *mahajans* likewise only assigned credit to profitable cash crop farming and thus promoted the cultivation of indigo, sugarcane and cotton. By the end of the Napoleonic Wars (1815), the increasing demand on the world markets for indigo and cotton sparked a boom and speculation on both commodities. A harbinger of the indigo market collapse in Bengal and Bihar at the beginning of the 1830s was the collapse of the Ganga-Yamuna Doab economy, which, on the economic fringe of British India, was the first to suffer under the withdrawal of credit. As a consequence of the disaster, British planters and Indian *banias* quickly shifted their focus to cotton and sugarcane production. The flexibility of the cash crop market was shown early on as whole areas were quickly forced to change their production from one crop to another for the cash economy.[59]

The consequence of the agronomic revolution, which the British had induced with their revenue system and systematic lending, was the persistent unrest that swept North India. Until the 1820s and 1830s the Central Doab area was repeatedly affected by local uprisings of *zamindars* and/or little kings, particularly those of Hatras and Mursan. Furthermore, one must not forget that the Great Rebellion of 1857–9 was carried out by desperate peasants of the region and often led by the socially deprived *taluqdars*. The amended revenue settlement in 1856 in the NWP had reduced the number of *taluqdars* from 23,550 to 13,650 which created significant potential for the marginalised local elite to rebel and which local peasants often joined.[60] Alongside the social and economic upheavals, the ecological changes also restricted agriculture in many places, if not making it all but impossible.[61]

After the Great Rebellion, the now conservative policy of the British led to a double structure of the entitled land ownership. In the NWP the Mahalwari Settlement continued to dominate, whilst in Awadh, annexed in 1856, the formerly dominant *taluqdar* rights were again strengthened in order to create a loyal class of landowners. In the former Awadh area alone, the British awarded land on the new revenue settlements to 24,000 *taluqdars* and 6,800 *zamindars* following its earlier confiscation.[62] In order to safeguard the tenants, the Bengal Act X of 1859 was extended to the NWP. Multiple improvements in the form of Rent Acts in 1873, 1881, 1886 and 1901, and finally the Agra Tenancy Act of 1926, transformed the tenant peasants to a type of "sub-owner" with state-guaranteed rights of possession. With the legislation of 1926 the British were able to integrate the previously disparate parts of the province by strengthening the protection of property alongside that of the tenant. By the mid-twentieth century just 1.3 per cent of the *zamindars* and *taluqdars* paid 52 per cent of the land revenue in the United Provinces of Agra and Oudh (former NWP plus Awadh).[63]

Whilst the legislation surrounding leases strengthened the landowning classes, it severely worsened the economic situation of the peasants. The uncertainties this produced were the most extreme for the land-poor peasants who could be ruined by further rent increases as well as the termination of the one-year leases. Aside from this, the divide between the land-poor and the landless was often narrow, since for these peasants small-scale land was often not sufficient to supply their families with food, and temporary agricultural work in fields of landowners had been made mandatory. Repeated local unrest was triggered from this latent insecurity. On account of the ongoing social deprivation, the tenant peasants of Awadh joined together, as they did in other regions of British India, in the Kisan Sabha (Peasants' Assembly) under local leaders such as Ram Chandra. He organised numerous resistance campaigns in 1920 and 1921 which were independent of the Congress and its ongoing movement of Non-Cooperation.[64]

The transformation of the agriculturally productive areas of the NWP–United Provinces to that of a cash crop area drove the British to continue the expansion of infrastructure in the region, the priority of which was the construction of canals for irrigation. The hub of the canal network was to be found in the plains of the Ganges and in the Panjab. A fundamental factor influencing government investment was the yield and efficiency that the canal projects would produce and the revenue income that they were likely to generate. In the NWP and in the Panjab the area of irrigated agricultural land increased from approximately 7 million hectares to nearly 9 million between 1880 and 1901. In the Panjab in 1901, 37 per cent of the agricultural area was irrigated and 26 per cent was irrigated in the NWP.[65] In order to repay the loans, and above all the water charges, peasants were now forced to grow the financially lucrative cash crops on the irrigated, better soils whilst food crops were increasingly relegated to marginal soils. This transformation could be seen in the Ganga-Yamuna Doab as early as during the first half of the nineteenth century.[66]

As a consequence of this revolutionary departure from the established farming practices, the irrigated areas slowly began to lose their fertility as insufficient drainage resulted in the salinisation and waterlogging of the soil. Canal, rail and road embankments also blocked the flow of water.[67] Often, topsoil on particularly dry ground was washed away through intensive irrigation or the standing water had the effect of ultimately hardening and compacting the soil surface. The continual deforestation of areas for agricultural expansion in the Ganga-Yamuna Doab had negative consequences on the agriculture of the region as rivers and wells that had hitherto run throughout the year soon ran dry just a few months following the monsoon rains. Salinisation increased on account of the standing surface water that evaporated quickly and fertile topsoil was lost as a result of water and wind erosion. The new farming practices were unable to ensure the self-sufficiency of food supply in times of a shortage of rainfall and led to drought-induced as well as the man-made famines in 1834, 1837–8, 1868–9, 1877 and 1880–81.[68]

Between 1880 and 1948 the agricultural land in the United Provinces was expanded from 29.4 million acres to 36.8 million acres. Despite the intensive canal irrigation in the western part of the region, the harvests here were always lower than in the eastern areas on account of the semi-arid climate which caused high evaporation rates within the irrigation system. This was in contrast to the eastern region which was subject to a shorter period of heat and abundant rainfall and where the positive effects of irrigation were therefore more sustainable. From Banares to Gorakhpur and Basti, agriculture was instead based on natural rainfall and state-sponsored irrigation wells.[69] Although expensive and labour intensive, well irrigation ensured higher yields than the low-cost canal irrigation (approximately seven times cheaper) which required low labour input over extensive areas, but produced comparatively modest returns. Ultimately, the deciding factor in irrigation method was cost; from 1922 only one-third of the agricultural area was supplied with well water. From a purely commercial perspective, the agrarian revolution was successful as by the mid-twentieth century almost 60 per cent of the agricultural land that was used for sugarcane cultivation in British India was found in the United Provinces.[70]

Panjab and Sind (Indus Valley)

In contrast to the foothill areas of the United Provinces, agricultural performance in the western Panjab was dependent on the availability and efficient control of surface water. In the eastern Panjab the 25 per cent higher precipitation levels and therefore higher overall water table allowed for more extensive well irrigation methods. However, despite the publicly funded British canal construction projects in western Panjab, privately funded irrigation systems continued to be built. The number of wells in the region rose from 137,000 to 347,000 between 1849 and 1947. In absolute terms, irrigation from well water increased faster than that of canal irrigation. By the end of British colonial rule about 70 per

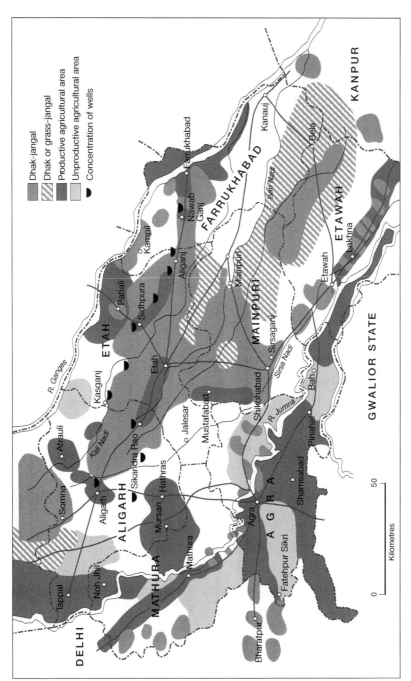

Map 4.2 Forests and agricultural infrastructure of the Central Doab (Ganga-Yamuna) c. 1800. Source: Michael Mann, *British Rule on Indian Soil* (Manohar: 1999), p. 114

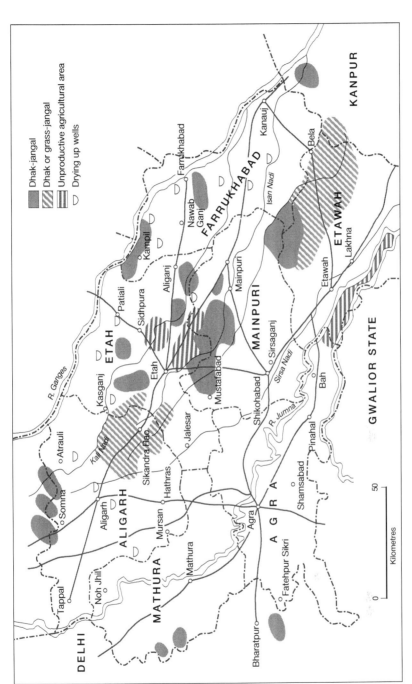

Map 4.3 Forests and agricultural infrastructure of the Central Doab (Ganga-Yamuna) c. 1850. Source: Michael Mann, *British Rule on Indian Soil* (Manohar: 1999), p. 142

cent of agricultural land was irrigated in the western Panjab whilst in the eastern Panjab this figure lay at only 44 per cent.[71]

Regular rainfall and artificial irrigation possibilities in the mountainous and foothill regions of the western Panjab persuaded the peasants of the Sikh principalities to increasingly cultivate cash crops in the eighteenth century, leading to the appraisal of the land as *zabt* from which revenues had to be paid in cash. The extent to which the expansion of world trade of Indian textiles affected this process of commercialisation remains, for the time being, unanswerable on account of a lack of data. The revenue system of the Mughals was maintained and organised along the lines of the *muqaddams* and *zamindars*. On account of the cultural and religious diversity in the Panjab there was a considerable amount of revenue-free *madad-i-ma'ash* or *dharmath* land that the Sikh princes often reconfirmed on festive occasions. During such occasions they also made new donations and endowments.[72] Because of the different revenue assessments and crop patterns, the composition of the agrarian society in the Sikh Raj in the mid-nineteenth century also differed depending on the region.[73]

After the annexation of the Panjab in 1849 the British formally created the Panjab Province from the territories stretching from the west of the Yamuna to the Indus. They took over the existing revenue system and combined it with the provisions of Mahalwari-Settlements, especially from the NWP, again to eliminate the intermediate layer of revenue contractors, mainly *zamindars*. Similarly as in the North-Western/United Provinces the British claimed large amounts of revenue-free land in the Panjab to increase revenue income. The claiming of this revenue-free land and the displacement of the *zamindars* was almost complete in 1870, so that by then rural social structure was represented by a predominant majority of small property owners (56 per cent) and a very small minority of large landowners (roughly 4 per cent), whilst the remaining 40 per cent was accounted for by small tenants.[74]

In the 1880s the yet untapped agrarian western Panjab attracted the attention of the British irrigation canal planners. Since the 1860s the British had only repaired the existing irrigation systems and constructed a handful of new canals.[75] The interfluvial areas of the Panjab seemed to be predestined for canal irrigation structures. The background to the engineering initiative was built on the concerns of the colonial treasury over the growing Home Charges which consisted mainly of the pensions for former British personnel in the colonial service. By the end of the nineteenth century this constituted a quarter of the annual revenues of British India. Since at this time the land revenue was still by far the largest single item in the India Budget, it made economic sense to use the Panjab's agricultural potential. In the following decades, the British systematically turned the Panjab into the "granary of India". Seen statistically, this expansion is impressive as in 1840 the agricultural area in the Panjab accounted for about 12 million acres and by the end of colonial rule this had been increased to 31.2 million acres. During the period from 1924–5 to 1933–4 an average of 35 per cent of the irrigable land was cultivated with wheat, 15 per cent with cotton and 2.5 per cent with sugarcane.[76]

In contemporary accounts, as well as the subsequent historiography, this success was based on economic, technological and political measures that had been introduced to a deserted, or at best underdeveloped, land in the Panjab, the potential of which was noticed and nurtured by the British to modernise and civilise the country and its people. In fact, the Panjab was inhabited by vibrant pastoral communities, which had developed complex small-scale irrigation systems for their agricultural activities which meant they were not exclusively dependent on the annual flooding of the monsoon rains. In contrast, the colossal canals of the British were systematically rolled out over the country almost levelling the local agriculture. Within just a few years the pastoral societies had all but disappeared from the region or had been forced to seek work as agricultural labourers.[77]

Through various annually operating irrigation canals, the interfluvial areas of the Panjab were opened up for an agricultural economy. This new land was categorised by the British as Crown Wasteland and it was selectively awarded to colonists mostly originating from the densely populated districts of the upper western Panjab. Almost 80 per cent of the arable land remained state property in the Canal Colonies that emerged between 1886 and 1925. Resistance to this high degree of state control was simmering in the villages of the Canal Colonies in 1906, when a law which stated that rates on loans could be unilaterally determined by British officials was passed and thereby increased the government's grip on the peasants. In return the settlers protested and demanded guaranteed property rights.[78] Only when the 1912 Colonisation of Land Act was passed were the small and medium-sized peasants able to acquire land ownership.[79] Former Indian military and civilian personnel who had been mainly recruited from the Panjab saw this new land for settlement as a basis for a fresh economic start. The settlers were used as internal colonists of the British Raj, which in turn received its strongest support from the Panjab.[80]

Despite the growing economy, land sales increased by 430 per cent between 1866 and 1900 due to delays in revenue payment and liabilities.[81] Regulatory acts to remedy the plight were late coming. The Punjab Tenancy Act of 1868 confirmed the first revenue assessment and the revision of 1887 brought no significant improvement, apart from giving new powers to the British revenue collectors to be able to set revenue and rent rates at their discretion. It was only with the Punjab Land Alienation Act of 1900 that land sales were halted to some extent due to the fact that the sale of agricultural land from peasants to non-agriculturists was prohibited. However, this did not bring an end to the rural indebtedness, but rather relocated the problem as from now on loans were offered from wealthy landowners. In 1929 a British Bank Commission in the Panjab realised that giving credit in the area was the most lucrative business opportunity. The lower classes were, however, excluded from this development. Outside the Canal Colonies, this discrepancy was even more explicit. Here in 1931 landowners accounted for only 5 per cent of the rural population, the various tenants on the other hand accounted for 80 per cent and the landless labourers 15 per cent.[82]

In the long term, the intensive irrigation of the formerly dry, high interfluvial areas led to serious ecological and agro-economic problems. Since adequate drainage was not put in place in the western Panjab, the areas suffered from residual water problems such as waterlogging. In the period from 1927–8 to 1946–7 this affected an area that increased from 11,500 hectares to 78,700 hectares. The problem of standing water and the threat of ponding was caused by wasteful water consumption as low fees had actually favoured the flooding of the fields. In western Panjab a quarter of cropland suffered from the effects of waterlogging which, by the mid-1890s, meant that 40 per cent of rural land could not be used any more. Although the government tried to counter the loss of arable land and also make concrete steps in the form of drainage canals as well as initiating and prompting the cleaning and unblocking of the existing irrigation systems, such actions rarely went beyond mere damage limitation. As a result, fertile soil was often irretrievably lost.[83]

In addition to the massive ecological problems, health issues also resulted from waterlogging. Official reports from the 1930s stated that the effects of canal irrigation had affected the whole area within a decade of their opening and the deleterious results of waterlogging included salinity and malaria. Especially in the semi-arid areas from the Doab to the Panjab the increased use of canal irrigation and the amount of marshy land increased the humidity of the region and offered water surfaces necessary for the *Anopheles* mosquitoes, transmitters of malaria, to breed. Due to malaria infections, the statistical data for the region west of the Yamuna recorded in the period 1890–9 show the highest mortality rate for the whole of British India. In the western Panjab, the spleen rates for endemic malaria rose markedly in the mid-1930s to 80–90 per cent instead of 15 per cent as had hitherto been measured. Warnings that further expansion of the irrigation system, especially with the Sukkur Barrage on the Indus, would lead to a dramatic increase in malaria infections and malaria deaths fell on deaf ears. Before long the predicted health problems had become a tangible issue.[84]

Gujarat-Maratha Desh

In central India, the Marathas took over the administrative structures, including the revenue administration, of the Mughal Empire, which were only slightly modified. However, revenue assessment in the coastal regions of the Konkan and in the southern Dekhan dated back to that used in the Vijayanagara Empire, thus hinting at fairly well-established systems of revenue assessment and collection. The *deshmukhs*, the incumbent elite, formed the foundation of the Maratha rule with their support of the tax and revenue system. In 1830, 90 per cent of the *deshmukhs* came from Maratha families. However, actual tax and revenue collection on the intermediate level was conducted by the state-employed *mamlatdars* who had been appointed by the Marathas from loyal families. However, the intended checks on the old and new revenue administrators functioned only in the centre of the state whilst on the periphery this led to frequent conflicts.[85]

In the villages the founding families (*mirasdars*) were concerned with the assessment and collection of the revenue amounts. On account of the ancient rights that the *mirasdars* enjoyed, a large proportion of the arable land belonged to them, which they were able to put out to rent; additionally their prominent status in village society often gave them the position of *patels* (village headman). After the *peshwa* of Pune had consolidated his rule in the mid-eighteenth century, he built upon this structure in the following two decades by updating revenue collection based on new calculations of the soil's quality. However, he still had to compromise with the local customs in Konkan, in southern Dekhan and Gujarat. Thus, as in many other parts of the Indian subcontinent, there existed no uniform revenue collection even within the different states of the Maratha Union as the *peshwa* was forced to vary his revenue assessment according to local conditions. A much more intensive revenue collection system was installed at the regional level by the Maratha Gaikwad of Baroda, in which the *patels* were forced to present a guarantee from a money-lender on the completion of a revenue assessment.[86]

Money-lenders known as *bania*, or *vanis* in the villages of Dekhan, secured the timely payment of revenues from their capital and credit. The higher the fiscal demands of the emergent states in the eighteenth century, the more important the position of the money-lender became. At the same time the debts of the peasants did not necessarily pose a problem to the system as long as the peasants remained creditworthy. Also land was only rarely confiscated because of debt. Instead, payment deferral, new loans or additional labour services were effective ways of stretching existing debt. The servicing of debt was a matter of honour and was observed across generations. Just as the land was annually auctioned to the highest bidding *mamlatdar* in other Indian states at the end of the eighteenth century, so too did the indebtedness of the central and western Indian peasants take on new dimensions at this time. This led to conflict between the *vanis* and the *kunbis*, the peasants. With 50 per cent of all peasants, the *kunbis* formed the backbone of the agricultural economy, which now threatened to break at any time on account of the high revenue and debt burdens, the relentless pressure of the British revenue collectors and the conflict with the *vanis*.[87]

A substantial change of the social structure and the foundation of revenue collection came following the annexation of parts of Gujarat and Maharashtra which were added to the Bombay Presidency in 1818. As usual, the British revenue collectors aligned themselves with the local conditions and structures showing the healthy pragmatism of the day.[88] The power of the revenue collectors, however, soon undermined the positions of *deshmukhs* as according to British ideals future revenues should be set exclusively with the *patels* and *mirasdars*.[89] The colonial administration kept the high level of revenue assessment which the *peshwa* had increased during the wars against the British at the beginning of the nineteenth century. Ultimately, this led to the growing indebtedness of peasants and their pauperisation to an extent hitherto unknown in this region.[90] Despite a partial revenue rebate as well as a slowly growing population, peasants often did not till their fields for unknown reasons, the result of which was a loss of up to a third of the agricultural land by the mid-nineteenth century.[91]

In Gujarat in 1801, the British annexed that part of the country it had previously economically penetrated on account of its profitability for cotton production.[92] In 1811, legal restrictions provoked a rapid accumulation of debt which especially affected the revenue-collecting *taluqdars* and resulted in social problems for the formerly powerful magnates and the British administration. The legal provisions introduced for the protection of the *taluqdars* in the second half of the nineteenth century succeeded only in stabilising the situation rather than introducing structural improvement of the society. In neighbouring Khandesh the British must have been amazed to discover that at the time of annexation only about 15 per cent of the arable land was used agriculturally. This was on account of a relatively high proportion of livestock and a relatively small population, meaning that only the best land had to be cultivated to provide for the inhabitants there. Due to this high productivity no detailed and direct revenue assessments were initially carried out. This had a positive effect on agriculture in Khandesh which expanded by 90 per cent by the second half of the nineteenth century whilst the population increased by only half.[93]

In the Bombay Presidency the British first implemented a systematic revenue evaluation in 1835 with the so-called Bombay Survey and Settlement System. Cadastral maps were drawn on the basis of soil fertility, yield and price development as well as irrigation possibilities. After over a decade of data collection, the revenue settlement was implemented in 1847; however, in many cases this was only completed during the 1870s.[94] Individual villages in Khandesh rebelled against the abolition of old privileges and the increased revenue amounts with the discontent culminating in the revolt of 1852.[95] In the Konkan the *khots* refused to cooperate with the British until the 1870s. The situation improved only after the Bombay Survey and Settlement System was replaced with the Khoti Settlement Act in 1880.[96]

However, the Deccan Riots of 1875 exhibited a far more menacing threat, the cause of which is seen to be the massive debt of most of the *kunbi* which was also exacerbated by the turmoil felt in the credit market. This credit market was, however, not dominated by the local money-lenders, the *vanis*, but by foreign *sahukars*, who in 1875 refused to grant credit for the revenues due on account of the shortage of capital. During the riots *kunbis*, *patels* and *deshmukhs* tried, not least, to destroy revenue records and loan books. The riots were not merely supported by the peasants and landowners, but shopkeepers, barbers and porters from the villages and towns also joined the thousands of rebellious peasants in a sign of solidarity and swore not to comply with the requirements of the *sahukars*. As usual, the British brutally defeated the rebellion.[97] A subsequent famine and a raging cholera epidemic between 1876 and 1878 desolated whole districts. Only the Deccan Agriculturalists' Relief Act of 1879 eased the lot of the peasants somewhat.[98]

In the end, however, the Act did not produce the desired and necessary relief. Until the end of the 1930s the spread of agricultural equipment, agricultural irrigation systems and numbers of livestock expanded steadily, just as the prices of agricultural products and agricultural land increased. Similarly, the sale of land due to the non-servicing of debt also increased. Meanwhile, no investment was given to technical innovations to increase crop yield, so that apart from the higher returns from the more intense irrigation of sugarcane, higher revenues were largely lacking. The consequences of agricultural revenue legislation in the Bombay Presidency were not as severe as in other provinces of British India. By 1947, 20 per cent, at most, of the agricultural land had changed hands, whilst regionally this equated to more than 10 per cent between 1881 and 1891. Another indicator of the nevertheless tight overall agro-economic conditions of production and living conditions of peasants was a more than 10 per cent increase in borrowing.[99]

In the decades that followed, the ongoing commercialisation of the agricultural sector accelerated this trend. Whilst at the end of the nineteenth century no serious change had come in the mode of cultivation for either food crops or cash crops, during the period from 1895–6 to 1926–7 the ratio of acreage of land dedicated to food crops and cash crops changed from 75:25 to 58:42 per cent of the arable land.[100] Such a structural change from a rather subsistence (local and regional) to a commercially (global) orientated agricultural sector could only be achieved through additional borrowing. By the late 1920s, an official enquiry commission established that 70 per cent of all cotton-growing peasants in Gujarat and Khandesh were indebted.[101] *Sarkar*, *zamindar* and *sahukar* all exerted pressure equally on their tenant peasants. In addition, the chronically weak credit market also put the wealthier peasants in a position to lend. This additional potential for securing loans proved to be the catalyst for a transformation process and accelerated the expansion of commercial agriculture from the late nineteenth century.[102]

Whilst the better-off peasants benefited from the fiscal and economic changes following the Deccan Riots, the situation of the poor peasants deteriorated rapidly. By 1904, the tenants of the *khots* in Konkan were still waiting for their guaranteed rights. The Bombay Tenancy Act, which categorised tenants for the first time and even assured the weakest among them legal protection of land they had tilled for a ten-year period, was not adopted until 1936.[103] In addition to these legal uncertainties, the government's loan policy exacerbated the situation of poor peasants, particularly during and after the famines of 1896 and 1902, as loans were preferentially given to established peasants. Market prospects for these established peasants were much greater than those of the poor, which was ultimately reflected in the distribution of land as between 1924 and 1925 12 per cent of the landowners farmed (or allowed the land to be farmed) 86 per cent of the total agricultural land of the region.[104]

At the end of the nineteenth century political and economic pressure from the colonial regime increased in Gujarat to such an extent that a peasant revolt was sparked in the Kheda District which had a number of similarities to that of the Titu Mir in Bengal. After the revision of the revenue settlements in the 1890s, the revenue burden of the Dharala society had doubled and thus, on account of their credit and revenue liabilities, peasants were forced to abandon their ancestral soil, making them landless agrarian labourers. Over half of the arable land available was hence no longer used. At the same time, the British strengthened the position of landowning *patidar* peasants so as to guarantee revenues. On 9 January 1898, Ranchod Vira (1848–99) declared independence from the British Raj, proclaimed himself king and spread this news via *patta* (letters) in the Kheda district. The legitimacy of the new monarchy was strengthened by revenue rebates which were based on the *chauth*, revenue demands introduced by the Marathas. Two days later this resulted in an armed uprising of about 600 peasants which was soon forcefully quelled by the British.[105]

The uprising was significant due to the fact that its social dynamics came from the society's lower strata and were directed at establishing an independent polity. This was based on the popular idea of traditional divine kingship, in which the king was worshiped as a deity or was viewed as being ritually homologous. Ranchod himself had acted as a priest and had sponsored the erection of a small *mandir*. Furthermore Ranchod Vira obviously knew about the bureaucratic administration of the colonial government as he was able to engage the colonial representatives in written communication, with which he was able to demonstrate that the monopoly of the colonial state on formalised documents no longer existed. Quite apart from this, the uprising is evidence of peasant resistance which was not led by the rural elite of *zamindars, taluqdars* or *patidars*, but rather was a rebellion against this elite and the state itself. Whether Ranchod recognised the context of colonial rule – which would mean that the uprising can be seen as an example of autonomous resistance against the colonial regime – remains unclear. Ultimately, Ranchod was sentenced to 14 years' rigorous imprisonment as a result of the rioting and conspiring against government. He died soon after his imprisonment.[106]

The Dharala resistance found new impetus during the famine of 1899–1901 when 20 per cent of the population died of malnutrition and disease. Around the same time Daduram became a much talked about figure and inspired thousands of the Dharala through his purist reform movement (including abstinence from meat, alcohol and theft) whilst oral culture and the media constituted a public sphere to further disseminate the ideas of the reform movement. The dramatic decline among the agricultural labour population made labour more expensive and resulted in an economic improvement of the region. This afforded the Dharala the chance to transform their hitherto customary labour relations (obligations) into contractual agreements. Between just 1907 and 1908 agricultural wages rose some 25–33 per cent. However, following the sudden death of Daduram in 1909 the movement ceased to continue in its actions. The majority in Dharala still found themselves in poverty and had no access to land due to the dominance of the *patidar*. Increasing violence against revenue officials in the region became a matter of deep concern for the administration.[107]

To put an end to the troubles caused by the uprising, some 250,000 Dharala were summarily declared a criminal tribe in 1911. This measure was based on the Criminal Tribes Act of 1871, which identified such non-sedentary, nomadic communities and societies as criminals. In order to settle these people and thereby transform them into revenue-paying peasants or urban industrial workers they were to be henceforth registered, monitored and controlled.[108] As already indicated above in connection with the "dacoits" and "thuggee", the Criminal Tribes Act embodied an almost century-long persistent political debate about how to effectively combat banditry and allegedly jointly committed crimes following the Great Rebellion of 1857–9. With price increases in British India as a result of the First World War, further economic deterioration followed which also severely affected the *patidars* in the Kheda District as well as the Dharala. At the beginning of 1918 Mohandas K. Gandhi arrived in Kheda and called for the "no revenue campaign" in March, which has since become known as Kheda-*satyagraha*.[109] However, although the revenue burdens of the *patidar* were central to the campaign, the fact that the Dharala, who still made up two-thirds of the region's agricultural labourers, were subject to the Criminal Tribes Act, was not discussed.[110]

Moreover, as the rural raids increased, the British Indian Government made Gandhi and the Indian national movement (Congress) responsible for the unrest. Gandhi then distinguished between the just concerns of *patidar* peasants and those of the Dharala that needed to be kept in check. It was evident to the colonial state, as well as to Gandhi, that the *patidars* were the pillars of the state which had to be protected. In 1923 Gandhi confessed that although the *patidars* had suppressed and exploited the Dharala, the *patidar* peasants should be forgiven for the good of the Indian nation. In a rare case of harmony the colonial state worked in cooperation with Congress to guarantee the suppression of the Dharala. No wonder then that the Dharala, in contrast to the *patidars*, showed no interest in the Indian nation, especially since they only lost their status as a Criminal Tribe within the Indian Union in 1951.[111] The second "Dharala episode" exemplifies that, first, resistance had become endemic in that region; and, second, that good reasons existed as a criminalised community not to support the major organisation of the Indian middle class, i.e. Congress, which was the centrepiece of the emergent Indian national movement. On the regional level, Congress also strove to secure organisational and ideological dominance, which, if necessary, would lead to the exclusion of "opponents".

Dekhan, Malabar Coast and Coromandel Coast

The British transformed the former Mughal province of Berar into a purely export-oriented region. After the war of the British and the *nizam* of Haiderabad against the Marathas the area was annexed in 1818 by the *nizam*. Due to its immediate proximity to Khandesh and the optimum climatic and geological conditions for the cultivation of cotton, the British forced the Haiderabad ruler to sign over Berar to them in 1853. From that point it became the

Hyderabad Assigned Districts administered by the Central Provinces before being fully incorporated into British Indian territory in 1903. One of the reasons for the annexation was the emerging tension between the northern and southern United States of America and an imminent decline in cotton exports to Lancashire. Within two decades, the British systematically developed Berar starting with cartographic surveys and the extension of the railway network from Khandesh to Nagpur via Berar which included a grid of paved roads to the stations as well as a telegraph and postal system. By 1884, a dense network of communication had been laid which linked the region to the world market.[112]

Apart from the Panjab Canal Colonies no other region in British India had been subjected to such rigid economic transformation. This development can be seen in the growth in acreage devoted to cotton cultivation which increased from 1.25 million acres in the mid-1860s to 2.44 million acres by the turn of the century. As observed in other regions, the proportion of the total agricultural land that was given over to cash crop production also grew in Berar from 21 per cent to 35.8 per cent. In some districts of Berar over half of the total land was planted with cotton, whilst exports of cotton also more than doubled in the same period. The dramatic expansion in the cultivation and export of cotton was the catalyst leading to the collapse of the local, mostly family-organised spinning sector responsible for processing the crop. By the end of the American Civil War (1865) this industry had completely disappeared as in the course of the war not only was the Berar cotton mostly exported, but so too were the weaving and spinning industries upon which a special tax had been levied. Thus the same fate as those in Bengal in the early nineteenth century befell the peasants of Berar who were often also weavers and spinners.[113]

Serious ecological consequences soon resulted from the profound economic changes that had developed as the events that had afflicted the Ganga-Yamuna Doab in the first half of the nineteenth century were repeated in a similar manner in Berar in the second half of the century. Due to massive deforestation for arable land gain, annual precipitation decreased and a warming of the region resulted. Consequently, many formerly year-round water-bearing streams and water sources dried up or dried out completely. In addition, the severe leaching of soil resulted from the cultivation of cotton as a monoculture. A British administration officer soon highlighted the fact that in order to strengthen the food crop cultivation, small-scale irrigation projects such as tanks, cisterns and anicuts would need to be built and that credit for the construction and maintenance would have to be made available. Such reports, however, were not welcome by the colonial administration and were shelved.[114] The drought and resulting famine of 1899–1901 had particularly tragic consequences for Berar. As food prices rose unabated, food crops and one-third of the usual cotton harvest were exported whilst up to 10 per cent of the population died from malnutrition and related diseases.[115]

In the second half of the nineteenth century an active state irrigation policy was started in Hyderabad State, which aimed to ensure food security and generate additional revenues. Despite this, net agricultural area decreased from 267,000 acres to 237,000 acres between 1922 and 1951 whilst the irrigable area of land increased from under 4 per cent to nearly 6 per cent. The increase in irrigation also led to an expansion of cash crop cultivation and the reciprocal dramatic decline in agricultural area where food crops could be grown. In spite of a 1942 government campaign to promote the cultivation of food crops, especially that of rice, the area devoted to food crops decreased further. This expansion of cash crops had further impact on the forest areas of the country, the proportion of which fell from 15 per cent to less than 12 per cent during the first half of the twentieth century. The environmental consequences soon became obvious in areas where the forests had been cleared to create farmland, as not only did the water table fall, but the highly fertile black soil was quickly eroded.[116]

Just as the northern half of the subcontinent is characterised by great geographic and climatic differences, so too is the south of India. In the west is the humid and rainy tropical Malabar Coast with the Western Ghats, a mountain chain that reaches heights of up to 2,000m. Behind this to the east lies the dry highlands of the Malnad, a flat plain from which the Maidan drops. This is followed by the Balanghat which eventually transforms into the lowlands of the water-rich river delta areas on the southern Coromandel Coast, the Payanghat. On this coastline, as on the Malabar Coast, soil was extremely fertile allowing for a highly productive agricultural sector which benefited from regular rainfall, meaning the region had historically been almost free of crisis. Until the second half of the nineteenth century a steadily growing agricultural sector, and, as a result, increasing economic prosperity, can be observed. It was not until the catastrophic famine of 1865–6 and especially that of 1876–8, during which four to five million people died (equivalent to about 10 per cent of the population), that the stability of the agricultural sector was brought to an abrupt end.[117]

The high plateau of southern Dekhan with its low rainfall was, in comparison, a much more crisis-prone area. Even the most secure access to land did not guarantee an economically sustainable livelihood, when labour, capital and materials for the agricultural sector were lacking. In times of drought it was often the cattle herds that first fell victim to the arid conditions before the peasants eventually migrated. On account of unstable weather conditions, large areas of land remained unfertilised and unploughed during the 1840s and 1850s, and again at the end of the nineteenth century. Despite such "fallow periods", the agricultural production and population of the area grew until the 1920s. However, by the mid-twentieth century yields of grain alone had fallen 30 per cent when compared to 1916 figures in the Madras Presidency. Dramatic demographic growth up to the 1920s is however not the sole factor to blame for this development as a number of colonial initiatives in the agricultural sector favouring the cultivation of cash crops must also be considered.[118]

Little is known about the principles of revenue settlement in southern India during the eighteenth century. Obviously the *naiks* and *palayakarars* established themselves as local and regional little kings following the fall of the

Vijayanagar Empire. At the village level *mirasdars* acted as revenue collectors and labour organisers for public projects such as the construction and maintenance of irrigation systems. In the eighteenth century in Malabar, the rule of the *zarmorin* of Khozikhode and the *raja* of Travancore formed a culturally and economically unique region in which the agricultural structures were largely determined by the *brahman-janmi*-property (*janmidar*) and the *kanam*-tenancy (*kanamdar*). As a result of the high agricultural yields, the income from the land revenue was of secondary importance as the state monopoly was based on pepper and other spices which composed the largest part of the state's fiscal income.[119]

The EIC expanded its territory in South India in the course of numerous wars and the subsequent annexation of areas between 1750 and 1799. Debates on a systematic revenue settlement began in the last decade of the eighteenth century. Until 1801, the EIC assessed the revenues of peasants (*raiyat*) on an individual basis and thus established what was to become named the Raiyatwari Settlement, which, as was the case with the Zamindari Settlement in Bengal and the Mahalwari Settlement in the NWP, was far from uniform and systematic. In addition to the Raiyatwari Settlement the Zamindari Settlement also existed which had been agreed upon by the British and the *naiks* and *palayakarars* between 1801 and 1807. In 1830 approximately one-third of all revenue assessments were subject to the Zamindari Settlement. As in the other territories of British India, the British Revenue Collector reserved the right to assess, calculate and demand revenues at his sole discretion, thereby making any systematic compilation a farce from the outset.[120]

The first half of the nineteenth century was marked by fiscal experiments as the British roughly sorted and organised the *zamindars* under the rubric of the Permanent Settlement and the *inamdars* under the Zamindari Settlement. In Tamil Nadu and the Telugu region they recognised the local *mirasdars* on account of their common land and the *janmdars* on the Malabar Coast (Malabar and Kanara) as landowners within the parameters of the Raiyatwari Settlement, which had been passed at the village level. Initially little changed in the duties owed by the peasants. Often they were left with as little as 20 per cent of the gross income of their crops, whilst in Thanjavur on the Coromandel Coast levels are recorded to have been between 25 and 33 per cent. The existing rent rolls of the peasants were not at first of interest to the British, nor the fact that the price decline in the mid-nineteenth century and the high revenues imposed severe burdens on the tenant peasants.[121]

In Haiderabad state, over half of the farmland was decreed to be *khalsa* land on which peasants were directly assessed for revenue and for which payment in cash was required. Furthermore, one-third of the land was possessed by the nobility or issued to *jagirs*. In the state of Maisur an almost identical mode of assessment was in place which, however, in this case the state claimed 50 per cent of the crop yield on irrigated land and 33 per cent on non-irrigated fields. Tipu Sultan had successfully reduced the rights of *palayakarars* and in some cases confiscated their rights in order to intrinsically link the land to the peasant and with this install fixed monetary revenue rates which would flow directly into Maisur's treasury. For the peasants, there seemed to have been a system of hereditary leasing in place which was limited to the right to tillage. As revenue liabilities and debts grew, this land was reclaimed by the state.[122]

When the British administrators recognised in the mid-nineteenth century that the previous administration in Madras was run to the detriment of agricultural development, they began to introduce reforms from 1855. These reforms initially focused on the *inamdars*. The 1858–69 appointed Inam Commission in cooperation with the Board of Revenue swept away almost 475,000 *inam* titles and nearly two and a half million *inamdars* by the end of the nineteenth century. Only those among them who could prove ownership of the land over the past 50 years were eligible to maintain their legal titles.[123] At the same time an increase in agricultural production and thus the long-term increase in revenue was the aim. To this end both a reassessment of land and a general reduction of duties within the Raiyatwari Settlement were undertaken. Ultimately in 1864 half of the net agricultural income was defined as revenue, the amount having been taken as a basis for further revenue assessments.[124]

For the poorer *raiyats* the provisions of the Act of 1864 proved to be fatal, as the government tightened measures relating the sale of land to revenue debts. By 1880, the number of tenancies that had been terminated had increased by 45 per cent; proof of the fact that, again, it was the layer of small tenants that fell victim to colonial legislation. A comparable land market as in North India or Bengal did not develop in the Madras Presidency. Whilst land sales continued on account of revenue debts from 1822, they never reached the extent they had in other British territories. It was only in the case of the *zamindars* that drastic changes could be observed as they saw their share of revenue settlements shrink from one-third of the total revenue contractors at the beginning of the nineteenth century to just one-fifth by the end of the century. This was obviously the result of their estates being divided and the land absorbed by a growing number of tenants and medium-sized granges.[125]

A year following the Act of 1864, the Madras Government once again took the legislative initiative and introduced the Rent Recovery Act which fixed the possibility of an annual termination of tenancy agreements. However, it was the famine during the 1870s and the recommendations of the Famine Commission that caused the Madras Government to introduce further legislative measures. That said, it took until 1887 before a bill was presented and which sparked a decade-long dispute between the Madras Government and the Government of India concerning the details of the bill so that the Madras Estate Act was not adopted until 1908. In principle the experts involved in the formulation of the Bengal Tenancy Act aimed to secure the right to the free market of land ownership as well as introducing slight modifications over the duration of leases. This act was supplemented with various provisions such as that in 1934 which finally regulated the contentious issue of the maintenance costs of irrigation systems.[126]

On the Malabar Coast, the structures of ownership, land and lease rights seemed utterly vague to the British who, through countless reports, tried to master the situation, but instead sank into a quagmire of incomprehensible information as no criterion existed that would have helped in their organisation. After decades of debate the Malabar Tenancy Act of 1930 was finally agreed upon. However, this brought little improvement for the tenants. Meanwhile the delayed implementation of most of the provisions which had been agreed upon were not introduced until after 1942 and thereby made a mockery of the entire legislation.[127] Just as before the law's introduction, the medium and large landowners remained in a powerful position. As in the Panjab and Gujarat, the new class of cash-crop peasants benefited most from the commercialisation of the agricultural sector that began to expand in the second half of the nineteenth century. In the course of this development, the long-established rural traders were also ousted in favour of their urban competition.[128]

In the dry zone of the highlands, the large estates soon fragmented to the benefit of the small and medium-sized peasant proprietors. Furthermore, the allocation of credit was not solely the domain of the big *zamindars* and *janmdars*, who accounted for about 4 per cent of the rural population, or that of the urban *mahajans*, but instead, money was easily accessible in the second half of the nineteenth century with low interest through credit institutions. This increased financial flexibility influenced the peasants' decision not to concentrate on the cultivation of cash crops. At the same time, general population growth exerted increasing pressure on the remaining forest and wasteland areas which led to their reclamation. Farming families were able to accumulate some wealth and were occasionally able to participate in economic development between 1890 and 1930. As in many other regions of India, access to land influenced economic livelihood. However, from 1930 to 1960 a stagnation and partial recession of the agricultural sector is to be observed.[129]

The formally independent state of Travancore is an example of how contemporary and adequate revenue assessments could be developed. Half of the land under rice cultivation and all wasteland was classified as belonging to the state and the revenue authorities directly assessed the so-called *sirkar raiyats*. The *kanamdars* who, as state tenants, initially had no property rights, received guarantee of their legal right to rent in 1829. The right to sell their land to tenants was finally granted in 1865. In the years 1867, 1896 and 1932 further laws strengthened these legal rights of tenants, gradually prompting an open land market to emerge. Compared to the tenants in British Malabar, those in Travancore, comprising approximately 4 per cent of the rural population, were in a significantly better legal situation. Apart from this, there were an estimated 15 per cent of agricultural labourers and landless peasants, which indicates agricultural property rights of about 80 per cent. This early landed property policy is certainly one reason for the relative prosperity of the present Indian state of Kerala.[130]

In the different regions of South India, the percentage of land-poor peasants and landless agricultural labourers at the beginning of the nineteenth century is estimated to have accounted for 10 to 15 per cent of the population. Parallel to this, different forms and degrees of dependent employment relations existed as in southern Malabar where up to 25 per cent of the agricultural labourers were either permanently bound or in slave-like employment conditions. A particularly blatant case is the Cherumar of Malabar, who, as field slaves, accounted for up to 15 per cent of the population. In Malabar the number of bonded labourers and slaves amounted to 10 per cent of the population whilst in northern Malabar this figure was approximately 5 per cent. Agricultural workers in such strictly controlled working conditions often belonged to particular social groups and were, according to their differing legal and economic status, characterised differently. Such labourers could be leased, rented or sold within a local region and its cultural context. The obligation to work, however, also included an entitlement of care during times of economic hardship.[131]

The Census of India, which had been taken place every ten years since 1871, presented the British with the problem of defining these social orders and social hierarchies which they reduced to the concept of "caste"; the word and concept of which had been adopted from the Portuguese. Often, the classification of "caste" depended on the individual understanding and definition of the officers responsible for the categorisation. This is exemplified in the case of the *palli* and *parayan* (from which the "Pariah" synonym for the casteless or untouchables is derived) which were listed as one "caste" in the censuses of 1871 and 1881 whilst in the following census they were listed as separate "castes". In the censuses of 1871 and 1901 the *pallis* were recorded as "agrarian labourers" whilst the 1871 Census also noted that 70 per cent of the *palli* were "cultivators" (with land ownership or leasehold), which, according to British understanding, was in stark contrast to the "agrarian labourers" who were landless. The removal of the *palli* from the category ("caste") of "agricultural labourers" saw their numbers reduced from 20 to 13 per cent. Administratively, however, this categorisation sidestepped the problem of inscrutable lease and ownership, describing the *palli* as mere agricultural labourers. Their duties were legally regulated and the British showed no interest in the annulment of employment relationships.[132] The case of the *palli* demonstrates that the Census of India is more telling of the administrative needs of the British than of the social reality for the people of British India.

The double-edged sword of the pressure of a growing population led to improvements in the use of existing farmland and its extension, but also had a negative impact on the agricultural labour market. In the last quarter of the nineteenth century wages in the agricultural sector decreased by 20 per cent; in some cases this figure was up to 50 per cent. At the beginning of the twentieth century work days were ultimately shortened as agricultural land per person decreased. Often the only way out of the economic malaise was temporary, seasonal or perennial migration. Many South Indian rural labourers, especially from the Malabar Coast and from Tamil Nadu, were attracted to the Ceylonese coffee, tea and rubber plantations. Meanwhile male and female kulis from the eastern Madras Presidency were usually shipped to

Mauritius, Malaya or the Caribbean, a topic that will be elaborated on in Chapter 6 on "Migration, circulation and diaspora". The dynamism of the trans-regional and intercontinental labour market helped ensure the preservation of the local labour market as its structures assisted with distributing the load on the economy in times of crisis whilst maximising the benefits from the landowning peasants and the British colonial government in better economic times.[133]

The British were always vigilant of the existing irrigation systems in improving agriculture and the resulting revenues. On account of the almost constant warfare during the second half of the eighteenth century most of the irrigation systems in the river deltas of Godaveri, Kaveri and Kolerun had fallen into disrepair.[134] In the 1830s, the British began to restore the derelict canals. Systematic planning began in the 1860s, which led to the centrally planned construction and expansion of state-run irrigation systems.[135] Because of the fairly high precipitation on the Coromandel Coast and the resulting large river systems, irrigation canals were only partially profitable as wells and tanks were relatively cheap and could be privately financed. As in other regions of India, the decentralised, private irrigation methods were also much more economical and ecologically sound.

Instead of investing in these small-scale irrigation projects, the British, as in Northern India and the Panjab, regarded the control of the major rivers of southern India and their "irregularities", i.e. flooding, to be much more important. As a result, embankments, weirs, dams and canals were among the arsenal of the British engineers who wanted to control the unpredictability of the monsoons. Apart from the engineers' technical ambitions to improve the irrigation systems by scientific means, it was the aim of the British-Indian Government and the provincial governments to develop the infrastructure of the agricultural economy for the best, albeit in accordance to their own understanding of what the "best" should mean. As in Northern India and the Panjab, however, these attempted agricultural improvements resulted in lasting economic and ecological damage, especially in the river deltas of southeast India.[136]

The cultivation of cash crops did not play a prominent role for South India's agricultural activities. By way of example, less than 10 per cent of the region's agricultural land was given over to cotton production whilst in the Nilgiri Hills of the Western Ghats, the coffee and tea plantations accounted for 15 per cent of the agricultural area. As a result of the favourable conditions along the flat and sandy coastline, the region was used for the cultivation of coconut trees. Yet, between 1900 and 1930 a significant leap was made in the cultivation of peanuts in South India and especially in the North Arcot District. In the period from 1924–8 alone, the acreage of peanut cultivation increased from 0.8 million hectares to 1.5 million hectares and across British India this amount increased to 1.9 million hectares. During the same period peanut yields increased from 0.7 million to 1.6 million tonnes and the export of peanuts accounted for 22 per cent of the total exports of the Madras Presidency.[137]

Ceylon/Sri Lanka

Although the British had occupied large parts of the Ceylonese flatlands since the beginning of the nineteenth century it took them until after the Great Rebellion of 1817–18 to administratively manage that region. At first they simply employed the existing revenue system they had inherited. Revenues initially equated to 10 per cent of the rental income of the land paid in crops. In some provinces, such as in Kandy, the so-called *aumani* system existed whereby government employees exacted revenues directly from the peasants. In a move to simplify the revenue system the British colonial government decided to collect revenues exclusively in cash rather than in kind. This was to be done on a voluntary basis in coordination with the Commutation Settlement; however, on account of the cumbersome bureaucracy it took the rest of the century to fully complete the new settlement. This is most probably the reason why a land market did not develop and that even in the decade with the highest rate of foreclosures less than 10 per cent of the arable land was auctioned.[138]

The occupation of Ceylon by the British hit Ceylonese agriculture hard. The "scorched-earth" tactics practised by the British during the Great Rebellion of 1817–18 saw the old irrigation systems in the northern "dry zone" fall into disrepair, and in some cases, completely destroyed. After the collapse of two dams in the Southern Province in the 1830s the local rice production fell by almost a third. Only with the 1856 Irrigation Ordinance was a policy of irrigation initiated by the colonial state. In addition to the restoration of a dilapidated dam, state aid was also used in combination with technical assistance and voluntary local labour services for small projects which made the irrigation scheme a success. In the 1870s, the British colonial government replicated the programme in the northern "dry zone" and restored a number of tanks and canals. The establishment of an Irrigation Department in 1900, parallel to the Irrigation Commission of India, exemplified the importance that the government now attributed to irrigation. However, by 1905 their interest in the programme waned significantly and funding was withdrawn. Although the newly built and restored irrigation systems improved the crop production for the immediate consumption of the rural population with basic food stuffs such as rice, Ceylon's rising population remained dependent on rice imports from Burma.[139]

The most substantial change in Ceylon's agriculture came with the expansion of coffee cultivation. Having been introduced by the Dutch and cultivated by the Ceylonese in their private gardens, the British increased the cultivation of coffee on the island following the increased demand for the crop from 1812. In the central highlands of Kandy, British planters and Ceylonese farmers set about clearing large forest tracts. Thereafter the systematic development of the highlands, which was accompanied by large-scale deforestation, was made possible through the accessibility offered by the increasing road network and the Colombo–Kandy railway which was opened in 1867. On account of the substantially lower freight costs and transport times afforded by the railway, even the more remote and distant regions became lucrative locations for plantations.[140] Legal measures such as the Ordinance Act of 1840 regulated the sale of Crown land, which was offered at rock-bottom prices to investors who were in many cases of British origin. Estimates suggest that up to 55 per cent of land that had been donated to Buddhist temples was confiscated and sold as Crown land. Between 1833 and 1886 alone, more than 10 per cent of the island's total area had been sold.[141]

Between 1867 and the early 1880s the area of agricultural land dedicated to coffee cultivation expanded from 168,000 acres to 252,431 acres. However, within a few years a fungus destroyed virtually every plant. A rapid and adequate replacement was found in tea, a hitherto marginally cultivated crop which similarly experienced exponential growth from just 13,500 acres in 1881 to 384,000 acres in 1900. Meanwhile, a new law on land reclamation paved the administrative and legal way into the highlands.[142] Since tea, in contrast to coffee, can be harvested year-round, the planters soon needed a permanent labour force. From the second half of the nineteenth century the social composition of the highlands changed fundamentally as not only had half a million South Indian tea pickers settled in the region, but the changing local economy also proved to be the catalyst for a shift in the social stratification.

The diversified village economy of rice cultivation on irrigated fields, grain and robust, sustainable food crops grown from the *chena* system (slash and burn), as well as fruits, vegetables and medicinal plants in the forest, ultimately had to give way to a highly commercialised and capitalised economy which the *chena* system could not compete with.[143] This change was not without opposition as the peasants of the highlands resisted their systematic disenfranchisement during the entire nineteenth century. However, long-established landowners also existed in colonial Ceylon who, despite the small land market, benefited from the British concept of property as they were able to considerably improve their economic position and social status. Access to land was increasingly unequally distributed and created a situation that was exacerbated by the insatiable thirst for land by the British planters.[144] In many ways, the agricultural development of Ceylon is typical of the plantation economy of the nineteenth century in South Asia and beyond.

Characteristics and consequences of colonial agrarian policy

In order to characterise the changes in South Asian agriculture that developed, in varying degrees in different regions and at different times, from the middle of the nineteenth century in British India, the globally oriented division of labour must also be highlighted. This division of labour made British India the supplier of raw materials originating from the primary sector whilst Great Britain became a supplier of products from the secondary sector. By 1900, the Indian agricultural sector had become dependent on and integrated in many regions of the world economy; this is especially true for the cash crops such as cotton, jute, sugarcane and indigo. The tonnes of cotton products exported by

British industries led to the mass impoverishment of peasants, spinners, weavers and dyers in Bengal and Gujarat. In comparison, the effects of the industrial exports from British workshops to South Indian markets were by no means as severe on account of the flexibility of the producers and a more varied product range. Despite such niches of production and consumption, commercialisation and globalisation caused further asymmetries as in the case of the indigo peasants (and planters) who lost business and income after BASF invented the artificial blue dye at the end of the nineteenth century.

A further feature of the colonially transformed agricultural sector was its under-capitalisation, which ultimately resulted in under-consumption. For more political than economic reasons, the strengthening of small and medium tenants was more often the exception rather than the rule, whilst the remaining landowners succeeded in continuing to accumulate capital, none of which however was reinvested into agriculture. This capital was mostly used as a credit to indebted peasants or as a means to acquire additional land. Thus it was not used innovatively which ensured the financial security of the investors, but did little to improve the economy of British India as a whole. The fact that land purchase was more lucrative than investment in the agricultural sector was a result of British colonial policy which showed little interest in economic innovation and social dynamics. However, the partial commercialisation of agriculture in some regions of India not only contributed to the diversification of crops and increased migration, but also to a rigid stratification of society. The colonial regime was hardly able to control these growing contradictions during, and following, the Great Depression (1929–39).

The Great Depression was, by far, the most dramatic event of the twentieth century for British India as for the first time the integration of the British-Indian economy into the world market affected the whole subcontinent. Whilst until that point a steady impoverishment of the majority of peasants had been observed, the Great Depression triggered the destitution of a broad stratum of the peasantry. External factors such as the credit crisis and stock speculation in the agricultural sector in the United States led to the stock market crash of 1929, whilst in London, the world's most important financial centre, banks refused to issue further loans. Furthermore, during the 1920s Japan had significantly expanded its acreage of rice and imposed an embargo on rice imports from India in 1928, resulting in huge economic repercussions. Borrowers began to panic about the repayment of the loans as the general credit crisis reached India. By the middle of 1931 prices of wheat and other agricultural products had fallen to half of the levels recorded in 1929, so that Indian peasants were forced to sell the harvested grain at low prices and often sell off parts of their land and, to an increasing amount, even gold jewellery.[145]

At the same time, creditors, banks and government also tried to collect their funds. Added to this, the British-Indian Government had difficulties in settling its remittances, especially the Home Charges, with London. This is why the enforced flow of peasant-debtors' gold into the revenue coffers of Calcutta suited the colonial state's financial needs. Capital soon flowed from

India at an unprecedented level. Until 1935, gold exports accounted for 30 per cent of the total annual exports and represented the largest single item. For the remainder of the decade the export of precious metals levelled off at between 8 and 19 per cent. These figures are testament to the desperate efforts made by the peasants to meet their debt obligations; however, in many cases this was, of course, in vain. Not surprisingly these peasants and small landowners were attracted by the INC which they joined in droves. Such rural support easily allowed Congress to increase its political influence which can be seen in the general elections of 1937.[146]

In some regions of British India in the nineteenth century a revolutionary restructuring of agricultural structures had been introduced, which focused increasingly on cash crop production and neglected food crop production. With this transformation and the progressive commercialisation and capitalisation of the agricultural sector, a corresponding spatial reorganisation of trade, transport and migration paths of agricultural as well as industrial labourers ensued. The clearest expression of this development of agricultural economy is in exports. For example, a port city such as Karachi adopted a completely new function, whilst Madras, Calcutta and Bombay, the erstwhile "bridgeheads" of the EIC, became maritime "termini" and export hubs for the country through infrastructural development such as the railway and its focus on these growing maritime metropolises.

The Green Revolution and the Gene Revolution (1960–2010)

In order to promote agriculture, politicians and economists in the independent states of South Asia recognised the benefits and necessity of planned large-scale canal and dam projects of the British colonial regime of the time. These construction projects were taken on against the backdrop not only of the political will of ruling parties and politicians, but also for the long-term security of food supply for the now rapidly growing population as soil was to be fertilised and productive through irrigation.[147] The economic limits of such comprehensive technological innovation were evident even during British rule as the state could not wholly control the use of water away from the main canals. Today, India and Pakistan still suffer from this colonial legacy. Even state-funded improvements to the water distribution have failed due to a lack of cooperative will of local communities as they refuse to be integrated into the larger hydraulic environment. Their fear is not unfounded as participation in such schemes would lead to higher costs and lower benefits.[148]

Since the 1960s, India, Pakistan and Ceylon (Bangladesh too since 1971) have built upon the foundation of these major British hydro-agricultural projects and started the Green Revolution. This revolution is defined as industrialised agricultural production by means of a mechanised agricultural sector in combination with new breeds of wheat and rice varieties that produce three- to four-fold higher yields. The use of large quantities of fertilisers, and thereby the massive consumption of water, is essential to ensure the maximum return on these now

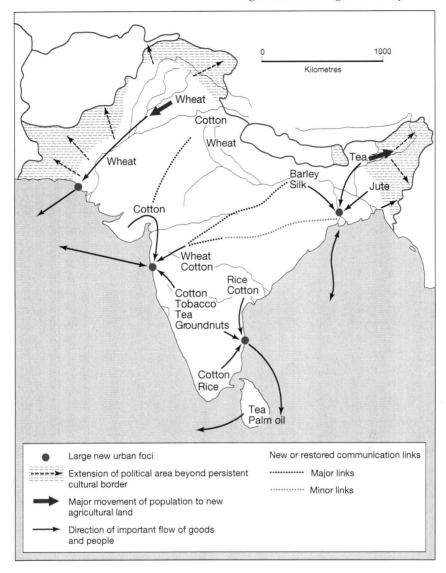

Map 4.4 Spatial reorganisation of economic and migration routes under the colonial rule. Adapted from B.R. Tomlinson, *The Economy of Modern India, 1860–1970* (Cambridge University Press: 2013), p. 56

densely packed standing cereals and vegetables. Furthermore, such cultivation methods require the use of pesticides to combat the infestation of bacteria and insects which threaten the intensive monoculture. Since the Green Revolution was built upon the existing agro-infrastructural structures, it triggered an intensification of the agricultural sector in the Pakistani and Indian Panjab, in parts of northern India and in the "rice bowls" in the river deltas in Tamil Nadu. The same also applies to the irrigation system in Ceylon/Sri Lanka and the natural river landscape of the Bengal delta.

It must also be considered that, contrary to the allegations of the Indian Government, it was not the Green Revolution based on the high yielding varieties of seeds, pesticides and technological equipment that, for the first time, brought additional agricultural wealth to the country, but rather the agricultural improvement schemes which the colonial regime had established as early as in the nineteenth century, aimed at improving British India as a whole.[149] In the 1950s the Ford Foundation, together with the Rockefeller Foundation, India's new cooperating partners with regard to industrial and agricultural development, continued the colonial rhetoric as well as (Orientalist) ideology maintaining that India's agriculture was utterly backward and static and not able to be improved by India's own capacities. Accordingly, only external aid would secure predictable food shortages and, more importantly, prevent revolutions, in particular socialist and communist, i.e. "red" revolutions.[150] Hence, the Green Revolution in India must also be read against this political background of the Cold War that became an omnipresent feature of international cooperation based on the economic interests of US companies as well as the US administrations and their common strategies in order to develop a global mastery.[151]

The history of the South Asian Green Revolution can be divided into two phases: the first which lasted from 1960 to about 1985; and the second from 1985 to the beginning of this millennium. The first phase saw the implementation of the Green Revolution which, in India, was initially dominated by the Nehru government's belief in development and progress. At first doubts about the revolution were regionally expressed; however, massive transformations of the agricultural sector came in the early 1970s. The debate about the benefits and foreseen damages caused by the Green Revolution were reignited during the second phase of the revolution and centred around the so-called Gene Revolution and the planned use of genetically modified rice and cotton. The Gene Revolution aimed to correct the deficits of the Green Revolution and introduce pesticide-resistant seeds to again increase food crop production and guarantee a sustainable agricultural sector.[152]

Over the years the public debates surrounding the Green Revolution as well as the Gene Revolution were also reflected in contemporary scientific literature. During the first phase (1960–81) opinion was divided roughly between two camps. On the one side were the proponents of the Green Revolution who mainly argued for food security, income improvements, economic progress and prosperity.[153] They were opposed by the critics who claimed such a revolution would lead to dire social consequences such as a growing inequality between rich and poor peasants/farmers and regional disparities as well as severe environmental consequences such as soil and water degradation.[154] During the second phase critics overwhelmingly warned of the economic consequences of India's integration into global economic structures and the world market as well as the biological consequences of using genetically modified seeds which was also being debated by agriculturalists worldwide at that time.[155]

The impact of the Green Revolution can be illustrated by the use of figures: the area of irrigated land for wheat cultivation in the Republic of India rose from 54 to 78 per cent between 1960 and 1990; meanwhile these figures for rice production also saw a rise from 38 to 45 per cent. At the same time the use of fertiliser increased from 2.2 million tonnes to 12.5 million tonnes. In order to promote the Green Revolution the Indian Government relaxed import regulations so that the amount of imported agricultural machinery doubled between 1950 and 1965.[156] A similar development can also be observed in Pakistan as in the districts of Lyallpur, Montgomery and Multan agricultural production between 1960 and 1965 alone increased by 9 per cent, almost twice as much as the national growth rate. By the early 1980s, 80 per cent of all of Pakistan's tractors and 88 per cent of all mechanical wells were in use in the Panjab. Between 1950 and 1990 the agricultural land of Pakistan grew from 11.4 to 15.0 million hectares whilst the crop yield of wheat increased from 3.9 to 14.3 million tonnes. During the same period, rice production increased from 0.8 to 3.2 million tonnes whilst the increase in cash crops was even more dramatic and saw the production of sugar alone escalate from 7.8 to 35.5 million tonnes.[157]

Whilst food production in both countries was now assured it came at the expense of soil quality. The concerns voiced by the initial critics that highlighted the possible consequences of pesticide use on the environment (water, air and soil) came to fruition within a decade in the decimation of many species, the increase of resistance among pest populations and the related increased risk of outbreaks of pest infestation in the monoculture crops. The genetically modified wheat and rice varieties that appeared during the 1990s offered a solution to these problems, at least superficially. However, their use again reduced the biodiversity of several hundred Indian rice varieties which, on account of their multiplicity, were effective in resisting infestations from pests. Predictably, the negative consequences of the long-term leaching of the land and the salinisation of the soil as well as the reliance on intense irrigation caused river levels and water tables to sink.[158] By the end of the 1990s about 40 per cent of the total arable land had already been exposed to serious soil degradation. Alarmingly, this resulted in the absolute decline of agricultural productivity in India when compared to figures from 1896.[159]

The situation further deteriorated following the turn of the millennium. To halt the ongoing deterioration of the soil quality the Indian Government promoted and, simultaneously, subsidised a mix of fertilisers which became a heavy burden on the national budget as the agriculturists paid only 25 to 40 per cent of the costs. However, it was not only food crops which received attention from the promoters of the Green and Gene Revolution, but cash crops as well. In India, the acreage of cotton fields expanded from 7.6 million hectares to 9 million hectares in 2004. This is mirrored by a remarkable increase of cotton yields which rose from 106kg/ha in 1970 to 324kg/ha in 2004. In other agricultural sectors similar rates of increase can also be observed. Milk production, for example, rose from 80.6 million tonnes in 1990 to 112 million tonnes in 2000. This increase, however, was not the result of the Green and Gene Revolution, but rather the fact that dairy farming had become an important source of income for landless labourers and cooperatives. In recent years this "White Revolution" has matched the results of the Green and Gene Revolution.[160]

Alongside the environmental effects of these genetically modified seeds the development also caused numerous economic and social consequences. Profitable returns were only possible on the large farms and, as a result, these agricultural "companies" were preferentially given credit. This led to the growing capitalisation of agriculture, albeit regionally, that was rationalised and modernised. The aim was to achieve greater efficiency, higher yields and cheaper food stuffs through the industrialisation and automatisation of the agrarian sector. Accordingly, in the course of the Green Revolution, the number of landless labourers increased by 20 million in just ten years from 1961 to 1971, whilst in the same period the number of farms fell by 15 million.[161] In the Panjab and parts of the south Indian river deltas these "farm deaths" were, and still are, the cause of persistent social unrest.[162] The economic and social impoverishments are reflected in the intensification of regional and national disparities that the Green Revolution induced.[163]

This is also reflected in the New Farmers' Movement in India, which responded to issues such as the transformation of the agricultural sector during the development decade of the 1960s to the globalised neo-liberal phase of capitalism in the early 1990s which also led to nationwide social formations, resistance movements and protests. Protests, which were particularly strong in Gujarat, Maharashtra, Karnataka and the west and south of Tamil Nadu, as well as the Panjab and Uttar Pradesh in the north, included demonstrations, blocking the food transportation system, denying officials access to villages, refusing to pay outstanding bills (tax arrears, electricity dues, bank loans) and withholding crops from local markets which all resulted in price rises. Meanwhile, it is assumed that the New Farmers' Movement significantly contributed to the downfall of Rajiv Gandhi's Congress Government in 1989 just as peasants brought down the NDA Government in 2004 when the BJP's election campaign motto of "India Shining" did not convince the rural population which felt itself to be the loser in the government's new economic policy.[164]

The second phase of the Green Revolution coincided with the growing integration of the Indian economy into the neo-liberal, global economy after 1991, the result of which led to further impoverishment and massive social protest movements in the Panjab.[165] Furthermore, the consequences of the Gene Revolution and the genetically modified cotton seeds were particularly striking: this was especially the case in eastern Maharashtra, and elsewhere, from the early 1990s. Hybrid cotton varieties had been in use by peasants and farmers of the region from the 1970s, but had become highly susceptible to pests such as the American bollworm during the 1980s. Repeated and indiscriminate pesticide treatment led to the development of resistance in the pest population whilst monocultural cultivation exacerbated the pest problem and caused heavy crop failures at the turn of the millennium. Additionally, the cost of cultivation had risen over the years and the remuneration the cotton farmers received was not enough to cover production costs. The rash of reported suicides of small-scale farmers and peasants turned them into the unfortunate victims of India's Gene Revolution.[166]

In Ceylon/Sri Lanka, the Senanayake Government made an effort in the years following the island's independence to free the country from the need to import food, especially rice. As in India under Nehru, political autonomy was followed by economic autarchy to ensure economic self-sufficiency. To achieve this, extensive state irrigation programmes were launched in the "dry zone" to enlarge the existing structures. Additionally an active government policy promoted the internal colonisation of fallow land and wasteland. In this way, in the first decade following independence and with a rising population of 2.8 per cent per annum, the Senanayake Government was able to increase paddy field yield from 16.7 million to 37.7 million bushels.[167] In addition to the small-scale irrigation projects, the overall success was attributed to the completion of the large-scale Gal Oya dam and irrigation scheme in the Eastern Province. Alongside the generation of hydroelectric power, the scheme also allowed an additional 40,000 hectares of land to be irrigated following the completion of the dam in 1956. However, the implementation of the programme also meant that some 250,000 people had to be resettled. The lack of involvement of stakeholders led, as elsewhere in Asia, to massive protests.[168]

After some delays, the Ceylonese Government launched its Green Revolution in 1967, which consisted mainly of the introduction of high-yield varieties in paddy fields and the necessary use of fertilisers and pesticides. Despite this, there was neither a capital-intensive mechanisation, nor an industrialisation of the agricultural sector.[169] Within just three years paddy field yield had been increased to 77 million bushels, a significant increase on the previous peak of 50 million bushels in 1964. However, despite the increases in rice production and the realistic possibility of becoming independent from rice imports, the region experienced a dramatic drop in rice crops until 1974. The reason for this was the withdrawal of government from state programmes, including the reallocation of management, administrative and scientific personnel. Only with the government reforms at the end of the 1970s did yields begin to rise again and reach the levels that had been recorded at the beginning of the decade.[170]

In East Pakistan, the Green Revolution was started in the middle of the 1960s; however, it only gained momentum after Bangladesh became independent from Pakistan in 1971. This is indicated, for example, by the sharp increase in the area sown with Modern Variety Seeds. The total area sown with these seeds amounted to 0.6 per cent of the total arable land in 1967, increasing to 4.6 per cent in 1971, sharply rising to 11.2 per cent the following year and reaching 30 per cent in 1986. Similar numbers demonstrate the impact of the Green Revolution on the water consumption for agricultural purposes. In 1970, the total number of deep tube-wells was 18,000; in 1985 the number had risen to 167,000 whilst shallow tube-wells had increased from zero in 1970 to 137,000 by 1985. During the same period the total area of irrigated land doubled from 12 per cent to 25.7 per cent.[171] However, due to the different ecological, climatic and agro-structural conditions in Bangladesh, the negative consequences of the Green Revolution were less dramatic than elsewhere in South Asia. Regular flooding and the heavy rainfall that covers large parts of the country stabilised the groundwater table and, more or less, ensured the quality of the water and the soil. Furthermore, because of the geological situation in the Ganga-Brahmaputra delta, large agro-industrial farms did not develop, thus reducing the negative impact of the Green Revolution on the social conditions of the peasants.[172]

Presently, the curse and blessing of the Green Revolution and the Gene Revolution continues to be hotly debated. Without doubt the Green Revolution contributed decisively to ensuring the supply of food to the growing population in all countries of South Asia which meant that catastrophes such as the famines that had occurred until the middle of the twentieth century could be avoided. However, the effects that the Green and Gene Revolutions have had on the environment, especially in soil and water quality, have now become obvious as local populations suffer from poor water quality caused by its contamination with pesticides and fertilisers that enter the groundwater unfiltered. Moreover, the lack of water treatment systems continues to exacerbate the problem. However, as in other regions of the world where an industrialised agricultural sector has successfully secured the food supply and drastically driven prices down, it seems that the inhabitants of the South Asian countries are able, and willing, to live with the negative effects of the agrarian revolution. Yet, at the same time, the dramatic changes in food production are having an effect on the consciousness of consumers here as well.

Notes

1 Moreland 1968.
2 Metcalf 1979; Reeves 1992; Robb 1992a.
3 Ludden 1994, 1996; Hardiman 1996.
4 Bhadani 1999.
5 Guha R. 1982–1992; Guha R. 1983; Hardiman 1992.
6 Mann 2002; Satya 2004; Iqbal 2010.
7 Stein 1980; Ludden 1985.
8 Ludden 1999.
9 Mann and Tobler 2012.
10 Chakravarti R. 1998: 87–105.
11 Kumar N. 1980: 211–15.
12 De Silva 1981: 27–34.
13 Wittfogel 1957; Worster 1985.
14 Bronger 1996: 359–61.
15 Robb 1983: 1–23, esp. 3.
16 Subrahmanyam 1994.

17 Rothermund 1978a: 1–9.
18 Datta 1996: 92–131, esp. 101–4.
19 Habib I. 1999: 240–71; Siddiqi 1970: 41–59; Frykenberg 1977; Frykenberg 1979.
20 Siddiqi N.A. 1970: 21–40.
21 Hasan S.N. 1998: 284–98.
22 Alam 1998: 449–73; Rana 198: 287–326.
23 Bayly 1983; Datta R. 1996: 114–5; Chowdhury-Zilly 1982.
24 Rothermund 1978a: 33–6; Pouchepadass 1983: 78–108; Robb 1983: 9–18; Charlesworth 1983: 182–216.
25 Dewey 1972: 291–328; Inden: 131–61.
26 *Journal of Peasant Studies* 26, 2–3 (1999); Prakash 1992: 12–19; Guha S. 1996: 251–61.
27 Chatterjee and Eaton 2006.
28 Siddiqi A. 1973: 51–4.
29 Prakash 1990.
30 Baden-Powell 1892.
31 Tomlinson 1993: 50–5.
32 Guha R. 1982.
33 Islam S. 1979; Chaudhury B. 1982: 87–118.
34 Bose S. 1993: 119.
35 Robb 1997; Rothermund 1978a: 86–115.
36 Bose S. 1993: 109–12.
37 Prakash 1990: 82–139; Prakash 1992: 1–46, esp. 21–8.
38 Chaudhuri B. 1994: 145–81; Datta R. 2000: 75.
39 Thorner 1996: 82–3; Chaudhuri B. 1969: 152–206.
40 Iqbal 2010: 117–39.
41 Ibid.: 140–59.
42 Chaudhuri B. 1996: 71–91; Bose S. 1993: 41–63.
43 Stokes 1983: 49–50; Yang 1989.
44 Kling 1966.
45 Goswami O. 1984: 335–64; Greenough 1982: 61–84.
46 Srimanjari 2009.
47 Iqbal 2010: 160–83.
48 Vaid, Merrill and Bage 1995.
49 Singh N.K. 2001.
50 Sharma J. 2011.
51 Mann 2000a: 213–45.
52 Ahmad Khan 1980: 1–74, esp. 7–15.
53 Ibid.: 21–40; Dasgupta A. 1983: 39–48; Naher 1976: 104–15.
54 Iqbal 2010: 67–92.
55 Rycroft 2006: 205–71.
56 Metcalfe T.R. 1979: 22–31; Siddiqi A. 1973: 66–86.
57 Siddiqi A. 1973: 15–25; Metcalfe T.R. 1979: 50–67.
58 Metcalfe T.R. 1979: 68–71, 125–32; Bhargava 1999: 96–191; Mann 2000a: 192–208.
59 Siddiqi A. 1973: 140–153; Mann 2000a: 113–34.
60 Kumar K. 1984: 6.
61 Stokes 1978; Stokes 1986; Metcalfe T.R. 1979: 143–158; Mann 2000a: 135–62.
62 Reeves 1991; Kumar K. 1984: 11.
63 Rothermund 1978a: 128–45; Kumar K. 1984: 17–35.
64 Stokes 1983: 58–65; Metcalfe T.R. 1990: 187–97.
65 Singh N.T 2005: 63–101; Singh P. 2011: 160–78.
66 Mann 2000a: 115–34.
67 Singh N.T. 2005: 157–64.
68 Mann 2000a: 162–83; Sharma S. 2001: 28–78; Whitcombe 197: 64–83.

182 Agriculture and agro-economy

69 Bhargava 1990: 35–53.
70 Thorner 1996: 68–77.
71 Ibid.: 60–2, 66–7.
72 Banga 1978; Banga 1997; Sachdeva 1997: 284–306.
73 Sharma R. 1978: 307–17.
74 Major 1997: 318–32; Major 1996: 155–69.
75 Islam M.M. 1997: 25–31, 37–55.
76 Thorner 1996: 64; Islam M.M. 1997: 73.
77 Agnihotri 1996: 37–58.
78 Barrier 1992: 227–58.
79 Ali 1978: 341–57.
80 Mazumdar R.K. 2003: 93–138, 202–57; Yong 2005.
81 Thorner 1996: 63, 67.
82 Bhattacharya 1985: 305–42; Rothermund 1978a: 148–53.
83 Islam M.M. 1997: 55–8.
84 Whitcombe 1996: 237–59.
85 Kumar R. 1968: 12–21; Charlesworth 1985: 25.
86 Wink 1986: 256–92; Gordon 1993: 140–4.
87 Fukazawa 1983: 178–83; Hardiman 1996: 96–117.
88 Stokes 1959: 81–139; Ambirajan 1978: 144–81.
89 McAlpin 1983: 84–103.
90 Ludden 1999: 200.
91 Kuma R. 1968: 56–72; Fukazawa 1983: 183–5; Hardiman 1996: 11–61.
92 Nightingale 1970.
93 Staubli 1994: 39–43; Charlesworth 1985: 73–4.
94 McAlpin 1983: 103–13; Charlesworth 1985: 43–52.
95 Jhirad 1968: 151–65; Staubli 1994: 121–7.
96 Charlesworth 1985: 65–8; Rothermund 1978a: 167–8.
97 Kumar 1968: 151–88; Charlesworth 1985: 95–115; Hardiman 1996: 202–19.
98 Charlesworth 1972: 401–21; Rodrigues 1998: 40–71.
99 Charlesworth 1985: 206–15; Staubli 1994: 166–8; Guha S. 1985: 85–160; McAlpin 1983: 113–43.
100 McAlpin 1983: 144–58; Thorner 1996: 114.
101 Fukazawa 1983: 197.
102 Guha S. 1985: 70–8.
103 Rothermund 1978a: 168–70; Fukazawa 1983: 202–4.
104 Fukazawa 1983: 193–203.
105 Chaturvedi 2007: 25–37, 58–61, 79–83.
106 Ibid.: 55–7, 69–74.
107 Ibid.: 103–19.
108 Radhakrishna 2001. For additional and detailed literature on the Criminal Tribes Act see Chaturvedi 2007: fn. 2, p. 235.
109 Hardiman 1981: 31–58, 138–56.
110 Chaturvedi 2007: 132–5.
111 Ibid.: 136–50.
112 Satya 1997: 52–70, 139–53, 204–46.
113 Ibid.: 180–94; Hossain 1988.
114 Satya 1997: 194–7, 283–88.
115 Satya 2009: 20–72, 161–223 *passim*.
116 Thaha 2009: 99–111.
117 Kumar D. 1982a: 207–9; Kumar D. 1982b: 353–5.
118 Kumar D. 1982a: 230–3; Charlesworth 1985: 78, 212.
119 Stein 1980: 259–64.
120 Kumar D. 1982a: 214–21; Sheik Ali 2004: 161–4; Dirks 1987.

121 Kumar D. 1965: 10–33; Stein 1989b: 24–138, 273–87.
122 Kumar D. 1982a: 224–6.
123 Kumar D. 1965: 13–14.
124 Kumar D. 1982a: 226–30.
125 Kumar D. 1965: 77–98.
126 Rothermund 1978a: 116–25.
127 Ibid.: 159–65.
128 Satyanarayana 1990.
129 Robert 1983: 59–78; Robert 1985: 281–306; Charlesworth 1985: 196.
130 Kumar D. 1982a: 238; Thorner 1996: 136.
131 Joseph 1987: 46–54; Mann 2012c: 89–93; Kumar D. 1965: 34–48.
132 Kumar D. 1965: 55–63.
133 Ibid.: 144–69; Baker 1984: 159–73.
134 Ahuja 1999: 130–45.
135 Schmitthenner 2011: 181–201.
136 D'Souza R. 2006: 51–96.
137 Thorner, 1996: 139; Rothermund 1988: 83.
138 Bandarage 1983: 124–31, 137–50.
139 De Silva 2005: 378–87, 500–4.
140 Webb 2002: 70–2, 76–9, 108–10; Meyer 1992: 321–61; Banderage 1983: 121.
141 Bandarage 1983: 89, 94–7, 109–14.
142 Webb 2002: 109–16, 134, 136.
143 De Silva 2005: 390–2.
144 Meyer 1998: 793–827.
145 Rothermund 1988: 94–102; Rothermund 1992: 79–134.
146 Tomlinson 1993: 68–70.
147 Werner 2013.
148 Gilmartin 1996: 210–36.
149 Mukherjee S.K. 1992: 445–52.
150 Strahorn 2009: 102–8.
151 Unger 2011: 121–42.
152 Bhardwaj 2010: 186–208, esp. 188–94.
153 Blyn 1979: 353–67; Farmer 1977; Parthasarathy S. 1994: 55–200.
154 Frankel 1971; Jacoby 1972: 63–9; Singh J. 1974.
155 Singh T. 2007: 1–15; Yapa 1993: 254–73.
156 Rothermund 1995: 493; Ludden 1999: 195; Husain M. 2007: 81–93.
157 Jaffrelot 2004: 18–19, 168–70.
158 Shiva 1993: 89–95.
159 Gadgil and Guha 1992: 24–7; Sanyal 2005: 699–763.
160 Economic Survey 2010–2011: 196–211.
161 Collins and Moore Lappé 1981: 155.
162 Dhanagare 1990: 266–88.
163 Chakravarti A.K. 1973: 319–30.
164 Brass T. 1995: 3–26.
165 Singh B.P. 2010.
166 Bhardwaj 2010: 194–5.
167 De Silva 2005: 617–22.
168 Uphoff 1992.
169 Herath 1981: 664–75.
170 De Silva 2005: 657, 666–8.
171 Hossain M. 1988: 25, 27.
172 Conway/Huq/Rahman 1990.

5 Silviculture and scientific forestry

Nature, culture and time

Whilst the agricultural history, especially in its evolution under the British colonial regime, has attracted major scientific attention, the management of forests has long been neglected by the historical sciences. Only in the last two decades of the twentieth century did this change following the particular impetus from the growing worldwide interest into environmental issues (and changes). Against this backdrop, environmental research into (British) India concentrated on the forest history of the subcontinent since the middle of the nineteenth century as it is here that the first and most serious interventions in the "natural" environment can be observed. Related to these interventions, and often as a direct result, are major changes in the human environment. The indigenous peoples of these forests are among those who were affected most by these changes and have also, to a much greater extent, seen their rights appropriated, transformed and suppressed by the colonial state. It is on this fact that the main historical focus of British India lies,[1] whilst the trade of forest goods and products has received somewhat less attention.[2] Only recently has the category of wildlife been added to the environmental research agenda.[3]

The strict division of the study of agriculture and forestry has hitherto only made sense from the perspective of those who imposed such a juxtaposition of terms (and fields). Thus, to distinguish between the two issues of agriculture and silviculture would run the risk of continuing an established discourse. However, such distinctions are not discursive remnants of the colonial-European origin, but rather have had a long tradition on the South Asian subcontinent. Both centrally organised governmental political systems, as well as agrarian settlers, have a veritable interest in differentiating between "peaceful" agricultural settlers and the forest with its "wild inhabitants". However, on closer inspection it becomes apparent that such a strict separation does not make sense as agricultural areas near forests always mark zones of transition and the intersecting use by peasants and forest dwellers including sylvan societies. Thus the rearing of cattle in forests was an essential part of agricultural production in South Asia just as it was in Europe, for example.

Nevertheless, the forest clearly presents a different ecosystem that must be dealt with accordingly. It is an ecosystem characterised by a rich biodiversity of flora and fauna that also renders the forest an adequate habitat for people. The notion perpetuated by the urban and agricultural societies that the dwellers of this habitat are, at best "tribal" societies and at worst, "savages", falls short of the reality as both conceptions are associated with a differing degree of civilisational backwardness. Although these perceptions have existed in South Asia since ancient times, the dimension of the notion was intensified during colonial rule and thereafter in the successor states, especially in India and Bangladesh. The ways in which the forest was used by its residents was, however, highly differentiated as slash-and-burn cultivation is only one, albeit the most common, form of sylvan agriculture. The collection of forest products for private consumption or processing and sale is another form of forest use. Sedentary societies each possessed a different picture of the forest. For example, the Tamils of South India were able to distinguish their natural environment in five (telling) categories: hill/forest country; forest/pasture; river areas allowing irrigation farming; coastal areas; and wasteland.[4]

With the arrival of the Aryans from about the twelfth century BCE and their gradual settling in North India from the tenth century BCE, a sharper distinction between civilised land and wild forest land began to crystallise. This distinction can be seen in the Mahabharata epos of the sixth century BCE which sang of the slash-and-burn method of clearance with help of the fire god Agni, as well as the gradual use of iron implements for clearing of jungle. The epos distinguished between human settlements and cultivated land with established social systems, and the wild and disordered (primary) forest, the habitat of hermits and of deities. However, immigrant Aryan *brahmans* did not only live as hermits in the forest, but with their ideas about social order they divided the world into a civilised (*kshetra*: field) and uncivilised sphere (*vana*: forest). From the Mahabharata it also becomes clear that the warlords (*kshatria*) and rulers (*raja*) had inherited the duty (*dharma*) to order the earthly universe, thereby distinguishing the wilderness of the forest in the cultivated area (*vana*) which marked a transition from this still arable landscape to the complete wilderness (*aranya*).[5]

From the twelfth century CE the Muslim rulers in South Asia made much more radical distinctions between the civilised city and uncivilised country than the Aryan immigrants had previously. As in many other countries the Muslim culture was also pronounced in urban South Asia, as can be seen in increasing urbanisation during the Mughal Empire.[6] The deforestation of the Ganges valley was now further advanced, which saw the *adivasi* (lit.: first inhabitants, aborigines) withdraw from the area and venture deeper into the forests where they still live today in the region that has become known at the Tribal Belt. This belt encompasses the current federal states of Madhya Pradesh, Jharkhand, northern Orissa, northwestern Chhattisgarh and western West Bengal. With the consolidation of colonial rule and the beginning of scientific forestry, the "tribals" were now not only categorised as backward, but often as criminals. In doing so, this categorisation was one instrument among many which secured state access to the forests in British India. Even today, the enforcement of forestry policies in the Indian state draws on the legal instruments introduced by the colonial state.

The history of the state's administrative access to the forests in South Asia dates back to the eighteenth century and can be divided into five phases. The first phase extends to the beginning of the nineteenth century as Indian rulers such as Tipu Sultan of Maisur and the British in South India, Gorkha rulers of Nepal/Gorkha and the Ahom in Assam, attempted to bring forests under central administration and to grant licences for logging and other uses of forest products. This system collapsed under British colonial rule on account of the under-staffed administrative workforce who were not experts in how to conduct silviculture in the forests of Malabar, Garhwal, Kumaon, Assam, Pegu and Tenasserim. Until the middle of the nineteenth century the British ceded rights to the Indian traders to trade in timber. This lack of governmental control led to extensive deforestation as, for the first time, commercial interests, such as the affordable provision of surplus quantities of wood, now dominated the management of forests. Such commercialisation of the forests came to characterise the second phase of forestry control, which lasted from 1820 until 1860.

The increased British demand for wood, driven by the onset of railway construction in the 1850s, saw the establishment of the Forest Department in 1864 and the beginning of the third phase of the British-Indian forest management. The management of the new scientific forestry aimed to satisfy the demand for wood and to initiate the long-term protection of forests. However, scientific forestry did not provide for the maintenance or expansion of forests, but was instead aimed only at securing the stock and the systematic conversion of primary forests into industrial (monoculture) forests. This conversion of forests was accompanied by a transformation of the sylvan societies whose rights to the forest and its products were systematically limited by the colonial state. However, this process was a long-term one as the colonial state was still too weak in terms of personnel to be able to immediately and comprehensively implement laws and regulations. Widespread resistance in Kumaon and Garwahl against state forest policy rose in the 1920s in response to the massive logging during the First World War. This ushered in the fourth phase of forest management which lasted into the 1990s.

This fourth phase is characterised by the continuous and partially soaring logging sector as well as by the gathering resistance of the local population against the growing central government's exploitation of local resources. The forest administration of independent India hardly differed from the colonial state in its claim on natural resources of the forest. Thus, from the administrative and constitutional points of view, as well as from the perspective of local residents and the view of the forest, the end of colonial rule in no way represented a departure from past policies. Although the law on Joint Forest Management in 1998 attempted to initiate a new policy and involve local people in the decision-making process, simply increasing participation in the decisions about sylvan resource utilisation did not necessarily contribute to the protection of the forests, let alone their expansion. On the contrary, continued population pressure and increasing demand for wood in the joint optimisation of resource utilisation have come to characterise the current, fifth phase.

Thus, continuities can clearly be seen from the pre-colonial to colonial and especially from the colonial to the post-colonial state. Hence to set the period of British colonial rule as a temporal limit offers few academic insights. Furthermore, it appears that it was only in the second half of the nineteenth century that the colonial state was in the position to initiate an all-India forest policy; however, its ultimate implementation was initially far from successful. This is not to say that the colonial state was not a tangible element in Indian society, but rather that its access to the forests and the rights of the local population varied greatly depending on the different regions and different times these actions were applied. As in other areas of colonial rule, such as revenue collection, it took several decades before new rules could not only be implemented, but were also followed. Where forest policy differs from that of revenue administration or jurisdiction, however, is that for the first time a comprehensive and far-reaching governmental initiative was envisaged to regulate an entire sector which was also accompanied by administration, including the British "modern" bureaucracy.

Forest management in South Asia until 1860

The huge biodiversity of tropical and subtropical humid forests in South Asia together with the adjacent semi-arid areas offered inhabitants a unique habitat. Semi-sedentary societies slashed and burned forest areas, which in turned offered them several years of food security before they had to relocate to a new area for cultivation. The semi-sedentary clans and sylvan settlers gathered fruits, roots, leaves and thin branches from the forest which were then utilised in a huge variety of daily chores. In contrast to the low biodiversity of the "industrial" forest of the late nineteenth century with its "pole wood", the rich variety of the "natural" forest was of considerable economic importance for the agro-sylvan cultural sphere. Peasants in the vicinity of forest areas regularly used the forest for the grazing of livestock and for their supply of firewood. In addition, the forests not only provided feed and fertiliser for the peasants, but were also the main sources of timber as well as providing edible and medicinal herbs. Thus already in Early India the local population which lived in the forest or in the border areas between forest, pasture and arable land was knowledgeable about the practicality of forest products and as such the forest was afforded a high social value.[7]

This knowledge and value of the forest as a resource of various products was demonstrated by the Maurya Emperor Ashoka (304–232 BCE), who, in the fifth of his famous Pillar Edicts, banned the burning of forests and prohibited the hunting of animals in and near forest areas. These laws, however, did not prevent the rulers of his centrally administered kingdom from pushing back the boundaries of the "open frontier" of the forests in the major river valleys such as the large tributaries of the Ganges. This often severely limited, if not destroyed, the livelihood of non-sedentary and semi-sedentary societies and made them dependent on the agricultural products of sedentary peasants. Since that time, a tense and often violent relationship between the settled peasant communities and nomadic societies can be observed.[8] The first forms of centralised governmental forest management through the implementation of institutions developed in South Asia in the eighth century. By the time of

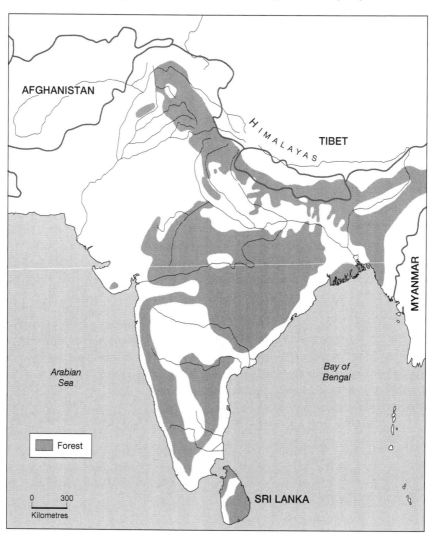

Map 5.1 Forest coverage in South Asia c. 1650. Adapted from I. Habib, *Man and Environment: The Ecological History of India* (Aligarh Historians Society: 2011), p. 96

the Mughal Empire in the seventeenth century, the silviculture had been further elaborated, showing characteristics of early forest management.[9] Careful reconstruction suggests that still during the middle of the seventeenth century about two-thirds of the subcontinent was covered in dense forest.[10]

Generally, access to the forest's resources was regulated by stately privileges and community interests (usufruct). Food stuff, firewood and other products, including spices such as pepper and cardamom, were collected and exchanged in the villages or sold to nearby market towns.[11] In the late eighteenth century, professional lumberjacks were granted licences to fell trees in the Malabar forests whilst monopolistic wholesalers closely organised the trade of wood and pepper.[12] The low forest population density allowed forest farmers to dictate licences and delivery times, as well as work that was to be performed, to local rulers and the merchants as other labourers were often not available. The same was true even under British colonial rule as the migration of labourers prevented both the short or medium term economic development of the forests.[13]

The relationship between the local rulers or their representatives and the forest dwellers was just as conflicted as their relationship to the rural subjects. Social and political status as well as economic position defined access to the natural resources of the forest and were the cause of sometimes violent confrontations between the local population and the authorities responsible for the collection of revenues. Thus an egalitarian or even peaceful sylvan pastoral community was not the case. On the contrary, potential conflict was always simmering below the surface for any number of reasons such as the economic, financial and fiscal access to the valuable forest products and the surrounding pasture. Moreover such conflict did not exist merely between sylvan communities, but also within them as disputes often arose over the rights to use sylvan resources.[14]

This situation was exacerbated by attempts to secure these resources, which, since the mid-eighteenth century and the South Indian wars of succession, consumed enormous quantities of raw materials and exerted extreme pressure on the forests in Malabar, Maratha Desh, on the Dekhan and in the Himalayas. In order to extract the maximum fiscal benefits possible from the forests and to ensure, in their mind at least, the optimum utilisation of natural resources, the *rajas* of Kochi annexed the hinterland of the region and confiscated the forests of the Ghats. In many cases they also expelled the local population from the area or deprived them of their rights to use the forest's resources as they set up a central forest administrative system.[15] Further to the north, the Marathas sanctioned strict forest laws, which included re- and afforestation to ensure increases in revenue and shipbuilding in particular. Similar measures were also taken by the *amir* of Sind.[16] Consequently, already in the pre-colonial period various attempts had been made by South Asian rulers to secure access to the forest's resources, to appropriate them and to establish a "forest line" as a sharp distinction between forest and agricultural land leading to different areas of revenue administration and access to natural resources.

However, as indicated above, this "forest line" was a source of constant controversy and, in the sense of an "open frontier", was regularly contested as those who lived in, or from, the forest attempted to defend their rights and privileges against the advances of external actors. On the other hand, according to the view of South Asian rulers, it was the clearing of the forest, as well as the access to forest resources, that made them conqueror the wilderness and the savages who lived within them as they became the colonisers and civilisers of the land. In this way these pre-colonial South Asian rulers hardly differed from other contemporary societies or the European, and especially British, colonisers. In the eighteenth century, the British considered the clearing of forests to be an act of civilisation, whereby the aim was to close the "open frontier" and to pacify the country, as had been the case in the Scottish Highlands.[17] Meanwhile forest policy on the other hand was a permanent attempt by the British rulers in South Asia to turn the "open frontier" into the demarcation of a borderline and thereby to define two clear zones of forest and agricultural land which could be militarily, administratively, economically and fiscally controlled.[18]

By the end of the eighteenth century, the British controlled large parts of Malabar and its forests. In the course of the military conflicts against Napoleon, the British Admiralty in London initiated a programme to build a fleet of warships which were to be constructed in Bombay from Malabar teak at the beginning of the nineteenth century. Within just a few years demand for the hardwood stocks of the Malabar forests increased to such an extent that the British Government in Bombay was prompted to initiate a forest administration according to the European model in order to secure the long-term supply of timber to the Bombay shipyards.[19] In doing so the administrators initially resorted to the local forms of forest management and practice of reforestation that had been introduced by the *raja* of Kochi. Such management of the forests is also testament to the forest management systems prior to the introduction of the European "science" of forestry that had already understood the principle of sustainability in terms of reforestation. This stood in stark contrast to the forest conservation methods employed by the British until the end of the nineteenth century which were confined to natural regeneration.

On account of an acute shortage and the growing demand for wood in Europe,[20] as well as the additional revenues promised from the centrally organised "scientific" forestry (based on mathematical, cartographic and regenerative principles), forest management started to emerge in Europe from the mid-eighteenth century in both Germany and France.[21] As a result, numerous small German states and France established an administrative forest management system. In India, the British seized this continental European expertise and applied it to a non-European territory for the first time as a number of Germans with experience in forest economy were commissioned to the British service to impart their knowledge and aid in the preservation of the forests in Malabar. In addition to the private economically organised, but state-controlled, logging, statistical data on tree species and the demarcation of areas in use were also gathered. Above all, the rights of the local population were to be defined and livestock grazing in the forest areas was to be strictly prohibited. After a few years, however, this attempt failed, partly because the divergent interests of the revenue administration, the forest conservation and shipbuilding fleet programme could not be harmonised.[22]

In Gorkha/Nepal, the *rajas* reforested the mountain slopes of the Siwalik region following their victory over the British in 1768 which the Gorkhas attributed to the dense forests and their hostile climate. Similarly, extensive reforestation was also initiated in Tarai following their defeat by the British in 1816. The wars of expansion of Gorkha in Garhwal and Kumaon (both territories were annexed in 1791 and correspond approximately to the present-day Indian federal state of Uttarakhand), put such pressure on the finances of the country that the economy could only be stabilised through a drastic revenue increase on sylvan and agricultural goods. The increased exploitation of natural and financial resources triggered an unrelenting deterioration of the environment, living conditions and the ultimate impoverishment of broad sections of the population that forced hundreds of thousands of people to migrate into the Ganges valley. Following the annexation of the territory by the British in 1816, more than 2,000 villages were deserted and countless fields were left untended and soon became wasteland.[23]

To the south of the Siwaliks is the Tarai, an ecologically unbroken area of wetland and forest that transcends into the present-day Indian federal state of Uttar Pradesh and Uttarakhand and into Nepal.[24] Whilst the "eastern" Tarai was much more inhospitable and, until the twentieth century, largely inaccessible, after the annexation of the "western" Kumaon and Garhwal the British began to systematically extract material from this forest region for the repair and maintenance of their ships; timber (such as pine) for ship masts was in particularly high demand. Despite the obvious demand, however, lack of both labour and local knowledge meant that success in this region was only moderate. As revenues were not reduced under the new regime, migration to North India continued. The agrarian landscape that had been sculpted out of the desolate landscapes over centuries was laid to waste within decades and partially reclaimed by the jungle.[25]

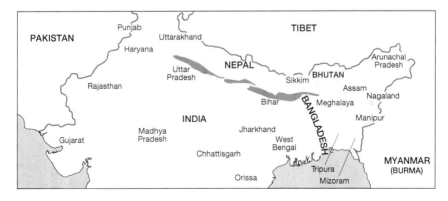

Map 5.2 The Tarai

According to British opinion in 1800, the forests of South Asia were inexhaustible. After the first British attempts to introduce regulated forest management had failed, an unprecedented onslaught of the forests began. By the 1830s in Malabar and Garhwal the consequences of deforestation had already become evident whilst the same was also true for the Pegu forests in Burma. Alongside the high demand for timber, firewood was also increasingly required for the firing of bricks which were used in the construction of British barracks. On account of this increasing demand, closed forests in Sind and the Central and Lower Doab regions of the Ganga and Yamuna rivers were cut down in the course of just a few decades.[26] The consequences of uncontrolled logging were so extreme in Garhwal and Kumaon that the local metal production came to an abrupt halt in the 1860s as wood required for the production of charcoal was not available for firing the furnaces.[27] The extent to which the forests were exploited was directly related to the fact that wood, now to proportions hitherto unknown, had become a commercial good that was traded through private companies and that the colonial state limited itself to the collection of revenue and duties.[28]

The impact of scientific forestry (1860–1920)

With the onset of railway construction in British India and the associated enormous demand for wood for sleepers from the mid-nineteenth century, the issue of securing a permanent supply of wood through state institutions was again raised. Future head of the Botanical Gardens at Kew (1865–85), Joseph D. Hooker (1817–1911), persuaded Governor-General Lord Dalhousie in 1848 of the urgent need for the state to manage the forests in order to ensure the long-term access to timber resources. Dalhousie took the first legislative action in this regard during his tenure (1848–56) as the British colonial administration relied, once again, on the knowledge of German scientific forestry experts.[29] The most famous of these German experts, Dietrich Brandis (1824–1907), campaigned for uniform forest legislation in British India from the mid-1850s. As Inspector-General of Indian Forests (1864–81), he founded the Forest Department in 1864 and ushered in the first legislation with Act 7 in 1865. This kept state control to a minimum which led to fierce debates in the following years.[30]

It was soon evident that a new law was needed that clearly defined the government's claims with regard to "ancient rights" and "ancient privileges" ultimately calling into question the ownership of the forest. The British claimed at the beginning of the nineteenth century that Tipu Sultan had confiscated entitlements to land in the Malabar forests, which, as a result, meant that they were now owned by the state. Meanwhile, the local population, and some British officers, assumed that the land and the forest belonged to those who lived in and from it.[31] Even after the withdrawal of state forest administration in 1823 the British did not relinquish their claim to the state ownership of the forests in Malabar. In Malabar, as with the forests of Kumaons and Garhwal, the British were ultimately forced into a fundamental debate about ownership and possession rights in the 1830s. Despite this widely unresolved legal issue, the British continued to enforce their vision of being the sole owners of the forest in Northern India in the mid-nineteenth century.[32] This followed some decades later in other regions of the subcontinent.

After long discussions the regulations of the India Forest Act of 1878 finally introduced the classification of forests in British India as either "reserved", "protected" or "village/communal" forests. The key provision of the act lay in the distinction between reserved and protected forests. In the former, no rights could be acquired unless explicitly ceded by the provincial government, whereas in the latter rights were to be recorded, but not settled. The Madras Government, however, opposed this law and adopted a separate Forest Act in 1882. The same was true for Burma, which had adopted its own specific legislation in 1881 whilst Berar did the same in 1886.[33] Thus it is hardly possible to speak of a uniform legislation in British India as overlapping governmental powers on the one hand, and differing legal rights of the local population on the other, resulted in difficulties in introducing a unified forest policy. However, this was also advantageous for the local custom of the regions that were more often taken into consideration and the laws that were implemented were "softer" versions of those that had been first planned.

With laws introduced in 1878, Brandis translated the principles of forestry in Europe north of the Alps (aimed at a minimal biodiversity, high economic efficiency and sustainability of the forests) to the forests of British India. The centuries-old, empirically derived ecological knowledge of the local population was overlooked in favour of the scientific and central forest administration, which, within a few decades, had brought the German scientific forestry vision of the *Normalbaum* and made it a reality in British India. European forestry methods were utilised to transform South Asian forests into hardwood forests. Brandis' successors in the position of Inspector-General (William Schlich, 1881–5 and Berthold Ribbentrop, 1885–99) soon realised that South Asian forests could not be managed with the same thoroughness as Central European forests on account of their sheer scale and the intricate layers of law that regulated them. Moreover, the differing interests between civil (revenue) and forest administration prevented the speedy and comprehensive implementation of forest laws.[34]

Garhwal and Kumaon, the region which, after the forests of Malabar, held the primary interest of the British in relation to forest management, saw the introduction of the classification of the sub-Himalayan forests between 1878 and 1893 and were predominantly demarcated as reserved forests. In this area, individual tree species such as *sal, sissu, khair* and *deodar* were all placed under special protection. Furthermore, the Forest Department was largely able to bring the forests of the inner Himalayas under colonial control until 1918. Since almost every resident of both the forest and land was affected and subject to the regulations of the Forest Department, resistance to the omnipresent state soon began to develop as regulations not only controlled the felling of trees, but also access to the forest for both humans and livestock. Cattle were counted, their movements recorded and grazing rights were limited and only awarded during certain seasons. The pastoralist societies such as the Gujars and Bhotiya particularly suffered under the new regulations. Consequently, the restrictive regimes of forest management resulted in pastoralists having to graze an increasing number of animals in an increasingly smaller space, ultimately causing severe environmental damage.[35]

From the 1860s the Forest Department also attempted to restrict the rights of access to the forests of the Central Provinces in order to secure its own access to certain types of wood such as *teak*, *sishan* and *saj* which were of considerable economic value. The executive power of the foresters was significantly strengthened in 1878 with the introduction of the Forest Act. Within the reserved forests of the Central Provinces there was a ban on the felling, girdling, lopping, tapping and burning of trees. Even the stripping of bark and the collection of leaves were prohibited. Exceptions made for the local population only confirmed these laws all the more. Increasingly, the foresters attempted to expand their influence in the privately owned forests, which covered one-fifth of the total forest area, and to regulate the types of trees found there. In individual cases where the government's access to particularly valuable trees was to be guaranteed, such as in the Singhbhum District in the Chotanagpur Division of the Bengal Presidency, the government even went as far as to expropriate private land ownership during the 1880s.[36]

The state's claim to the forests in British India was formulated even more clearly with the passing of the Indian Forest Act in 1893. The grazing of cattle and the collection of firewood now became strictly forbidden in all reserved forests throughout the Central Provinces whilst in other regions of British India foresters endeavoured to implement tougher regulations. By the turn of the century, however, the strategy of strict exclusion became the subject of strong criticism as it was now argued that the burning of small forest and meadow areas was the most conducive for the recultivation of such areas. The same was also acknowledged for cattle grazing as cattle do not consume hardwoods such as teak, but rather everything else around these trees, in this way creating a natural young forest plantation. Of course these paradigm shifts were less about securing old local privileges and ensuring the protection of the forests, and more about optimising the colonial timber industry.[37] It was obvious that, just as in Europe, in India the forests were becoming ever more meaningless as habitats of humans and animals and the boundary between silviculture and agriculture gradually became more pronounced.[38]

In many cases, sedentary, semi-sedentary and nomadic societies living from or in the woods became the victims of the government's access to their living and working space. Whole villages and sylvan societies were marginalised or displaced, without payment of any compensation in the form of municipal land for their resettlement. It was soon evident that nomadic or semi-sedentary ways of life were not to be willingly accepted by the colonial state. According to colonial rhetoric of the time, these nomadic and semi-sedentary societies, as well as non-sedentary pastoralists, caused lasting damage to the forests with their *jhum* (slash-and-burn) cultivation methods. As a result the "wasteful" practice was banned. This judgmental assessment of the local beneficiaries of forests was based on the European understanding of scientific forestry, which, in the context of political economy, sought a greater common good through improvement and emancipation and thus raised the welfare of the population and the nation as a whole.[39] In response to the encroaching British-Indian Government, the sylvan societies, such as the Baiga in the Central Provinces, retreated ever further into the mountains.[40] Meanwhile, in other regions, as in the Chittagong Hills, local societies such as the Chakma and Marma were transformed into sedentary peasants after a quarter of their land was declared a reserved forest in the 1880s.[41]

The British staff of the Forest Department partially coordinated the stereotypes of the sylvan land use as they claimed that the grazing of sheep was solely responsible for environmental damage such as soil erosion, floods, desertification of agricultural land and the degradation of forests. Apocalyptic scenarios based on unreliable data heralded the destruction of civilisation by these people and their livestock which could only be stopped by consistent, centrally controlled forestry policies and strict forest laws.[42] At the same time it showed that despite the regulations by the Forest Acts, local societies had their own agency when it came to negotiating their ancestral and customary rights.[43] Testament to the self-consciousness is the emergence of sylvan societies' self-designation as *adivasi* in the eastern Indian region of Chotanagpur in the 1930s. The term was used by political activists with the aim of forging a new sense of identity against the *dikus* (lit.: outsiders) among different "tribal" peoples. The tactic enjoyed considerable success.[44]

This strategy was also the first result of a new self-assurance in reaction to the continuing external threat. In order to counter the colonial regime's denomination of the "tribe" and break with its negative associations, local kin-based societies gave themselves the name of *adivasi* as an expression of social, economic and cultural independence. For the Kol, Santhals, Hos, Birhors, Munda, Baiga and many other *adivasi* in the Tribal Belt, the forest was not only a source of wood, food, medicine and other resources, but its significance was equally important to faith and worship, and thus their entire environment. The forest was consequently an economic, political, social and cultural habitat. Their understanding of the landscape and its history differed fundamentally from the scientific perception of the colonial *dikus*.[45] The colonialist's intrusion into this area was often countered with resistance. This was especially so in the second half of the nineteenth century as resistance grew and threatened to spread uncontrollably in the Santhal Hol rebellion of 1855–6. The Birsa Munda uprising in the 1890s was the culmination of this first period of resistance.[46]

Resistance continued until the 1920s, which increased its initial local support in ever-widening circles. At that time the Tana Bhagat Movement had acquired disturbing links with the Congress's campaigns in Bihar.

Santhals and Mundas demanded the restoration of access to forests and freshwater fisheries, resulting in a wave of protest lasting well into the 1930s. The Chotanagpur Unnati Samaj, founded in 1915, was reorganised and renamed Adivasi Mahasabha in 1937 and became the political representation of the *adivasi* after the enactment of the India Act of 1935, and ahead of the general elections of 1937. However, the overwhelming success of Congress in the 1937 general elections demonstrated to the *adivasi* that the INC represented the urban and rural elites as well as the peasants, yet not their societies. In response, the Adivasi Mahasabha tried to both establish a pan-*adivasi* identity whilst simultaneously opening membership of the organisation to non-*adivasi* groups. Coinciding with this political organisation of the party, an invention of tradition took place.[47] The despoliation of the forested landscape and the transformation of the people's relationship with their environment in the nineteenth century was a powerful memory that was revived in periods of cultural and, ultimately, political resistance.[48]

South of the Tribal Belt lies the state of Haiderabad with its deciduous forests which run along the Godaveri and Krishna rivers and on into the north-western border of the state. It was first in the second half of the nineteenth century that an active forest management policy was introduced to the area, but after which the clearing of the forests for arable land continued, as elsewhere, for the maximisation of agricultural production and the maximisation of revenues. The growing demand for timber in British India also led to an uncontrolled felling of trees in Hyderabad State. The government responded in 1867 with the Hyderabad State Forest Department, but was forced to follow the British line due to its lack of expertise. Thus at first a British Inspector of Forests managed the forests in Haiderabad according to the Imperial Forest Act of 1878 without the strict implementation of its regulations. The following Forest Act of 1900 merely copied the legislation of the Imperial Forest Department and remained ineffective. Attempts to classify and protect the forests failed. Not even the revised versions of the law in 1917 and 1946 were able to change a great deal. Access for peasants and tribal societies was so strictly monitored and prohibited that the Forest Department was known as an unofficial police department by those affected.[49]

As such, virtually no forest management was to be found in Haiderabad until the mid-twentieth century. Rather, the state became another arena where the British-owned Revenue Department rivalled the Forest Department in the continuing expansion of agricultural land at the expense of forest areas. Alone in the first half of the twentieth century the ratio of forest area to total area of the state fell from 15 to 12 per cent. Dwindling forests also partly triggered ecological disaster as fertile black soil was eroded and the water table sank in some formerly forested areas. Reduced rainfall and increasing temperatures as well as an increase in the velocity of winds were also recorded by the British geologist, Leonard Munn, at the end of the nineteenth century. With this Munn proved to be a representative of the "Desiccation Theory" which had evolved out of a group of British colonial and European administrators, botanists, geologists and geographers from the second half of the eighteenth century.[50] Furthermore, Munn concluded that the catastrophic famine of 1876–8 in Hyderabad State was due, in part, to these changing climatic and environmental conditions as although natural in occurrence, the extreme effects were apparently a man-made disaster.[51]

The construction of the railway in British India soon allowed the imperial arm of the British to extend into Nepal. The wood required for this expansion, primarily for the railway sleepers, was sourced from the Tarai region. In order to coordinate the trade in timber, the Gorkha/Nepalese Government instigated the first supervisors of forests in the 1860s. Thanks to this coordination, the government was able to secure the second highest revenue returns from timber sales which continued until the turn of the century. In 1923 the British Imperial Forest Department sent supervisors from the Indian Forest Service to monitor the impact of felling in Nepal and the transport of wood to British India for which a specially designed railway line was constructed. Once the valuable timber had been extracted, the Gorkha Government often grew cash crops such as cotton, jute and tea in the deforested areas that were left. The impact and effects of the British colonial forestry and agricultural methods soon became all too obvious in the Nepalese Tarai.[52] Similar to the effects in neighbouring Garhwal and Kumaon, the hitherto uncultivated Tarai jungles with their rich biodiversity were systematically opened up to deforestation and the creation of agricultural land, including irrigation systems, during the late nineteenth century.[53]

Increasing exploitation and growing resistance 1920–90

The exploitation of the South Asian forests enacted during the two world wars reached hitherto unimaginable dimensions. The British not only stationed Indian troops on all fronts, but also exported millions of sleepers to extend the railway network in order to ensure the supply and mobility of troops. In the 1940–41 period alone, 440,000 sleepers were exported, exceeding pre-war demands by 65 per cent. Exceptions concerning the access to the forests were subsequently overridden in order to meet British war interests. This increasing activity is exemplified in Kumaon where between 1942 and 1945 the felling of trees exceeded annual yields six-fold; similarly the income of the Hyderabad State Forest Department skyrocketed between 1940 and 1945 from ₹1.4 million to ₹11.4 million.[54] The end of the Second World War and colonial rule did not mean a reprieve for the forests. As early as 1952, the Government of India decreed that the use of the forests was forbidden to village communities as this was against national interests. In a clear continuation of the colonial forest policy both rights of use and customary rights were confiscated and converted, if at all, into "concessions". More and more forest areas were declared as reserved forests, so that in Bihar alone nearly all the forested areas had come under state control within just two decades.[55]

The management of the forests of Assam is a revealing example of the continuities with the past two centuries.[56] Colonial rule clearly established a previously unknown level of commercial exploitation of the forests. However, it is the "set" of actors who took part in the exploitation that is remarkable as they included the colonial state, the planters who reclaimed land for the creation of tea plantations, local and immigrating peasants in search of new territory and land speculators. The specific problem in Assam lay in the fact that the colonial state as well as the post-colonial state had to balance the interests of all. Despite the strict demarcation of forest boundaries neither the colonial state, nor the post-colonial (successor) state, were successful in providing the valve to release the peasants' pressure on farmlands. This had the effect, among other things, that the peasant-settlers were not entitled to the land they worked and thus were forced to maintain their own claim to the forests and the ground through resistance in both the colonial and post-colonial regimes.[57]

By the end of the nineteenth century the colonial state had demarcated all uncultivated land in Assam, including jungle areas, as wasteland. In these areas as well as in the woodlands that had been declared as reserved forests the pressure of peasants and planters grew constantly. The aforementioned competition between the Forest and Revenue Departments exacerbated the situation as the latter transformed the "forest frontier" into an "agricultural frontier" allowing the felling of the forests of little economic worth, which also included parts of the reserved forests. In this way between 1870 and 1950 some 700,000 hectares of dense forest and woodland were converted to agricultural land which immigrating peasants had to share with a sizeable portion that was earmarked for the increasing acreage of jute cultivation.[58] As in other regions of British India the commercialisation and integration of the cash crop economy into the world economy proved to be the catalyst for the impoverishment of peasants which in many cases turned them into landless agricultural labourers. After independence, their number increased due to the unchanged forest policy of the Indian Government.[59]

Part of the ongoing expansion of the cash crop economy in Assam was based on the Settlement Scheme for the Brahmaputra Valley that the British had initiated in 1928. Since the late nineteenth century about 150,000 settlers from eastern Bengal had settled here and had cleared the grassland and forest areas around the river courses to create rice and jute fields. Within a decade, approximately 500,000 Bengalis came to Assam, most of whom settled in the Brahmaputra valley leading to another huge clearing of grass and jungle land to cultivate jute. This transformation of the landscape meant that the annual floods, which the local population had previously learnt to live with developing an ecological cycle for the cultivation of various crops, now led to the erosion of the reclaimed land. Official government estimates at the end of the 1930s recorded that about two-thirds of new agricultural land had been lost through erosion and thereby had increased the impoverishment of the peasants, consequently increasing the pressure on the forests of the mountains as potential agricultural land.[60]

After independence, pressure on the forests of Assam was increased further following the peasant movements between 1948 and 1954. Meanwhile the

Congress Government had attempted to implement peasant-friendly policies in which it sought to relieve the situation of the peasants in lieu of a comprehensive land reform. After Nagaland became a separate federal state in 1963, a hitherto unprecedented onslaught on the forests of Assam/Nagaland began in the 1970s and 1980s to provide agricultural land for immigrating peasants. The new measures such as the Wildlife Protection Act of 1972 and the Forest Conservation Act of 1980 which allowed such clearing under certain conditions had far-reaching consequences in this process. The situation was aggravated further by the state border conflicts between Assam and Nagaland. Although resistance to the colonial and post-colonial forest policy had been omnipresent, this escalated following the violent clashes in the mid-1980s during which many peasants were killed.

The Joint Forest Management Act of 1990, which provided for the participatory management of forests by all parties involved, additionally promoted deforestation for land reclamation as small farmers were now actively involved in the commercial exploitation of forest resources and land reclamation. This became particularly evident when the collective ownership of the *adivasi* was replaced by private ownership in Assam, Jharkhand and Chhattisgarh and the rights to forest products, especially wood, were leased to entrepreneurs such as sawmill owners for a fixed period of time. In this way, a new class of local capitalists had developed in a short period of time which commercially exploited the valuable timbers. At the same time, the social and gender structures of the *adivasi* societies were transformed, if not destroyed, leading to their progressive deprivation.[61] Attempts to improve the economic, environmental and social dislocation through government aid programmes of horticulture and garden farming, proved to be of little success.[62] Thus, it is hardly surprising that the debates concerning forest management and land use have continued into the new millennium.[63]

In the Chittagong Hill Tracts in present-day Bangladesh, a similar process can be observed. A serious issue aggravating the population's pressure on the forests of the district – of which 90 per cent was, until the beginning of the nineteenth century, forested – was the damming of the Karnafuli River to create the Kaptai reservoir in the 1960s, whilst Bangladesh was still the Eastern Wing of Pakistan. In creating the reservoir some 40 per cent of the arable land in the region was flooded and more than 100,000 people were displaced. In many cases peasants migrated to the mountains where they cleared the forest and began the cultivation of crops. This massive deforestation led to substantial soil erosion affecting almost a quarter of the land in the Chittagong Hills and it was now that the *jhum* cultivation methods truly became an ecological problem. As the available forest was constantly shrinking, the shifting cultivators were forced to reduce their "fallow" periods. At the beginning of the twentieth century cultivation cycles lasted for between 10 and 15 years; however, by the early 1970s this had been reduced to just 3–4 years. A vicious circle began for the sylvan, semi-sedentary and non-sedentary societies concerning the sustainability of forests as their food security, since the governments of Bangladesh

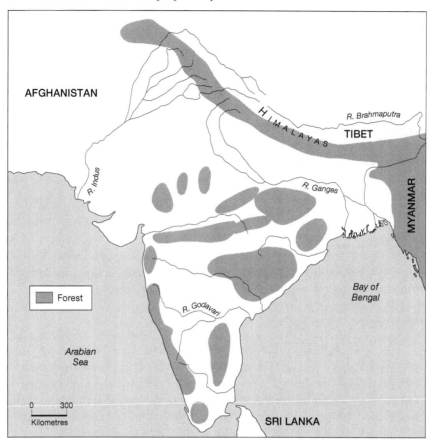

Map 5.3 Forest cover in British India, c. 1900. Adapted from Arup Jyoti Saikia, *Forests and Ecological History of Assam* (Oxford University Press: 2011), p. 59 and Irfan Habib, *Man and Environment*, p. 134

looked to the forests as providing potential land for settlement, as exemplified in the Resettlement Scheme from 1978.[64]

State protection of forests in the Republic of India meant nothing other than to exert exclusive control over its natural resources as seen in the example of Assam whereby the existing legislation from the colonial period and the related legal claims were upheld. As the Republic of India aimed to catch up with the process of industrialisation, the progressive commercial and industrial exploitation of forests led to additional plundering of forests. Industrialisation was seen by the political class as the most important measure and almost as a symbol of decolonisation in itself. The proliferation of the commercialisation of forests was an integral part of this development strategy in the context of Western-style modernisation ideology with its growth-led economic pursuits. The result of this, among other things, was that all sectors of the industrial

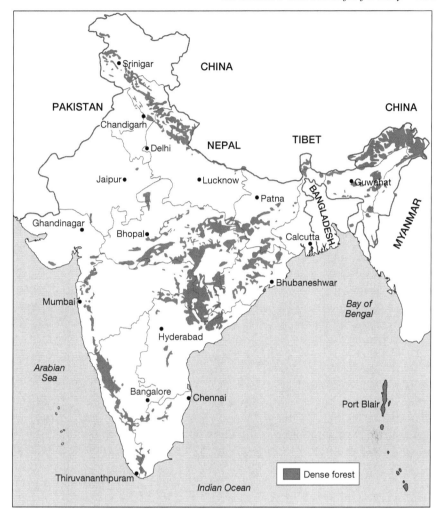

Map 5.4 Forest cover in the Republic of India, c. 2010

timber industry were subsidised by the state whilst local forest users were poorly, or not at all, supported.[65]

An example of this is the use of bamboo as a base substance for pulp in paper mills, the potential of which had already been recognised by the British colonial government.[66] In 1925 approximately 5,800 tonnes of bamboo had been cut for the production of paper and cardboard; by 1939 this had increased to 58,000 tonnes and by 1987 to about 5 million tonnes. The extent of this dramatic increase was only made possible by the independent Indian state's subsidising of bamboo between 1972 and 1992 so that it could be made available below the market price.[67] The high extraction rates of bamboo alone are evidence of the rapidly increasing industrial plundering of Indian timber resources, not least because market economy rules had been suspended. It is therefore not surprising that according to the forest surveys of India, the forest area declined from 17 to 11 per cent of the total land, whilst the proclaimed "ideal" level of 33 per cent seemed to be a distant wish. At the same time, the state of the forests continued to deteriorate in terms of biodiversity, density and regenerative capacity.[68]

Local and regional resistance formed in many areas of India against the state's industrial forest policies.[69] In the 1970s in Kumaon and Garhwal the *chipko* movement (*chipko*: hug, in this case trees) rose from the tradition of the local resistance movements in the area and their re-formation in the 1950s. The specific catalysts leading to this resistance movement were the devastating floods of 1971 which were attributed to the massive deforestation that had occurred in recent decades. Since the 1830s representatives of the "Desiccation Theory" had repeatedly claimed that the impact of the deforestation in the region would have long-term negative consequences on rainfall levels and would lead to the desertification and increased wind erosion whilst short and intense downpours would cause floods, mud slides and severe erosion of topsoils. However, these experts' claims fell on deaf ears. In the 1970s, these ecological predictions became terrible reality on the edge of the Himalayas as torrential rainfall caused mountain slopes to slip in enormous mud slides that blocked the surrounding valleys.[70]

The *chipko* movement started its agitation in 1973 as a reaction to the unequal treatment of villagers by government. Repeatedly, raw materials necessary for local industries had been denied to them. The movement quickly gained popularity, in part because it was also supported by women who were responsible for the collection of firewood and were forced to travel ever-increasing distances to procure the supply they required. In addition, the women no longer wanted to sit idly by as their husbands made short-term financial gain decisions about the forest's resources without considering the associated long-term consequences, for alongside firewood collection the women also collected other forest products for home consumption and local sale. Thus they acutely saw their and their family's economic base begin to shrink. The unexpected ferocity of the resistance movement directed at the government as well as the extent of environmental damage eventually led to a gradual redrawing of policies. A clear indication of this shift was the decision to reduce timber extraction from the area which resulted in a decline from 66,000 cubic meters in 1971 to 40,000 cubic meters in 1981.[71]

So-called state development projects in Assam also caused problems as, according to unofficial estimates, between 1947 and 2000 almost two million *adivasi* were displaced, whilst official data indicate only about 400,000 displacements. Often the *adivasi* received no compensation for the land they had inhabited and worked. As the *adivasi* usually jointly owned their land and jointly farmed it, they were unable to produce any individual private property titles which the Indian state, represented by the Assamese Government, took as justification to classify the *adivasi* as "encroachers" and to confiscate the land for development programmes. It is from this undertaking that the discrepancy above of 1.6 million displacements of "encroachers" can be attributed. With the loss of access to land, the *adivasi* subsequently also lost access to work. Displacement often resulted in migration, either to urban centres or industrial plants as they became cheap labourers in dangerous jobs in the aluminium, cement or nuclear industries.[72]

Continuities with the colonial state can also be seen in the Indian state of Chotanagpur where it was the mining sector that led to the massive changes in the forest landscape. In 1894 the large-scale mining of coal in Hazirabagh in present-day Jharkhand began with the number of coal miners rising from about 25,000 to 175,000 in 1919. Most of these miners were *adivasi* from the surrounding areas and worked in an "enclave economy", isolated almost entirely from the general economy.[73] After 1947, most British owners sold their coal mines to Indian coal traders. As these new owners expected the mines to be nationalised they did not invest in the improvement and extension of the mines. When the Indian Government nationalised the mines in 1973 they were in a very bad condition. Production increased slowly until 1980 and it was only in the following two decades that the output of coal increased from roughly 100 million tonnes per year to 310 million tonnes in 2000 and 380 million tonnes in 2010.[74] Open-cast mining contributes to about 70 per cent of the total coal production, transforming densely forested areas into lunar landscapes.

In neighbouring Orissa plans for an integrated aluminium industry were outlined in the early 1930s as several of the large mountains there were identified as sources of good quality bauxite. This early mining undertaking meant that many dense forests on Chotanagpur's hilltops were felled for the extraction of more "valuable" raw materials. Within just a few decades the established ecological balance of the region had been destroyed. At the end of the nineteenth century the humid climate of Ranchi and Hazaribagh that had been considered ideal for tea cultivation had been transformed into a dry and hot climate by the beginning of the twentieth century. This produced a new, completely different ecological balance in the area which is, in any case, far less humid, less biodiverse and consequently less habitable. Furthermore, deforestation caused severe soil erosion which was exacerbated by the excavation of coal from underground seams.[75]

Prime Minister Nehru continued and emphasised the erstwhile colonial development policy whereby the *adivasi* were again stigmatised as backward people which therefore justified their forceful eviction from their ancestral land. Industrial plants such as that in Rourkela which had been erected with foreign help in the 1960s within the *adivasi* habitat are, alongside the big dams, among many instances exemplifying this policy.[76] As a result the *adivasi* were forced into open-cast mining in southern Bihar (Jharkhand) where, in addition to coal, mainly bauxite was extracted, the extraction of which increased from 74 million tonnes in 1960 to 2,653 million tonnes by the end of the 1980s.[77] The *adivasi* stood in the way of the state's development policy in the truest sense of the word. However, the *adivasi* did not only use physical resistance in response to the attempts to deprive them of their culture and habitat, as in the latter half of the twentieth century specific cultural images of the landscape were evoked through ritual festivals of the sacred grove and, at the same time, emerged as a factor of protest. Thus, in the face of the growing threat an "invention of tradition" came to the fore. Meanwhile a successful network of local and regional NGOs had been created that included the famous ACCORD which was founded in 1985.[78]

The degradation of natural resources also destroyed primary forests in other parts of India and created new landscapes. The post-colonial forest policy altered the landscape permanently in the Tarai of Uttar Pradesh. Whilst the "western" Taria had already been largely deforested, settled and channels for irrigation had been created under British rule, the "eastern" Taria with its sylvan ecosystem had been initially spared this massive intervention.[79] On account of its dense forests (*jangal*), its marshes, the large population of wild animals such as tigers, elephants and wild boar as well as the high rates of malaria, the area of the Pilibhit and Kheri districts were deemed uninhabitable. The British described the area in their literature as untouched, wild and perfect for game sports. This meant that by 1912, when the Wild Birds and Animals Protection Act was introduced, about a quarter of the region's wild animals had been lost. Furthermore, as the law was not implemented, the shooting of animals continued unabated until the end of colonial rule. The establishment of the Hailey National Park in 1935 offered little protection to the endangered animals.[80]

This decimation of wild animals can be observed throughout British India. Between 1870 and 1920 alone, some 65,000 tigers were killed and in some regions, such as the Panjab and on the southern peninsula, lions had become extinct by the mid-twentieth century. These high figures demonstrate that the slaughter and extinction of predatory species like tiger, lion, cheetah and rhino were not solely the results of the expansion of agricultural land, but were also due to the government funding for hunting. This was implemented either in the granting of licences to "sport hunters" or by offering a premium for the shooting of a predatory animal, both of which were completely new in the South Asian context. Despite this, progressive deforestation had increasingly restricted the habitat of predators and made them prey upon the grazing cattle of the human settlements that had begun to encroach on their natural environment. In turn this served as a justification to introduce hunting quotas and to increase licensing, as was particularly the case in the Tarai.[81]

In both western and eastern Tarai, the Government of India initiated settlement programmes in the early 1950s as refugees from Pakistan and demobilised soldiers from India were to be located here. The clearing of the *jangal* was finally made possible through American aid that had brought the bulldozer to India in 1948. As a preparatory measure, the Indian Government launched a programme to combat malaria in 1946 during which the widespread use of DDT was deployed for the first time. By the mid-1950s the Tarai was reported to be malaria free. With the conclusion of the second five-year plan, the Government of Uttar Pradesh also ended the land reclamation programmes in the Tarai in 1961. In the context of the Green Revolution irrigation and drainage system projects were undertaken in the new agricultural areas of the Tarai with the aim to boost yields. On account of this massive "modernisation", the physical landscape in eastern Tarai had been completely transformed by the end of the 1970s.[82]

In the following two decades the wildlife conservation projects also contributed to a further change in the scenery as the Wildlife Protection Act of 1972 led to the creation of several national parks, especially for the protection of the tiger. This did not prevent the fact that by the turn of the millennium their number had been reduced to 3,000. Buffer zones were established in order to protect the surrounding villages from the tigers, wild boars and other wild animals. This, however, had only limited success on account of the population pressure. In this way a patchwork landscape, characterised by forests, farms, wildlife sanctuaries, reserved forests, buffer zones and cultivated country came to exist by the turn of the millennium.[83] Moreover, the government began a scheme of reforestation on all reclaimed land that was not considered cultivable. Thus, on designated areas fast-growing trees were planted which were envisaged to serve peasant-settlers as fuel and fodder reserves. Yet this was only of limited success as the tree species leached minerals from the soil and had to be frequently watered, thus demanding intensive and time-consuming care.[84] For the same reasons the ambitious reforestation schemes in other parts of northern India also failed.[85]

Although it seems the Indian Government was aware of the consequences of its role in the forestry and settlement policies, it made no attempt to improve the agro-sylvan situation. The previous forest policy was not only unable to prevent the plundering of forests but was also unable to reduce the potential for conflict between the government and the local communities. As in neighbouring Bangladesh, the shortcomings of the established forestry methods were all too obvious in India. In Bangladesh, the local population considered the Forest Department to be part of a custodian government and paramilitary service which led a bureaucratic, revenue-orientated forest management regime. At the same time the governments undermined existing local structures, ignoring local knowledge and isolating the population largely through corruption, connivance and collaboration with external commercial companies. Ultimately this resulted in the alienation of the state and its population.[86]

It was in response to this ongoing process of alienation and the continuing and growing opposition from local communities, that the Social Forestry policy was introduced in the Indian Government's five-year plan from 1976 to 1981. The principal emphasis of Social Forestry was on the wider participation of local communities in the protection and regeneration of forest resources. Local people were to be allowed to participate in the planning, implementation and management of local forests for their own benefit. At the same time, Social Forestry was also charged to monitor environmental degradation, enhance the socio-economic status of the local population, improve their income, and to foster the development of local cooperative institutions. In short, Social Forestry was primarily about empowering the local population and enhancing their welfare; thereafter it aimed to promote social equity through equitable sharing of decisions and profits. An instrument for the implementation of this ambitious programme was the so-called forest farms which were promoted through the government's distribution of free or subsidised seedlings and the offer of technical assistance.[87]

However, the forest farms quickly aligned themselves to the industrial capitalist environment and produced fast-growing trees, which were based more on market needs than on the regeneration of the forests. Not without grounding, this form of forest management has been described as a method of monocultural agriculture whose main crops were, and still are, eucalyptus and bamboo, and to which has been attributed environmental damage such as soil degradation and increased water consumption.[88] Therefore results of the scheme are highly ambivalent. For example, on account of the new forest policy (Social Forestry, Joint Forest Management after 1990) in Tamil Nadu, the extent of the reserved forests increased from 14.1 to 16.6 per cent between 1960 and 2000, whilst the overall forest area has in fact decreased. Pressure from land-seeking peasants and the rehabilitation programme for the resettlement of repatriated Tamils from Sri Lanka in the 1970s have led to further loss of forest.[89]

During the 1990s the Joint Forest Management Support Programme was initiated in other regions of India, which aimed at increasing the local population's cooperation and offered assistance for self-help programmes. However, the number of villages and communities involved in such programmes is fairly low and is concentrated on a few areas in western Uttaranchal, Nepal, Orissa and Jharkhand as well as in Gujarat, Kerala and Tamil Nadu. Obviously this programme targets areas that are still partially covered with forest. In Pakistan, the problem is less extreme as the country only has 4.3 per cent forest land registered under the working plan of the Forest Department.[90] However, the few forests that are located in the Himalayas and the North-West Frontier Province are also threatened with destruction due to human and animal activities. The small area of forest probably causes a lack of interest in that environment which is mirrored by the lack of scientific research and publication on forestry in Pakistan.

By the end of the last millennium the new Forest Policy/Social Forestry had failed to produce more than a few positive results. In particular, its role as a participatory development practice has been insignificant. Though there has been some achievement in the physical and quantitative targets, the crucial participatory goals such as participation, empowerment and equity have remained largely unfulfilled. Instead of reducing the alienation between state and population concerned, the schemes have succeeded in producing the opposite. One reason for this was that the programme of participation was bureaucratic in its conception and enactment and consequently excluded the population from decision-making processes. Furthermore, the participation of the population in the new forestry policy and the distribution of the celebrated benefits has only been moderately successful. This trend is true for all regions in India and

Bangladesh where Social Forestry was initiated and practised. Ultimately it seems that Social Forestry, pointedly formulated, has merely come to imply another form of technical land use whereby "people" are, at best, a new economic "input".[91] Social Forestry has given the state a grassroots façade behind which it has reacted more harshly against "uncooperative" communities.

The new millennium

Taking the above into consideration, it is clear that the independent Indian and Bangladesh governments have pursued the same kind of forest policy as the colonial government before them. Only recently does there seem to have been a slight shift in forest policy with regards to the perseverance of the environment and the supply of the local population with fodder and food for their consumption. The revised National Forest Policy of 1988, being the second amendment to the Forest (Conservation) Act of 1980, strengthened the rights of the people participating in the Social Forestry/Joint Forest Management. Local knowledge and expertise is accordingly expected to be utilised for the benefit of cooperating communities. However, the centralised national Indian forest policy (as, again, indicated by the 1980 legislation) simultaneously undermines the 1988 policy to encourage local participation in the management of forests. It remains to be seen whether the recently launched National Forest Action Programme of 1999, which emphasised the extension of forests on hitherto non-forest lands and wastelands as well as wasteland reclamation schemes, will bear fruit. The Area-Orientated Fuelwood and Fodder Scheme seems an appropriate means to achieve this aim.[92]

On one hand, small advances in forest policy have been made in as far as local projects are concerned that are for the benefit of the many stakeholders. Beneficiaries of this have particularly been the population along the Himalayan border. To remove some of the political pressure from the resistance movements, the central government under the leadership of the BJP was prepared to release the regions Kumaon and Garhwal as Uttarakhand from Uttar Pradesh, as well as Jharkhand from Bihar and Chhattisgarh out of Madhya Pradesh at the turn of the millennium. As separate states they are largely removed from the central authority. However, the political aspiration of the BJP to combine the additional federal states and to increase their electorate and thus enter government there was not met. The attempt to wipe out the term *adivasi* from the lexicons and to replace it with *vanvasi* (lit.: forest dwellers) in order to support the Hindutva ideology in which it was not the *adivasi* but the Aryans who were the first inhabitants of the subcontinent was just as unsuccessful.[93]

Nevertheless, the new federal states in central India were also unable to reach a mutual agreement and control the fundamental problem of the degradation of natural resources in the Tribal Belt as their governments also pursued "development" of the country through the means of national and international mining companies. As part of their ideology and programme of modernisation the federal governments supported, and still support, the regional operations of international aluminium cartels to increase the extraction of bauxite from the large area of forested mountains in Orissa in order to "develop" the nation. Furthermore, the 1970 Environmental Impact Assessment was undermined in Jharkhand when a *carte blanche* was given to mining projects to lease up to 25 hectares, widen the highways and modernise irrigation without the displaced people's prior informed consent or public hearing.

Mining further increased after the Foreign Direct Investment Act of 1993 and the regulations of the National Mining Policy allowed international companies to invest in Indian mining enterprises to an amount of up to 50 per cent. In 2006 this was raised to 100 per cent.[94] Meanwhile the extraction of iron ore and production of iron and steel have joined the mining of bauxite and aluminium production industry. In order to ensure and provide the enormous amounts of energy required for this, new hydro-electric plants and mega dams (and power stations operated with coal) have been planned, which will mean the loss through flooding of forest land in the valleys of Jharkhand, Orissa and Chhattisgarh. In order to fulfil these plans, the centralised state, as well as federal governments, have seemed willing to use force to break any resistance.[95]

Already, forests are being cut down on a huge scale and tens of thousands of *adivasi* are being once again displaced and relocated. Critical opponents, including the affected *adivasi*, have quickly been stigmatised as opponents of "development" and as enemies of the nation during the clashes. In the course of an open paramilitary campaign Chhattisgarh police – in an operation euphemistically entitled "Operation Green Hunt" in 2009 – set about pursuing the so-called Communist Naxalites as the government could hardly camouflage its brutal ground-clearing operation against the *adivasi* designed to open up India's forested heartland for mining corporations.[96] The violent clashes have since taken the form of a civil war and are thus an example of the curse that lies on the state protection of natural resources and which, as a result, triggers a breakdown of all social and ethical standards. Some extremely brutal attacks carried out by the state have led critical observers to consider the dimension of violence as genocidal.[97] The coming years will show if there is a balance of interests on the "forest frontier", or whether the "mining frontier" remains open.

For Bangladesh governmental statistics show that the forest area of the mid-1980s accounts for only 2 per cent of the total land area despite the forest-rich areas in the Chittagong Hills and the Sunderbans in the Ganges-Brahmaputra Delta. It is in this area where deforestation has increased tremendously. Subsequently, a task force was set up in 1987 charged with addressing the problem of sylvan resources. The model of Social Forestry, as it had already been implemented in neighbouring India, was its inspiration.[98] The Social Forestry plan was then brought into line with the National Forestry Policy in 1994 and Forestry Sector Master Plan in 1995. Additionally, the Forest Act of 1927 was amended in 2000 to protect the Social Forestry and its cooperation with the Forest Department, the Local Community Organisations (LCO) and the NGOs. Already in 2003 the Government of Bangladesh stated that it was important to strengthen the LCOs in order to accomplish the project of sustainable forest management and participatory forestry.[99]

In effect Social Forestry was only implemented in the new millennium so that what was suggested in the 1990s was not manifest until the end of the first decade of the twenty-first century. Meanwhile local organisations increasingly complain about the role of bureaucrats who attempt to join local meetings to manipulate decisions taken whilst the foreign NGOs have little chance to act against the actions of the government's bureaucrats because of local power relations. Even the participation of women, one of the main concepts of Social Forestry, has had only partial success as the daily workload of women made participation in such projects unrealistic from the outset, unless the women were offered some support. Meanwhile, the barely existing provisions for (school) education goes yet one step further in restricting the participation of women, as being illiterate means that they have very limited access to information. These factors, taken together, make Social Forestry in Bangladesh currently extremely unattractive.[100]

Here, as in neighbouring India, a credible move by the state and its institutions, in close cooperation with the NGOs, is needed in order to show the local population that the ambitious programme of Social Forestry is not a waste and not a new form of manacles. Social Forestry currently seems to be the only strategy that will help prevent the progressive deforestation and exploitation of forest resources, whether that be open or concealed, local-private or international-industrially driven, of the remaining forest areas of the two countries. The forthcoming substantial problems that are certain to affect the two countries cannot be overcome through bureaucratic administrative manipulation or through violence against their "enemies". Not that Social Forestry would not be a good instrument with which a modern, that is contemporary, scientific forestry could be fulfilled, but for this to succeed the political will of a new governance and the implementation of laws that guarantee benefits of all involved down to the local level is needed.

Notes

1 Grove, Damodaran and Sangwan 1998; Chakrabarti R. 2007; Rangarajan and Sivaramakrishnan 2012.
2 Mann 2001a: 403–25.
3 Rangarajan 2012: 95–142.
4 Sontheimer 1989: vii–viii, 107.
5 Haynes E.S. 1998 734–92; Thapar 2012: 105–26.
6 Moosvi 1987: 299–316.
7 Habib I. 2010: 47–110.
8 Parasher-Sen 2012: 127–52.
9 Das 1976: 105–15; Grove 1998: 187–209.
10 Habib I. 2010: 95–96.
11 Morrison 2006: 43–64.
12 Frenz 2003: 108–10; Mann 1996: 79–88.
13 Rangarajan 1998: 575–95.

14 Guha R. 1989: 9–25, 62–9; Guruani 2001: 170–90, esp. 183.
15 Grove 1995a: 387.
16 Pouchepadass 2002: 116–43, esp. 131; Grove 1995a: 456–7.
17 Richards E. 1982.
18 Rangarajan 1996: 10–18.
19 Grove 1995a: 388–90.
20 Radkau 1996: 63–76.
21 Raja 2006: 35–54.
22 Mann 2001b: 1–28.
23 Dangwal 2007: 46–9, 63.
24 Strahorn 2009.
25 Rangan 2001: 23–46.
26 Rangarajan 1996: 24–9; Mann 1999: 145–51.
27 Tucker 2012: 73.
28 Dangwal 2007: 116–9.
29 Barton 2002: 38–93.
30 Rangarajan 1996: 55–9, 61–2.
31 Mann 1996: 55–64; Cederlöf 2012: 374–430.
32 Dangwal 2007: 119–26.
33 Guha R. 1990: 65–84; Rangarajan 1996: 29–47; Hesmer 1975.
34 Rajan 2006: 39–40, 82–6.
35 Dangwal 2007: 137–88.
36 Damodaran 2007: 127–66, esp. 132–3.
37 Rangarajan 1996: 74–94.
38 Harrison R.P. 1993: 115–6.
39 Rajan 2006: 48–50.
40 Rangarajan 1996: 95–118, 120–2; Pouchepadass 1996: 123–51; Ahmed S. 2007: 263–78.
41 Rasul 2010: 220–39, esp. 224–6.
42 Saberwal 1999.
43 Saberwal and Lele 2004: 273–303; Cederlöf 2005: 247–69.
44 Damodaran 2007: 130.
45 Oraon 2002; Parkin 1992; Beutner 2009.
46 Singh K.S. 1983.
47 Hobsbawm and Ranger 2010.
48 Damodaran 2007: 138–52.
49 Thaha 2009: 14–94.
50 Grove 1995a: 255–82; Rajan 2006: 55–74.
51 Thaha 2009: 81–2, 103, 108–11.
52 Donovan 2011: 231–61.
53 Dangwal 2007: 67–80.
54 Guha R. 1989: 48; Thaha 2009: 80–1, 85.
55 Devalle 1993: 62.
56 Saikia A. 2005.
57 Saikia A. 2011: 114–204.
58 Ibid.: 326–9.
59 Saikia A. 2005: 154–8.
60 Goswami R. 2012: 27–52.
61 Mishra D.K. 2012: 137–65.
62 Krishna S. 2012: 308–22.
63 *Agenda 21: An Assessment* 2002: 161–8; Divan and Ronsencranz 2001: 288–91.
64 Rasul 2010.
65 Khan N.K 1998: 446–9.
66 Pearson R.S. 1913.

67 Savur 2003.
68 Gadgil and Guha 1992: 198; Mann 2001b: 11–12.
69 Gadgil and Guha 1989: 41–77; Tucker 2012: 161–90.
70 Grove 1995a: 425–62; Skaria 1998: 598–605.
71 Linkenbach 2007: 43–92; Guruani 2001: 181–2; Gadgil and Guha 1992: 178.
72 Fernandes 2012: 119–34.
73 Rothermund 1978b: 1–20.
74 Economic Survey 2010–2011: 269.
75 Damodaran 2010: 170–1.
76 Meher 2004.
77 Damodaran 2010: 175.
78 Adivasi Munnetra Sangam (AMS) 2013.
79 Dangwal 2007: 69–70, 79.
80 Strahorn 2009: 20–35.
81 Rangarajan 2012: 95–142.
82 Strahorn 2009: 59–77, 101–12.
83 Greenough 2012: 316–56.
84 Strahorn 2009: 114–23.
85 Mann 2012a: 431–55.
86 Khan N.A. 1998: 52–3, 60–8.
87 Ibid.: 70–2, 282–6.
88 Poore and Fries 1987; Barooah 2009.
89 Saravanan 2007: 723–67.
90 Amjad and Mohammad 1982: 3, 9, 16.
91 Khan N.A. 1998, 117–8.
92 *Agenda 21: An Assessment* 2002: 161–8; Divan 2001: 288–91.
93 Damodaran 2007: 155.
94 Damodaran 2010: 177.
95 Ibid.: 178.
96 Padel and Das 2010.
97 Padel and Das 2006.
98 Khan N.A. 1998: 1–3.
99 Chowdhury S.A. 2010: 46–60.
100 Ibid.: 73–4, 92–3, 105, 115.

6 Migration, circulation and diaspora

Theories and thoughts

The search for better living conditions for individuals, families, clans, communities and societies has been an omnipresent aspect of human history. In this search, migration has become a universal historical phenomenon that has occurred throughout time and across space. Migration, therefore, is neither a phenomenon of the modern industrial state and its almost permanent labour shortages, nor is it a crisis of modern capitalism. That said, the migration of people from the mid-sixteenth century in the form of slaves, indentured servants, indentured labourers, convicts and colonists saw a considerable increase in the trans-continental dimensions of migration.[1] Recent research has therefore understood the modern era as a period in human history during which the foundations were laid for a global labour market, which has been increasingly supplied with circulating and migrating labourers. Migration history can thus be seen as an integral part of the economic, social and cultural history of humankind.[2]

Questions as to the extent to which permanent and temporary migration has taken place – and still takes place, either voluntarily or under duress – can only be answered in relation to the various contexts of each case. In the narrow sense, migration is forced when the life of each human is under threat through discrimination, political persecution, or because of wars, as they are made refugees. In the broader sense, any form of migration can be seen as being forced on account that very few would voluntarily choose to leave their family and familiar surroundings unless compelling reasons such as economic, social, political and ecological issues affect them. Potentially anyone may become a migrant at any given time.[3] Thus, against such a background, the current nation-state, as it has developed across the globe in the previous 150 years, should not be the sole point of reference for the analysis of the causes and occasions of migration.[4]

Furthermore, migration is not only confined to horizontal mobility, but also has vertical mobility elements. More often than not, people migrate from their regions for long-term economic and social gain rather than to replicate the conditions of their home region in their destination area. In order to achieve this dual objective, migration cannot be explained solely with simple "push and pull" factors or a basic "cost-benefit analysis" of factors such as wage differential. Nor is the "rational choice model" adequate in explaining migration as it fails to account for the diverse processes involved in deciding whether or not to emigrate.[5] Instead socio-economic factors across macro-, meso- and micro-levels together with theoretical research approaches from disciplines that deal with migration (Sociology, Political Science, History, Anthropology, Demography, Economics and Law) must be considered in order to adequately analyse the phenomenon of migration, circulation and diaspora.[6]

Results stemming from these research debates can be summarised as follows. First, a dual labour market has been recently triggered in industrially developed countries which have experienced migration from poorer countries. As a result of industrial mass production the national, and increasingly global, labour market seems to have been divided into two segments in recent decades which have been conceptually referred to as a "formal sector" and "informal sector" since the 1970s. The "formal sector" is characterised by regulated wage labour in industrial companies, government offices and large-scale establishments. It is mostly financially lucrative, legally secured and connected with social prestige. On the other hand, the "informal sector" is defined as an area characterised by low wages, uncertain legal standings, a lack of social protection and poor social status. By definition, the "informal sector" lies outside the organised labour market and is frequently marshalled under the all-inclusive term of "self-employment" which does not need any or, at best, only little organisation.[7]

The informal sector is especially attractive to migrants, since it offers low skilled employment and easy entry opportunities into the urban as well as the peri-urban labour market. In the cities of the global South, the informal sector now accounts for more than 50 per cent of the total employment. Aside from the low acquisition opportunities and security, the sector is often assumed to be criminal and illegal, dominated by mafia-like organisations. At the same time, the informal sector is self-regulating and an economically dynamic, innovative and open "business unit". Other than these distinctions, the strict separation into these two separate sectors does not seem helpful as the regulations and working relationships transcend both, thereby blurring the boundaries of each.[8] It is precisely this fluidity that causes a permanent labour shortage which is, in turn, filled by migrants. Migration is in most cases a movement from the countryside to the city and less often from a city to another city or from the countryside to a city located in another country. This worldwide trend began at the end of the nineteenth century, and is currently undergoing a geographically varying degree of quantitative increase, and, above all, qualitative change.

Second, migration is primarily characterised not through individuality, but rather through the collective as local family ties, group membership and regional family and friendship networks significantly influence the decision to migrate or circulate. Circulation itself, defined as the temporary, often seasonal migration of one or more family and/or village members to a particular area of work that is repeated, is the hallmark of the modern, capitalist organised global labour market.[9] An important aspect of this collective is the imagination of social betterment or overall benefits in the destination country or the home country through better marriage opportunities, better education and better economic standards. Furthermore, initial opportunities offered by family and friendship networks as well as reduced initial financial burden – for example, on account of shared living spaces – generate a certain risk mitigation in the form of systematic risk diversification.[10]

Third, "mass migration", which has been observed since the nineteenth century, became an essential feature in the development of the world capitalist economic system. To some extent, capitalism itself, with its "power of integration", provided for a steady stream of migrants and circulants as previously untapped economic regions were opened up to the system. This led to the economic disintegration of the now unprofitable small and family-owned agricultural and artisanal enterprises which released surplus labour. This formed a pool of cheap labourers and flooded the labour market in Europe's former Asian and African colonies. However, as the difference in pay had not set workers in motion, their movement had to be stimulated and organised through recruitment efforts. More recently, the globalisation process has rapidly accelerated this development, most specifically in the informal sector.[11]

In both the migration and circulation processes different networks are of the utmost importance.[12] As a result, the diversity of information they offer along with the decreasing risks and the increasing opportunities in integration as well as the possibility of a pre-selection in the labour supply led to a higher willingness of individuals to undertake long-distance and long-term migration.[13] Consequently, migration occurs even if no labour shortages in the corresponding destination area exist. This is also the reason why there is the geographic concentration of immigrants and a "niche formation" in professional disciplines. This trans-local binding of families promotes the formation of identities and communities of a certain nationality, regional background or religious or cultural community in the immigration country. As such, Indians will only become aware of a specific Indian identity through the circumstances created in emigration. These ethnic, cultural and religious "enclaves", often caused by racial marginalisation in the country of immigration, regularly lead to the formation of their own traditions in the sense of preserving tradition in a "multiculturalist" environment.[14]

In some countries of immigration, especially in the cities, such tradition formation has come to form a diaspora. As a result of global migration movements, the term diaspora has, in the last two decades, come to be a collective term for migration, exile, asylum, migrant workers and ethnic or religious communities scattered in a foreign land and, ultimately, all over the globe.[15] The question as to which immigrants or foreign groups can claim the status of a diaspora is the subject of intense debates that are often ideologically, emotionally and politically highly charged. In its narrowest definition, which emphasises the "victim" as a result of a traumatic expulsion, only the Jews, Armenians and Greeks are included. By broadening this definition to include the category of the voluntary formation of a community for the mutual safeguarding of interests would also add the Chinese, Indians and Africans to this list. However, a purely ethnic approach is not sufficient to take into account all of the strategies for the formation of a diaspora.[16]

On account of these many differences, little consensus has been made in the definition of the term diaspora. It is undisputed that the definition of the term includes the voluntary emigration and forced exile for which the Jewish diaspora is used as the reference point of the term following their expulsion from Palestine and the destruction of the temple in Jerusalem in 70 CE. Their specific case has led to a diaspora formed in trans-local networks with an often mythical reference back to their country of emigration. In order to develop these relationship networks, a common consciousness is required which can be generated through the manifestation of marginalisation and otherness. This awareness is constituted by cultural and social ties which are permanently reshaped and handed down – the reference point of which is a common origin, common region, language and culture,[17] or, from the nineteenth century onwards, a common nation. Additionally, the now emerging tradition in the diaspora is the intensified use of symbols and "rituals of remembrance".[18] The central task of constructing this new cultural identity and preserving it falls to the elites of the respective diaspora.[19]

However, this formation of consciousness has its limits; by way of example are the South Asian religious organisations and their diaspora-targeted identification campaigns for the Hindu and Muslim cultures, most notably in the United States, Canada and Great Britain. Here, these organisations have only been of moderate success as Muslims from Pakistan have not readily identified with Muslims from India. South Indian Muslims, whilst sharing the faith, do not share the same community values with North Indian Muslims. Therefore, it is not possible to speak of either a homogeneous South Asian or a homogenous Muslim community.[20] As with other forms of constructed collective identities, the identities of the diaspora must be understood on a situational basis. As such the different regional and social identities in India, Pakistan, Bangladesh and Sri Lanka as well as various periods and destinations of emigration offer only a limited capability to uniformly characterise the communities in the immigration countries with the concept of diaspora.[21]

In the past two decades, South Asian migration and the formation of diaspora in the Indian Ocean and beyond has attracted significant scientific interest.[22] However, only few historical studies have focused on the causes, motives and scope in relation to the subcontinental internal migration.[23] This, together with the related migration in the Indian Ocean, requires a comprehensive examination in order to better explain the emergence of the colonial-capitalist global labour market.[24] In some ways, the current research takes South Asian diasporic communities and societies in the Indian Ocean and beyond in the former Caribbean colonies of the British Empire as an almost avant-garde feature, as no other group of migrants–indentured labourers, so-called coolies (kulis) is as well documented as this.[25]

Early South Asian migration and diaspora communities

As in other regions of the world, the history of the South Asian subcontinent is characterised by recurrent immigration and emigration of families, clans and societies and migration from within the geographical boundaries on the subcontinent.[26] Trade in the Arabian Sea to the Arabian Peninsula and East Africa as well as in the Bay of Bengal to the Indo-Malayan Archipelago can be traced back to around the second century CE. These cultural and trade contacts remained intact over a number of centuries and intensified in many places along the Indian Ocean rim. Occasionally this also developed into the formation of community structures which have all the features of a diaspora. For example, the *bania* (traders, bankers) community seems to have formed a diaspora in Mozambique which maintained strong ties with their origin in the Gujarat region. This is especially true for the Jain (religious) community to which many of the overseas trading *banias* belonged to.[27]

However, traders were far less concerned about their regional origin or their religious background, but rather the origin of the commodities they sold. The goods of Gujarat were mostly shipped to Africa by Persian and Arabic, and later European, traders.[28] As cargo capacity increased through the introduction of European ships from the sixteenth century, South Asian traders were increasingly found along the Swahili coast, where communities with a separate cultural life soon emerged. It is assumed that the majority of traders stayed for several years in the cities as an annual round voyage was not possible south of Zanzibar on account of the monsoon. In addition to this circulation of traders and labourers, the permanent settlement of migrants increased in the course of the following centuries.[29] By the mid-nineteenth century, 1,500 Gujaratis had settled in Muscat alone; in Zanzibar figures equalled over 4,000 whilst some 8,500 had settled in Aden.[30]

The development in the eastern Indian Ocean saw almost the opposite occur. As in the Arabian Sea the specific geographic proximity determined the direction of trade in the Bay of Bengal. As such, the Chettiyars and Chulias trading communities mastered South Indian maritime transport over a number of centuries.[31] The appearance of the Portuguese and subsequently the Dutch and English East India Companies with their fierce battle for monopsonies and monopolies in spices and textiles led to the creeping decline of the Indian trade activities. This particularly affected the port and trade cities of Khambhat and Surat in Gujarat; Hugli in Bengal; Masulipatnam, Katalur and Nagapatnam along the Coromandel Coast; Pegu and Syriam in Burma; and Banten, Acheh, Johor and Melaka on the islands of the Indonesian archipelago. In the long run, South Asian traders and merchants were almost entirely forced out of the trans-continental business as South and Southeast Asian goods were mainly transported on European ships. Finally, by the end of the eighteenth century, the EIC came to dominate the major trading routes in the Indian Ocean.[32]

All ports in the Indian Ocean were integrated into local, regional, inter-regional and inter-continental, that is trans-local, networks of merchant communities and zones of commodity exchange. Some cities specialised in local coastal trade, whilst others concentrated on the inter-regional and transcontinental trade. All acted as the link between the heartlands of the continent to the sea and vice versa. By the eighteenth century these links gave rise to a commercial space, which was structured by micro-, meso- and macro-regions, as shown in the map below. These trading regions are defined by the concentration of commodities and the range of exchange as a chain of marine transport. The increasing dominance of European, and especially the EIC shipping, from the mid-eighteenth century did not change this orientation to the sea.

Coastal shipping continued to control the South Asian merchants on a local and supra-regional scale. Teams of numerous merchant ships were manned with *lascars* who had been recruited from the neighbouring coastal regions and had settled in the port cities to await recruitment and hire there.[33] Then, during the wars against Revolutionary and Napoleonic France (1792–1815) and contrary to the provisions of the English Navigation Acts, in India manned ships began calling at British ports with the result that for the first time *lascars* were granted temporary stay in the East End of London. This brought very real problems such as dress, eating and living habits of the foreign seamen to the fore.[34] Although at this time it is not possible to speak of an Indian community in London, the *lascars* who arrived in London laid the foundations in the city as a place of business for the future generations of immigrants so that today the East End continues to be one of the major centres of South Asian communities in Great Britain.

Individual traders soon began to use the structures of the British Empire for their own purposes or withdrew from them and created their own niches to suit their trading interests. *Banias* from Shikarpur and Haiderabad, both cities located in the lower Indus valley, built regional trading networks during the nineteenth and twentieth centuries. The metaphor of the network being the radial spider's web lends itself as a precise and workable definition in this context as it describes a system with a centre where the capital-raising competent people are located, from which offices in key hubs of trade routes are scattered and are connected by travelling employees. An intense and interactive resource flow consisting of personnel, capital, goods and information accompanied the network.[35] A characteristic of these networks is that they ushered in not only a quantitative expansion of existing structures but also qualitative changes which are of the utmost importance at this point as they indicate the catalyst towards increasing globalisation.

The network of the South Indian Chettiyars is also comparable to that above. Since the tenth century, merchants and bankers had been active in the Chola Empire in Tamil Nadu and had built links to Lanka. Even before the First Anglo-Burmese War (1824–6) the Chettiyars had held offices in the Irrawaddy Delta. Following the British annexation of Lower Burma in 1852 they found new areas of activity, as most of the South Indian labourers were recruited for the expansion of rice cultivation in Burma from the second half of the nineteenth century. The Chettiyars then set about systematically expanding their existing connections. As maritime trade lay in the hands of the Chinese and

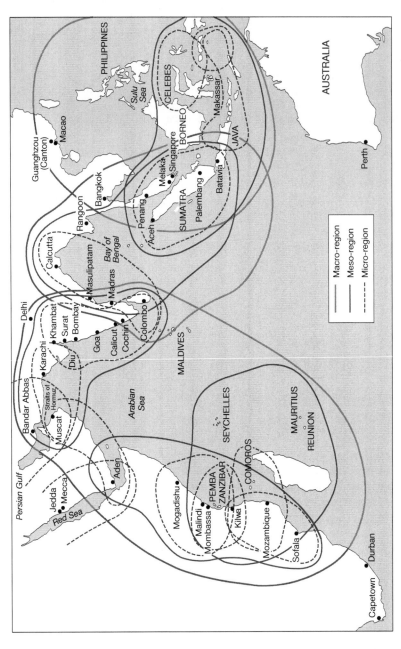

Map 6.1 Trading zones of the Indian Ocean in the mid-eighteenth century. Michael Mann, *Sahibs, Sklaven und Soldaten: Geschichte des Menschenhandels rund um den Indischen Ozean*. (Darmstadt: Wissenschaftliche Buchgesellschaft/Darmstadt-Mainz: Verlag Philipp von Zabern, 2012), p. 35

land trade was controlled by the Burmese, the Chettiyars soon found their economic niche as money-lenders as they offered cheap loans against high collateral.[36] By the end of the nineteenth century it is estimated that some 100 Chettiyar companies were located in Burma and their informal rules contributed to a high compliance in the management and cooperation between the companies. This was also reflected in the foundation of a common temple in Yangon (Rangoon), which operated under the name Chettiyar Exchange, where financial transactions were regularly handled.[37]

Nevertheless, the sporadic and sometimes isolated branch of traders from a family or a clan did not constitute a diaspora. That said, such small units succeeded in creating structures that would become essential for the formation of a diaspora. Crucially, a South Asian community living in a foreign country must feel itself to be, and define itself as a diaspora, for example through day-to-day cultural practices. However, until well into the nineteenth century it was often difficult to provide proof of such common feeling. Even the indentured labourers in Mauritius, South Africa and the Caribbean were not initially perceived as people living as a diaspora. In many cases, it seems appropriate to speak of various South Asian communities which remained rather isolated and did not sociologically and politically collectivise and homogenise all South Asians in their immediate vicinity. By the twentieth century, however, this development certainly looked different.

South Asians on the new subcontinental and global labour markets

In the nineteenth century, the scope of the plantation economy had taken on a new worldwide scale. Until then, plantations had almost exclusively been confined to the Caribbean and the Americas along with Mauritius and Reunion in the Indian Ocean. Now a wave of new large-scale plantations in Asia and Africa were established. Old and new natural resources and cash crops (sugar, cotton and rubber on the one hand, tea and palm oil in addition to metal ores on the other) were fed into a rapidly expanding world economy. The foundation for this development was the ideology of free trade in the context of the new global peace order following the Napoleonic wars known as Pax Britannica. Free trade ultimately brought about the abolition of the slave trade in the British Empire as it was announced in 1807/11 and slavery was finally eradicated in 1834. Since the former slaves did not want to work as indentured labourers on the plantations of their former owners, the imminent shortage of labour force caused the owners of the plantations within the British Empire to seek another more or less controllable labour force.

In British India the establishment of the first tea plantations in Assam soon saw the plantation owners call for cheap and reliable agricultural labourers as Chinese labourers, regarded as particularly strong and diligent workers, who were originally recruited in Malaya and Singapore, rebelled against lack of wage payments and were consequently dismissed.[38] Added to this was the emerging industrialisation of British India, even if it was localised and limited to the textile sector, which dramatically increased the demand for industrial labour in the cities of Bombay, Ahmedabad, Kanpur, Calcutta and Dhaka. Against the background of this chronic shortage of labourers, various forms of labour organisation were discussed, of which the most common became the system of so-called indentured labour. This system set millions of people in temporary or permanent motion, bringing them to geographically and culturally uncharted areas within and outside the South Asian subcontinent from 1840 onwards.[39]

Indentured labour is, however, not an invention of the agro-industrial world of the nineteenth century, but rather it existed in England from as early as the fourteenth century. With the English settlement of North America, some 60 per cent of the colonists were indentured servants. These servants, as indentured labourers later, were contractually obliged to complete a fixed number of years working for their employer, who, in turn, was required to pay regular wages. However, employers were in the position to drastically restrict the mobility of their labourers and their rights. The employer was also entitled to use coercive measures to ensure the contractual obligations were fulfilled whilst the indentured servants had few legal means to counter such action. Such a pattern also began in the 1830s for the contracts of the indentured labourers who were more commonly referred to as "coolies" (kulis)[40] and were employed on the plantations across the British Empire. Such recruitment and employment was then also adopted in Mauritius in the 1840s, in Natal from the 1860s and Jamaica, Trinidad and Fiji from 1879.

The contracts initially tied the kulis to three- to five-year contracts to their work overseas or the employer during which time it was not possible to change their employment. Extensions to contracts were possible, although such an extension was limited to just a one- or two-year period. After ten years of service an indentured labourer was entitled to be transported back to British India at the expense of the plantation owner. In quite a few cases kulis permanently settled in the new environment and made it their "new home". As with the indentured servants, contracts were asymmetric since the employer had a number of restraints that he could employ to fulfil the contractual fixed labour services. Kulis had little access to legal services; should a kuli breach his contract in any way he could be criminally sentenced, whereas a breach from the employer's side would be prosecuted civilly. Whilst a gradual easing of the legislation towards workers was undertaken in the 1870s in Great Britain, the opposite was the case in the colonial context.[41]

With the onset of the globally organised migration and circulation of contract labourers from 1840, South Asian labourers, who had been put to work on the plantations and in mines during the first half of the nineteenth century, composed, by far, the largest group. In the second half of the nineteenth century a further wave of migration of people from the middle and upper strata of society had evolved as the so-called Passenger Indians established themselves in the service sector. Meanwhile, from the end of the centrury students of British Indian upper classes formed another group of migrants who, especially after the First World War, sought training in the Western industrial countries.

After the Second World War numerous Indian artisans migrated in the 1950s and 1960s, mostly to Great Britain and increasingly to Australia, Canada and the United States. The 1970s saw a wave of so-called twice migrants who fled as refugees from Suriname, Guyana and Fiji, as well as Uganda and Kenya. Additionally, a growing number of people from South Asian countries migrated as guest workers to the Gulf States. From the 1990s migrants had begun to travel through multiple countries before arriving at their destination country; for example, travelling from India to Britain and from there on to the United States or Canada.[42]

The first major wave of emigration began in the 1830s. In the period between 1840 and 1930 about 32 million South Asians left the subcontinent. This migration trend was not confined to the Asian subcontinent, but was rather part of a global mobility movement that can be observed on almost all continents. The result of this was that some 52 million people emigrated from their homes in South Asia and southern China between the nineteenth century and the beginning of the Second World War. In Europe this number is recorded to be as high as 58 million whilst an additional 51 million emigrated from northwestern Asia and Russia.[43] No estimates exist for such numbers from Africa. However, when the Boer migration in the southern part of the continent as well as the expanding slave trade and plantation economy in the nineteenth century is taken into account,[44] it is likely that here too millions of people migrated within or emigrated from the area, if not to the same extent that has been identified for the other continents.

A broad overview illustrates the dimensions in which the migration and circulation took place. Of the Indian migrants about 14 million went to Burma, up to eight million to Ceylon, some three million to the islands of the Caribbean and approximately the same number to Mauritius and Eastern Africa. Approximately two million Indians went as indentured labourers to Malaya. Additionally, up to two million traders, merchants and lawyers lived abroad.[45] As is the case with all migration numbers, it is unlikely that these are complete as they only refer to official numbers. The amount of informal migration organised by private recruiting agencies remains obscure. Nevertheless, existing numbers reflect a high mobility among Indians. Members of this new labour force mainly stemmed from shifting agriculturists, poor and middling peasants as well as from demobilised soldiers, and even *brahmans* joined the migrants.[46]

After labour contracts had expired and kulis were shipped back to British India, some returnees entered into new employment contracts as indentured labourers. Often several members of a family and residents of a village committed themselves to contracts as indentured labourers, with the effect that circulatory networks of migration, information and labour were formed, which in turn might have led to the permanent settlement in the plantation colony. Thus some 2,321,000 South Asians remained in Ceylon, 1,911,000 in Malaya, 1,164,000 in Burma, 455,000 in Mauritius, 153,000 in Natal, 75,000 in La Reunion and 39,500 in East Africa. Corresponding figures for the Caribbean and the Pacific saw 239,000 South Asians stay in British Guiana, 150,000 in Trinidad, 79,000 in the French Caribbean, 35,000 in Dutch

Guiana and 61,000 in Fiji.[47] The majority of the indentured labourers (more than 25 million) returned to British India on account of the terms of the indentured labour contract they were subject to. Despite the enormous number of returnees, very few studies exist on the economic, cultural and social impacts in the local *adivasi* societies, village communities, clans, kin and families, from which indentured labourers originated.[48]

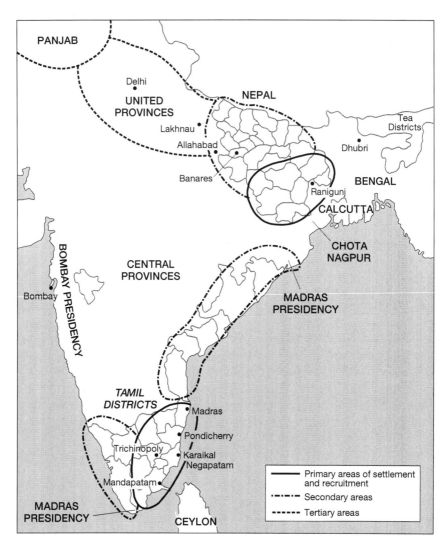

Map 6.2 Spaces of circulation. Michael Mann, "Migration – Re-migration – Circulation: South Asian Kulis in the Indian Ocean and Beyond, 1840–1940." In *Connecting Seas and Connected Ocean Rims. Indian, Atlantic, and Pacific Oceans and China Seas Migrations from the 1830s to the 1930s*, Donna R. Gabaccia and Dirk Hoerder (eds) (Brill, 2011), p. 118

According to some reports, migrants returning from Mauritius in 1842 possessed sums of between ₹10 and ₹50 after a five-year contract. At the end of the nineteenth century many kulis had saved between ₹150 and ₹250.[49] In comparison, annual wages for labourers in the cotton mills of Bombay at the beginning of the twentieth century were between ₹95 and ₹108, indicating that the savings of the migrants were relatively high.[50] However, a considerable number of kulis returned to British India without any savings. For example, from 3,271 returnees in 1876, 713 (22 per cent) had no savings at all. The year 1885 was worse still as 57 per cent of the returnees claimed to possess no money when they arrived back in British India. In many cases money had been remitted by banks, local recruiters or previously returning family members. Some claimed they had been robbed on their way to the harbour, others said they had to spend all their money on food and medicine during the time of indenture, whilst others had to repay debts to the recruiters who often acted as money-lenders to the kulis.[51]

Savings and remittances may have caused tremendous changes in the social stratification and economic situation of the returnees' home villages and families. To date, only a few case studies of remittances to pre-independence British India exist which are focused on the early twentieth century circulation and emigration of Sikhs to Canada. Remittances caused a significant change in the outward appearance of village houses as families with emigrants in, and returnees from, Canada were able to buy land and to build masonry houses, thus investing in primary and secondary agro-economic values. The total amount of annual remittances by Sikhs varied from ₹42,000 up to ₹2,000,000 between 1910 and 1914. This sum was further enhanced by the money returnees brought back home. For all selected Panjabi villages this amounted to an annual average sum of approximately ₹230,000. As a consequence, land prices increased four-fold between 1914 and 1926 which was significantly higher than in the remaining districts of the province.[52]

Three groups of South Asian migrants can be distinguished based on their region of origin and the different destination areas. First, the indentured labourers of the nineteenth century who were to be found on the plantations, in the mines and on the railway construction projects of the colonial powers, where they represented a significant proportion of the local population. Second are the migrants from British India's successor states and the "twice-migrants" from the former British colonies who went to Europe and North America in the 1960s where they became significant minorities. Third, the temporary guest workers who circulated in the Gulf States from the 1970s, where Indians, Pakistanis, Bangladeshis and Lankans, although unable (and forbidden) to form a single community because of their foreign status, were a prominent group in the society of the given Gulf state where they were located.[53]

Apart from these official numbers a large number of people exist who are not categorised as migrants because they have not emigrated from the South Asian subcontinent. For example, only rarely would refugees of war be categorised as migrants, which is inappropriate in demographic as well as in social and economic aspects. The end of British colonial rule proved to be the catalyst for a then unprecedented migration in the late 1940s in South Asia as population exchange of approximately 12 million people took place between the two successor states of British India. Still today in Pakistan the Muslim refugees from the North Indian cities are perceived as a distinct group known as *muhajirs*, lit.: "migrants". As already shown in Chapter 3, in Karachi currently about half of the urban population has formed a political and cultural identity over the course of the previous decades.[54]

Far less well documented, in part as it is less spectacular and therefore attracted less political and media attention, has been the immigration of millions of Nepalese over the open border to India since 1951. Estimates currently point to a number of between six and ten million people who were born in Nepal and now live permanently in India. Several hundred thousand people, including many Muslims, have emigrated from Myanmar (Burma), primarily to Bangladesh and also to India.[55] To this twentieth-century migration in South Asia, the resettlement of more than 350,000 Highland Tamils and descendants of former indentured labourers must also be taken into account who had to be repatriated to Taminlandu in four phases on account of the ethno-racial riots in 1983 and subsequent bilateral agreements between India and Sri Lanka from 1984 to 2002.[56] Thus, a high proportion of South Asian (e)migrants have been forced to leave their homes following the region's independence from the British colonial regime.[57] Most people, however, as will be shown below, emigrated, in the first place, for economic reasons followed by political reasons.

It should be observed that generally people on the subcontinent migrated to the cities as both seasonal and industrial workers. Thus, scientists must deal with temporary rural–urban migration tendencies. On the other hand, there were also a significant number of migrants who moved around the subcontinent as migrant seasonal agricultural labourers from the labour-intensive regions such as Assam with its plantations to the cotton fields of Berar, thereby creating rural–rural migration patterns. In contrast to state-organised migration, as in the case of recruitment made specifically for the tea plantations in Assam, documentation referring to internal migration is generally quite poor as such migratory movements were hardly ever registered by the British authorities. However, it can be assumed that the regional migration was far more extensive than was recorded in contemporary documents such as the Census of India. Because of such sparse figures, only a handful of scientific studies on migration in the agricultural sector are available. However, these do provide evidence that the South Asian rural population was highly mobile.[58]

This agrarian–rural, or agrarian–urban, internal migration should be seen as a horizontal movement within the primary sector and between the primary and secondary sectors. However, these movements, when examined in detail, show significant differences in terms of the decision to migrate as well as in relation to the direction and the target sector.[59] In contrast, the focus of overseas emigration was first on the primary sector (rural–rural migration).

Meanwhile, the share of the tertiary sector grew as lawyers, physicians, publishers, merchants and craftsmen settled in the cities (inter-urban migration).[60] People originating from different regions could find themselves in very different areas, the result of which was that both rural and urban areas could not be distinguished by either an ethnic, social, religious or cultural homogeneity. This, of course, also applies for the internal migration. Thus a distinction between internal and external migration is only useful in the specific context. This would be the case with regard to national laws and administrative regulations as well as recruitment patterns and remittances flows. Only in such cases can the nation-state be, and sometimes must be, the reference point.

From the end of the eighteenth century indigo and sugar plantations began to emerge in North India that remained the exclusive property of the British colonialists. By the nineteenth century tea plantations in Assam developed which were partly owned by Indians. British entrepreneurs and Indians in the independent territories such as South Indian Maisur and Kurg founded coffee and rubber plantations. As a result, labourers were in demand more than ever before in both the overseas plantations, some of which had already existed for a century and were now expanded, and on the numerous new plantations that emerged after 1820 in the subcontinent. Since the immediate areas surrounding the plantations had never had the need for such high numbers of labourers, the additional demand for labourers could not be covered from the surrounding area and therefore they had to be recruited from distant regions. As land was still in abundance, but labour was scarce, aggressive recruitment in the highly competitive South Asian labour market resulted.

Recruitment of indentured labourers

In the nineteenth century two large recruitment regions emerged. One such region consisted of the "rice bowls" in the hinterland of the Coromandel Coast. Since the late eighteenth century the colonial power had set about restructuring land ownership by replacing communal land use rights with private ownership in order to intensify agriculture. This considerably strengthened the landlords and rich peasants. Subsequently, it was only these landlords and rich peasants who were in the position to achieve the conversion to irrigation agriculture and thus instil a capital-intensive cash crop economy. In the long term this commercialisation of agriculture prevented the small peasants and tenants from expanding. The colonial state's political control over the redistribution of agricultural resources caused food shortages and the stress of malnutrition on the population in times of scarce harvests and droughts which could only be relieved through temporary or permanent migration of those affected in such extreme times.[61]

The other big recruitment region was the mountain region in Chhattisgarh and Chotanagpur in southern Bihar with its hills, poor soils and extensive forests. The colonial state's economic intervention and its social consequences were felt even more apparently here. As noted in the previous chapter, shifting cultivation and the general use of forest products formed the economic basis of the *adivasi* population. The forest legislation of British India – in particular in the second half of the nineteenth century – sparked a dramatic redistribution of ownership and agrarian resources in these forested mountain regions as large forest areas were declared state property and, as a consequence, communal use and rights of use were abolished, thereby removing the *adivasis*' economic base. The legal dispossession followed by an economic impoverishment ultimately created a large labour force that became the reservoir of available labourers for the plantation owners in British India and the Empire at large.[62]

In order to control the labourers, the British colonial government put together a package of legislative measures in which the contracts of kulis were specified. The first was the Workman's Breach of Contract Act from 1859, which criminalised workers defaulting on their contracts in British India. This law, which included both economic and non-economic constraints of work, was implemented in most provinces in British India where it remained in place until the 1930s. It provided for the management of the plantations and allowed them to become ever more profitable business enterprises. Furthermore, this law allowed payment below the level of general wages, and, in extreme cases, below the poverty line. When plantation owners made plots of land available to plantation workers (mostly families), they were forcing the plantation workers to grow staple food crops which, in many cases, did not cover their basic food needs. Deficiency and malnutrition resulted, negatively affecting, among other things, the reproductive capacity of the labourers.[63]

Among this catalogue of measures is also the disciplinary power of the plantation owners to punish those workers who breached their contracts, making the plantation world comparable with a prison regime as draconian punishments such as flogging for the refusal to or absence from work were imposed. The high mortality rates during transport of labourers to Assam prompted the colonial government to install statutory regulation of transport conditions in 1863. However, in 1882 all the provisions concerning the transport and disciplinary power were relaxed under pressure from the plantation owners. This provoked the resistance of the labourers during which the collective response was for large groups to leave the plantations. Increasingly difficult recruitment, together with continued scarce sources of labour, led to the paradoxical phenomenon that cheap labour caused high costs. This in turn increased plantation owners' pressure on the kulis and consequently reinforced their willingness to resist. Ultimately the harsh, often violent labour regime led to the reform of the labour and recruitment market for the tea plantations in Assam.[64]

In the 1830s and 1840s Mauritius acted as a laboratory for the development of an imperial legislation on overseas plantations which made the recruitment of Indian indentured labourers a viable workforce. In the first decades of the nineteenth century French planters brought contract labourers from their South Asian settlements on the Malabar Coast to Mauritius. With the abolition of slavery in 1834 the global availability of labour was thereafter not only organised by a private sector as during the slave trade, but the labour market in the colonies was increasingly regulated through the concerted effort made by government and the local plantocracy. In Mauritius the local French and British planters, local colonial administrators, the British-Indian Government and the government in London experimentally tested the transition of the management of plantations from slave labour to that of strictly controlled wage workers in the form of indentured labourers. After successful trials on this British "island laboratory" the system was finally able to be applied within, and also outside, the British Empire.[65]

Once the legislative hurdles had been cleared, overseas migration began after 1842. In particular, the methods of recruitment and transportation involved in this had been regulated in such a way that comparisons with the Atlantic Slave Trade and its infamous Middle Passage were not to be immediately exposed. Already by 1843, 30,000 men, women and children had emigrated from British India to Mauritius. In the following decades, the British Indian colonial state developed more packages of legislation that ensured the control of recruitment, transportation and medical care. Recruitment was regulated for the first time with the legislation of 1871. This legislation ensured that in the future all agents had to be registered and the newly created office of the Protector of Emigrants which was situated in the three port cities of Calcutta, Bombay and Madras was to make sure that agents, kulis, depots and ships were regularly inspected. Furthermore, the newly recruited kulis were from then on subjected to various medical examinations before departure and upon arrival.[66]

Initially, the recruitment market was regulated more or less by itself. Informal migration functioned and developed through family and rural information networks. Additionally, former contract labourers could act as recruiters on behalf of their plantation owner in their home villages and bring both family and clan members, as well as residents of the village and surrounding villages, to the plantation colony. With the prestige associated with such a position, these temporary returnees qualified as overseers (*sirdars*) and recruiters and thereby improved their own social status. Former contract kulis used the opportunity to elevate their social status and became mediators between workers and employers whilst, as was soon to be seen in Mauritius, they simultaneously formed the nucleus of a future Indian community.[67]

The ever-growing demand for labour from both within and from outside of India soon meant that the professional recruitment of labourers was needed. During the second half of the nineteenth century recruitment structures emerged that were initially geared to existing migration patterns, but were then gradually aligned along specific needs. Internal migration structures, apart from the early systematic recruitment of labourers for the tea plantations of Assam, which was still largely based on informal structures, remained more or less in place whilst new recruitment agencies for overseas workplaces soon replaced the existing methods of recruitment. This network of Indian recruitment agencies succeeded in almost completely supplying the demand for kuli workers.[68] However, the British repeatedly criticised the alleged lack of efficiency within the recruitment system as it was "Indian" and therefore *eo ipso* unreliable and inefficient. In fact, the British were attempting to impose their own control.[69]

Agencies were hierarchically structured and consisted of the agents who were centrally located together with sub-agents in the districts, followed by *daffadars*, *sirdars*, *mukaddams* and *maistries* (names for the local recruiters) depending on the region. In the case of the *mukaddam* this implied the village headman whilst the other notations indicated positions as foreman and overseers on the plantations. The *arkatis* were specifically employed to manage recruitment matters. The social and economic basis of the recruiters was thus rather heterogeneous; yet one commonality of all was that they worked on a commission basis.[70] However, the importance of the labour agent went beyond these mere logistical and organisational needs as the recruiters were deeply integrated in the local economy. The tension between the involvement of established recruiters and the emerging capitalist-led labour setting created contradictions that were typical and constitutive of a colonial regime.[71]

The entire personnel that had been assembled acted on three levels. The *arkatis* concentrated on the operational base for the recruitment serving the villages whilst all others focused more on the market towns and pilgrimage centres of the districts, religious festivities and the train stations. Sub-agents collected the recruited kulis in cities that had rail connections and transported them to the port cities of Madras, Bombay and Calcutta, where agents took care of their shipment. However, from the first contact of the kulis' recruitment to shipment a loss of nearly 30 per cent was recorded as they were either "dismissed" according to the regulations of the colonial state's control apparatus or they simply "deserted" as the journey from the depot to the ship was poorly monitored. On their way to the port kulis came into contact with fellow experienced labourers making newly recruited kulis revise their decision to migrate based on accounts of the type of work expected of them and the distance they would have to travel.[72]

The highly competitive labour pool drove competition among the agencies, often culminating in illegal action as whole groups of kulis were taken to different ports due to false promises made by competing agencies in other shipping depots. Furthermore, it was often the case that even after departure from India destinations could be changed so that kulis originally bound for Mauritius unexpectedly found themselves in Fiji. Moreover kulis who had secured a second contract of work were often not granted a position in their favoured region or the specified plantation. Further confusion was caused among the migrants by the competition between the British public administration and the private British agencies as district magistrates and revenue collectors often interfered with kuli recruitment since migrant workers would pose a shortage for the local agricultural labour market. Furthermore, the conservative Indian landowners did not support the exodus of peasants. Indian landowners and British officials alike were concerned that a dwindling workforce would have implications for the production of cash and food crops as agricultural products formed the basis of the revenue system in British India.[73]

However, a further form of labour recruitment was offered by the so-called *kangany* system. In contrast to state-regulated recruitment system which placed recruitment more or less in private hands whilst the maritime passage, medical and sanitary issues came under state control, the *kangany* system left the entire organisation and procedure of emigration in the hands of Indian agents. In order to be allowed to legally operate this recruitment system, agents had to possess a state licence. The significant difference between indentured labourer and those kulis enlisted from the *kangany* system was the amount of contracted work time they were bound to as, whilst indentured labourers were committed from the outset to five years of service, the *kangany*-kulis had a right to cancel their contract after four weeks. That said, however, the *kangany*-kuli was far more dependent on the financial advances of the *kangany*.

On account of their intermediate position between plantation owners and kulis, the *kanganies* secured a prominent position for themselves. In this way they were able to retain up to one-third of all of the designated financial and nutritional support for themselves by cutting such rations to the Indian kulis. On the other hand, on account of the advances and loans received, the kulis often found themselves in debt to the *kangany*, thereby creating a situation of debt bondage. Also, *kanganies* often bought Tamil workers out of their local debt bondage using advance funding, only to then reproduce almost identical conditions for the labourers. Apart from the recruitment and organisation of the emigration, the transportation of labourers and formalities of immigration, the organisation of work on the plantations also rested on the *kangany*. This gave the *kanganies* an indispensable, and at the same time uncontrollable position as they could act as a social mediator between planters and kuli-workers. The *kanganies* were confirmed in this role by the behaviour of the plantation owners who did not want direct contact with their workers.[74]

Empty promises, along with various dishonest methods used by recruiters such as assurances of advance payments, free board and lodging and generous working conditions, engendered a lack of willingness to migrate. Deceit and premeditated disinformation about destinations and working conditions there were also part of the recruiters' repertoire. Open kidnapping, however, seems to have been the exception rather than the rule.[75] Despite such scheming, kulis were far from the unsuspecting and defenceless victims of an overwhelming recruitment mafia. It has not only been Indian historiography that has contributed to this pathetic stereotype, but also the kulis themselves who occasionally presented themselves as victims in order to compensate for the loss of status or the trauma of "expatriation" they experienced.[76]

Ex-soldiers (*sipahi*/sepoy) of the British Indian Army, who after the Great Rebellion, at least from the British perspective, had doubtful loyalties, were systematically demobilised and lost status. The *sipahis* came primarily from the upper *varna*/*jati* of the often impoverished *brahmans* and the *kshatriyas* of Hindustan, but had found a new social status as well as a fiscally lucrative position in the British army. From 1860 the number of kulis recruited from this region rose, as former soldiers found their new economic niche as contract labourers, although this implied a considerable loss of social prestige.[77] Occasionally *brahmans* in overseas South Asian communities were called on as specialists in ritual affairs, an opportunity which could not be missed, especially since their return was virtually impossible because of the ship's passage through *kalapani* (lit. black water) in which purity requirements could not be met.[78] Contrary to popular and long-time scientific opinion, it has been documented that a considerable number of migrants and emigrants came from such middle and upper strata of society.

Kulis also became the target group of Christian missionaries on the plantations; this is especially true for the Caribbean. In Trinidad alone, the number of so-called rice Christians rose by 20 per cent in the last third of the nineteenth century, whilst numbers on the other islands and the South American mainland are recorded to have been between one and four per cent. At the same time a notable Sanskritisation can be observed whereby the former *adivasis* and *dalits* who had been largely excluded from the Hindu rituals and beliefs were gradually integrated into an emerging syncretic form of Hinduism. In the broadest sense this also, for example, included the abandonment of goat sacrifices as practised by some South Indian Hindu communities. Some emigrants easily succumbed to the campaigns of reform groups such as the Hindu Arya Samaj or the Muslim Ahmadiyya movement, which were particularly attractive to the uprooted and disoriented because of their egalitarian social visions.[79]

According to the contemporary Indian and the British perception, kulis were also the victims of their migration. Often by virtue of their mostly tribal origin, they were denoted as uncivilised and as the dregs of urban slums even before their departure on account of the British and Indian bourgeois-elite ideas of morality and standards of living and were thus stigmatised as the "Other" of Indian society. This outsider label remained in the destination country whose people and plantation owners had no interest in integrating the foreign labourers into the established creole society. It was the exploitation of the labour force and not issues of acculturation or assimilation that was on the contract agenda.[80] The kuli system remained almost unchanged until the First World War. Following massive agitation of the INC with respect to indentured labour, the British forbade it in 1917 in order not to suffer any uprisings from the "workers' front" in the colonies important to the war effort. However, the measures were not successfully implemented until 1922–3.[81]

The quickly established stereotype of backward, simple-minded and easily influenced peasants and mountain-dwellers referred not only to the generally lower status of kulis, but also marked the border in the self-perception of migrants. Kulis in overseas colonies and plantations were challenged more explicitly than any plantation workers in British India with regards to their own dignity and self-confidence. Doubtlessly, this was related to the traumatic experiences of their passage and the fear of not ever being able to return home. It was partly determined by the perception on the part of the creole, mestizo and British, as well as the French and Dutch-influenced plantation societies. Even today this presents a huge problem in the identity formation of

South Asians in the overseas communities and new nation-states. The literary and political concept of *Coolitude* – apparently borrowed from *Négritude* of the 1930s – attempts to counteract this by encouraging later generations to be aware of (or rediscover) their historical roots and thereby draw strength from them to form an identity, with the aim of accepting the hybridity of their local society and developing it further.[82]

Migration and settlement

If the kulis had had bad experiences with their recruiters on the transport over land and during their stay in the urban depots, this was further enhanced with the shipment and work on the plantations. The hard, prison-like regimes of the tea plantations of Assam have already been mentioned. Maritime transport, however, proved to be an experience that seemed downright traumatic for many kulis as it was coupled with the fear of losing all familiar bonds and an uncertain future in a foreign country which oppressed all seafaring migrants as they became aware, perhaps for the first time, of how far the distances between their homes and the plantations were. Added to this was the initial experience of the sea crossing for emigrants as people who had never even heard of an ocean, let alone seen one, believed that crossing such an ocean would lead to the exclusion of both *jati* and *varna* culminated in uncertainty and despair.[83] The food, or rather lack thereof, on board did the rest to set the sombre mood of the crossing. Food rations were mostly tight and consisted of fish and rice twice a day, with which putrid water was served. The inadequate diet along with the additional effects of exhaustion caused by seasickness suffered by many of the kuli increased the risk of disease on board.[84]

Despite regulations, hygiene on the ships was often deficient. Overcrowding of up to 20 per cent above capacity served as preventive compensation for deaths en route, but in effect contributed to the poor sanitary conditions on board and drove the mortality rate up. On some transport ships the mortality rate reached 4 per cent.[85] Additionally, the behaviour of officers, like that of many of the sailors, was rather appalling; both were usually drunk and either incompetent or untrained for the situations they met with and both subjected the kulis to a great deal of everyday brutality. Particularly striking was the behaviour of the ship's doctors. Women on board the ships were subject to particular suffering as doctors misused the trust they built with them to sexually assault and rape them. Women were also victims of sexually motivated attacks from the sailors who took advantage of the separate accommodation of the women below deck. Only in a handful of cases did such attacks have serious consequences for the criminal behaviour of the offenders. British court documents show that stereotypes of "Oriental" women as always sexually willing served to exclude rape in the contemporary understanding of civil law.[86]

Upon arrival on the islands and the plantations, the kulis were soon faced with the rigours of the labour regime. Following the ship's relatively short passage to Ceylon, the South Indian kulis were met with a 220-kilometre trek to the plantations in the highlands. The roads were often in a state of disrepair and inadequately equipped with facilities and possibilities to replenish rations. On the Mascarene Islands, the kulis were usually housed in the former lodgings that had been used for slaves. Since medical care on the plantations was far from the best and any medical costs the kulis incurred would be deducted from their wages (in stark contrast to the free medical care given to the former slaves), chronic diseases soon became part of their everyday life. Furthermore, food supply was poor and many kulis quickly succumbed to exhaustion through the hard, physical work. The plantations of Ceylon were notorious as seasonal or annual intervals saw many circulating kulis succumb to physical exhaustion on the journey back to their South Indian villages due to malnutrition.[87]

The system of indentured labour is generally characterised by its hardships in terms of work and human effects; however, women, as kulis, were far worse off than their male "colleagues". In most plantation colonies they were initially seen with reluctance, as they were viewed to be a burden. Their physical strength was considered inadequate for the heavy physical work. Furthermore, on account of their puritan morals, British planters were suspicious of single women. Instead, young, fit and strong men were demanded and the share of workers in the 20- to 30-years age group is estimated at 60 per cent of the total workforce. Yet soon plantation owners realised that women's work could be systematically valorised and be made an integral part of the plantation system, without which it would not have been a profitable enterprise. This was first achieved by paying women lower wages, having the effect of keeping overall average wages down. In this way men's wages on many plantations could be reduced by 10 per cent in the second half of the nineteenth century.

Second, the stabilisation of the "social order" was achieved by having women present on the plantations as they married, started a family and developed family bonds. This often led to the permanent settlement of the workers and resulted in partial control over them. Thus, the stabilisation of the working class as well as the so-called reproductive work of women became an integral part of the plantation labour system. Third, plantation owners transferred parts of the remuneration costs directly onto the working families as they were allowed (or forced) to grow extra food on small plots, and this in turn contributed to further capital accumulation on the plantation owners' side. Despite the aforementioned reasons, single women were undesirable labourers on the plantations in an attempt to hinder the development of prostitution. Despite this fact, only 41 per cent of emigrating women were married. This suggests that unmarried women were not generally frowned upon as workers and as sexual partners and that they were tolerated by the plantation owners because of the sexual "stabilising function" they created.[88]

Aside from this functional role, from an economic point of view, women experienced the usual double burden of being a wife, and possibly a mother, having to complete the household chores, tending to the garden and children after having completed an arduous day of work in the fields. Women were often only used by the plantation owners and administrators as casual workers or for seasonal activities with the effect that their wages, set by law at half that of the men's wages, were once again cut. Little consideration was given to pregnant women, or to those who had recently given birth. As a result, the mortality rate of malnourished mothers and infants was high. In addition to this economic exploitation, women were also under constant threat of the continuing sexual exploitation from plantation owners, administrators, their husbands and other male kulis.[89]

The British perception of female Indian labourers who had emigrated for work purposes saw them enter a lower social stratum whereby they were simply classified as starving widows, abandoned or runaway wives and were stereotyped as prostitutes. Only dishonourable women would emigrate, and if they did they would be accompanied by their husbands or a close relative.[90] This reputation impacted the picture of the women working abroad, seeing them as prostitutes.[91] This corresponds to the colonial perception of the women from villages who worked in the textile factories in Bombay and Calcutta.[92] Although the share of single women workers in the industrial cities was far greater than in the plantations, there was still a considerable surplus of men. In order not to become victims of rape, many women entered into temporary relationships with "colleagues" or administrators for protection.

However, many kuli women were forced into prostitution in order to supplement their meagre wages. Often plantation owners refused wage rises of female labourers with the reasoning that they could easily increase their earnings through prostitution. Indian women who were in the position of wardens often forced their female workers into prostitution; the bulk of the profit that these women earned often ended up back in the hands of the warden. It is not, however, scandalous that kuli women worked as prostitutes, but rather that wages were kept so low because of the "character of an extra (family) income" that was available to them. Women's wages were simply not enough to survive, so in order to earn their livelihood they had not only to sell their labour, but also to sell their bodies and to become part-time sex workers.[93] Moreover, it is obvious that the plantocratic regime as well as that in the mines bore unique structures of exploitation and violence.

In general migration, and specially emigration, did little to help women achieve any freedom, but rather it subjected them to new and enhanced forms of dependencies, exploitations and humiliation on the part of men – both European and South Asian. If differences existed, then it was mostly between the internal and external migration, as in the industrial cities women could often choose between different tasks which were contractually forbidden on the plantations.[94] Even for the men, migration and circulation did not often lead to significant improvements as despite wages, the foreign external environment, the hard work and the brutal punishments posed a constant danger to their health and well-being. The prospect of savings from years of hard work and, related to this, the change of upward social mobility does however seem to have been the motivation to take this risk.

It seems that kulis were not merely passive in this process, but rather shapers of their own lives. On the plantations kulis often fought to reclaim their contractually guaranteed rights as they quickly realised that common action was more effective than individual protest. Additionally, during such action participants inevitably found solidarity with other kulis, and formed friendships that would be the beginning of a permanent community away from home. The end of the contract period afforded the kulis some bargaining power. As plantation owners saw the benefit of having at least a partly stable workforce, they were willing to grant small concessions in the renewal of contracts. Under certain circumstances this renewal of contracts improved some kulis' lives so much that they decided to permanently settle in this new region where they acquired land. They were able to start a small existence as vegetable farmers, artisans and petty traders and create a new local community.[95]

South Asian communities overseas

Mauritius

Some 450,000 of all the indentured labourers in Mauritius settled there permanently between 1840 and 1917. The majority of the emigrants came from Bihar and to a lesser extent from Bengal and the North-Western Provinces/ United Provinces, whilst only a small minority came from the southern regions of the subcontinent.[96] The regional origin and the specific cultural differences of these migrants determined the life of the South Asian communities on the island from the outset. Of the current population of 1.2 million, approximately two-thirds have their origins in South Asia, nearly 30 per cent are descendants of former slaves from Africa and 2 per cent are of former Chinese origin. Since 1962, six years before the island's independence, South Asians have been officially distinguished as Hindus (52 per cent of the population) and Muslims (16 per cent). The Creoles, descendants of Europeans and Africans, remained close to the Roman Catholic faith. As in good British tradition, which had arisen in British India, this led to the societal division of the island's inhabitants solely into communities of religious denominations that still persist.

Today, numerous Hindus have converted to Catholicism. The term Hindu does not represent an endogamous ethnic group, but rather constitutes different cultural communities, each with its own history and culture. Although Islam creates a common faith for Muslims, no homogeneous community of Muslim faith formed in Mauritius. Seen politically, a common faith did not offer reason to pursue common goals as Muslim organisations instead followed different strategies in the context of independence. From the 1970s, Muslims oriented themselves less with South Asian Muslim communities (i.e. Pakistani or Bangladeshi), but rather more with the Arab-Muslim communities which resulted in a certain "Arabisation" of the Mauritian Muslims.[97]

The South Asian communities in Mauritius are characterised, above all, by their "ancestral languages" of Hindi, Tamil, Telugu, Urdu and Marathi.

However, only a minority of the former kulis' descendants now understand these languages. Hindi has been influenced by French Creole and is mostly used as a second language, whilst Tamil has become something of a sacred language because of its exclusivity in religious rituals. Identity formation along these "ancestral language" lines is actively promoted in government schools and is hence a state-furthered process. Whilst Hindu organisations such as the RSS and the VHP have attempted to promote the protection of Hindi in order to safeguard Hinduism, attempts to utilise the language for political and religious purposes have been unsuccessful. The uniform state support for languages not only afforded languages an official positive reification of their role; the government itself was able to utilise this as a foundation for a substantial part of its own legitimacy.[98]

The permeability of social hierarchies of Mauritian society added to its stabilisation. Former indentured labourers were able to start small subsistence lives early on, establishing themselves as craftsmen and tradesmen in order to accumulate a little capital, acquire wealth and provide the next generation with access to education and thus career opportunities in the agricultural sector as well as prestigious professions and in politics.[99] The liberal political system finally came into fruition with the electoral declaration in 1968 which expressed that each individual who did not want to be officially assigned to the Hindu, Muslim and Chinese communities would be included into the fourth category, the "General Population". It is therefore not surprising that Mauritius experiences hardly any ethnic, religious or communal tensions. The state ensures that none of the groups represented are in the position to dominate over another, thus relatively peaceful co-existence seems assured.[100]

French Mascarene

In 1848, only 3,440 Indians lived on Réunion. During the 1850s, the number of kulis there averaged just 1,700. It was the contracts of 1860–61 which resulted in the subsequent need for labour to manage the plantations of the islands. Yet by 1885 the British Indian government had banned recruitment for Réunion following reports of the brutal recruitment methods of the French agencies. The British-Indian Government alleged that the French seemed to use significantly more force, often extending as far as abduction, than their British and Indian counterparts. Aside from such brutal recruitment, the British were also particularly appalled by the conditions in the recruitment camps of the French settlements in Karikal and Pondicherry which were reported to have been particularly dreadful, exemplified in the regular outbreak of epidemics such as cholera and the high mortality rate among the kulis in the overfilled deportation camps.[101]

In total, approximately 118,000 South Asians came to Réunion between 1829 and 1924, of whom about 88,000 were recorded to have stayed on the island.[102] Réunion Island has been a French overseas administrative department since 1946. The descendants of the kuli immigrants still mainly live in rural areas as small farmers, with only a few having moved in the vicinity of commercial and industrial areas. On the one hand a strong Hinduisation has taken place in the last decades whilst on the other Muslim consciousness has begun to grow as in neighbouring Mauritius. This is partly due to the geographical proximity of the island to the South Asian subcontinent which has facilitated communication. This is in contrast to the Caribbean where the distance has also had the effect of promoting a certain "creolisation". At the same time the French central government-led "assimilation" in recent years has increased tensions between the Creole-African majority and the South Asian minority, mainly because the South Asian families refuse to submit to the state-imposed cultural policy and instead stress their "Indianness".[103]

South Africa

In fact, South Africa did not need supplementary kulis from abroad as enough workers from within the Zulu society were easily available to be recruited. However, Sir Theophilus Shepstone, Secretary for Native Affairs in Natal, implemented a system of racial segregation in which Africans were allowed to keep their cultural, social and economic (separate) autonomy. The state made enough land available to them, meaning that there was no reason for Africans to look to the sugar plantations in Natal for work. For this reason, the mainly British planters looked to the experiment in Mauritius for inspiration and methods of recruitment. The first kulis arrived in Durban in 1860 following agreements with the British-Indian Government. By 1911, a total of 152,184 people had emigrated from British India, prompting the Government of Natal to decide to cease further referrals. In the interwar period, some 38,000 former kulis were "repatriated". Despite this, approximately one million decedents from South Asian emigrants continue to live in the Union of South Africa.[104]

Most South Asian kulis were employed as labourers on the South African sugar plantations whilst a handful found employment in households and hotels as well as for the Natal Railway Company. At times owners of South African coal mines also employed kulis from British India. The latter two industries in particular required specifically trained employees resulting in a relatively high proportion of skilled kulis. Once their contracts expired most could quickly establish themselves in South Africa as vegetable and fruit growers in the vicinity of urban centres. Already by 1893 some 24,459 former kulis lived alongside 16,051 indentured labourers.[105] Added to these figures were the Passenger Indians, most of whom originated from Gujarat, Bombay and Surat, exhibiting the typical behaviour of chain migration. Well over 20,000 Passenger Indians were found to be living in Natal alone by 1911. Here they manoeuvred themselves into the positions of merchants and traders among the middle and upper segments of the South Asian immigrants.[106] From the perspective of the British merchants and shopkeepers, the new competition was perceived as an economic threat which was countered with racist state measures. This perceived or actual economic threat was soon expressed demographically as the 8.8 per cent proportion of "Whites" in the total population of Natal was soon outnumbered by 9.1 per cent of "Indians" early in the twentieth century.[107]

As the "White" settlers in Natal were given the right to self-government in 1893, successive laws were issued that systematically discriminated against the "Indian" and other "Non-white" populations. Among these laws was the decree that "Indians" who, for whatever reason, did not extend their work contracts upon expiry, were subject to an annual poll tax of £3, a sum that most could not afford. A general English language test for kuli immigrants posed an additional, almost insurmountable, hurdle. Additionally, since 1897 municipal authorities had been given the power to grant commercial licences which followed in the open discrimination of "Indian" competitors.[108] It was in this political constellation that Mohandas K. Gandhi stepped onto the stage of history. His more than 20 years of experience in South Africa has been given little attention, since most biographies treat this period as a kind of prelude to Gandhi showing himself in India.[109]

M.K. Gandhi, who had studied law in London, took on the mandate of a Gujarati businessman in Durban in 1893. Gandhi initially only wanted to move there for this mandate but was soon joined by his family. For the duration of his South African career Gandhi remained true to his rich South Asian business clientele, only representing the kuli miners and women in his political actions towards the end of his stay. This became clear in the Natal Indian Congress (NIC) which was launched in 1894 by Gandhi and whose founding members and donors came almost exclusively from the Indian merchant class.[110] However, he lost the sympathy he had enjoyed among the business clientele as he mobilised 20,000 South Asian miners in the fight against the discriminatory poll tax. In the course of this campaign Gandhi observed, for the first time, the effect of a politically active, broad stratum of the ("Indian") population, although a minority, which ultimately put him in the position to negotiate with the South African Government and force the withdrawal of the £3 poll tax in 1914. This experience led the way for his later career in British India.

In addition to the broad involvement of religious, social and moral standards, this political campaign and its success was decisive for the great support that Gandhi experienced at the end of his South African days. For the first time, he awoke the consciousness of having common interests among the Indian minority in Natal. The power of this strategy was so immense that Gandhi had the ability to break through social, religious and cultural barriers and align the thus rudimentarily homogenised Indians toward a common goal. In this way he was able to create an Indian community in South Africa. It was these social competences that Gandhi showed by leading the people of the INC that developed his role as a social activist. Although Gandhi's actions were only short-lived in South Africa, the impact of the experiments he undertook there became permanently embossed on his life and laid the foundations for all his work in British India.[111]

The position of the Indian minority in South Africa worsened once again in the interwar period as the commercial elite used its supremacy in the NIC to pursue its own individual concerns. As it was not willing to represent the indentured labourers, a new elite was soon created which came from those Indians who had been born in South Africa. This group consisted of approximately 300 people, mostly employees, freelancers or teachers. Through organisations such as the Young Men's Hindu Association this group succeeded in producing a socio-cultural reference back to India that was simultaneously interested in the structure and design of the current situation in South Africa. This ultimately allowed them to establish solidarity relations with the Indian indentured labourers. Thus, this new elite soon gathered wide support, which it deployed in direct competition with the NIC. This dual constellation was to dominate the political situation of the Indians in South Africa for a long time.[112]

Although many kulis became small peasants following the expiration of their contract period, this step was, for many, merely a stopover on their way to the cities as life in the agricultural sector did not offer the chances of a secure livelihood for a prolonged duration. It was not only the big cities such as Johannesburg that benefited from this development (over 70 per cent of all Indians in South Africa lived in the greater Durban area alone) but Indians began to settle widely across all of the country's urban centres.[113] Their migration to the cities increased in the 1930s and 40s. The proportion of male South Asian labourers grew from 30 to 53 per cent in the decade between 1936 and 1946 alone. By the 1980s, 91 per cent of all Indians in South Africa had settled in cities, a number that makes them the highest percentage of urban settlers among all South African population groups.[114]

The discrimination against Indians as indentured labourers was followed by the discrimination dedicated to apartheid policy of the South African regime after 1946 once the political class of the country dispensed with the war-related politics of "holding still". In 1950 the Group Area Act prohibited Indians from living in the inner cities and instead relocated their residential areas to the outskirts.[115] From Durban alone 250,000 Indians were forcibly relocated to Phoenix and another 300,000 to Chatsworth.[116] For most this expulsion from the urban centres meant the end of their business activities, which had been the intention of the law in the first place.[117] Only with the gradual abolition of the Group Area Act were the foundations for a gradual economic rise of the Indians laid so that by the early 1990s only 10 per cent of them were still below the poverty line; a drop from almost 71 per cent at the beginning of the 1940s.[118]

Even after the end of apartheid in South Africa, many Indians felt threatened on account of their relatively good social and economic position. This resulted in the high number of emigrants to the United States, Australia, Canada and Great Britain. The high level of uncertainty that prevails among the Indians of South Africa was particularly noticeable during the celebrations of the 150th Anniversary of Indian immigration in 2010. Alone the question

Migration, circulation and diaspora 239

of whether celebration, commemoration or commiseration indicates the difficulties that the Indian communities have in, and with, the post-apartheid regime in South Africa. Whilst Indians in the professional and business sectors identify more closely with the regime, as both groups belong to the economic winners, working-class Indians feel increasingly isolated as they have been economically marginalised and are therefore unable to participate in the new regime.[119]

East Africa

The South Asian immigration to East Africa represents a special situation in South Asian migration history. On the one hand is the small trading community along the Swahili coast from the mid-nineteenth century, which not only focused on the cultivation of cloves, but was also engaged as financier and entrepreneur in the trade of ivory and slaves; and, on the other hand, the 37,000 Indians who were recruited in the 1890s who profited from the construction of the Uganda Railway from Mombasa to Lake Victoria. Most of these migrants were Sikhs from the Panjab who were repatriated after their contracts expired. However, nearly 20 per cent (about 7,000) remained in Kenya and Uganda, where they settled as artisans and small entrepreneurs in the cities along the new railway lines. Connections to family and friends soon induced a process of chain migration.

In many cases urban–urban migration can be observed as many immigrants migrated for a second time after they or their parents had previously migrated to a city from the countryside in South Asia. Gradually, the Panjabi Sikhs established themselves as informal financiers of European plantation owners and colonial civil servants as well as importers of various goods. Even doctors, lawyers, engineers, teachers and accountants (that is the Passenger Indians) started to migrate to East Africa. Until the eve of the First World War some 20,000 further South Asian migrants had come to Kenya alone so that their total number now lay at 34,000. In 1921, this figure equalled 54,000, and a decade later it reached nearly 100,000. Between the end of the Second World War and the independence of Kenya in 1963 another 260,000 emigrants from the Indian Union entered the country. However, their share of the total population has never reached more than 2 per cent.[120]

The composition of these immigrants was highly heterogeneous. The Chotara Muslims (Sunni) immigrated before the mid-nineteenth century and had become almost indistinguishable from the local population a century later. Muslim merchants from Baluchistan became almost completely assimilated with the adoption of clothing, ceremonies and language. Shiite Muslims from North India such as the Istn Astheris and the Ismailis were by far the largest immigrant group until the First World War. Alongside all of the different Muslim faiths, Hindus, Jains, Christians from Goa, Jats, Sikhs and Parsi all formed their own communities to pursue their particular interests by building separate schools, hospitals, recreational facilities, mandirs, mosques, churches and cemeteries. Strong bonds back to their South Asian region of origin helped to preserve the cultural identities of individual communities.[121]

These various communities were only united following the bitter legal battles with the British colonial power over equal access to land. Demands ranged from political representation to land acquisition and culminated in the demand for an independent East African settlement area that was to be regulated by British India. Instead, however, with the Devonshire Declaration of 1923 the British introduced a systematic exclusion policy as Indians were prohibited not only from purchasing land, but they were also forced out of various economic positions and limited to certain professions. Natural growth and further immigration from British India soon led to overcrowding in the cities. Indians were now increasingly perceived as an alleged or real affluent urban minority. They became the target of racist attacks from the African majority who felt as if they had been socially and economically disadvantaged and targeted their resulting frustrations at the "foreign" Indians.[122]

Four years after independence, the Kenyan Government introduced an "anti-Asian" legislative campaign in 1967 as part of a citizenship law that forced all Indians to accept the citizenship of Kenya and surrender their British nationality. Just a few years later, the neighbouring Ugandan dictator, Idi Amin, issued an ultimatum in 1972 for all "Asians" to leave the country within a few months. An exodus of more than 300,000 "Asians" followed. The causes of this expulsion can be found in the structural (de-)formation of the colonial era. As in Kenya (where 90 per cent of Indians lived in the 16 largest cities in the country before independence) the adjoining states of Tanganyika and Uganda saw up to 60 per cent of Indians living in urban areas. Their concentration in a handful of professions led to African economic discontent directed at the relatively affluent Indians after independence which ultimately provided the pretext for their expulsion.[123] Their situation was made even more difficult on account of the diplomatic dispute between Britain and India as to the reception of these displaced persons.[124]

Malaya

Compared to South Africa and Mauritius, the British colonies in Southeast Asia and the research on the indentured labourers from British India have not been studied as intensively. An example of this is British Malaya where the coffee plantation owners were initially uninterested in importing labourers from British India. This changed abruptly when at the end of the nineteenth century coffee prices plummeted, whilst the demand for rubber for the production of tyres at the beginning of the twentieth century opened a new economic sector. Now labourers were urgently needed in Southeast Asia too. Around 1900, just 2,000 hectares were used throughout Southeast Asia for the production of rubber; by 1910 and 1911 this had increased to 260,000 hectares. In addition to the European producers, Chinese manufacturers were becoming increasingly involved in the rubber business. Thus, whilst the scope of the

European plantations increased from 68,000 hectares in 1907 to 425,000 hectares in 1918, the area of Chinese-owned plantations increased from 810 to 338,000 hectares during the same period. The government-funded infrastructure was instrumental in this rapid expansion as were the preferential rates with the Straits Settlements and subsidising of the recruitment of Indian kulis.[125]

Local agencies had been recruiting kulis on a small scale from the 1870s. With this now huge demand for labour in 1907, the British coordinated the recruitment through the central Indian Immigration Committee and the Indian Immigration Fund, in this way optimising the *kangany* system. Between 1870 and 1919, 249,832 kulis arrived in Malaya. When the Malaysian Government officially prohibited recruitment in 1910, the official migration rate of kulis fell from 70 per cent of all immigrants from British India to just 6 per cent within a couple of years. However, the number of South Indian migrants continued to rise. Between 1900 and 1911 alone, the number of Indians in Malaya doubled; the following decade saw a further doubling of their numbers so that by 1921 they accounted for approximately 10 per cent of the total population. The privately organised recruitment through the still-functioning *kangany* system made this increase possible.[126]

The decline in the rubber production during the Great Depression meant that of the 206,000 kulis employed on the plantations in 1929, only 104,000 remained three years later. A total of 190,000 unemployed Tamils were repatriated at the government's expense. Thus, unwanted costs and the potential for unrest were reallocated as the burden of the integration of returning unskilled and unemployed kulis was imposed on the British-Indian Government since plantation owners as well as the Malaysian state managed to evade the financial and social problems of the geographic displacement of people. A small number of surplus labourers remained in order, as already seen in the sugar plantations, to suppress the wages of workers.[127] Until the Second World War, few Indians were particularly interested in the political affairs of Malaya and Singapore. Seen from a national identity perspective they could, until then, be mobilised in only two ways: first through language policies; and, second, through the Indian National Army under the command of Subhas Chandra Bose who, as has been shown in Chapter 2, had recruited the soldiers among the local kulis and started his march on British India from Singapore.[128]

In 1946, the then Indian Malayans and Singaporeans were organised into the Malayalam Indian Congress, which fought together with the United Malay National Organisation and the Malaysian Chinese Association for the independence of the Federation of Malaysia, and, in an alliance with these parties, formed a government until 1969. However, many Indians also joined non-national parties such as the Labour Party in Malaya and the People's Action Party in Singapore, the latter of which pushed for the non-caste orientated ethnic society as the basis of the federation.[129] This goal was in contrast to the coalition government and the parties it represented which insisted on a representation of the "ethnic" communities. At the same time one of the most powerful organisations in the federation, the National Union of Plantation Workers, missed its opportunity to act on a wide scale and thus to become another political power in the country.[130]

Finally, in the 1960s, the South Indian language movement found its representation in two political organisations, the Drawidian Progressive Movement and the Dravida Kazhagam Mumettra. However, both groups were paralysed by their dispute over identity establishing celebrations. Nevertheless, in the late 1970s, the Tamil language movement again found momentum as it now no longer emphasised Tamil as a distinct cultural entity, but rather as a contribution to the South Indian multicultural society of Singapore and Malaya. Of course, the sole claim for representation through the agitators for Tamil enraged the Panjabis and Sindis as well as the Malayalam speakers.[131] At this point, the heterogeneity of the South Asian immigrant groups in Singapore and Malaya can again be seen in various ways.

Ceylon/Sri Lanka

A distinction is usually made in the scientific and political literature on Ceylon/Sri Lanka between the immigration of South Indian Tamil merchants, traders, monks, priests and peasant settlers who permanently settled in the north and east of the island in the tenth to thirteenth centuries and the immigration of poor, job-seeking Tamils who migrated as temporary labourers on the coffee and later tea plantations in the highlands around Kandy from the 1820s. However, such a distinction is no longer justifiable. Instead a permanent circulation of working people, merchants, traders and monks from South India to Ceylon/ Lanka organised through the *kangany* system and funded by the South Indian Chettiyar traders-cum-bankers existed long before the development of the British plantation economy of the nineteenth century.[132]

Seasonal South Indian workers were recruited as early as the 1820s and 1830s to provide the labour force for the burgeoning demand for coffee; however, for the most part, the coffee harvest was carried out by the local village population.[133] Yet, once the plantation economy had been converted from coffee to tea in the 1880s, the local labour force was no longer sufficient to manage the year-round crop harvest of tea (in contrast to seasonal coffee harvest) which sparked intensive discussions between the British planters and the Ceylonese colonial government around the provision of additional recruitment of labour from South India. Nevertheless, the geographic proximity of the island to India made government control with regard to human traffic all but impossible. Furthermore, the long trading relationships as well as the established migration routes resulted in the influx of labourers being regulated almost by itself, making state help superfluous at this point.

It was the British plantation owners, not the colonial state, that seized the *kangany* system and invested funds to recruit plantation labourers. Economic liberals argued for a strict restraint of the state and urged for the purely private organisation of labour recruitment through the *kanganies*. Against this background, the Ceylonese colonial government initially saw no need to interfere with the recruitment of labourers, in contrast to the kuli recruitment in British India. Only one Ordinance from 1841 governed employment relationships and became known as the Master and Servant Law. Further restrictions were introduced in 1865 and 1889 which, among other things, criminalised the breach of labour contracts as had also been done in the kuli legislation in British India.[134]

The uncontrolled recruitment by the *kanganies* ultimately triggered the high annual number of migrant workers. Due to the lack of supplies available in Ceylon on the journey to the highlands – a problem the colonial government, the recruiters and planters did little to resolve – an extremely high mortality rate resulted among migrants. Only now did the British colonial government see the need to regulate the immigration in Ceylon in order to bring the humanitarian disaster which regularly affected those on the routes up and down the mountains under control with the establishment of services such as rest areas, wells and hospitals.[135] The medical care of the circulating migrants on the plantations was to be ensured by hospitals that were to be built in the vicinity. However, these institutions quickly developed into hospices as they were either still too far removed from the plantation or labourers were usually brought there too late to offer effective medical assistance and as a result were often avoided.[136]

According to official estimates nearly three million South Indians, mostly Tamils, migrated to Ceylon between 1839 and 1886 whilst only 2.2 million left the island. The difference can be explained by the number of those who had entered into multi-year contracts, had settled permanently or died on the plantations or on the hike to their place of work.[137] As in previous centuries, merchants, shopkeepers and boatmen also came to the island adding to the number of migrants for the plantations. As immigration became regulated between the colonial governments of British India and Ceylon, the number of immigrants decreased continuously from 1922. In 1924, 154,000 people had migrated to Ceylon with government support; by 1930 this number had dropped to 91,000. Meanwhile the figures of return migration began to rise from 46,000 to 101,000 people. In the same time period non-subsidised immigration increased from 88,000 to 133,000 people. In the first three years of the Great Depression alone (1930 to 1933) nearly 460,000 Tamils left the island.[138]

Just as in Malaya, the question of repatriation surfaced in the aftermath of the Great Depression. In 1938, government-sponsored recruitment was stopped and further immigration was prohibited. Shortly after, the first violent uprisings of Tamil labourers against this policy were recorded and were led by the *kanganies*. The Second World War interrupted any manifestations of these tense social relations, but the independence of Ceylon in 1948 saw them vehemently surface once again. The unsettled question of national affiliation of the South Indian plantation workers also led to bilateral conflicts between the new nation-states in which Ceylon insisted on the repatriation of Highland Tamils whilst the Indian Union had no desire to bear the financial and social costs of such action. Government initiatives led to an agreement in 1964 to award the remaining 975,000 "stateless" people Ceylonese (300,000) and Indian (525,000) citizenship. The remainder were to be negotiated at a later date which only occurred in 1983 following further violent clashes.

According to the population census of 1981, over 800,000 Tamils of South Indian origin lived in Lanka, a figure that represents 5.6 per cent of the total population. By 1989, some of the Tamils had decided to return voluntarily.[139] At the same time, the existing migration between the two countries came to a standstill. The forced repatriation exacerbated the question of identity for the South Indian tea pickers, some of whom were fourth generation decendants of the initial migrants. As such they were just as foreign in their native Tamil Nadu "origin", which they had never seen, as they were in this Ceylonese "enclave" which had become their home. From the 1980s Lanka has been the country of South Asia which has the largest number of circulating migrants in proportion to its population. On account of global economic shifts Lanka has now become a country of emigration in stark contrast to the centuries-long role it played as an immigration country. Most of the migrants from Lanka now circulate between the island and the Gulf States. Today, more than 1.3 million Lankans, about 7 per cent of the population, either migrate temporarily or have permanently emigrated. In addition to the Gulf States, preferred destinations of emigration include the United States, Canada, Great Britain and Germany.[140]

Burma

After the annexation of Lower Burma in 1852, the British encouraged the systematic expansion of the Irrawaddy Delta as an area for cultivating rice which was destined for export. In 1856–7 a total area of 662,000 acres was recorded as arable land, of which 616,000 acres were under rice cultivation. This area grew to over 6 million acres by 1935 from a total agricultural area of 8.7 million acres. Export volumes of rice also increased from 162,000 tonnes in 1855 to over two million tonnes in 1905–06. The main importers of rice were found in Colombo, London, Liverpool, Hamburg and Bremen. Such economic data reflect the region's demographic development. In 1850 it is estimated that about one million people lived in the delta region; however, in the period of 1881 to 1901 alone, the population of Lower Burma increased from 2.6 million to 4.1 million. Between 1872 and 1931 the Indian population grew from 136,500 to nearly 850,000, representing about 11 per cent of the total population. During the same period the number of kulis throughout Burma increased from 136,500 to just over one million, evidence of the fact that the vast majority of kulis worked in the delta region.[141]

Two reasons can be identified for this development. On the one hand, the colonial state's economic development strengthened internal migration of Burmese from the Dry Zone in Upper Burma to the Delta region. On the other hand, in the period 1852 to 1937 an estimated 2.6 million, mostly South Indian kuli men, immigrated to Burma after having been shipped from Madras. Most kulis came from the well-known recruitment areas of South India from where 60 per cent of all migrants originated. Approximately 25 per cent came from Bengal and were usually shipped from Calcutta.[142] The kulis worked in Burma for an average of between one and four years and were concentrated in and around the major cities of Burma, Yangon, Mulmein and Bassein. About a quarter of all circulating kulis settled permanently there. Yangon became a particularly Indian city as already in 1901 about 50 per cent of its population came from British India (however, only in 1936 did Burma become a separate colony and was, until then, a province of British India).[143]

Recruitment was based on the *maistry* system in which the recruiter acted as an intermediary and took over the recruitment process, then handing over to the labour contractor. The latter was only responsible for the transport and allocations of the future workplaces. The kulis remained under the *maistries'* supervision whose recruitment methods, over the course of decades, developed in a multi-layered system, which was hardly controllable by the government and employers.[144] In comparison to the *kangany* system, the *maistries* in the *maistry* system worked at their own expense and risk whilst the *kanganies* were often controlled by government agencies and private institutions. A commonality between both recruitment agencies is that they took on relatively powerful and influential positions as intermediaries.

The high migration numbers refer to the appeal that emanated from the Burmese labour market. In contrast to the domestic and overseas plantations, kulis were able to accept work here without having to previously enter into contractual commitments. Furthermore, employment opportunities were much more diverse as they were able to find work not merely as harvest labourers but also as port and industrial workers. Wages were also better in comparison to both other plantations as well as in relation to the Indian labour market. The transfer of savings to British India is recorded to have been between 40 and 80 per cent of the salary which equated to ₹30 million annually in the 1930s. Members of Chettiyar companies acted as agents in the financial affairs of the kulis by making loans available to them and allocating permanent jobs to those who wanted to settle permanently. Some immigrants succeeded, not least through the Chettiyar financial aid, in purchasing property in the delta region. In this way, by 1930 just 2 per cent of the population (former kulis) of Lower Burma owned almost 10 per cent of the agricultural area of the region. The Chettiyar also offered assistance in the commercial and artisanal sectors, although this was far from the extent of support they had shown in the agricultural sector.

The economic and social advancement was brought to an end following the drastic decline in agricultural prices during the Great Depression. Burgeoning social tensions between Burmese and Indians resulted in anti-Indian agitations, which targeted the "Indian exploitation" and the "Indian immigration problem". The first bloody conflicts between Burmese and Indians came in the late 1920s and culminated in the 1930s in prolonged street battles between the two population groups which the British were unable to bring under control in the following years. It was not until the Japanese invasion of Burma in

1942 that the British colonial elite left the country with some 400,000 Indian settlers fleeing the country behind them.[145]

Migrants, twice migrants, guest workers

The end of the official recruitment of indentured labourers from British India in 1923 did not terminate contract labour. On the contrary, the highest migration and circulation figures were recorded in 1936. It was only after the Second World War and the independence of British India that the kuli system definitively came to an end. Until then the INC felt responsible for the fate of the expatriate Indians and saw itself as their representative. This also explains its commitment to the abolition of indentured labour during the First World War. This is in stark contrast to the policy adopted in 1947 by Nehru's Congress Party government which not only excluded the issue of overseas Indians totally from Indian foreign and domestic policy, but actively encouraged expatriates to integrate into their host societies. Only legislation in the Indian Union in 1973 focused on the expatriate Indians in which, as with the Foreign Exchange Act, the question of foreign remittances was to be clarified. It classified the then guest workers in the Gulf States as well as Indians living in Britain and elsewhere as Non-Resident Indians (NRI). In the 1980s a number of different names appeared for these expatriate Indian such as "Indians Abroad" and "People of Indian Origin" (PIO). Since 1991, the Government of India has accepted all such terms indiscriminately, with the result that, even in the scientific literature, the NRI and PIO has since been used synonymously.[146]

After 1947 the expatriate Indians were something of a lost generation to whom the new nation-state had cut off any legal connections. Despite this, the migration of people from all countries of South Asia continued unabated. This was partly on account of the post-colonial situation that led to the aforementioned expulsion of Indians from the young nation-states of East Africa. Some Indians who had come to East Africa in their youth as railroad workers were forced to leave the country in later life, thus making them so-called twice-migrants. At the same time any children of these migrants who had been born in these East African countries had to leave, forcing them into their first migratory experience. Destination countries of these migrants were Great Britain, followed by Canada and the United States. New emigrants from South Asian countries joined these aforementioned migrants in the countries above and this increased their numbers further. Furthermore, the so-called oil crisis of 1973 saw the Gulf States' wealth grow rapidly, coupled with the rapid growth of the construction sector which significantly increased the recruitment of guest workers from South Asian countries.

Great Britain

The first migrants arrived in Europe and particularly Great Britain in the 1950s and 1960s.[147] Three types of migrants can be distinguished therein.

First were the "trader" migrants who settled as peddlers in the larger cities of London, Manchester, Birmingham, Leeds and Newcastle, most of whom came from the Canal Colonies of Pakistan's Panjab. The second group was composed of students, who often remained in Great Britain after their education, though some returned to their home countries. The third group was made up of the "worker" migrants who only arrived after the previous two groups were already well established. In cities such as Manchester, migrants found work as peddlers and small shopkeepers as well as in the public transport services. On the one hand they found and occupied economic niches and on the other they filled the gaps in the labour market which had become unattractive for British employees and workers on account of the gradually expanding economies of post-war employment and the better terms this offered workers.[148]

The mostly male immigrants initially shared cheap accommodation, bringing their family members over to join them once they had established themselves. Pakistanis developed a special kind of network as they focused on established forms of giving with the circle of friends and confidants which was now extended so that economic ties could be strengthened. In this way communities gradually emerged based on division of wages and salaries for the joint financing of housing and food. In the long term this formed the foundation for self-regulatory, interest-free loans, which ultimately led to the economic success of many Pakistanis. Moreover, communities emerged that were based on local origin as well as on Muslim identity and developing a decidedly Pakistani identity that can be understood as a patchwork of different communities.[149]

At the beginning of the 1960s the first secondary migrants from the Caribbean and East Africa appeared in Great Britain and Canada. Most of these migrants were able to migrate to Great Britain on account of their dual nationality which had been provided for by the post-colonial nation-states.[150] In addition to the initially peasant Jat group, the most prominent among these migrants were the small-town artisans from Ramgarhia who were classified as Sikh immigrants and faced the same experience as twice-migrants coming to Britain from British India via East Africa.[151] At the same time they represented a transnational urban–urban migration trend. In contrast to the temporary first-time immigrants to Britain in the 1960s and 1970s and their regular visits home, or regular visits from relatives to Great Britain, these twice-migrants were determined to settle permanently following their immigration.[152]

These Sikh and Gujarati twice-migrants were much more conservative, if not more traditionalist, than the first wave of migrants from the South Asian subcontinent. This phenomenon may be related to the fact that twice-migrants often migrated in complete family groups, whilst first-time immigrants exhibited the more typical pattern of individual migration with the possibility of future reunification of families. Whilst the first-time migrants were initially forced into poorly paid jobs with low social prestige, the twice-migrants had the advantage of being able to use their previously acquired knowledge again in a familiar urban environment. This also resulted in a different pattern of settlement.

Instead of spatial separation, immigrants dispersed in the city quarters, settling mostly in areas which were already dominated by migrants from diverse countries.[153]

As some women in the second generation of immigrants had gained independent access to economic resources, hitherto established and defined gender roles began to be changed. This often led to extreme tensions within Sikh families.[154] Often attitudes shown in factories and offices changed the structures of the old, and the formation of new identities. For example, Jats usually found work in industrial businesses whilst Ramgarhias were mainly employed as offices workers. Meanwhile, identities of class and caste, as they existed in India and Pakistan, were given a new context in the British social and working environment. The consequence of this was that migrants' own perceptions of the new environment led to a sharper formation of class along old and current lines whilst constructions based on projected differences emerged and still do so.[155]

On the other hand, the events of 1984 regarding the storming of the Golden Temple in Amritsar, the assassination of Indira Gandhi by her Sikh bodyguard and the subsequent pogrom-like riots against Sikhs in Delhi have led to British Sikhs becoming part of a Sikh diaspora. In part, this community has become more aware of its identity, including the invention of new traditions such as the increasing trend that orange turbans are worn by all Sikh groups.[156] In this respect, the question of the constructed realities and imagined identities is entirely justified. Related to this is also the issue of the actual existence of a Sikh diaspora. To be Sikh, especially as the displaced victims of British India's partition dividing the Panjab Province home of most Sikhs, is to be inextricably linked with the history of "Sikhism". Yet "Sikhism" also consists of externally constructed identities such as the martial and loyal race of British India as well as the internally imagined community through the rediscovery of the Gurus' writings and teachings in Britain and Canada.[157] Accordingly, the British colonial state, the independent Indian state and the British state provided the basis for such a heightened awareness of a separate communal and, in short, diasporic identity.[158]

Economic globalisation starting in the 1970s brought with it worldwide distortions within the rapidly globalising labour market as well as the formation of new identities among migrants. One such example is the textile sector. After the Second World War, the rise in wages in the textile production of the Western industrialised nations gave the recently decolonised countries a significant competitive advantage on account of their cheap and abundant labour supply. This prompted the industry into a global regulation of the textile market. The Multi-Fibre Arrangement of 1974 finally took into account quotas concerning the import of textiles from low-wage countries. Subsequently, textile producers then began to search for countries that did not fall under such regulation. The newly independent Bangladesh became the target of many international investors. In 1976 just a handful of textile factories existed in Bangladesh; by 1985 this had increased to more than 700 in Dhaka and Chittagong. It is estimated that this has created up to 250,000 new jobs, which were predominately filled by young, unmarried women. During the same period, the textile market collapsed in Great Britain resulting in a loss of a third of the textile workers, directly affecting Bangladeshi immigrant women in this cheap labour sector.[159]

The popular Orientalist stereotype held by international investors of the hardworking, willing and humble worker in turn helped to mobilise young women in Bangladesh. Most originated from the same few districts, particularly from Sylhet to the east of the country. However, the Commonwealth Immigration Bill of 1962 and 1968 with its stricter immigration rules meant that the influx of immigrants gradually dried up. Since this regulation did not apply to those already established immigrants, Bangladeshis were able to bring their families. This explains their concentration on the East Bengal districts and villages. In London, men mostly worked in restaurants or set up their own restaurants. Meanwhile women began to work from home for the textile sector as work processes were increasingly outsourced to these cheap production sites. The boom in this sector can be seen in the figure from 1981 for London where 29,000 officially registered "formal" jobs in the textile sector were recorded which were supplemented by 40,000 "informal" workers who operated at home.[160]

According to the last Census of England and Wales in 2011, the number of Indian immigrants in Great Britain was recorded to be over 1.4 million persons. In the meantime, the number of immigrants from Pakistan had also grown from about 10,000 in 1951 to almost 1.2 million in 2011. According to the same figures, the number of Bangladeshis equalled just fewer than 450,000 representing an increase from 1981, ten years after the country's independence from Pakistan, from just 64,500.[161] The information derived from the Census is based on minorities ascribing themselves to certain ethnic groups from their own perceptions and cultural backgrounds. As such, these figures deviate significantly from those of the Indian Ministry of Overseas Indians, as will be seen at the end of this chapter. This is partly due to the fact that the Ministry's figures are not based on the self-ascription of immigrants, but rather depend on the Ministry's own understanding of emigrants, NRIs and PIOs. In this attribution of constructed identity more Indians can be seen as being part of the global Indian diaspora.

Canada

Although just 5,800 Indians lived in Canada in 1908, the Canadian Government nevertheless saw it necessary to legally prevent their further influx. This was done with success as in 1941 only 1,465 Indians lived in Canada. Only after the last racial immigration laws were abolished in 1970 did the immigration of Indians begin to rise again. In 1971 alone their number increased from just a few thousand to more than 67,000.[162] Canada was a particularly popular destination among second-migrants so that by 1980 the some 130,000 Sikhs from East Africa and the nearly 100,000 immigrants from the Caribbean formed the largest groups of Indian immigrants in the country. Meanwhile, approximately

700,000 Indians live in Canada. Three-quarters of all immigrants secured good academic and technical training making their transition to careers relatively seamless.[163] On account of the timescale involved in this immigration, two phases of migration can be distinguished with 1970 as the point of division.

In the first phase, the Sikhs who had mainly settled in British Columbia and in Vancouver became almost completely isolated. This led to the situation that they sometimes replicated their social and family structures in Canada as they had existed in the Panjab so that Sikh communities in Canada often became known as a "Little Panjab".[164] Since the Sikhs primarily found employment in the woodworking industry due to discriminatory legislation they were quickly categorised and stereotyped as manual workers within Canadian society. Most Sikhs who were part of the second phase of immigration had a good education, and the gradual abolishment of discriminatory laws gave them access to middle-class jobs. Of the 350,000 Indians living in Canada in late 1987, including the descendants of immigrants from British India, 115,000, or 33 per cent, were Sikhs. In British Columbia, Sikhs made up 50 per cent of the resident Indian population.[165]

In contrast both to the situation in Great Britain and to the first phase of immigration to Canada, Sikhs were no longer pushed into economic niches. As such, most Canadians hardly noticed Sikhs as a special immigrant group. However, the increasing competition in the Canadian labour market led to an increase in discriminatory statements against Indians in the 1970s and 1980s. The Sikhs showed no resistance to this discrimination. Instead they established trans-national networks to other Sikh communities that were often aligned with religious institutions. Such trans-national networks included organisations such as the World Sikh Organisation, founded in 1984, and International Sikh Youth Federation which were making local Hindu communities aware of their own identity in Canada, the United States and Great Britain.[166] This fact is evident in the literature produced by Sikhs about their own identity.[167]

The attempt to establish a "national" pan-Indian representation in Canada failed. In reaction to the foundation of the National Association of Canadians of Origin in India (NACOI), the Sikhs refused to be subsumed into a generic organisation of Indian immigrants by forming the Shiromani Akali Dal of Canada. Demonstratively they answered the call of the Panjab Sikh nationalists to form an autonomous Khalistan Sikh state before the Indian events of 1984.[168] At the same time a proliferation of Hindutva activities and the dissemination of Indian nationalism among the Indians in Canada can be observed. In addition to the existing reorientation of the Sikh community-diaspora to the regions of their Panjab origin and their radicalisation in Canada, a valorisation now also took place among the Indian immigrants by national and religious organisations of the Indian "mother country", in particular from the VHP and RSS, in which the Indian diaspora was allegedly the bearer of the true, and at the same time vulnerable, Hinduism.[169]

United States of America

The first emigrants from British India arrived in the United States after 1820 and by 1900 almost 700 migrants had arrived in the country. As the number of Indian immigrants increased to over 1,000 by 1907, the American Association of Labour took the initiative to prevent any further immigration of Indians to the country to save the American people from being swept away in a "tide of turbans". Apart from such exaggerations and prejudice that Indians were supposedly the least efficient workers, Indian immigrants generally accepted the lowest wages. Not without reason, the American public feared that the overall level of wages would be suppressed on account of the Asian and particularly Indian immigrants. The Barred Zone Act of 1917 and the Asian Exclusion Act of 1924 prohibited the immigration of people of Asian origin with the result that the number of resident "Indians" in the United States declined constantly until the 1940s.[170]

After several unsuccessful campaigns this finally changed in 1946 as the immigration law for Indians was liberalised following the crucial agitation furthered by a certain "J.J." Singh. Thereafter until 1965 some 7,000 people migrated to the United States from the Indian Union, including an increasing number of women. The previous lack of Indian women had led to many Indians, who settled as farmers and had acquired land, to marry Hispanic women of mostly Mexican-American farmer family origins. Due to the acute shortage of skilled labour and specialised staff in 1965, immigration laws were partially abolished under the premise of "occupational immigration" which served to increase the total number of immigrants to 75,000 in 1970. A decade later, nearly 400,000 Indians lived in the United States during which time in the period of 1972–6 the number of women exceeded that of men.[171]

This issue also marks a crucial difference relating the immigration patterns of Indians into Britain. Whilst in Britain legal restrictions sidelined identity formation and fostered a certain ghettoisation, resulting in the stark isolation of immigrants from South Asian countries by the population surrounding them, the United States's special "way of life" with its better income and generous family policies was (and remains) more attractive for South Asians and their dispersion in American society. This does not mean that this has not led to the formation of communities; in fact quite the opposite is true. In New York alone, Indians succeeded in organising themselves over the years into more than 100 associations of different kinds. Immigrants from India quickly learned the benefits of a pluralistic society as they were able to use their status as minorities in pressure groups to pursue their own specific goals.[172]

According to US Census records from 1990, some 94,000 Indians lived in New York. A closer examination of the behaviour of South Asian immigration to the United States shows that New York as an urban area is seen as a type of mirror of the Indian communities in the United States. In New York, the settlement behaviour of Indians has shifted both geographically and demographically from Manhattan to Queens since the 1980s. Together with other

Asians, Africans and Hispanics, they have formed the so-called "majority minority". Queens offered first-time migrants direct access to the public transport network system which is important for economic progress; meanwhile an infrastructure that is tailored to the needs of South Asian immigrants has developed. National barriers have fallen as shops and companies advertise Indo-Pak-Bangla products reaffirming Queens' popularity as the first point of contact for South Asians.

Aside from the religious differences that are so obvious from the number of mandirs and mosques, class differences remain visible within the South Asian communities as middle and upper classes dominate the classical Indian cultures and pan-Indian activities whilst the lower classes take part more in popular festivals such as the Temple Car Festival and India Day Parade. Additionally cross-class events held in the public sphere also exist which includes the festival of Diwali, for example.[173] Furthermore, in more private spheres Indian movie and cooking nights also bring people together. It is the development of this individual cultural life which characterises the Indian communities in their entirety, and which has become so sustainable in New York City that Queens is known as "Little India". This contributes to the multicultural appearance of Queens in particular and New York as a whole and is therefore not without national significance. Seen from a different perspective, however, it shows that despite all of the assimilation, let alone integration, efforts, as long as Indian communities remain exclusive on the one hand – and the vandalism of Indian private property and harassment against Indians continues on the other – a truly multicultural society will not develop.[174]

Great Britain, Canada and the United States were, in this order, the most popular countries of immigration for people from South Asian countries in the second half of the twentieth century. Between 1951 and 2001 almost 470,000 people from India alone migrated to Great Britain, 322,000 migrated to Canada and 141,000 to the United States. The peak of the migration to Great Britain was reached in the 1960s when between 15,000 and 23,000 migrants arrived annually. The United States saw a huge influx of Indian immigrants which lasted until the new millennium and grew from 10,000 immigrants in 1970 to 42,000 immigrants annually in 2001. However, when one takes into account all Indian immigrants, including the second-migrants, the figures increase enormously. According to official estimates of the Indian Government nearly 5 million registered people of Indian origin (NRI, PIO) were recorded to be living in Great Britain whilst 5.6 million were registered in Canada and 1.3 million Indian immigrants in the United States at the beginning of the twenty-first century.[175]

The reason for the growing popularity of the United States as an immigration destination is attributed to the relaxation of immigration rules for Asians, which facilitated, among other things, the reunification of family members. Furthermore, the coveted green card helped in making the United States attractive as Indians could offer the much-needed skills which the US economy demanded, creating an attractive opportunity for immigration and settlement along with their families. The IT sector in particular benefited from this fact. Canada and Australia also favoured Indians with higher education and professional standing and attracted immigrants from India.[176] In contrast, the immigration of Pakistanis and Bangladeshis has played a much less significant role. Additionally, the terror attack of 9/11, the ensuing "war on terrorism" and the Muslim-phobia it created in the United States has seen the attractiveness of the United States decline considerably as an immigration destination for people from these two countries, as well as the willingness of the US immigration authorities to allow such an influx of migrants from these states.

The Gulf States

Alongside immigration to the industrialised and post-industrialised countries of the North, the geographically closer region of the Gulf States has become increasingly more attractive as a migration destination. This has been especially true for the unskilled male workers who first migrated to work in the oil industry in the 1930s and then during a second wave of migration to the construction sector from the mid-1970s, as well as a number of women who have recently begun to migrate to this area to be employed as domestic servants. Since all contracts were limited to one year with the possibility of renewal, which was often done, the migration trends of the guest workers to the Gulf States reflect more of a case of circulation rather than migration *per se*. Workers soon formed a network that stretched across families, villages and regions in South Asia. By 1990 about two million workers had come from India alone, approximately 1.5 million had come from Pakistan, 200,000 from Bangladesh and about 70,000 from Lanka.[177] By the turn of the millennium, the number of Indian guest workers alone had increased to 3,000,000. It is of interest to note here that of this figure almost 80 per cent had come from Kerala and 50 per cent were under 35 years of age.[178]

The organisational continuity in the recruitment of workers is also noteworthy. In the 1930s, with the help of British and American oil companies, the structure of the oil industry in the Gulf States began to take shape. In order to meet the high demand for labour and the shortage of locally available workers, labourers were recruited from British India. The strong British influence in the Gulf secured the legal regulation necessary for the recruitment of workers from British India. Thus, it is not surprising that the terms of the contracts were fairly similar to those of the indentured labourers. These structural continuities meant that mostly male workers were employed in the Gulf; according to estimates, in 1950 alone almost 15,000 workers from the new states of South Asia were working here. The governments of the Gulf States showed a preference for Muslim workers, and they accounted for about 60 per cent of the total South Asian labourers and craftsmen in the region. However, the independence of British India and the establishment of Israel led to a reorientation in the recruitment of workers as they were now increasingly recruited from the Levant.[179]

A second phase of recruitment of workers began in the 1970s which saw a focus on female employees. This phase mirrors the substantial changes in global political and economic relations that took place in the mid-1970s. Among these changes was the "oil shock" which saw the price of a barrel of oil rise significantly in 1973–4, 1979 and 1981 from $3 to $34. For the Gulf States, however, the price increases of the 1970s did not represent a "shock", but rather were accompanied by a "boom" which powered infrastructure development in their countries. On account of the chronic local labour shortages, they therefore had to recruit workers from other countries.[180] Initially these vacancies were offered again to the Muslim regions of South Asian states, where the Liberation War of Bangladesh in 1971 had resulted in the fact that Pakistan now increasingly turned westward, at least politically, to the Gulf region. This was evident in the deployment of 10,000 troops to Saudi Arabia. Conversely, Pakistan now temporarily became the main beneficiary of financial and material assistance from Arab countries, which was made possible thanks to the drastic increase in oil prices.[181]

The number of South Asian migrant workers rose continuously until it reached its peak in 1983 when nearly 221,000 workers from India came to the Gulf region, 128,000 came from Pakistan and a further 60,000 from Bangladesh. At the same time temporary workers were recruited from Southeast Asia; however, their number hardly increased.[182] In order to exclude immigration from the outset, labourers were attributed the status of guest workers whilst any similarities to the colonial kulis were deliberately concealed. However, similarities and parallels cannot be denied between these guest workers and the former indentured labourers. Like the indentured labourers, guest workers also received a temporary contract, during which they were subjected to a rigid labour regime with strict working hours, work performance and enclosed living areas.[183] It was against these poor working conditions and discrimination against other workers, and in particular the level of wages, that demonstrations began in 1974 among the South Asian guest workers in Bahrain, followed by unrest in Saudi Arabia in 1976 and finally, a year later, in Dubai.

In reaction to this unrest, the governments in the Gulf States increasingly recruited workers from East Asia, whose working conditions were regulated even more strictly. South Koreans were specifically recruited as temporary workers and the contract packages that resulted between the governments of the Gulf States and the Korean entrepreneurs became closely intertwined. The continuing demand for labour was thus met by the "disciplined" circulation of workers. For similar reasons to the influx of Korean workers, the number of Filipino emigrants has also soared whilst those of South Asian origin has been in constant decline.[184] Nevertheless, the number of South Asian second-migrants has increased within the Gulf States since the 1980s. The most popular countries for these migrants are Jordan, Oman and the United Arab Emirates where not only can they find work as unskilled labourers, but also increasingly in permanent positions as teachers and nurses.[185]

The recruitment was organised through private recruitment agencies which were supervised by state institutions in Pakistan and initially also in Bangladesh. Agencies attempted to respond to the specific requests for specific workers that ranged from unskilled and skilled workers to mid-level staff and academics and to closed contracts with detailed agreements on working hours and benefits, wage and salary for a period exceeding the officially stipulated one year to sometimes two and even up to five years. Soon well-known patterns of informal recruitment of former indentured labourers developed out of this official system of recruitment as workers were permitted periods of home leave or returned home indefinitely.[186] The same is also observed for the circulation of workers from India, Bangladesh and Lanka. In many cases, social networks provide(d) the initial information whilst the final implementation of migration, such as arranging visas, tickets and choosing the job was and still is arranged by private recruiting agencies.[187]

Meanwhile, a two-class system among South Asian circulating workers has emerged with working-class immigrants comprising unskilled, semi-skilled and skilled workers on the one hand and the middle-class professional immigrants such as engineers, doctors, bankers, architects, lawyers and teachers on the other. The latter have formed clubs and schools as well as operating hotels and restaurants. According to figures from the year 2000 the ratio between the two groups was roughly two-thirds workers to one-third professionals, showing that depictions of a purely "worker regime" is far from accurate. However, the strict immigration regime in the Gulf States ensures that there will be little, or no, integration in the local societies as migrants are only integrated into the economic structures, not social structures. The policy in relation to the guest workers is one of separation and segregation, not integration and assimilation. For this reason social contact between Arabs and South Asians was limited from the outset and has not been welcomed since.[188] Meanwhile, the high death toll on the building sites for the football World Cup in Qatar in 2022 has brought the treatment of South Asian guest workers to the world's attention.

As with the former indentured labour system, most Pakistani workers, as those of other South Asian origins, returned to their home country at the end of their contracts. However, on account of the barely controllable borders and the levels of unofficial migration, the number of circulating workers and immigrants is difficult to ascertain. Exact figures are only available for individual years; thus in 1984, some 100,500 immigrants are recorded to have entered the region whilst 94,000 left.[189] Due to the relatively good wages in the Gulf States and the high savings rate, the impact on the mobility of the rural–rural societies was often considerable. The relative wealth of the circulating workers sparked a building boom that was either focused on the restoration or improvement of the old buildings or in the construction of new real estate. This alone accounted for 44 per cent of all real estate in the 1970s. This influx of capital not only changed the appearance of villages; the face of some urban suburbs also changed considerably. Agricultural production methods also seem to have been improved, although these failed to penetrate deep enough into the rural society to initiate substantial structural change.[190]

During and after their time in the Gulf States, a noticeable increase in workers' and employees' consumption rates were recorded, especially in the field of electronics. In some regions of Pakistan, as in the Pashtun region, the rate of education rose significantly, especially in the case of young girls. Changes in health through better diets and health care can also be observed. With this growing prosperity, the position of women in the family and village communities also changed. During the long absence of their husbands, women were forced to take over the responsibility for the house and land and make decisions for themselves. It was a role that they would not give up readily when their husbands returned. This growing self-understanding was expressed in a new self-confidence, as female farmers were now seen more often in colourful and more refined clothes that had either been sent from the Gulf or bought at home. Such changes make it easy to understand how the potential for family and social conflict increased significantly.[191]

Similar phenomena can also be observed in the regional migration trends in South India, where female workers circulated between villages and cities causing anger on account of their newly purchased expensive cosmetics. Social tensions occurred in the same region where the (untouchable) *dalits*, whose women and men were forced by the *brahmans* to cover themselves with just a loin cloth until the 1930s, were now in the position to buy flamboyant clothing with the money they had earned on urban construction sites of industrial enterprises and thus provoked the population in the countryside.[192] In the same way the poor Gulf migrants from Kerala in southern India – from where about 50 per cent of all Indian workers in the Gulf originate – became the thorn in the side of the elite as they used public space to demonstrate their wealth, thereby causing the traditionalists to reassess the old morals and values.[193]

The last example shows that even opposing "orthodox" processes of self-assurance were introduced which were of course just as contemporary and innovative as the "progressive" provocateurs. So it was that poor Muslim women from Lanka would work in the Gulf States as maids and take on the social habits of the middle class, including such orthodox forms of Islam as *pardah* and Arab clothing styles that they then took with them back to their homes as they held these forms as "modern" in the sense of the times.[194] It is, however, inappropriate to refer to these women as active agents of Islamisation[195] and assign them the role of potential terrorist mothers as current global security discourse does. Similar to the Lankan maids, Muslim seamen and ship-owners from Gujarat adapted new, yet orthodox forms of Islam distancing themselves from their local worship of saints and shrines which was now regarded as backward.[196]

From the 1970s Lanka rapidly transformed itself from an "importing" country to an "exporting" country of circulating workers. What is striking within this development is the high proportion of women who were employed as housekeepers. From 1979 figures of female emigration increased rapidly from 47 per cent to 52 per cent in 1981 and finally to 79 per cent of all circulating workers from Lanka in 1991.[197] The high proportion of female circulants changed the domestic and social status of women, particularly in the villages of Lanka. Just as Pakistani women were forced to learn (self) responsibility in the absence of their husbands, the Lankan women returning from abroad now took over negotiations with banks, carried out financial transactions and completed administrative procedures. The impact that this had on family structures varied hugely. Some men could not accept or cope with the growth of competence of their wives and insisted on the old "rights". Often such conflicts saw families disintegrate and separate. On the other hand, it can also be observed that these initial conflicts created greater cohesion, especially in circulating families.[198]

Generalisations about the impact of migration and circulation on individuals, families, clans, villages and regions are not possible. The above examples show only trends which led to different results at different times and in different localities.[199] In as far as an actual increase in the financial resources is concerned, this induced an immediate improvement of living conditions among the immigrant workers. Such improvements included diet, land acquisition, house expansion, improvement or construction and health care, and was followed by electronic equipment, education and clothing. However, only sporadic statements can be made about the internal changes of a family unit. Nevertheless, the examples show the dimensions which the changes within a circulatory working regime can play when additional financial resources are available. The basis for these changes was, and still is, remittances which have become the focus of attention in the course of the process of current globalisation.

A global Indian diaspora?

With the growing number of circulatory workers and migrants from the South Asian countries the number of remittances also grew. In the 1980s alone remittances from Bangladeshi workers overseas grew from $421 to $628 million and currently lie at over $1 billion. Data for Pakistani workers are estimated to have been $2.5 billion in the early 1980s and have exceeded the $10 billion mark in 2010.[200] Since the mid-1980s, remittances of Indian immigrants in the United States exceeded those of the workers in the Gulf States and were of the same magnitude as the Pakistani remittances. As shown above, the Foreign Exchange Act of 1973 invented and established the category of NRI, thereby facilitating remittance payments of Indians working abroad whilst the Indian Emigration Act of 1983 attempted to organise the state-controlled migration on a global scale. In 2008, India became the country with the world's highest remittances as it recorded payments equalling $52 billion. Of note is also the share of remittances in relation to GDP which can account for up to 8 per cent in the three countries.[201]

Just as the actual number of migrants and circulatory workers can never be determined on account of unofficial and informal migration, the actual amount of remittances is also difficult to definitively determine; this, despite the fact that the South Asian states have introduced financial and technical instruments legalising remittances and thus channelling taxes. However, in doing so, payments to the treasury are bypassed. Overall, however, a "win-win" situation for the state, national economies and the private wealth of expatriates is likely to materialise. Therefore it would be wrong to view South Asian migrants who went abroad as failures, or as the helpless and flotsam of their societies, or as inherently problematic people, either on the subcontinent or wherever they settled. Migrants, i.e. mobile persons, are a dynamic part of any society as they contribute to the prosperity of the country of immigration as well as to their home country's economy.[202]

All that now remains is the question posed at the outset of the chapter as to whether an Indian or South Asian diaspora has emerged through the global migration and circulation trends. In answering this, one is first met with the dilemma of emigration itself, as on the one hand emigrants seek to forge a dedicated cultural life of their own built, among other things, on an exclusionary tradition of marriage. On the other hand, they seek to build loyal relationships with the new majority society where they find themselves and prove themselves to be good citizens. Compared to other immigrant groups, people from South Asia, and particularly Indians, show a certain selfishness that sets *a priori* limits to their assimilation. With the outgoing of the twentieth century especially, a sense of "Indianness" was spread across the breadth of the Indian emigrants, defined in Indian music, Indian films, Indian food and Indian fashion. However, it cannot be assumed that a global feeling exists among all of these emigrants as lifestyles in the various countries and their societies are far too diverse, just as the social and economic conditions of migrants.[203]

The relative isolation of the South Asian communities may also be a reason why most Indian immigrants are characterised by an increased mobility. Modern means of transport have made it increasingly easier to come together, bring scattered acquaintances, friends and relatives across the globe closer. Additionally, modern means of communication create a "virtual diaspora" between families, friends and business partners, which is formed through emails, online contacts and photos, videos, Skype and phone calls. These different forms of communication make the migrants constantly aware of their attachment to, and within, an Indian community wherever in the world they may find themselves. A lively debate about the existence of an Indian diaspora has been raging among intellectuals of Indian origin as well as Indian politicians since the beginning of the 1990s.[204] It must however first be considered whether there is a pan-Indian diaspora, or even a Hindu diaspora.[205] Nevertheless, it is unlikely that each of the various South Asian communities would constitute a distinct diaspora as in this case only the Sikh community would qualify.

Quite different is the case of the political construction and ideology of a supposedly global Indian diaspora. The origins of this category are, as seen, to be found in the NRI, to which the PIO came in the 1990s. Between 1998 and 2004 the Hindu nationalist BJP coalition government of the National Democratic Alliance significantly contributed to a sharpening of the diaspora consciousness. In 2000, the government established the High-Level Committee on the Indian Diaspora which was tasked with checking the status of NRIs and PIOs around the world. In order to align all of these Indians, the Committee organised the annual Pravasi Bharatiya Divas (Non-resident Indian Day) in 2003. The crowning act of this diaspora ideology was the establishment of a Ministry of Overseas Indian Affairs in 2004. Since then, all overseas Indians have been eligible to apply for Indian citizenship.[206]

The BJP was supported by extra-parliamentary organisations such as the RSS and the VHS in their goal to spread the ideology of the diaspora. All met to discuss the worldwide spread of Hindu values that were supported by the Hindutva ideology. An ethnic "Hinduness" now came to be combined with the cultural "Indianness" which aimed to create and increase awareness of a global Indian diaspora. According to information stated by the Ministry of Overseas Indians, this consisted of about 25 million "Indians" in 2009, whereby no distinction was made for descendants of indentured labourers in Mauritius or Trinidad, migrants in England, twice-migrants in Canada or guest workers in Saudi Arabia as they were all subsumed under this single category.[207] It should also be considered that such a construction of cultural and ethnic identity is highly problematic, as, for example, in the case of the overseas Indian Muslims. As remittance payers, they are, on the one hand, welcome citizens in building the nation, whilst on the other hand, as Muslims they are seen as potential terrorists who threaten the unity of (Hindu) India.

But such inconsistencies are common to all ideologies, especially those of a nation-state, that target the homogeneity and uniformity of a society. This is evident in the political exploitation of Indian emigration, which was still referred to in the sense of continuing post-colonial exploitation as a national "brain drain" in the 1980s, but is now seen as a global "brain bank". This diaspora ideology is partly constructed by the Indians themselves who are overseas. Thus, the participants and organisers of the First Global Convention of People of Indian Origin, which took place in 1989 in New York and which saw several hundred Indians from all over the world attend, came to the common (self) agreement that a pan-Indian identity did indeed exist.[208] However, the vast majority of overseas Indians knew very little of this category as it did not, or only marginally, affected their worlds. The potential development of the diaspora ideology is, however, not excluded as this may yet advance in the future.

Notes

1 Boogaart and Emmer 1986: 3–15.
2 Lucassen and Lucassen 1999: 9–40, esp. 9–10.
3 Amrith 2011: 2–4, 89–94,110–16.
4 Green 1999: 57–72.
5 Parnreiter 2000: 27–8.

6 Brettell and Hollifield 2000: 1–26.
7 Hart 1973: 66–82.
8 Breman 2009: 81–102.
9 Markovits, Pouchepadass and Subrahmanyam 2003: 1–22.
10 Parnreiter 2000: 28–32.
11 Ibid.: 32–6.
12 Glick Schiller, Basch and Szanton Blanc 1992: 1–24.
13 Brettell 2000: 97–135.
14 Parnreiter 2000: 36–41.
15 Cf. *Diaspora*, a journal published by Khachig Tölölyan since 1991.
16 Tölölyan 1991: 3–7, esp. 4; Dabag and Platt 1993: 130; Cohen R. 1997: 57.
17 Cohen R. 1997: 57–8.
18 Schwalgin 2000: 205–23; Safran 1991: 83–99.
19 Tölölyan 1996: 3–36.
20 Leonard 2001: 224–44; Nave 2001: 87–108.
21 Veer 1995: 1–16; Brown 2006: chs 3–5 *passim*.
22 Bates 2001; Emmer 1986a.
23 Mann 2011a: 108–33.
24 Ahuja 1999: 125–74; Haan 1994; Sen S. 1999: 21–53.
25 Carter 2002: 91–100.
26 Ratnagar 2002; Habib I. 2002.
27 Pearson M.N. 1998: 227–49; Curtin 1984: 2–3.
28 Newitt 1987: 201–23.
29 Dias Antunes 1995: 301–32; Pearson M.N. 1998: 230–1.
30 Pankhurst 1974: 453–97.
31 Jain P.C. 2003: 102–22, esp. 103; Arasaratnam 1998: 210–26; Mukund 1999.
32 Das Gupta A. 1987: 240–75; Arasaratnam 1986: 95–163; Arasaratnam 1994.
33 Broeze 1981: 43–67; Ahuja 2006: 111–41; Ahuja 2009a: 13–48.
34 Dixon 1980: 265–81; Bulley 2000: 235–6.
35 Markovits 2000: 24–6.
36 Evers 2000: 197–221; Rudner 1994.
37 Adas 1974a: 113–8; Adas 1974b: 385–401.
38 Sharma J. 2006: 429–55; Sharma J. 2009: 1287–1324.
39 Bose S. 2006: 72–121.
40 Breman and Daniel 1992: 268–95.
41 Hay and Craven 2004; Steinfeld 2001.
42 Vertovec 1992: 1.
43 McKeown 2004: 155–89.
44 Mann 2012c: 123–49.
45 Davis 1951: 99; Sandhu 1969: 373–80; Driesen 1997; Carter 1996: 22–3.
46 Carter 1996: 42–4; Jain R.K. 1993: 23–7.
47 Bose S. 2006: 76–7.
48 Mann 2011a: 108–33.
49 Carter 1995: 281–2.
50 Morris 1965: 50.
51 Carter 1995: 281–3.
52 Verma 2002: 182–203.
53 Jain R.K. 1993: 2–4.
54 Richards J.J. 1993; Siddiqi F.H. 2012.
55 Ghosh P.S. 2001: 1–27.
56 Bass 2013.
57 Banerjee, P. 2013.
58 Staubli 1994: 143–56; Yang 1989: 190–205; Pouchepadass 1990: 11–27; Bhattacharya 1996: 49–85.

59 Bates 1985: 573–92; Omvedt 1980: 185–212.
60 Gregory 1971; Gregory 1993.
61 Kumar D. 1965: 128–43.
62 Mohapatra 1985: 247–303; Bates and Carter 1993: 159–85.
63 Das Gupta R. 1992: 173–98.
64 Behal and Mohapatra 1992; Behal 2010; Varma 2006.
65 Kale 1995; Singaravélou 1990; Hoefte 1984.
66 Sarup 2004: 257–631.
67 Carter 1996: 84–7; Carter 1995; Jain K.R. 1993: 8–9, 11–12.
68 Carter 2000.
69 Emmer 1986b: 187–207.
70 Carter 1996: 37; Carter 1995: 35–76.
71 Roy T. 2008: 971–98.
72 Emmer 1986b: 189.
73 Carter 1996: 38–9, 45.
74 Heidemann 1992: *passim*.
75 Ibid.: 67–83.
76 Cf. Tinker 1974, 1976, 1977 vs Emmer 1986b: 189–90; Lal B.V. 1979: 12–39; Carter 1992.
77 Carter 1996: 42–4.
78 Lal B.V. 1979: 15–16.
79 Jain K.R. 1993: 23–7.
80 Carter 1996: 45–61, 183–227.
81 Tinker 1974: 335–66.
82 Carter and Torabully 2002: 17–53.
83 Arp 2000: 5–85, 160–197.
84 Carter and Torabully 2002: 37–44.
85 Tinker 1974: 116–9.
86 Carter 1996: 94–6; Shepherd 2002.
87 Driesen 1997.
88 Emmer 1986b: 198.
89 Beall 1990: 57–74.
90 Carter 1996: 51–2.
91 Chatterjee S. 2001: 206–23.
92 Sen S. 1999: 177–212.
93 Breman and Daniel 1992: 285–6.
94 Sen S. 1999: 212; Beall 1990: 70–3.
95 Carter and Torabully 2002: 89–106.
96 Carter 1996: 20, 44.
97 Jahangeer-Chojoo 2002: 115–126.
98 Eisenlohr 2006.
99 Carter 2002: 91–100.
100 Nave 2001: 87–108.
101 Gerbeau 1986: 209–36, esp. 223–4.
102 Singaravélou 1990: 76.
103 Ibid.: 84–87.
104 Brijlal 1989: 23–39, esp. 26.
105 Bhana 1990: 3.
106 Padayachee and Morrell 1991: 71–102; Bhana 1985: 235–63.
107 Guest 1996: 7–20, esp. 11.
108 Bradlow 1970: 38–53; Huttenback 1971: 141, 154–60.
109 Huttenback 1971; Brown and Prozesky 1996.
110 Swan 1985; Bhana 1990: 9–17.
111 Gandhi M.K. 1925.

112 Swan 1985: 10–19; Bhana 1990: 22.
113 Lemon 1990: 131–48, esp. 132.
114 Freund 1994: 11–28.
115 Mesthrie 1993: 177–202.
116 Freund 1994: 50–63.
117 Bozzoli 1993: 215–39.
118 Jain P.C. 1999: 94; Vahed 1997: 1–36, esp. 11–12.
119 Maharaj 2012: 77–95.
120 Gregory 1993: 10–15.
121 Bhattia 1973: 14–18, 43, 57; Twaddle 1990: 152–5.
122 Twaddle 2001: 109–12, 118–9.
123 Patel 1973–1974: 9–12.
124 Lall 2008: 116–9; Brown 2006: 46–8.
125 Sundaram J.K. 1993: 288–313, esp. 288–93.
126 Arasaratnam 1970: 28–9; Kaur A. 2006: 425–75.
127 Sundaram J.K. 1993: 299–301.
128 Amrith 2011: 104–7.
129 Stockwell 1992: 329–82, esp. 361–80.
130 Sandhu 2006: 785–7.
131 Mani 2006: 799–805.
132 Meyer 2003: 55–88.
133 Pebbles 2001: 30.
134 Wenzelhuemer 2007: 575–602.
135 Driesen 1997.
136 Wenzelhuemer 2007: 591–96.
137 Driesen, 1997: 22, 80, 121, 173.
138 Meyer 2003: 85; Heidemann 1992: 99–105.
139 Heidemann 1989.
140 Meyer 2003: 87–8.
141 Kaur A. 2006: 430–1.
142 Adas 1974: 85–93.
143 Ibid.: 21–54, 58, 98–101.
144 Kaur A. 2006: 434–5.
145 Ibid.: 154–65, 185–08; Adas 1998.
146 Lall 2008: 1–2.
147 Brown 2006: 40–1.
148 Werbner 1990: 331–47.
149 Werbner 1995: 213–36.
150 Twaddle 1990: 156–58.
151 Dusenbery 1989: 1–28, esp. 7.
152 Kelly 1990: 251–67.
153 Bhachu 1993: 163–83.
154 Bhachu 1988: 76–102.
155 Bhachu 1993: 171–3.
156 Ibid.: 176.
157 Ballantyne 2012.
158 Dusenbery 1995: 17–42; Cohen R. 1997: 105–14.
159 Kabeer 2000: 2–15.
160 Ibid.: 193–201, 421–2.
161 Office for National Statistics 2012.
162 Walker 2003: 66–82.
163 Jain R.K. 1993: 43–7; Narayan 2003: 25–47, esp. 26.
164 Verma 2002.
165 Buchignani and Indra 1989: 141–84, esp. 142–51.

166 Brown 2006: 163.
167 Singh B. 2001.
168 Dusenbery 1995: 32–3.
169 Lele 2003: 66–119.
170 Daniels 1994: 83–103.
171 Ibid.: 83–103; Kumar A. 2002: 167–8; Jain R.K. 1993: 35–8.
172 Jain R.K. 1993: 38–43.
173 Lessinger 1995: 56–67.
174 Khandelwal 1995: 178–96.
175 Rajan S.I. and Kumar P. 2010: 1–29, esp. 10–12.
176 Brown 2006: 54–6.
177 Gardezi 1991: 179–94.
178 Jain P.C. 2003: 105–6.
179 Secombe and Lawless 1986: 548–74.
180 Kerr B. 1990: 173–94, esp. 173–8.
181 Addleton 1992: 45–8.
182 Gardezi 1991: 179–94, esp. 189–90.
183 Secombe and Lawless 1986: 548–74; Jain P.C. 2003: 108.
184 Gardezi 1991: 189–90; Kerr B. 1990: 178.
185 Jain R.K 1993: 47–51.
186 Addelton 1992: 63–9, 82–3.
187 Oomen 2014: 17–19.
188 Jain P.C. 2003: 119–11, 116.
189 Addelton 1992: 190.
190 Gardner and Osella 2004: xi–xlviii.
191 Addelton 1992: 175.
192 Gidwani and Sivaramakrishnan 2004: 339–67.
193 Osella and Osella 2004: 109–40; Nair G. 1986: 66–109, esp. 70–5.
194 Thangarajah 2004: 141–61.
195 Gardner and Osella 2003: xviii.
196 Simpson 2004: 83–108.
197 Gamburd 2000: 35.
198 Ibid.: 148–54, 239; Gunatilleke 1986: 206–10.
199 Brown 2006, 157–9.
200 Oomen 2014: 6–14.
201 Brown 2006: 154–5; Index mundi 2013a, 2013b; Blogs.worldbank.com 2013.
202 Mallick 2010: 30–67; Brown 2006: 156–8.
203 Brown 2006: 81–93.
204 Vertovec 1991; Daniels 1994: 83–103.
205 Vertovec 2000.
206 Rajan S.I. and Kumar P. 2010: xv; Brown 2006: 159–60.
207 Rajan S.I. and Kumar P. 2010: xv.
208 Lessinger 1995: 94–5.

7 Urbanisation and industrialisation

General observations on urban history and urban development

In 2011, the urbanisation rate in India and Bangladesh reached just over 30 per cent whilst in Pakistan the figures were recorded to have been more than 40 per cent. It is estimated that by the mid-twenty-first century, more than 50 per cent of the South Asian population will live in cities. By way of comparison, the urbanisation rate in the European Union in 2011 was about 74 per cent. Despite the relatively low urbanisation, in terms of area and population most of the world's megacities are found in South Asia with the cities of Karachi, Mumbai, Delhi, Bengaluru, Chennai, Haiderabad, Kolkata and Dhaka each having more than 10 million inhabitants. The megacities, as well as some 50 other cities each with a population of over one million inhabitants, are the greatest attraction for migrants from the countryside. However, the population growth of the cities is not solely attributed to the increasing rural–urban migration, but is also due to the natural reproduction rates within the cities themselves.[1]

This uneven urban development is in part a product of the current process of globalisation with its growing global economic inequalities in the sectors of production and service. The inequalities are found at the global level just as they are at the regional or state levels and are expressions of the same dialectical process of de-territorialisation and re-territorialisation, i.e. the ongoing reorganisation of territorial, economic and social spaces.[2] Moreover, the political developments in South Asia, which have, for example, caused the rapid growth of Karachi through the immigration and settlement of several million refugees from Afghanistan during the last 20 years, are expressions of the changing global structures following the collapse of the Soviet Union in 1991 and the ongoing international "war on terrorism" initiated by the United States after 9/11 which has placed Pakistan and Afghanistan, particularly, in a continued state of crisis.[3]

Furthermore, the contemporary disparities in urban development can also be traced, in part, back to the British colonial era where from the 1830s a notable de-urbanisation can be observed which persisted, in some instances, into the twentieth century. Among other things this process contributed to the

Orientalist stereotype of India being a land of villages.[4] Rapid industrialisation and urbanisation began almost simultaneously from the second half of the nineteenth century, especially in the colonial metropolises Bombay and Calcutta.[5] Both developments are expressions of the then incipient process of globalisation with its reorganisation of space and the diversification of the division of labour. The rapid demographic growth and the appalling hygienic conditions found especially in Bombay at the end of the nineteenth century contributed to the forming of the Orientalist stereotype of the dirty and chaotic Indian city of the twentieth century that has survived until today.[6]

A first, albeit modest revision of these Orientalist perceptions came in the 1920s by virtue of the archaeological excavations in Harappa and Mohenjo Daro which unearthed something of a sensation. The excavations showed that alongside the Sumerian and Akkadian civilisations in Mesopotamia (3200–1800 BCE) the Harappan civilisation had settled in the northwest region of South Asia from about 2800 BCE. On account of its geographical expansion, the notion of a "fertile crescent" is also used to describe the Harappan civilisation in reference to the Egyptian-Mesopotamian civilisations. Cities of different sizes and functions defined this urban civilisation which was based on a network of connections between one another and further links to the cities of Central Asia and Mesopotamia. These civilisations were further characterised by a high degree of planning, the separate upper and lower town areas, a regular street grid, standardised bricks, water supply and sewerage systems, urban stores of food, and bathing facilities in private homes as well as a functional breakdown of districts into residential, commercial and administrative areas, all demonstrating a high level of organisation.[7]

In the field of urban planning, early written sources exist which document a second phase of urban development in South Asia.[8] In this context, the first theoretical text for the ideal-typical city originated from the Arthashastra, most probably written by Kautilya, around 300 BCE. According to this, cities were an expression and reflection of a cosmological order. An ideal of the hierarchy of cities and their functions has also been discovered in the excavations. As far as archaeological results show, few cities developed along these ideal lines beyond the rudimentary classification of quarters. An exception to this rule can however be found in the example of Pataliputra in which its area was organised as a parallelogram. In contrast to the early Harappan cities none of the towns here had a water supply or sewerage system.[9] Similarly massive urban development also began in Lanka in the middle of the first millennium BCE with the highlight being the development of the royal cities of Anuradhapura, Polonnaruwa and Sigiriya.[10]

In the early modern period, urban development reached its peak under the Mughals in the seventeenth century as the urbanisation rate is estimated to have reached 15 per cent. In comparison, the urbanisation rate in Europe during the same period is calculated to have reached just 10 per cent. Meanwhile, a new type of city had developed on the subcontinent which was to become known as the "Islamic city". Its main characteristics and structural

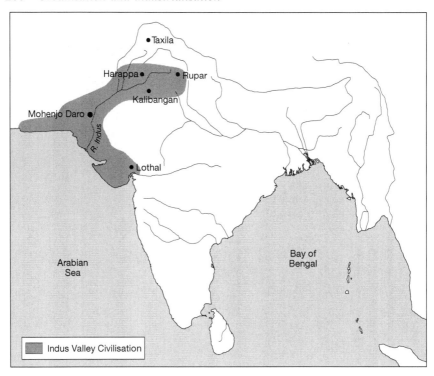

Map 7.1 South Asia's fertile crescent

features consisted of the Friday Mosque (*jama masjid*) and institutions such as the *madrassah* and the *hamam* which formed the cultural and intellectual centres of the city. Crafts and trades were sorted according to occupations in the adjacent bazaars (*suq*). The population lived in different neighbourhoods (*mohallas*) according to their faith and occupation, each of which had their own sub-centres, including mosques, mandirs and bazaars whilst a hierarchical road system linked the different parts of the city. City centres and gates were connected via main roads. From these main thoroughfares, side streets and crossroads led to each quarter as they branched out into dead-end alleys.[11]

A new phase of urban development began with the urbanisation of the nineteenth century as the expansion of industries on the periphery of cities soon attracted millions of job-seekers from the countryside to the cities within just a few decades. In England, where the effects of industrialisation had already begun to be felt at the beginning of the nineteenth century, more than half of the population was recorded to be living in cities by the middle of the century. A certain time lag can be observed in this process of urban development among the Western industrialised nations where it also sparked political action in terms of municipal organisation and town planning.[12] In South Asia, however, the British prevented almost any comparable industrialisation process with their systematic policy of protective tariffs, due to the fact that they viewed the region rather more as a supplier of raw materials and as a market for its own industrial products than an equal member of the emerging global market. Only in the core areas of cotton and jute cultivation did the British allow regionally concentrated industrialisation which had consequences for urban development in general and the urbanisation of a number of smaller cities in particular.[13]

This economic asymmetry distorted the development of the cities which can be seen in the various features of the Indian colonial city. One such fundamental characteristic of the colonial city in India, as in any other colonial territories, is its dual structure, which is reflected in the segregation of the European and Indian parts of a city. Whilst the European parts of the city could be places of diverse cultural variety, the Indian and residential areas, were, at least from the perspective of the Europeans, merely a source of labour and a supply station for food.[14] The connection to the railway network further distorted the urban development of the city as railway embankments were constructed as separating *cordons sanitaire*. Additionally, the British urban tax policies that stimulated and supported the European residential quarters whilst disproportionately neglecting the Indian quarters led to a redistribution of financial means from the lower layers of the Indian society to the upper layers of the British colonial society.[15]

Wasteful use of land by Europeans in the construction of striking administrative, office and representative buildings as well as spacious residential areas corresponded with the simultaneous compression of the residential areas in the Indian quarters of the city. This space-filling, combined with expansive architecture and urban development, has become the hallmark of the morphological changes in many South Asian cities in which the British constructed their military (cantonment) and civilian (station) settlements. This was especially noticeable in northern India, where colonial transformations continue to determine urban development. However, the large majority of the other cities in British India remained virtually untouched by these developments.[16] Thus, the dual structure of the colonial city came to legitimise colonial rule, as on the one side of the city were the clean and orderly British settlements that stood as a mark of modernity, in stark contrast to the dirty and chaotic Indian quarters on the other side which were attributed to civilisational backwardness.

Whilst attempts were made in the industrialising Western world to address the problems of urbanisation through urban planning, the first systematic investigation into the growing problems of the growing Indian cities was not conducted until the early twentieth century, by the Scottish urban sociologist Patrick Geddes, the outcome of which did not yield any concrete results.[17] This lack of professional urban planning continues to have dire consequences today in the now rapidly increasing urbanisation of South Asian cities in the wake of growing industries and commerce. City planners and urban designers continue, just as their former colonial colleagues did, to concentrate almost exclusively on cities of over 100,000 inhabitants. Only since the 1990s can a slow change in attitudes be discerned. Far more problematic, however, is the fact that town planning continues to be based, as before, on Western concepts and experiences of urbanisation, which are often meaningless or superfluous in the South Asian environment and the habits of the South Asian urban inhabitants.[18]

Overall trends in crafts and industries

In the eighteenth century the South Asian subcontinent was the coveted goal of European trading companies, as it was here that the inexpensive yet high-quality white and coloured textile products as well as spices could be bought and then resold on the European markets at high profits. The textile industry in South Asia was an economic sector in which some degree of monetisation already existed. A growing number of labourers, such as spinners, dyers and weavers, were involved in the production process and often received financial and material advances from the merchants or their agents (*gomashtas*). A differentiated labour market also existed with different forms of wage labour. However, such a labour market depended on the high degree of mobility within the population. Moreover, a certain professional flexibility also existed as working peasants and numerous *parayyars* (Pariah: untouchables) also seasonally joined the different sections of the textile industry.

The growing monetisation and commercialisation, the beginning of differentiation of the labour market and greater occupational flexibility point towards large economic and social dynamics.[19] These dynamics, however, originated without European influence. This means that South Asian societies responded to contemporary transformations and changes without external encouragement and consequently were anything but static, as is often claimed in contemporary reports and in the historiography of South Asia. The development of bazaars and *qasbas*, small country towns that were aligned to the local trade to supply the agricultural hinterland and its administration, also shows that considerable economic and social dynamics were at play in these small and medium-sized cities from the eighteenth until well into the twentieth century.[20]

Much of the textiles were not manufactured in towns, but rather in the country, leading to the scientific term "rurbanity" as rural settlements took on the urban form of production.[21] Villages regularly produced more than would be required for subsistence agricultural economics, thereby indicating involvement in a trans-regional market. The expanding textile industry and the export of textiles to Southeast Asia and Europe led to a concentration of weaving villages in Tamil Nadu. The same can also be observed in the northern region around the commercial port of Masulipatnam.[22] Whilst the villages were the places of textile production, the sale of such products took place almost exclusively in the cities. In addition to numerous inner-Indian cargo handling areas such as Jallandar in the Panjab and Varanasi (Banaras) in Hindustan, Kasimbazar and Dhaka in Bengal, and Burhanpur and Ahmedabad in western India, from the mid-eighteenth century port towns such as Hugli in Bengal, Masulipatnam and Chennai/Madras on the Coromandel Coast and Surat on the Gulf of Khambhat ensured export trade links.

Whilst one side of the textile industry began to become increasingly commercialised, the production methods of the sector remained virtually unchanged from the methods of the eighteenth century. Seen from a technological perspective, the Indian looms were far simpler than those used in contemporary European textile production. This was reflected in a lower productivity of the Indian workforce, who nevertheless were able to produce high-quality textiles from this simple equipment. The English manufacturers were only able to defend their products and be competitive against the producers in Bengal, Gujarat and Tamil Nadu through the implementation of protectionist laws.[23] South Asian weavers were unable to access more efficient looms as such significant outlays would have required capital-intensive investment that was rarely available. This resulted in differentiation in the production sector. Highly skilled weavers in the textile-rich region of Masulipatnam worked on fine and high-quality textiles in small villages with low social differentiation. At the same time, large amounts of medium-quality materials could be produced in larger settlements, where wealthy "chief-weavers" employed wage workers.[24]

The demise of a portion of the Indian textile industry in the nineteenth century has numerous causes. First, the British colonial power, after consolidating its rule following the final war against the Maratha Union in 1818, demobilised the numerous militia of local little kings in the course of its pacification actions. These local and regional rulers had been customers of various textile products for uniforms, and the collapse of this military market resulted in significant sales crises in the textile sector. The same was also true of the demand for finer fabrics for the local rulers, who, now no longer in a position of power following their disempowerment, were unable to afford the expensive luxury fabrics, thereby halting the segment's production. The decline of the small and medium-sized residential cities could not be compensated for by the rise of the British coastal cities as transit points for goods and as centres of the textile industry.[25]

While the weavers in South India were able to respond with relative flexibility to the increasing economic pressure from the British textile imports in the first half of the nineteenth century, by reducing the number of looms in operation and concentrating on the coarser types of fabric, in Bengal the textile trade became fragmented. In contrast to the South Indian textile industry, the Bengali weavers were rarely organised in guilds. In the event that the weavers in Tamil Nadu were successful in acting against the dictating conditions of production imposed upon them and defended themselves by refusing to work or emigrating collectively, Bengali textile crafts, especially in the cities of Dhaka and Murshidabad, collapsed because they had been exposed to the control of the EIC from the late eighteenth century.[26] In the cities of Gujarat, the textile industry did not suffer to the same extent from the decline in production because the producers had come to specialise in coarse cotton fabrics for the domestic market. The same can also be observed in the Panjab, where the Swadeshi Movement after 1905 contributed considerably to the increased production of domestic textiles.[27]

Finally, from the 1820s, industrially spun yarn as well as woven textiles from England began to enter the South Asian markets. Both products were not only able to be produced cheaper because of the mechanical production, but they were also able to be imported free of duty at the instigation of the English textile entrepreneurs. This combined political and economic penetration of the Indian market by the colonial power rendered the Indian producers defenceless. However, the Indian textile industry never collapsed completely. On the contrary, as mentioned above, the Indian market was especially successful in the segment of rough and simple cotton cloth produced for the rural population, as it was able to respond with flexibility and speed to the cheap imports and compete against the English competition which had instead focused on the better, globally marketable products and distributed them to the wealthier, more urban populations of South Asian countries.[28]

In addition to the textile crafts, other trades and handicrafts also existed on the subcontinent such as the production of gold thread for brocade embroidery, brass finishing, tanning and carpet weaving, each with regional points of production.[29] It can be assumed that the process of industrialisation and the growing involvement of Indian crafts in the global economy after 1869 (opening of the Suez Canal) to the beginning of the Great Depression in 1929 did not lead to major changes in the structure, organisation and technology of these sectors. Since structural transformations did not occur and were not initiated by the state and the economy until well into the post-colonial era, labour-intensive forms of production persisted at the level of proto-companies which inhibited the structural changes necessary to initiate industrialisation on the basis of rationalisation. In some instances the division of labour increased as contract and wage work also penetrated these economic sectors.[30]

Nevertheless, it would be wrong to assume a uniform development in all commercial sectors. Even within sectors different developments were common and identifiable. Some industries, such as iron and steel production (often carried out by semi-nomadic smelters), were unable to operate under the intense global pressure due to their inefficiency and high cost of production, leading to their disappearance by the beginning of the twentieth century. Others were able to survive, albeit in a weakened state, as in the example of the weavers of coarse textiles shows. Still others, such as blacksmiths, even managed to expand into niches such as the railway workshops by adapting to new technologies. Various attempts by the British to enter into the production and processing of iron in British India failed. In part, this was because of the open resistance led by the local *zamindars* against foreign industry, but also because the British entrepreneurs focused only on the colonial army and railway market rather than opening up new markets.[31]

The leather manufacturing sector shows that substantial transformations of an economic, technological and social nature could be implemented successfully. The leather industry, including numerous skilled professionals, had been located in the northern Indian villages surrounding the cities of Lakhnau and Kanpur since the beginning of the eighteenth century. After the British occupied Kanpur in 1778 and created one of the largest cantonments in India there, they transformed the city over a number of decades into a military base with supplier trades such as saddleries and cobblers. By the mid-nineteenth century it is estimated that some 300 families worked in the leather processing sector. This in turn attracted the *jati* of the *chamars*, skinners and tanners, whose settlement in the area intensified. In 1867 the British military government decided to make Kanpur one of the largest military bases and industrial sites in British India and as such cotton and leather processing plants were located in the city. However, whilst the textile industry was slow in coming, the leather industry received investment in the form of government incentives to relocate to Kanpur or was immediately established as a state enterprise.[32]

The Government Harness and Saddlery Factory was founded in 1876 and soon employed up to 2,800 workers. The private company Cooper, Allan & Co., also known as Bangla Hazari, followed in 1880 and employed some 3,000 workers who produced specially tanned leather and saddles. Finally, in 1892 the Northwest Tannery opened after additional railway lines had created new opportunities for trade capacity and the supply of raw materials such as hides and bark for tanning. Within a few years, saddles and bridles, shoes and boots were being delivered to all of the British Indian military bases along with raw products, including tanned skins that were now also exported, mainly to South Africa and China. With growing imperial involvement of the British in the world, the leather industry in Kanpur, as well as the small businesses organised in Delhi, also expanded to a total of 2,500 workers, as did those in Lakhnau, Calcutta, Madras and Maisur.[33]

The leather processing industry was transformed at the turn of the nineteenth century with the introduction of chemical tanning and dyeing processes in industrial production that was located in towns connected to the railway network.[34] As a result the villagers, often nomadic *chamars*, lost their common right to the skins of dead animals to the urban, permanent resident and were thus easier to be controlled as contract workers. Sometimes *chamars* could accumulate capital in towns by opening their own tanneries and, in a few cases, thereby creating the basis for modest economic and social advancement. The *chamar* never disappeared entirely from the villages as it was here that his economic and social base was located. Aside from this, the industrially manufactured leather products were not intended for village use, but rather for the military market meaning that the village *chamars* were almost entirely unrivalled.[35] Thus this points towards a characteristic of the industrialisation in British India which was highly export-oriented on the one hand, whilst on the other Indians continued to supply the domestic subcontinental markets not yet covered by the European companies by operating conventional methods and techniques.

Industrialisation and de-industrialisation

Until recently, South Asian economic history has focused on the topics of de-industrialisation, the development and under-development as well as the under-capitalisation of the economy and the society. The pre-colonial production conditions and social relations, that are sometimes described as either being partly or completely backward – or, in contradistinction, glorified (and romanticised) as primordial and therefore "paradisiacal" – have served as a starting point for many such studies.[36] Currently, the focus of these topics is rather more on the small industries such as the processing of leather, metal, wood, silk and wool, whose production facilities were outside the British metropolises and therefore often allow and provide more information about transformations and continuities in South Asian crafts industries.[37]

However, it is also important to consider industrialisation in British India, as it allows the impetus of developments that lasted until the end of the twentieth century. The British were very reluctant to initiate the industrialisation of India as they were concerned about the potentially uncontrollable consequences of a transfer of technology and, as a consequence, the similarly uncontrollable increase of competition. As a result, the importation and introduction of steam engines was delayed for several decades. Although initial enquiries had been made from British India at the end of the eighteenth century for the import of such engines, they were only delivered after considerable delay for various reasons. These included general reservations based on cultural and of climatic differences (such as "modern" technology does not work in South Asia/tropical countries) and were paired with prejudice ("Indians" do not understand "modern" technology), resulting in the fact that British machinists were sent to British India to oversee the introduction. As such, the transfer of know-how to the Indian society was systematically prevented.[38]

First attempts by Europeans to establish a textile industry in British India in collaboration with Indian investors in the 1820s and 1830s failed due to lack of capital, lack of equipment and repair personnel and a general inexperience in the face of strong British competition. The same was also true of the attempt to establish ironworks. Furthermore, the unwillingness of the colonial state to take over the guarantees on loans that were required for these projects proved to prevent the development further. The initially promising approaches of Dwarkanath Tagore in the 1830s and 1840s to establish banking and industrial enterprises in Bengal collapsed with the financial crisis of 1846. From then on Indian elites fled from the field of British capital investors. However, Indian capitalists did invest their capital in industrial enterprises when the British founded the textile mills in Bombay and Calcutta after the mid-nineteenth century.[39]

In 1873 four jute mills existed in Calcutta along with 1,000 looms; by the 1880s this had increased to 23 jute processing enterprises and 6,000 looms employing some 48,000 workers. In Bombay, a Maratha investor founded the first cotton mill. Between 1872 and 1878, 32 new factories were added. The

Bengali and Maratha entrepreneurs' aim was to gradually substitute the English textile imports with local products and to eventually dominate the market in the long run. Whilst this strategy seemed to work for cotton and jute production, the same does not hold true for leather processing in Kanpur or the iron and steel industry, with the exception of Jamshed Tata. A major obstacle to the industrialisation of the subcontinent was the lack of South Asian capital markets. The aforementioned under-capitalisation of industry resulted from the ongoing financial commitments that the Indian tax and revenue-payers were forced to pay to the colonial exchequer. Between 1859 and 1878 alone, almost ₹5.5 billion was remitted to the UK in the form of pension funds and dividend payments in the so-called Home Charges.[40]

After 1870, industrialisation began to progress in a few locations in British India. Production increased proportionally with the rising national income whilst the growth in value per worker and the productivity in the secondary sector (industry) increased further relative to that in the primary sector (agriculture). Judged by the production figures of cotton and jute, India, at the beginning of the nineteenth century, had become a global competitor and by the country's independence in 1947 had become the tenth largest manufacturer of consumer goods. However, on closer inspection it is obvious that this resulted in only a small per capita increase in income. Moreover, there was a general lack of mechanisation throughout the country. Thus, the rate of industrialisation in the first half of the twentieth century remained at a modest 12 per cent whilst the share of industry in the national product stood at just three per cent and the share of industrial workers in the total workforce ranked below two per cent. Despite a flourishing and partially export-oriented cotton industry, British India remained a net importer of textiles in 1939.[41]

Industrialisation was also asymmetrically implemented according to geographical factors. In the west of the subcontinent around Bombay and Ahmedabad industrial centres specialising in the processing of cotton developed, whilst jute production was centred around Calcutta in the east. From the beginning of the twentieth century iron and steel works developed around Jamshedpur, adding another industrial centre located in the "Tribal Belt" of the subcontinent's east. However, no structural connections linked these regions, meaning that any advantageous synergistic effects failed to materialise. In 1947 the two textile production regions generated two-thirds of all British Indian industrial production, a fact that must be seen as another indicator of the asymmetrical industrialisation of the colony causing long-term inequalities in the primary sector.[42]

The same disparity is also reflected in the railway network. In contrast to the industrialised countries in Europe and the United States, hardly any "locomotive effect" dissipated out from the hub of the rail network influencing the surrounding industries. Only a handful of cities in the interior of the continent were able to benefit economically from the construction of the railways, provided of course that they were located at strategic railway junctions. Moreover, the railway network usually reproduced the existing road links without expanding the country's infrastructure. Missing connecting roads to the railway stations further inhibited the efficiency of the rail system instead of modernising a communication and transport system in the contemporary British understanding which aimed at compacting space and time. Finally, the rail system also failed on account of the one-sided orientation of the rail network's development for the military and economic needs of the colonial power along the coastal metropolises to the disadvantage of the people of the country as the network ultimately generated economic and social disparities and inequalities.[43]

The industrial sector's logistical shortcomings added to the geographical disparities and the various administrative directives. There existed a lack of willingness from the British side to provide sufficient repair facilities, including replacement materials. The barely existing urban energy supply presented a constant problem, so that companies were forced to produce their own electricity. From the Indian side, a lack of willingness existed to invest in developing their own machines and training courses to develop a base of skilled workers. Not until 1888 did the Indian entrepreneurs institute a professional training centre in the form of the Victoria Jubilee Technological Institute in Bombay. However, this initiative was rather more the exception than the rule, especially since it led Bombay factories to be distinguished by Indian professionals unlike in the rest of the country where factories relied on European professionals until the twentieth century.[44]

Alongside the aforementioned urban centres that emerged in the regions of the established textile sector, smaller textile processing industry enterprises were founded in Surat, Kanpur, Nagpur, Delhi, Lahore and in Madurai during the 1860s. A number of smaller cities also benefited from the general cotton boom. Taken from a countrywide perspective, the sporadic distribution of industrial sites remained a long-negligible factor for the general Indian economy. Within a short time the British Indian textile industry exceeded the market segment demand for coarse cotton cloth that was produced from the rough South Asian cotton and began to move from the threshold of import substitution towards export-oriented production.[45] Fine cotton yarn and cotton textiles continued to originate from Great Britain. The village textile craft industries were only able to withstand the growing industrial pressure by making massive cuts in production; the cost of a meagre and troubled life under the British colonial economy.[46]

However, in a few major textile centres industrialisation progressed rapidly, the extent of which can be seen in Table 7.1 and Table 7.2. The long rows of figures show an almost uninterrupted growth in the jute processing industries in India that spans almost a century. The development began modestly with only five jute mills in Calcutta until 1873. Thereafter a wave of firms were formed in the 1880s, making it possible to rapidly conquer the British market after the Indian jute products had been sold almost exclusively to Australia, America and Egypt in the 1870s.[47]

The rows of figures cannot of course hide the fact that there was a notable difference in regional and local growth within which Bombay and Calcutta,

Table 7.1 Development of the cotton industry in India, 1875–6 to 1918–19

Years	Companies	Spindles	Looms	Labourers
1875–6	47	1,100,000	9,100	n.a.
1883–4	79	2,002,000	16,300	60,000
1893–4	142	3,650,000	31,100	130,000
1903–4	191	5,118,000	45,300	185,000
1913–14	271	6,779,000	104,200	260,000
1918–19	258	6,690,000	118,000	293,000

Source: Adapted from D. Morris (1982) 'The Growth of Large-Scale Industry to 1947', in Dharma Kumar (ed.) *The Cambridge Economic History of India. Vol 2: c. 1757–1970.* (Cambridge University Press: 1982), p. 567. © Cambridge University Press, reproduced with permission.

Table 7.2 Development of the jute industry in India, 1854–5 to 1938–9

Year	Companies	Looms	Labourers
1854–5	1	n.a.	n.a.
1868–9	5	950	n.a.
1883–4	23	6,132	47,863
1893–4	28	9,580	69,179
1903–4	38	18,400	123,869
1913–14	64	30,050	216,288
1918–19	76	40,043	275,500
1923–4	89	49,088	330,408
1928–9	95	52,409	343,868
1933–4	99	59,501	257,175
1938–9	107	67,939	295,162

Source: Adapted from D. Morris (1982) 'The Growth of Large-Scale Industry to 1947', in Dharma Kumar (ed.) *The Cambridge Economic History of India. Vol 2: c. 1757–1970.* (Cambridge University Press: 1982), p. 569. © Cambridge University Press, reproduced with permission.

as well as Ahmedabad, occupied the top positions which drove figures up. Despite this, the "success story" of Calcutta's jute industry paradigmatically highlights the forms and consequences of colonial economic relations. Factories, shipping companies and insurance companies were almost exclusively in British hands and cooperated closely with the colonial state institutions. Meanwhile, industry, capital and the state worked together in a colonial orientated constellation to ensure the transfer of maximum profits out of the country.[48]

The system of managing agencies in Calcutta formed the economic and logistical base of the colonial industrial enterprises. Initially, the European managing agent had been used on the plantations, in the mines and industrial enterprises as an administrator with comprehensive skills to run the business for the absentee owner.[49] A managing agency was permitted to offer its services to several businesses, thereby gradually obtaining a monopoly position as a management consultant. Over time successful agencies became independent, sold shares and became companies specialising in the raising of capital, the provision of expertise, modern management and specialists in specific colonial organisational forms. Thus the managing agencies offered British capital investors a service package which made their business run smoothly.

Manipulation of the company's businesses and speculation on the credit market were only part of the other side of the same coin when financial dealings offered more profit than could be gained through the agreed service package. In such situations, technical and business innovations were neglected as they required too much unnecessary time and energy for minimal returns. It is hardly surprising then that Indian agencies and capital investors also wanted to maximise their profits through cooperation with the managing agencies who in turn were dependent on the cooperation with domestic Indian merchants, bankers and industrialists. Ultimately the managing agencies became so successful and powerful in 1927 that they controlled the economy, cartel-like, without meeting any opposition from the colonial government.[50]

A watershed in British India's economic development came in 1923. Until this point British India had been opened up to free trade, which promoted the export-oriented structures and the British held, *a priori*, an advantageous situation.[51] After 1923 the protectionist colonial government promoted a few large investors in the key industries of cotton and steel. In addition, the colonial state's involvement influenced the economic development of British India, as can be seen in the decrease of public spending due to the effects of the Great Depression in the 1930s. The government showed little interest in reallocating capital from the primary sector and reinvesting it in the secondary sector during this economically and fiscally strained period. Instead, capital continued to be sunk into the Indian soil. In 1913, peasants were indebted to a total of about ₹5 billion, whilst the value of the soil was estimated to equal approximately ₹40 billion. In contrast, investment in industry was recorded at just ₹300 million.[52]

Indian-owned industries

Bombay's cotton industry is, in many ways, an exception, as for the most part its investors and factory owners were Indians. In 1924 only 11 of the 81 textile enterprises there were in European hands.[53] After 1918, the Indian industrial production grew faster than that of Britain, Germany or the United States and ranked above the world average. Whilst the effects of the Great Depression in South Asian agriculture were catastrophic (seeing a fall in prices by 50 per cent between 1929 and 1930 alone), the integrity with which the industry survived the crisis years and was still able to expand is remarkable. This was however often at the expense of the workers who were committed to increased performance at lower wages as well as the better utilisation of the machines. Due to the increased demand for textiles, numerous small businesses established themselves in the cities in the interior of the subcontinent as direct competitors to the large textile processing centres in the coastal metropolises on account of the lower food and living costs found in these smaller cities. On account of these price and wage relations, hand-spun cotton textiles also now became competitive.[54]

This regional distribution of cotton farms had dramatic consequences for Bombay, as the city was now exposed to intra-Indian production and commercial trading pressures. Between 1913–14 and 1938–9 Bombay's share of factories fell from 31.4 per cent to 17.5 per cent whilst the percentage of those employed in daily production tasks fell from 42.3 per cent to 25.7 per cent. In order to remain competitive, the industries in Bombay and Ahmedabad were forced to cut wages by up to 15 per cent.[55] Despite these drastic measures massive social conflicts could not be prevented from the steadily rising unemployment levels that were compounded further by the closing of a total of 22 of the 77 surviving cotton factories between 1929 and 1934. In the period from 1919 to 1940 eight general strikes took place in Bombay, equalling a loss of some 48 million work hours. However, the increased demand for industrial products during the Second World War eased the economic situation and allowed the country to develop from a debtor to Great Britain to the sum of £385.1 million in 1934 to a creditor of £1.3 billion by the year of independence in 1947.[56]

The asymmetric industrialisation is mirrored by the textile industry in North India and by Delhi in particular. The first factory, the Delhi Cloth and General Mills, was founded here in 1889 and was soon followed in 1893 by the Krishna Cotton Mills and New Mofussil Co., as well as the Ram Bilas Jari Mal Cotton Mills. Around the turn of the century in the Panjab almost 9,000 workers were employed and worked the 143,000 spindles in eight textile mills. By 1912 only the Delhi Cloth and General Mills remained. Furthermore, whilst the number of cotton mills in the Panjab had risen from 114 to 202 between 1904 and 1912, the number quickly fell back to 115 by 1915. The Swadeshi Movement was certainly a major reason which had led to the significant increase in business formation, but the precarious capital was the main reason that prevented the development of companies and, as a consequence of that, the overall economy from expanding in the long run. In all, this indicates the misery that befell the Indian textile industry when it lay outside the three systematically funded British enclaves.[57]

The founding of the company by Jamshed N. Tata reads as something of a success story of private Indian entrepreneurship. After careful locational site assessment and of the various industries, Tata decided to form an iron and steel plant in the form of the Tata Iron and Steel Company (TISCO) in southern Bihar.[58] Located near abundant coal seams, rich iron ore mines and reliable water supplies, Tata soon began to build both his industry and city at the beginning of the twentieth century. Within half a century, 218,000 people were living in Jamshedpur. Unlike with other Indian initiatives the British-Indian Government supported the company's undertaking by agreeing to purchase 20,000 tons of iron rails annually for a decade. Despite this government guarantee and his personal presence in London in 1906–7, Tata was unable to secure the necessary start-up capital from the London credit market. It was only with the support of Indian capital providers, who saw it as part of the Swadeshi Movement and thereby part of their patriotic duty to invest private funds in a "national" company, that Jamshed Tata was able to raise the required credit. In 1911 he had about 11,000 small investors, whilst 13 per cent of the capital came from the coffers of several Indian monarchs and four members of the Tata family had invested a further 13 per cent.[59]

The Tata Technical Institute was founded in 1921, followed by the Research and Control Laboratory in 1937, to ensure the sufficient training of the workforce whose staff soon consisted entirely of Indians. In this way Tata provided the possibility that the foreign experts and specialists within his operation could be replaced by native specialists. Of course, this does not necessarily mean that patriotic attitudes played a role in this decision, but rather that it made pure entrepreneurial calculus sense as salaries and wages of Indian professionals were often half those of their European and American counterparts. The general sales crisis in the 1920s, caused among other things by a lack of government contracts, made such savings all the more necessary along with the more effective utilisation of equipment, technical innovations and the expansion of exports of cheap pig iron to Japan, the United States and Great Britain.

Between 1923–4 and 1932–3 Tata was able to expand his share in the iron and steel market in India due to the favourable conditions of production and rising domestic Indian demand for iron and steel which rose from 17.6 per cent to 72.3 per cent. With this drastic change of consumption patterns in the 1920s, Tata developed sales strategies which aimed at the reduction of information asymmetries between the company, the end-user and the intermediary merchant. The development of a sales network based on specific consumer information enabled TISCO to cultivate an emerging demand in domestic outlets thus being able to survive after the 1920s.[60] Additionally, protective tariffs and increased government orders helped TISCO to weather the economic storms of the Great Depression – as well as the low-cost competition from Belgium and Germany – almost unscathed.[61]

In comparison to other major Indian companies TISCO took a special position concerning the recruitment of its workers. To a large extent the easy recruitment of workers and labourers was possible because of the British forest legislation. It consisted of sometimes rigid forest laws, which were introduced with the Imperial Forest Act of 1878 and the consequent disenfranchisement of local communities. As seen in Chapter 5, numerous *adivasi*s from the wooded area of Jharia (Jharkhand) fell victim to the forest legislation of 1878 and again more intensely in 1917 and they could now be easily recruited and moved to the settlement in Jamshedpur. Thus it was less about the lucrative wages and more about their poor living conditions that drove people into the arms of TISCO. Apart from this, TISCO was also provided with many skilled workers after the local iron industry collapsed and the local living conditions and social spaces had thus been destroyed. Many men found themselves as wage labourers in TISCO's blast furnaces and rolling mills.[62]

There are, of course, other interesting, if somewhat less spectacular accounts, of industrialisation, such as the Marwari trader-cum-bankers. They originated from the area of present-day Rajasthan and migrated from there to the big cities on the subcontinent, including Delhi, Lahore, Nagpur, Haiderabad, and later Bombay and Calcutta from the eighteenth century onwards. In the cities where the Marwari settled they formed separate commercial communities with a strong cultural life that endures today.[63] During the course of their migration they established family-based networks, which consisted of a conglomerate of integrated companies. According to the 1921 Census, the number of Marwari was recorded to be about 300,000, and there were around 1,000 family units. Apart from ancillary businesses such as brokers and speculators it was the "great firms" that participated in the modest industrialisation in British India. Among these was the Tarachand Ghanshymdas company, whose multifunctional roles as banker, consultant, selling and purchasing agent, large stockholder and company owner can be compared to the aforementioned managing agencies. The Bansilal Abirchand company from Bikaneer had branches in Nagpur and Indor from which it led the operations from its two cotton textile mills, 20 cotton gins and presses, and a multi-branch banking business.[64]

The industrialisation in the Indian monarchies and principalities remained at markedly lower levels compared to the rest of British India and was especially noticeable in the first three decades of the twentieth century. On the one hand, this was due to the agricultural structures of the areas that had grown out of historical development in which a high percentage of the rural elite skimmed off the capital with the result that industrial investment capital in the region was lacking. On the other hand, the unwillingness of the British to lend to Indian companies meant that here too the aspired projects and investment in railway construction as well as the establishment of industrial enterprises could not be implemented. Moreover, British Residents occasionally meddled in the internal affairs of a state, enforcing the abolition of transit duties or obtaining concessions for railway lines emanating from the British territory that were to be routed through the Indian State.[65]

In Maisur in 1884, a British syndicate was granted generous terms to the mining rights in the mines of Kolar by the Maharaja and his prime minister where gold had also been discovered in the same year. The rights, however, brought only profits into the coffers of the ruling house without having any direct benefit to the state of Maisur itself. Moreover, the development costs, the imported machinery and the British engineering personnel as well as the recruitment of workers in the Madras Presidency were expensive and the monarch was obviously not ready to make such investments. Thus, all profits went to the British investors.[66] In 1893 a railway line was built in Maisur and in 1902 a hydroelectric plant was erected. A similar situation was replayed in Haiderabad where the discovery of coal in Warangal and Godaveri in 1872 roused the interest of the British-Indian Government which wanted to replace the expensive imported English coal with cheaper Indian coal. In 1880, government employees from Calcutta and Haiderabad aimed to combine the rights of the railways and mines and, despite warnings from the India Office in London, they received exceptionally favourable conditions from the *nizam*. Then the investors drove shares of Nizam's Guaranteed State Railway up exponentially, benefited greatly on the London Stock Exchange and nearly caused the bankruptcy of Haiderabad.[67]

Thirty years after the first textile factory in Bombay was founded, the Mysore Spinning and Manufacturing Mills opened in Maisur, and two years later the Woollen, Cotton and Silk Mills in Bengaluru/Bangalore. From the outset, a missing business class, the lack of capital and the British tariff policy prevented the successful development of the two industrial plants. M. Visvesvaraya, an engineer who had received training in Pune and was employed until 1909 in the Public Works Department in Bombay, attempted to meet government-sponsored enterprises through large-scale projects that were based on their own infrastructure and foreign capital. As a minister in Maisur, he founded the Mysore Bank in 1913, the Mysore Chamber of Commerce in 1916 as well as the Mysore University. With the help of J.N. Tata and the British-Indian Government, he succeeded in bringing the Indian Institute of Technology to life in 1911. He also initiated the highly capital-intensive Kauvery Dam Project and the Mysore Iron and Steel Works.

Visvesvaraya's successor, Mirza Ismail, continued this policy of industrialisation. With the help of a wealthy ship-owner, Walchand Hirachand, he worked on plans to develop an automobile company in Maisur and to build Chrysler cars under licence. The British, however, quickly banned the factory's construction for fear of competition to their own automobile industry. A welcome contrast to this British position came in 1940 with the establishment of Hindustan Aircraft in Bengaluru as the Indian engineers and producers could then be included in their war aims. In contrast to these large projects, Alfred Chatterton, who had been made the first director of the Department of Industries and Commerce in Maisur in 1912, preferred the less capital-intensive, small-scale industrial projects such as the Experimental Weaving Factory, the Sandalwood Oil Factory and a soap factory. An ammonium sulfate plant was built in 1937 which initiated the production of artificial fertiliser on the South Asian subcontinent.[68]

Three phases of industrialisation can be distinguished over the long term in Bangalore/Bengaluru. First, from around 1880 to 1940 as "classical" companies were established in the field of textile processing. Second, from 1940 to 1960 during which companies such as the Hindustan Aircraft Factory, Indian Telephone Industries, Hindustan Machine Tools and Bharat Electronics Limited were created, bringing the logistical and personnel requirements for a technology centre to be based in Bangalore. Third, from 1980 to the beginning of the twenty-first century, as the arrival of Texas Instruments saw the number of IT companies and suppliers grow from 100 to over 3,000. However, it was only in the late 1990s that the early reputation of Bangalore/Bengaluru as the Indian "Silicon Valley" came true as the number of employees in the IT sector grew from just 2,600 in early 1990 to nearly 70,000 within a decade.[69]

What is noticeable in this long-term development is that already at the time of colonialism in Mysore State, state bureaucracy forged a kind of nation-ness primarily based in the economic domain well before independence from colonial rule came, although it refrained from any overt critique of colonial modernisation. The bureaucracy provided a vehicle for the state to enter that domain and act as a mobiliser and manager of investible resources. Thus the state addressed the most serious internal impediments to economic progress and capitalist development through administrative and economic incentives. Although Maisur did not gain its economic autarchy within the British Raj that Visvesvaraya and Ismail had imagined, they not only planted the seed of the contemporary Indian IT sector with their various institute and industry foundations and the state administrative initiative, but they were also the forerunners of a state-controlled and subsidised economy, at a time when the INC had yet to take a clear position.[70]

A similar process can be observed in Haiderabad, with results that are more reminiscent of those areas directly administered by the British in British India. Even in Haiderabad there was an industrial development that was initially induced by the state administration. The financial means to do so came from the massive increase in the land revenue (up 160 per cent) as well as the customs revenue (up 700 per cent) from the 1850s to the 1870s. The attempt to create an economically viable rail network that would connect the coal fields and cotton fields to the capital, where the processing industry had been built up, was quashed by the British-Indian Government. Meanwhile, investors from Bombay established the first textile mills in Haiderabad in 1874. However, this impetus was not sustainable due to the conservative-aristocratic social structures that prevented the emerging of an industrial capitalist class. Nevertheless, the state invested millions of rupees in industrial plants from the 1930s that were accompanied by five-year plans until its violent integration into the Indian Union at the beginning of the 1950s. Statistics show an increase of trade and industry which had little or no impact on the economic and social structures of the region.[71]

The Gaekwad of Baroda also wanted to "modernise" his country with governmental help. For this purpose he established a Ministry of Trade and Industry and the Bank of Baroda which extended the credit base and customs duties in the course of the Swadeshi Movement. The 11 textile factories in the country were organised in the Baroda Millowner's Association in 1918, from which the Federation of Gujarat Mills and Industries later emerged. Meanwhile an import company for tractor spare parts was transformed into the Hindustan Tractors and Bulldozers Company. The Gaekwad invited specific investors, such as the Sarabhai family of Ahmedabad, for whom he guaranteed specific land acquisition and attractive fiscal terms which thus laid the foundation for a future chemical and pharmaceutical industry in India from the 1940s. In addition the Second World War had the effect of stimulating the expansion of production in many Indian states after imports largely failed and had to be substituted.[72]

Catching up with industrialisation was high on the new Indian state's priority list following British India's independence. In the framework of the economic five-year plans, Jawaharlal Nehru had vigorously driven the expansion of the iron and steel industry for import substitution since 1951. Whilst steel production during the Second World War reached one million tonnes, it increased to some three million in 1960 and further increased in 1964 to six million. Similar increases were also seen in the capital goods sector where a number of processing machines were produced. In stark contrast was the stagnation of the textile processing sector, where, despite increasing the strength of the labour force, production increased only marginally. This hints at the structural imbalance between the production of consumer and of capital goods as the mass-produced, high-quality fabrics created little demand due to the lack of workers' purchasing power who instead invested their money in the fulfilment of their basic needs. The situation was further exacerbated with the rise in food prices after the drought of 1966.[73]

The textile industry remained the problem child of Indian economic planning. Whilst industrial production rose, in part, considerably between 1960 and 1980, particularly in the crude steel, crude oil and electricity sectors along with the increased production of consumer goods, the results of the stagnating jute processing and the decline of the cotton processing sectors seriously affected the balance of the entire state's economy. Once again, the small weavers and textile companies in the country were competitive as the focus on coarse materials had the advantage of being located in the cheaper inland regions. This partially initiated a reversal in the development of the centralisation process which had started with the expansion of the textile industry as the steel industry grew in a way that was not foreseen. On account of global overcapacity in the production of steel and the subsequent declining steel prices, the industry fell far short of what was expected of it. Since the Indian Government had subsidised the steel industry, it was the government that ultimately shouldered the costs and lack of marginal gains alone.[74]

Furthermore, the massive economic control introduced with the five-year plans did not produce the desired results in the long run. Reforms in the economic sector were first made in the 1980s. Prime Minister Rajiv Gandhi, in particular, attempted to finalise the numerous licences, permits and assessments that the previous governments had started and which had earned them the nickname of the "license raj". Large parts of the economy were already deregulated in the 1980s.[75] Furthermore, it was Rajiv Gandhi's economic and political ideology to prepare India for the twenty-first century in which IT was to play a central role. In addition, the consumer products industry and the automotive industry were to be expanded. The gradual liberalisation of the Indian economy was accompanied by a highly critical press sector which had experienced something of a media revolution initiated by the Emergency Rule period (1975-7) and saw the number of press products between 1975 and 1995 increase from about 600 to almost 1,100 as well as the creation of a public sphere that became part of an emerging civil society.[76]

The acute cash crisis proved to be the catalyst for Prime Minister Narasimha Rao (in office 1991–6) of the then Congress Government to embark on additional economic reforms as he took out a loan from the International Monetary Fund in 1991 as a stabilising measure and as a way to effect structural reforms. More bureaucratic barriers were eliminated in the following years; however, this only represented a first step towards the further liberalisation of the Indian economy.[77] Additional decentralisation and deregulation measures were planned, although these were to be enacted slowly so as to avoid any economic shock. The financial crisis of 2008 showed that this strategy had been well founded as India was not nearly as badly affected by the fiscal and economic dislocations of the following years as other regions, such as the United States or the European Union.

The labour market and labourers' organisations

It was not solely the process of industrialisation that set the rural–urban migration in motion, since alongside the numerous industrial and commercial cities in north India a growing population can be observed in the metropolises of Calcutta, Bombay and Madras from the mid-eighteenth century. However, despite the continuing influx of migrants, complaints remained about the lack of manpower. The British found the expansion of Calcutta and the large-scale construction of nearby Fort William in the 1760s to be a difficult task for which they had to attract more than 30,000 workers from the nearby rural areas who were set to work, alongside countless professionals from Dhaka and the smaller towns of Bengal, on the building sites in and around the city. Even high wages did not serve as an effective "pull factor" as the working conditions remained too unattractive whilst rural life was relatively stable and ensured social ties.[78]

The industrialisation of large urban centres reinforced the previously existing domestic migration of Indian job seekers. Their livelihoods in the country had increasingly worsened on account of the substantial colonial restructuring; thus the city was increasingly considered an economic beacon of hope. Due to the continuing influx of migrants, the population of Calcutta and Bombay grew from 180,000 and half a million, respectively in 1820, to more than one million each by the beginning of the twentieth century.[79] Calcutta and Bombay were characterised in their roles as trade, textile, port, service and industrial centres, whilst Kanpur and Ahmedabad in comparison were industrial cities with complementary trade and commerce. According to statistics, the number of factories in British India increased between 1894 and 1914 from about 800 to almost 3,000, whilst the average daily number of employees rose from 350,000 to 950,000. This proves that the overwhelming majority of migrants did not find work in factories.[80]

A large proportion of migrants and circulants arrived in the big cities without the aid of professional recruiters. In Bombay, especially, vacancies were so numerous that immigrants easily found employment in the textile processing industry as well as dockers after the opening of the Suez Canal in 1869, which led to rapidly expanding port operations and a demand for labourers. The same trend is also noticeable in Calcutta. As machine-made cotton products were imported from England to Bengal from the 1820s, numerous weavers found themselves unemployed and poured into Calcutta from the neighbouring districts along with countless other impoverished artisans. During the mid-nineteenth century the majority of the immigrants to Calcutta came from the surrounding region; however, by the end of the century these regions accounted for just half of the immigrants who had settled in the city. Instead immigrants and circulants were now coming from as far afield as Bihar and the United Provinces of Agra and Oudh.[81]

The railway links that had been laid to develop the Ganges valley helped ease the situation in the labour market somewhat following the competitive recruitment of workers among the numerous jute mills in Calcutta which had caused tensions on the labour market in the 1880s. Alongside the well-established informal recruitment of workers, migrants were now actively recruited as workers. They were attracted by financial benefits such as salary advances, travel and commission. Whilst the rate of immigration to Calcutta equalled some 12 per cent of the resident population in the 1880s, this proportion increased in the following decade to just over 40 per cent and lay at 32 per cent during the first decade of the twentieth century. This shift in the regional origin of the workers led to social tensions and often violent riots among the various regional groups. Seasonal workers – whether temporary immigrants living in the city for large parts of the year or regularly circulating labourers – were dependent on wages from the urban industrial centres in order to maintain or improve their social position in their rural homes.[82]

The Calcutta ratios were replicated in Bombay as workers first poured out of the neighbouring districts in the city. Only in the first decades of the twentieth century did workers increasingly come from the United Provinces. In 1911 almost 50 per cent of the workers originated from Ratnagiri (Konkan) and by 1931 the region accounted for some 25 per cent of the labour force in Bombay. Conversely, the influx of northern Indian workers increased during the same period from a modest 3 per cent to almost 12 per cent. Most migrants came from a distance of 150–300km away. At the same time, the proportion of those workers born in Bombay increased from nearly 11 per cent to about 26 per cent.[83] A rather atypical, however comprehensible, migration behaviour can be seen in the example of the peasants in Khandesh, a district in the hinterland of Bombay. As seasonal workers, they were not attracted to the textile industry in Bombay and Ahmednagar, but rather to the cultivation of cotton in Central India, which was much more attractive to them because of the familiar rural environment and more familiar way of working.[84]

Unlike in Calcutta, the factory owners in Bombay rarely complained about a lack of manpower as the diverse employment opportunities attracted many rural labourers and poor peasants to the city. As more workers were needed, professional recruitment became more urgent. Aside from the recruitment of workers for the tea plantations in Assam and the overseas sugar plantations, the managing agencies controlled and organised the labour market and directed the migration flows to the desired sectors. The temporary migrants showed a greater interest in employment in the industrial cities, not only because of the possibility of circulation, but also because the wage level in the city was higher than that on the plantations of Assam or Mauritius. In addition, the concentration of the working class in the cities led to legal working arrangements. The first labour laws for men, women and children were adopted in British India in Calcutta and Bombay.[85]

Women were, as was generally the case, paid less. One would imagine, for this reason, that they were systematically recruited as industrial workers, yet this was not the case in the large Indian cities. Initially, some factory owners were impressed by the female workers because they were more sociable and less strike-prone. However, this positive image shifted to their disadvantage as they soon became seen as not as resilient and inefficient workers to be used only in the manual, low-tech areas of production.[86] The extent to which the legislation of the Factory Acts of 1891 and 1911, with its strict work arrangements for women (and children), influenced the image of the female workers is questionable. Despite the negative adjustment women accounted for between one-fifth to one-quarter of the workforce in the cotton mills of Bombay between 1884 and 1931, after which their numbers dropped to 11 per cent by 1947. This was related to the increase of shifts against the backdrop of the Great Depression, during which additional night shift work was introduced from which women were prohibited.[87]

As seen above, Indian peasants, in many cases, were artisans often employed in the textile sector. As they migrated and circulated as seasonal workers to the industrial centres, simultaneously wanting to remain firmly embedded in the economic and social structures of the village, the industrial enterprises benefited from a skilled workforce as they brought with them at least a basic knowledge of cotton and jute cultivation and processing.[88] The riots in Calcutta from 1926 document how strong the family and emotional bonds of the seasonal workers could be in relation to their rural region of origin. Within days, the number of train tickets sold in Calcutta with destinations in northern Bengal and Bihar rose dramatically as the unrest also eventually was manifest in the villages.[89] Town and country were in many cases two compatible areas of working and living places. Permanent settlement in the city was just one option, the other was circulation.

Apart from the circulation of workers to work in the industries and the thus often associated difficulties felt by the employees in controlling the workers, there was the aforementioned large area of non-industrial sector and the fact there was a large potential for employees to show resistance. This was particularly the case in the small-scale artisanal enterprises that would today be attributed to the informal sector. For the regions of Gujarat and Maratha Desh, the size of the independent textile businesses ranged from family businesses with five or more pairs of working hands to small factories with at least 30 labourers within which the division of labour was organised according to age and sex. Working conditions varied greatly, ranging from custom to contract. However, non-contractual relationships based upon family, kinship, *jati* and patronage continued to be central to the maintenance of control and discipline over artisan labour and was, at the same time, subjected to processes of transformation.[90]

Such small businesses were to be found in the country, but during the period between 1880 and 1940 were concentrated increasingly in small towns. It was in these small towns that the distribution of textiles via the so-called *gujari* system took place and was organised by *adatiyas* (brokers). Through these small enterprises *sahukars* were able to gain extensive control by offering loans. They often acted as master weaver for 25 to 125 weaving families. With an increasing number of businesses this resulted in the *sahukars* having little presence in the place of production and they consequently possessed only a limited ability to exercise regular and intense control over the production process.[91] Alongside these dependent households were independent companies, the so-called *karkhanas* that were small businesses with 10 to 20 looms and an average of 30 employees. The *karkhanas* were highly dependent on the influx of skilled labour. However, this group of labourers also had a high mobility rate with their home villages. Similar to the *sahukars,* the *karkhanadars* also practised lending, especially for the financing of social events such as weddings, as well as advancements of material, thereby exerting influence over the labourers. Such social structures are evidence of a few horizontal allegiances that only seldom criss-cross the still strong vertical ties.[92]

The emerging workers nevertheless struggled to organise themselves. This was true not only for the structures mentioned above, but also for the industrial workers in the major production centres. The first union, the Bengal Press Workers' Union, was founded during the Swadeshi Movements in 1905. However, one can only speak of a trade union movement in British India following the establishment of the Madras Labour Union in 1918. By 1920 almost 125 trade unions had been formed representing some 250,000 members among which the textile industry and the railroad workers were prominently represented. The first All India Trade Union Congress (AITUC) was held in the same year. Strikes of the industrial workers were now increasingly organised by the trade unions, as was the case with the railway strike of 1922.[93] This prompted the founder of the Communist Party of India (1920), M.N. Roy, to draw parallels with the contemporaneous railway strike in Germany and the miners on the Rand in South Africa. Against this background, Roy saw the emergence of an Indian working class in the context of an international industrial workforce.[94]

The increasing number of trade unions and strikes that had been organised prompted the British-Indian Government to enact the Indian Trade Union Act in 1926. Whilst this made the foundation of a trade union relatively easy, it made most of the unions' activities questionable in the eyes of the law. Despite this, this did not prevent the massive strikes in the textile centres of

Bombay, Ahmedabad and Calcutta in 1928–9. In the case of the Calcutta general strikes, the workers' militancy ultimately affected the whole jute mill belt of Bengal. This developed from the tense interaction of workers and trade unionists, and by the intervention of colonial and local authorities.[95] Even the steel mills of Jamshedpur went on strike, whilst the railway union in Haiderabad, where the first trade union was founded in 1927 and the railway workers had by now formed a single trade union, also joined the struggle.[96] Given the massive perceived threat from the formation of the industrial workforce, the colonial government struck back with the Meerut Conspiracy Case in 1929, seeing a total of 31 trade unionists, including three Englishmen, arrested and accused of organising the Indian railway strike.

The court case took the form of a show trial against the Communists and Bolsheviks, which should also be seen in connection with the bombings of the revolutionaries around Bhagat Singh in the same year, as shown above in Chapter 2. The colonial government used the Meerut Conspiracy Case to help it achieve its aim of depriving the trade unions of their communist leadership whilst simultaneously sinking many of the communist activities in British India. However, the harsh penalties that were imposed and which were publicised in 1933 had the opposite effect of that intended and led to a consolidation of the Communist Party. The defence had in fact succeeded in turning the courtroom into a public forum and was able to generate a general sympathy for the accused and for the cause of the communists, thereby publicising their political aim and making their cause nationally known.[97]

A disadvantage to the trade union movement was manifest in the first division of the AITUC along the lines of radical and reformists following the Nagpur Session at the end of the year. Jawaharlal Nehru had been elected as President of the Assembly and yet could not prevent the split into the two factions. Although he sympathised with the radicals, he stressed that the Indian trade unions would have to distance themselves from the Comintern and its radical-revolutionary aims. The following year, against the backdrop of the Great Depression and Gandhi's civil disobedience agitations, came the second split when the Red Trade Union Congress was founded. Whilst the first fracture had been a conflict between the left and right wings of the AITUC, the second secession was a conflict within the left wing. Along with the colonial legislation and the disinterest shown by Congress in social conflicts, these divisions have contributed to the fact that trade unions have not been able to take a prominent role in the organisation of industrial workers on an all-India level. Yet also on the regional and local level, the workers in the small industrial establishments were only reached by the trade unions in the 1940s.[98]

The case of the Sholapur strike, a small industrial city in western India, between 1937 and 1939 shows the dilemma the trade unions were to face in future. Gandhi's civil disobedience campaign of 1930 compelled the colonial government to impose martial law on account of the scale and intensity of civil unrest which had caused the breakdown of the district administration. As the first general elections after the India Act of 1935 formed the Congress

Government, Congress also raised the workers' expectations of a policy that would grant them concessions. These expectations were mainly related to the withdrawal of the Criminal Tribes Act, as a quarter of the workers belonged to peoples classified as such. The withdrawal of this act became a central demand of the local Batwa Lal Girni Kamgar Union election campaign, the support of which had helped the INC come to power.[99]

However, the two organisations pursued divergent strategies. On the one hand, the Communists sought to expand their influence on the workers using the trade unions whilst Congress continued, on the other hand, to eliminate the influence of the trade unions and the Communists. Congress finally succeeded in 1938 during a strike in the textile mills in Sholapur as almost the entire union leadership was arrested on charges of criminal intimidation. In alliance with the colonial bureaucracy, the Communist leaders were convicted and removed from political life as they were sentenced to many months of imprisonment.[100] As in the case of the Dharala in 1923, mentioned in Chapter 4, the alliance between the colonial British and Indian elites stabilised the colonial system. However, whilst the colonial government supported Congress for strategic reasons of maintaining power, the collaboration of Congress with organs of the colonial state allowed the Congress to successfully pursue its political claim to be the sole representation of all Indians in British India.

It is against this background that the 1937 alliance between the Ahmedabad Millowners Association (AMA, founded in 1891) and the Textile Labour Association (TLA, founded in 1920), on the one hand, and Congress on the other must be seen as they had taken over government offices at the provincial level in the same year. Since the strikes of 1918 Mahatma Gandhi, who had settled close to Ahmedabad following his return from South Africa, occasionally led the workers, and recommended the TLA to desist from class struggle and, instead, pursue politics of material and moral betterment. Thus, during the 1937 strikes wage increases were much less of a problem for the TLA than the socialist involvement in synthesis of these demands. The aforementioned alliance of entrepreneurs, trade unionists and politicians successfully rallied against the Mill Kamdar Union, founded in 1930, which aimed to induce a radical class struggle. The TLA finally achieved its long-term political representation in the Bombay Legislative Assembly with the help of Congress and two reserved seats.[101]

The position of the trade unions in India, as well as in Pakistan, did not however improve following the Second World War and the gaining of Independence. Whilst the number of trade unions had risen considerably to 1,230, representing some 1.4 million unionised workers in British India in 1946, the fragmentation of the union movement also increased. Thus the establishment of the Indian National Trade Union Congress (INTUC) in 1947 by the government aimed to stand as a model for the moderate Gandhian policy of the TLA at the national level and to ensure an alliance there.[102] The Nehru-led governments drove an increasingly tough line against the trade unions as they targeted continuing industrialisation; plans which were not to be halted by the allegedly unqualified demands. The demand for minimum wages, debated on a nationwide scale in 1959–60, was rejected by the government on the grounds that this would exceed the financial capacity of the industry. Nehru denounced the 1960 strikes as "civil rebellion" which led to the arrest of 20,000 workers, of which 1,500 were convicted. The climax of strikes organised by the trade unions was, however, reached in the early 1970s.[103] The railway strike of 1974, which involved 17 million workers, was particularly significant as it paralysed the entire country for 20 days, and resulted in Indira Gandhi enforcing Emergency Rule in the following year.[104]

In Pakistan, the overdeveloped apparatus of the former colonial government supported state intervention in the labour organisation. When compared with India, Pakistan had, by far, the worst starting prospects in terms of catching up with the industrialisation process on account of the fact that a mere 3 per cent of British India's industrial plants were located there. A working class emerged following a government economic policy, which, as in India, led to the licensing of entire sectors of the country's economy. The textile industry grew into an all-dominant economic sector until the 1970s which covered nearly 40 per cent of all exports, in which almost 40 per cent (350,000 workers) of the labour force was employed. After 1947 the labour force in Karachi unified from its two groups; the aforementioned *mohajirs* who had migrated to the city in a relatively short period of time and had permanently settled there, and the peasants from Sind who often established a regime of circulating workers. This made the formation of a labour class difficult from the very beginning. Furthermore, company structure ensured that more of a clientelistic, factory class consciousness developed.[105]

Thus at the company level, the organisation of the working class was relatively good. However, a powerful trade union was lacking at the regional and national levels. The Sindh Trade Union Coordination Committee, for example, was unable to rise above this provincial status in 1975. Already in 1950, the Pakistani Government had, as a preventive measure, established the All Pakistan Confederation of Labour, the chairmen of which warned the workers in his inaugural speech not to demand wage increases as that was against the interests of the nation. In India, as demonstrated above, the INTUC was founded by the government for similar purposes, namely to hinder workers from enacting stoppages, strikes and disruption. However, in Pakistan the suppression of the trade union movement escalated when section 144 of the Pakistan Penal Code was enacted in the course of martial law which was sometimes declared for several years. It was a relic dating from colonial legislation prohibiting the gathering of more than five people at any time in any place. Thus it is no surprise that the police and military were often called upon to break up the numerous strikes and beat down the demonstrations by force, leading to the death of dozens of people in the first half of the 1970s.[106]

The obvious weakness of the British-Indian labour movement has sparked a vehement discussion in academic circles in recent years around the ability of the workers in urban environments in forming class consciousness. On the one hand, the position is held that the Indian workers were unable to develop separate social structures in the city due to their rural origins and their strong continued involvement in the rural social structures and spaces that were oriented to the family, clan, kin, *jati* and community. It is argued that the dual identity of peasants and workers would have been suppressed by the spatially and socially different worlds of city and country. On account of their conservative base, it is assumed that the peasants were not flexible and thus not adaptable enough to have created such social structures.[107] Moreover, class formation would have been impossible from the outset on account of the pre-colonial structures that were in place. It is claimed that this triggered a "clash of cultures" within the industrial sectors of society which ultimately sparked the social tensions and led to the violent clashes of the twentieth century which were termed "communal riots" by the British authorities.[108]

The opposing view, on the other hand, considers the fact that the circulating workers would have been able to create a class consciousness in the urban environment. That said, the Indian working classes were clearly anything but homogeneous and did not pursue common goals. Instead the specific neighbourhood structures cast newly emerging working quarters as well as social relationship networks such as the organisation of work and collective action.[109] The active proportion of workers who were involved in the design of the urban society and their choice and agency within this is highlighted, the result of which was that they were able to constantly realign their networks of relationships within and between classes. It was not only the communal living conditions in the city that led to these shifting relationships, but also the regional origins, common cultures, customs, beliefs, history and similar experiences that played a crucial role.[110] Meanwhile, it is this latter argument that has achieved prominence in the academic research.

Urbanisation

From a vernacular scientific perspective, the term "urbanisation" has a double meaning. On the one hand, the term points towards a quantitative parameter measuring the rapid growth of cities in the nineteenth and twentieth centuries in terms of space and population, particularly in industrialising countries. On the other hand urbanisation can be seen as the qualitative extent to which a specific urban society and an urban lifestyle have formed. From a sociological viewpoint, urbanisation is concerned with the expression and shaping of different areas of life and behaviour whereby a strong differentiation and high intricacy are characteristics of the urban area. Urbanisation asks questions of urban planning to produce orderly settlements for the growing population, which in turn implied a multitude of municipal management requirements such as urban water supply, waste water disposal, waste disposal, sewage disposal, public bathing facilities, educational institutions (schools, libraries, universities) and health care (hospitals, health departments). The acquisition, organisation and institutionalisation of new urban functions are all hallmarks of a tendency towards the centralisation of municipal administration.[111]

Seen historically, the population growth in the major cities of British India is not due solely to the rural–urban migration flow but, as elsewhere in the world, also a result of natural population increase. Various estimates place the all-India population from 1750 to the 1800s between 150 and 200 million people. By 1850 estimates of British India and adjacent regions held that the population had reached roughly 240 million people. Meanwhile, the first Census of India, which was conducted by the British in their provinces in 1871 and complemented by estimates from the monarchies and principalities, resulted in a total population of 250 million people, whilst the Census of India of 1901 saw the population grow to 285 million inhabitants.[112]

These general figures from the beginning of the nineteenth century show a trend of steady population growth that is also reflected in the growing number of inhabitants in the cities of the subcontinent. In big cities such as Bombay, the population in 1814 was recorded to be about 180,000 people; in 1846 this had increased to little more than half a million inhabitants and in 1864 had reached 816,000 persons. After years of larger demographic fluctuations, the population of the city grew steadily after 1901 from 776,000 to 1,176,000 people in 1921.[113] Similar gains can also be seen in Calcutta where in 1821 the population is estimated at about 180,000. In 1850 this number had increased to 413,000, the first reliable Census of India in 1881 recorded that the population had risen to 433,000, and in 1911 it stood at almost one million inhabitants.[114] Such increases in the urban population are also observed in the other colonial cities of Madras and Colombo, albeit to a lesser extent.[115]

Even in cities such as Kanpur, Dhaka, Ahmedabad and Delhi population rates grew steadily. From the mid-nineteenth century the emerging industrialisation of Kanpur had noticeable demographic effects on the city as the population increased from 109,000 in 1841 to over 210,000 in 1921. By 1971, the population had grown to 1.15 million people.[116] In Dhaka, a city that had once been the residence of the *nawabs* of Bengal and had since fallen to a provincial town, the population rates grew between 1872 and 1941 from almost 70,000 to over 210,000 inhabitants.[117] Similar growth can also be seen in Ahmedabad despite the decimation of the textile industries on account of the rail connections that had been created; the city's population nevertheless grew from about 80,000 people in 1817 to over 270,000 in 1921 as the city became a hub for imported goods.[118] Even in Delhi – once the residence of the Mughals which had suffered under the British occupation – population increased during the nineteenth century from 100,000 residents to over 200,000 by 1900.[119]

This population increase was interrupted at the turn of the century as population growth in the cities, especially in western India, seemed to decline on account of extreme famine and the disease epidemics that broke out, resulting in high mortality rates which were particularly noticeable in the middle-sized and small towns. In Satara, for example, the population fell from 26,000 to 19,000 between 1901 and 1911, whilst during the same period Dharwar's population fell from 32,000 to 30,000.[120] The continued decline in political and cultural aspects was eventually reflected demographically in

Lakhnau, whose population was estimated to be around 400,000 people at the time of Awadh's annexation in 1856. After the demolition of many inner-city quarters as a result and punishment of the city's involvement in the Great Rebellion, the urban population totalled just 285,000 people according to the census of 1871; by 1911 this had fallen further to 260,000 inhabitants and ten years later further still to 240,000.[121]

The steady decline in Lakhnau's population mirrors the decline of the urban sector, which took place at the expense of the rise of the industrial city of "nearby" Kanpur. An indicator of this shift is reflected in the conduct of the grain and vegetable peasants of the area who until the second half of the nineteenth century brought and sold their products in the Lakhnau markets that were within 10km of where the products were grown. However, from the 1880s these peasants instead travelled up to 60km to Kanpur to sell their products. Whilst Lakhnau barely benefited from the connection to the north Indian railway network in 1864, Kanpur in contrast experienced a marked increase in craft, commerce and industry following the connection. As a result, and at least because of the massive support from the colonial state, Kanpur became one of the most important industrial centres within a matter of decades, and continued to grow after the independence of British India as the construction of iron and steel works was subsidised by the independent Indian state.[122] The same can also be observed in Maharashtra where the population of Sholapur increased dramatically following the connection to the railway network and the establishment of the Spinning and Weaving Company in 1877, whilst Satara, which was not connected, witnessed a dramatic demographic collapse during the same period.[123]

Such accelerated urban growth had begun in the large colonial cities and in some major provincial cities already during the first half of the nineteenth century; thus before the beginning of industrialisation. The negative effects of urbanisation were soon recorded in the growing cities. One such negative effect was the rise of overpopulation which was caused by a scarcity of housing and the high density in which people were forced to live. An often uncontrolled growth of the city outskirts began, caused by an equally increasing trend of land speculation. Poor sanitary conditions dramatically increased the mortality rate in urban centres, which only gradually led to the view that city planning was seen as a public responsibility. Even though it sometimes seemed that the colonial port cities were not subject to any planning, let alone aesthetic concepts, some systematic town planning and the performance of public functions by municipal institutions did begin to be shaped at the beginning of the nineteenth century, much of which, however, remained confined to the European quarters of the said cities.[124]

The fire of Bombay in 1803 provided an opportunity to redesign the layout of the city and to rebuild it. To this end, a town committee was founded to plan the development of the city. The basis of these plans was the determination of the inner-city ownership according to which the future tax charges were calculated, from which in turn the future municipal duties were to be paid.

Although a line of segregation existed in the city since the late seventeenth century in the understanding of the European population, such a strict separation by British and Indian residential areas could never be maintained. However, the planned full reconstruction of Bombay was limited almost exclusively to the wealthy European-Indian living areas that stood out with their opulent façades and clean thoroughfares. Meanwhile, in the purely Indian quarters, the spaces between the houses were gradually filled in as meandering alleys with open gutters developed.[125] Although attempts were made by the town committee to relocate the unwelcome (Indian) trading competition to areas beyond the city's boundaries, this move failed as a result of concerted actions of resistance.[126]

In 1803, Governor-General Richard Wellesley began with the imperial expansion and the architectural transformation of Calcutta. Until then the city was infamous for the seemingly random collection of some magnificent buildings, whilst at the same time was also dangerously narrow and densely populated on account of a severe lack of living space. Wellesley appointed an improvement committee that was charged with halting unapproved construction activities and the systematic planning of the city. Within a few years the British had transformed a part of Calcutta into a "City of Palaces", where they could lead the grand lifestyles that were otherwise only to be found in aristocratic circles.[127] Accordingly such was also the contemporary figurative representation of the city that was portrayed mainly in Great Britain.[128] Despite this one-sided representation of Calcutta as a "white city", the British also failed here to establish a distinct segregation to the "black town", aside from the fact that Calcutta was hardly a city of palaces.[129]

During the nineteenth century the population density of the city increased dramatically, especially in the northern areas which were the districts that the majority of the Indians inhabited. Even beyond the Circular Road, the former Maratha Ditch, which had been filled in in 1799, a densely populated residential area had developed which was soon classified as *basti* (slum). Official British opinion regarded such areas as a stronghold of diseases which prevented the expansion of the city.[130] Reports on the sanitary and hygienic condition of the city from the 1840s reinforced the aspect of disease. This was also reflected in the representation of the city that no longer appeared as a colonial picturesque view of the Orient, but rather maps showed the locations where hygiene and sanitation were lacking and thus were hotbeds of potential epidemics. This new perception of the city as a pathological space made it, as a consequence, an object of constant surveillance, monitoring and control.[131]

In the north of the inner city wealthy Indian merchants and traders had established bazaars that became the hallmark of this area. Its development hugely varied. Alongside *pakka* houses (of permanent building materials) there were a variety of *kacha* dwellings (non-durable materials) made of mud and with thatched roofs that only disappeared from the cityscape in the mid-nineteenth century.[132] It is highly likely that numerous working-class Europeans such as sailors, servants, workers and clerks were also attracted to these neighbourhoods on account of the cheap accommodation.[133] Moreover, rich Indians also rented numerous houses to the wealthy Bengalis and Europeans in the south of the city with its magnificent buildings. The "City of Palaces", however, accounted for only a small portion of Calcutta and dominated only the core area of the city with its architecturally and politically representative buildings. Just as striking were the mixed neighbourhoods of Europeans and Indians and the often job-specific composition of the residents and the corresponding appearance of the streets.[134]

Urban development measures were to be financed by additional public revenues, which were funded by the lottery committee. The reports of the lottery committee overwhelmingly focused on the sanitation measures of the city during the second half of the nineteenth century. Leaking tanks were to be repaired or filled in, roads were to be widened for better ventilation and large trees felled for the same reason. In addition, large, parallel north–south running roads were to be created. Similarly the issue of the drainage of waste water was also on the priority list. Although a report from 1840 claimed that the health and cleanliness of the city had improved significantly, the thoroughfares in the northern districts of the city had become even more densely populated in the remaining area of this part of the inner city, and consequently had led to in an increase in mortality rates.[135]

Although the so-called Presidency Towns (Calcutta, Bombay, Madras) were organised, according to English law, with a mayor, aldermen and the Justice of the Peace, they remained limited to purely administrative scope and jurisdiction on the lower level due to the lack of financial self-reliance. Ultimately, urban policy was determined solely by the British Governors and the Governor-General. Indian cities in areas of British control were subject to a *zamindar* or the revenue collector and the district magistrate or a commissioner. In this way the British reduced the Indian city to a source of state revenue, which was subordinate to a tax officer, whilst formerly Indian rulers placed the city under a town administrator, the *kotwal*, who was responsible for matters like security, trade and business. In order to finance urban tasks, formerly private-publicly organised guards were transformed into publicly funded British-Indian police units. Such new city government control occasionally led to violent resistance, as in Delhi, Calcutta and Varanasi.[136]

In the late eighteenth century the city limits of the three Presidency Towns were drawn for the first time, thereby defining the juridical and administrative responsibilities, leading later to the incorporation of conurbations or their definition as suburbs. On this basis, the definition of the urban administrative districts, known as municipalities, was formed during the nineteenth century. Such measures were also carried out in the second half of the nineteenth century in many other Indian cities in an attempt to delineate the formal and informal sectors of cities into the categories of core city, suburbs as and surrounding hinterland, and to simultaneously control each of them. This policy was quite similar to contemporaneous urban politics regarding European cities and towns. With the definition of city limits and inner-city areas, whether in British India or in Europe, urban projects such as roads, sewers and other such measures were able to be broached and were implemented from the perspective of urban sanitation and hygiene.[137]

Municipality and urban planning

In the nineteenth century the guiding principle for the solution of urban problems was the awakening of the importance that hygiene played. In Great Britain, urban authorities and scientists alike realised as early as the 1840s the problem that ensued from rapidly deteriorating hygienic conditions. Through the public health movement politicians, administrators and physicians formed public opinion significantly to realise that economic and social problems, including rising crime and the violent clashes at the lower strata of the population, stem from unhealthy living conditions.[138] Urban hygiene reforms were not only enacted to improve health conditions, but also to begin to control some of the social problems it implied. Consistent public health legislation and its strict implementation by means of an efficient administration were seen by scientists and politicians as appropriate solutions to urban problems. However, social and health policy issues only had priority as long as they allowed poorer sections of society to be brought under control. Consequently city hygiene became a means of social discipline.[139]

In the colonial metropolises of British India, urban problems were far more serious than those in contemporary Europe. Compared to London, there lived about seven times more people in Bombay despite being cities of a comparable area. Living conditions in Bombay deteriorated within the first few decades of the nineteenth century to such an extent that many residents preferred instead to sleep on the street rather than in the utterly congested dwellings. After the outbreak of the plague in 1896 and because of the high mortality rate of 35 to 60 per cent between 1904 and 1912, Bombay had developed a reputation of being one of the most dangerous cities in terms of health in the world. Of course, the problem of the high mortality rate and lack of hygiene was not new. In 1852 the British administration had commissioned a study into the sanitary conditions of the city. The report concluded that an efficient water supply and sewerage system could reduce the mortality rate by up to 20 per cent. Furthermore, a comparison with contemporary European cities, where similar measures to reduce the mortality rates in the densely populated neighbourhoods had been successful, supported the argument. Influenced by these shining European examples of the hygiene and sanitation movement, the die was cast to solve the problems of Bombay and other Indian cities.[140]

The already functioning water supply projects that had been in place in Bombay since 1845 were now adapted to the latest developments, all of which were funded through an increased housing tax. However, due to technical and financial difficulties, the plans had to be revised several times. Clean drinking water finally became available from the 1890s. However, the geological and ecological conditions of the island had the consequence that the drainage systems of the city failed to cope with the now excessive water inflow into the low-lying parts of the city, meaning that the population began to sink in its own wastewater. This resulted in an increased mortality rate. Just as with the outbreak of the plague in 1896, the cause of the increasing mortality rate was quickly identified: it was the unhealthy lifestyle of the poor in their crowded residential areas which was considered the cause of the epidemic. This diagnosis simply succeeded in drawing attention away from the lack of sanitation infrastructure that had been installed in the city and the actual cause of the epidemic. Moreover, evacuating those affected and disinfecting areas served only to treat the symptoms rather than target the causes of the outbreak.[141]

After it was determined at the international health conference in Constantinople in 1867 that Bombay was a hotbed of disease, the British were called for a second time to the international dock as it was noted at the Tenth World Health Congress in Venice in 1897 that the world's rampant plague had originated in Bombay. This statement not only named the British as those responsible for the outbreak, but also held that the British had not adequately fulfilled their colonial mission of civilising India.[142] Suddenly the problems of urbanisation became a question of the legitimacy of colonial rule. Urban planning in British India seemed now to be an urgent bid by the British not to be permanently in the international focus as a colonial power. Thus, quarantine regulations were adopted following the opening of the Suez Canal, mainly to protect European and North American ports against "oriental diseases" such as plague and cholera and prohibited the landing and unloading of goods and people. With the world's largest merchant fleet and by far the largest navy, the British had to be careful not to be moved further into the international spotlight.[143]

In the other Presidency Towns urban tasks were now being addressed. Plans had existed in Calcutta since 1828 to supply the city with filtered river water, but these were not enacted upon until 1843 after having been subjected to numerous modifications. In the first decades of the nineteenth century the city council ordered that the open sewers in the city centre be filled. From 1855 the city council planned an extensive sewage system that was completed in 1870 and today continues to be the core of the city's urban sewage disposal.[144] The background for the ongoing sanitation measures was the intensified debates on the sanitary conditions prevailing in the capital of British India since the 1840s as the colonial elite lived in growing fear that the city could sink into unhygienic chaos. The shanty settlements (*basti; jhuggi-jhompri*) especially attracted attention. They were regarded as a hotbed of disease and therefore had to be eliminated. To this end, slum clearance in the context of town improvement henceforth became a hallmark of colonial town planning.[145]

Whilst the decades after 1890 until the First World War became a formative phase in comprehensive urban planning in Europe and America, the British neglected almost all cities in South Asia which were not of military or commercial interest. The British rarely showed any interest in providing anything more than a purely municipal administration and ensuring basic urban needs. Moreover, they often attempted to solve the problems of urbanisation in British India with the urban planning concepts from Europe. As a result, legislation on urban planning in British India was based on the laws of the German Reich from 1893, 1911 and 1913 as well as the English laws enacted between 1909 and 1910. At the end of the nineteenth century the British formed Town Improvement Trusts as administrative institutions for the development of Indian cities. The improvement trusts were charged with, among other things, buying undeveloped land on the outskirts of towns and cities, to divide it and monitor its proper development after its sale.[146]

The improvement trusts were aligned with the British National Housing Reform Council, which gave special attention to improving the living conditions of the poor. In the long term, and over the colonial period, the improvement trusts in British India developed into instruments of marginalisation as they drove out the poor from the centres to the edges of the city and converted their homes into residential areas for the rich. Bombay was the first Indian city to establish an improvement trust in 1898 in order to respond to the effects of the dissipating plague epidemic. However, within a short time it became clear that the work of the improvement trust extended far beyond the containment of outbreaks and instead massive slum clearances took place without making replacements available for those inhabitants who lost their living space. It is not surprising that, as a result, the housing situation subsequently became compacted in the other quarters of the city and led to further deterioration in living standards.[147] The improvement trust was obviously not interested in the general improvement of living conditions. Social disciplining in British India had by far a greater precedence over the sound cause of fighting disease and death than in Western European countries. To put it another way, social discipline became a public health prophylaxis.[148]

The same is also true for Calcutta, where an improvement trust was established in 1911.[149] After the plague had broken out in the city in 1898, the Calcutta Municipality also began searching for lasting solutions to the problem. Several plans recommended the complete demolition of all areas defined as slums according to Western hygiene ideas and the construction of wide thoroughfares. Against the background of radical urban renewal of Baron Haussmann and the destruction of the historic urban landscape of Paris in the 1860s, such plans received only limited recognition. Because of the expected resistance of the population by those affected, only a handful of proposals were implemented. Nevertheless, the townscape within the Circular Road had changed fundamentally by the end of the colonial period. However, instead of heralding a disentanglement of the population, the creation of a network of wide roads led to a further compaction of space in northern Calcutta so that the image of the congested "black town" was rather more the result of the urban "sanitation" measures in the first half of the twentieth century than it is a historical fact of the eighteenth and nineteenth centuries.[150]

Essentially the work of the improvement trust was limited and continues to be limited to this day to the demarcation of potential building land in urban peripheral areas and urban centres, the sale of land and the resettlement of *basti* dwellers. They are continually evolving into an institution that aims to police the "dangerous classes" of the urban poor.[151] As long as the improvement trusts existed, but also after they were integrated into the Municipal Corporations, a nearly unbroken continuity of colonial policy can be observed in many cities in India as inner-city slums were cleared – most recently for the Commonwealth Games in Delhi 2010 – to make room for expensive housing units, parks and thoroughfares, and to forcibly relocate inhabitants of villages to the urban fringes in order to provide space for rural parks for the metropolitan elite.[152] Among the continuities is also the fact that the establishment of the improvement trust in Delhi in 1936 saw the simultaneous resistance of those affected to radical politics and their sometimes violent enforcement that continues today.[153]

There was a considerable time lag before the other major cities in British India had plans for a publicly organised water supply and sanitation network. The first systematic investigation from 1885 in Ahmedabad found that on account of the population increase in urban areas the sanitary conditions were in fact worse than had been feared. The most positive factor to come from the report was the supply of water from house cisterns, which dated back to the Mughal period. The assessment of Ahmedabad's waste disposal system failed not only to meet European standards, but was also far from sufficient in serving the pressures of a growing population. Moreover, it was found that legal measures from the 1870s had failed to bring improvement. Significant improvements in sanitary conditions only began to materialise following the municipally organised removal of "nightsoil" from 1884. That said, it would take decades before an extensive sewage system was finally installed in the various neighbourhoods of the city.[154]

The developments in Lakhnau, Allahabad and Delhi all followed similar lines. British stations and cantonments were built in the immediate vicinity of these cities and especially around British India's new capital New Delhi after 1912. In 1863, the Royal Commission on the Health of the Anglo-Indian Army had pointed out that it was impossible to separate the the troops' health from the sanitary conditions of the local population.[155] Thus with momentum caused by military-medical need and for the reasons of city hygiene, the dual process of separation and segregation of Indian and European populations was finally given priority in colonial town planning. The culmination of the process was to create New Delhi that was strictly planned according to this dual system. Thus, almost systematically, "Old" Delhi's/Shahjahanabad's infrastructure was now neglected, whilst attention focused on the development of the new city.[156]

With reference to sanitary reforms, British officials clung to the notion that Indians generally did not understand the meaning of sanitation and this served as evidence not to introduce them to new technologies. This type of clouded thinking was reflected, among other things, in the mechanisation of the removal of rubbish and excrement. By way of example, whilst in Old

Delhi no trucks were used for the removal of debris and *dalits* continued to perform manual labour as sweepers, New Delhi was equipped with five trucks. Seen socially, this has led to the consequence that the social structures of old have been preserved, as *dalits* today continue to work as "rag pickers", the collectors and separators, on the rubbish dumps of the city. A lack of funding and poor planning resulted in the water supply system and sewerage system being equipped with inadequate technology to cope with the growing water consumption that could not be satisfied as the two systems leaked badly. Moreover, on account of the inferior materials used to construct these systems, an outbreak of diseases began to affect Old Delhi in the mid-twentieth century.[157]

From a topographical perspective the two parts of Delhi differ dramatically. New Delhi was built as a spacious-looking city, taking advantage of numerous parks, open spaces, wide roads and large buildings in spacious compounds, whilst Old Delhi remained tight, congested and cramped. Additionally, with the planning of New Delhi numerous historical monuments in the wider urban area of Delhi such as Safdar Jang's Mausoleum or Purana Qila – dating over 3,000 years of settlement history in the Delhi area, and with its highly visible Jama Masjid built in the middle of the seventeenth century – served the function of follies in an English landscape garden. Thus, the construction of New Delhi not only turned Shahjahanabad into "Old Delhi", as the city was now referred to on official maps and in tourist guides, but reduced the unique historic landscape to a picturesque decoration of the British Empire in India.[158]

Allahabad offers an example of a variation in urban planning where segregation was not as openly enforced as in Delhi. Outwardly this segregation was visible in the tarmacked, wide tree-lined streets and the spacious design of the British neighbourhoods in Allahabad whilst inwardly such city areas had a functioning water-supply system including toilets. By contrast, the city administration saw fit to establish publicly accessible toilets for the Indian wards that were cleaned by staff and the construction of such amenities took on several experimental models over a number of decades. A regulated water supply for the growing city was first introduced in 1894. Despite the negative experiences witnessed in Bombay stemming from an abundant water supply with insufficient drainage, Allahabad experienced the same problems within just a few years, yet these were not officially approached until 1904.[159] A similar dual development of separation and segregation can also be seen in Lahore, which the British gave special attention to, being the provincial capital of Panjab.[160]

In Dhaka, the segregation was not immediately achieved through the water supply which, thanks to the geological location of the city, posed few problems in serving the population. Instead the city council levied higher prices for the installation of water pipes through the winding streets of the old town where the Indian population predominantly resided, whilst the straight roads in British neighbourhoods were charged lower installation prices. For this reason, only the easily accessible roads received a municipal water supply.

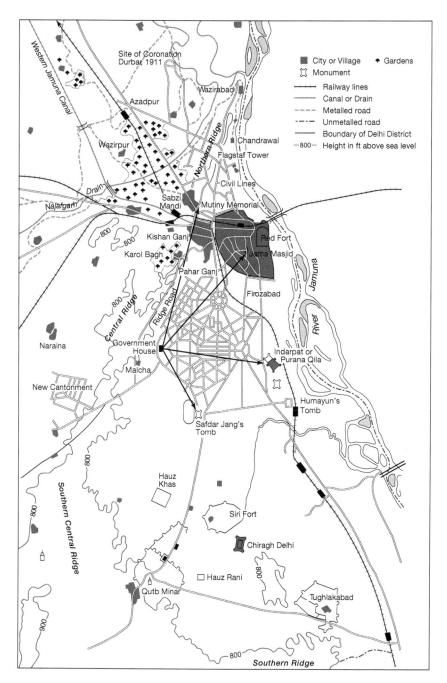

Map 7.2 New Delhi–Old Delhi: English landscape gardening in India. Michael Mann and Samiksha Sehrawat: "A City with a View: The Afforestation of the Delhi Ridge, 1883–1913", MAS 43.2 (2009)

Segregation could also be seen from the supply of electricity of the city. As curious as it may seem, the *nawab* of Dhaka funded the electrification of the city in the 1920s under the condition that the city administration took over the cost of further maintenance. However, the grotesque reality of this could be seen in the nightscape of the city as the wards of the local population were lit only by oil and kerosene lamps and the streets themselves remained dark, whilst the parts of the city where the British lived shone at night in the brightest of electric lights, especially at the racecourse where alone 100 electric lights had been installed.[161]

It was not only the lack of political will that prevented the implementation of structural measures in the cities, but also, and above all, financial obstacles that could easily destroy all planning. Whilst the urban regeneration of European city infrastructure projects had been funded through public borrowing, such funding opportunities were non-existent in British India. Until well into the twentieth century the *octroi*, the direct tax from imports of goods into a city, formed the financial backbone of a city's budget.[162] The rest was achieved by the regulatory, but unpredictable "official channels" to the top of the provincial administration which prevented many a project by the conditions imposed by the British central administration. Most infrastructural improvement financing plans were classified as dubious.[163]

The background for these tight fiscal policies was that the British were unwilling to further burden the already weak Indian capital market and to primarily ensure tax revenue, thereby securing their military and civil institutions as well as the Home Charges – military budget 1878–1910 average: 27 per cent of the India budget, including pensions, expenses of imperial wars in Asia and Africa, etc., in addition to Home Charges for civil establishment and pensioners[164] – and less about providing safe living conditions for Indians. By way of comparison, at the beginning of the twentieth century approximately £6 million had been invested in the previous two decades in Calcutta's urban redevelopment; in Paris this figure equated to £40 million with a further £35 million sanctioned for the continuation of the measures. Meanwhile, in Washington the US administration had just approved funding of £10.5 million for a single sanitation project.[165]

It is therefore hardly surprising that throughout the first half of the twentieth century, the majority of Indian cities were dark, dirty and stank beyond measure. The financial disparities alone clearly highlight the substantive disadvantages and structural asymmetries suffered in the cities of British India in the course of urbanisation. These asymmetries in infrastructure continue to be apparent in the present day as, for example, only 35 per cent of all 550 Class 1 cities (those with over 100,000 inhabitants) have functioning sewerage systems (most of the major metropolitan areas have functioning sewerage systems), a figure which falls to just 18 per cent of the 410 Class 2 cities (between 50,000 and 100,000 inhabitants).[166] Two things become clear from these figures: first, the high number of large cities compared to medium and small cities; second, the causally connected and persistent asymmetry in urban development.

A major reason for this structural deficit can be seen in the lack of reform of local self-government in which little has changed from the British Indian Municipality Act of 1850. As a result of the act, cities were assigned the role of night-soil removal and development of road lighting without, as already seen, having the necessary financial resources in place. The Municipality Act of 1858 was implemented in 352 cities whilst also including a number of villages, each with several thousand inhabitants. Obviously, the "town" and "city" were not yet clearly defined in the political structure of British India.[167] Apart from this insufficiency, the British often allowed many local institutions to remain, merely changing the top administration to include their own representative. This pattern was to be found, albeit in variations, in numerous cities of British India which determined the role of urban "self-government" until the establishment of the municipal boards in 1864. In general, the British managed the existing urban bodies as their predecessors had without however striving to enhance efficiency.[168]

Given the empty public coffers, the colonial government was forced to allow reforms at least in urban self-government after the Great Rebellion. The content of these reforms was initially left to the individual provinces of British India. In 1864 the new Municipal Act was passed, which was then gradually introduced in the provinces of Bengal and Awadh (1864), in the Panjab, the North-Western Provinces and the Central Provinces (1865). After that the municipal boards were composed of appointed members of the urban *panchayats* and respectable citizens. The municipal board was granted the right to levy taxes and found administrative institutions. However, its responsibilities were limited to measures to repair. Since the control of the finances remained in the hands of the British authorities, the scope and room for manoeuvre was not enlarged. The municipal boards were therefore not seen to be very popular among the urban population who saw in them institutions of colonial control. The collection of new taxes, which continued not to benefit the city budgets, offered the public the opportunity to voice displeasure, which in time turned violent.[169]

The Resolution on Local Self-Government was introduced in 1882 under the label of liberal reforms. It had been initiated by Viceroy Lord Ripon (in office: 1880–4) and led to representative elections for the municipal board. However, the reforms were only to be initially introduced in the most advanced cities where even here their introduction was to be gradual as all reforms were to maintain an experimental character, and not represent a final settlement. All checks and controls were still to be held by the British-Indian colonial state and not given over to the Indian representative. This restrictive representation was reflected in elector turnout, which was less than 2 per cent of the urban population. As a result of the provisions, huge differences began to develop in urban self-government. For the year 1885, some 197 municipal boards were reported to be active in the Panjab, of which just over 42 per cent of its members had been elected, with the rest having been appointed. In the North-Western Provinces 109 municipal boards were registered, of which nearly

80 per cent of their members had been elected. In comparison, in the Bombay Presidency, there were 162 municipal boards, just under a mere 11 per cent of which had elected members.[170]

The urban public showed little interest in the municipal institutions which were regarded more as an irrelevant political arena than as a communal institution for urban design concerns. The 1907-9 policy of decentralisation changed little as ultimately the control of the executive organs of self-government always remained in British hands. That said, the Morley-Minto reforms of 1909 triggered a growing interest in local and regional politics. In the following year, the elections became increasingly competitive as professional men attempted to gain positions in offices from which they fought for access to the scarce financial resources of the cities. One contributing factor was also that fewer British were installed as chairmen of the municipal boards. Confused by a perplexing mixture of concessions and constraints, new and old urban institutions alike often found themselves trying to align administratively to the colonial state and all too often enacting contradictions.[171]

The contradiction between centralised and decentralised elements of local government can be discerned in the cities of British India following the colonial era. On the one hand were a number of bodies and institutions whose range of expertise often overlapped, sometimes crippling their efforts and certainly interfering with their work. On the other hand, the successor states India and Pakistan maintained the external political and financial control of the cities. For example, the still existing Governor of a former province of British India, now federal state, can immediately interfere in the municipal affairs of a city, in particular with respect to financial matters. Still today, the administrator in Delhi is seen as the successor of the former Commissioners and has the authority to suspend decisions of the various committees on behalf of the central government. This not only leads to disadvantages in the administrative field, but also dictates planning and project specifications.

As can be seen from the examples of the city administration and town planning, the academic research of the topic thus far rather follows the colonial discourse, namely to represent the city in the colony as a screen for measures of discipline and civilisation. In this way, the colonial state assumes the role of an actor, whilst the Indian population is usually only assigned the role of passive recipient. A handful of studies exist which show how an urban Indian agency developed in this radically changing environment. For Bombay, for example, it has been demonstrated that the inhabitants had quite a commitment to cultural, social and economic activities. The foundation of economic representation, charitable organisations, educational institutions and cricket clubs indicate the high social involvement of the population in the context of an emerging civil society.[172] The same can also be stated for Calcutta where the members of the *bhadralok* developed new forms of public sphere and, for example with *adda*, established a great culture of discussion and debate.[173]

The urban poor in Banaras/Varanasi, Allahabad, Kanpur and Lakhnau, despite the policing of the interwar period, developed a considerable space to pursue their own interests in which they were not defined by a class, but rather they formed their own identities in the urban context according to different forms of labour, culture, region, *jati* and religion. The urban public sphere as an arena of political debate has been transformed by the urban poor, especially, into a highly contested field, which is far from dominated by solely middle-class and elite organisations or Congress. Urban labour should no longer only be seen as merely a way of improving the socio-economic status of the rural–urban circular workers in the country, as it was at the beginning of the twentieth century. It should now be understood from the perspective of urban residents who fought for the city with reference to it as a social, economic, cultural and political space of identity.[174] The history of urban communities, identities, cultures, social and economic conditions from the times of British colonialism has yet to be written.

Urban development after 1947: metropolises, megacities, middle towns

The partition of British India at the end of colonial rule caused a demographic disaster as millions of people migrated back and forth between the newly created states, and the border cities such as Calcutta to East Pakistan and Delhi to West Pakistan experienced unexpected population growth. Whilst some 918,000 inhabitants lived in Delhi in 1941, by 1951 this number had grown to 1,744,000, a population growth rate of 90 per cent.[175] In the same period, the population of Calcutta grew from 3.62 million people to 4.67 million.[176] In Pakistan, Karachi's population increased from 360,000 in 1941 (which corresponded to just half of the population of Lahore) to over 1.1 million residents by 1951. Most of the *mohajirs*, who originated from North India, settled in other cities of Sind, especially in Haiderabad and Sukkur where they accounted for 65 and 55 per cent of the populations, respectively, and 57 per cent in Karachi. Urban Pakistan was considerably affected by the extent to which Indian immigrants settled in the cities.[177]

Since the 1950s new housing developments were pursued in the existing cities and particularly in Delhi, Karachi and Lahore as well as the development of new towns that were built for the immigrant refugees, five of which were found in Uttar Pradesh alone and four in the Panjab. In addition, industrial cities such as Rourkhela, Bhilai, Durgapur and Bokarao emerged with more than 100,000 inhabitants each as well as refinery-orientated cities including Barauni, Haldia and Ankleshwar. A characteristic of these newly developed cities were the chemical and aluminium production or coal mining industries.[178] This urban development is reflected by the overall increase in the rate of urbanisation. Between 1951 and 2007, the rate of urbanisation increased in India from 17 per cent to 33.4 per cent, in Pakistan from 17.5 per cent to 41.4 per cent, in Bangladesh from 4.2 per cent to 32 per cent and in Sri Lanka from 15.3 per cent to 25 per cent. At the end of 2010, 56 cities with over one million inhabitants were to be found among these South Asian states. Moreover, ten of these cities are recorded as megacities (cities with over 10 million inhabitants), the largest of which is Mumbai with nearly 20 million inhabitants, followed by Delhi and Kolkata each with about 15 million inhabitants and Karachi and Dhaka with more than 13 million inhabitants.[179]

In recent years, these megacities in the global South have received increased attention from the fields of science and politics. In contrast to the "global cities" of the North, these "megacities" seem to occupy a category of their own as they are characterised by uncontrolled in-migration, uncontrolled growth, inadequate infrastructure, unpredictable environmental problems and the aforementioned notorious yet dominant informal sector. Based on such characteristics, megacities have been turned into a problem area that needs investigation as they are in stark contrast to the global cities that seem to pose few problems in these same areas.[180] It must however be remembered that the current political and scientific perception of the megacities is also subject to a continued colonial discourse, as the cities of Asia (and Africa) are often seen to be in need of monitoring and policing and are made the object of surveillance, because of the potential threat they pose to the world. Among other places, this discourse is reflected in scientific literature as well as global media coverage which focus rather more on emphasising the unsolvable problems rather than the pioneering potential of the megacity.[181]

Part of this ongoing discourse is the study of the rapidly growing "ugly" appearance of the South Asian megacities which focuses on the slums and their poor living conditions. In 1981, it was estimated that about 28 million people were living in urban slums in the Indian Union; by 1991 the figure had increased to 46 million. At the beginning of this millennium it was estimated that by the year 2020 the slum population would "become at least 100 million [...] which, *if unchecked*, will multiply to 300 million by 2050."[182] The biggest problem of South Asian cities seems to be that of an uncontrolled growth of slums/*bastis-jhuggis* and their role in the cause of the urban plight.[183] A consequence of this is that the major focus of policies is on the consistent and partly radical control of slum development, including violent slum clearance, as well as an aggressive state-sponsored birth control system. Delhi, as the capital of the Indian Union, has attracted its share of attention for its strict "resettlement schemes" and crude sterilisation campaigns in the 1970s. However, neither the policies of urban slum clearance nor the state birth control scheme have produced the desired results which is why they remain objects of open criticism.[184]

Slums/*batis-jhuggis* are by no means an aesthetic problem that cannot be corrected with the help of "beautification" measures as the official parlance calls for. In addition, it has been shown that *bastis-jhuggis* are socially and economically, culturally and politically heterogeneous formations, which constitute an important part of the overall urban fabric. Dharavi (Mumbai), the world's largest *basti*, with an estimated one million inhabitants, is a more or less shining example of urban governance through the participation of all groups, such as local residents, city government, and local and urban industry that is regulated together. Meanwhile recent attempts to implement a giant private–public redevelopment project of Dharavi have failed on account of huge popular resistance.[185] In Ahmedabad too, promising attempts at community-based partnerships exist in the context of urban governance.[186] Great opportunities would be available for the *basti* dwellers in Bengaluru if the diversity of professional skills that are so often found in the informal sector were to be supported through the issuing of small loans, which in turn would trigger an economic boom.[187]

Chennai has been able to improve the quality of life of individual neighbourhoods of low-income classes through the help of the so-called "street beautifier" programme and the aid given by NGO Exnora. The "street beautifier" programme, financed by small donations of the local community, not only promotes the regular collection of refuse, but also the sorting and further selling of this "raw material", thereby generating additional income. Aside from waste removal, the scheme has also swept the streets, planted trees and cultivated small gardens. The efficiency of this programme is guaranteed through its decentralised and small-scale organisation. The paradox is striking, that it is the low-income communities that are far more willing to act voluntarily (and independent of the city itself) and to cooperate than those communities of the middle and high-income classes. Moreover, it is the young members of these low-income communities that have contributed the most in the implementation of the programme.[188] However, the real potential of the *basti* residents and low-income quarters are obviously still not officially recognised and promoted accordingly or legitimised by city officials.

Numerous plans exist for the development of South Asian cities away from the "problem areas". At the national level, the government under Jawaharlal Nehru quickly entered debates surrounding the issue of urban planning. With its new role as the capital of the nation, Delhi, as a refugee town and as a future trade, commercial and industrial city, was a prominent example of a city that needed to resolve the seemingly unmanageable social problems. Within a few years, the national government responded by implementing a far-sighted plan of unique dimensions for the control of urban development in the Delhi Master Plan of 1962. With the help of international town planners and scientists as well as support from the US Ford Foundation, a large-scale urban plan was drafted based on decentralised urban development and an optimal road network. The measure of all planning was (and still is) the Western industrial city with its high individual and motorised mobility of inhabitants, that was not, however, the reality in India at that time.[189]

Meanwhile more than 1,000 master plans have been developed for Indian cities, which account for about one-third of all cities. In general the master plans attempted to specify the allocation of land for residential, commercial, industrial, recreational and public use and to commit to the development of the city within a fixed planning period of 10 to 20 years. As with all the far-sighted planning attempts, various drawbacks are bound to arise. The first is the time-consuming act of preparing the plans for all statutory procedures.

Second, the goal of decentralisation makes commuting necessary, which in turn leads to the contrary drawback of increased reliance on private transport, traffic congestion and pollution. Third, the master plans lack the necessary flexibility to react quickly to changing circumstances. Finally, the focus of the master plans, as in the case of the improvement trusts, is on land use, thus the claim of urban planning to include the residents and their ideas of a city thereby raising the terms of public participation is unachievable. The result is a deep cleft between planning and implementation.[190] The dilemma of this deficit is that the planning regime is, itself, an informalised entity, one that is in a constant state of deregulation, ambiguity and exception.[191]

The 74th Constitutional Amendment Act of 1993 granted Indian cities a little more political autonomy for the first time since independence. So-called urban local bodies such as the municipalities and the *panchayats* were to initiate new forms of urban planning in cooperation with state institutions, organisations of civil society and the public–private sector. After more than a decade, hardly any progress has been recorded. The fact remains that the autonomy of municipal bodies has continued to be restricted, as is their financial self-sufficiency. At the beginning of the twenty-first century just 3.4 per cent of the municipal budget originated from its own taxes. Due to the extreme levels of urbanisation and on account of the international competitiveness of attractive cities, the Indian Government felt compelled to call the New Urban Planning to life. The development of the Jawaharlal Nehru Urban Renewal Mission (JNURM) from 2005 stands as an alternative to the existing principles of the master plans for a number of selected cities.[192] In addition to financial assistance, the close cooperation with public–private partnerships is critical for this development to function.[193] Currently, the peri-urban villages have now also been involved in the planning and development, thereby reinforcing the scheme.[194]

The Master Plan 2015 for Bengaluru, published in 2007, attempts to implement the directives of the JNURM. In the nineteenth century, Bengaluru/Bangalore developed into a colonial dual city with the establishment of the Civil and Military Station (CMS) and was based on the infrastructural differences and building segregation described above. However, in Bangalore urban planning based on the principles of segregation reproduced social hierarchies of *jati*/*varna* in the form of the British "caste system", thus cementing social structures.[195] Nevertheless, the aforementioned settlement of technological industries between 1940 and 1956 and the establishment of ancillary industries brought an influx of workers (to cover the more than 100,000 new jobs that were created by 1961), as well as bringing new social groups and strata into the urban population structure. Additionally, more industrial, engineering and technological companies settled in the city during the 1960s and 1970s.[196]

Even before the city earned its reputation as a global IT city in the late 1980s, key industries demanding qualified workers to be resident in the city were important. However, despite this, neither the city nor its society has truly been able to assert the claim of being an "information society" given the unevenness of the economic and political transition.[197] This transition is also reflected in the planning design of the city. In this way, the slogan of "Bring Back Beauty to Bangalore" is meant to reintroduce the administrative separation between Bangalore and CMS as it existed until 1949. Following the example of Singapore as a global city and "world-class city", Bengaluru now works in close cooperation with Singapore to form the International Technology Park Bangalore, which, according to the most recent plans, will aim to transform itself into an "IT corridor" to the east of the city. Integral infrastructure for the success of this plan includes six residential townships, a highway to the logistic centre, an international airport and a ring road, as well as the surrounding greenbelt area.[198]

Here, as in other urban agglomerations, big cities and megacities, the victims of the plans are, time and again, the residents of the slums, who account

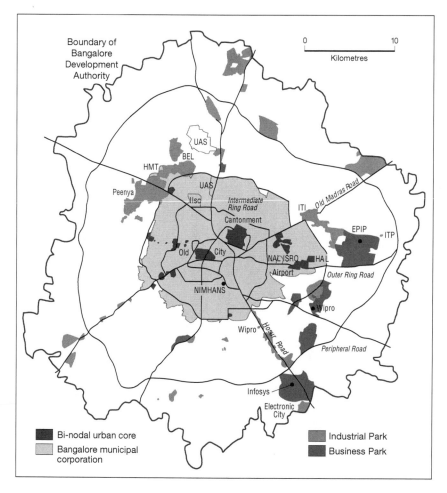

Map 7.3 Industrial and Business Park of Bangalore, c. 2005. Adapted from James Heitzman, *The City in South Asia* (Routledge: 2008), p. 219

for almost 20 per cent of the urban population, as well as the villages in the outlying areas of the city. Both population groups find themselves excluded from the planning process and are often overlooked in the plans themselves. In this respect the master plans reinstate the dualistic structure that was established during the colonial period of legal/illegal, opening up urban space for higher-income groups and corporate economies, whilst closing options for the urban poor and economies that support them. Thus the city has become a dichotomous space of rich and poor, formal and informal, green and spacious on the one hand and dirty and congested on the other. Planning the urban environs means ordering space rather than promoting social welfare or, at least, providing access to social and economic opportunities.[199] Seen from a historical perspective, there seems hardly any difference between the colonial improvement trusts and the current master plans as the redistribution of urban space still has priority on the town planning agenda.

Major cities in South Asia, as elsewhere, are becoming increasingly similar urban agglomerations with clusters of town centres, urban expansion projects, settlements, satellite towns, industrial zones, airports, railways, motorways and so on. Bengaluru is a good example of such an emerging urban agglomeration which has transformed and continues to transform an entire region. Meanwhile, even larger plans are being made within the Indian Union as the so-called "knowledge corridors" that will link the widely spaced urban agglomerations with each other is the latest form of urban planning. The corridors aim to disentangle two compacted urban spaces and concentrate the establishment of industries and universities, cutting-edge research centres, additional to the founding of residential new towns alongside highways. The Andhra Pradesh knowledge corridor is such an urban mega-project, as is the Bangalore–Mysore corridor, which breaks with all previous notions of town and urbanity.[200] Added to this concept, which can be seen in the context of "world-class cities", is the claim of the capital city Delhi – since the construction of the Delhi Metro and the hosting of the Commonwealth Games in 2010 – to be such a "world-class city" and a showcase for the nation and the world.[201]

With all the modern design and planning focused on the 56 cities with one million inhabitants, the 550 cities with over 100,000 inhabitants and the countless middle towns between 10,000 and 100,000 inhabitants fall almost completely by the wayside as they are subject to their own social, economic and cultural problems which arise for small towns as a result of their transformation into larger urban units.[202] Although these towns are not growing as rapidly as the prominent megacities, the hardly existing government attention given to these middle towns, the even more dire possibilities of securing finance and barely existing urban planning, means that these towns and cities have much larger problems to fight. Many of these towns are embedded in an agrarian structure and therefore serve the rural population as sub-regional headquarters for a predominantly agrarian economy in which courts of law, central post offices and insurance companies, as well as shopping facilities for jewellery, clothing and footwear, complete the middle town's function as a rural supply centre.[203]

Thus, the urbanisation of South Asia seems to be a two-speed process. The high-speed track is occupied by the rapid transformation of big cities, metropolises and megacities. This development, as seen in the example of the knowledge corridors, is partly funded by the state. Meanwhile, in the slow lane, the middle-sized towns are found floundering as their involvement in the rural hinterland creates little political, media and scientific attention which instead is focused almost exclusively on the megacities. Given its dramatic population growth in the last five decades in the wake of post-colonial industrialisation, which was based on the Green Revolution as well as steel plants and hydraulic projects, and more recently, the post-modern knowledge society, which is based on media and technology, the development of these cities is not, of course, *a priori* to be characterised as problematic or as chaotic.

In comparison, no city in the western countries of Europe and North America has had to cope with such population growth in such a short time during industrialisation between 1850 and 1950 as have many of the Indian cities during the last decades. Aside from this fact, the cities of Europe and America had the financial means in place and had developed adequate administrative structures with which they could deal with such challenges. However, as shown above, South Asian cities have been administratively and fiscally conserved at the level of the late eighteenth and early nineteenth centuries due to colonial rule and by staying under the direct control of a central government. As such, autonomy and self-government, legitimised by public participation, were generally not desired in British India, and certainly not at the urban level. Thus the many shortcomings of urbanisation in present-day South Asian states can therefore be attributed to the colonial regime. This is not to say that the current South Asian states, which find themselves still in many of these structures, cannot rid themselves of these shackles in order to give the cities the leeway they need to plan and, ultimately, to give such plans a chance to be implemented and realised.

Notes

1 Statista 2013; Paul 2010: 1–10, esp. 5; Heitzman 2008: 176.
2 Middell and Naumann 2010: 149–70.
3 Gayer 2007: 515–44.
4 Mann 2000b: 166–82.
5 Tomlinson 1993: 4.
6 Kidambi 2007: 49–70.
7 Ratnagar 2001; Ratnagar 2002; Jansen 1986: 22–37, 45–92.
8 Heitzman 2008: 12–34.
9 Ratnagar 2002: 5–9.
10 Coningham and Allchin 1995: 152–83.
11 Moosvi 1987: 303–5; Ehlers and Krafft 1993: 9–25.
12 Friedrichs 1985; Zimmermann 1996: 9–38.
13 Rothermund 1988: 50–60.

14 King 1980: 1–19.
15 Grewal R. 1994: 173–90.
16 Broeze 1992: 245–72.
17 Meller 1979: 330–50.
18 Ramachandran 1989: 6–18.
19 Tchitcherov 1998: 167–252.
20 Yang 1998; Hasan M. 2007.
21 Perlin 1994: 72.
22 Ahuja 1999: 26–7.
23 Aiolfi 1987: 7–105.
24 Brennig 1994: 66–89.
25 Bayly 1988: 106–68; Bayly 1983: 303–69.
26 Hossain 1988; Specker 1984: 93–106, 130–70.
27 Divekar 1982: 332–52, esp. 347; Parshad 2007: 30, 42, 48–52.
28 Specker 1984: 117–91.
29 Subba Rao 2007: 17–21.
30 Roy T. 1999; Parshad 2007: 67–74.
31 Roy T. 2009: 579–613.
32 Bellwinkel-Schempp 1982: 133–57; Yalland 1987.
33 Parshad 2007: 84–8.
34 Mann 2012a: 431–55.
35 Walton 1903: 28; Roy T. 1999: 155–96; Parshad 2007, 84–8.
36 Parthasarathi P. 2001.
37 Roy T. 1999; Parshad 2007.
38 Tann and Aitken 1992: 199–214.
39 Morris 1982: 553–676, esp. 572–83.
40 Rothermund 1988: 56–8, 67–8; Tomlinson 1993: 98–9.
41 Tomlinson 1993: 92–3; Charlesworth 1982: 39.
42 Tomlinson 1993: 96; Gillion 1982: 46–49, 74–104.
43 Ahuja 2009: 48–60; Thorner 1950: 69–182; Kerr I. 1995; Kerr I. 2001.
44 Morris 1982: 556–7, 572, 583, 599–600.
45 Ibid.: 578.
46 Specker 1984.
47 Rothermund 1988: 56–60.
48 Ghosh P. 2000: 10–12, 35–44.
49 Kling 1992: 83–98.
50 Rothermund 1988: 62–4; Morris 1982: 613, 623; Tomlinson 1993: 116–8.
51 Bagchi 1972: 3–25.
52 Rothermund 1988: 60.
53 Ibid.: 58.
54 Rothermund 1992: 136–38, 154–67; Morris 1982: 602–16; Tomlinson 1993: 115–6.
55 Morris 1982: 616–24.
56 Tomlinson 1993: 114–5, 153–4, 160–1.
57 Parshad 2007: 131–6.
58 Heitzman 2008: 144–6.
59 Bagchi 1982: 291–321.
60 Nomura 2011: 83–116.
61 Tomlinson 1993: 9, 130–1; Bagchi 1972, 321–8; Lala 1981.
62 Bahl 1995: 92–8.
63 Hardgrove 2004.
64 Timberg 1992: 126–56; Timberg 1971: 264–83.
65 Hurd 1975a: 169–81; Hurd 1975b: 490–524; Haynes E.S. 1980: 25–42.
66 Nair J. 1998.
67 Ramusack 2004: 198–9.

68 Ibid.: 199–201.
69 Nair J. 2005: 81–6.
70 Nair J. 2011: 13–6.
71 Subba Rao 2007: 25–7, 40–50, 71–5.
72 Ramusack 2004: 201; Erdman 1971.
73 Rothermund 1988: 133–7.
74 Ibid.: 147–56.
75 DeLong 2003: 195–7; Rodrik and Subramanian 2005: 197–9.
76 Jeffrey 2000: 211.
77 McCartney 2010: 55; Mohanty and Reddy 2010: 47–58; Ahluwalia 2002: 67–88.
78 Marshall 1987b: 23–38.
79 Datta P. 2012: 59, 164; Kidambi 2007: 22.
80 Sen S. 1977: 36.
81 Datta 2012: 132–6.
82 Sen S. 1999: 22–8.
83 Morris 1965: 62–4.
84 Staubli 1994: 144–8.
85 Morris 1965: 44–62.
86 Sen S. 1999: 29–31.
87 Morris 1965: 65–71.
88 Ghosh P. 2000: 79–85.
89 Chandavarkar 1998.
90 Haynes D.E. 2008: 1–30.
91 Haynes D.E. 2001: 170–198.
92 Haynes D.E. 2008: 32–45.
93 Datta P. 1993: 57–84.
94 Sinha N. 2008: 999–1033, esp. 1017.
95 Sailer 2013: 207–55.
96 Sen S. 1977: 36–285 *passim*; Subba Rao 2007: 97.
97 Singh D. 1990.
98 Sen S. 1977: 292–13; Haynes D.E. 2008: 40.
99 Shaheed 2007: 70–83.
100 Kamat 2010: 99–119.
101 Breman 2004: 40–52, 65–9, 70–5.
102 Ibid.: 80–3.
103 Sen S. 1977: 433–6.
104 Sherlock 2001.
105 Shaheed 2007, *passim*.
106 Ibid., *passim*.
107 Olbrecht 2000.
108 Chakrabarty 1989; Ghosh P. 2000.
109 Chandavarkar 1998.
110 Bahl 1995; Gooptu 2001.
111 Zimmermann 1996: 11–13.
112 Visaria and Visaria 1982: 463–532, esp. 466.
113 Morris 1965: 13, 20.
114 Thankappan Nair 1990a: 10–23.
115 Ahuja 1999: 39–41.
116 Bellwinkel-Schempp 1982: 152; Oldenburg 1984: 18.
117 Hussain N. 1980: 197–223, esp. 198.
118 Gillion 1982: 53–4, 103–4.
119 Gupta N. 1981: 46–7.
120 McDonald-Gumperz 1974: 581–601, esp. 585; McAlpin 1983: 47–83.
121 Oldenbourg 1984: 18–19.

122 Thomas 1982: 68–80.
123 Heitzman 2008: 126.
124 Mitter 1986: 95–114.
125 Tindall 1982: 127.
126 Dossal 1992: 227–44; Burnell 1997: 20–8.
127 Lotsy 1990.
128 Chattopadhyay 2005: 54–62.
129 Ibid.: 77–92.
130 Datta P. 2012: 13–34, 137–40.
131 Chattopadhyay 2005: 62–75.
132 Heitzman 2008: 138.
133 Fischer-Tiné 2009: 90–121.
134 Gupta S. 1993: 29–33.
135 Datta P. 2012: 89–127; Mukherjee R. 1990: 45–51; Chatterjee M. 1990: 133–47.
136 Gillion 1982: 108–21; Heitler 1972: 239–57.
137 Masselos 1992: 273–316.
138 Chadwick 1965.
139 Berndt 1987: 140–63; Schubert 1997: 7–8; Yelling 1986: 10–15.
140 Klein 1986: 725–54, esp. 732; Dossal: 1991: 125–48.
141 Kidambi 2007: 49–70.
142 Dossal, 1991: 143; Klein 1986: 740, 743–5; Harrison M. 1994: 133–6.
143 Goodman 1952; Mann 2005c: 80–106.
144 Thankappan Nair 1990b: 224–37; Biswas A.B. 1990: 160–6; Nath and Majumdar 1990: 167–72.
145 Datta P. 2012: 127–70.
146 Meller 1979.
147 Kidambi 2007: 71–113.
148 Masselos 1992: 305–11.
149 Chatterjee M. 1990: 133–47.
150 Datta 2012: 184–275; Meller 1979.
151 Gooptu 2001, 66–139.
152 Soni 2000: 75–94.
153 Tarlo 2003; Mann 2005d: 251–78.
154 Gillion 1982: 129–33, 138–43.
155 Oldenburg 1984: 99.
156 Legg 2007.
157 Prashad V. 2001: 113–55; Mann 2007: 1–31; Sharan 2011: 425–62.
158 Mann and Sehrawat 2009: 543–70.
159 Harrison J. 1980: 167–95.
160 Vandal and Vandal 2006: 54–95.
161 Hussain N. 1980: 212–8.
162 Tinker 1954: 74.
163 Ibid.: 69.
164 Simon 1974: 30–41.
165 Datta P. 2012: 243.
166 Tewari, Raghupathi and Ansari 2007: 41–76, esp. 48.
167 Tinker 1954: 28–30.
168 Gillion 1982: 10–118; Bayly 1975: 52–120, esp. 92–4.
169 Tinker 1954: 31–5, 50; Bayly 1975: 157–8; Gillion 1982: 118–9.
170 Tinker 1954: 45–50.
171 Bayly 1975: 93; Bayly 1971: 289–311.
172 Kidambi 2007: 157–233.
173 Chattopadhyay 2005: 186–216.
174 Goopto 2001: 141–364.

175 Datta V.N. 1993: 287–306; Kaur R. 2005: 229–249.
176 Chatterjee M. 1990: 135.
177 Jaffrelot 2004: 17; Khuhro 1997: 95–111.
178 Ramachandran 1989, 69–71; Rothermund, Kropp and Dienemann 1980.
179 Heitzman 2008: 175–8
180 McTarlane and Waibel 2012.
181 Fuchs R.J. 1994; Keizai-Kenkyūsho 2001; Siddiqui 2004, 2010; Yagnik and Sheth 2011.
182 Bijulal 2004: 4.
183 Bhatnagar 2010.
184 Tarlo 2000: 51–73; Gulati, Tyagi and Sharma 2003.
185 Fuchs M. 2005: 103–23.
186 Mathur and Bazaz 2010: 114–40.
187 Kamath, Dasmohapatra and Patkar 2010: 283–308.
188 Tewari, Raghupathi and Ansari 2007: 62–3.
189 Sundaram R. 2010: 28–66; Jain A.K. 1990.
190 Ravindra 2010: 11–29, esp. 12–15.
191 Roy A. 2009: 76–87.
192 Government of India 2005.
193 Banerjee 2012: 93–118.
194 Ravindra 2010: 15–16; Asher and Vasudevam 2010: 177–205.
195 Nair J. 2005: 38–76.
196 Nair J. 2005: 78–89, 127–8.
197 Heitzman 2004.
198 Heitzman 2005: 219–20; Nair J. 2005: 161–4; 333–43.
199 Nair J. 2005, 124–6; 140–52.
200 Heitzman 2008: 220–3
201 Delhi 2010 XIX Commonwealth Games 2010; Mann 2012d: 136–61.
202 Weiz 2005: 151–75; Heitzman 2008, 178.
203 Heitzman 2008: 209–10.

8 Knowledge, science, technology and power

Themes, theories and subjects

The term science often goes hand in hand with the attribute of "modern". In research, science, as a term, is used almost exclusively in the West for a certain humanism and the explanation of specific sciences. The term entails that modernisation is understood as a process based on advanced technology and scientific spirit, rational attitude towards life, a secularised image of society, justice as a measure of public affairs and the idea of the nation-state. This culminates occasionally in the view that modern science and technology found its immediate expression in industrialisation and thereby contributed directly to the progress of society building and the nation-state, especially of European origin. Such a concept of science is of course self-referential.[1]

It seems that in "Western" research discourse, a consensus existed with regard to the European expansion of the modern era which has gone hand in hand with five centuries of a monopoly on knowledge that was held by the colonial powers. Ideological constructions of rational, technical and social superiority and the systematic exclusion of non-European-American sciences have been the long-lasting result.[2] The non-European world not only represented the "Other", but the European colonies and their inhabitants served as laboratories in which sociopolitical, labour and racial considerations were experimentally conceptualised. Such concepts found their way into the discourse on science and politics.[3] Only recently has the role of colonies been critically scrutinised with respect to the rational-scientific self-understanding as well as in the formation of the nation-state in Europe.

In this constellation, British India occupied a special role in the British Empire as well as in the formation of the European scientific landscape. Currently there are two different approaches in research which explain the development of the sciences in South Asia. First is the diffusion model to explain the contemporary Indian sciences as having gradually grown out of European influence from the former "colonial sciences". Despite some valuable insights such as in the concept of "colonial science" and its mutation into "national science", it still leaves a rather Euro-centric perspective and hence a European-dominated discourse on science as it focuses on European actors reducing Indians to the role of passive "recipients".[4] The second model is based on the sciences as an expression of the modern world to be observed on the basis of mutual perception, influence and exchange.[5] In this way the Indian actors are attributed a greater deal of agency who took up the challenge posed by the Western forms of sciences, self-critically questioning their own forms and thus advancing their own understanding of "modern" science and "modernity".[6]

It is striking, however, to notice that almost all previous books on the history of science of South Asia start out from a point of scientific concept that is limited to the natural sciences as the "exact" sciences. There is hardly an account of South Asia's history of science in which the social and human sciences are discussed[7] – other than in the historical scientific studies into Indology-Sanskrit whereby the scientific and political ramifications for Europe are emphasised rather than the impacts in South Asia[8] – despite the fact that they may have more sustainable and far-reaching effects on the society. This bias is reflected, among other things, in the creation of numerous Indian Institutes of Technology in independent India in response to the selective neglect of the sciences through the colonial education policy. This bias also mirrors the neglect of South Asia's various conventional education systems and institutions.

Education: schools, colleges, universities

In the eighteenth century, India's education system was divided into two levels. At the primary education level were the local elementary institutions such as the *pathshalas* and *maktabs*. At the higher education level were the *tol*s and the *madrassas*. The British initially changed little in this scheme with their territorial domination of the subcontinent. In 1781 the Calcutta Madrasah was founded with state funding and this was followed by the Sanskrit College in Varanasi in 1792. In both cases, the EIC proved to be a generous sponsor of local educational institutions and donated books and scholarships. In this formative stage, the standardisation of curricula was innovative whilst the bureaucratisation of the administration was a new concept. However, the content of education was not changed for two reasons: on the one hand the British had to rely on the cooperation of indigenous specialists such as translators, judicial text interpreters and revenue administrators, whilst on the other hand a certain respect for Indian cultures and institutions still existed.[9]

In the 1830s, the upcoming judicial reforms and the question of future judicial and administrative language sparked an educational policy offensive. In this context, the first Law Member of the Govenor-General's Council Thomas B. Macaulay (1800–59), completed a dossier on Indian history, culture, literature and languages. He came to the conclusion that the entire literature in Sanskrit and Persian was not comparable to a single bookshelf of European literature and thereby felt justified – indeed calling it a British duty – to abolish the Indian legal, administrative and especially the educational institutions on account of their linguistic and cultural deficits. According to Macaulay's opinion, India's modernisation could only be guaranteed through the introduction of English legal institutions and the English language as well as the educational content of European culture which would also lead to the success of the envisaged legal reforms.[10]

In addition, Macaulay called for the formation of a small Indian elite, who were to be Indian according to "colour and blood", but British according to "tastes and morals". Ideally, a gradual diffusion of the British educational content was sought that would result in the overall uplift of Indian society. Apart from the introduction of Persian as the language of the Mughal government and courts, such a realignment of Indian education policy can be seen as undoubtedly the biggest paradigm shift of modern South Asian intellectual history. Parts of the Indian elite, especially the new *bhadralok* in Calcutta, welcomed this radical reform, as they recognised for themselves the benefits of English in colonial enterprises and therefore advocated not only the introduction of British educational institutions, but also protested against the promotion of indigenous institutions.[11]

Whilst it seemed that the Anglicists (radical modernisers according to "Western" ideas) had gained the upper hand with the decision by Governor-General Bentinck (in office 1828–35), the Orientalists (moderate modernisers combining "Eastern" and "Western" ideas) did not give in and forced a compromise in the 1840s. The Bengalis were also involved in this process and fought, with the support of Orientalists, through numerous petitions for the preservation of Sanskrit schools and *madrassas*. On account of the agitation they were able to secure not only the future of these indigenous schools, but also a small number of government scholarships for them too. Apart from this, the teaching in local schools was to be done through the use of regional languages. The debate surrounding the appropriate language for the dissemination of scientific and educational content finally settled on the British side of the argument at the end of the nineteenth century. However, up until 1882 their experts were unsure whether or not exclusively English or Indian languages were best suited for the distribution of knowledge.[12]

In 1854, the EIC introduced a three-tier education system in the image of the British system that consisted of primary and secondary and higher education schools, the latter of which was the only one to receive funding. Three years later universities were established in Calcutta, Bombay and Madras, followed by a further two in Lahore and Allahabad in 1882 and 1887, respectively. They consisted of colleges, the numbers of which in 1857 reached 27, and grew to 72 in 1881 and 150 in 1921. However, the universities were rather more mere degree-granting machines than research facilities. Science courses were first offered in the three British coastal metropolises in 1868 and it took until the University Act of 1904 to establish post-graduate education and research facilities. Engineering was taught at separate institutions such as Roorkee and Sibpur in order to train Indian subaltern personnel who then found employment in subordinate positions in the Public Works Departments (PWD) which were established after 1854 in the provinces of British India.[13]

However, university curriculum was limited and unbalanced. Still in the 1930s M.A. programmes were made up of some 230 classes in English, yet only 65 in mathematics. Furthermore, it was not until the 1930s that training in mechanical, electrical and mining engineering took place in the civil engineering colleges of the PWDs. No wonder then that before the turn of the century massive criticism of the British-Indian universities and engineering education came to a head, prompting the establishment of two technical colleges in 1906 in the wake of the Swadeshi Movement in Calcutta, namely the Bengal Technical Institute and the Bengal National College. Since the British did not recognise the qualifications awarded by these institutions, they were short-lived. However, the call for an adequate education in science and technology was not quietened. There was added demand for education for industrialisation purposes, especially during the 1930s, in which, with the help of a stronger institutionalisation, academic research and industrial needs were to be coordinated.[14]

The British regarded the establishment of independent universities in the cities of Maisur, Haiderabad and Baroda with suspicion. Many monarchs intentionally distanced themselves from the Western educational content whilst others operated on a selective adaptation of this very educational content to promote integration into the British Raj. Most rulers however understood the term "modern education", as many educational reformers of the nineteenth century in Calcutta did, to be a blend of Indian and European scientific education.[15] Sometimes Indian rulers proved to be more "modern" than the British as they, on account of their understanding of dominion (*rajadharma*), opted for both the "traditional" as well as the "modern" sciences for state promotion, thereby increasing their overall social prestige. Since this was not on the political agenda of the British, the colonial state hardly paid any attention to primary education. As a result the number of primary schools ended up in decline by the end of the nineteenth century, with the result that the literacy rate of the population did not equal even one per cent.[16]

At the same time, an unforeseen dilemma affected educational policy: despite the difficult entrance and final exams at colleges and universities, a glut of graduates had developed. Graduates found employment in adequate professional fields to be increasingly difficult and instead became more and more engaged in political work. The British watched this development with concern. After the turn of the century, the public debate on the shortcomings of the British-Indian education system grew significantly. Finally, the British retreated from the educational policy with the constitutional reforms of 1919, leaving it to the judgement of the newly established provincial ministries which were occupied by Indians. Growing dissatisfaction with educational policy and the desire to delineate themselves from the British educational model led to patriotic and nationally minded Indians to form their own education programmes and establish independent educational institutions.

The most famous of these was the Gurukul Kangri founded in 1902 in Hardwar in northern India. Superficially this resembled the teaching of *pathshala*, but was in fact a hybrid variant of the English public schools whilst the curriculum of courses in Sanskrit and Vedic literature were complemented by subjects such as chemistry and physics. Spiritual strength, character building and physical exercise were envisaged to contribute to the virility of the newly forming nation.[17] Meanwhile, the establishment of the Jamia Millia in Delhi in 1920 by Zakir Hussain added a significant accent against the orthodoxy of the Deobandi school.[18] The reform movements at the turn of the century were also felt in the arena of primary education. The reforms were part of a globally significant education reform known as New Education and represented a reaction to the established educational institutions and educational content. Directed against authoritarian and alien educational concepts, these reforms ushered in a nature-based, practice-oriented educational system focused on hands-on learning. Rabindranath Tagore founded such an experimental school in Shantiniketan. Gandhi's Nai Talim was a similar experiment which also aimed at a fundamental transformation of society.[19] This led to extensive educational debates in different regions of British India that lasted until well past the end of colonial rule.[20]

The situation also changed at the universities in the 1920s, as scientific branches were established at the new universities in Allahabad and Lakhnau as well as at the other institutions. This move made it possible for Indian scientists to gain access to higher education facilities, and also gave them access, albeit highly limited access, to prestigious academic institutions such as The Royal Society. The first demands for a nationalisation of academic institutions came during the last quarter of the nineteenth century and were quickly implemented with the Indian Association of Cultivation of Science, founded in 1876, whose mission was to disseminate scientific results nationally. Moreover, official publications for science in Indian languages also increased following the founding of the Journal of the Asiatic Society in 1836; however, by 1895 just 18 articles had been written by Indian scientists, whilst more than 1,021 had been published by European scientists.[21]

The first recognition of Indian sciences came in 1930 as Chandrasekhara Venkata Raman was awarded the Nobel Prize for Physics. At the same time, the Indian scientific traditions experienced a renaissance, especially in the fields of chemistry and medicine (in particular Ayurveda), which were now seen as complementary to Western medical knowledge. This new self-consciousness found its institutional expression in 1924 as the School of Indian Medicine was established in Madras and was immediately awarded the status of a College of Indian Medicine after independence.[22] The National Institute of Science was founded explicitly to promote and disseminate scientific knowledge and for the representation of Indian scientists at both a national and international level. Moreover, an increasing number of academic textbooks were published in South Asian languages.[23]

However, Indian scientists complained of a lack of financing for the institutes and laboratories as well as of a lack of equipment and international contacts in the 1940s. It is this financial structural disadvantage that explains why the scientific level of Indian academics remained generally low. The nationalisation of the sciences was consistently demanded, not for the lack of resources, as claimed, but because both human and natural resources were simply not being used appropriately. This demand was, in part, realised when Jawaharlal Nehru became Prime Minister of India as he promoted the natural sciences primarily. Between 1947 and 1986, the number of universities increased from 20 to 160. The development of a knowledge society, especially at the Indian Institutes of Technology, became based on goal-oriented research as in the famous Massachusetts Institute of Technology.[24] The successes of the pharmaceutical industry, as well as in the IT industry, were based on this scientific policy initiative. Ultimately, this initiative included the development of nuclear technology and the testing of nuclear devices in 1974 and 1998.[25] A similar "development policy" can also be seen in Pakistan, although here development is rather more motivated by competition with India.[26]

Indians were therefore not helpless victims of a dominant colonial discourse in which they had no room for manoeuvre and were not given the chance to influence the forms and their own institutions in education and science. Furthermore, Indian scientists were not in particular favour of European academia, and they did not bow to this constant discrimination in colonial academia.[27] There is now consensus that the "modern" science only partially came to South Asia through the Europeans whilst it has been emphasised that the South Asian scientists massively influenced the so-called "modern sciences", as will be shown below in particular reference to medical knowledge production.[28] Meanwhile, Indian scientists, especially, have created a science of their own, particularly in the fields of mathematics, computer science, physics and chemistry as well as original contributions to the now global science culture.[29]

History and historiography

South Asia is a world region in which literacy developed relatively late (c. 270 BCE) and did not lead to a recording of history as we know it in Europe by the Greek Herodotus and Livy for the Romans. Moreover, when compared to China and the Ottoman and Persian empires, the historiography of South Asia is rather modest. However, we do benefit from various forms of historiographical evidence which include the so-called Vedic texts that were handed down orally for thousands of years, especially the Rigveda (c.1200–1000 BCE). These texts are now no longer understood as a collection of theoretical discussions, but rather as parts of a historical narrative. This also applies to the epics of the Mahabharata and the Ramayana, even if they are confined, to a large extent, to heroic myths and genealogies of dynasties that were compiled in the second century BCE from different storylines.[30]

From CE 300 the text genre of the Puranas is discernible, the content of which is of historical importance insofar as it describes the rights and obligations of a ruler (*rajadharma*) and hands down the standards of those rulers considered exemplary. The substance of the Puranas, as well as that of the epics, has remained a part of the cultural traditions of South Asia and continues to be of political relevance. In general, the authors associated with the epics and Puranas subordinate history to literature. For this reason courtly literature contains many dramas and ballads with a historical core without actually being historiographical works. In general, the historical account was tied to a regional court. From these courts chronicles were also produced, such as the Rajatarangini of Kalhana in Kashmir from the mid-twelfth century CE or the Mahavamsa in Lanka which recounts the history of the island and its Buddhist shrines from the third century BCE, making it the oldest historiographical testimony of South Asia.

Generally it can be observed that the stronger the regionality or locality of the political events, the larger the historical core that can be discerned. Indian rulers did not feel compelled to bring their own history into conjunction with that of their neighbours. Rather, defeated dynasties were systematically hidden and replaced with the genesis and genealogy of the new dynasty, its allocation of privileges and land rights in either oral or written form. Written by local poets for a local audience, this literature, which was still produced at the beginning of the nineteenth century in some places of South India, reconstructing individual events of the fifteenth century, won ever more legitimation. On account of their local connection and the historiographical unity they represent, the texts constitute what has been termed endo-history.[31]

In addition to this specific form of South Asian historiography further various forms of historiography emerged with the Muslim rulers from the thirteenth century which were aligned inter-regionally. The early historical works present biographies or annals of Muslim princes, written in Arabic or Persian languages. Without doubt Zia du Din Barani (b. 1285) is one of the most important of the early writers. In his Tarikh-i-Firoze-Shahi he tells the story of the Sultanate of Delhi from an analytical and critical perspective.[32] The most significant historiographical work was compiled by Akbar (r. 1556–1602): the Akbarnama. In his role as courtly historiographer, Abu'l Fazl represents the ruler-friendly contemporary historiography with this work. Various schools of historiographical writing, including court history, as well as a quite critical history writing, document the fairly tolerant scientific activities in Akbar's times.[33]

With the gradual expansion of territorial rule, the British claimed sovereignty over the country's history. From the mid-eighteenth century India was no longer described as the land of inexhaustible wealth. Increasingly, the "oriental despotism", the alleged decadence of the disintegrating Mughal Empire and the contemporary anarchic conditions were highlighted in these historical representations.[34] The British implemented their own, two-fold, historical construct against this disenchanted vision of India. On the one hand, Robert Orme (1728–1801) established in his *History of the Military Transactions of the British Nation in Hindustan* (1778) the myth of Robert Clive as the conqueror of Bengal and in the long run the image of an always victorious Britain. On the other hand was the Orientalists' deconstruction of Indian history, emphasising the glorious scientific achievements of the Vedic Age, from then on termed the "Indian Ancient Times", which was followed by an ongoing period of "medieval" decline which accelerated with the advent of the Muslim invaders at the beginning of the thirteenth century followed by the British "Modern Time".[35]

Since the beginning of the nineteenth century, the utilitarianism of philosophical radicals in Britain sustained the employees of the EIC.[36] A pioneer of this radical position was James Mill (1773–1836), an executive of the EIC in London and a man who had never set foot on Indian soil. As a representative of the aforementioned Anglicists, in his *History of British India*, published in 1817, he did away with any Indian history and culture and took the view that India had at no time possessed a glorious history; on the contrary, he argued the country had always been at a lower level of civilisation.[37] This difference of civilisation and the self-imposed obligation to civilise the Indians was understood as the historically derived legitimacy of colonial rule in what was to become the civilising mission.[38]

For all the differences between Orientalists and Anglicists, they did however share the assumption of a civilisation gap between India and Europe and the necessary reforms required to modernise India. The differences were only in the methods by which the civilisation project should be achieved. The positions of the Orientalists and Anglicists would be roughly divided according to the differentiation in contemporary scientific disciplines at the time in Europe. Whilst the Orientalists promoted a rather more humanities-based approach, the Anglicists increasingly wanted to use the natural sciences to achieve modernisation. During the nineteenth century the modernisation of British India was increasingly understood as a rational-technical innovation that could only be accomplished by the British.[39] With the simultaneous introduction of Anglo-European education, which was limited to the humanities, "Indian" history began to be integrated into British history. According to this understanding, since the founding of the EIC settlements, Indian history was an integral part of the British history whilst the "rest" of South Asia's history was demoted to mere pre-history. Until the mid-twentieth century little changed in the British historiography, which was often a mere military history, written by mostly retired military officers and civil administrators.[40]

With the onset of the national movement in the late nineteenth century, Bengali and Marathi writers, journalists and politicians first began to remember their own history.[41] In doing so, the Indian nation did not at first stand at the centre of the narratives, but rather the regional stories of Bengal and Maharashtra, followed by Orissa, Sind, Hindustan and Tamil Nadu.[42] The question as to what and who the Indian nation constituted was first broached in 1918 with the 14-point programme of US President Woodrow Wilson as it included the self-determination of nations. A longstanding debate broke out in the INC as to whether India was already a nation and therefore could demand independence or whether it was still on the path of nation-building. Yet, the question as to what would constitute the Indian nation remained unresolved until the independence of British India and continues to be a subject of debate today.[43]

The construction of a Hindu national history became ever more clearly distinguishable from the end of the nineteenth century. It focused on a view that not only stressed the self-equivalence of India's past as a reassurance of the national presence, but also postulated civilisational primacy of Indian culture in comparison to the European. To this end technical inventions and democratic systems were identified in the Vedic scriptures which thus predated European antiquity. Educational reformers such as Dayanand Saraswati (1824–83), writers such as Bankimchandra Chatterjee (1838–94) and politicians such as Bal Gangadhar Tilak (1856–1920) deliberately referred to such an imagined past in order to advance social renewal of the Indian society as historians in all nation-states at that time did. They all worked on highly influential historical constructions with the aim of freeing India from its current dependence. In search of useful topics and figures for a national history to be written, regional history books gradually became meaningless, sometimes surviving in their own small niche.[44]

As arguments about social, cultural and religious identities increasingly occupied political debates in the 1920s, history and historiography were considered as an ideological source and as a means of politics. More and more professional historians now entered the national Indian stage, including most prominently Jadunath Sarkar (1870–1951). The ruling qualities of the Maratha king Shivaji (1630–80) were reinforced as he was now portrayed as a Hindu ruler fighting the despotic regime of the Muslim Mughal Aurangzeb, and declared general Hindu characteristics. These characteristics were to act as reference points for politicians, especially in the fight for an independent India. From now on the British and the Muslims were seen as foreign rulers, both of which carried blame for the current plight of the Indian nation. Coincidently, this histor(iograph)y took the periodisation and characterisation of South Asian history from that of the colonial historiography.

The first concise, Hindu nationalist, draft of Indian history was written by Vinayak D. Savarkar. With his interpretation of the "Mutiny" as an "Indian War of Independence", he initiated a paradigm shift in the historiography of South Asia whereby Indians were no longer passive objects, but rather active subjects of history. Savarkar explored this further in his pamphlet *Hindutva: Who is a Hindu?* in 1923. As a pupil of the radical Bal Tilak, Savarkar took the concept of the primordial Hindu civilisation of India as the basis and constructed from this an already existing Indian nation from the Vedic scriptures. Compared to most Western national historiographies, such a historiography brought the advantage of only having to recall the old common values for the construction of the imagined Hindu nation. Savarkar used Italy's Risorgimento (1815–70) as a model of such a process and the reminder of that country's former cultural greatness.[45]

A new addition to the programmatic treatise was the definition of Hindu, Hinduism and Hinduness as Hindutva, under which Savarkar attributed the entire history of the Hindus. They were regarded the inhabitants of Hindustan, which encloses the entire continent of South Asia. Beyond mere territoriality,

Aryan blood had linked all Hindus since the Vedic age (c. 1200 BCE). This had since been led astray by the Islamic-Mongol and Christian-British rule. Jews, Christians and Muslims who held their central religious shrines outside of India were generally seen as foreign.[46] Just as the interpretation of the "Mutiny" as Indian War of Independence had little immediate effect, the same was also initially true of this concept of Hindutva, which nevertheless remained present. The idea of the Aryan-Indian nation quickly became the common property of many Indian historians. Decades later these ideological seeds began to sprout following the riots in Ayodhya in 1992, and the subsequent pogroms against Muslims. A wave of Hindu-nationalist historiography then began to build in educational policy.[47]

In comparison to the historiography of independent India which had continued almost unabated, Pakistan had to reinvent itself as a nation, a point that had stood at the top of the political agenda of the Muslim League since the Lahore resolution in 1942. Muhammad Ali Jinnah laid the foundation stone for this with his Two-Nation Theory which he presented at the annual meeting of the Muslim League in 1942, in which he proclaimed that Hindus and Muslims were two fundamentally different nations that neither a common history nor a common culture would connect. As a result it was only natural that they live separately. Although Jinnah did not speak of a clearly defined territory for Pakistan, it gradually transpired that the future Pakistan would lie in the northwest of British India. Implicitly, it was, as the acronym implies, to be composed of the provinces of **P**unjab, **A**fghania (Pakhtun-area), **K**ashmir, **S**ind, Baluchis**tan**. Here, in the land of the *ashraf*, the Muslim immigrants, as an historic construction, would be able to retreat from their imperial expansion between 1200 and 1858 and again live undisturbed. It remained unresolved as to how the rest, the *aslaf*, the converted Muslims, in the other successor state(s) of British India would be included and organised.[48]

However, despite all the efforts to establish homogeneity, a unified narrative of Pakistan's national history failed to emerge. Even the question as to when the history of Pakistan began has yet to be resolved and debate surrounds whether it should be set at the first Muslim conquest of Sind in CE 711 or indeed with the founding of the Delhi Sultanate in 1206. In addition to these two versions of a "long history", a "short" version has also been put forward which traces the origins of Pakistan to the fall of the Mughal Empire which forced the Muslim elite to reorientate itself following the massive collapse of tradition. New editions of history textbooks and new works from the 1960s have perpetuated both variants to the present day.[49]

Aside from both of these versions, the Islamisation that was sought under President Zia ul Haq (1977–88) represents an important addition. The Western terminology of "modern" and "scientific" were, for the first time, utilised to create a historiography which had of course to serve the ideological needs of the state. Yet each historiography legitimates a political regime, including Western democracies, and therefore is never free of ideology. A further boost to the Islamisation came in 2002, creating a certain course correction as the historiography of Pakistan was distanced from the Western historiographical methods now placing humans in the centre of consideration.[50] However, in 2007 Ayesha Jalal presented an alternative view of Pakistan's historiography with her work in which she firmly places individuals and identities at the centre of attention.[51]

It took until the late 1970s for South Asian history scholars to criticise the conventional historiography of India, leading the Subaltern School to generally question the previous Indian historiography. It was presumed that, just as the imperial British historiography had been, it was an elitist historiography which utilised the same sources as the British and therefore could not arrive at any new results. This historiography is characterised as questionable on account of the paradigm of modernity and progress for which a "history from below" is forwarded as an alternative. Instead of permanently interpreting macro-level events, micro studies into the people have now been made which have usually been written out, or indeed do not even surface, in the previous historiography. The Subaltern School aims to provide a mosaic of a more nuanced picture of modern Indian history. Initially such histories were strongly focused on resistance movements against colonial rule; however, their focus then shifted in the 1990s to more cultural analysis.[52]

The research field into the social and economic history of the 1970s and 1980s has recently expanded considerably. A prominent addition to this, as seen in Chapter 6, is environmental history which is experiencing intensive engagement in India like nowhere else in the academic world. Moreover, the field of labour history has also been established in which Indian historians working on South Asian history provide important contributions. In Pakistan, Sri Lanka, Bangladesh and Nepal, this field, as well as that of environmental history, still remains largely fallow. The same also applies for gender studies, studies on the urban poor and the marginalised of society in general, in contrast to India where such fields of research are more or less densely sown. However, research universities have improved the situation in these aforementioned countries since the beginning of the new millennium.

Natural sciences: botany, geography and geology

A wealth of botanical knowledge existed among the indigenous societies of South Asia during the eighteenth century which related to the culinary, medicinal and, in parts, commercial exploitation of flora. European scientists, the number of which increased in British India at the turn of the nineteenth century, built on this knowledge. Before this point, Indian scholars' botanical knowledge decisively influenced early European compilations regarding botanical classification systems. The Portuguese physician Garcia de Orta (c. 1499–1568) built upon the local medicinal and botanical knowledge from Malabar and wrote his *Coloquios dos simples e drogas he cousas medicinais da India* (Goa 1563) whilst Hendrik Adriaan van Rheede tot Draakestein, Governor in Kochi (Cochin) composed the 12-volume *Hortus Malabaricus* (Amsterdam 1678–93). Carl von Linné (1707–78), founder of the modern botanical classification system, took some 240 new species from this work of the Dutch governor in 1740. Moreover, Linné's work was also influenced by German physician Paul Hermann's (1646–95) *Musaeum Zeylanicum* (1717) about Ceylon/Lanka.[53]

The same can also be observed in the field of geography and cartography as knowledge gained by European scholars, missionaries and travellers came almost exclusively from Indian informants.[54] The earliest maps of India originated from the Japanese in the fourteenth century. As the Europeans penetrated into the interior of the subcontinent from the mid-eighteenth century, they sought original Indian cartographic material, but soon realised that any maps that they came across were of a European cartographic origin. Indian-made maps, if at all available, were concerned with representations of religious places and were not, according to European understanding of science, "scientific". The first European depictions of the Indian subcontinent dated from the sixteenth century whilst more detailed maps of individual regions were produced from the mid-eighteenth century.[55] However, the Maratha drew quite a few maps for administrative and military purposes in the first half of the eighteenth century depicting geographical specifics, overland routes and fortresses in different colours which demonstrates that cartography in Maratha Desh pursued the same targets as cartography in contemporary European states, namely to strengthen the central power of the emerging early modern state.[56]

At the turn of the eighteenth century, Governor-General Richard Wellesley forged the beginnings of a comprehensive geographical survey of British India. After he had redirected EIC credit intended for trading investments for the war against Tipu Sultan in 1798–9, Wellesley was forced to justify his actions to the Court of Directors and made a report on the fiscal gains and the economic performance of the annexed territories which would prove compensation enough in the long term for the redirected finances. To this end he sent the botanist Francis Buchanan (1762–1829) on an expedition to South India in 1800. The report was so successful that the Court of Directors in London decided to commit his *A Journey from Madras through the Countries of Mysore, Canara and Malabar* to print in 1807. Buchanan was considerably influenced by Sir John Sinclair's Statistical Account of Scotland and the therein formulated doctrine about a general "improvement" which had become a central European leitmotiv from the late eighteenth century and which was echoed in his own report.[57]

Between 1799 and 1810 Colin Mackenzie (1754–1821) compiled a survey of Maisur which brought important new geographical discoveries and more information about the area's natural resources. Thus, the EIC was supplied with commercially valuable data and simultaneously improved its scientific knowledge.[58] Under these guidelines Francis Buchanan wrote a report on various geographical districts in Bengal and Bihar in 1807.[59] The reports and surveys increasingly resembled what has been referred to in the contemporary European scientific community as Natural History and gathered comments on geography, geology, mineralogy, zoology, botany and meteorology. The commercial fervour occasionally led to the fact that, without the EIC's cognition, scientists gathered information about raw materials and infrastructure outside the British territories that then served to prepare the annexation of neighbouring territories, as in the case of Gujarat between 1787 and 1803.[60]

With this accumulated knowledge the employees of the EIC laid the foundation for a scientific enterprise that was simultaneously ignited in Europe. William Jones, for example, also followed his botanical interests alongside that of his philological studies as he worked closely with a Danish student of Linné, Johann Gerhard Koenig (1728–85), who was appointed as the first botanist employed in the EIC in 1778. Koenig introduced Linné's binary nomenclature according to the genus and species for the South Asian flora. William Jones founded the Asiatic Society of Bengal in 1784 according to the model of academic societies in Europe as a forum for the various scientific activities of the region. The *Asiatic Researches* (in publication 1789–1838) provided him with a publication medium which was aimed at a broad readership.[61] In 1790 he published his *Treatise on the Plants of India*, in which he insisted on the general fixing of Indian plant names in Latin, and only in exceptional cases in Sanskrit. This triggered a debate that continued until the end of the nineteenth century.[62]

Botanical knowledge was seen as essential for the overall improvement of living conditions as with its help the food supply of the population could be ensured. To this end Colonel Robert Kyd (1746–93), secretary to the military department of inspection in Bengal from 1782 until his death, established the first of numerous botanical gardens in India and Ceylon in 1786 in Calcutta and became its honorary superintendent in 1787. The main focus of these gardens was on productive agricultural and commercial horticultural products. Scientific botany developed rather slowly in comparison, finally receiving impetus from the director of the Botanical Gardens at Kew, Sir Joseph Banks (1743–1820),[63] to develop this field by appointing Kyd's successor, the experienced botanist William Roxburgh (in office 1793–1820). In this way the Botanical Gardens in Calcutta developed into a general collection of plants to which both Francis Buchanan and the Danish physician Nathaniel Wallich (1786–1854), who had been in the service of the EIC since 1809, contributed. Within a few decades, the structural change from ambitious amateur to institutionally based professional scientists took place, though not without personal animosities and scientific rivalries.[64]

The botanical garden of Saharanpur located at the foot of the Himalayas won particular importance after its founding in 1817 because plants were able to be cultivated here that perished in Calcutta. Following the first successful experiments with the acclimation of tea, further experiments were also undertaken with cotton, tobacco and other crops. John Forbes Royle, the technical manager of the garden from 1823 to 31, developed a novel botanical classification system as a clear demarcation to Linné's gender-based principles of organisation which he deliberately aligned to the local ecological conditions and experimentally implemented in northern India. The scientific enterprise in the colony was therefore not an annex to the London-based "control centre", but the colony was in many instances independently researched; this fact was true not only in the field of botany, but also for other fields of science.

The global networking of botanical gardens under the aegis of Sir Joseph Banks generally promoted not just the botanical sciences. Their practical application took on a rather more avant-garde position compared to that in Europe, especially in the field of forestry. The information and knowledge exchange to the Botanical Gardens in St Vincent, St Helena and Mauritius, as well as in Cape Town and in British India, documented the increasing scale of global deforestation. On account of the high level of knowledge acquired in the colonies, the awareness about the ecological consequences of the massive interventions made in the natural environment were developed earlier and more efficiently than in Europe. At the end of the eighteenth century the first forest conservation laws were adopted in St Helena to ensure the supply of docks and the production of commercial crops; this was soon followed by the introduction of similar laws on the islands in the Caribbean and in British India. Consequently, the legislative initiative was based in the colonies even though the local policy was initially anything but consistent, as described above in Chapter 5. The authorities in London reacted decades later and the Imperial Forest Department was not established until 1924.[65]

In addition to a comprehensive description of annexed territories, geography and the development of cartographic material was of a high importance.[66] Robert Clive, two-time Governor of Bengal (1757–60 and 1765–7) stressed the military value of having accurate maps at the beginning of a process of territorial expansion he had launched in 1757. In order to secure a cartographic survey of the newly acquired territories in Bengal he appointed James Rennell (1746–1830) to the newly created position of Surveyor General of the EIC's dominions in Bengal. As Colin Mackenzie had surveyed South India, so did Rennell embark upon his own measurements of British Bengal, often using local informants and local maps. The extent to which Rennell used local maps remains obscure, which is also true for later British cartography in South Asia. After Rennell had published his maps of Bengal in 1780, he was commissioned to make a map of the entire Indian subcontinent. In 1783 Rennell published the Map of Hindustan, the basis of which, in addition to numerous accounts of local information, consisted of four maps that showed the Panjab, Gujarat, Bundelkhand and Malabar.[67]

However, the wars led by the EIC in the Indian subcontinent soon called for more detailed maps which finally led to the institutionalisation of cartography in Madras as part of the military establishment at the beginning of the nineteenth century.[68] It is from here that all the efforts to survey the entire subcontinent have their origin. By means of triangulation the area between the Coromandel Coast and the Malabar Coast was measured on the initiative of William Lambdon between 1799 and 1817. One year after the successful completion of the survey, Lambdon established the Great Trigonometrical Survey which aimed to extend the already initiated triangulation across the subcontinent. However, despite the existence of countrywide cartographic institutions their activities could not be synchronised in the 1820s and 1830s and huge problems ensued in the implementation of the collected astronomical and geodetic measurements as well as the disclosures of local informants into meaningful, accurate cartographic representation. In order to justify the huge expense of the project, as well as to ease a certain publication pressure, a general map of India was ultimately published.[69]

Governor-General William C. Bentinck was an avid utilitarian and was inspired by the idea of reforming and modernising Indian society and this led him to enthusiastically participate in the project of a general map. Bentinck commissioned George Everest to take on such a project in the form of the Great Trigonometrical Survey at the beginning of the 1830s. When he finally retired in 1843 the Great Arch of the southern tip of the subcontinent, Cape Kanyakumari (Cape Comorin), to Dehra Dun at the foot of the Himalayas had been measured. Further measurements were made from this nearly 2,000km stretch so that at the beginning of the 1860s a basic trigonometric network spread over the subcontinent. It seems that Everest aimed at a plain surface (and literally superficial) representation of the subcontinent and thus at the mere applicability of "scientific cartography", rather than producing detailed cartographical material useful for administrative and military purposes.[70]

The survey was undertaken without the scientific support of the London authorities. The political and topographical diversity of the subcontinent had to be shaped into a rational (or at least rationally looking) system, in order to document the prudence of the colonial administration and ultimately colonial rule in Calcutta to the London authorities in government and the Court of Directors. However, in reality the cartographic material gathered in many areas remained rather poor. Certainly, British India had come to be represented as a unit, but too many inaccuracies resulted from the only rough survey methods which resulted in inconsistencies in the map series, which, along with the sheer size of the subcontinent, made mapping the entire subcontinent illusory from the outset.[71]

However, the few results that were secured were perfectly suited for use in science and policy setting in Great Britain. The territorial domination of India and the survey of the Great Arch as a hitherto unmeasured longitudinal section of the earth's surface gave British national science a clear advantage in the face of the competition posed by the other European countries in being able to calculate the circumference of the globe because of their own, more accurate, data. Despite all of the inaccuracies in the triangulation measurements, political intent had been satisfied. British contemporaries noted that the mountains of the Himalayas would now bow before the British flag.[72] The Great Trigonometrical Survey demonstrated the academic performance and force of the British Empire in India. Subsequent survey work only served to complement and complete the existing maps.

Geology too, as another geography-related science, came to take on a direct colonial-imperial function as it literally put the reference to the ground, its history and its usefulness. In contrast to the fields of botany and geography, geology was not initially considered by the academic institutions in London. This lack of interest in the geological resources in India is explained by the fact that India had been regarded primarily as a land of agricultural commodities. However, the extensive alluvial sediments in the river valleys and the enormous depth of the lava flows on the Dekhan offered a unique scientific field of study.[73] The first ventures into geological research came at the beginning of the nineteenth century as Governor-General Earl of Minto (in office 1807–13) personally ordered geological investigations in the coal mining area of Raniganj in 1808. However, expertise was initially lacking for the mineralogical analysis of coal quality.[74]

Yet, the introduction of steam navigation on the Ganges and Indus changed the hesitant attitude to geology in general and to coal in particular. In 1827 experts of the English and German coalfields were enlisted to analyse the coal reserves and a Committee for Investigating the Coal and Mineral Resources of India was established in 1836. Finally Thomas Oldham, former director of the Geological Survey of Ireland, succeeded in 1851 to bundle all of these activities into the Geological Survey of India. The systematic development of coal resources now began as a part of the mineralogical opening of the subcontinent. The most immediate expression of this can be seen in the establishment of the Museum of Practical Geography in the same year as the successful transfer of the Museum of Economic Geology from the Asiatic Society to the Geological Survey of India in 1856.[75]

In order to reflect on the onset of intense geological activity in British India, the Asiatic Society of Bengal decided to publish the *Journal of the Asiatic Society of Bengal* in 1831 alongside that of the *Asiatic Researches* which had first been published in 1786. Other geographical and geological journals highlighted the differentiation within the discipline as the Geographical Survey of India published its findings from 1856 in its *Memoirs* and then from 1868 in *The Records of the Geological Survey of India*. The progressive specialisation was eventually reflected in the *Palaeontologia Indica* published from 1862. Oldham's attempts to establish the study of geology in the newly founded universities nonetheless failed. Instead, in a move similar to that in Dehra Dun which established the Central Forest School in 1881, the Civil Engineering College in Shibpur was founded in 1856 where subaltern Indian employees were trained.[76]

Research-based geologists found wide acceptance in the scientific world from their roles in British India, and South Asia often served as a career springboard. The subcontinent was geologically unknown terrain which made it attractive for both individual researchers as well as for scientific disciplines. Geological finds not only led to the economic benefit of the colony, but, together with paleontological finds, they also gave tantalising insights into the age of the earth. Following territorial annexation, scientists now embarked on a "secondary annexation" story of "India". Now, the discoveries of the natural past of the continent offered the geological and geographical sciences the chance to complete that story of the subcontinent by submitting it completely through the medium of natural history according to their own understanding and to their own perception.

The Indian colony therefore proved to be an ideal field of research in which botany, geography, cartography and geology went hand in hand in arranging and bringing in new forms of understanding of both the interior and exterior of the country. Systematic expeditions were now made in the "hinterlands" of British India and above all to Kashmir, Tibet and Central Asia, on the one hand in order to explore the unknown natural resources and, on the other, to explore the possible access routes to the Chinese market which was considered as inexhaustible. The knowledge created in this way guaranteed and justified the previous "primary" territorial annexations of military and political leaders. In addition, it also supported Britain's position as a competing nation-state on Europe's scientific "battleground".[77]

The case of Ceylon, which the British annexed in 1802 from the Dutch, was handled quite differently as here colonial science aimed to serve the colonial state in a specific way. Whilst the Indian geographical survey consisted of three departments (one for trigonometrical, one for topographical and one for revenue or cadastral surveying), the Ceylon Survey Department focused almost exclusively on the block survey of forests in order to parcel the land for the creation of coffee plantations from the 1830s. In addition, surveys were also undertaken for road construction. This difference in scientific exploration reflects the different forms of colonial rule and resulting asymmetries. In British India, administrative focus lay on revenue settlement, hence the focus on cadastral surveys, whereas in Ceylon the plantation economy was at the centre of colonial rule which ultimately led to the concentration in the parcelling of estates. Because of these diverse interests, the staff used in each colony were often qualified in different areas. Whilst the Trigonometrical Survey in British India could celebrate its triumphs, in Ceylon this was far from the case because the necessary personnel and equipment were seriously lacking.[78]

This partial mapping hindered the systematic cartographic survey of the island. A map of Ceylon was not produced until the mid-nineteenth century, but it was so incomplete that it was totally inappropriate for administrative purposes as not once were the provincial boundaries precisely located. The extent to which the island had only partially been surveyed showed itself in the planned construction of a road from Colombo to Kandy following the annexation of the highlands of the island in 1815 and where the Great Rebellion was militarily suppressed in 1818 after strenuous marches. The then Governor, Edward Barnes (twice in office: 1820–22, 1824–31) provided the stimulus for the construction of the road link. However, in order even to reach the planning phase, his cartographers were reliant on the cooperation of Ceylonese informants to an extent that was unknown to contemporary cartographers in British India. Apart from this, the resistance of the local population against the road project would hardly have been broken without the knowledge of local informants.[79]

The subdivision of blocks of land for public auction systematically prevented the exploration of the entire island. The fact that the limited cadastral survey, as well as the block survey, were run according to financial aspects served to aggravate this further. However, only the block survey proved worthwhile in contrast to the cadastral survey which was carried out by Burghers, who were descendants of Dutch and Ceylonese. Due to the disrespect shown by local land-owners to this "colonial class", the costs of the survey could often not be recovered from them. Block surveys, however, completed by the British subaltern personnel, were remunerated by investment-willing British buyers. It is hardly surprising that with such asymmetrical structures the first general map of Ceylon was completed on the findings of a survey based on just two-thirds of the land area between 1898 and 1903. It was only after Ceylon's independence in 1948 that a National Atlas was prepared in 1971 and finally published in 1988.[80]

From medical knowledge to scientific medicine

In South Asia, physicians from the Himalayas to Lanka possessed a profound botanical and medical awareness based on the exchange of knowledge in local and regional networks.[81] This knowledge can roughly be divided into two systems that developed over the course of millennia. First, Unani Tibb, based on a hybrid of Graeco-Arab and local tradition, the practitioners of which (physicians and surgeons) were known as *hakim*, *tabib* and *jarrah*. Second, Ayurveda, based on hybrid local knowledge and practices, whose practitioners were called *vaidya*, or *tibb-i-hindi* in Persian documents. However, what is presently known as Ayurveda came only into existence as a "coherent" medical system between 1880 and 1930. It was part of the Indian national movement, its agitators looking for a national Indian medicine opposing colonial or Western medicine.[82] A central premise to the medical schools in South Asia was the balance of humors and the importance of environmental miasma for general physical and mental well-being. The balance of humors refers to a general balance including the weather, food, emotional agitation, sins against wisdom, and so on. Whilst Ayurvedic practitioners, in contrast to some of their Unani colleagues, may have been inaccurate in their knowledge of human physiology, they were extremely skilled in plant morphology, its pharmacological functions and therapeutics.[83]

Although many different schools of thought are identifiable, numerous overlaps were recorded including the mutual acquisition of healing which can be seen in the literature and the translations of Sanskrit works and Persian books, among other records.[84] In the eighteenth century especially, the publication of medical texts increased beyond that of the two other much more esteemed sciences of astrology and mathematics. Since the European medicine of the time was based on the same principles of humoral balances, diagnosis and treatments differed only slightly from those in South Asia. By way of example, the European physicians prescribed the analysis of stools and the practice of blood-letting whilst *vaidyas* gained their knowledge from urine analysis and prescribed urine therapy. In the sixteenth century the respect for the diagnosis and treatment of South Asian physicians was so high that European physicians advised their colleagues who went to South Asia, in as far as they possessed no deep knowledge of local diseases and their cure, acknowledging and following the recommendations of the Indian physicians there.[85]

Physicians generally had a good reputation in the Mughal Empire and in the courts of kings, princes and nobles they were held in a patron–client relationship. In addition to these "official" appointments physicians often worked in hospitals (*shifakhana* or *darush-shifa*) where connected pharmacies (*darukhana*) had been established in various towns of the Mughal Empire. A chief physician acted as superintendent (*daroga*) and headed a strict hierarchical order. Countless privately practising physicians were engaged in activities outside the hospitals such as in the bazaars.[86] There was also a kind of ethical "code" for physicians which had been in place since the sixteenth century, which, aside from a casual reference to God and the Quran, explicitly stressed the ethical and moral responsibility of the physician. Other than the reading of medical texts to acquire knowledge and experience, a good physician was seen as one who would see to all ailments and was especially committed to the poor.[87]

Indian medicine became of model system in the field of preventative health care through prophylactic vaccine. Whilst smallpox was endemic in many regions of South Asia in the seventeenth century, and frequently epidemic in some places, experiments were performed in Bengal meaning that epidemic disease outbreak could be combated relatively successfully in the eighteenth century. This was achieved through preserving the pus from smallpox pustules of people who were infected in the year before and was administered by applying the pus to a cut in the upper arm (variolation). Smallpox vaccination appears to have been practised in other regions of the subcontinent in this way. J.Z. Holwell described the theory and practice of smallpox vaccination in Bengal in a short essay in 1767 with which he then addressed the College of Physicians in London. With his essay Holwell contributed to the changing European medical discourse because he stressed the "technical" aspects of the variolation denying its cultural context in Bengal which included the veneration of the personified disease in the goddess Sitala.[88]

The reception of this essay marks a clear paradigm shift in the history of European medicine in British India. Following Edward Jenner's publication in 1798 of a method of smallpox vaccination which consisted of inoculation with bovine lymph, the Bengal vaccination method, which was partially being applied in Europe at the time, was systematically discredited. This prompted a targeted vilification of India's medical knowledge. Indian vaccination methods were now marred with the image of superstition on account of their integration with religious rituals and attributes, whilst the English method of vaccination was praised for its alleged rationality. The British aimed to demonstrate the superiority of their medical knowledge specifically in the case of smallpox; however, this was not possible in Bengal due to the high acceptance of variolation by the population. Thus, the new method of vaccination was first introduced in 1802 in the Madras Presidency where variolation was almost unknown. However, this was with limited success, since the disease continued to break out on a regular basis.[89]

In its role of "ruling knowledge" (*Herrschaftswissen*), medicine in British India took on a central position. European doctors had first come to India almost exclusively as ships' doctors and were sporadically assigned to the three colonial coastal cities from the seventeenth century. The general medical care of the Europeans was therefore in the hands of local physicians until well into the eighteenth century. It was only with the territorial expansion of the British that European physicians were brought to India from 1763 who were, however, explicitly responsible for the civilian employees and military units of the EIC. In 1785, some 234 physicians were in the EIC's service; this figure grew to 630 by 1824 and fluctuated between 650 and 820 until the end of colonial rule.[90] In the 1860s a high degree of conformity and an esprit de corps was formed which drew sharp institutional distinctions to the Indian Medical Service and the Indian physicians.

In addition to the Indian Civil Service (ICS), the Indian Medical Service (IMS) represented an archetype of colonial institutions which was primarily focused on the military needs of the colonial state. The functions of the IMS were not extended until the end of the nineteenth century when the consequences of urbanisation brought with it a growing occurrence of epidemics such as cholera and the plague which challenged both medical research and practice alike. Health and hygiene were not only key concepts of the Europeans, but were given specific functions in the colony which was particularly evident in maintaining the health of European city dwellers, soldiers and settlers. This manifested itself in the now apparently scientifically demonstrable need for the segregation of Indians and Europeans. From the 1890s, British doctors were introduced to all the major health commissions, and with their periodic reports had a significant impact on the urban development in British India.[91]

As with the British employees of the ICS, a certain disinterest in service in British India was discernible in British doctors even before the First World War. Therefore the British Indian government was compelled to open both the ICS and the IMS to Indian candidates. In 1922 the number of Indian applicants for the IMS exceeded that of British applicants.[92] In order to meet the constant shortage of staff, a Native Medical Institution was formed in 1824 in Calcutta, and two years later in Bombay, to train subaltern Indian doctors in assistive positions such as surgeons and pharmacists. Indian higher education institutions were included in the training. The Calcutta Sanskrit College offered courses in Ayurveda whilst the Calcutta Madrassa offered lectures in Unani Tibb (thereby contributing to the colonial image of two different schools and systems).[93] Apart from this, a public debate was held in the nineteenth century which led to the practical application of knowledge of Unani medicine in the *Oudh Akhbar*. This public debate was based on an increasing number of medical texts written in Urdu which brought forth a new type of *hakim* and simultaneously triggered the confrontation of theorists from the established Unani Tibb families.[94]

Nevertheless, William Jones already claimed, at the end of the eighteenth century, that none of the Indian languages known to him originally described scientific and medical treatises. He also held that almost all Ayurvedic knowledge had been lost in the last centuries. Moreover, there was a significant absence of scientific experiments. However, he saw an opportunity to help reinvent Indian medical knowledge through European instructions.[95] Long before the Anglicists entered the Indian stage, the ideological shift from the limited cooperation of British and Indian physicians had already been carried out in a systematic rejection of Indian medical traditions by colonial policy. Finally the Anglicists gained dominance in the scientific as well as political debate, rejecting all forms of Indian medical analysis, diagnosis and treatments which they characterised as quackery, pleading instead for an exclusive Western medical system. Amid their growing influence, Governor-General Bentinck founded the Medical College in 1835.[96]

Despite high completion figures seeing some 1,000 Indians in top medical positions and more than 4,000 at the lower end of the medical service in the 1920s, European medicine in British India remained an insular phenomenon as Western medical knowledge was hardly spread beyond the major cities, military institutions and some princely residences. British doctors sometimes encountered resistance from the local population, such as during the mass vaccination against smallpox in the early nineteenth century in South India, as the population simply withdrew from the British health authorities. Massive public campaigns were launched during the last decades of the nineteenth century and in some selected regions led to forced vaccinations, forcing the number of vaccinations to eventually rise. Despite this, statistics pertaining to the number of infections continued to rise. Although these numbers fell in the 1920s, it was not until the 1970s that the disease was considered to be defeated.[97]

Two significant breaks can be seen in the medical health care of British India. The first came after the Great Rebellion (1857–9) and the second after the plague in Bombay (1896–7). The Great Rebellion saw a high mortality rate among the British, including non-combatant soldiers, as they contracted infectious diseases from the civilians in besieged Lakhnau and other cities, which alarmed the British public. This was compounded by the alarm caused by the mortality among non-combatants during the Crimean War (1853–6). Although British doctors had warned for many years of the sometimes catastrophic hygienic conditions in the barracks of the British Indian army, it was not until after the Crimean War, the Great Rebellion and the activism of Florence Nightingale that the mortality rate was given the necessary attention which was recorded as being three times the rate of soldiers stationed in Britain. As a result, the English Parliament passed the Contagious Diseases Act in 1864.[98]

Meanwhile, the fight against venereal diseases among European soldiers had grown to an imperial security problem. Whilst somewhere between 10 and 20 per cent of all soldiers had been treated for syphilis in hospitals before the Great Rebellion, the number of those infected then rose to more than one-third, seeing some 16,200 of 45,000 soldiers (37 per cent) in medical treatment in 1862 alone. In order to achieve greater "stability" among the troops, prostitution became strictly controlled whilst the number of most sexually active soldiers (i.e. those under 25 years old) was reduced. After initial minor successes, numbers of infected soldiers rose again from 33 to 55 per cent and hundreds of soldiers were invalided home to Great Britain every year. Superficially it seemed that it was only the promiscuous male sexual behaviour and its consequences in the form of emasculation through failure of the sexual organs that stood in opposition to this health issue, but in fact it seriously threatened the entire function of the army and therefore the foundations of the British Empire in India.[99]

In the same year a Sanitary Commission was set up in each province of British India which produced annual reports on the sanitary conditions in the cities. The establishment of municipal corporations in the major cities of British India in 1865 promoted the medical control of the state at the city level. However, priority was given to the barracks whose medical-sanitary regulations pertaining to the regulation of sewers and surrounding land use were soon extended to the neighbouring Indian bazaars, until, in 1877, sanitary commissioners were given visitation rights for villages within a five-mile radius. Despite these extensive measures, the mortality rate of British soldiers still lay far beyond that of Indian soldiers at the end of the nineteenth century.[100] In general, medical health policy fell short of expectations and, rather pathetically, short of their actual possibilities. As a purely investigative authority, British doctors and officials ended up combatting epidemics rather than actively preventing them. This became glaringly obvious in the case of cholera prevention, as despite a successful test series on soldiers, the military leadership did not allow a mass vaccination.[101]

Especially in the fight against cholera and the plague – both of which were stigmatised as being archetypal Indian diseases by the British – European physicians were unable to extend beyond a mere description of symptoms until well into the second half of the nineteenth century.[102] Scientists were equally challenged and equally unsuccessful in the study of malaria despite the fact that the sanitary commissioner of Bengal recorded some one million malaria deaths in 1889 alone. By turning the facts around, the British medical professionals claimed biological proof of racial and cultural superiority in which the Europeans were seen as the strong and dominant peoples in contrast to the depiction of the Indians as weak and degenerated peoples. Even when cholera broke out simultaneously in English and Indian cities, it was succinctly noted that diseases in India were not diseases in England.[103]

As shown in the previous chapter, the British came under increasing pressure in the globalising world to establish international control as the plague broke out in Bombay and Calcutta at the end of the nineteenth century. Cholera too was a disease with origins that can be traced back in South Asia. From here it spread in 1817, during the then British war campaign in central and western India, as an epidemic across Bengal and the whole of the subcontinent, reaching Europe in the 1830s. The more cholera was found outside of British

India, or the higher the risk, the more the British were pressured to develop control mechanisms. Yet despite the fact that cholera took the land route to Europe via the Caucasus, Central Asia and Russia, the official policy of various European governments was to regulate the sea route, in particular the route via the Red Sea. Altogether 17 international sanitary conferences between 1851 and 1938 tried to protect Europe from an invasion of cholera on ships from the "East".[104] This included, among other things, the medical-sanitary control of the Haj pilgrimage to Mecca, which was sometimes an unbearable burden for the pilgrims as ships were often held for weeks in preventive quarantine or passengers were forced to remain in quarantine camps.[105] Meanwhile, troop transporters returning to Britain were exempted from such regulations.[106]

The powers of the police were greatly expanded in order to implement the control of pilgrims travelling to, from and within British India. The police units were occupied by Indians to a greater extent than the British Indian Army was. As such, they became an important executive organ which, unlike in contemporary England, was used for the prevention of diseases (less of crime!).[107] The arsenal of the colonial regime consisted of directing streams of pilgrims to Puri to be checked along with the monitoring of "pilgrim masses" in Hardwar, both of which demonstrated the regime's alleged superiority in terms of discipline.[108] The arm of political control, however, reached far beyond British India as in the wake of the Great Game, the British forced the Amir of Afghanistan to close its borders to Muslim pilgrims from the Central Asian Russia.[109]

Apparently, medicine, medical science and imperial politics went hand in hand. However, the more preventive measures seemed to be lacking, the more British doctors reacted negatively to their Indian counterparts. British doctors and administrators increasingly made reprisals against *hakims* and *vaiydas* whose restricted rights were legally fixed in the Registration of Medical Practitioners Act of 1912. Bombay played a leading role after the British authorities determined that only 10 per cent of the population consulted doctors with European training which showed that there remained an unbroken trust in Indian medical knowledge and its practical application. This was also the result of the decreasing willingness of British physicians to settle in Bombay. The number of registered European doctors fell in the last quarter of the nineteenth century from 11 to 2, whilst conversely Indian doctors rose from 37 to 61. In order to also secure their privileged position in the pharmaceutical field, all Indians were excluded from the pharmacist profession by government decree in 1884. However, this did not prevent indigenous pharmaceutical knowledge being disseminated through local practitioners.[110]

Medical science ultimately widened the cleft between Europeans and Indians. Whilst during the eighteenth century Europeans believed that, in principle, it was possible to acclimatise to foreign climates and unknown environmental conditions, increasing exceptions to this belief were "discovered" after the turn of the century. The previously stated and constructed difference to peoples outside Europe, which was based on cultural prejudices and stereotypes, was now continued in the medical justification of the "white race" holding biomedical superiority over all other races. Race and gender were new categories of knowledge that stood out from the Linnaean natural history and its superficial description of genetic "depth". It was not the climate alone that made the acclimatisation of Europeans in tropical India impossible, but rather a superior genetic predisposition qualified them as rulers of the region, although this might mean they would not be permanent settlers there.[111]

India, particularly at the beginning of the twentieth century, was conceived as a laboratory for "racial sciences" as national-imperialist rivalry between the European states approached its first peak in the field of anthropology. Herbert H. Risley (1851–1911), organiser of the Census of India in 1901 and 1911, who had introduced a thus far unchallenged strict categorisation and classification for castes, clans and tribes based on biological (i.e. racial) criteria, also expressed the fear that Britain could fall behind the other European countries, especially Germany, in the field of anthropology and racial theory as they received too little support from politicians and academic circles. Britain would have to use its Indian potential of different races and castes to reassert itself as the superior power among the European competitors. Anthropological studies were by no means the only solution to the colonial state's administrative problems as in "the everlasting battle of all races" sciences also had to contribute to the evidence of one's own race's (and people's) superiority. This was especially true in medicine, which, along with hygiene, increasingly explored the maintained racial differences.[112]

Irrigation systems and hydraulic constructions

The earliest forms of irrigation systems in the Indus Valley date back to the time of the Harappan civilisation (2500–1800 BCE) which were typical of the hydro-agriculture across the northern South Asian subcontinent. Easily constructed flood channels that directed the abundant rainfall of the monsoon on distant fields formed the backbone of agriculture over thousands of years. In modern times, an elaborate system of canals was created by Indian rulers to increase the extension and intensification of agricultural land and agricultural output along with the revenue incomes of the state. In Rajasthan, as elsewhere in South Asia, the growing administration of the seventeenth and eighteenth centuries had an impact on the efficiency of the irrigation systems which contributed to the ongoing processes of state formation.[113] Thus, individual Sikh *rajas*, the *nawab* of Bahawalpur and the *amir* of Sind ordered the repair of old irrigation canals and the construction of new systems in the eighteenth century. In northern India, the Ruhelas reutilised the smaller channel systems, which had been built in the seventeenth century under the Mughals, at the end of the eighteenth century.[114]

In the first half of the nineteenth century, the British repaired many of the smaller dams in the South Indian river deltas whilst from 1847, the colonial government addressed projects for dams and canals in the Godaveri delta.[115] Meanwhile, the British also showed a greater commitment in the Northern India Ganga-Yamuna Doab, where after just a few years of the annexation of the Ceded and Conquered Provinces of 1801 they started to repair the dilapidated canals such as the Western Yamuna Canal and Eastern Yamuna Canal. New construction projects took place from 1836 as Sir Proby Cautley (1802–71) planned a large-scale hydraulic project on the Ganges Canal that would irrigate the entire Doab. The Ganges Canal was an engineering feat of its time as it measured nearly 500km in length flowing from Hardwar in the Himalayas, over numerous aqueducts, some up to 250m long, to Kanpur. Ultimately the canal system, measuring nearly 7,000km, irrigated an area of more than a million acres.[116]

This masterpiece of British engineering in British India was opened in 1854 and 40 years later it still held its place in direct comparisons with the irrigation structures in Egypt, Italy and the United States as it remained by far the world's largest hydraulic system. As for all canal projects, the planning work had been carried out by British engineers who were, as with most contemporary scientists, technicians and doctors, recruited from the army. Even when the PWD was established as a central coordination and planning office in 1854, engineers continued to come from the military for decades to come. The British engineers selectively employed the knowledge of Indian engineers in their approaches, which was admitted by one of the most famous canal engineers in British India, Sir Arthur Cotton (1803–99), who otherwise stressed the superiority of European construction design.[117] However, as with botany, cartography and medicine, this knowledge was absorbed into the "imperial science" without due recognition.[118]

A second phase of canal planning began immediately after the defeat of the Great Rebellion. Now, rather than state planning, financing and construction, private investors were sought to lead and fund projects. The colonial state guaranteed a return of 5 per cent on capital investments. This led to the establishment of the East India Irrigation Canal Company in 1861 and the Madras Irrigation Company two years later. In the early 1870s, Arthur Cotton designed a gigantic irrigation system that would ultimately connect the major rivers of the subcontinent through numerous canals.[119] In addition to these irrigation possibilities, Cotton also planned to expand transport routes. This was an important argument that had been high on the political agenda since the famines of the 1830s and was instrumental in securing capital from the British financial market, which was increasingly invested in the railways of British India. However, Arthur Cotton was unable to secure political support, so his gargantuan canal project ultimately failed.[120]

The Agra Canal was envisaged as a major new project in the Ganga-Yamuna Doab after 1863. However, the most extensive canal systems were built in the Panjab, which, in the decades around the turn of the century, were the most prestigious objects of the canal constructors. The technical feats in the process of measurable progress can also be expressed statistically. By 1920, almost

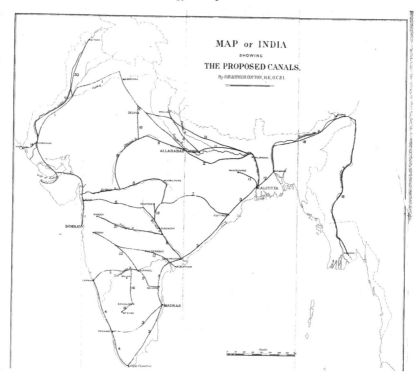

Map 8.1 Sub-continental canal system as envisaged by Sir Arthur Cotton. *The Indian Problem Solved: Undeveloped Wealth in India, and State Reproductive Works: The Ways to Prevent Famines and Advance the Material Progress of India* (London: Virtue & Co 1874), 252–72

3,000km of main canals had been constructed in British India, along with more than 20,000km of secondary, lateral canals. Whilst in 1878–9 only 4.6 million acres were irrigated by canals, by 1900–1 this had risen to nearly 11 million acres. However, from a fiscal perspective, the canal projects were initially not, or barely, profitable since investments were often short of what was in fact required and returns often fell short of expectations. Only in the long run, such as up to the 1945–6 financial year, could irrigation systems be described as remunerative.[121] Despite this, large individual projects such as the gigantic Sukkur Barrage, built between 1923 and 1932 on the Indus, emerged as triumphs of "imperial sciences".[122]

Technical challenges were linked to organisational performance of politicians, administrators and engineers who were of the opinion that only the British colonial power was capable of such feats and they were, as the technology itself, evidence of superior civilisation. Each section of the British canals required the efficient use of thousands of workers along the construction route. On the Ganges Canal, for example, one engineer was responsible for the organisation in daily work columns of up to 5,000 men, women and children in addition to hundreds of oxen carts. Alongside the recruitment of workers was also the logistical task of the procurement of construction materials. The logistical and organisational structures were borrowed from the PWD's experience in work assignments during famine, when thousands of people were employed in famine relief works. Many canal and railway embankment projects, as well as other projects of public utility, were created during such times of desperation and indigence.[123]

However, the intensive irrigation did not bring only benefits. As already mentioned in Chapter 4, intense irrigation and inadequate drainage led to waterlogging and salinisation. This resulted, on the one hand, to the consequence that in many regions with irrigation, such as in the North-Western Provinces, up to 10 per cent of agricultural land was destroyed, and, on the other hand, from the perspective of health, that in the second half of the nineteenth century the infection and mortality rates for malaria increased dramatically in the Panjab and Sind. These facts were often downplayed in official reports which instead highlighted the great technological innovation, which, when applied correctly, would lead to a general improvement of the food supply. These different interpretations of the consequences of canal irrigation projects continue to be reflected in recent research discussions.[124]

Since the annexation of large parts of Orissa in 1803, the British partially repaired many of the existing embankments along Mahanadi River. In the mid-nineteenth century a raging debate began which remained unanswered until the end of colonial rule between the Revenue Department and Military Department as to the correct policy towards peasants and embankments. The creation of private property by the Revenue Department had in fact led the peasants to erect embankments so as to protect their fields against flooding and to increase their income. However, additional embankments constructed by the colonial state produced a delta demarcated by protected, semi-protected and unprotected enclaves. Military experts reported on the geological and ecological features and called for a dismantling of the embankments as their unsystematic construction would trigger a growing risk of flooding in other areas.[125]

The contradictory policies substantially transformed the delta region of the Mahanadi within half a century. From a system of agriculture that was in sync with frequent flooding and the corresponding threats to cultivation, a different system of agriculture emerged that was constantly threatened by more frequent floods and crop damage. At the beginning of the twentieth century, the whole system of colonial water control collapsed. In 1901, the Irrigation Commission, which had been established throughout the whole of British India, recommended that the state should refrain from the construction of embankments. In addition, it became clear that the ambitious goals of irrigation could not be reached. Instead of the proposed extent of the irrigated area reaching some 2.5 million acres, a mere 250,000 were achieved by the late 1920s. Above that, the existing canals, dams and embankments deeply influenced the ecological conditions of the delta since, as in North India, soil fertility diminished and, as a result, so did crop yields. Waterlogging of low-lying lands also became a serious problem.[126]

Like the Tennessee Valley Authority which was established to overcome the effects of the Great Depression in the United States, the Mahanadi Valley Scheme, founded in 1944, and the Damodar Valley Authority of 1947–8, comprised a multitude of embankments, dams and canals which was to combine environmental improvement, technological (hydrological) development and economic growth with political power to develop British India's economy.[127] This debate took place at a time when the British and the Indians increasingly discussed the opportunities for rural reconstruction and industrial development in British India through "nation-building".[128] However, instead of damming the river on its way to the delta it was resolved to regulate the water from its head. The Hirakud Dam became the heart of the Mahanadi scheme and in the end the only major project which was completed. Initiated and planned in the 1930s, the independent Indian government under Prime Minister Nehru pursued the project with even more ambition. After 20 years of planning and construction the dam was opened in 1958 as one of Nehru's many "Temples of Modern India".[129]

The almost relentless warfare in the river delta regions of Kaveri and Colerun during the second half of the eighteenth century meant that irrigation system projects were never enacted upon. Furthermore, the fleeing and migrating rural population no longer invested in wells, tanks and sewer systems.[130] In the 1830s, the British gradually began to repair the canals; however, systematic planning began only in the 1860s.[131] That said, on account of the relatively high precipitation amounts on the Coromandel Coast and the great rivers that run through the area, irrigation channels were only partially profitable since wells and tanks could both be constructed relatively cheaply by private individuals. As in many other regions of British India, the decentralised, private-led irrigation projects were much more economical and ecologically meaningful and therefore more attractive. Currently 120,000 of the 208,000 tanks in India still remain in Karnataka, Tamil Nadu and Andhra Pradesh.[132]

The dam projects of Tungabhadra, Godaveri, Krishna and Caveri have permanently changed the South Indian landscape. In the Krishna-Godaveri Delta alone arable land acreage increased from 24,500 to 163,500 acres between 1883 and 1897. This massive transformation of the natural environment and the dramatic changes in agricultural structures is exemplified in the transformation of space. Between 1850 and 1930 the colonial administration significantly increased both revenue assessments and water tax. This not only changed ownership and tenure rights, but also the methods of cultivation as expensive canal water, for example, could only be used by wealthy owners and tenants. At the same time a political formation of stakeholders was created which joined forces in various organisations and initiated resistance. An awareness of the region was simultaneously created which was manifested in the formation of the federal state of Andhra Pradesh after the independence of British India. This regional formation documents the transformation and creation of economic, political and social spaces.[133]

Despite the questionable and sometimes inappropriate technology, not to mention the incalculable social and ecological consequences, a further gigantic dam was envisaged in the 1940s on the Godaveri as South India was, in the long term, to become independent from Burmese rice imports with the expansion of its own rice cultivation area. At the same time, British and Indian politicians promised the new dam project would guarantee industrialisation, modernisation and the supply of food to all. Likewise, the first designs of the Narmada dam project are a clear indicator of this new thinking. Guided by the idea of using the river valleys for irrigation, navigation and electricity production, the British used these projects as evidence of their enduring ability in predictive and central planning. However, the INC once again had set up a working group to help answer the question of multi-functional dam projects in the framework of a future national economic programme to mobilise Indian capital investors for the modernisation of the country. In this way the die would be cast for hydraulic projects that would come to dominate the post-colonial India.[134]

The first considerations for the expansion of state irrigation systems in Hyderabad State were discussed in 1894 and a comprehensive survey was carried out between 1898 and 1903. Contrary to the recommendations of the Irrigation Commission of India, which had suggested the construction of large-scale irrigation systems to prevent famine in the growing population, the *nizam* decided to promote the development of small, medium and large-scale irrigation projects. Thus, with financial support from the state, the irrigable area of land grew from one million acres to 1.4 million acres between 1922 and 1951. Of this, private tanks, wells and reservoirs account for 84 per cent of the total whilst 16 per cent was served by government canals. Yet, the percentage increase in the share of small-scale irrigation systems also preserved the feudal agrarian structures in Hyderabad State as the agricultural and irrigation facilities were concentrated in the hands of *patels, patwaris* and *jagirdars*. As in the case of Andhra Pradesh, irrigation schemes transformed social spaces, albeit in a different "direction".[135]

Many of the major dam and canal projects in Godaveri, Tungabhadra and Krishna, however, remained stuck in the planning stage as these rivers do not affect merely the Haiderabad territory, but, depending on the river, the border of the Bombay Presidency, Madras Presidency or Maisur. From a British perspective, many of these river projects on the Godaveri and Krishna threatened their own water use.[136] The British feared a drop in the water table in the lower reaches of the rivers if the water was to be used agriculturally in the upper reaches. The *nizam*, however, was not prepared to flood land in joint irrigation projects and thereby lose area and be worse off in terms of irrigable area. The Krishna project was shelved in 1917. The Tungabhadra project was completed in 1958 after no agreement could be reached until after the independence of British India. All of the major dam projects were only completed by the independent Indian state.[137]

These post-independence irrigation systems, of which the Indira Gandhi Canal in Rajasthan and the Tehri Dam in the Himalayas are two notable large-scale projects, allowed India to demonstrate its own technological expertise. The colonial debate of "improvement", and most recently of "development", became post-colonial "development" and "modernisation", which, in principle, continues the old colonial discourse. However, massive popular resistance formed against these politically prestigious projects which criticised Western provenance and the dramatic intrusions in nature and societies. The Nehruvian model of modernisation was set against the Gandhian model of resistance of the population as can be seen in the formation of resistance against the Tehri Dam.[138] This process was evident over decades, particularly on the Narmada dam project. Even more so than in the case of the Tehri Dam project, the Narmada became almost a beacon of political will and broad public local, regional, national and international resistance.[139]

In the 1960s, the Indian government took over the British ideas for the Narmada project. Whilst concrete plans were still taking shape, Prime Minister Rajiv Gandhi (in office 1984–91) gave approval to the project in the second half of the 1980s and instructed the participating states of Gujarat, Maharashtra and Madhya Pradesh to implement the project. More than 3,200 dams were to be built, the construction of which would have taken more than 100 years. In addition, approximately 75,000km of canals were to be built, primarily to supply the state of Gujarat with water. Because of the sheer size of the project, attention focused initially on the two main dams: the Sardar Sarovar and Narmada Sagar, both of which would hold back more water than all the then existing Indian reservoirs. According to plans, the turbines of the dam facilities would, in the long term, supply 275 megawatts of energy annually and provide water for nearly 1.8 billion hectares of land.[140]

Once again, technical high performance data were utilised as the foundation of modernisation of (all of) the post-colonial state(s), ensuring the production of food and energy. However, these figures ignore what was to become of the some 300,000 people who would need resettling, not to mention the endangered flora and fauna and the changing of landscapes. Moreover, after the Yamuna and Ganga, the Narmada River is revered as sacred and numerous famous pilgrimage sites of India, such as Maheshwar, are found along its banks. As early as 1988, opponents to this project formed the Narmada Bachao Andolan (Save the Narmada Movement) led by Mehta Patkar. The Indian writer, Arundhati Roy, also emerged as an opponent of the dam project. However, at the end of 1999 the hopes of the movement were dashed by a Supreme Court judgment which approved the continued construction of the dam.[141]

In a similar process to the mining of resources in Jharkhand and Chattisgarh, as has been shown in Chapter 5, the ideology of "Progress and Patriotism", to which the discourse surrounding development has now been elevated, has stigmatised the affected population as enemies of the nation.[142] The internationalisation of the Narmada project, however, led to the World Bank withdrawing its loan of $450 million in 1993 and German companies such as

Siemens pulling out of the project. Nevertheless, the Sardar Savorar dam was put into operation in 2007. As the reservoir was flooded to levels higher than was agreed, 51 displaced individuals took an unusual form of action in June 2012. They remained in their houses despite the slowly rising water and announced their resistance in a dramatic appeal that they would, if necessary, drown (*drown-satyagraha*). Joined by numerous solidarity actions, the demonstrators succeeded after 16 days of protest to have the level of the reservoir lowered and received a promise that the displaced persons would receive replacement land and other compensation.

However, such successes do not prevent further controversial hydraulic plans from being envisaged and filed on the record shelves of ministries of the Government of India. One such plan is the Indian River Inter-Link Project. Exactly 100 years after Sir Arthur Cotton had presented his plan to join the major rivers of the Indian subcontinent, the Government of India took up these plans again in 1974. In the course of the next 20 years it was developed into a project with the aim to divert the water wealth of the eastern regions of India through a system of hundreds of dams and thousands of miles of canals to the west and south to increase agricultural yields through increased irrigation. The project has most recently been touted by the BJP-led National Democratic Alliance government at the beginning of this millennium and propagated through extensive media involvement. However, on account of the moderate estimated construction cost of $140 billion and the still unresolved technical problems, the project remains shelved, yet continues to resurface from time to time, most recently in 2013.[143]

It became clear that the massive intrusions that were made in natural habitats and ecosystems in construction of canals and dams caused a rearrangement of space which was not without its implications. For example, the Narmada valley was once a place of religious significance in which one could embark upon a two-year pilgrimage. However, the building of the dam has turned this region into a water reservoir that has created completely new social, familial, economic and cultural areas. Irrigation channels are fed from the water reservoir, developing new agrarian land, whilst other areas further downstream in the Narmada valley have disappeared. Those affected are resettled in new areas that are cut off from the existing habitats as well as from agricultural and social spaces which were created through circulatory movements. Furthermore, the habitats of those in the lower reaches of the Narmada are also in danger of losing their livelihoods (such as the fishermen) through falling river levels and marshy water.

Large-scale irrigation in Gujarat has expanded, intensified and transformed agricultural land. Even the industries of Ahmedabad and other medium-sized towns have been said to have benefited from this additional water supply in the improved power supply leading to geographic and demographic expansion. Technical innovations of the small-scale tank irrigation systems in southern India (such as bore wells/groundwater instead of tanks/surface water) as well as the conversion of old weirs, which previously

Map 8.2 Indian River Inter-Link Project

regulated the steady inflow of tank cascades and now supply only the larger tanks along the main arteries, have led to a reorganisation of hydro-agriculture and thus a reorganisation of agricultural and social spaces. In general, this means that the control of water, composed of technical, organisational and socio-economic control, is crucial for the composition and transformation of social spaces which will be explored in more detail at the end of this chapter.[144]

Railway construction and railway networks

The British constantly lamented the poor transport routes in India, yet they themselves did little to eliminate the grievances. On the occasions they took it upon themselves to develop the road system, it was often against the backdrop of military-strategic and/or commercial importance. In this they differed little from contemporary Indian road construction which was often funded from private funds rather than public money. Local magnates and princes commissioned streets and sarais as a way of increasing their social status and displaying their piety and power. As shown in the case of Bengal and Orissa in the first half of the nineteenth century, the British indeed planned and constructed roads, but mainly to improve communication between their three Presidency towns and to facilitate the transportation of raw materials such as cotton. However, in general, the British invested too little in the construction and maintenance of roads, so most fell into disrepair within a few years and became impassable.[145]

An exception to this rule was the Grand Trunk Road, the old military and trading route of the Mughals, which once stretched from Kabul to Dhaka. The British rebuilt this northern Indian communication artery between 1833 and 1855 and made it navigable for faster harnessed horse teams. However, it was not until after the Great Rebellion that initial plans were made for the operation of a state road system. In a move to complement the already emerging railway network that was to open up the subcontinent, "imperial roads" were envisaged to penetrate and join British India at the district and regional level. However, the British administration constructed the road network with different densities which led to the emergence of infrastructural asymmetries and different circulatory regimes. Despite the ambitious plans and projects, road construction remained labour intensive and did not benefit from technological innovation; instead, penal punishment work groups were replaced by labour gangs of the Famine Relief Works.[146]

This one-sided development was mirrored by the construction of the railways in British India which was given priority from the 1850s onwards. Initial doubts about the technology transfer were quickly eliminated. As in the case of canal projects, the EIC, at the instigation of the British government in London, once again had to guarantee a 5 per cent return on capital investment. Private enterprise thus once again profited from public income. The projects were administered by the Government of India, and the actual construction work carried out by private companies.[147] However, the colonial state built and operated railway lines publicly after 1869. The expansion of the railway network by the colonial state received a significant boost after 1880 as the Famine Commission, which had been established after the devastating famine catastrophes of the previous decade, recommended refocusing the development of the railway lines to aid the rapid distribution of food. In this respect 30,000km of track were laid. A change in railway policy was once again enacted after 1925 as the government took over expiring contracts with railway companies simultaneously creating mergers of state and private enterprises.[148]

In an article in the *New-York Daily Tribune* on 8 August 1853 Karl Marx analysed the locomotive effect that the construction of the railway had created in Europe which brought with it supply industries and led to the establishment of further trade en route. For India especially, Marx saw the train as the engine driving the modernisation of society.[149] It was the same belief in science and technology propelling the modernisation of a society which led Governor-General Lord Dalhousie to argue for the development of India. In British India, the railway was, at least from the government's and constructors' perspective, almost exclusively associated with mobility as an indispensable means of modernisation with regard to society. At the same time, as contemporary British literary works demonstrate, Indians were to be impressed by the wonder that the machine represented and not to comprehend its technical functions.[150]

This is not to deny that the British Indian government clearly had security and commercial interests in mind when introducing the railway to British India, yet official arguments always pointed towards the civilisational character of the railway. What Bentinck was to the development of canalisation, so was Dalhousie for the development of the railway. Dalhousie was one of the decisive protagonists involved in the rapid railway construction in British India: it was a network which was to extend over the entire subcontinent. At the end of Dalhousie's tenure the network comprised a few hundred kilometres. During the next decades it grew from 1350km in 1860 to 7700km by 1870 and almost 25,500km by 1890. By 1947 the rail network was eventually expanded to over 65,000km. Despite these impressive figures it is not possible to speak of systematic expansion of the network as political, military and economic interests were often in conflict with one another. Alone the endless discussions about the proper track gauge led to unnecessary delays in construction and later to exasperating transhipment operations.[151]

Technologically speaking, four types of design work can be distinguished: first, route planning; second, the embankment construction; third, tunnel excavation; and fourth, bridge building. Each stage remained under the sole supervision of the British. Engineers not only controlled the plans in the drawing offices, but also on site. Additionally, technicians had to prove their capabilities as practitioners, as they took over the entire logistics of the procurement of materials and the organisation of the labour force. Indians were merely assigned subordinate roles, among other things including the recruitment of workers along the construction route. The large extent of excavation works was done exclusively by Indian men, women and children workers who were employed most frequently as unskilled labourers on the earthworks sites of embankment and tunnel construction. However, British designers also needed a considerable number of skilled craftsmen such as carpenters, blacksmiths, welders, trackmen, stonemasons, bricklayers, tillers and divers. Machines were hardly used in the construction of the railways, meaning that the sector remained highly labour intensive until well into the twentieth century – a stark contrast to Europe and the United States.[152]

The Indian subcontinent presented a challenge for the engineers from a technological perspective as the geological conditions often pushed their knowledge to the limits. These limits were tested less in tunnel construction –

thanks in part to the employment of British explosives experts – and more in the erection of bridges. The significantly fluctuating water levels of rivers and the softer ground along the river banks necessitated special designs that were initially mastered only by Indian engineers and only machined following the development of adequate techniques. Thus, a characteristic of the Indian railway bridges became long iron bridge segments embedded on few, yet deeply sunk pillars. Similarly, the targeted narrowing of the river courses was also specially designed to aid bridge construction. The colony once again proved a laboratory in terms of technical construction methods as various construction pillars were experimentally tested and then successfully applied throughout the colonies in Asia and Africa.[153]

The locomotive effect of the railroad failed to hit India for six primary reasons. First, the Indian railway network was, in principle, the continuation of the English network in Lancashire and London as the routes systematically tapped the fertile agricultural regions specialising in export-oriented cash crops and thereby enacting further commercialisation. Second, cargo regulations systematically promoted exports and imports. Freight charges for comparable domestic routes were always more expensive meaning, for example, that it was cheaper to buy imported matches from Britain in northern India than those produced in Kanpur. Long-distance tariffs were more favourable than for short distances whilst block tariffs additionally promoted the transformative import–export structures. Thus, for the reason of protectionist measures, the export of wheat to distant regions remained more lucrative even during times of famine than distributing it to famine victims located just a few hundred kilometres away.[154]

Third, the ineffective development of the rail network infrastructure created inefficiency across the entire transport system as bad and insufficient roads used by conventional ox-driven carts were often the only regional feeder links to the railway stations. Thus, the innovative system of the railway remained, at least partially, dependent on the old transport facilities. Fourth, the various track gauges which had arisen from private sector competition and state needs in many cases prevented rapid rail transport.[155] Fifth, just about every building material from rails, switches, iron beams and signal systems as well as other technical materials were imported from Great Britain. In addition, just about every other piece of rolling stock was purchased from abroad deliberately preventing the establishment of local industries, facilities and expertise.

By independence, British India had imported a total of 14,420 locomotives from Great Britain whilst just over 707 had been produced locally. Approximately 3,000 locomotives had been purchased from other industrial nations such as Germany. However, German locomotives threatened British interests on account of their performance and competitive pricing, forcing the British government in London to decree protectionist measures and thereby forcing the railway companies in British India to purchase only British engines by law.[156] The Chittranjan Locomotive Works, founded in 1950, eventually produced the first series of Indian engines and was followed in 1955 by the Integral Coach Factory which constructed passenger carriages in Perambur, near Madras. Diesel locomotives were manufactured in Varanasi from 1964. Despite this, the Indian railway companies continued to purchase their wheels and axles from abroad until well into the 1980s. Only from 1984 was the Wheel and Axle Plant in Bangalore able to meet demands.[157]

Finally, the sixth reason for failure was the economic and technological asymmetries between India and Britain. Indian coal mines were owned by private railway companies which, due to the low cost enterprise of open-cast mining, could have produced cheap coal. However, due to the artificially held high prices, Indian coal was so unattractive that imported English coal remained competitive. Apart from this, Indians were rarely taken into account in the technical training of the railways as they were not considered suitable to use the technology. The Great Indian Peninsular Railway Company was the first to employ an Indian locomotive driver in 1942. Although Indian mechanics were occasionally credited with a certain skill in the mechanical issues of the railway, they were nevertheless kept away from the technical professions. In the 1920s only 45 Indians were accepted annually to attend advanced training programmes. Instead, large numbers of Indians found employment in simple mechanical trades such as in the railway workshops in Lahore where more than 10,000 Indians were engaged in repair work in 1914. There was a clear lack of technology transfer promoted by British industry, technology, science and, of course, politics.[158]

However, the railroads not only created jobs, but also destroyed many. In 1865 some 34,000 employees and workers were employed by the British Indian railway companies; by 1895 this had grown to 273,000 and to about 790,000 by the late 1920s before reaching just over a million during the last year of colonial rule in 1946–7. However, at the same time many job opportunities were lost in overland transport as, for example, the Banjara caravans of pack oxen, which consisted of up to 20,000 animals, were now surplus to requirements as rail transport was not only cheaper and faster but also more reliable. The same can be observed in the sector of water transportation as at the end of the nineteenth century the railway network caused the river transportation system on the Mahanadi in Orissa to decline.[159] The expansion of the railway network also had an impact on the industrial sector and caused distortions in the labour market. As shown in the chapter on industrialisation, there was a significant decline in population in cities that were cut off from old ways of communication by the railway, causing massive losses in the labour market.[160] In the agricultural sector, the combination of large canal and dam construction projects along the Mahanadi on coastal Orissa transformed the region into an agricultural zone that became connected to the city of Calcutta and disconnected with the hinterland.[161]

Despite massive government intervention, the railway companies did not become profitable until long after the turn of the century as passenger numbers rose from 19 million in 1871 to 183 million in 1901 and to 630 million in

1930. The same trend can also be observed in the transport of goods which amounted to some 3.6 million tonnes in 1871 and grew to 42.6 million in 1901 before reaching 116 million in 1930.[162] Despite this, it was not possible to speak of profitability as the productivity of the railways in British India declined as a whole. The three shocks in price and freight payments between 1884 and 1939 significantly contributed to this. A long decline in real freight rates took place between 1884 and 1919, which was followed by a rapid increase in 1923 to the levels of 1884, and an explosive increase in prices of up to 90 per cent by 1939. Simultaneously, operational costs began to increase and created a falling output of railway workers which meant that the railways were increasingly running at a deficit. A similar trend, unlike in the United States and Germany, was also occurring in Britain, prompting contemporaries to term the downturn the "British disease" which had obviously been contracted in British India.[163]

The expansion of the rail network, however, saw the spread of more than just this economic disease as the spread of epidemic diseases such as cholera, typhoid and malaria followed the rail network. Infectious diseases regularly broke out in the labourers' camps which were then carried back to the neighbouring villages by those labourers from the surrounding area who had found work on the construction sites. At times, up to a third of the workforce was decimated by such epidemics. Previously cholera-free areas became susceptible to the disease following their connection to the railway network. Rail embankments and a lack of drainage led to water retention creating marshy land and waterlogging; a biotope for the larvae of malaria-bearing mosquitoes. Contemporary estimates suggest that one person died from malaria or other such diseases for each railway sleeper that was laid on account of the physical debilitation of individuals through hard manual labour.[164]

Against all odds, the British colonial government always emphasised the civilisational character of railway construction which has been stylised into a beacon of its efforts to modernise the subcontinent. Designers, administrators, politicians and even writers, such as Rudyard Kipling, constantly emphasised the immense organisational benefits that were associated with the construction and operation of the railway. As with the construction of canals, they pointed out the efficient construction methods, the rational organisation of work, and now, newly, the superior materials and machinery. However, the use of large, disciplined work groups as well as the manufacturing of special materials on the Indian subcontinent was no British innovation as the construction of large irrigation systems, fortresses and palaces during the time of the Mughals, for example, demanded the same logistics and similar technologies. The only difference then was in the number of labourers which is likely to have increased; however, this is more a quantitative rather than a qualitative criterion.

With reference to their alleged superiority of civilisation, the British forbade any criticism of the railroad. As pilgrims to Puri complained of frequent delays, inadequate food supply and lack of sanitation in the trains at the beginning of the twentieth century, the British railway managers reported in official statements that the train was basically a comfortable means of transport and the Indians' familiarity with it was too short to be able to understand deviations from its normal state. As mentioned above, the British judged Indians as ignorant and unreasonable towards technology. This in turn derived the need for a paternalistic leadership. It is therefore easy to understand why the British regarded the railway as a useful tool of the civilising mission and therefore did not give up that means of control until the end of colonial rule.[165]

Furthermore, in Ceylon the British made sure to keep control of the railroad in their hands. However, as in the case of cartography, the development of the transport infrastructure resulted in a different system to that in India. Road construction in the first half of the nineteenth century was primarily for the military development of the island. This included the road connection from Colombo to Kandy and the inland route from Colombo to Trincomalee, both of which were emphatically promoted by Governor Barnes. As the only natural port of the British Empire in the Indian Ocean, Trincomalee was important for the deployment and redeployment of forces on the island independent of the monsoons. It was only after the establishment of the plantation economy from the 1840s and the Colombo–Kandy rail connection after 1867 that the rapidly growing rail network linked the highlands to the roads, which were systematically built as feeder links to the main stations. By the end of the nineteenth century, 75 per cent of the newly constructed roads were in the highlands of Ceylon.[166]

In contrast to British India, the colonial state in Ceylon put the railway network almost exclusively in economic terms as it served primarily for the import of machinery for the production of tea and, of course, for the transportation of tea from the main stations in the highlands for shipping to Colombo. Railway lines in the southwest of the island as well as the inland lines to Trincomalee and Jaffna to the north were also used to transport colonial goods, particularly spices, palm oil and the growing import of Burmese rice to supply the population. The railway reduced freight costs of rice by 14 per cent and coffee by almost 25 per cent, making the production of coffee (and later tea) in Ceylon competitive on the emerging global market. The large asymmetry of the infrastructural network is blatantly obvious. As the network was aligned so perfectly to the needs of the plantation economy, its one-sidedness remained in Ceylon longer than it did in British India, evident still today in tea being the main export commodity of the Lankan economy.[167]

Telecommunication systems and networks

Until the nineteenth century, the dissemination of information was only ever as fast as the fastest man-made transport. Exceptions to this rule were acoustic and visual communication systems, but these were not suitable for the transmission of extensive and complicated issues and were also dependent on the weather. The Mughals introduced a regular postal system (*dhak chaukis*) to their empire for means of communication with its peripheries. Alongside this there was also a network of local informants and news writers who, like the town police chief (*kotwal*), the judges (*kazis*), censors (*muhtasibs*), village clerks (*qanungos*) and local police chiefs (*barkandazis*), collected, selected and delivered information. Spies also procured information from monasteries, from the official residence of provincial governors, from the urban bazaars and in the sarais on the highways. A complementary, highly efficient network of runners (*harkaras*) ensured the reliable weekly reporting in the Mughal court.[168]

State formation in the eighteenth century differentiated and intensified these structures as the Marathas and Afghans introduced a mounted communication service. Whilst in the Mughal Empire it is estimated that there were some 4,000 *harkaras*, some 20,000 are estimated to have been in the service of the *nawab* in Awadh alone in 1770. Additionally thousands of *harkaras* ran for *zamindars*, *taluqdars*, *mahajans* and *banias*. Following the gradual annexation of South Asian territories by the British in the second half of the eighteenth century, the existing information and communication systems were adopted and supplemented by their own runners and riders and new routes were established as they hoped to become independent of the Indian informants; a policy which, however, achieved only limited success. The colonial power was only able to secure a communication advantage for a few decades following the introduction and state monopoly it held over the telegraph system, which in many ways contributed to the expansion of its rule on the subcontinent.[169]

The first proposals for the construction of a telegraph system in British India were put forward by Adolphe Bazin in 1838 to the Asiatic Society. As a visionary, Bazin aimed to connect London and Calcutta. However, the incumbent Vice President of the Asiatic Society, Dr William O'Shaughnessy, rejected the proposal due to a perceived lack of profitability. Whilst this criticism only held as partially true, it cannot be overlooked that with this decision O'Shaughnessy eliminated a competitor from the field. O'Shaughnessy had come to Bengal in 1833 as an assistant surgeon and was appointed Professor of Chemistry at the newly founded Calcutta Medical College two years later. Since then, he had experimented with electromagnetic devices. By 1839 his efforts had advanced to such an extent that he envisaged introducing his system to the public. O'Shaughnessy was among scientific researchers from around the world who had been working on the concept of a wire-based data transmission since the 1820s. Among them was Samuel F.B. Morse, who was able to produce a working telegraph in 1837. Morse later claimed to have invented the telegraph alone, a historic myth which stubbornly persists to this day.[170]

An experimental line was laid between Calcutta and Diamond Harbour in 1851. The military advantage it afforded the British in the second Anglo-

Burmese War (1852) convinced the technophile Governor-General Lord Dalhousie who now vehemently argued for the construction of telegraph lines alongside the construction of the railway network in India. A year later, the laying of overground cables began, mostly parallel to the course of the railway lines and often in anticipation of their proposed routes. As elsewhere in the world where railway lines were built, track and signal systems could not operate efficiently without telegraphic communication links. By 1855 a rudimentary network had been created. It consisted of three main axes that were exclusively aligned to the military needs of the colonial state. Priority was given to the connection of the Calcutta–Delhi–Lahore–Peshawar line to help secure the new border with Afghanistan. A second line ran from Bombay–Indore–Gwaliar to Agra and a third from Madras via Bangalore and on to the Bombay–Agra line; the three lines thus roughly shaping a "Z". According to contemporaries, much more reasonable alternatives existed but Dalhousie was determined to protect his annexations and prepare for new ones.[171]

The experience O'Shaughnessy had with his first telegraph lines was partially integrated into the envisaged all-India system as he predominantly used bamboo poles as supports, which had the advantage of being resistant to weathering and were flexible and able to withstand the monsoon winds. Also he employed local specialists to install the lines. O'Shaughnessy laid the first underwater cable in the world in Calcutta through the Hugli at a distance of almost 700m. Just as in the case of the construction of the railways, technical equipment was imported from Great Britain. In addition to the technical apparatus required for construction, iron wire – which was gradually replaced by copper wire from 1886 – was also imported. The laying of the cables was not technically challenging since only small construction crews were needed. This may be one reason why the silent telegraph has, in contrast to the noisy steam engines in ships and trains, only recently been discovered in historical technological research.[172]

The shortcomings of the rudimentary telegraph network were felt during the Great Rebellion. Whilst it succeeded in delivering a message to Calcutta vaguely reporting the arrival of the rebels in Delhi, the lines were almost immediately cut by the rebels, causing a communication blackout. The British failed to repair the network sufficiently enough to give them a crucial logistical and organisational advantage before the end of the rebellion. The lack of communication from Calcutta to Madras also meant the badly needed troops from Madras had to be summoned by runners and riders. Meanwhile, the few steamboats that existed could only transport the army at the speed that the slowest sailing ship could sail. The Great Rebellion made the technological shortcomings of the British in British India clear in that it became evident that the chain of different transport and communication systems was only as strong as its weakest link.[173]

The desired benefits of the information networking slowly came following the systematic expansion of the network, which was funded by loans and state guarantees from London, as well as the successful laying of the world's first functioning submarine telegraph line from Bombay to Suez in 1865. Conversely complaints about the inadequacies and losses during data transmission gradually decreased, despite the fact that, for example, misreporting in the Austro-Prussian War of 1870–1 had led to grotesque contradictions.[174] Inaccurate economic data on prices for cash crops created a paradoxical situation in the speed of data transfers as when important and fast decisions were needed, wrong decisions were often made. Still during the First World War too much or too little transmitted information could trigger panic and confusion among the colonial administration.[175]

The much praised speed of data transfer by telegraph made civilians demand its use, and especially so in the sectors of industry and the press. Civilian use was permitted in 1855 as cables were made public for companies, private individuals, traders, merchants, bankers, opium speculators, journalists and shareholders. Already in 1859 more than a third of all telegrams originated from Indians; by 1860 this had reached almost two-thirds.[176] Although the telegraph in British India, as elsewhere in the world, never became a means of mass communication, it nevertheless led to a revolution in journalism and print media reporting. Moreover, the telegraph was decisive in the gradual emergence of a public sphere in British India from the 1880s as debates surrounding what should constitute an Indian nation, and whether this already existed, were passionately played out in newspapers, journals and nationally organised meetings including the INC debates at its annual meetings.[177]

The telegraph hardly made an impact on the colonial administration as although all British administrative offices were part of the telegraph network, the telegram could not replace the actual decision-making process which was still based on hand-written or machine-written correspondence. Thus, although telegrams helped prepare decision-making, they usually became mere attachments to the official correspondence. Therefore, it is not possible to speak of a much faster, let alone more efficient colonial bureaucracy.[178] However, the telegraph, as in the case of the resignation of Lord Curzon as Governor-General in 1905, succeeded in settling decisions quickly, here to the Viceroy's surprise as the English king accepted his resignation; which then, of course had to be followed up with official written confirmation. At the end of colonial rule some 770,000 miles of telegraph lines had been laid across the Indian subcontinent whilst a further 5,300 miles surrounded it. Although the network appears to be dense and uniform at first glance, 95 per cent of the total British Indian telegrams went via Calcutta and Bombay, thus demonstrating the high asymmetry of the communication.[179]

Whilst the overland telegraph was a medium that connected cities to one another, the telephone was initially an urban communication tool and this was particularly true for British India. In stark contrast to the United States, where in the last decades of the nineteenth century the telephone network had been systematically developed as a means of mass communication, this was not the case in Europe. Great Britain in particular lay under a certain "technological inertia" of the day. Politicians, and public opinion, were of the view that the phone lent itself only as a medium for intra-house communication, and possibly even inter-house, but not as a tool for country-wide communication. This perspective was exacerbated in British India. The first telephone lines were laid in 1881, and in 1883 the colonial state had ensured its monopoly. By 1933–4 there were some 55,000 telephone connections, half of them with licensed private companies. Thus, calculated as a proportion of the population of the subcontinent, this results in one telephone to 8,500 inhabitants. By way of comparison the ratios in the United States was 1:8 and 1:47 in Great Britain.[180]

Initially, only trunk lines that linked individual cities were laid. The network roughly copied the "Z" of the early telegraph network until the 1930s when the coverage of the network was concentrated on the northwestern regions of British India. During the British and Russian imperial expansion into Central Asia, the telephone was specifically to secure the British border to Afghanistan whilst the transfer of the capital of British India from Calcutta to New Delhi after 1912 made the northwest the centre of political decision-making. Obviously, the telephone network served purely military (and political) security needs whilst within the few cities where telephone lines existed it was basically used for commercial purposes. As the aesthetic design of New Delhi shows, the British not only considered the environs of the imperial city as a kind of oversized estate dotted with historical monuments, but this was also applicable to India as a whole, whose entrances were now secured by (military) guards equipped with the latest electronic device.[181]

In 1952, five years after independence, there were fewer than 200,000 telephone extensions in the Indian Union, half of which were located in the three cities of Bombay (46,200), Calcutta (36,000) and Delhi (15,000).[182] In 1989, India had some 4 million telephones for a population, then, of 800 million people resulting in a ratio of 1:200. Four years later, the number of telephones had increased to 7 million and an additional 2.8 million connections had been applied for. Compared with the preceding years, this was an impressive figure; however, at the same time the ratio of 1:125 was still lamentable when compared with industrialised countries.[183] To improve the situation, the Congress government under Rajiv Gandhi set up the Telecom Commission in early 1989. Headed by Satyanarayan Gangaram Pitroda – better known as Sam Pitroda, a US-based businessman and close confidant of Rajiv Gandhi – the Telecom Commission was to circumvent the bureaucracy with its strangling licence system. Within a few years Pitroda and the Telecom Commission were successful in setting up a wide network of (urban) public telephones.[184] From then on, the usage of telephones in India multiplied.

The telephone industry was deregulated during the 1990s. However, the liberalisation of telecommunications was only partially implemented in 1997 and again in 2003. The Telecom Regulatory Authority of India Act of 1997 (TRAI) regulated private telecommunication services including wireless mobile telephones, telephones and other wire-based services. As there had been no further legislation since colonial times, the law had to refer back to the Indian Telegraph Act of 1885 and the Indian Wireless Telegraphy Act of 1933 which regulated

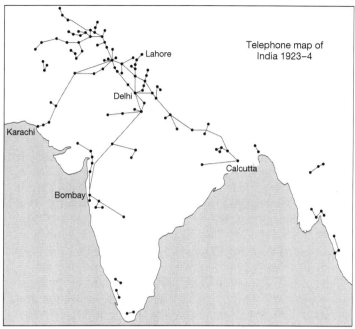

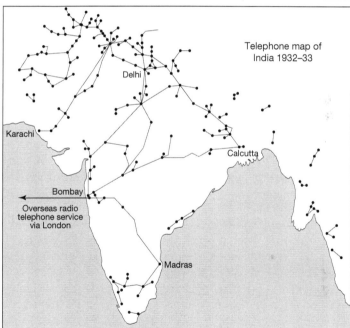

Map 8.3 Telephone network 1923–24 and 1932–33. Michael Mann, "The deep digital divide. The telephone in British India, 1883–1933", *Historical Social Research/Historische Sozialforschung* 35, 1 (2010), p. 203

state monopoly and had set up the licence system for private enterprises. Ultimately, the Indian Telegraph (Amendment) Act of 2003 stipulated that the recommendations of the TRAI were to be implemented.[185] Meanwhile, the mobile network represents more than 750 million mobile phones in 2011 and has expanded so quickly that it has since replaced the wire-based communication system in many areas.[186] Consequently, the last telegraph message was sent on 15 July 2013.

Finally, a brief look at television is merited as the post-independent Indian central government envisioned its use as a broadcasting tool of public education in the sense of progress and betterment of the Indian population at large. Moreover, broadcasting was seen as an appropriate technical means to create the Indian nation and the nation-state. In line with its policy to use broadcasting as a tool to manipulate and control, the central government supported the creation of its first public service broadcaster, Doordarshan (DD) in 1959. Officially DD was to educate the vast majority of the illiterate population in the rural parts of the country on issues such as parenting, rights of women and agriculture. Crucial in the execution of the government's control over the institution was its financial structure. Until 1976 the funding of public broadcasting was based on a mixture of television licences and an allocation from the annual central budget. In this way, the central government steered the DD's programming policy, operation and maintenance.[187]

The overall cable and satellite boom starting in the late 1970s saw the proliferation of TV ownership and credit networks. Between 1984 and 1990 numbers of televisions rose from 3.6 million to 27.8 million. In 1988, five TVs were said to be sold every minute and as many as 30 television brands tried to attract the buyer's attention.[188] Apparently an increasing number of Indians, mostly belonging to the so-called middle class, actively participated in the consumerism generated by the Indira Gandhi regime of the 1970s and early 1980s to promote the nation on the technological front. It is against this background that Indira Gandhi and her government organised the Asian Games (Asiad) in Delhi in 1982. From the very beginning the games were designed as a spectacular showcase of technology and nationalism. The media spectacle was to unite the country through a common network. The nation was to be forged, among many other things, by technological modernity signified through TV broadcasting on a national scale which materialised on 15 August 1982 (significantly on Independence Day). In popular Indian memory the 1982 Asiad is remembered as a caesura marking media urbanism and the beginning of the national colour TV era.[189]

In 1991, the first non-Indian broadcast operator went into business from outside the country as it was still prohibited to broadcast from Indian soil. The Hong Kong-based STAR TV used the existing urban-based rudimentary cable network to deliver its programmes. In the same year CNN started to deliver coverage of the First Gulf War.[190] This was the very first time that news reporting and broadcasting was transmitted independent of government control. In the following year, Zee TV started to operate entertainment programmes such as soap operas and game shows. Although they were mostly conceptual acquisitions of American series, a specific Indian form of reality TV soaps and 24/7 news soon developed, creating an "Indian-ness" which continues to be produced by Indian TV channels today.[191] In the beginning, however, the new programmes also caused critique, accusing the new (foreign) media of "Western imperialism" and the corruption of India's cultural values. Yet, in spite of the critique, and after many lawsuits being fought over TV programmes and delivery services, government passed the Broadcasting Bill in 1997, thus opening the sluices for infinite broadcasting.[192]

Licences were given to over 600 registered TV channels in 2012. These private operators provided an opportunity for the development of regional and, even more importantly, multi-lingual programming.[193] Finally, and at the same time somewhat ironically, the private media quietly created what DD and official government politics had failed to achieve, namely an increasing national thinking and a middle class struggling over issues like the definition of an "Indian culture" or even an "Indian national culture", or just an "Indian-ness" on the one hand; and yet, at the same time, over questions of regional and local identities.[194] It is therefore nothing more than the public negotiation of old and new, but in any case taking place in the changed, and changing, social spaces which are achieved through human interaction, communication and circulation.

Notes

1. Paty 1999: 171–204.
2. Adas 1989.
3. Mann 2005e: 27–53.
4. Basalla 1967: 611–22.
5. Irschick 1994.
6. Arnold 2000: 13–16; Cohn 2006; Raj 2007: 1–26, 159–80; Prakash 1999.
7. Raj 2011: 55–82.
8. Sengupta I. 2005.
9. Fischer-Tiné 2003a: 90–112, esp. 93–4; Pernau 2006; Robinson 2002: 41–102.
10. Dharampal 1983: 1–79.
11. Zastoupil and Moir 1999: 23–6.
12. Kumar D. 1995: 143–5.
13. Sarkar S. 2013: 99–124.
14. Kumar D. 2013: 45–61; Mukherjee H. and Mukherjee U. 2000: pt I, 19–175.
15. Sarkar S. 2013: 99–124.
16. Zastoupil and Moir 1999: 36–50, 54–66; Ghosh S.C. 1995: 6–99; Sharma R.N. and Sharma R.K 1996: 74–143.
17. Fischer-Tiné 2003b.
18. Ganehan 2008; Metcalf B.D. 1982.
19. Dash and Dash 2009; Mann 2015.
20. Oesterheld and Kumar 2007.
21. Krishna V.V. 1992: 57–72.
22. Arnold 2000: 169–85.
23. Sangwan 2000: 13–53.
24. Francis 2011: 293–326.

25 Perkovich 2000; Malik P. 2010.
26 Arnold 2000: 190–8, 208–10; Raina and Habib 2004: 214–20.
27 Kumar D. 1995: 180–227.
28 Fischer-Tiné 2013.
29 Raina and Habib 2004: 60–80; Raina 2003.
30 Kulke 2005: 105–14.
31 Rao, Shulman and Subrahmanyam 2001; Berkemer 1998: 145–90.
32 Conermann 2002.
33 Moosvi 1999: 181–7.
34 Gottlob 2002.
35 Kopf 1969; Embree 1962: 141–57.
36 Stokes 1959.
37 Majeed 1992.
38 Mann 2004: 1–26, 2011b: 317–28.
39 Zastoupil and Moir 1999:1–72.
40 Guha R. 1988; Mann 2009: 28–50.
41 Lal V. 2006: 27–78.
42 Kulkarni 2006b; Mohanty 1982; Mishra P.K 2001; Bandhyopadhyay 2001.
43 Ali D. 1999.
44 Zutshi 2011: 99–122; Frese 2003: 95–106.
45 Savarkar 1923; Mann 2009: 65–9, 126–7.
46 Jaffrelot 1996: 25–33.
47 Lal V. 2003: 141–85.
48 Mann 2009: 139–55, 169–78, 190–9.
49 Sayeed 2007; Hussain J. 2006; Burke and Quraishi 1995.
50 Parvez 2002: 77–95.
51 Jalal 2007.
52 Lal V. 2003: 186–230. Cf. the publications of *Subaltern Studies*, 1982ff; Chaturvedi 2000; Ludden 2001.
53 Grove 1995a: 77–8, 80–90; Raj K. 2007, 27–59.
54 Raj K. 2003: 23–54; Mann 2010b: 115–39.
55 Gole 1983.
56 Gogate and Arunachalam 2006.
57 Vicziany 1986: 625–60.
58 Robb 1998: 181–206.
59 Edney 1997: 45–7.
60 Arnold 2000: 22.
61 Kejariwal 1988.
62 Baber 1998: 156.
63 Desmond 1995: 85–126.
64 Sangwan 1998: 210–36; Arnold 2007: 899–928.
65 Grove 1995b: 36–41.
66 Withers 1993: 255–64.
67 Mann 2003: 25–46.
68 Edney 1994; Edney 1997: 91–102, 124–8, 165–95.
69 Edney 1997: 2, 21–23, 199–235.
70 Ibid.: 250–68; Barrow 2003: 135–43.
71 Barrow 2003: 30.
72 Stafford 1990: 67–89, esp. 71.
73 Arnold 2000: 45.
74 Grout 1990: 1–18.
75 Kumar D. 1990: 59–60; Sangwan 1991: 35–41.
76 Sangwan 1991: 35–41; Sangwan 1999: 187–237.
77 Stafford 1990; Stafford 1984: 5–32; Raj K. 2007: 181–222.

78 Barrow 2008.
79 Sivasundaram 2007: 925–65, esp. 946; Barrow 2008: 96–102.
80 Barrow 2008: 62–9, 165–86.
81 Chakrabarti P. 2010: 49–82.
82 Fischer-Tiné 2013: 45–7.
83 Kumar D. 2001: xi–xxiii, esp. xv–xvii.
84 Wujastyk et al. 2013.
85 Rezawi 2001: 40–65, esp. 53–6; Zoysa and Palitharatna 1992: 111–20, esp. 112–3.
86 Rezawi 2001: 40–51.
87 Moosvi 2001: 66–70.
88 Naraindas 2001: 94–119; Arnold 1993: 125–33.
89 Brimnes 2004: 191–204.
90 Harrison M. 1994: 6–35.
91 Arnold 2000: 59–60.
92 Harrison M. 1994: 10, 22–23.
93 Arnold 2000: 60–2.
94 Alavi 2005: 101–29.
95 Sangwan 1991: 3–4.
96 Harrison M. 2001: 37–87.
97 Arnold 2000: 75; Harrison M. 1994: 82–7.
98 Harrison M. 1994: 60–72, 76–8.
99 Mishra S.S.R. 2001: 166–79.
100 Arnold 1993: 68–9, 75–7.
101 Arnold 2000: 85–6.
102 Harrison M. 1999: 177–203; Ramanna 2004: 205–25.
103 Arnold 2000: 79–80.
104 Howard-Jones 1975.
105 Mishra S. 2011.
106 Howard-Jones 1975: *passim*.
107 Khalid 2009: 45–73.
108 Ahuja 2004: 95–116; Pati 2001: 270–98; Lochtefeld 2010: 49–102.
109 Dutta 2009: 74–92.
110 Ramanna 2002: 18, 23, 48–82; Kumar A. 1998.
111 Harrison 1999: *passim*.
112 Bayly S. 1999: 119–43.
113 Kumar M. 2008: 211–33.
114 Whitcombe 1982: 677–737, esp. 678–9; Gilmartin 1994: 1127–49, esp. 1129–30.
115 Rao G.N. 1988: 25–60.
116 Stone 1984: 13–19; Arnold 2000: 117–18.
117 Arnold 2000: 115, 118–19.
118 Gilmartin 1994: 1136.
119 The Indian Problem Solved 1874: 252–72 and inlaid map.
120 Stone 1984: 19–31.
121 Whitcombe 1982: 692–717, 727–30; Stone 1984: 31–4.
122 Gilmartin 1994: 1132.
123 Stone 1984: 57–60; Mann 2012a: 431–55.
124 On the one hand: Whitcombe 1996: 237–59; Klein 2001: 147–79 and on the other hand: Stone 1984: 68–104.
125 D'Souza R. 2006: 51–96.
126 Singh N.T. 2005: 86–110.
127 Klingensmith 2003: 122–40.
128 Zachariah 2005.
129 D'Souza R. 2006: 127–47, 182–214.
130 Ahuja 1999: 130–45.

131 Schmitthenner 2011: 181–201.
132 Manimohan 2013: 284–311, esp. 284.
133 Stoddart 2011: 1–54.
134 D'Souza R. 2003: 81–105.
135 Thaha 2009: 95–9; Vaikuntham 2010: 50–65, 94–104.
136 Rao B.E. 2011: 145–59.
137 Vaikuntham 2010: 123–95.
138 Werner 2013.
139 Alvares and Billorey 1988; Singh S. 1997.
140 Alvares and Billorey 1988: 11–25.
141 Dwivedi 2000; Agarwal, Jain and Singh 2007: 513–59.
142 D'Souza D. 2002.
143 Shukla and Asthana 2005.
144 Manimohan 2013: *passim*.
145 Ahuja 2009: 196–204.
146 Ibid.: 204–23; Arnold 2000: 106–7.
147 Thorner 1950: 1–21, 168.
148 Hurd 1982: 737–61, esp. 738–9; Thorner 1950: 44–168.
149 Marx 2001: 62–7.
150 Aguiar 2010: 24–47.
151 Arnold 2000: 111; Hurd: 1982, 739.
152 Derbyshire 1995: 177–215, esp. 185–6.
153 Kerr 1995: 127–47; Derbyshire 1995: 201.
154 Hurd 1982: 745–7, 756.
155 Derbyshire 1995: 187–190; Arnold 2000: 110.
156 Lehmann 1965: 297–306.
157 Khosla G.S 2001: 216–56.
158 Lehmann 1977: 49–61; Arnold 2000: 111.
159 Ahuja 2009: 247–9.
160 Hurd 1982: 748, 757.
161 Ahuja 2009: 255–8.
162 Hurd 1982: 754.
163 Hurd 2007: 314–62.
164 Kerr 1995: 159–66.
165 Ahuja 2004: 112–15.
166 Munasinghe 2002: 6–29, 65–97.
167 Ibid.: 117–62.
168 Bayly 1996: 10–20, 60–6; Habib I. 1986: 236–52.
169 Bayly 1996: 30–6, 69–76.
170 Choudhury D. 2000: 335–41; Gorman 1968: 184–214.
171 Gorman 1971: 581–601; Ghose 1995: 153–76.
172 Choudhury D. 2000: 346–8; Shridharani 1953: 25, 74.
173 Choudhury D. 2010: 31–49; Wenzelhuemer 2013: 217–20.
174 Bonea 2010: 167–87.
175 Choudhury D. 2010: 179–208.
176 Ibid.: 65–7.
177 Mann 2013: 197–222.
178 Fletcher 2010: 90–107.
179 Wenzelhuemer 2013: 231–6.
180 Mann 2010c: 188–208, esp. 197–201.
181 Ibid.: 202–5.
182 Shridharani 1953: 112–14.
183 Mann 2010c: 189.
184 Menon and Nigam 2007: 9.

185 Sridhar 2013.
186 Munshi 2012: 26.
187 Sinha S.K. 2006a: 1–38; Sinha S.K. 2006b: 39–47.
188 Shah 1997: 41.
189 Sundaram R. 2010: 83–4.
190 Butcher 2003; Sinha N. 1998: 22–37.
191 Munshi 2012.
192 Campbell 2007: 140–71.
193 Mehta 2008: 1–12.
194 Desai and Agrawal 2009.

Afterthought and prospect

The new technologies, from the railways, telegraph, telephone and television – now extended with the addition of the internet – have led to profound far-reaching changes in the spatial structures across the world, and specifically in South Asia since the mid-nineteenth century. New communication systems have created new economic as well as new political spaces which have been subjected to constant transformations. The dynamics of these spaces depends on who is connected to each network and who can participate in them and, perhaps more importantly, who cannot. The circulation of people and information, which in turn determines the circulation of goods and capital, has created completely new spatial orders that are referred to as social spaces. These are based on densities as well as disparities that result from the shift, reorganisation and recreation of spaces. They are therefore the result of sustained processes of deterritorialisation and reterritorialisation which are characteristic of the historical development that has been increasing in quantity and quality since the mid-nineteenth century, in short: globalisation.

Two examples can emphasise this fact. First, the railway grid in North India linked the most important pilgrimage centres for followers of the Hindu forms of belief from which the British created a Hindu pilgrimage area of their own understanding. In response to this, the writer and journalist Bharatendu Harischandra created his own literary space in the 1870s, specifically designed as being beyond the "religious space" defined by the British, as he deliberately added pilgrimage centres that were not connected and reachable with rail connections thus creating a new social space.[1] Second, British nationalist historiography has constantly attempted to depict the telegraph as a global communication network and to emphasise the national-imperial interests as well as the firm control this afforded the empire, the centre of which was in London. Meanwhile, however, it has transpired that international cartels were operating beyond the nation-state, which controlled much of the space covered by the telegraph, and divided it according to vested interests.[2]

Social spaces are obviously (among others other things) constantly recreated, ideologically constructed and sometimes also scientifically established through technical innovation but simultaneously questioned, renegotiated and redefined.

Afterthought and prospect 365

This process of circulatory ordering (and reordering) and organisation (and reorganising) of social spaces has continued, unabated, and with different dynamics until the present day. These dynamics have manifested themselves in the emergence of new public spheres since 2010 with the spread of internet and mobile technologies that have played an integral role in the Arab Spring revolutions and NSA surveillance. These social spaces are also part of a global process of deterritorialisation and reterritorialisation that has been ongoing from the mid-nineteenth century. In short: changes, transformations and reorganisations of space(s) constitute and define globalisation. Contrary to many assumptions, predictions and hopes with regard to the effects of globalisation, these changes have produced more injustices and inequalities than equality and justice, which is clear merely from looking at events since the turn of the millennium.

Although the topics presented in this book could not be processed with the same depth, it is hoped that a general overview and introduction to the various topics and questions about the history, society, culture, economics and politics of people and countries in South Asia has been presented. Certainly the themes, weightings and perspectives presented here are not an exhaustive list and other additions would have been possible; however, the issues presented reflect those which have concerned me as a researcher and teacher over the past 30 years. It has been important for me to write an "open history" which allows for development, change, transformation and evolution from any direction. In this sense I look to the thoughts of Fareed Zakaria in his article "India Rising" from 2006 and modify them for the current people and countries of South Asia.[3]

Currently, in the countries of the South Asian subcontinent, there may be several Silicon Valleys, Special Economic Zones, Metro Line systems, multi-lane motorways and glittering shopping malls, which are quite comparable to some European or American counterparts, but simultaneously there are numerous comparisons that can be drawn with the Nigerias and Somalias of the world as nearly a third of South Asia's 1.5 billion people live below the poverty line. Furthermore, every South Asian country suffers, to some degree, from a lack of government control, autonomy movements, state and regional terrorism and even anarchic conditions in addition to deeply patriarchal structures.

The societies and communities in South Asia will certainly take away from all these "contradictions" something in the future and their people will undoubtedly create many new forms. Changes, not only in the shopping malls, but also in the slums and villages, are already becoming visible, whereby the rapid changes in telecommunications and transport are certainly just the obvious indications. Meanwhile, the image of the family unit is under much criticism, especially following the 2012 Delhi rape case and its aftermath which is testament to the public pressure applied on the Indian Government, forcing it to respond in a very short period of time and to legislate over the case in response to public outcries.

From the outside looking in, these changes look largely messy, chaotic, spontaneous and unplanned. Furthermore, these changes will never occur

Afterthought and prospect

with the same intensity in all states and for all people in South Asia. Nevertheless, in every case these changes are not instigated from the top–down, but rather bottom–up, and this happens in a large part not because of the governments but rather in spite of them. As stated in the beginning of the first chapter on State Formation, this characteristic bottom–up transformation, transition and change seems to be the great historical continuum of South Asian societies and polities.

Notes

1 Bury 2007: 1–38, esp. 20–2.
2 Boyce 2000: 39–70; Winseck and Pike 2007.
3 Zakaria 2006.

Bibliography

Adas, Michael (1974a) *The Burma Delta: Economic Development and Social Change on an Asian Rice Frontier, 1852–1941*, Madison: University of Wisconsin Press.
——(1974b) 'Immigrant Asians and the Economic Impact of European Imperialism: The role of the Indian Chettiars in British Burma', *Journal of Asian Studies*, 33: 385–401.
——(1989) *Machines as the Measures of Men: Science, Technology and Ideologies of Western Domination*, Ithaca: Cornell University Press.
——(1998) 'Ethnic Pluralism and Conflict on the Frontiers of South Asian Migration', in: Michael Adas (ed.) *State, Market and Peasant in South and Southeast Asia*, Aldershot: Ashgate.
Addleton, Jonathan S. (1992) *Undermining the Centre: The Gulf Migration and Pakistan*, Karachi: Oxford University Press.
Adeney, Katherine and Sáez, Lawrence (eds) (2005) *Coalition Politics and Hindu Nationalism*, London: Routledge.
Adhikari, Di Pi (1998) *The History of Nepalese Nationalism*, Kathmandu: Romila Adhikari Acharya.
Adivasi Munnetra Sangam (AMS) (2013) *Adivasi Munnetra Sangam, (AMS)*. Available online at www.adivasi.net (accessed 5 August 2013).
Agarwal, Pushpendra K., Jain, Sharad K. and Singh, Vijay P. (2007) *Hydrology and Water Resources of India*, Dordrecht: Springer.
Agenda 21: An Assessment (2002) *Agenda 21: An Assessment, Chapter 9, Forests*, Ministry of Environment and Forests, New Delhi: Government of India. Available online at http://envfor.nic.in/divisions/ic/wssd/doc2/main.html (accessed 13 October 2013).
Agnihotri, Indu (1996) 'Ecology, Land Use and Colonization: The Canal Colonies of Punjab', *Indian Economic and Social History Review*, 33(1): 37–58.
Aguiar, Maian (2010) *Tracking Modernity: India's Railway and the Culture of Mobility*, Minneapolis: University of Minnesota Press.
Ahmad Khan, Main-ud-din (1980) *Titu Mir and his Followers in British Indian Records (1831–1833 A.D.)*, Dacca: Islamic Foundation Bangladesh.
Ahmad, Syed Sami (2008) *The Trial of Zulfikar Ali Bhutto and the Superior Judiciary in Pakistan*, Karachi: Royal Book Company.
Ahmed, Ishtiaq (1999; 2nd edn 2005) 'The 1947 Partition of Panjab: Arguments put Forth before the Panjab Boundary Commission by the Parties Involved', in: Ian Talbot and Gurharpal Singh (eds) *Region and Partition: Bengal, Punjab and the Partition of the Subcontinent*, Karachi: Oxford University Press.

Ahmed, Sahara (2007) 'Conflicting Claims: The Colonial State Forests and Forest Dwellers in the Jalpaiguri District, 1869–1947', in: Ranjan Chakrabarti (ed.) *Situating Environmental History*, New Delhi: Manohar.

Ahuja, Ravi (1999) *Die Erzeugung kolonialer Staatlichkeit und das Problem der Arbeit: Eine Studie zur Sozialgeschichte der Stadt Madras und ihres Hinterlandes zwischen 1750 und 1800*, Stuttgart: Franz Steiner Verlag.

——(2004) '"The Bridge-Builders": Some Notes on Railways, Pilgrimage and the British "Civilizing Mission" in Colonial India', in: Harald Fischer-Tiné and Michael Mann (eds) *Colonialism as Civilizing Mission: Cultural Ideology in British India*, London: Anthem Press.

——(2006) 'Mobility and Containment: The Voyages of South Asian Seamen, *c.* 1900–1960', *International Review of Social History*, 51: 111–41 (Supplement).

——(2009a) 'Networks of Subordination–Networks of the Subordinated: The ordered Space of South Asian Maritime Labour in an Age of Imperialism (*c.* 1890–1947)', in: Ashwaini Tambe and Herald Fischer-Tiné (eds) *The Limits of British Colonial Control in South Asia: Spaces of Disorder in the Indian Ocean Region*, London: Routledge.

——(2009b) *Pathways of Empire: Circulation, 'Public Works' and Social Space in Colonial Orissa, c. 1780–1914*, Hyderabad: Orient BlackSwan.

Aiolfi, Sergio (1987) *Calicos und gedrucktes Zeug: Die Entwicklung der englischen Textilveredelung und der Tuchhandel der East India Company 1650–1750*, Wiesbaden: Franz Steiner Verlag.

Alam, Muzaffar (1986) *The Crisis of Empire in Mughal North India: Awadh and the Punjab, 1707–48*, New Delhi: Oxford University Press.

——(1998) 'Aspects of Agrarian Uprising in North India in the Early Eighteenth Century', in: Muzaffar Alam and Sanjay Subrahmanyam (eds) *The Mughal State, 1526–1750*, New Delhi: Oxford University Press.

Alam, Muzaffar and Subrahmanyam, Sanjay (1998) 'Introduction', in: Muzaffar Alam and Sanjay Subrahmanyam (eds) *The Mughal State, 1526–1750*, New Delhi: Oxford University Press.

Alavi, Seema (1995) *The Sepoys and the Company: Tradition and Transition in Northern India, 1770–1830*, New Delhi: Oxford University Press.

——(2005) 'Unani Medicine in the Nineteenth-Century Public Sphere: Urdu Texts and the *Oudh Akhbar*', *Indian Economic and Social History Review*, 42(1): 101–29.

——(ed.) (2002) *The Eighteenth Century India: Debates in Indian History and Society*, New Delhi: Oxford University Press.

Aleem, Shamim (1985) *Personnal Management in a Princely State*, New Delhi: Gitanjali Publishing House.

Ali, Daud (ed.) (1999) *Invoking the Past: The Uses of History in South Asia*, New Delhi: Oxford University Press.

Ali, Imran (1978) 'Canal Colonization and Socio-economic Change', in: Indu Banga (ed.) *Agrarian System of the Sikhs, Late Eighteenth and Early Nineteenth Century*, New Delhi: Manohar.

Ali, Syed Mahmud (2010) *Understanding Bangladesh*, New Delhi: Foundation Books.

Alvares, Claude and Billorey, Ramesh (1988) *Damming the Narmada: India's Greatest Planned Environmental Disaster*, Penang: Third World Network.

Ambirajan, S. (1978) *Classical Political Economy and British Policy in India*, Cambridge: Cambridge University Press.

Amjad, Mohammad and Mohammad, Iqbal (1982) *The State of Forestry in Pakistan*. Peshawar: Pakistan Forest Institute.

Amtith, Sunil S. (2011) *Migration and Diaspora in Modern Asia*, Cambridge: Cambridge University Press.

Andersen, Walter K. and Damle, Shridhar D. (1987) *The Brotherhood in Saffron: The Rashtriya Swayamsevak Sangh and Hindu Revivalism*, Boulder, Colorado: Westview Press.

Ansari, Sarah (2005) *Life after Partition: Migration, Community and Strife in Sindh 1947–1967*, Karachi: Oxford University Press.

Anwar, Firdoz (2001) *Nobility Under the Mughals (1628–1658)*, Delhi: Manohar Publishers.

Arasaratnam, Sinnappah (1970) *Indians in Malaya and Singapore*, Kuala Lumpur: Oxford University Press.

——(1986) *Merchants, Companies and Commerce on the Coromandel Coast, 1650–1740*, New Delhi: Oxford University Press.

——(1988) 'The Rice Trade in Eastern India, 1650–1740', *Modern Asian Studies* 22(3): 531–49.

——(1994) *Maritime India in the Seventeenth Century*, New Delhi: Oxford University Press.

——(1998) 'The Eastward Trade in India in the Eighteenth Century', in: Rudrangshu Mukherjee (ed.) *Politics and Trade in the Indian Ocean World*, New Delhi: Oxford University Press.

Ariyaratne, R.A. (1977) 'Communal Conflict and the Formation of the Ceylon National Congress', *Ceylon Journal of Historical and Social Studies*, 7: 57–82.

Arnold, David (1993) *Colonizing the Body: State Medicine and Epidemic Disease in Nineteenth Century India*, New Delhi: Oxford University Press.

——(2000) *Science, Technology and Medicine in Colonial India*, Cambridge: Cambridge University Press.

——(2007) 'Plant Capitalism and Company Science: The Indian Career of Nathaniel Wallich', *Modern Asian Studies*, 42(5): 899–928.

Arp, Susmita (2000) *Kalapani: Zum Streit über die Zulässigkeit von Seereisen im kolonialzeitlichen Indien*, Stuttgart: Franz Steiner Verlag.

Ashton, Stephen R. (1982) *British Policy towards the Indian States, 1905–1939*, London: Curzon.

Athar Ali, Muhammad (1966; revised edn 1997) *The Mughal Nobility Under Aurangzeb*, New Delhi: Oxford University Press.

Ayres, Alyssa (2009) *Speaking Like a State: Language and Nationalism in Pakistan*, Cambridge: Cambridge University Press.

Baber, Zaheer (1998) *The Science of Empire: Scientific Knowledge, Civilization, and Colonial Rule in India*, New Delhi: Oxford University Press.

Baden-Powell, Baden H. (1892) *The Land-Systems of British India; Being a Manual of the Land-Tenures and of the Systems of Land-Revenue Administration Prevalent in the Several Provinces*, 4 Vols, Oxford: Oxford University Press.

Bagchi, Amiya K. (1972) *Private Investment in India, 1900–1939*, Cambridge: Cambridge University Press.

Bahl, Vinay (1995) *The Making of the Indian Working Class: The Case of the Tata Iron and Steel Co., 1880–1946*, New Delhi: Sage Publications.

Bajpayi, Anandita (2012) 'Imagining a "Secular" India: Roots, Offshoots and Future Trajectories of the Secularism Debate in India', *Südasien-Chronik/South Asia Chronicle*, 2: 198–218. Available online at http://edoc.hu-berlin.de/suedasien/band-2/189/PDF/189.pdf (accessed 12 October 2013).

Bajracharya, Bhadra R. (1992) *Bahadur Shah: The Regent of Nepal (1784–1795A.D.)*, New Delhi: Anmol Publications.
Baker, Christopher J. (1984) *An Indian Rural Economy, 1880–1955: The Tamilnad Countryside*, New Delhi: Oxford University Press.
Ball, Charles (1859) *The History of the Indian Mutiny, Vol. 2*, London: Printing and Publishing Company.
Ballantyne, Tony (2012) 'Migration, Cultural Legibility, and the Politics of Identity in the Making of British Sikh Communities', in: Anush Malhotra and Farina Mir (eds) *Punjab Reconsidered: History, Culture and Practice*, New Delhi: Oxford University Press.
Bandarage, Asoka (1983) *Colonialism in Sri Lanka: The Political Economy of the Kandyan Highlands, 1833–1886*, Berlin: Mouton.
Bandhu, Deep C. (ed.) (2003) *History of Indian National Congress (1885–2002)*, New Delhi: Kalpaz Publications.
Bandhyopadhyay, Sekhar (ed.) (2001) *Bengal: Rethinking History: Essays in Historiography*, New Delhi: Manohar.
Banerjee, Paula (2013) *Unstable Populations, Anxious States: Mixed and Massive Population Flows in South Asia*, Kolkata: SAMYA.
Banga, Indu (1978) *Agrarian System of the Sikhs: Late Eighteenth and Early Nineteenth Century*, New Delhi: Manohar.
——(ed.) (1997) *Five Panjabi Centuries. Polity, Economy, Society and Culture, c. 1500–1990*, New Delhi: Manohar.
Barnett, Richard B. (1987) *North India between Empires: Awadh, the Mughals, and the British 1720–1801*, New Delhi: Manohar.
Barns, Margarita (1940) *The Indian Press: A History of the Growth of Public Opinion in India*, London: Allen & Unwin.
Barooah, Chandra (2009) *Bamboo in the Culture and Economy of Northeast India*, Noida: Vigyan Prasar.
Barrier, N. Gerald (1992) 'The Punjab Disturbances of 1907: The Response of the British Government in India to Agrarian Unrest', in: David Hardiman (ed.) *Peasant Resistance in India, 1858–1914*, New Delhi: Oxford University Press.
Barrow, Ian J. (2003) *Making History, Drawing Territory: British Mapping in India, c. 1756–1905*, New Delhi: Oxford University Press.
——(2008) *Surveying and Mapping in Colonial Sri Lanka, 1800–1900*, New Delhi: Oxford University Press.
Barton, Gregory A. (2002) *Empire Forestry and the Origins of Environmentalism*, Cambridge: Cambridge University Press.
Baruah, Sanjib (1999) *India against Itself: Assam and the Politics of Nationality*, Philadelphia: University of Pennsylvania Press.
Basalla, George (1967) 'The Spread of Western Science', *Science* 156(3775): 611–22.
Basran, Gurchan S. and Bolaria, B. Singh (2003) *The Sikhs in Canada: Migration, Race, Class, and Gender*, New Delhi: Oxford University Press.
Bass, Daniel (2013) *Everyday Ethnicity in Sri Lanka. Up-Country Tamil Identity Politics*, London: Routledge.
Bates, Crispin (1985) 'Regional Dependence and Rural Development in Central India: The Pivotal Role of Migrant Labourers', *Modern Asian Studies*, 19: 573–92.
——(2007; reprint 2010) *Subalterns and the Raj: South Asia since 1600*, London: Routledge.
Bates, Crispin (ed.) (2001) *Community, Empire and Migration: South Asians in Diaspora*, Basingstoke, UK: Palgrave Macmillan.

Bates, Crispin and Carter, Marina (1993) 'Tribal and Indentured Migrants in Colonial India: Modes of Recruitment and Forms of Incorporation', in: Peter Robb (ed.) *Dalit Movements and the Meanings of Labour in India*, New Delhi: Oxford University Press.
Bawa, Vasant K. (1992) *The Last Nizam: The Life and Times of Mir Osman Ali Khan*, New Delhi: Penguin.
Bayly, Christopher A. (1971) 'Local Control in Indian Towns: The Case of Allahabad 1880–1920', *Modern Asian Studies*, 5(4): 289–311.
——(1975) *The Local Roots of Indian Politics: Allahabad, 1880–1920*, Oxford: Clarendon Press.
——(1983) *Rulers, Townsmen and Bazaars: North Indian Society in the Age of British Expansion, 1770–1870*, Cambridge: Cambridge University Press.
——(1988) *Indian Society and the Making of the British Empire*, Cambridge: Cambridge University Press.
——(1989) *Imperial Meridian: The British Empire and the World, 1780–1830*, London: Longman.
——(1994) 'The British Military-fiscal State and Indigenous Resistance: India 1780–1820', in Lawrence Stone (ed.) *An Imperial State at War: Britain from 1689 to 1815*, London: Routledge.
——(1996) *Empire and Information: Intelligence Gathering and Social Communication in India, 1780–1870*, Cambridge: Cambridge University Press.
——(1998) *Origins of Nationality in South Asia: Patriotism and Ethical Government in the Making of Modern India*, New Delhi: Oxford University Press.
——(2004; 14th edn 2009) *The Birth of the Modern World, 1780–1914: Global Connections and Comparisons*, Malden: Blackwell.
——(2010) *Recovering Liberties: Indian Thought in the Age of Liberalism and Empire. The Wiles Lectures given at the Queen's University of Belfast, 2007*, Cambridge: Cambridge University Press.
Bayly, Susan (1999) *Caste, Society and Politics in India from the Eighteenth Century to the Modern Age*, Cambridge: Cambridge University Press.
Beall, Jo (1990) 'Women under Indenture in Colonial Natal 1860–1911', in: Colin Clarke, Ceri Peach and Steven Vertovec (eds) *South Asians Overseas. Migration and Ethnicity*, Cambridge: Cambridge University Press.
Behal, Rana P. (2010) 'Kuli Drivers or Benevolent Paternalists? British Tea Planters in Assam and the Indenture Labour System', *Modern Asian Studies*, 44(1): 29–51.
Behal, Rana P. and Mohapatra, Prabhu P. (1992) "Tea and money versus human life': The rise and fall of the indenture system in the Assam tea plantations 1840–1909', *Journal of Peasant Studies*, 19(3/4): 142–72.
Bellwinkel-Schempp, Maren (1982) 'Kanpur 1830–1973: Eine koloniale Industriestadt und ihre Arbeiterschaft', in: Hermann Kulke, Hans Christoph Rieger and Lothar Lutze (eds) *Städte in Südasien: Geschichte, Gesellschaft, Gestalt*, Stuttgart: Franz Steiner Verlag.
Berkemer, Georg (1998) 'Literatur und Geschichte im vormodernen hinduistischen Südasien', in: Jörn Rüsen, Michael Gottlob and Achim Mittag (eds) *Die Vielfalt der Kulturen. Erinnerung, Geschichte, Identität 4*, Frankfurt am Main: Suhrkamp.
Berkemer, Georg and Schnepel, Burkhard (2003) 'History of the Model', in: Georg Berkemer and Margret Frenz (eds) *Sharing Sovereignty: The Little Kingdom in South Asia*, Berlin: Klaus Schwarz Verlag.
Berndt, Heide (1987) 'Hygienebewegung des 19: Jahrhunderts als vergessenes Thema von Stadt-und Architektursoziologie', *Die alte Stadt* 14: 140–63.

Berthet, Samuel and Girish, Kumar (eds) (2011) *New States for a New India: Federalism and Decentralization in the States of Jharkhand Chhattisgarh*, New Delhi: Manohar.

Besant, Annie (1925) *Shall India Die or Live*, Madras: National Home Rule League.

Beutner, Stephan (2009) *Baigas und Briten – Bewar im kolonialpolitischen Kontext von 1861–1900 im Mandla Distrikt (Central Provinces/Indien)*. Available online at http://archiv.ub.uni-heidelberg.de/savifadok/volltexte/2012/2386/ (accessed 5 August 2013).

Bhachu, Parminder (1988) '*Apni Marzi Khardi* Home and Work: Sikh Women in Britain', in: Sallie Westwood and Parminder Bhachu (eds) *Enterprising Women: Ethnicity, Economy, and Gender Relations*, London: Routledge.

——(1993) 'Twice and Direct Migrant Sikhs: Caste, Class and Identity in pre- and post-1984 Britain', in: Ivan H. Light and Parminder Bhachu (eds) *Immigration and Entrepreneurship: Culture, Capital and Ethnic Networks*, New Brunswick: Transaction Publishers.

Bhagavan, Manu (2003) *Sovereign Spheres: Princes, Education and Empire in Colonial India*, New Delhi: Oxford University Press.

Bhalla, Alok (2006) *Partition Dialogues: Memories of a Lost Home*, New Delhi: Oxford University Press.

Bhana, Surendra (1985) 'Indian Trade and Traders in Colonial Natal', in: Bill Guest and John M. Sellers (eds) *Enterprise and Exploitation in a Victorian Colony: Aspects of the Economic and Social History of Colonial Natal*, Pietermaritzburg: University of Natal Press.

——(1990) *Gandhi's Legacy: The Natal Indian Congress 1894–1994*, Pietermaritzburg: University of Natal Press.

Bhardwaj, Asmita (2010) 'From the Green Revolution to the Gene Revolution in India 1965–2008', in: John McNeill, José Augusto Pádua and Mahesh Rangarajan (eds) *Environmental History: As if Nature Existed*, New Delhi: Oxford University Press.

Bhargava, Meena (1999) *State, Society and Ecology: Gorakhpur in Transition, 1750–1830*, Delhi: Manohar.

Bhattacharya, Neeladri (1985) 'Lenders and Debtors: Punjab Countryside: 1880–1940', *Studies in History*, 1(2): 305–42.

——(1996) 'Pastoralists in a Colonial World', in: David Arnold and Ramachandra Guha (eds) *Nature, Culture, Imperialism: Essays on the Environmental History of South Asia*, New Delhi: Oxford University Press.

Bhatterjee, Anil C. (1978) *The Constitutional History of India, Vol. III, 1919–1977*, Delhi: Macmillan.

Bhattia, Prem (1973) *Indian Ordeal in Africa*, New Delhi: Vikas Publishing House.

Biswas, Anil Baran (1990) 'Water Supply in Calcutta', in: Sukanta Chaudhuri (ed.) *Calcutta, The Living City, Volume 2: The Present and Future*, New Delhi: Oxford University Press.

Biswas, Sukumar (ed.) (2005) *The Bangladesh Liberation War: Mujibnagar Government Documents 1971*, Dhaka: Mowla Brothers.

——(2007) *History from Below: Accounts of Participants and Eyewitness*, Dhaka: Muktijuddo Gobeshona Kendro.

Blackburn, Terence R. (ed.) (2008) *The Extermination of a British Army: The Retreat from Cabul*, New Delhi: APH Publications.

Blogs.worldbank.com (2013) 'India is the Top Recipient of Remittance'. Available online at http://blogs.worldbank.org/peoplemove/india-is-the-top-recipient-of-remittances (accessed 5 May 2013).

Blume, Michael (1987) *Satyagraha: Wahrheit und Gewaltfreiheit, Yoga und Widerstand bei Gandhi*, Gladenbach: Hinder und Deelmann.
Blyn, George (1979) 'The Green Revolution and Rural Social Structure in India', *Contributions to South Asian Studies*, 13: 353–67.
Bohle, Hans-Georg (1995) 'Ökologische Grundlagen: Naturraum und Klima', in: Dietmar Rothermund (ed.) *Indien. Kultur, Geschichte, Politik, Wirtschaft, Umwelt: Ein Handbuch*, Munich: Beck Verlag.
Bonea, Amelia (2010) 'The Medium and Its Message: Reporting the Austro-Prussian War in the Times of India', Special Issue: Roland Wenzelhuemer (ed.) *Global Communication: Telecommunication and Global Flows of Information in the Late 19th and Early 20th Century*, Historical Social Research/Historische Sozialforschung 35(1): 167–87.
Boogaart, Ernst van den and Emmer, Piet C. (1986) 'Colonialism and Migration: An Overview', in: Piet C. Emmer (ed.) *Colonialism and Migration; Indentured Labour before and after Slavery*, Dordrecht: Nijhoff.
Bose, Anima (1994) 'The Rowlatt Act and Gandhian Satyagraha', in: Subrata Mukherjee and Sushila Ramaswamy (eds) *Facets of Mahatma Gandhi, Volume 1, Non-violence and Satyagraha*, New Delhi: Deep & Deep Publications.
Bose, Subhas Chandra (2005) *Netaji Subhas Chandra Bose: The Last Hero. A Special Number on Netaji Subhas Chandra Bose*, New Delhi: Netaji Subhas Mela.
Bose, Sugata (1993) *Peasant Labour and Colonial Capital: Rural Bengal since 1770*, Cambridge: Cambridge University Press 1993.
——(2006) *A Hundred Horizons: The Indian Ocean in the Age of Global Empire*, Cambridge: Harvard University Press.
——(2011) *His Majesty's Opponent: Subhas Chandra Bose and India's Struggle against Empire*, Cambridge: Belknap Press of Harvard University Press.
Bose, Sugata and Jalal, Ayesha (1998; 2nd edn 2004) *Modern South Asia: History, Culture, Political Economy*, New York: Routledge.
Boyce, Robert W.D. (2000) 'Imperial Dreams and National Realities: Britain, Canada and the Struggle for a Pacific Telegraph Cable, 1879–1902', *English Historical Review* 115: 39–70.
Bozzoli, Belinda (1993) *Town and Countryside in the Transvaal – Capitalist Penetration and Popular Response*, Johannesburg: Ravan Press.
Bradlow, Edna (1970) 'Indentured Indians in Natal and the £3 Tax', *South African Historical Journal* 2(1): 38–53.
Brass, Paul R. (2003) *The Production of Hindu-Muslim Violence in Contemporary India*, Oxford: Oxford University Press.
Brass, Tom (1995) 'Introduction: The New Farmers' Movements in India', in: Tom Brass (ed.) *New Farmers Movements in India*, Newbury Park: Frank Cass.
Breman, Jan (2004) *The Making and Unmaking of an Industrial Working Class: Sliding Down the Labour Hierarchy in Ahmedabad, India*, New Delhi: Oxford University Press.
——(2006; 2nd edn 2009) 'Dualistic Labour System? A Critique of the Informal Sector Concept', in: Sujata Patel and Kushal Deb (eds) *Urban Studies*, New Delhi: Oxford University Press.
Breman, Jan and Daniel, E. Valentine (1992) 'Conclusion: The Making of a Coolie', *Journal of Peasant Studies* 19(3/4): 268–95.
Brennig, Joseph J. (1994) 'Textile Producers and Production in Late Seventeenth Century Coromandel', in: Sanjay Subrahmanyam (ed.) *Merchants, Markets and the State in Early Modern India*, New Delhi: Oxford University Press.

Brettell, Caroline B. (2000) 'Theorizing Migration in Anthropology', in: Caroline B. Brettell and James F. Hollifield (eds) *Migration Theory: Talking Across Disciplines*, New York: Routledge.

Brettell, Caroline B. and Hollifield, James F. (2000) 'Introduction', in: Caroline B. Brettell and James F. Hollifield (eds) *Migration Theory: Talking Across Disciplines*, New York: Routledge.

Bridge, Carl (1986) *Holding India to the Empire: The British Conservative Party and the 1935 Constitution*, London: Oriental University Press.

Brijlal, P. (1989) 'Demographic Profile', in: Karl P. Magyar and Gerald J. Pillay (eds) *The Indian South Africans: A Contemporary Profile*, Pinetown: Owen Burgess.

Brimnes, Niels (2004) 'The Sympathizing Heart and the Healing Hand: Smallpox Prevention and Medical Benevolence in Early Colonial South India', in: Harald Fischer-Tiné and Michael Mann (eds) *Colonialism as Civilizing Mission: Cultural Ideology in British India*, London: Anthem Press.

Brittlebank, Kate (1997) *Tipu Sultan's Search for Legitimacy: Islam and Kingship in a Hindu Domain*, New Delhi: Oxford University Press.

Broeze, Frank (1981) 'The Muscles of Empire: Indian Seamen under the Raj, 1919–1939', *Indian Economic and Social History Review*, 18(1): 43–67.

——(1992) 'The External Dynamics of Port City Morphology: Bombay 1815–1914', in: Indu Banga (ed.) *Ports and their Hinterlands in India (1700–1950)*, New Delhi: Manohar.

Bronger, Dirk (1996) *Indien: Größte Demokratie der Welt zwischen Kastenwesen und Armut*, Gotha: Perthes.

Brown, Judith M. (1985) *Modern India: The Origins of an Asian Democracy*, New Delhi: Oxford University Press.

——(2006) *Global South Asians: Introducing the Modern Diaspora*, Cambridge: Cambridge University Press.

Brown, Judith M. and Prozesky Martin (eds) (1996) *Gandhi and South Africa: Principles and Politics*, Pietermaritzburg: University of Natal Press.

Bryant, Gerald J. (1986) 'Pacification in the Early British Raj, 1755–85', *Journal of Imperial and Commonwealth History*, 14(1): 3–19.

Buchignani, Norman and Indra, Doreen M. (1989) 'Key Issues in Canadian–Sikh Ethnic and Race Relations', in: N. Gerald Barrier and Verne A. Dusenbery (eds) *The Sikh Diaspora: Migration and the Experience beyond Punjab*, Delhi: Chanakya Publications.

Buckler, Frederick W. (1985) 'The Political Theory of the Indian Mutiny', in: Michael N. Pearson (ed.) *Legitimacy and Symbols: The South Asian Writings of F. W. Buckler*, Ann Arbor: University of Michigan.

Bulley, Anne (2000) *The Bombay Country Ships, 1790–1833*, Richmond: Curzon Press.

Burke, Samuel M. and Quraishi, Salim Al-Din (1995) *The British Raj in India: An Historical Review*, Karachi: Oxford University Press.

Burki, Shahid J. and Baxter, Craig (1991) *Pakistan under the Military: Eleven Years of Zia ul-Haq*, Boulder: Westview Press.

Burnell, John (1933; reprint 1997) *Bombay in the Days of Queen Anne: With an introduction by Samuel T. Sheppard*, New Delhi: Munshiram Manoharlal.

Bury, Harriet (2007) 'Novel Spaces, Transitional Moments: Negotiating Texts and Territory in Nineteenth-Century Hindi Travel Accounts', in: Ian J. Kerr (ed.) *27 Down: New Departures in Indian Railway Studies*, New Delhi: Permanent Black.

Busch, Briton C. (1971) *Britain, India, and the Arabs 1914–1921*, Berkeley: University of California Press.

Butcher, Melissa (2003) *Transnational Television, Cultural Identity and Change: When STAR Came to India*, New Delhi: Sage.
Calkins, Philip B. (1970) 'The Formation of a Regionally Orientated Ruling Group in Bengal: 1700–1740', *Journal of Asian Studies*, 29(3): 799–806.
Campbell, Dennis (2007) 'India', in: Dennis Campell (ed.) *International Telecommunications Law*, Salzburg: Yorkhill Law Publishing.
Cannadine, David (2001) *Ornamentalism: How the British saw their Empire*, Oxford: Oxford University Press.
Carter, Marina (1992) 'Strategies of Labour Mobilisation in Colonial India: The Recruitment of Indentured Workers for Mauritius', *Journal of Peasant Studies* 19(3/4): 229–45.
——(1995) *Servants, Sirdars and Settlers: Indians in Mauritius, 1834–1874*, New Delhi: Oxford University Press.
——(1996) *Voices from Indenture: Experiences of Indian Migrants in the British Empire*, London: Leicester University Press.
——(ed.) (2000) *Across the Kalapani: The Bihari Presence in Mauritius*, Port Louis: Centre for Research on Indian Ocean Societies.
——(2002) 'Subaltern Success Stories: Socio-Economic Mobility in the Indian Labour Diaspora – Some Mauritius Cases', *Internationales Asienforum* 33(1/2): 91–100.
Carter, Marina and Torabully, Khal (2002) *Coolitude: An Anthology of the Indian Labour Diaspora*, London: Anthem Press 2002.
Cashman, Richard (1975) *The Myth of the Lokamanya: Tilak and Mass Politics in Maharashtra*, Berkeley: University of California Press.
Cederlöf, Gunnel (2005) 'The Agency of the Colonial Subject: Claims and Rights in Forestlands in the Early Nineteenth Century Nilgiris', *Studies in History*, 21(2): 247–69.
——(2012) 'Narrative of Rights: Codifying People and Land in Early Nineteenth Century Nilgiris', in: Mahesh Rangarajan and Krishna Shivaramakrishnan (eds) *India's Environmental History. Vol. 1, From Ancient Times to the Colonial Period. A Reader*, New Delhi: Orient BlackSwan.
Chadwick, Edwin (1842; reprint 1965) *Report on the Sanitary Condition of the Labouring Population of Great Britain*, Edinburgh: Edinburgh University Press.
Chakrabarti, Hiren (1992) *Political Protest in Bengal: Boykott and Terrorism 1905–1918*, Calcutta: Papyrus.
Chakrabarti, Pratik (2010) 'Networks of Medicine: Trade and Medico-Botanical Knowledge on the Eighteenth-Century Coromandel Coast', in: Arun Bandopadhyay (ed.) *Science and Society in India, 1750–2000*, Delhi: Manohar.
Chakrabarti, Ranjan (ed.) (2007) *Situating Environmental History*, Delhi: Manohar.
Chakravarti, A.K. (1973) 'Green Revolution in India', *Annals of the Association of American Geographers* 63(3): 319–30.
Chakravarti, Ranabir (1998) 'The Creation and Expansion of Settlements and Management of Hydraulic Resources in Ancient India', in: Richard H. Grove, Vinita Damodaran and Satpal Sangwan (eds) *Nature and the Orient: The Environmental History of South and Southeast Asia*, New Delhi: Oxford University Press.
Chamberlain, Muriel E. (1988) *'Pax Britannica': British Foreign Policy, 1789–1914*, London and New York: Longman.
Chandavarkar, Rajnarayan (1998) *Imperial Power and Popular Politics: Class, Resistance and the State in India, c. 1850–1950*, Cambridge: Cambridge University Press.

Chandraprema, Candauda A. (1991) *Sri Lanka, the Years of Terror: The J.V.P. Insurrection, 1987–1989*, Colombo: Lake House Bookshop.
Charlesworth, Neil (1972) 'The Myth of the Deccan Riots of 1875', *Modern Asian Studies* 6(4): 401–21.
——(1982) *British Rule and the Indian Economy, 1800–1914*, London: Palgrave Macmillan.
——(1983) 'The Origins of Fragmentation of Landholdings in British India: A Comparative Examination', in: Peter G. Robb (ed.) *Rural India*, London: Curzon Press.
——(1985) *Peasants and Imperial Rule: Agriculture and Agrarian Society in the Bombay Presidency, 1850–1935*, Cambridge: Cambridge University Press.
Chatterjee, Indrani and Eaton, Richard M. (eds) (2006) *Slavery and South Asian History*, Bloomington: Indiana University Press.
Chatterjee, Joya (1999; 2nd edn 2005) 'The Making of a Borderline: The Radcliffe Award for Bengal', in: Ian Talbot and Gurharpal Singh (eds) *Region and Partition: Bengal, Punjab and the Partition of the Subcontinent*, Karachi: Oxford University Press.
Chatterjee, Monidip (1990) 'Town Planning in Calcutta: Past, Present and Future', in: Sukanta Chaudhuri (ed.) *Calcutta, The Living City. Volume 2: The Present and Future.* New Delhi: Oxford University Press.
Chatterjee, Sunita (2001) 'Communitarian Identities and the Private Sphere: A Gender Dialogue amongst Indo-Trinidadians (1845–1917)', in: Crispin Bates (ed.) *Community, Empire and Migration: South Asians in Diaspora*, New York: Palgrave Macmillan.
Chattopadhyay, Swati (2005) *Representing Calcutta. Modernity, Nationalism, and the Colonial Uncanny.* London: Routledge.
Chaturvedi, Vinayak (2007) *Peasant Pasts: History and Memory in Western India*, Berkeley, Los Angeles, London: University of California Press.
——(ed.) (2000) *Mapping Subaltern Studies and the Postcolonial*, London: Verso.
Chaudhuri, Binoy B. (1969) 'Agricultural Production in Bengal, 1850–1900: Co-existence of Decline and Growth', in: *Bengal Past and Present* 88(2): 152–206.
——(1982) 'Eastern India', in: Dharma Kumar (ed.) *The Cambridge Economic History of India, Vol. 2, c. 1757–1970*, Cambridge: Cambridge University Press.
——(1994) 'Growth of Commercial Agriculture in Bengal 1795–1885', in: David Ludden (ed.) *Agricultural Production and Indian History*, Delhi: Oxford University Press.
——(1996) 'The Process of Commercialisation in Eastern India during British Rule: A Reconsideration of the Notions of "Forced Commercialisation" and "Dependent Peasantry"', in: Peter G. Robb (ed.) *Meanings of Agriculture: Essays in South Asian History and Economics*, New Delhi: Oxford University Press.
Chaudhuri, Kirti N. (1978) *The Trading World of Asia and the English East India Company, 1660–1760*, Cambridge: Cambridge University Press.
——(1990) *Asia before Europe: Economy and Civilisation of the Indian Ocean from the Rise of Islam to 1750*, Cambridge: Cambridge University Press.
Chaudhuri, Sushil (1995) *From Prosperity to Decline: Eighteenth Century Bengal*, Delhi: Manohar.
Cheema, G. Shabbir (2005) *The Forgotten Mughals: A History of the Later Emperors of the House of Babar (1707–1857)*, Delhi: Manohar.
Choudhury, Deep K.L. (2000) 'Beyond the Reach of Monkeys and Men'? O'Shaughnessy and the Telegraph in India, c. 1836–56', *Indian Economic and Social History Review*, 37(3): 335–41.

—— (2010) *Telegraphic Imperialism: Crisis and Panic in the Indian Empire, c. 1830*, Basingstoke, UK: Palgrave Macmillan.
Chowdhury, Saber A. (2010) *Participation in Forestry: Social Forestry Policy in Bangladesh. Myth or Reality?* Dhaka: A.H. Development Publ. House.
Chowdhury-Zilly, Aditee N. (1982) *The Vagrant Peasant: Agrarian Distress and Desertion in Bengal 1770 to 1830*, Wiesbaden: Franz Steiner Verlag.
Cohen, Robin (1997) *Global Diasporas: An Introduction*, London: UCL Press.
Cohen, Stephen P. (2004) *The Idea of Pakistan*, Washington: Brookings Institution Press.
—— (2011) 'Pakistan: Arrival and Departure', in: Stephen P. Cohen (ed.) *The Future of Pakistan*, Washington: Brookings Institution Press.
Cohn, Bernard S. (1962) 'Political Systems in Eighteenth Century India: The Banaras Region', *Journal of American Oriental Society*, 82(3): 312–20.
—— (1987a) 'Regions Subjective and Objective: Their Relation to the Study of Modern Indian History and Society', in Bernard S. Cohn (ed.) *An Anthropologist among the Historians and other Essays*, Delhi: Oxford University Press.
—— (1987b) 'Political Systems in Eighteenth-Century India: The Benares Region', in Bernard S. Chon (ed.) *An Anthropologist among the Historians and other Essays*, Delhi: Oxford University Press.
—— (1987c) 'Representing Authority in Victorian India', in: Bernard S. Cohn (ed.) *An Anthropologist among the Historians and other Essays*, Delhi: Oxford University Press.
—— (2006) *Colonialism and its Forms of Knowledge: The British in India*, Princeton: Princeton University Press.
Collins, Joseph and Moore Lappé, Frances (1981) *Vom Mythos des Hungers: Die Entlarvung einer Legende. Niemand muß hungern*, Frankfurt am Main: Fischer Taschenbuch-Verlag.
Conermann, Stephan (ed.) (2002) *Geschichtsdenken der Kulturen/Südasien – von den Anfängen bis zur Gegenwart. 2, Die muslimische Sicht (13. bis 18. Jahrhundert)*, Frankfurt am Main: Humanities Online.
Coningham, Robin A.E. and Allchin, Frank R. (1995) 'The Rise of the Cities in Sri Lanka', in: Frank R. Allchin (ed.) *The Archaeology of Early Historic South Asia: The Emergence of Cities and States*, Cambridge: Cambridge University Press.
Conrad, Dieter (1999) 'Von der Teilung Indiens zur Teilung Pakistans' in: Jürgen Lütt und Mahendra P. Singh (eds) *Zwischen den Traditionen: Probleme des Verfassungsrechts und der Rechtskultur in Indien und in Pakistan. Gesammelte Aufsätze aus den Jahren 1970–1990*, Stuttgart: Steiner Verlag.
Conway, Gordon R., Huq, Saleemul and Rahman, Atiq A. (eds) (1990) *Environmental Aspects of Agricultural Development in Bangladesh*, Dhaka: University Press.
Cooper, Randolf G.S. (2004) *The Anglo-Maratha Campaigns and the Contest for India: The Struggle for Control of the South Asian Military Economy*, Cambridge: Cambridge University Press.
Copland, Ian (1982; reprint 1987) *British Raj and the Indian Princes: Paramountcy in Western India, 1857–1930*, Bombay: Sangam Books.
—— (1993) 'Communalism in Princely India: The Case of Hyderabad, 1930–40', in: Mushirul Hasan (ed.) *India's Partition: Process, Strategy and Mobilization*, New Delhi: Oxford University Press.
—— (1999) *The Princes of India in the Endgame of Empire, 1917–1947*, Cambridge: Cambridge University Press.

Curtin, Philip D. (1984) *Cross-cultural Trade in World History*, Cambridge: Cambridge University Press.
Dabag, Mihran and Platt, Kristin (1993) 'Diaspora und das kollektive Gedächtnis: Zur Konstruktion kollektiver Identitäten in der Diaspora', in: Mihran Dabag and Kristin Platt (eds) *Identität in der Fremde*, Bochum: N. Brockmeyer.
Dale, Stephen F. (1980) *The Mappilas of Malabar 1498–1922: Islamic Society on the South Asian Frontier*, Oxford: Clarendon Press.
Dalrymple, William (2006) *The Last Mughal: The Fall of a Dynasty, Delhi, 1857*, New Delhi: Penguin/Viking.
Damodaran, Vinita (2007) 'Tribes in Indian History', in: Ranjan Chakrabarti (ed.) *Situating Environmental History*, New Delhi: Manohar.
——(2010) 'Globalization and Tribal Histories in Eastern India', in: John McNeill, José Augusto Pádua and Mahesh Rangarajan (eds) *Environmental History: As if Nature Existed*, New Delhi: Oxford University Press.
Dangwal, Dhirendra D. (2007) *Himalayan Degradation: Colonial Forestry and Environmental Change in India*, New Delhi: Cambridge University Press.
Daniels, Roger (1994) 'The Indian Diaspora in the United States', in: Judith M. Brown and Rosemary Foot (eds) *Migration: The Asian Experience*, New York: St Martin's Press.
Das Gupta, Ashin (1987) 'The Maritime Trade of Indonesia: 1500–1800', in: Ashin Das Gupta (ed.) *India and the Indian Ocean*, Calcutta: Oxford University Press.
Das Gupta, Ranajit (1992) 'Plantation Labour in Colonial India', *Journal of Peasant Studies*, 19(3/4): 173–98.
Das Gupta, Sanjukta (2010) 'Remembering Gonoo: The Profile of an Adivasi Rebel of 1857', in: Biswamoy Pati (ed.) *The Great Rebellion of 1857 in India: Exploring Transgressions, Contests and Diversities*, London: Routledge.
Das, Diprakanjam (1976) *Economic History of the Deccan*, New Delhi: Munshiram Manoharlal.
Dasgupta, Atis (1983) 'Titu Meer's Rebellion: A Profile', *Social Scientist*, 11(10): 39–48.
Dash, B.N. and Dash, Nibedita (2009) *Thoughts and Theories of Indian Educational Thinkers*, New Delhi: Dominant Publ.
Datta Vishwa N. and Settar, Shadashari (eds) (2000) *Jallianwala Bagh Massacre*, New Delhi: Pragati Publications and Indian Council of Historical Research.
Datta, Nonica (2009) *Violence, Martyrdom and Partition: A Daughter's Testimony*, New Delhi: Oxford University Press 2009.
Datta, Partho (1993) 'Strikes in the Greater Calcutta Region, 1918–1924', *Indian Economic and Social History* Review, 30(1): 57–84.
——(2012) *Planning the City: Urbanization and Reform in Calcutta c. 1800 – c. 1940*, New Delhi: Tulika.
Datta, Rajat (1996) 'Peasant Production and Agrarian Commercialism in a Rice-growing Economy: Some Notes on a Comparative Perspective and the Case of Bengal in the Eighteenth Century', in: Peter G. Robb (ed.) *Meanings of Agriculture: Essays in South Asian History and Economics*, New Delhi: Oxford University Press.
——(2000) *Society, Economy and the Market: Commercialization in Rural Bengal c. 1760–1800*, Delhi: Manohar.
Datta, Vishwa N. (1993) 'Panjabi Refugees and the Urban Development of Greater Delhi', in: Robert E. Frykenberg (ed.) *Delhi through the Ages: Selected Essays in Urban History, Culture and Society*, New Delhi: Oxford University Press.

Davis, Kingsley (1951) *The Population of India and Pakistan*, Princeton: Princeton University Press.
De Silva, Kingsley M. (1967) 'The Formation and Character of the Ceylon National Congress 1917–1919', *Ceylon Journal of Historical and Social Studies*, 10(1/2): 70–102.
——(1981; 2nd revised and enlarged edn 2005) *A History of Sri Lanka*, Colombo: Vijitha Yapa Publications.
Debes, Ernst, Kirchhoff, Alfred and Kropatschek, Hermann (1905) *Schul-Atlas für Ober-und Mittelklassen höherer Lehranstalten*, Leipzig: Verlag von Wagner & Debes.
DeLong, J. Bradford (2003) 'India since Independence: An Analytical Growth Narrative', in: Dani Rodrik (ed.) *Search of Prosperity: Analytic Narratives on Economic Growth*, Princeton: Princeton University Press.
Derbyshire, Ian (1995) 'The Building of India's Railways: The Application of Western Technology in the Colonial Periphery 1850–1920', in: Roy MacLeod and Deepak Kumar (eds) *Technology and the Raj*, New Delhi: Oxford University Press.
Derrett, John D.M. (1968; 2nd edn 1999) *Religion, Law and the State in India*, London: Oxford University Press.
Desai, Mira K. and Agrawal, Binod Ch. (2009) *Television and Cultural Crisis: An Analysis of Transnational Television in India*, New Delhi: Connect Publ.
Desmond, Ray (1995) *Kew: The History of the Royal Botanic Gardens*, London: Havill Press.
Destradi, Sandra (2012) *Indian Foreign and Security Policy in South Asia: Regional Power Strategies*, London: Routledge.
Devalle, Susana B.C. (1993) 'Beyond Ecology? Indigenous Territories and Natural Resources (Jharkhand, India)', in: Wolfgang L. Werner (ed.) *Aspects of Ecological Problems and Environmental Awareness in South Asia*, Delhi: Manohar.
DeVotta, Neil (2004) *Blowback: Linguistic Nationalism, Institutional Decay, and Ethnic Conflict in Sri Lanka*, Stanford: Stanford University Press.
——(2011) *From Civil War to Soft Authoritarianism: Ethnonationalism and Democratic Regression in Sri Lanka*, London: Routledge.
Dewaraja, Lorna S. (1972; 2nd revised edn 1988) *The Kandyan Kingdom of Sri Lanka, 1707–1782*, Colombo: Lake House Investments.
Dewey, Clive (1972) 'Images of the Village Community: A Study in Anglo-Indian Ideology', *Modern Asian Studies*, 6(3): 291–328.
Deyell, John S. and Frykenberg, Robert E. (1982) 'Sovereignty and the SIKKA under the Company Raj: Minting Prerogative and Imperial Legitimacy in India', *Indian Economic and Social History Review*, 19(1): 1–25.
Dhanagare, Dattatraya N. (1990) 'Green Revolution and Social Inequalities in Rural India', in: Kadur S. Krishnaswami (ed.) *Poverty and Income Distribution*, Bombay: Oxford University Press.
Dhar, Prithvi N. (2000) *Indira Gandhi, the 'Emergency', and Indian Democracy*, Delhi: Oxford University Press.
Dharampal (1983) 'Introduction', in: Dharampal (ed.) *The Beautiful Tree: Indigenous Indian Education in the Eighteenth Century*, New Delhi: Biblia Impex.
Dias Antunes, Luis F. (1995) 'The Trade Activities of the *banyans* in Mozambique: Private Indian Dynamics in the Portuguese State Economy (1686–1777)', in: Kuzhippalli S. Mathew (ed.) *Mariners, Merchants and Oceans: Studies in Maritime History*, Delhi: Manohar.

Dirks, Nicholas (1987) *The Hollow Crown: Etnhohistory of an Indian Kingdom*, Cambridge: Cambridge University Press.

Divan, Shyam and Ronsencranz, Armin (eds) (2001) *Environmental Law and Policy in India: Cases, Materials and Statutes*, New Delhi: Oxford University Press.

Divekar, Vasudev D. (1982) 'Regional Economy 1757–1857: Western India', in: Dharma Kumar (ed.) *The Cambridge Economic History of India, Vol 2: c. 1757–1970*, Cambridge: Cambridge University Press.

Dixon, Conrad (1980) 'Lascars: The Forgotten Seamen', in: R. Ommer and G. Pantma (eds) *Working Men who got Wet*, St Johns: Maritime History Group, Memorial University of Newfoundland.

Domin, Dolores (1977) *India in 1857–59: A Study in the Role of the Sikhs in the People's Uprising*, Berlin: Akademie Verlag.

Donovan, Deanna G. (2011) 'Forests at the Edge of Empire: The Case of Nepal', in: Deepak Kumar, Vinita Damodaran, and Rohan D'Souza (eds) *The British Empire and the Natural World. Environmental Encounters in South Asia*, New Delhi: Oxford University Press.

Doornbos, Martin and Kaviraj, Sudipta (eds) (1997) *Dynamics of State Formation: India and Europe Compared*, New Delhi: Sage Publications.

Dossal, Miriam (1991) *Imperial Designs and Indian Realities: The Planning of Bombay City 1845–1875*, New Delhi: Oxford University Press.

——(1992) 'Knowledge for Power: The Significance of the Bombay Revenue Survey, 1811–1827', in: Indu Banga (ed.) *Ports and their Hinterlands in India (1700–1950)*, Delhi: Manohar.

Draper, Alfred (1981) *Amritsar: The Massacre that Ended the Raj*, London: Cassell.

Driesen, Ian van den (1997) *The Long Walk: Indian Plantation Labour in Sri Lanka in the Nineteenth Century*, New Delhi: Prestige.

D'Souza, Dilip (2002) *The Narmada Dammed: An Inquiry into the Politics of Development*, New Delhi: Penguin Books.

D'Souza, Rohan (2003) 'Damming the Mahanadi River: The Emergence of Multi-purpose River Valley Developments in India (1943–46)', *Indian Economic and Social History Review*, 40(1): 81–105.

——(2006) *Drowned and Dammed: Colonial Capitalism and Flood Control in Eastern India*, New Delhi: Oxford University Press.

Dusenbery, Verne A. (1989) 'Introduction : A Century of Sikhs beyond the Punjab', in: Norman G. Barrier and Verne A. Dusenbery (eds) *The Sikh Diaspora: Migration and the Experience beyond Punjab*, Delhi: Chanakya Publications.

——(1995) 'A Sikh Diaspora? Contested Identities and Constructed Realities', in: Peter van der Veer (ed.) *Nation and Migration: The Politics of Space in the South Asian Diaspora*, Philadelphia: University of Philadelphia Press.

Dutta, Sanchari (2009) 'Plague, Quarantine and Empire: British Indian Sanitary Strategies in Central Asia, 1897–1907', in: Biswamoy Pati and Mark Harrison (eds) *The Social History of Health and Medicine in Colonial India*, London: Routledge.

Dwivedi, Ranjit (2000) *Resource Conflict and Collective Action: The Sardar Sarovar Project in India*, Maastricht: Shaker Pub.

Eaton, Richard M. (1993) *The Rise of Islam and the Bengal Frontier, 1204–1760*, Berkeley: University of California Press.

Economic Survey (2010–2011), New Delhi: Government of India.

Edney, Matthew H. (1994) 'British Military Education, Mapmaking and Military, "Map-mindedness" in the Later Enlightenment', *Cartographical Journal* 31(1): 14–20.

——(1997) *Mapping an Empire: The Geographical Construction of British India, 1765–1843*, Chicago: The University of Chicago Press.
Ehlers, Eckart and Krafft, Thomas (1993) 'Islamic Cities in India? – Theoretical Concepts and the Case of Shahjahanabad/Old Delhi', in: Eckart Ehlers and Thomas Krafft (eds) *Shahjahanabad/Old Delhi: Tradition and Colonial Change*, Stuttgart: Franz Steiner Verlag.
Eisenlohr, Patrick (2006) *Little India: Diaspora, Time and Ethnolinguistic Belonging in Hindu Mauritius*, Berkeley: University of California Press.
Embree, Ainslie T. (1962) *Charles Grant and British Rule in India*, New York: Columbia University Press.
Embree, Ainslie T. and Wilhelm, Friedrich (1967; reprint 11th edn 2002) *Geschichte des Subkontinents von der Induskultur bis zum Beginn der englischen Herrschaft*, Frankfurt am Main: Fischer Taschenbuchverlag.
Emmer, Piet C. (1986a) *Colonialism and Migration, Indentured Labour before and after Slavery*, Dordrecht: Nijhoff.
——(1986b) 'The Meek Hindu: The Recruitment of Indian Indentured Labourers for Service Overseas, 1870–1916', in: Piet C. Emmer (ed.) *Colonialism and Migration, Indentured Labour before and after Slavery*, Dordrecht: Nijhoff.
Erdman, Howard L. (1971) *Political Attitudes of Indian Industry: A Case Study of the Baroda Business Elite*, London: Athlone Press.
Evers, Hans D. (2000) 'Chettiar Moneylenders in Southeast Asia', in: Denys Lombard and Jean Aubin (eds) *Asian Merchants and Businessmen in the Indian Ocean and the China Sea*, New Delhi: Permanent Black.
Farmer, Betram H. (1977) *Green Revolution? Technology and Change in Rice-Growing Areas of Tamil Nadu and Sri Lanka*, London: Palgrave Macmillan.
——(1983; 2nd edn 1993) *An Introduction to South Asia*, London: Routledge.
Faruqui, Munis D. (2009) 'At Empire's End: The Nizam, Hyderabad and Eighteenth-Century India', *Modern Asian Studies* 43(1): 5–43.
Fay, Peter W. (1993) *The Forgotten Army: India's armed Struggle for Independence, 1942–45*, Ann Arbor: University of Michigan Press.
Fernandes, Walter (2012) 'Land, Environmental Degradation and Conflicts in North-eastern India', in: Sumi Krishna (ed.) *Agriculture and a Changing Environment in Northeastern India*, London: Routledge.
Fisch, Jörg (1983) *Cheap Lives and Dear Limbs: The British Transformation of the Bengal Criminal Law 1769–1817*, Wiesbaden: Franz Steiner Verlag.
Fischer-Tiné, Harald (2000) '"Kindly Elders of the Hindu Biradri": The Arya Samaj's Struggle for Influence and its Effects on Hindu–Muslim Relations, 1880–1925', in: Antony Copley (ed.) *Gurus and Their Followers: New Religious Reform Movements in Colonial India*, New Delhi: Oxford University Press.
——(2003a) 'Vom Wissen zur Macht. Koloniale und 'nationale' Bildungsmodelle in Britisch Indien, ca. 1781–1920', in: Karin Preisendanz und Dietmar Rothermund (eds) *Südasien in der "Neuzeit". Geschichte und Gesellschaft, 1500–2000*, Wien: Promedia.
——(2003b) *Der Gurukul Kangri oder die Erziehung der Arya-Nation: Kolonialismus, Hindureform und 'nationale Bildung' in Britisch-Indien (1897–1922)*, Würzburg: Ergon.
——(2009) *Low and Licentious Europeans: Race, Class and 'White Subalternity' in Colonial India*, Hyderabad: Oriental BlackSwan.
——(2013) *'Pidgin-Knowledge': Kolonialismus und Wissenszirkulation*, Berlin: Diaphenes Verlag.

Fischer-Tiné, Harald and Mann, Michael (eds) (2004) *Colonialism as Civilizing Mission: Cultural Ideology in British India*, London: Anthem Press.

Fisher, Michael H. (1981) 'British Expansion in North India: The Role of the Resident in Awadh', *Indian Economic and Social History Review* 18(1): 69–82.

——(1984) 'Indirect Rule in the British Empire: The Foundation of the Residency System in India (1764–1758)', *Modern Asian Studies* 18(3): 393–482.

——(1987) *A Clash of Cultures: Awadh, the British, and the Mughals*, Delhi: Manohar.

——(1991) *Indirect Rule in India: Residents and the Residency System, 1764–1858*, Delhi: Oxford University Press.

Fletcher, Paul (2010) 'The Uses and Limitations of Telegrams in Official Correspondence between Ceylon's Governor General and the Sectretary of State for the Colonies, ca. 1870–1900', Special Issue: Roland Wenzelhuemer (ed.) *Global Communication: Telecommunication and Global Flows of Information in the Late 19th and Early 20th Century*, Historical Social Research/Historische Sozialforschung 35(1): 90–107.

Foley, Tadhg and O'Connor, Maureen (ed.) (2007) *Ireland and India: Colonies, Culture and Empire*, Dublin: Irish Academic Press.

Förster, Stig (1992) *Die mächtigen Diener der East India Company: Ursachen und Hintergründe der britischen Expansionspolitik in Südasien 1793–1819*, Stuttgart: Franz Steiner Verlag.

Fox, Richard G. (1971) *Kin, Clan, Raja and Rule: State-Hinterland Relations in Pre-Industrial India*, Berkeley, CA: University of California.

Francis, Sabil (2011) 'The IITs in India: Symbols of an Emerging Nation', *Südasien-Chronik/South Asia Chronicle*, 1: 293–326. Available online at http://edoc.hu-berlin. de/suedasien/band-1/293/PDF/293.pdf (accessed 10 October 2013).

Frankel, Francine R. (1971) *India's Green Revolution: Economic Gains and Political Costs*, Princeton: Princeton University Press.

Frenz, Margret (2000) *Vom Herrscher zum Untertan: Spannungsverhältnis zwischen lokaler Herrschaftsstruktur und der Kolonialverwaltung in Malabar zu Beginn der britischen Herrschaft (1790–1805)*, Stuttgart: Steiner Verlag.

——(2003) *From Contact to Conquest: Transition to British Rule in Malabar, 1790–1805*, New Delhi: Oxford University Press.

Frese, Heiko (2003) 'Strategische Historiographie? Anmerkungen zu Orissa und der Mackenzie Collection', in: Stephan Conermann and Jan Kusber (eds) *Studia Eurasiatica*, Schenefeld: EB-Verlag.

Freund, Bill (1994) *Insiders and Outsiders: The Indian Working Class of Durban, 1910–1990*, Portsmouth: Heinemann.

Friedrichs, Jürgen (ed.) (1985) *Stadtentwicklung in West-und Osteuropa*, Berlin: de Gryter.

Frykenberg, Robert E. (ed.) (1977) *Land Tenure and Peasant in South Asia*, New Delhi: Orient Longman.

——(1979) *Land Control and Social Structure in Indian History*, New Delhi: Manohar.

Fukazawa, Hiroshi (1983) 'Western India', in: Dharma Kumar (ed.) *The Cambridge Economic History of India, Vol. 2, c. 1757-c. 1970*, Cambridge: Cambridge University Press.

Gadgil, Madhav and Guha, Ramachandra (1989) 'State Forestry and Social Conflict in British India', *Past and Present* 123(1): 41–77.

——(1992) *This Fissured Land: An Ecological History of India*, New Delhi: Oxford University Press.

Gamburd, Michaele R. (2000) *Transnationalism and Sri Lanka's Migrant Housemaids: The Kitchen Spoon's Handle*, New Delhi: Vistaar Publications.

Gandhi, Mohandas K. (1925) *An Autobiography or The Story of my Experiments with Truth*, Ahmedabad: Navajivan Press.
——(1930) "The Cult of the Bomb", *Young India*, 2 January 1930, in *Young India 1919–1931: In Thirteen Volumes, Vol. XII*, Ahmedabad: Navajivan Publishing House.
Ganehan, Noorjehan N. (2008) *Educational Philosophy of Dr Zakir Husain*, New Delhi: Global Vision.
Gardezi, Hassan N. (1991) 'Asian Workers in the Gulf States of the Middle East', *Journal of Contemporary Asia*, 21(2): 179–94.
Gardner, Katy and Osella, Filipo (2004) 'Migration, Modernity and Social Transformation in South Asia: An Overview', in: Filippo Osella and Katy Gardner (eds) *Migration, Modernity and Social Transformation in South Asia*, New Delhi: Sage Publications.
Gayer, Laurent (2007) 'Guns, Slums, and "Yellow Devils": A Genealogy of Urban Conflicts in Karachi, Pakistan', *Modern Asian Studies*, 41(3): 515–44.
Gerbeau, Hubert (1986) 'Engagees and Coolies on Réunion Island: Slavery's Masks and Freedom's Constraints', in: Piet C. Emmer (ed.) *Colonialism and Migration*, Dordrecht: Nijhoff.
Ghassen-Fachandi, Pavis (2012) *Pogrom in Gujarat: Hindu Nationalism and Anti-Muslim Violence in India*, Princeton: Princeton University Press.
Ghose, Saroj (1995) 'Commercial Needs and Military Necessities: The Telegraph in India', in: Roy MacLeod and Deepak Kumar (eds) *Technology and the Raj: Western Technology and Technical Transfers to India, 1700–1947*, New Delhi: Sage Publications.
Ghosg, Nityapriya (ed.) (2005) *Partition of Bengal: Significant Signposts 1905–1911*, Kolkata: Sahitya Samshad.
Ghosh, Parimal (2000) *Colonialism, Class and a History of the Calcutta Jute Millhands, 1880–1930*. London: Sangam Books.
Ghosh, Partha S. (1999) *BJP and the Evolution of Hindu Nationalism: From Periphery to the Centre*, New Delhi: Manohar.
——(2001) *Migrants and Refugees in South Asia: Political and Security Dimensions*, Shillong: North-Eastern Hill University.
Ghosh, Suresh C. (1995) *The History of Education in Modern India, 1757–1986*, New Delhi: Orient Longman.
Gidwani, Ninay and Sivaramakrishnan, K. (2004) 'Circular Migration and Rural Cosmopolitanism in India', in: Filippo Osella and Katy Gardner (eds) *Migration, Modernity and Social Transformation in South Asia*, New Delhi: Sage Publications.
Gillion, Kenneth L. (1982) *Ahmedabad: A Study in Urban History*, Berkeley: University of California Press.
Gilmartin, David (1994) 'Scientific Empire and Imperial Science: Colonialism and Irrigation Technology in the Indus Basin', *Journal of Asian Studies*, 53(4): 127–49.
——(1996) 'Models of Hydraulic Environment: Colonial Irrigation, State Power and Community in the Indus Basin', in: David Arnold & Ramachandra Guha (eds) *Nature, Culture, Imperialism: Essays on the Environmental History of South Asia*, New Delhi: Oxford University Press.
Glick Schiller, Nina, Basch, Linda and Szanton Blanc, Christina (1992) 'Transnationalism: A New Analytical Framework for Understanding Migration', in: Nina Glick Schiller, Linda Basch and Christina Szanton Blanc (eds) *Towards a Transnational Perspective on Migration: Race, Class, Ethnicity, and Nationalism Reconsidered*, New York: New York Academy of Sciences.

Godbole, Madhav (2006) *The Holocaust of Indian Partition: An Inquest*, New Delhi: Rupa & Co.

Gogate, Prasad P. and B. Arunachalam, B. (2006) 'A Maratha Map of South India', in: Lotika Varadarajan (ed.) *Indo-Portuguese Encounters: Journeys in Science, Technology and Culture, Volume 1*, New Delhi: Indian National Science Academy; Lisboa: Centro de Historia de Alem-Mar, Universidad Nova de Lisboa; New Delhi: Aryan Books International.

Gole, Susan (1983) *India within the Ganges*, New Delhi: Manohar.

Gommans, Jos J.L. (1999) *The Rise of the Indo-Afghan Empire, c. 1710–1780*, Oxford: Oxford University Press.

Goodman, Neville M. (1952) *International Health Organizations and their Work*, London: Churchill.

Gooptu, Nandini (2001) *The Politics of the Urban Poor in Early Twentieth-Century India*, Cambridge: Cambridge University Press.

Goradia, Nayana (1993) *Lord Curzon: The Last of the British Moghuls*, Delhi: Oxford University Press.

Gordon, Stewart (1993) *The Marathas 1600–1818*, Cambridge: Cambridge University Press.

—— (1994) *Marathas, Marauders, and State Formation in Eighteenth-Century India*, Delhi: Oxford University Press.

—— (1998) 'Legitimacy and Loyalty in some Successor States of the Eighteenth Century', in John F. Richards (ed.) *Kingship and Authority in South Asia*, Delhi: Oxford University Press.

—— (2002) 'Symbolic and Structural Constraints on the Adoption of European-style Military Technologies in the Eighteenth Century', in: Richard B. Barnett (ed.) *Rethinking Early Modern India*, Delhi: Manohar.

—— (ed.) (2003) *Robes of Honour: Khil'at in Pre-Colonial and Colonial India*, Delhi: Oxford University Press.

Gorman, Mel (1968) 'An Early Electric Motor in India', *Society for the History of Technology*, 9(2): 184–214.

—— (1971) 'Sir William O'Shaughnessy, Lord Dalhousie, and the Establishment of the Telegraph System in India', *Technology and Culture*, 12(4): 581–601.

Gossman, Patricia A. (1999) *Riots and Victims: Violence and the Construction of Communal Identity among Bengali Muslims, 1905–1947*, Boulder, Colorado: Westview Press.

Goswami, Manu (2004) *Producing India: From Colonial Economy to National Space*, Chicago and London: Chicago University Press.

Goswami, Omkar (1984) 'Agriculture in Slump: The Peasant Economy of East and North Bengal in the 1930s', *Indian Economic and Social History Review*, 21(3): 335–64.

Goswami, Ritupan (2012) 'Floods and Fields in the Brahmaputra Valley: 20th Century Changes in Historical Perspective', in: Sumi Krishna (ed.) *Agriculture and a Changing Environment in Northeastern India*, London: Routledge.

Gottlob, Michael (ed.) (2002) *Historisches Denken im modernen Südasien (1876 bis heute), Geschichtsdenken der Kulturen – Eine kommentierte Dokumentation: Südasien – Von den Anfängen bis zur Gegenwart*, Frankfurt am Main: Humanities Online.

Gourgey, Percy S. (1996) *The Indian Naval Revolt of 1946*, Hyderabad: Orient Longman.

Green, Nancy L. (1999) 'The Comparative Model and Poststructural Structuralism: New Perspectives from Migration Studies', in: Jan Lucassen and Leo Lucassen (eds) *Migration. Migration History, History. Old Paradigms and New Perspectives*, Bern: Peter Lang.

Greenough, Paul R. (1982) *Prosperity and Misery in Modern Bengal: The Famine of 1943–1944*, Oxford: Oxford University Press.
——(2012) 'Bio-Ironies of the Fractured Forest: India's Tiger Reserves', in: Mahesh Rangarajan and K. Sivaramakrishnan (eds) *India's Environmental History, Vol II, Colonialism, Modernity and the Nation*, New Delhi: Orient BlackSwan.
Gregory, Robert (1971) *India and East Africa, 1890–1939: A History of Race Relations within the British Empire*, Oxford: Clarendon Press.
——(1993) *South Asians in East Africa: An Economic and Social History, 1890–1980*, Boulder: Westview Press.
Grewal, Jaspal S. (1990) *The Sikhs of the Punjab*, Cambridge: Cambridge University Press.
Grewal, Jyoti (2007) *Betrayed by the State: The Anti-Sikh Pogrom of 1984*, New Delhi: Penguin Books India.
Grewal, Reeta (1994) 'Urban Morphology under Colonial Rule', in: Indun Banga (ed.) *The City in Indian History, Urban Demography, Society and Politics*, Delhi: Manohar.
Grout, Andrew (1990) 'Geology and India, 1775–1805: An Episode in Colonial Science', *South Asia Research*, 10(1):1–18.
Grove, Richard H. (1995a) *Green Imperialism: Colonial Expansion, Tropical Island Edens and the Origins of Environmentalism, 1600–1860*, Cambridge: Cambridge University Press.
——(1995b) 'Imperialism and the Discourse of Desiccation: The Institutionalisation of Global Environmental Concerns and the Role of the Royal Geographical Society, 1860–1810', in: Morag Bell, Robin Butlin and Michael Heffernan (eds) *Geography and Imperialism, 1820–1940*, Manchester: Manchester University Press.
——(1998) 'Indigenous Knowledge and the Significance of South-west India for Portuguese and Dutch Constructions of Tropical Nature', in: Ridchard H. Grove, Vinita Damodaran and Satpal Sangwan (eds) *Nature and the Orient: The Environmental History of South and Southeast Asia*, New Delhi: Oxford University Press.
Grove, Richard H., Damodaran, Vinita and Sangwan, Satpal (eds) (1998) *Nature and the Orient: The Environmental History of South and Southeast Asia*, New Delhi: Oxford University Press.
Guest, Bill (1996) 'Indians in Natal and Southern Africa in the 1980s', in: Judith M. Brown and Martin Prozesky (eds) *Gandhi and South Africa: Principles and Politics*, Pietermaritzburg: University of Natal Press.
Guha, Ramachandra (1989) *The Unquiet Woods: Ecological Change and Peasant Resistance in the Himalayas*, New Delhi: Oxford University Press.
——(1990) 'An early Environmental Debate: The Making of the 1878 Forest Act', *Indian Economic and Social History Review*, 27(1): 65–84.
Guha, Ranajit (1963; reprint 1982) *A Rule of Property for Bengal: An Essay on the Idea of Permanent Settlement*, New Delhi: Orient Longman.
——(1983) *Elementary Aspects of Peasant Insurgency in Colonial India*, Delhi: Oxford University Press.
Guha, Ranjit (ed.) (1982–1992) *Subaltern Studies: Writings on South Asian History and Society*, New Delhi: Oxford University Press.
——(1988) *An Indian Historiography of India: A Nineteenth-century Agenda and its Implications*, Calcutta: K.P. Bagchi & Co.
——(1997) *Dominance without Hegemony: History and Power in Colonial India*, Cambridge: Harvard University Press.

Guha, Sumit (1985) *The Agrarian Economy of the Bombay Deccan, 1818–1941*, New Delhi: Oxford University Press.
—— (1996) 'Time and Money: the Meaning and Measurement of Labour in Indian Agriculture', in: Peter G. Robb (ed.) *Meanings of Agriculture: Essays in South Asian History and Economics*, New Delhi: Oxford University Press.
—— (1999) *Environment and Ethnicity in India, 1200–1991*, Cambridge: Cambridge University Press.
Gunaratna, Rohan (1990) *Sri Lanka – A Lost Revolution? The Inside Story of the JVP*, Kandy: Institute of Fundamental Studies.
—— (ed.) (2005) *Peace in Sri Lanka: Obstacles and Opportunities*, London: World Alliance for Peace in Sri Lanka.
Gunatilleke, Godfrey (1986) *Migration of Asian Workers to the Arab World*, Tokyo: United Nations University Press.
Gupta, Hari R. (1999) 'Declaration of Sikh Sovereignty', in: Indu Banga and Jaspal S. Grewal (eds) *The Khalsa over 300 Years*, New Delhi: Tulika.
Gupta, Narayani (1981) *Delhi between Two Empires, 1803–1931: Society, Government and Urban Growth*, New Delhi: Oxford University Press.
Gupta, Samita (1993) 'Theory and Practice of Town Planning in Calcutta, 1817–1912: An Appraisal', *Indian Economic and Social History Review*, 30(1): 29–33.
Guruani, Shubhra (2001) 'Regimes of Control, Strategies of Access: Politics of Forest Use in the Uttarakhand Himalaya, India', in: Arun Agrawal and K. Sivaramakrishnan (eds) *Social Nature: Resources, Representations, and Rule in India*, New Delhi: Oxford University Press.
Haan, Arjan de (1994) *Unsettled Settlers: Migrant Workers and Industrial Capitalism in Calcutta*, Hilversum: Verloren.
Habib, Irfan (1963: 2nd rev. edn 1999) *The Agrarian System of Mughal India, 1556–1707*, New Delhi: Oxford University Press.
—— (1986) 'Postal Communications in Mughal India', in: Indian Historical Records Commission (ed.) *Proceedings of the Indian Historical Congress, 46th Session*, New Delhi: India Press.
—— (2010) *Man and Environment: The Ecological History of India*, New Delhi: Tulika.
—— (ed.) (2002) *The Growth of Civilizations in India and Iran*, New Delhi: Tulika.
Habib, Irfan S. (2007) *To Make the Deaf Hear: Ideology and Programme of Bhagat Singh and His Comrades*, New Delhi: Three Essays Collective.
Hanif, Mohammed (2009) *A Case of Exploding Mangoes*, Noida: Random House India.
Hansen, Anders B. (2002) *Partition and Genocide: Manifestation of Violence in Punjab, 1937–1947*, Delhi: India Research Press.
Hardgrove, Anne (2004) *Community and Public Culture: The Marwaris in Calcutta*, New Delhi: Oxford University Press, 2004.
Hardiman, David (1981) *Peasant Nationalists of Gujarat: Kheda District, 1917–1934*, Delhi: Oxford University Press.
—— (1994) 'Power in the Forests: The Dangs 1820–1940', in: David Arnold and David Hardiman (eds) *Subaltern Studies VIII*, Delhi: Oxford University Press.
—— (1996) *Feeding the Baniya: Peasants and Usurers in Western India*, New Delhi: Oxford University Press.
—— (ed.) (1992) *Peasant Resistance in India, 1858–1914*, New Delhi: Oxford University Press.
Harrison, John (1980) 'Allahabad: A Sanitary History', in: Kenneth Ballhatchet and John Harrison (ed.) *The City in South Asia, Pre-modern and Modern*, London: Curzon Press.

Harrison, Mark (1994) *Public Health in British-India: Anglo-Indian Preventive Medicine 1859–1914*, Cambridge: Cambridge University Press.
——(1999) *Climates and Constitutions: Health, Race, Environment and British Imperialism in India, 1600–1850*, New Delhi: Oxford University Press.
——(2001) 'Medicine and Orientalism: Perspectives on Europe's Encounter with Indian Medical Systems', in: Biswamoy Pati and Mark Harrison (eds) *Health, Medicine and Empire: Perspectives on Colonial India*, New Delhi: Orient Longman.
Harrison, Robert P. (1993) *Forests: The Shadow of Civilization*, Chicago: Chicago University Press.
Hart, Keith (1973) 'Informal Income Opportunities and Urban Employment in Ghana', in: Richard Jolly *et al.* (eds) *World Employment: Problems and Strategy*, Harmondsworth: Penguin.
Hasan, Mubashir (2002) *The Mirage of Power: An Inquiry into the Bhutto Years, 1971–77*, Karachi: Oxford University Press.
Hasan, Mushirul (2007) *From Pluralism to Separatism: Qasbas in Colonial Awadh*, New Delhi: Oxford University Press.
——(ed.) (1993, 6th edn 2003) *India's Partition: Process, Strategy and Mobilization*, New Delhi: Oxford University Press.
Hasan, S. Nurul (1998) 'Zamindars under the Mughals', in: Muzaffar Alam and Sanjay Subrahmanyam (eds) *The Mughal State, 1526–1750*, New Delhi: Oxford University Press.
Hashmi, Taj-ul-Islam (1999, 2nd edn 2005) 'Peasant Nationalism and the Politics of Partition: The Class-Communal Symbiosis in East Bengal', in: Ian Talbot and Gurharpal Singh (eds) *Region and Partition: Bengal, Punjab and the Partition of the Subcontinent*, Karachi: Oxford University Press.
Hay, Douglas and Craven, Paul (eds) (2004) *Masters, Servants, and Magistrates in Britain and the Empire, 1562–1955*, Chapel Hill: University of North Carolina Press.
Haynes, Douglas E. (2001) 'Artisan Cloth Producers and the Emergence of Powerloom Manufacture in Western India', *Past and Present*, 172: 170–198.
——(2008) 'The Labour Process in the Bombay Handloom Industry, 1880–1940', *Modern Asian Studies*, 42(1): 1–30.
Haynes, Edward S. (1980) 'Comparative Industrial Development in 19th and 20th-Century India: Alwar State and Gurgaon District', *South Asia: Journal of South Asian Studies*, 3(2): 25–42.
Haynes, Edward S. (1998) 'The Natural and the Raj: Customary State Systems and Environmental Management in Pre-integration Rajasthan and Gujarat', in: Richard H. Grove, Vinita Damodaran and Satpal Sangwan (eds) *Nature and the Orient: The Environmental History of South and Southeast Asia*, New Delhi: Oxford University Press.
Heathcote, Thomas A. (1995) *The Military in British India: The Development of British Land Forces in South Asia 1600–1947*, Manchester: Manchester University Press.
Heehs, Peter (1993; 2nd edn 2004) *The Bomb in Bengal: The Rise of Revolutionary Terrorism in India, 1900–1910*, New Delhi: Oxford University Press.
Heesterman, Jan C. (1998) 'The Conundrum of the King's Authority', in John F. Richards *Kingship and Authority in South Asia*, Delhi: Oxford University Press.
Heidemann, Frank (1989) *Die Hochland-Tamilen in Sri Lanka und ihre Repatriierung nach Indien: Ethnologische Überlegungen zur selbstbestimmten Entwicklung von Tagelöhnern*, Göttingen: Edition Re.
——(1992) *Kanganies in Sri Lanka and Malaysia: Tamil Recruiter-cum-Foreman as a Sociological Category in the Nineteenth and Twentieth Century*, Munich: Anacon.

Heitler, Richard (1972) 'The Varanasi House Tax Hartal of 1810–11', *Indian Economic and Social History Review*, 9(3): 239–257.
Heitzman, James (2008) *The City in South Asia*, London: Routledge.
Hellmann-Rajanayagam, Dagmar (1994) *The Tamil Tigers: Armed Struggle for Identity*, Stuttgart: Franz Steiner Verlag.
Herath, H. M. Gamini (1981) 'The Green Revolution in Rice: The Role of the Risk Factor with Special Reference to Sri Lanka', *Asian Survey*, 21(6): 664–75.
Herbert, Christopher (2008) *War of no Pity: The Indian Mutiny and Victorian Trauma*, Princeton: Princeton University Press.
Hesmer, Herbert (1975) *Leben und Werk von Dietrich Brandis, 1824–1907: Begründer der tropischen Forstwissenschaft, Förderer der forstlichen Entwicklung in den USA, Botaniker und Ökologe*, Bonn: Westdeutscher Verlag.
Hobsbawm, Eric and Ranger, Terence (eds) (1983; reprint 2010) *The Invention of Tradition*, Cambridge: Cambridge University Press.
Hodges, Kip (2006) 'Climate and the Evolution of Mountains', *Scientific American* 295(2): 72–79.
Hoefte, Rosemarijn (1984) *In Place of Slavery: A Social History of British Indian and Javanese Labourers in Surinam*, Gainesville: University Press of Florida.
Hossain, Hameeda (1988) *The Company Weavers of Bengal: The East India Company and the Organization of Textile Production in Bengal 1750–1813*, New Delhi: Oxford University Press.
Hossain, Mahabub (1988) *Nature and Impact of the Green Revolution in Bangladesh*, Washington: International Food Policy Research Institute.
Howard-Jones, Norman (1975) *The Scientific Background of the International Sanitary Conferences, 18511–1938*, Geneva: World Health Organization.
Hurd, John (1975a) 'The Economic Consequences of Indirect Rule in India', *Indian Economic and Social History Review*, 12(2): 169–81.
——(1975b) 'The Influence of British Policy on Industrial Development in the Princely States, 1890–1933', *Indian Economic and Social History Review*, 12(4): 490–524.
——(1982) 'Railways', in: Dharma Kumar (ed.) *The Cambridge Economic History of India, Vol. 2: c. 1757–1970*, Cambridge: Cambridge University Press.
——(2007) 'A Huge Railway System But No Sustained Economic Development: The Company Perspective, 1884–1939: Some Hypotheses', in: Ian J. Kerr (ed.) *27 Down: New Departures in Indian Railway Studies*, New Delhi: Permanent BlackSwan.
Husain, Intizar (2002) *A Chronicle of the Peacocks: Stories of Partition, Exile and Lost Memories.* Translated from Urdu by Alok Bhalla and Wishwamitter Adil, New Delhi: Oxford University Press.
Husain, Iqbal (1994) *The Ruhela Chieftaincies: The Rise and the Fall of Ruhela Power in India in the Eighteenth Century*, Delhi: Oxford University Press.
——(2008) 'The Rebel Administration of Delhi', in: Shireen Moosvi (ed.) *Facets of the Great Revolt 1857*, New Delhi: Tulika Books.
Husain, Majid (2007) 'Green Revolution in India and the Performance of Major Cereal Crops. An Appraisal', in: Hifzur Rehman *et al.* (eds) *Fifty Years of Indian Agriculture. Vol. 1: Production and Self-Sufficiency*, New Delhi: Concept Publishing Company.
Husain, Sayed Mahdi (1958; reprint with a new pref. by Mushirul Hasan 2006) *Bahadur Shah Zafar and the War of 1857 in Delhi*, Delhi: Aakar Books.

Hussain, Jane (1979, 3rd edn 2006) *A History of the Peoples of Pakistan: Towards Independence*, Karachi: Oxford University Press.

Hussain, Nazia (1980) 'The City of Dacca, 1921–1947: Society, Water and Electricity', in: Kenneth Ballhatchet and John Harrison (eds) *The City in South Asia, Pre-modern and Modern*, London: Curzon Press.

Huttenback, Richard A. (1971) *Gandhi in South Africa. British Imperialism and the Indian Question, 1860–1914*, Ithaca and London: Cornell University Press.

Ikegame, Aya (2013) *Princely India Re-Imagined: A Historiographical Anthropology of Mysore from 1799 to the Present*, London: Routledge.

Inden, Ronald B. (1990) *Imagining India*, Oxford: Blackwell.

Index mundi (2013a) 'Bangladesh – Workers' Remittances and Compensation of Employees'. Avalaible online at www.indexmundi.com/facts/bangladesh/workers%27-remittances-and-compensation-of-employees (accessed 5 May 2013).

——(2013b) 'Pakistan – Workers' remittances'. Available online at www.indexmundi.com/facts/pakistan/workers%27-remittances (accessed 5 May 2013).

Iqbal, Iftekhar (2010) *Bengal Delta: Ecology, State and Social Change, 1840–1943*, Basingstoke, UK: Palgrave Macmillan.

Iqtidar, Humeira and Gilmartin, David (2011) 'Secularism and the State in Pakistan', *Modern Asian Studies*, 45(3): 491–99.

Irschick, Eugene (1994) *Dialogue and History: Constructing South India, 1795–1895*, Berkeley: University of California.

Islam, M. Mufakharul (1997) *Irrigation, Agriculture and the Raj: Punjab, 1887–1947*, Delhi: Manohar.

Islam, Sirajul (1979) *The Permanent Settlement in Bengal: A Study of its Operation, 1790–1819*, Dacca: Bangla Academy.

——(ed.) (1992) *History of Bangladesh, 1704–1971, 3 Vols*, Dhaka: Asiatic Society of Bangladesh.

Jacoby, Erich H. (1972) 'Effects of the 'Green Revolution' in South and South-East Asia', *Modern Asian Studies*, 6(1): 63–9.

Jaffrelot, Christophe (1996) *The Hindu Nationalist Movement and Indian Politics 1925 to the 1990s: Strategies of Identity-Building, Implantation and Mobilisation (with special reference to Central India)*, London: C. Hurst & Co. Ltd.

——(ed.) (2002; 2nd edn 2004) *A History of Pakistan and its Origins*, London: Anthem Press.

Jafri, A.B.S. (ed.) (2002) *The Political Parties of Pakistan*, Karachi Royal Book Comp.

Jafri, Saiyid Z. (1998) *Studies in the Anatomy of a Transition: Awadh from Mughal to Colonial Rule*, New Delhi: Gyan Publishing House.

Jahan, Rounaq (2000) 'Bangladesh: Promise and Performance', in: Rounaq Jahan (ed.) *Bangladesh: Promise and Performance*, Dhaka: The University Press.

Jahangeer-Chojoo, Amenah (2002) 'Islamisation Process among Mauritian Muslims', *Internationales Asienforum* 33(1/2): 115–126.

Jain, Mahabir P. (2nd edn 1966) *Outlines of Indian Legal History*, Bombay: N.M. Tripathi Private Ltd.

Jain, Prakash C. (1999) *Indians in South Africa: Political Relation of Race Relations*, Delhi: Kalinga Publications.

——(2003) 'Culture and Economy in an 'Incipient' Diaspora: Indians in the Persian Gulf Region', in: Bhikhu Parekh, Gurharpal Singh and Steven Vertovec (eds) *Culture and Economy in the Indian Diaspora*, New York: Routledge.

Jain, Ravindra K. (1993) *Indian Communities Abroad: Themes and Literature*, New Delhi: Manohar.
Jalal, Ayesha (1990) *The State of Martial Rule: The Origins of Pakistan's Political Economy of Defence*, Cambridge: Cambridge University Press.
——(2007) *Self and Sovereignty: Individual and Community in South Asia since 1850*, Lahore: Sang-e-Meel Publications.
Jansen, Michael (1986) *Die Indus-Zivilisation: Wiederentdeckung einer frühen Hochkultur*, Köln: DuMont.
Jeffrey, Robin (2000) *India's Newspaper Revolution: Capitalism, Politics and the Indian Language Press, 1977–1999*, London: Hurst.
Jha, Prem S. (2003) *Kashmir 1947: The Origins of a Dispute*, Delhi: Oxford University Press.
Jhirad, J.F.M. (1968) 'The Khandesh Survey Riots of 1852: Government Policy and Rural Society in Western India', *Journal of the Royal Asiatic Society*, 100(2): 151–65.
Joseph, Sebastian (1987) 'Slave Labour of Malabar in the Colonial Context', in: Sabyasachi Bhattacharya, (ed.) *Essays in Modern Indian Economic History*, New Delhi: Munshiram Manoharlal Publishers.
Joshi, Puran C. (ed.) (1957) *Rebellion 1857: A Symposium*, Calcutta and Delhi: K.P. Bagchi & Company.
Journal of Peasant Studies 26(2/3) (1999) 'Special Issue: Rural Labour Relations in India', *Journal of Peasant Studies*, 26(2/3).
Juergensmeyer, Mark (2006) *The Oxford Handbook of Global Religions*, Oxford: Oxford University Press.
Kabeer, Naila (2000) *Bangladeshi Women Workers and Labour Market Decisions: The Power to Choose*, New Delhi: Vistaar Pub.
Kale, Madhav (1995) 'Projecting Identities: Empire and Indentured Labour Migration from India to Trinidad and British Guiana, 1836–1885', in: Peter van der Veer (ed.) *Nation and Migration: The Politics of Space in the South Asian Diaspora*, Philadelphia: University of Philadelphia Press.
Kamat, Manjiri (2010) 'Disciplining Sholapur: The Industrial City and its Workers in the Period of the Congress Ministry, 1937–1939', *Modern Asian Studies*, 44(1) 99–119.
Kannangara, A.P. (1984) 'The Riots of 1915 in Sri Lanka: A Study in the Roots of Communal Violence', *Past and Present*, 102: 130–165.
Kanungo, Pralay (2003) *RSS's Tryst with Politics: From Hedgewar to Sudarshan*, Delhi: Manohar Publishers.
Karim, Sayyid A. (2005) *Sheikh Mujibur Rahman: Triumph and Tragedy*, Dhaka: Dhaka University Press.
Kaur, Amarjit (2006) 'Indian Labour, Labour Standards, and Workers' Health in Burma and Malaya, 1900–1940', *Modern Asian Studies*, 40(2): 425–75.
Kaur, Raminder (2003) *Performative Politics and the Cultures of Hinduism: Public Uses of Religion in Western India*, New Delhi: Permanent Black.
Kaur, Ravider (2005) 'Planning Urban Chaos: State and Refugees in Post-partition Delhi', in: Evelin Hust and Michael Mann (eds) *Urbanization and Governance in India*, Delhi: Manohar.
——(2007) *Since 1947: Partition Narratives among Punjabi Migrants of Delhi*, Delhi: Oxford University Press.
Kaviraj, Naharari (1972) *A Peasant Uprising in Bengal 1783: The First Formidable Peasant Uprising against the Rule of the East India Company*, New Delhi: People's Publishing House.

Kearney Robert N. (1970) 'The 1915 Riots in Ceylon. A Symposium', *Journal of Asian Studies*, 29(2): 219–66.
Keethaponcalan, Soosaipillai I. (2008) *Sri Lanka: Politics of Power, Crisis and Peace*, Colombo: Kumaran Book House.
Kejariwal, Om P. (1988) *The Asiatic Society of Bengal and the Discovery of India's Past, 1774–1838*, New Delhi: Oxford University Press.
Kelly, Elinor (1990) 'Transcontinental Families – Gujarat and Lancashire: A Comparative Study of Social Polity', in: Colin Clarke, Ceri Peach and Steve Vertovec (eds) *South Asians Overseas: Migration and Ethnicity*, Cambridge: Cambridge University Press.
Kerr, Bétrice (1990) 'South Asian Countries as Competitors on the World Labour Market', in: Colin Clarke, Ceri Peach and Steven Vertovec (eds) *South Asians Overseas: Migration and Ethnicity*, Cambridge: Cambridge University Press.
Kerr, Ian J. (1995) *Building the Railways of the Raj, 1850–1900*, Oxford: Oxford University Press.
——(ed.) (2001) *Railways in Modern India*, New Delhi: Oxford University Press.
Khaldun, Talmiz (1957) 'The Great Rebellion', in P. C. Joshi (ed.) *Rebellion 1857: A Symposium*, Calcutta and Delhi: K.P. Bagchi & Company.
Khalid, Amna (2009) '"Subordinate" Negotiations: Indigenous Staff, the Colonial State and Public Health', in: Biswamoy Pati and Mark Harrison (eds) *The Social History of Health and Medicine in Colonial India*, London: Routledge.
Khan, Abdul S. (2012) 'Sindh Population Surges by 81.5 pc, Households by 83.9 pc', *The News International* (02.04.2012). Available online at www.thenews.com.pk/Todays-News-13–13637-Sindh-population-surges-by-81.5-pc,-households-by-83.9-pc (accessed 30 October 2012).
Khan, Hamid (2001) *Constitutional and Political History of Pakistan*, Karachi: Oxford University Press.
Khan, Niaz Ahmed (1998) *A Political Economy of Forest Resource Use: Case Studies of Social Forestry in Bangladesh*, Aldershot: Ashgate.
Khan, Yasmin (2007) *The Great Partition: The Making of India and Pakistan*, New Haven: Yale University Press.
Khandelwal, Madhulika S. (1995) 'Indian immigrants in Queens, New York City: Patterns of Spatial Concentration and Distribution', in: Peter van der Veer (ed.) *Nation and Migration: The Politics of Space in the South Asian Diaspora*, Philadelphia: University of Pennsylvania Press.
Khosla, G.S. (2001) 'A History of Indian Railways', in: Ian J. Kerr (ed.) *Railways in Modern India*, New Delhi: Oxford University Press.
Khosla, Gopal D. (1989) *Stern Reckoning: A Survey of the Events Leading up to and Following the Partition of India*, Delhi: Oxford University Press.
Khuhro, Hamida (1997) 'The Capital of Pakistan', in: Hamida Khuhro and Anwer Mooraj (eds) *Karachi: Megacity of our Times*, Karachi: Oxford University Press.
Kidambi, Prashant (2007) *The Making of an Indian Metropolis: Colonial Governance and Public Culture in Bombay, 1890–1920*, Aldershot: Ashgate.
King, Anthony D. (1980) 'Colonialism and the Development of the Modern Asian City: Some Theoretical Considerations', in: Kenneth Ballhatchet and John Harrison (eds) *The City in South Asia, Pre-modern and Modern*, London: Curzon.
Kinger, Michael K. (2005) *Punjab Politics and Congress, 1947–66*, New Delhi: Commonwealth Publications.

Klein, Ira (1986) 'Urban Development and Death: Bombay City, 1870–1914', *Modern Asian Studies*, 20(4): 725–754.
——(2001) 'Development and Death: Reinterpreting Malaria, Economics and Ecology in British India', *Indian Economic and Social History Review*, 38(2) 147–79.
Kling, Blair B. (1966) *The Blue Mutiny: The Indigo Disturbances in Bengal, 1859–1862*, Philadelphia: University of Philadalphia Press.
——(1992) 'The Origin of the Managing Agency System in India', in: Rajat K. Ray (ed.), *Entrepreneurship and Industry in India, 1800–1947*, New Delhi: Oxford University Press.
Klingensmith, Daniel (2003) 'Building India's Modern Temples: Indians and Americans in the Damodar Valley Cooperation, 1945–60', in: K. Sivaramakrishnan and Arun Agrawal (eds) *Regional Modernities*, New Delhi: Oxford University Press.
Kolff, Dirk H.A. (1990) *Naukar, Rajput, and Sepoy: The Ethnohistory of the Military Labour Market in Hindustan, 1450–1850*, Cambridge: Cambridge University Press.
Kolsky, Elizabeth (2010) *Colonial Justice in India*, Cambridge: Cambridge University Press.
Kopf, David (1969) *British Orientalism and the Bengal Renaissance: The Dynamics of Indian Modernization, 1773–1825*, Berkeley: University of California Press.
——(1988) *The Brahmo Samaj and the Shaping of the Modern Indian Mind*, New Delhi: Archive Publishers.
Kostal, Rande W. (2005) *A Jurisprudence of Power: Victorian Empire and the Rule of Law*, Oxford: Oxford University Press.
Koteswara Rao, M.V.S. (2003) *Communist Parties and United Front Experience in Kerala and West Bengal*, Hyderabad: Prajasakti Book House.
Krishna, Sumi (2012) 'The Potential of Horticultural Interventions for Livelihood Enhancement and Biodiversity Conservation in Tripura, Mizoram and Arunachal Pradesh', in: Sumi Krishna (ed.) *Agriculture and a Changing Environment in Northeastern India*, London: Routledge.
Krishna, Venni V. (1992) 'The Colonial "Model" and the Emergence of National Science in India: 1876–1920', in: Patrick Petitjean, Catherine Jami and Anne Marie Moulin (eds) *Science and Empires: Historical Studies about Scientific Development and European Expansion*, Dordrecht: Kluwer.
Kulkarni, Anant R. (2006a) *Explorations in the Deccan History*, New Delhi: Pragati Publications.
——(2006b) *Maratha Historiography*, Delhi: Manohar.
Kulke, Hermann (2005) *Geschichte Indiens bis 1750*, Munich: Beck.
——(1995) 'The Early and the Imperial Kingdom: A Precessural Model of Integrative State Formation in Early Medieval India', in: Idem (ed.), *The State in India, 1000–1700*, Delhi: Oxford University Press, 233–62.
Kulke, Hermann and Rothermund, Dietmar (1986; 5th edn 2010) *A History of India*, London: Routledge.
Kumar, Amitava (2002) *Bombay – London – New York*, New York: Routledge.
Kumar, Anil (1998) *Medicine and the Raj: British Medical Policy 1835 – 1911*, New Delhi: Sage Publications.
Kumar, Deepak (1995) *Science and the Raj, 1857–1905*, New Delhi: Oxford University Press.
——(2001) 'Social History of Medicine: Some Issues and Concerns', in: Deepak Kumar (ed.) *Disease and Medicine in India: A Historical Overview*, New Delhi: Tulika.

——(2013) '"New" Knowledge and "New" India: Lessons from the Colonial Past', in: Deepak Kumar *et al.* (eds) *Education in Colonial India: Historical Insights*, New Delhi: Manohar.
Kumar, Dharma (1965) *Land and Caste in South India: Agricultural Labour in the Madras Presidency during the Nineteenth Century*, Cambridge: Cambridge University Press.
——(1982a) 'South India (Agrarian Relations)', in: Dharma Kumar (ed.) *The Cambridge Economic History of India, Vol. 2*, Cambridge: Cambridge University Press.
——(1982b) 'South India (Regional Economy)', in: Dharma Kumar (ed.) *The Cambridge Economic History of India, Vol. 2*, Cambridge: Cambridge University Press.
Kumar, Kapil (1984) *Peasants in Revolt: Tenants, Landlords, Congress and the Raj in Oudh 1886–1922*, New Delhi: Manohar.
Kumar, Mayank (2008) 'Situating the Environment: Settlement, Irrigation and Agriculture in Pre-colonial Rajasthan', *Studies in History*, 24(2): 211–33.
Kumar, Nand K. (1980) 'Hydraulic Agriculture in Peninsular India (*c*. 300 BC to 1300 AD)', in: Sumit Sakar (ed.) *Proceedings of the Indian History Congress, 1979*, New Delhi: Delhi Metha.
Kumar, Raj (2008) *Pakistan Peoples Party: Zulfikar Ali Bhutto to Benazir Bhutto*, Delhi: Sumit Enterprises.
Kumar, Ravinder (1968) *Western India in the Nineteenth Century: A Study in the Social History of Maharashtra*, Canberra: Australian National University Press.
Lal, Brij V. (1979) 'Fiji Girmitiyas: The Background to Banishment', in: Vijay Mishra (ed.) *Rama's Banishment: A Centenary Tribute to the Fiji Indians, 1879–1979*, London: Heinemann.
Lal, Vinay (2003; 2nd edn 2006) *The History of History: Politics and Scholarship in Modern India*, New Delhi: Oxford University Press.
Lala, Russi M. (1981) *The Creation of Wealth*, Bombay: IBH Publ.
Lall, Marie C. (2008) *India's Missed Opportunity: India's Relationship with the Non Resident Indians*, Aldershot: Ashgate.
Lawoti, Mahendra (ed.) (2010) *The Maoist Insurgency in Nepal: Revolution in the Twenty-first Century*, London: Routledge.
Lebra-Chapman, Joyce (2008) *The Indian National Army and Japan*, Singapore: Inst. of Southeast Asian Studies.
Legg, Stephen (2007) *Spaces of Colonialism: Delhi's Urban Governmentalities*, Malden: Blackwell.
Lehmann, Fritz (1965) 'Great Britain and the Supply of Railway Locomotives to India', *Indian Economic and Social History Review*, 2(4): 297–306.
——(1977) 'Railway Workshops, Technology Transfer and Skilled Labour Recruitment in Colonial India', *Journal of Historical Research*, 20(1): 49–61.
Lele, Jayant (2003) '"Indian" Diaspora's Long-Distance Nationalism: The Rise and Proliferation of "Hindutva" in Canada', in: Sushma J. Varma and Radhika Seshan (eds) *Fractured Identity: The Indian Diaspora in Canada*, Jaipur: Rawat Publications.
Lemon, Anthony (1990) 'The Political Position of Indians in South Africa', in: Colin Clarke, Ceri Peach and Steven Vertovec, *South Asians Overseas Migration and Ethnicity*, Cambridge: Cambridge University Press.
Leonard, Karen (2001) 'Hyderabadis in Pakistan: Changing Nations', in: Crispin Bates (ed.) *Community, Empire and Migration: South Asians in Diaspora*, Basingstoke, UK: Palgrave Macmillan.

Lessinger, Johanna (1995) *From the Ganges to the Hudson: Indian Immigrants in New York City*, Boston, United States: Allyn and Bacon.
Leue, Horst-Joachim (1981) *Britische Indien-Politik 1926–1932: Motive, Methoden und Mißerfolg imperialer Politik am Vorabend der Dekolonisation*, Wiesbaden: Franz Steiner Verlag.
Lieven, Anatol (2011) *Pakistan. A Hard Country*, London: Allen Lane.
Linkenbach, Antje (2007) *Forest Futures: Global Representations and Ground Realities in the Himalayas*, London, New York, Calcutta: Seagull.
Little, J.H. (1920) 'The House of Jagatseth – I', *Bengal Past and Present*, 20: 111–200.
——(1921) 'The House of Jagatseth – II', *Bengal Past and Present*, 22: 1–119.
Llewellyn-Jones, Rosie (1985; reprint 2001) 'A Fatal Friendship: The Nawabs, the British and the City of Lucknow', in: Rosie Llewellyn-Jones and Veena T. Oldenburg (eds) *The Lucknow Omnibus*, Delhi: Oxford University Press.
——(2007) *The Great Uprising in India 1857–58: Untold Stories, Indian and British*, Woodbridge: The Boydell Press.
Lloyd, Tom (2008) 'Thuggee, Marginality and the State Effect in Colonial India, circa 1770 – 1840', *Indian Economic and Social History Review*, 45(2): 201–37.
Lochtefeld, James G. (2010) *God's Gateway: Identity and Meaning in a Hindu Pilgrimage Place*, Oxford: Oxford University Press.
Lotsy, Jeremiah P. (1990) *Calcutta. City of Palaces. A Survey of the City in the Days of the East India Company, 1690–1858*, London: The British Library, Arnold Publishers.
Lucassen, Jan and Lucassen, Leo (1999) 'Migration, Migration History, History: Old Paradigms and New Perspectives', in: Jan Lucassen and Leo Lucassen (eds) *Migration, Migration History, History: Old Paradigms and New Perspectives*, Bern: Peter Lang.
Ludden, David (1999) *Agrarian History of South Asia*, Cambridge: Cambridge University Press.
——(2002) *India and South Asia: A Short History*, Oxford: Oneworld Publication.
——(2012) 'Spatial Inequity and National Territory: Remapping 1905 in Bengal and Assam', *Modern Asian Studies*, 46(3): 483–525.
——(ed.) (2001) *Reading Subaltern Studies: Critical History, Contested Meaning, and the Globalization of South Asia*, New Delhi: Permanent Black.
Mahajan, Sucheta (2000) *Independence and Partition: The Erosion of Colonial Power in India*, New Delhi: Sage Publications.
Maharaj, Brij (2012) 'Commemoration, Celebration or Commiseration? 150th Anniversary of Indentured Labourers in South Africa', in: Sujata Patel and Tina Uys (eds) *Contemporary India and South Africa: Legacies, Identities, Dilemmas*, London: Routledge.
Majeed, Javed (1992) *Ungoverned Imaginings: James Mill's The History of British India and Orientalism*, Oxford: Oxford University Press.
Major, Andrew J. (1996) *Return to Empire: Punjab under the Sikhs and British in the Mid-Nineteenth Century*, New Delhi: Sterling Publishers.
——(1997) 'Land Revenue and Peasant Protection in early British Punjab', in: Indu Banga (ed.) *Five Panjabi Centuries: Polity, Economy, Society and Culture, c. 1500–1990*, Delhi: Manohar Publishers.
Malik, Jamal (1989) *Islamisierung in Pakistan: Untersuchungen zur Auflösung autochthoner Strukturen*, Stuttgart: Franz Steiner Verlag.
Malik, Priyanjali (2010) *India's Nuclear Debate: Exceptionalism and the Bomb*, London: Routledge.

Mallick, Hrushikesh (2010) 'Remittances, Consumption, Investment, and Economic Growth', in: S. Irudaya Rajan (ed.) *Governance and Labour Migration: India Migration Report 2010*, London: Routledge.

Mani, A. (2006) 'Indians in Singapore Society' in Kernial S. Sandhu and A. Mani (eds) *Indian Communities in Southeast Asia*, Singapore: Institute of Southeast Asian Studies.

Manimohan, R. (2013) 'The Political Economy of Tank Management in Tamil Nadu', in: Dik Roth and Linden Vincent (eds) *Controlling Water: Matching Technology and Institutions in Irrigation Management in India and Nepal*, New Delhi: Oxford University Press.

Mann, Michael (1996) *Flottenbau und Forstbetrieb in Indien 1794 – 1823*, Stuttgart: Franz Steiner Verlag.

——(1999) *British Rule on Indian Soil: North India in the First Half of the Nineteenth Century*, New Delhi: Manohar.

——(2000a) *Bengalen im Umbruch: Die Herausbildung des britischen Kolonialstaates 1754–1793*, Stuttgart: Steiner Verlag.

——(2000b) 'Max Webers 'Konzept' der indischen Stadt', in: Hinnerk Bruhns und Wolfgang Nippel (eds), *Max Weber und die Stadt im Kulturvergleich*, Göttingen: Vandenhoeck und Ruprecht.

——(2001a) 'Timber Trade on the Malabar Coast, 1792–1840', *Environment and History*, 7(4): 403–25.

——(2001b) 'German Expertise in India? Early Forest Management on the Malabar Coast, 1792–1805', in: Hermann Kulke, *et al.* (eds) *Explorations in the History of South Asia,* New Delhi: Manohar.

——(2003) 'Mapping the Country: European Geography and the Cartographical Construction of India, 1760–1790', *Science, Technology and Society*, 8: 25–46.

——(2004) '"Torchbearers upon the Path of Progress": Britain's Ideology of a "Moral and Material Progress" in India. An Introductory Essay', in: Harald Fischer-Tiné and Michael Mann (eds) *Colonialism as Civilizing Mission: Cultural Ideology in British India*, London: Anthem Press.

——(2005a) 'Turbulent Delhi: Religious Strife, Social Tension and Political Conflicts, 1803–1857', *South Asia*, 28(1): 5–34.

——(2005b) 'Pomp and Circumstance in Delhi, 1877–1937 or: Die hohle Krone des British Raj', in: Peter Brandt, Arthur Schlegelmilch and Reinhard Wendt (eds) *Symbolische Macht und inszenierte Staatlichkeit: 'Verfassungskultur' als Element der Verfassungsgeschichte*, Bonn: Dietz Verlag.

——(2005c) 'Kolonialismus in den Zeiten der Cholera: Zum Streit zwischen Robert Koch, Max Pettenkofer und James Cuningham über die Ursachen einer epidemischen Krankheit', *Comparativ* 15, 5/6 (2005), 80–106.

——(2005d) 'Town Planning and Urban Resistance in the Old City of Delhi, 1937–1977', in: Evelin Hust and Michael Mann (eds) *Urbanization and Governance in India*, Delhi: Manohar.

——(2005e) 'Empirische Eilande: Inseln als Laboratorien der europäischen Expansion', *Jahrbuch für Europäische Überseegeschichte* 5 (2005), 27–53.

——(2007) 'Delhi's Belly: The Management of Water, Sewerage and Excreta in a Changing Urban Environment during the Nineteenth Century', *Studies in History*, 23(1): 1–31.

——(2009) *Sinnvolle Geschichte: Historische Repräsentationen im neuzeitlichen Südasien*, Heidelberg: Draupadi Verlag.

—— (2010a) 'Der ungeliebte Krieg: Compagnie des Indes und East India Company als Kombattanten in einem globalen Konflikt, 1742–1763', in: Sven Externbrink (ed.) *Der Siebenjährige Krieg als (europäischer) Weltkrieg*, Berlin: Akademie-Verlag.

—— (2010b) 'Geografie in Wissenschaft und Unterricht: Die Glauchaer Anstalten zu Halle, die Missionare in Tranquebar und die Kartografie Indiens im 18. Jahrhundert', in: Heike Liebau, Andreas Nehring, Brigitte Klosterberg (eds) *Mission und Forschung: Translokale Wissensproduktion zwischen Indien und Europa im 18. und 19. Jahrhundert*, Halle: Verlag der Franckeschen Stiftungen.

—— (2010c) 'The Deep Digital Divide: The Telephone in British India, 1883–1933', Special Issue: Roland Wenzelhuemer (ed.) *Global Communication: Telecommunication and Global Flows of Information in the Late 19th and Early 20th Century*, Historical Social Research/Historische Sozialforschung, 35(1): 188–208.

—— (2011a) 'Migration – Re-migration – Circulation: South Asian Kulis in the Indian Ocean and Beyond, 1840–1940', in Donna R. Gabaccia and Dirk Hoerder (eds) *Connecting Seas and Connected Ocean Rims: Indian, Atlantic, and Pacific Oceans and China Seas Migrations from the 1830s to the 1930s*, Leiden: Brill.

—— (2011b) 'Afterword: Improvement, Progress and Development', in: Carey A. Watt and Michael Mann (eds) *Civilizing Missions in Colonial and Postcolonial South Asia*, London: Anthem Press.

—— (2012a) 'Forestry and Famine in the Chambal-Jamna Doab, 1879–1919', in: Mahesh Rangarajan and K. Sivaramakrishnan (eds) *India's Environmental History. Vol. I. From Ancient Times to the Colonial Period*, New Delhi: Orient BlackSwan. (reprint from *Studies in History* 19(2) 2003: 253–77).

—— (2012b) 'Bauernaufstände auf dem Indischen Subkontinent im späten 18. und frühen 19. Jahrhundert Annäherungen an eine Sozialgeschichte Südasiens von unten', in: Michael Mann and Hans-Werner Tobler (eds) *Bauernwiderstand: Asien und Lateinamerika in der Neuzeit*, Wien: Mandelbaum Verlag.

—— (2012c) *Sklaven, Sahibs und Soldaten: Geschichte des Menschenhandels rund um den Indischen Ozean*, Wiesbaden: Philipp von Zabern Verlag.

—— (2012d) 'Delhi-Metro-Polis: Public Transport, Public Opinion and National Politics', in: Andreas Hilger and Corinna R. Unger (eds) *India in the World since 1947: National and Transnational Perspectives*, Frankfurt am Main: Peter Lang.

—— (2013) 'Telegraphy and the Emergence of an All-India Public Sphere', in: Michaela Hampf and Simone Müller-Pohl (eds) *Global Communication Electric: Business, News and Politics in the World of Telegraphy*, New York: Peter Lang.

Mann, Michael (ed.) (forthcoming) *Shantiniketan-Hellerau: New Education in India, Germany and Beyond*, Heidelberg: Draupadi.

Mann, Michael and Sehrawat, Samiksha (2009) 'A City with a View: The Afforestation of the Delhi Ridge, 1883 – 1913', *Modern Asian Studies*, 43(2) 543–70.

Mann, Michael and Tobler, Hans Werner (2012) *Bauernwiderstand. Asien und Lateinamerika in der Neuzeit*, Wien: Mandelbaum Verlag.

Manning, Catherine (1996) *Fortunes a Faire: The French in Asian Trade, 1719–48*, Aldershot: Ashgate.

Markovits, Claude (2000) *The Global World of Indian Merchants, 1750–1947: Traders of Sindh from Bukhara to Panama*, Cambridge: Cambridge University Press.

—— (ed.) (2002) *A History of Modern India, 1480–1950*, London: Anthem Press.

Markovits, Claude, Pouchepadass, Jacques and Subrahmanyam, Sanjay (2003) 'Introduction: Circulation and Society under Colonial Rule', in: Claude Markovits, Jacques Pouchepadass and Sanjay Subrahmanyam (eds) *Society and Circulation:*

Mobile People and Itinerant Cultures in South Asia, 1750–1950, Delhi: Permanent Black.

Marshall, Peter J. (1975) 'Economic and Political Expansion: The Case of Oudh', *Modern Asian Studies*, 9(4): 465–82.

——(1987a) *Bengal: The British Bridgehead: Eastern India 1740–1828*, Cambridge: Cambridge University Press.

——(1987b) 'The Company and the Coolies: Labour in early Calcutta', in: Pradip Sinha (ed.) *The Urban Experience: Calcutta*, Calcutta: Riddhi-India.

——(2003) 'Introduction', in: Peter J. Marshall (ed.) *The Eighteenth Century in Indian History: Evolution or Revolution?* Delhi: Oxford University Press.

——(2005) *The Making and Unmaking of Empires: Britain, India, and America c. 1750–1783*, Oxford: Oxford University Press.

Marx, Karl (2001) 'The Future Results of British Rule in India', in: Ian J. Kerr (ed.) *Railways in Modern India*, New Delhi: Oxford University Press.

Masselos, Jim (1986) *Indian Nationalism: A History*, London: Oriental University Press.

——(1992) 'Changing Definitions of Bombay: City State to Capital City', in: Indu Banga (ed.) *Ports and Their Hinterlands in India (1700–1950)*, Delhi: Manohar.

Mazumdar, Rajit K. (2003) *The Indian Army and the Making of the Punjab*, New Delhi: Orient BlackSwan.

Mazumdar, Shaswati (ed.) (2011) *Insurgent Sepoys: Europe Views the Revolt of 1857*, London, New York, New Delhi: Routledge.

McAlpin, Michelle B. (1983) *Subject to Famine: Food Crises and Economic Change in Western India, 1860–1920*, Princeton: Princeton University Press.

McDonald-Gumperz, Ellen (1974) 'City-hinterland Relations and the Development of a Regional Elite in Nineteenth Century Bombay', *Journal of Asian Studies* 33(4): 581–601.

McKeown, Adam (2004) 'Global Migration, 1846–1940', *Journal of World History* 15(2): 155–89.

McLane, John R. (1977) *Indian Nationalism and the Early Congress*, Princeton: Princeton University Press.

——(1993) *Land and Local Kingship in Eighteenth-Century Bengal*, Cambridge: Cambridge University Press.

McLeod, John (1999) *Sovereignty, Power, Control: Politics in the States of Western India, 1916–1947*, Leiden: Brill.

McPherson, Kenneth (1998) *The Indian Ocean: A History of People and the Sea*, Delhi: Oxford University Press.

McTarlane, Colin and Waibel, Michael (eds) (2012) *Urban Informalities: Reflections on the Formal and Informal*, Farnham: Ashgate.

Meeto (Bhasin-Malik, Kamaljit) (2007) *In the Making: Identity Formation in South Asia* Gurgaon: Three Essays Collective.

Meher, Rajkishor (2004) *Stealing the Environment: Social and Ecological Effects of Industrialization in Rourkela*, New Delhi: Manohar.

Mehta, Nalin (2008) 'Introduction: Satellite Television, Identity and Globalisation in Contemporary India', in: Nalin Mehta (ed.) *Television in India: Satellites, Politics and Cultural Change*, London: Routledge.

Meller, Helen E. (1979) 'Urbanization and the Introduction of Modern Town Planning Ideas in India, 1900–1925', in: Kirti N. Chaudhuri and Clive J. Dewey (eds),

Economy and Society, Essays in Indian Economic and Social History, New Delhi: Oxford University Press.
Mendis, Garrett C. (ed.) (1956) *The Colebrooke-Cameron Papers: Documents on British Colonial Policy in Ceylon, 1796–1833*, 2 Vols, London: Oxford University Press.
Menon, Nivedita and Nigam, Aditya (2007) *Power and Contestation: India since 1989*, London: Zed Books.
Menon, Vapal P. (1956; reprint 1999) *The Story of Integration of the Indian States*, Mumbai: Orient Longman Limited.
Menon, Visalakshi (2003) *From Movement to Government: The Congress in the United Provinces, 1937–42*, New Delhi: Sage Publications.
Mesthrie, Uma Sh. (1993) 'Tinkering and Tampering: A Decade of the Group Areas Act', *South African Historical Studies* 28(1): 177–202.
Metcalf, Barbara D. (1982) *Islamic Revival in British India: Deoband, 1860–1900*, Princeton: Princeton University Press.
Metcalf, Barbara D. and Metcalf, Thomas R. (2002) *A Concise History of India*, Cambridge: Cambridge University Press.
Metcalf, Thomas R. (1964; 2nd edn 1990) *The Aftermath of Revolt: India, 1857–1870, with a new introduction*, New Delhi: Manohar Publishers.
——(1979) *Land, Landlords and the British Raj: Northern India in the nineteenth century*, Berkeley: University of California Press.
——(2007) *Imperial Connections: India in the Indian Ocean Arena, 1860–1920*, New Delhi: Permanent Black.
Meyer, Eric (1992) 'From Landgrabbing to Landhunger: High Land Appropriation in the Plantation Areas of Sri Lanka during the British Period', *Modern Asian Studies*, 26(2): 321–61.
——(1998) 'Forests, Chena Cultivation, Plantations and the Colonial State in Ceylon, 1840–1940', in: Richard H. Grove, Vinita Damodaran and Satpal Sangwan (eds) *Nature and the Orient. The Environmental History of South and Southeast Asia*, New Delhi: Oxford University Press.
——(2003) 'Labour Circulation between Sri Lanka and South India in Historical Perspective', in: Claude Markovits, Jacques Pouchepadass, Sanjay Subrahmanyam (eds) *Society in Circulation. Mobile People and Itinerant Cultures in South Asia, 1750–1950*, Delhi: Permanent Black.
Middell, Matthias and Naumann, Katja (2010) 'Global History and the Spatial Turn: From the Impact of Area Studies to the Study of Critical Junctures of Globalization', *Journal of Global History*, 5(1): 149–70.
Minault, Gail (1982; 2nd edn 1999) *The Khilafat Movement: Religious Symbolism and Political Mobilization in India*, New Delhi: Oxford University Press.
Mishra, Deepak K. (2012) 'Livelihood Diversification: Farming, Forest-Use and Gender in Northeastern India', in: Sumi Krishna (ed.) *Agriculture and a Changing Environment in Northeastern India*, London: Routledge.
Mishra, Prabodh K. (2001) *Historians and Historiography in Orissa*, Delhi: Indian Publishers & Distributors.
Mishra, Sabya S.R. (2001) 'An Empire "De-masculinized!" The British Colonial State and the Problem of Syphilis in Nineteenth-century India', in: Deepak Kumar (ed.) *Disease and Medicine. A Historical Overview*, Delhi: Tulika.
Mishra, Saurabh (2011) *Pilgrimage, Politics, and Pestilence: The Haj from the Indian Subcontinent, 1860–1920*, New Delhi: Oxford University Press.

Mitra, Subrata K. (2011) *Politics in India: Structure, Process and Policy*, London: Routledge.
Mitter, Partha (1986) 'The Early British Port Cities of India: Their Planning and Architecture, circa 1640–1757', *Journal of the Society of Architectural Historians*, 45(2): 95–114.
Mohan, Surendra (1997) *Awadh under the Nawabs: Politics, Culture and Communal Relations, 1722–1856*, Delhi: Manohar Publishers.
Mohanty, Nivedita (1982) *Oriya Nationalism: Quest for a United Orissa, 1866–1936*, New Delhi: Manohar.
Mohapatra, Prabhu P. (1985) 'Kulis and Colliers: A Study of the Agrarian Context of Labour Migration from Chotanagpur, 1880–1920', *Studies in History*, 1(2): 247–303.
Mojumdar, Kanchanmoy (1973) *Political Relations between India and Nepal (1877–1923)*, Delhi: Manoharlal.
Moon, Penderel (1961) *Divide and Quit*, London: Chatto & Windus.
Moore, Robin J. (1988) *Endgames of Empire: Studies of Britain's Indian Problem*, Delhi: Oxford University Press.
Moosvi, Shireen (1987) *The Economy of the Mughal Empire, c. 1595. A Statistical Study*, New Delhi: Oxford University Press.
——(1999) 'Making and Re-ordering History – Akbar and the *Akbar-nāma*', in: Iqtidar Alam Khan (ed.) *Akbar and his Age*, New Delhi: Northern Book Centre.
——(2001) 'A Sixteenth-Century Code for Physicians', in: Deepak Kumar (ed.) *Disease and Medicine in India: A Historical Overview*, New Delhi: Tulika.
——(2008) 'Rebel Press, Delhi 1857', in: Shireen Moosvi (ed.) *Facets of the Great Revolt 1857*, New Delhi: Tulika Books.
Moran, Arik (2007) 'From Mountain Trade to Jungle Politics: The Transformation of Kingship in Bashahr, 1815–1914', *Indian Economic and Social History Review*, 4(2): 147–77.
Moreman, Tim R. (1998) *The Army in India and the Development of Frontier Warfare, 1849–1947*, Basingstoke, UK: Palgrave Macmillan.
Morris, Morris D. (1965) *The Emergence of an Industrial Labour Force in India: A Study of the Bombay Cotton Mills, 1854–1947*, Berkeley: University of California Press.
——(1982) 'The Growth of Large-Scale Industry to 1947', in: Dharma Kumar (ed.) *The Cambridge Economic History of India. Vol 2: c. 1757–1970*, Cambridge: Cambridge University Press.
Morrison, Kathleen D. (2006) 'Environmental History, the Spice Trade, and the State in South India', in: Gunnel Cederlöf and K. Sivaramakrishnan (eds) *Ecological Nationalism: Nature, Identities and Livelihoods in South Asia*, New Delhi: Permanent.
Mukherjee, Haridas and Mukherjee, Uma (2000) *The Origins of the National Education Movement*. Calcutta: National Council of Education, Bengal.
Mukherjee, Rudrangshu (1990) '"Forever England": British Life in old Calcutta', in: Sukanta Chaudhuri (ed.) *Calcutta, The Living City. Volume 1: The Past*, New Delhi: Oxford University Press.
Mukherjee, S.K. (1992) 'Progress of Indian Agriculture: 1900–1980', *Indian Journal of History of Science*, 27(4): 445–52.
Mukhopadhyay, Subhas Ch. (1990) *British Residents at the Darbar of Bengal Nawabs at Murdhidabad (1757–1772)*, Delhi: Gian Publishing House.
Mukund, Kanakalatha (1999) *The Trading World of the Tamil Merchant: Evolution of Merchant Capitalism in the Coromandel*, Chennai: Orient Longman.

Munasinghe, Indrani (2002) *The Colonial Economy on Track: Roads and Railways in Sri Lanka, 1800–1905*, Colombo: Social Scientists' Association.

Munshi, Shoma (2012) *Remote Control: Indian Television in the New Millennium*, New Delhi: Penguin Books India.

Naher, Shamsun (1976) 'The Agrarian Uprising of Titu Mir: The Economics of a Revivalist Movement', *Journal of the Institute of Bangladesh Studies*, 1(1): 104–15.

Nair, Gopinathan P.R. (1986) 'India', in: Godfrey Gunatilleke (ed.) *Migration of Asian Workers to the Arab World*, Tokyo: United Nations University.

Nair, Janaki (1998) *Miners and Millhands: Work, Culture and Politics in Princely Mysore*, Walnut Creek: AltaMira Press.

——(2005) *The Promise of a Metropolis: Bangalore's Twentieth Century*, New Delhi: Oxford University Press.

——(2011) *Mysore Modern: Rethinking the Region under Princely Rule*, Minneapolis: University of Minnesota Press.

Nair, Neeti (2011) *Changing Homelands: Hindu Politics and the Partition of India*, Cambridge: Harvard University Press.

Naraindas, Harish (2001) 'Of Therapeutics and Prophylactics: The Exegesis of an Eighteenth-century Tract on Smallpox', in: Deepak Kumar (ed.) *Disease and Medicine in India: A Historical Overview*, New Delhi: Tulika.

Narayan, N. (2003) 'The Indian Diaspora in Canada: An Analytical Introduction to Themes and Subjects', in: Sushma J. Varma and Radhika Seshan (eds) *Fractured Identities: The Indian Diaspora in Canada*, Jaipur: Rawat Publications.

Narayana Rao, Velcheru, Shulman, David and Subrahmanyam, Sanjay (2001) *Textures of Time: Writing History in South India 1600–1800*, Delhi: Permanent Black.

Nath, K.J. and Majumdar, Arunaya (1990) 'Drainage, Sewerage and Waste Disposal', in: Sukanta Chaudhuri (ed.) *Calcutta, The Living City, Volume 2: The Present and Future*, New Delhi: Oxford University Press.

National Atlas & Thematic Mapping Organisation (2nd edn 2007) *National Atlas of India, Vol. 3, Climate and Weather*, Kolkata: National Atlas & Thematic Mapping Organisation, Dept. of Science & Technology, Govt. of India.

Nave, Ari (2001) 'Nested Identities: Ethnicity, Community and the Nature of Group Conflict in Mauritius', in: Crispin Bates (ed.) *Community, Empire and Migration: South Asians in Diaspora*, Basingstoke, UK: Palgrave Macmillan.

Nayar, Baldev R. and Paul, Thazha V. (2004) *India in the World Order: Searching for Major-Power Status*, Cambridge: Cambridge University Press.

Newitt, Malyn D. (1987) 'East Africa and Indian Ocean trade', in: Ashin Das Gupta and Michael N. Pearson (eds), *India and the Indian Ocean, 1500–1800*, Calcutta: Cambridge University Press.

Nightingale, Pamela (1970) *Trade and Empire in Western India, 1784–1806*, Cambridge: Cambridge University Press.

Nomura, Chikayoshi (2011) 'Selling Steel in the 1920s: TISCO in a Period of Transition', *Indian Economic and Social History Review*, 48(1): 83–116.

Noorami, Abdul G. (1996; reprint 2005) *The Trial of Bhagat Singh: Politics of Justice*, New Delhi: Oxford University Press.

Oddie, Geoffrey A. (2003) 'Constructing "Hinduism": The Impact of the Protestant Missionary Movement on Hindu Self-Understanding', in: Robert E. Frykenberg (ed.) *Christians and Missionaries in India: Cross-Cultural Communication since 1500 with Special Reference to Caste, Conversion, and Colonialism*, Grand Rapids: W.B. Eerdmans Publishing.

Oesterheld, Joachim and Kumar, Krishna (eds) (2007) *Education and Social Change in South Asia*, New Delhi: Orient Longman.

Office for National Statistics (2012) '2011 Census: Ethnic Groups, Local Authorities in England and Wales: Ethnic Group Classifies People according to their own perceived Ethnic Group and Cultural Background'. Available online at www.ons.gov.uk/ons/search/index.html?pageSize=50&sortBy=none&sortDirection=none&newquery=ethnic+group+local+authority+in+england+and+wales (accessed 15 May 2013).

Ogura, Kiyoko (2008) *Seeking State Power: The Communist Party of Nepal (Maoist)*, Berlin: Berghof-Stiftung für Konfliktforschung.

Oldenburg, Veena T. (1984) *The Making of Colonial Lucknow 1858–1877*, Princeton: Princeton University Press.

——(1991) 'Lifestyle as Resistance: The Case of the Coutesans of Lucknow', in: Douglas Haynes and Gyan Prakash (eds) *Contesting Power: Resistance and Everyday Social Relations in South Asia*, Delhi: Oxford University Press.

Omissi, David (1998) *The Sepoy and the Raj: The Indian Army, 1860–1940*, London: Palgrave Macmillan.

Omvedt, Gail (1980) 'Migration in Colonial India: The Articulation of Feudalism and Capitalism by the Colonial State', *Journal of Peasant Studies*, 7(2): 185–212.

Oomen, Ginu Zacharia (2014) *South Asia-Gulf Migratory Corridor: Emerging Patterns, Prospects and Challenges*, New Delhi: Nehru Memorial Museum and Library.

Oraon, Karma (2002) *Dimension of Religion, Magic, and Festivals of Indian Tribe the Munda*, New Delhi: Kanishka Publishers.

Osella, Filippo and Osella, Caroline (2004) 'Migration and the Commoditisation of Ritual: Sacrifice, Spectacle and Contestation in Kerala, India', in: Filippo Osella and Katy Gardner (eds) *Migration, Modernity and Social Transformation in South Asia*, New Delhi: Sage Publications.

Padayachee, Vishnu and Morrell, Robert (1991) 'Indian Merchants and dukawallahs in the Natal Economy, c. 1875–1914', *Journal of Southern African Studies*, 17(1): 71–102.

Padel, Felix and Das, Samarendra (2006) *Anthropology of a Genocide: Tribal Movements in Central India against Over-Industrialisation*, London: South Asia Analysis Group. Available online at http://sanhati.com/wp-content/uploads/2008/08/felixpadel-samarendradas.pdf (accessed 23 October 2013).

——(2010) *Out of This Earth: East India Adivasis and the Aluminium Cartel*, New Delhi: Orient BlackSwan.

Page, David (1982) *Prelude to Partition: The Indian Muslims and the Imperial System of Control 1920–1932*, Delhi: Oxford University Press.

Pandey, Gyanendra (1990) *The Construction of Communalism in Colonial North India*, Delhi: Oxford University Press.

——(2001) *Remembering Partition: Violence, Nationalism and History in India*, Cambridge: Cambridge University Press.

Pankhurst, Richard (1974) 'Indian Trade with Ethiopia, the Gulf of Aden and the Horn of Africa in the Nineteenth and early Twentieth Centuries', *Cahiers d'Etudes Africaines*, 14(3): 453–97.

Parasher-Sen, Aloka (2012) 'Of Tribes, Hunters and Barbarians', in: Mahesh Rangarajan and K. Sivaramakrishnan, (eds) *India's Environmental History. Vol. I: From Ancient Times to the Colonial Period*, New Delhi: Orient BlackSwan.

Parkin, Robert (1992) *The Munda of Central India: An Account of their Social Organization*, New Delhi: Oxford University Press.

Parnreiter, Christof (2000) 'Theorien und Forschungsansätze zur Migration', in: Karl Husa, Christof Parnreiter und Irene Stacher (eds) *Internationale Migration. Die globale Herausforderung des 21. Jahrhunderts?* Frankfurt am Main: Brandes & Apsel.

Parshad, Gopal (2007) *Industrial Development in Northern India (A Study of Delhi, Punjab and Haryana 1858–1918)*, New Delhi: National Book Organisation.

Parthasarathi, Prasannan (2001) *The Transition to a Colonial Economy: Weavers, Merchants and Kings in South India, 1720–1800*, Cambridge: Cambridge University Press.

Parthasarathy, S. (1994) 'Green Revolution in India: Impact Assessment', in: Centre on the Integrated Rural Development for Asia and the Pacific (ed.) *Impact of Green Revolution in Selected Countries of South Asia and South-East Asia*, Dhaka: Centre on Integrated Rural Development for Asia and the Pacific.

Parvez, Mahfuz (2002) 'Search for Islamization of History: A South Asian Perspective', *Quarterly Journal of the Pakistan Historical Society*, 50(4) 77–95.

Patel, Hasu H. (1973–1974) *Indians in Uganda and Rhodesia: Some Comparative Perspectives on a Minority in Africa*, Denver: University of Denver.

Pati, Biswamoy (2001) '"Ordering" "Disorder" in a Holy City: Colonial Health Interventions in Puri during the Nineteenth Century', in: Biswamoy Pati and Mark Harrison (eds) *Health, Medicine and Empire: Perspectives on Colonial India*, New Delhi: Orient Longman.

——(2010) 'Beyond Colonial Mapping: Common People, Fuzzy Boundaries and the Rebellion of 1857', in: Biswamoy Pati (ed.) *The Great Rebellion of 1857 in India: Exploring Transgressions, Contests and Diversities*, London: Routledge.

——(ed.) (2007; 2nd edn 2008) *The 1857 Rebellion*, New Delhi: Oxford University Press.

——(ed.) (2010) *The Great Rebellion of 1857 in India: Exploring Transgressions, Contests and Diversities*, London: Routledge.

Paty, Michel (1999) 'Comparative History of Modern Science and the Context of Dependency', *Science, Technology and Society*, 4(2): 171–204.

Paul, Samuel (2010) 'Urban Growth and Governance in India. An Overview', in: G. Ramesh (ed.) *Urban Infrastructure and Governance*, London: Routledge.

Peabody, Norbert (2003) *Hindu Kingship and Polity in Precolonial India*, Cambridge: Cambridge University Press.

Pearson, Michael N. (1998) 'Indians in East Africa: The Early Modern Period', in: Rudrangshu Mukherjee and Lakshmi Subramanian (eds) *Politics and Trade in the Indian Ocean World*, New Delhi: Oxford University Press.

——(2003) *The Indian Ocean*, London: Routledge.

Pearson, Ralph S. (1913) *Note on the Utilization of Bamboo for the Manufacture of Paper-Pulp*, Calcutta: Superint. Gov. Press.

Pebbles, Patrick (2001) *The Plantation Tamils of Ceylon: New Historical Perspectives on Migration*, London: Leicester University Press.

Perkovich, George (2000) *India's Nuclear Bomb: The Impact of Global Proliferation*, New Delhi: Oxford University Press.

Perlin, Frank (1983) 'Proto-industrialization and Pre-colonial South Asia', *Past and Present* 98(1): 30–95.

——(1985) 'State formation reconsidered: Part Two', *Modern Asian Studies* 19(3): 415–80.

——(1994) *Unbroken Landscape: Commodity, Category, Sign and Identity. Their Production as Myth and Knowledge from 1500*, Aldershot: Variorum.

——(2003) 'The Problem of the Eighteenth Century', in: Peter J. Marshall (ed.) *The Eighteenth Century in Indian History: Evolution or Revolution?* Delhi: Oxford University Press.
Pernau, Margrit (ed.) (2006) *The Delhi College: Traditional Elites, the Colonial State, and Education before 1857*, Oxford: Oxford University Press.
Pernau-Reifeld, Margrit (2000) *The Passing of Patrimonialism: Politics and Political Culture in Hyderabad, 1911–1949*, Delhi: Manohar.
Pieris, Paulus E. (1920) *Ceylon and the Portuguese, 1505–1658*, Tellippalai: American Ceylon Mission Press.
——(1950) *Sinhale and the Patriots 1815–18*, Colombo: The Colombo Apothecaries Comp.
Pomeranz, Kenneth (2000) *The Great Divergence: China, Europe and the Making of the Modern World Economy*, Princeton: Princeton University Press.
Pomeranz, Kenneth and Topik, Steven (2006) *The World Trade Created: Society, Culture, and the World Economy*, New York: M.E. Sharp.
Poore, M.E.D. and Fries, C. (1987) *The Ecological Effects of Eucalyptus*, Dehra Dun: Natraj Publishers.
Potter, David C. (1996) *India's Political Administrators: From ICS to IAS*, Delhi: Oxford University Press.
Pouchepadass, Jacques (1983) 'Land, Power and Market: the Rise of Land Market in Gangetic India', in: Peter G. Robb (ed.) *Rural India*, London: Curzon Press.
——(1990) 'The Market for Agricultural Labour in Colonial north Bihar, 1860–1920', in: Mark Holmström (ed.) *Work for Wages in South Asia*, Delhi: Manohar.
——(1996) 'British Attitudes Towards Shifting Cultivation in Colonial South India: A Case Study of South Canara District, 1800–1920', in: David Arnold and Ramachandra Guha (eds) *Nature, Culture, Imperialism. Essays on the Environmental History of South Asia*, New Delhi: Oxford University Press.
——(1999) *Champaran and Gandhi. Planters, Peasants and Gandhian Politics*, Delhi: Oxford University Press.
——(2002) 'Colonialism and Environment in India: A Comparative Perspective', in: Alice Thorner (ed.) *Land, Labour & Rights. Ten Daniel Thorner Memorial Lectures*, London: Anthem.
Powell, Avril A. (2010) *Scottish Orientalists and India: The Muir Brothers, Religion, Education and Empire*, Woodbridge: The Boydell Press.
Powell, Geoffrey (1974; reprint 1988) *The Kandyan Wars: The British Army in Ceylon 1803–1818*, New Delhi: Navrang.
Prakash, Gyan (1990) *Bonded Histories: Genealogies of Labor Servitude in Colonial India*, Cambridge: Cambridge University Press.
——(1992) 'Introduction: The History and Historiography of Rural Labourers in Colonial India', in: Gyan Prakash (ed.) *The World of the Rural Labourer in Colonial India*, New Delhi: Oxford University Press.
——(1999) *Another Reason: Science and the Imagination of Modern India*, Princeton: Princeton University Press.
Prashad, Vijay (2001) 'The Technology of Sanitation in Colonial Delhi', *Modern Asian Studies*, 35(1): 113–55.
Price, Pamela G. (1996) *Kingship and Political Practice in Colonial India*, Cambridge: Cambridge University Press.
Prinz, Thomas (1990) *Die Geschichte der United National Party in Sri Lanka*, Wiesbaden: Franz Steiner Verlag.

Punia, Sumandeep K. (2009) *Electoral Politics in Punjab: Emerging Trends and Changing Patterns, 1966–2009*, New Delhi: Mohit.

Pye, Lucian W. and Pye, Mary W. (1985) *Asian Power and Politics: The Cultural Dimensions of Authority*, Cambridge, MA: Harvard University Press.

Qasmi, Ali Usman (2010) 'God's Kingdom on Earth? Politics of Islam in Pakistan, 1947–1969', *Modern Asian Studies*, 44(6): 1197–1253.

Qureshi, Iqbal H. (1999) 'Tipu Sultan's Embassy to Constantinople', in: Irfan Habib (ed.) *Resistance and Modernization under Haidar Ali and Tipu Sultan*, New Delhi: Tulika.

Radhakrishna, Meena (2001) *Dishonoured by History: 'Criminal Tribes' and British Colonial Policy*, New Delhi: Orient Longman.

Radkau, Joachim (1996) 'Wood and Forestry in German History: In Quest of an Environmental Approach', *Environment and History*, 2(1): 63–76.

Raghavan, Srinath (2010) *War and Peace in Modern India*, London: Palgrave Macmillan.

Rahman, Shamimur (2002a) 'Pakistan Peoples Party', in: A.B.S. Jafri (ed.) *The Political Parties of Pakistan*, Karachi: Royal Book Company.

——(2002b) 'Muttahida Qaumi Movement', in: A.B.S. Jafri (ed.) *The Political Parties of Pakistan*, Karachi: Royal Book Company.

Rahman, Tariq (2009) 'The Events of 1857 in Contemporary Writings in Urdu', *South Asia*, 32(2): 212–29.

Rai, Animesh (2008) *The Legacy of French Rule in India (1674–1954): An Investigation of a Process of Creolization*, Pondicherry: French Institute of Pondicherry.

Rai, Lala Lajpat (1915) *The Arya Samaj: An Account of its Aims, Doctrines and Activities with a Biographical Sketch of the Founder*, London: Green and Co.

Rai, Mridu (2004) *Hindu Rulers and Muslim Subjects: Islam, Rights, and the History of Kashmir*, Delhi: Permanent Black.

Raina, Dhruv (2003) *Images and Contexts: the Historiography of Science and Modernity in India*, New Delhi: Oxford University Press.

Raina, Dhruv and Habib, S. Irfan (2004) *Domesticating Modern Science: A Social History of Science and Culture in Colonial India*, New Delhi: Tulika.

Raj, Kapil (2003) 'Circulation and the Emergence of Modern Mapping: Great Britain and Early Colonial India, 1764–1820', in: Claude Markovits, Jacques Pouchepadass and Sanjay Subrahmanyam (eds) *Society and Circulation: Mobile People and Itinerant Cultures in South Asia, 1750–1950*, New Delhi: Permanent Black.

——(2007) *Relocating Modern Science: Circulation and the Construction of Knowledge in South Asia and Europe, 1650–1900*, Basingstoke, UK: Palgrave Macmillan.

——(2011) 'The Historical Anatomy of a Contact Zone: Calcutta in the Eighteenth Century', *Indian Economic and Social History Review*, 48(1): 55–82.

Rajan, S. Irudaya and Kumar, Prabhat (2010) 'Historical Overview of International Migration', in: S. Irudaya Rajan (ed.) *Governance and Labour Migration: India Migration Report 2010*, London: Routledge.

Rajan, S. Ravi (2006) *Modernizing Nature: Forestry and Imperial Eco-Development 1800–1950*, Oxford: Clarendon.

Ram, Raja (1969) *The Jallianwala Bagh Massacre: A Premediated Plan*, Chandigarh: Panjab University, Publication Bureau.

Ramachandran, R. (1989) *Urbanization and Urban Systems in India*, Delhi: Oxford University Press.

Ramakant (1968) *Indo-Nepalese Relations 1816–1877*, Delhi: S. Chand.
Ramani, Shrikant Y. (2008) *Operation Vijay: The Ultimate Solution*, Panjim: Broadway Book Centre.
Ramanna, Mridula (2002) *Western Medicine and Public Health in Colonial Bombay*, New Delhi: Orient Longman.
——(2004) 'Perceptions of Sanitation and Medicine in Bombay, 1900–1914', in: Harald Fischer-Tiné and Michael Mann (eds) *Colonialism as Civilizing Mission: Cultural Ideology in British India*. London: Anthem.
Ramusack, Barabara (2004) *The Indian Princes and their States*, Cambridge: Cambridge University Press.
Rana, R.P. (1981) 'Agrarian Revolts in Northern India during the Late 17th and Early 18th Century', *Indian Economic and Social History Review*, 18(3/4): 287–326.
Rangan, Haripriya (2001) 'State Economic Policies and Changing Regional Landscapes in Uttarakhand Himalaya, 1818–1947', in: Arun Agrawal and K. Sivaramakrishnan (eds) *Social Nature. Resources, Representations, and Rule in India*, New Delhi: Oxford University Press.
Rangarajan, Mahesh (1996) *Fencing the Forests: Conservation and Ecological Change in India's Central Provinces, 1860–1914*, New Delhi: Oxford University Press.
——(1998) 'Production, Desiccation and Forest Management in the Central Provinces 1850–1930', in: Richard H. Grove, Vinita Damodaran, Satpal Sangwan (eds) *Nature and the Orient. The Environmental History of South and Southeast Asia*, New Delhi: Oxford University Press.
——(2012) 'The Raj and the Natural World: The Campaign against "Dangerous Beasts" in Colonial India, 1875–1925', in: Mahesh Rangarajan and K. Sivaramakrishnan, (eds) *India's Environmental History. Vol II, Colonialism, Modernity and the Nation*, New Delhi: Orient BlackSwan.
Rangarajan, Mahesh and Sivaramakrishnan, K. (eds) (2012) *India's Environmental History: A Reader. 2 Vols*, New Delhi: Orient BlackSwan.
Rao, B. Eswara (2011) 'Taming "Liquid Gold" and Dam Technology: A Study of the Godavari Anicut', in: Deepak Kumar, Vinita Damodaran and Rohan D'Souza (eds) *The British Empire and the Natural World: Environmental Encounters in South Asia*, New Delhi: Oxford University Press.
Rao, G.N. (1988) 'Canal Irrigation and Agrarian Change in Colonial Andhra: A Study of Godavari District, *c.* 1850–1890', *Indian Economic and Social History Review*, 25(1): 25–60.
Rao, Velcheru, Shulman, David and Subrahmanyam, Sanjay (2001) *Textures of Time: Writing History in South India 1600–1800*, Delhi: Permanent Black.
Rasul, Golam (2010) 'Policy Root in Environmental Degradation: The Case of Chittagong Hill Tracts of Bangladesh', in: John McNeill, José Augusto Pádua and Mahesh Rangarajan (eds) *Environmental History: As if Nature Existed*, New Delhi: Oxford University Press.
Ratnagar, Shereen (2001) *Understanding Harappa: Civilization in the Greater Indus Valley*, New Delhi: Tulika.
——(2002) *The End of the Great Harappan Tradition*, New Delhi: Manohar.
Ravikant and Saint, Tarun K. (eds) (2001) *Translating Partition: Stories by Attia Hosain, Bhisham Sabni, Joginder Paul, Kamleshwar, Saadat Hasan Manto, Surendra Prak*, New Delhi: Katha.
Ray, Rajat K. (2003) *The Felt Community: Commonality and Mentality before the Emergence of Indian Nationalism*, Delhi: Oxford University Press.

Reddy, K. Jayasudha and Joseph, Joy V. (2004) 'Executive Discretion and Article 356 of the Constitution of India: A Comparative Critique', *Electronic Journal of Comparative Law*. Available online at www.ejcl.org/81/art81-4.html (accessed 31 March 2013).

Reetz, Dietrich (2006) *Islam in the Public Sphere. Religious Groups in India, 1900–1947*, New Delhi: Oxford University Press.

Reeves, Peter (1991) *Landlords and Governments in Uttar Pradesh: A Study of their Relations until Zamindari Abolition*, Bombay: Oxford University Press.

Rezawi, S. Ali Nadeem (2001) 'Physicians as Professionals in Medieval India', in: Deepak Kumar (ed.) *Disease and Medicine in India: A Historical Overview*, New Delhi: Tulika.

Richards, Eric (1982) *A History of the Highland Clearances: Agrarian Transformation and the Evictions, 1746–1886*, London: Croom Helm.

Richards, John F. (ed.) (1998) *Kingship and Authority in South Asia*, Delhi: Oxford University Press.

Richards, Julian J. (1993) *Mohajir Subnationalism and the Mohajir Qaumi Movement in Sindh Province, Pakistan*, Cambridge: Cambridge University Press.

Risso, Patricia (1986) *Oman and Muscat: An Early Modern History*, London: Croom Helm.

Robb, Peter G. (1983) 'Introduction. Land and Society: The British 'Transformation' in India', in: Peter G. Robb (ed.) *Rural India*, London: Curzon Press.

——(1992) *The Evolution of British Policy towards Indian Politics, 1880–1920. Essays on Colonial Attitudes, Imperial Strategies, and Bihar*, Delhi: Manohar Publishers.

——(1997) *Ancient Rights and Future Comfort. Bihar, the Bengal Tenancy Act of 1885 and British Rule in* India, Richmond: Curzon Press.

——(1998) 'Completing "Our Stock of Geography", or an Object "Still More Sublime": Colin Mackenzie's Survey of Mysore, 1799–1810', *Journal of the Royal Asiatic Society*, 8(2): 181–206.

——(2002) *A History of India*, Basingstoke, UK: Palgrave Macmillan.

Robert, Bruce L. (1983) 'Economic Change and Agrarian Organization in "Dry" South India 1890–1940: A Reinterpretation', *Modern Asian Studies*, 17(1): 59–78.

——(1985) 'Structural Change in Indian Agriculture: Land and Labour in Bellary District, 1890–1980', *Indian Economic and Social History Review*, 22(3): 281–306.

Roberts, Michael (2004) *Sinhala Consciousness in the Kandyan Period 1590s to 1815*, Colombo: Vijitha Yapa.

Robinson, Francis (2002) *The Ulama of Farangi Mahal and Islamic Culture in South Asia*, Lahore: Ferozsons.

Rodrigues, Livi (1998) *Rural Political Protest in Western India*, New Delhi: Oxford University Press.

Rodrik, Dani and Subramanian, Arvind (2005) 'From Hindu Growth to Productivity Surge: The Mystery of the Indian Growth Transition', *IMF Staff Papers, Vol. 52, No. 2*, Washington: International Monetary Fund.

Rose, Leo O. and Sisson, Richard (1990) *War and Secession: Pakistan, India and the Creation of Bangladesh*, Berkeley: University of California Press.

Rösel, Jakob and Jürgenmeyer, Clemens (2002) 'Entstehung und Struktur des indischen Parteiensystems seit der Unabhängigkeit', in: Werner Draguhn (ed.) *Indien 2002. Politik, Wirtschaft, Gesellschaft*, Hamburg: Institut für Asienkunde.

Rothermund, Dietmar (1965) *Die politische Willensbildung in Indien, 1900–1960*, Wiesbaden, Germany: Franz Steiner Verlag.

——(1978a) *Government, Landlord, and Peasant. Agrarian Relations under British Rule, 1865–1935*, Wiesbaden: Franz Steiner Verlag.

—— (1978b) 'The Coal Field – An Enclave in a Backward Region', in: Dietmar Rothermund and Charan D. Wadhwa (eds) *Zamindars, Miners and Peasants: Studies in an Indian Coal Field and its Rural Hinterland*, New Delhi: Manohar.
—— (1988) *An Economic History of India*, London: Croom Helm.
—— (1992) *India in the Great Depression, 1929–39*, Delhi: Manohar Publishers.
—— (2002) *Geschichte Indiens. Vom Mittelalter bis zur Gegenwart*, Munich: Beck Verlag.
—— (ed.) (1995) *Indien. Kultur, Geschichte, Politik, Wirtschaft, Umwelt. Ein Handbuch*, Munich: Beck Verlag.
Rothermund, Dietmar, Kropp, Erhard and Dienemann, Gunther (eds) (1980) *Urban Growth and Rural Stagnation: Studies in the Economy of an Indian Coalfield and its Rural Hinterland*, Delhi: Manohar.
Roy, Franziska, Liebau, Heike and Ahuja, Ravi (eds) (2011) *'When the War Began We Heard of Several Kings': South Asian Prisoners in World War One Germany*, New Delhi: Social Science Press.
Roy, Samaren (1998) *M.N. Roy: A Political Biography*, Hyderabad: Orient Longman.
Roy, Tapti (1994) *The Politics of a Popular Uprising: Bundelkhand in 1857*, Delhi: Oxford University Press.
Roy, Tirthankar (1999) *Traditional Industry in the Economy of Colonial India*, Cambridge: Cambridge University Press.
—— (2008) 'Sardars, Jobbers, Kanganies: The Labour Contractor and Indian Economic History', *Modern Asian Studies*, 42(5): 971–98.
—— (2009) 'Did Globalisation Aid Industrial Development in Colonial India? A Study of Knowledge Transfer in the Iron Industry', *Indian Economic and Social History Review*, 46(4): 579–613.
Rudner, David W. (1994) *Caste and Capitalism in Colonial India: The Nattukottai Chettiars*, Berkeley: University of California Press.
Russell, Jane (1982) *Communal Politics under the Donoughmore Constitution 1931–1947*, Colombo: Tisara Prakasakayo.
Russell, William H. (1860) *My Diary in India in the Year 1858–9*, London: Routledge.
Rycroft, Daniel J. (2006) *Representing Rebellion: Visual Aspects of Counter-Insurgency in Colonial India*, New Delhi: Oxford University Press.
Saberwal, Vasant K. (1999) *Pastoral Politics: Shepherds, Bureaucrats and Conservation in the Western Himalaya*, New Delhi: Oxford University Press.
Saberwal, Vasant K. and Lele, Sarachchandra (2004) 'Locating Local Elites in Negotiating Access to Forests: Havik Brahmins and the Colonial State 1860–1920', *Studies in History*, 20(2): 273–303.
Sachdeva, Veena (1997) 'Agrarian Production and Distribution in the late Eighteenth Century', in: Indu Banga (ed.) *Five Panjabi Centuries. Polity, Economy, Society and Culture, c. 1500–1990*, Delhi: Manohar Publishers.
Sachsenmaier, Dominic (2011) *Global Perspectives on Global History: Theories and Approaches in a Connected World*, Cambridge: Cambridge University Press.
Sáez, Lawrence and Singh, Gurharpal (eds) (2012) *New Dimensions of Politics in India: The United Progressive Alliance in Power*, London: Routledge.
Safran, William (1991) 'Diasporas in Modern Societies', *Diaspora: A Journal of Transnational Studies*, 1(1): 83–99.
Saikia, Arupjyoti (2005) *Jungles, Reserves, Wildlife: A History of Forests in Assam*, Guhawati: Wildlife Areas Development and Welfare Trust.
—— (2011) *Forests and Ecological History of Assam, 1826–2000*, New Delhi: Oxford University Press.

Saikia, Yasmin (2010) 'Listening to the Enemy: The Pakistan Army, Violence and Memories of 1971', in: Naveeda Khan (ed.) *Beyond Crisis: Re-evaluating Pakistan*, London: Routledge.

Sailer, Anna (2013) ' "Various Paths Are Today Opened": The Bengal Jute Mill Strike of 1929 as a Historical Event', in: Ravi Ahuja (ed.) *Working Lives and Worker Militancy: The Politics of Labour in Colonial India*, Delhi: Tulika.

Samarth, Anil (1975) *Shivaji and the Indian National Movement: Saga of a Living Legend*, Bombay: Somaiya Publications.

Sandhu, Kernial S. (1969) *Indians in Malaya*, Cambridge: Harvard University Press.

——(2006) 'Indian Immigration and Settlement in Singapore', in Kernial S. Sandhu and A. Mani (eds) *Indian Communities in Southeast Asia*, Singapore: Institute of Southeast Asian Studies.

Sangwan, Satpal (1991) *Science, Technology and Colonialism: An Indian Experience, 1757–1857*, New Delhi: Anamika Prakashan.

——(1998) 'From Gentlemen Amateurs to Professionals: Reassessing the Natural Science Tradition in Colonial India, 1780–1840', in: Richard H. Grove, Vinita Damodaran, Satpal Sangwan (eds) *Nature and the Orient: The Environmental History of South and Southeast Asia*, New Delhi: Oxford University Press.

——(1999) 'Making of a Popular Debate: The Indian Forester and the Emerging Agenda of State Forestry in India, 1875–1914', *Indian Economic and Social History Review*, 36(2): 187–237.

——(2000) 'Science and its Public in British India: Problematic of Diffusion and Social Appropriation', in: Narender K. Sehgal, Satpal Sangwan and Subodh Mahanti (eds) *Unchartered Terrains: Essays on Science Populatrisation in Pre-independence India*, New Delhi: Vigyan Prasar.

Sanyal, Manoj K. (2005) 'Policy, Environment and Agricultural Trends: Post Independence India', in: Binay Bhushan Chauduri (ed.) *Economic History of India from Eighteenth to Twentieth Century*; New Delhi: Centre for Studies in Civilizations.

Saran, Vishnu (ed.) (2008) *Laljpat Rai, the Unknown: With an Appreciation by T. N. Chaturvedi*, Bhopal: Directorate of Swaraj Sansthan, Dept. of Culture, Govt. of M.P.

Saravanan, Velayutham (2007) 'Environmental History of Tamil Nadu State, Law and Decline of Forest and Tribals, 1950–2000', *Modern Asian Studies*, 41(4): 723–67.

SarDesai, Damodar R. (2007) *India: The Definitive History*, Boulder, CO: Westview Press.

Sarkar, Sumit (1983; reprint 2003) *Modern India, 1885–1947*, Delhi: Palgrave Macmillan.

——(1992) 'The Fascism of Sangh Parivar', *Economic and Political Weekly*, 30 January: 163–167.

——(2nd edn 2000) 'The Logic of Gandhian Nationalism: Civil Disobedience and the Gandhi–Irwin Pact 1930–31', in: Sumit Sakar (ed.) *A Critique of Colonial India*, Calcutta: Papyrus.

Sarkar, Suvobrata (2013) '*Bhadralok* Aspirations and the Quest for Technical Knowledge, 1830–1900', in: Deepak Kumar *et al.* (eds) *Education in Colonial India: Historical Insights*, New Delhi: Manohar.

Sarup, Leela G. (2004) *Indentured Labour: Slavery to Salvation. Colonial Emigration Acts 1837–1932*, Kolkata: Aldrich International.

Satya, Laxman D. (1997) *Cotton and Famine in Berar, 1850–1900*, New Delhi: Manohar.

——(2009) *Medicine, Disease and Ecology in Colonial India: The Deccan Plateau in the Nineteenth Century*, New Delhi: Manohar.

Satyanarayana, Adapa (1990) *Andhra Peasants under British Rule: Agrarian Relations and the Rural Economy 1900–1940*, New Delhi: Manohar.

——(1996) *History of the Wodeyars of Mysore (1610–1748)*, Mysore: Directorate of Archaeology and Museums.

Savarkar, Vinayak D. (1923) *Hindutva – Who is a Hindu?* Nagpur.

Savur, Manorama (2003) *And the Bamboo Flowers in the Indian Forests: What did the Pulp and Paper Industry do?* New Delhi: Manohar.

Sayeed, Khalid bin (1968; 13th edn 2007) *Pakistan: The Formative Phase, 1857–1947*, Karachi: Oxford University Press.

Schendel, Willem van (2000) 'Bengalis, Bangladeshis and Others: Chakma Vision of a Pluralist Bangladesh', in: Rounaq Jahan (ed.) *Bangladesh: Promise and Performance*, Dhaka: The University Press.

——(2004) *The Bengal Borderland: Beyond State and Nation in South Asia*, London: Anthem Press.

——(2009) *A History of Bangladesh*, Cambridge: Cambridge University Press.

Schmitthenner, Peter L. (2011) 'Colonial Hydraulic Projects in South India: Environmental and Cultural Legacy', in: Deepak Kumar, Vinita Damodaran, and Rohan D'Souza (eds) *The British Empire and the Natural World: Environmental Encounters in South Asia*, New Delhi: Oxford University Press.

Schubert, Dirk (1997) *Stadterneuerung in London und Hamburg: Eine Stadtbaugeschichte zwischen Modernisierung und Disziplinierung*. Braunschweig: Vieweg.

Schwalgin, Susanne (2000) 'Rituale des Gedenkens an den Genozid. Eine Situationsanalyse', in: Thomas Hengartner, Waltraud Kokot, Kathrin Wildner (eds) *Kulturwissenschaftliche Stadtforschung: Eine Bestandsaufnahme*, Berlin: D. Reimer.

Schwerin, Kerrin von (1980) *Indirekte Herrschaft und Reformpolitik im indischen Fürstenstaat Hyderabad 1853–1911*, Wiesbaden: Steiner Verlag.

Secombe, J. and Lawless, R.I. (1986) 'Foreign Worker Dependence in the Gulf, and the International Oil Companies: 1910–1950', *International Migration Review*, 20(3): 548–74.

Sehrawat, Samiksha (2009) '"Prejudices Clung to by the Natives", Ethnicity in the Indian Army and Hospitals for Sepoys, c. 1870s-1890s', in: Biswamoy Pati and Mark Harrison (eds) *The Social History of Health and Medicine in Colonial India*, London: Routledge.

Sen, Asok (1977) 'A pre-British Economic Formation in India of the Late Eighteenth Century: Tipu Sultan's Mysore', in: Barun De (ed.) *Perspectives in Social Sciences I. Historical Dimensions*, Calcutta: Oxford University Press.

Sen, Samita (1999) *Women and Labour in late Colonial India: The Bengal Jute Industry* Cambridge: Cambridge University Press.

Sen, Satadru (2000) *Disciplining Punishment: Colonialism and Convict Society in the Andaman Islands*, New Delhi: Oxford University Press.

Sen, Snigdha (1992) *The Historiography of the Indian Revolt of 1857*, Calcutta: Punthi-Pustak.

Sen, Sukomal (1977) *Working Class of India: History of the Emergence and Movement 1830–1970*, Calcutta: KP Bagchi.

Senaveratna, John M. (1924) *The Story of the Sinhalese: From the Most Ancient Times*, Colombo: Times of Ceylon.

——(1930) *The Story of the Sinhalese: From the Most Ancient Times up to the end of "The Mahavansa or Great Dynasty" Vijaya to Maha Sena, BC 543 to AD 302*, Colombo: W.M.A. Wahid.

Sengupta, Debjani (2006) 'A City Feeding on Itself: Testimonies and Histories of 'Direct Action' Day', in: *Sarai Reader*, New Delhi: The Sarai Programme.

Sengupta, Indra (2005) *From Salon to Discipline: State, University and Indology in Germany 1821–1914*, Würzburg: Ergon.

Sengupta, Nitish K. (2007) *Bengal Divided: The Unmaking of a Nation (1905–1971)*, New Delhi: Penguin.

Seth, Mesrob J. (1937; reprint 1992) *Armenians in India: From the Earliest Time to the Present Day*, New Delhi: Asian Educational Services.

Shah, Amrita (1997) *Hype, Hypocrisis, and Television in Urban India*, New Delhi: Vikas.

Shaha, Rishikesh (1996) *Modern Nepal: A Political History, 1769–1955*, Delhi: Manohar.

Shaheed, Zafar (2007) *The Labour Movement in Pakistan: Organization and Leadership in Karachi in the 1970s*, Karachi: Oxford University Press.

Shaik, Farzana (2007) *Making Sense of Pakistan*, London: Hurst & Company.

Shani, Giorgio (2008) *Sikh Nationalism and Identity in a Global Age*, London: Routledge.

Sharan, Awadhendra (2011) 'From Source to Sink: "Official" and "Improved" Water in Delhi, 1868–1956', *Indian Economic and Social History Review*, 48(3): 425–62.

Sharar, Abdul H. (1975; reprint 2001) '*Lucknow: The last Phase of an Oriental Culture*', in: Rosie Llewellyn-Jones and Veena T. Oldenburg (eds) *The Lucknow Omnibus*, Delhi: Oxford University Press.

Sharma, Jayeeta (2006) 'British Science, Chinese Skill and Assam Tea: Making Empire's Garden, *Indian Economic and Social History* Review, 43(4): 429–55.

——(2009) '"Lazy" Natives, Kuli Labour and the Assam Tea Industry', *Modern Asian Studies*, 43(6): 1287–1324.

——(2011) *Empire's Garden: Assam and the Making of India*, Durham: Duke University Press.

Sharma, Radha (1978) 'Agrarian Society in Transition: Mid-nineteenth Century', in: Indu Banga (ed.) *Agrarian System of the Sikhs: Late Eighteenth and early Nineteenth century*, New Delhi: Manohar.

Sharma, Ram N. and Sharma, Rajendra K. (1996) *History of Education in India*, New Delhi: Atlantic Publishers and Distributors.

Sharma, Sanjay (2001) *Famine, Philanthropy and the Colonial State: North India in the Early Nineteenth Century*, New Delhi: Oxford University Press.

Sharma, Sita R. (2005) *Life and Works of Lala Lajpat Rai*, Jaipur: Book Enclave.

Sheik Ali, Belagodu (1963) *British Relation with Haidar Ali, 1760–1782*, Mysore: Geetha Book House.

——(1982) *Tipu Sultan. A Study in Diplomacy and Confrontation*, Mysore: Geetha Book House.

——(1999; 2nd end 2004) 'Developing Agriculture: Land Tenure under Tipu Sultan', in: Irfan Habib (ed.) *Confronting Colonialism: Resistance and Modernization under Haidar Ali and Tipu Sultan*, New Delhi: Tulika.

——(2002) 'A Critique of Tipu Sultan's Political Economy', in: Arinuddha Ray (ed.) *Tipu Sultan and His Age: A Collection of Seminar Papers*, Kolkata: The Asiatic Society/New Asian Printers.

Shepherd, Verene A. (2002) *Maharani's Misery: Narratives of a Passage from India to the Caribbean*, Trinidad and Tobago: The University of the West Indies Press.

Sherlock, Stephen (2001) *The Indian Railways Strike of 1974: A Study of Power and Organised Labour*, New Delhi: Rupa.

Sherman, Taylor C. (2007) 'The Integration of the Princely State of Hyderabad and the Making of the Postcolonial State in India, 1948–56', *Indian Economic and Social History Review*, 44(4): 489–516.
—— (2009) *State Violence and Punishment in India*, London: Routledge.
Shiva, Vandana (1993) *The Violence of the Green Revolution: Third World Agriculture, Ecology and Politics*, London: Zed Books.
Shridharani, Krishnanlal (1953) *Story of the Indian Telegraphs: A Century of Progress*, New Delhi: Govt. of India Press.
Shukla, A.C. and Asthana, Vandana (2005) 'Anatomy of Interlinking Rivers in India: A Decision in Doubt', *University of Illinois, ACDIS Occasional Paper*. Available online at https://ideals.illinois.edu/bitstream/handle/2142/42/Shukla-AsthanaOP.pdf?sequence=1 (accessed 10 August 2013).
Siddiqa-Agha, Ayesha (2007) *Military Inc.: Inside Pakistan's Military Political Economy*, London: Pluto Press.
Siddiqi, Asiya (1973) *Agrarian Change in a Northern Indian State: Uttar Pradesh 1819–1833*, Oxford: Oxford University Press.
Siddiqi, Farhan H. (2012) *The Politics of Ethnicity in Pakistan: The Baloch, Sindhi and Mohajir Ethnic Movements*, London: Routledge.
Siddiqi, Norman Ahmad (1970) *Land Revenue Administration under the Mughals (1700–1750)*, New Delhi: Munshiram Manoharlal.
Sikka, Ram Prakash (1984) *The Civil Service in India: Europeanisation and Indianisation under the East India Company – (1765–1857)*, New Delhi: Uppal Publishing House.
Silvestri, Michael (2007) *Ireland and India: Nationalism, Empire, and Memory*, London: Palgrave Macmillan.
Simon, Werner (1974) *Die britische Militärpolitik in Indien und ihre Auswirkungen auf den britisch-indischen Finanzhaushalt 1878–1910*, Wiesbaden: Franz Steiner Verlag.
Simpson, Edward (2004) 'Migration and Islamic Reform in a Port Town of Western India', in: Filippo Osella and Katy Gardner (eds) *Migration, Modernity and Social Transformation in South Asia*, New Delhi: Sage Publications.
Singaravélou, Pierre (1990) 'Indians in the French Overseas Departments: Gouadeloupe, Martinique, Reunion', in: Colin Clarke, Ceri Peach and Steven Vertovec (eds) *South Asians Overseas. Migration and Ethnicity*, Cambridge: Cambridge University Press.
Singh, Ajay K. (ed.) (2009) *Federal Perspective, Constitutional Logic and Reorganisation of States*, New Delhi: Manak.
Singh, Anita I. (1987) *The Origins of the Partition of India, 1936–1947*, Delhi: Oxford University Press.
Singh, Bhagat (2001) *Canadian Sikhs through a Century (1897–1997)*, Delhi: Gyan Sagar Publications.
Singh, Birinder P. (ed.) (2010) *Punjab Peasantry in Turmoil*, New Delhi: Manohar.
Singh, Devendra (1990) *Meerut Conspiracy Case and the Communist Movement in India, 1929–35*, Meerut: Research India.
Singh, Harkirat (2003) *The INA Trial and the Raj*, New Delhi: Atlantic Publishers & Distributors.
Singh, Indramani K. (2009) *Politics of Presidential Rule in India*, New Delhi: Akansha.
Singh, Jagtar (2011) *Khalistan Struggle: A Non-Movement*, Delhi: Aakar Books.
Singh, Jasbir (1974) *The Green Revolution in India: How Green it is*, Kurukshetra: Vishal Publications.
Singh, Kumar S. (1983) *Birsa Munda and His Movement, 1874–1901: A Study of a Millenarian Movement in Chotanagpur*, Calcutta: Oxford University Press.

Singh, Navinder K. (2001) *Role of Women Workers in the Tea Industry of North East India*, New Delhi: Classical Publ.

Singh, Nitmal T. (2005) *Irrigation and Soil Salinity in the Indian Subcontinent: Past and Present*, Bethlehem: Lehigh University Press.

Singh, Praveen (2001) 'Flood Control for North Bihar: An Environmental History from the 'Ground-Level' (1850–1954)', in: Deepak Kumar, Vinita Damodaran, and Rohan D'Souza (eds) *The British Empire and the Natural World: Environmental Encounters in South Asia*, New Delhi: Oxford University Press.

Singh, Satyajit (1997) *Taming the Waters: The Political Economy of Large Dams in India*, New Delhi: Oxford University Press.

Singh, Tapeshwar (2007) 'Green Revolution, Food Security and Agricultural Sustainability in India. The Conflicts and Solutions', in: Hifzur Rehman *et al.* (eds) *Fifty Years of Indian Agriculture. Vol.1: Production and Self-Sufficiancy*, New Delhi: Concept Publishing Company.

Singh, Upinder (ed.) (2011) *Rethinking Early Mediaval India. A Reader*, New Delhi: Oxford University Press.

Singha, Radhika (1998) *A Despotism of Law: Crime and Justice in Early Colonial India*, Delhi: Oxford University Press.

Sinha, Nikhil (1998) 'Doordarshan, Public Service Broadcasting and the Impact of Globalization: A Short Story', in: Monroe E. Price and Stefaan Verhulst (eds) *Broadcasting Reform in India – Media Law from a Global Perspective*, New Delhi: Oxford University Press.

Sinha, Nitin (2008) 'The World of Workers' Politics: Some Issues of Railway Workers in Colonial India, 1918–1922', *Modern Asian Studies*, 42(5): 999–1033.

Sinha, Shashank S. (2010) '1857 and the Adivasis of Chotanagpur', in: Biswamoy Pati (ed.) *The Great Rebellion of 1857 in India: Exploring Transgressions, Contests and Diversities*, London: Routledge.

Sinha, Sushil K. (2006a) 'Introduction', in: Sushil K. Sinha (ed.) *Globalization of Indian Broadcasting*, New Delhi: Raj Publications.

——(2006b) 'Doordarshan and Satellite Channels: A Profile', in: Sushil K. Sinha (ed.) *Globalization of Indian Broadcasting*, New Delhi: Raj Publications.

Sivaramakrishnan, K. (1999) *Modern Forests. Statemaking and Environmental Change in Colonial Eastern India*, Stanford: Stanford University Press.

Sivasundaram, Sujit (2007) 'Tales of the Land: British Geography and Kandyan Resistance in Sri Lanka, c. 1803–1850', *Modern Asian Studies*, 41(5): 925–65.

Six, Clemens (2006) *Hindi-Hindu-Hindustan: Politik und Religion im modernen Indien*, Wien: Mandelbaum-Verlag.

Skaria, Ajay (1998) 'Timber Conservancy, Desiccationism and Scientific Forestry: the Dangs 1840s–1920s', in: Richard H. Grove, Vinita Damodaran, Satpal Sangwan (eds) *Nature and the Orient: The Environmental History of South and Southeast Asia*, New Delhi: Oxford University Press.

——(1999) *Hybrid Histories: Forests, Frontiers and Wilderness in Western India*, Delhi: Oxford University Press.

Sobhan, Rehman (1993) *Bangladesh: Problems of Governance*, New Delhi: Konark Publishers.

Soni, Anita (2000) 'Urban Conquest of Outer Delhi. Beneficaries, Intermediaries and Victims: The Case of Mehrauli Countryside', in: Véronique Dupont, Emma Tarlo, Denis Vidal (eds) *Delhi: Urban Space and Human Destinies*, New Delhi: Manohar.

Sontheimer, Günter-Dietz (1989) *Pastoral Deities in Western India*, Oxford: Oxford University Press.
Specker, Konrad (1984) *Weber im Wettbewerb: Das Schicksal des südindischen Textilhandwerks im 19. Jahrhundert*, Wiesbaden: Franz Steiner Verlag.
Sridhar, Varadharajan (2013) *The Telecom Revolution in India: Technology, Regulation and Police*, New Delhi: Oxford University Press.
Srimanjari (2009) *Through War and Famine Bengal, 1939–45*, New Delhi: Orient BlackSwan.
Stafford, Robert A. (1984) 'Geological Surveys, Mineral Discoveries, and British Expansion, 1835–1971', *Journal of the Imperial and Commonwealth History*, 12(3): 5–32.
—— (1990) 'Annexing the Landscapes of the Past: British Imperial Geology in the Nineteenth Century', in: John M. MacKenzie (ed.) *Imperialism and the Natural World*, Manchester: Manchester University Press.
Stang, Friedrich (2002) *Indien*, Darmstadt: Wissenschaftliche Buchgesellschaft Gesellschaft.
Statista (2013) 'Grad der Urbanisierung in der Europäischen Union von 2001 bis 2011'. Available online at http://de.statista.com/statistik/daten/studie/249028/umfrage/urbanisierung-in-der-europaeischen-union-eu/ (accessed 11 October 2013).
Staubli, Maurus (1994) *Reich und arm mit Baumwolle: Exportorientierte Landwirtschaft und soziale Stratifikation am Beispiel des Baumwollanbaus im indischen Distrikt Khandesh (Dekkan) 1850–1914*, Stuttgart: Franz Steiner Verlag.
Stein, Burton (1980) *Peasant State and Society in Medieval South India*, New Delhi: Oxford University Press.
—— (1985) 'State Formation and Economy Reconsidered: Part One', *Modern Asian Studies* 19(3): 387–413.
—— (1989a) *Vijayanagara: The New Cambridge History of India I, 2*, Cambridge: Cambridge University Press.
—— (1989b) *Thomas Munro: The Origins of the Colonial State and his Visions of Empire*, New Delhi: Oxford University Press.
—— (1998) *A History of India*, Oxford and Malden: Blackwell.
Steinfeld, Robert J. (2001) *Coercion, Contract, and Free Labor in the Nineteenth Century*, Cambridge: Cambridge University Press.
Stern, Philip J. (2011) *The Company-State: Corporate Sovereignty and the Early Modern Foundations of the British Empire in India*, Oxford: Oxford University Press.
Stockwell, Arthur J. (1992) 'Southeast Asia in War and Peace: The End of European Colonial Empires', in: Nicholas Tarling (ed.) *The Cambridge History of Southeast Asia. Vol. 2*, Cambridge: Cambridge University Press.
Stoddart, Brian (2011) *Land, Water, Language and Politics in Andhra: Regional Evolution in India since 1850*, London: Routledge.
Stokes, Eric (1959) *The English Utilitarians and India*, Oxford: Clarendon Press.
—— (1978) *The Peasant and the Raj: Studies in Agrarian Society and Peasant Rebellion in Colonial India*, Cambridge: Cambridge University Press.
—— (1983) 'Northern and Central India', in: Dharma Kumar (ed.) *The Cambridge Economic History of India, Vol. 2, c. 1757-c. 1970*, Cambridge: Cambridge University Press.
—— (1986) *The Peasant Armed: The Indian Revolt of 1857*, Oxford: Clarendon Press 1986.
Stone, Ian (1984) *Canal Irrigation in British India: Perspectives on Technological Change in a Peasant Economy*, Cambridge: Cambridge University Press.

Strahorn, Eric A. (2009) *An Environmental History of Postcolonial North India: The Himalayan Tarai in Uttar Pradesh and Uttaranchal*, New York: Peter Lang.

Subba Rao, C.V. (2007) *Hyderabad: The Social Context of Industrialisation, 1875–1948*, New Delhi: Orient Longman.

Subrahmanyam, Sanjay (1994) (ed.) *Money and the Market in India 1100–1700*, New Delhi: Oxford University Press.

Sundaram, Jomo Kwame (1993) 'Plantation Capital and Indian Labour in Colonial Malaya', in: Kernial S. Sandhu and A. Mani, *Indian Communities in Southeast Asia*, Singapore: Times Academic Press and Institute of Southeast Asian Studies.

Sundaram, Ravi (2010) *Pirate Modernity. Delhi's Media Urbanism*, London: Routledge.

Swan, Maureen (1985) *Gandhi: The South African Experience*, Johannesburg: Ravan Press.

Taban, Faruqui A. (2008) 'The Coming of the Revolt in Awadh: The Evidence of the Urdu Newspapers', in: Shireen Moosvi (ed.) *Facets of the Great Revolt 1857*, New Delhi: Tulika Books.

Talbot, Ian (1998; enlarged and updated edn 2005) *Pakistan: A Modern History*, London: C. Hurst & Co.

——(2006) *Divided Cities: Partition and its Aftermath in Lahore and Amritsar 1947–1957*, Karachi: Oxford University Press.

Talbot, Ian and Singh, Gurharpal (2009) *The Partition of India*, Cambridge: Cambridge University Press.

Talbot, Ian and Thandi, Shinder (eds) (2004) *People on the Move: Punjabi Colonial, and Post-Colonial Migration*, Karachi: Oxford University Press.

Tann, Jennifer and Aitken, John (1992) 'The Diffusion of the Stationary Steam Engine from Britain to India, 1790–1830', *Indian Economic and Social History Review*, 29 (2): 199–214.

Tarlo, Emma (2003) *Unsettling Memories: Narratives of the Emergency in Delhi*, London: Hurst & Company.

Tchitcherov, Alexander I. (1998) *India: Changing Economic Structure in the Sixteenth to Eighteenth Centuries: Outline History of Crafts and Trade*, Delhi: Manohar.

Tewari, Vinot, Raghupathi, Usha and Ansari, Jamal Husain (2007) 'Improving Housing and Basic Services for the Urban Poor in India', in: Aprodicio A. Laquian, Vinod Tewari, and Lisa M. Hanley (eds) *The Inclusive City: Infrastructure and Public Services for the Urban Poor in Asia*, Baltimore: John Hopkins University Press.

Thaha, S. Abdul (2009) *Forest Policy and Ecological Change: Hyderabad State in Colonial India*, New Delhi: Foundation Books.

Thangarajah, Cecil Y. (2004) 'Veiled Constructions: Conflict, Migration and Modernity in Eastern Sri Lanka', in: Filippo Osella and Katy Gardner (eds) *Migration, Modernity and Social Transformation in South Asia*, New Delhi: Sage Publications.

Thankappan Nair, Parameswaran (1990a) 'The Growth and Development of Old Calcutta', in: Sukanta Chaudhuri (ed.) *Calcutta, The Living City, Volume 1: The Past*, New Delhi: Oxford University Press.

——(1990b) 'Civic and Public Services in old Calcutta', in: Sukanta Chaudhuri (ed.) *Calcutta, The Living City, Volume 1: The Past*, New Delhi: Oxford University Press.

Thapar, Romila (2012) 'Perceiving the Forest: Early India', in: Mahesh Rangarajan and K. Sivaramakrishnan (eds) *India's Environmental History. Vol. I: From Ancient Times to the Colonial Period*, New Delhi: Orient BlackSwan.

The Indian Problem Solved (1874) *The Indian Problem Solved: Undeveloped Wealth in India, and State Reproductive Works. The Ways to Prevent Famines and Advance the Material Progress of India*, London: Virtue & Co.

Thenews (2012) 'Sindh Population Surges by 81.5 pc, Households by 83.9 pc', thenews.com, 2 April 2012. Available online at www.thenews.com.pk/Todays-News-13-13637-Sindh-population-surges-by-81.5-pc,-households-by-83.9-pc (accessed 12 December 2013).

Thomas, David A. (1982) 'Lucknow and Kanpur 1880–1920: Stagnation and Development under the Raj', *South Asia: Journal of South Asian Studies*, 5(2): 68–80.

Thorner, Daniel (1950) *Investment in Empire: British Railway and Steam Shipping Enterprise in India 1825–1849*, Philadelphia: University of Philadelphia Press.

——(ed.) (1996) *Ecological and Agrarian Regions of South Asia, circa 1930*, Karachi: Oxford University Press.

Timberg, Thomas A. (1971) 'A North Indian Firm as Seen Through its Business Records, 1860–1914: Tarachand Ghanshyamdas, A "Great" Marwari Firm', *Indian Economic and Social History Review*, 8(3): 264–83.

——(1992) 'Three Types of Marwari Firm', in: Rajat K. Ray (ed.) *Entrepreneurship and Industry in India, 1800–1947*, New Delhi: Oxford University Press.

Tindall, Gillian (1982) *City of Gold: The Biography of Bombay*, London: Temple Smith.

Tinker, Hugh (1954) *The Foundation of Local Self-Government in India, Pakistan and Burma*, London: University of London.

——(1974) *A New System of Slavery, the Export of Indian Labour Overseas 1830–1920*, London: Oxford University Press.

Tölölyan, Khachig (1991) 'The Nation-state and its Others: in Lieu of a Preface', in: *Diaspora: A Journal of Transnational Studies*, 1(1): 3–7.

——(1996) 'Rethinking Diaspora(s): Stateless Power in the Transnational Moment', *Diaspora: A Journal of Transnational Studies*, 5(1): 3–36.

Tomlinson, Brian R. (1993) *The Economy of Modern India, 1860–1970*, Cambridge: Cambridge University Press.

Toor, Saadia (2011) *The State of Islam: Culture and Cold War Politics in Pakistan*, London: Pluto Press.

Travers, Robert (2007) *Ideology and Empire in Eighteenth-Century India: The British in Bengal*, Cambridge: Cambridge University Press.

Tucker, Richard P. (2012) *A Forest History of India*, New Delhi: Sage Publications.

Twaddle, Michael (1990) 'East Africans Through a Hundred Years', in: Colin Clarke, Ceri Peach and Steven Vertovec, *South Asians Overseas: Migration and Ethnicity*, Cambridge: Cambridge University Press.

——(2001) 'The Development of Communalism among East African Asians', in: Crispin Bates (ed.) *Community, Empire and Migration: South Asians in Diaspora*, New York: Palgrave Macmillan.

Umar, Badruddin (2003) *The Emergence of Bangladesh. Vol 1: Class and Political Struggle in East Pakistan, 1947–1958*, Oxford: Oxford University Press.

——(2006) *The Emergence of Bangladesh. Vol. 2: The Rise of Bengal Nationalism, 1958–1971*, Oxford: Oxford University Press.

United Nations Statistics Division (2012) *Composition of Macro Geographical (Continental) Regions, Geographical Sub-regions, and selected Economic and other Groupings.* Available online at http://millenniumindicators.un.org/unsd/methods/m49/m49regin.htm#asia (accessed 2 January 2012).

Upadhya, Samjay (2012) *Nepal and the Geo-Strategic Rivalry between China and India*, London: Routledge.

Uphoff, Norman T. (1992) *Learning from Gal Oya: Possibilities for Participatory Development and Post-Newtonian Social Science*, Ithaca: Cornell University Press.

Uprety, Prem R. (1980) *Nepal-Tibet Relations, 1850–1930: Years of Hopes, Challenges and Frustration*, Kathmandu: Puga Nara.
——(1984) *Nepal: A Small Nation in the Vortex of International Conflicts, 1900–1950*, Kathmandu: Pugo Mi.
Uyangoda, Jayadeva (1999) 'A State of Desire? Some Reflections on the Unreformability of Sri Lanka's Post-colonial State', in Marcus Meyer and Siri Hettige (eds) *Sri Lanka at Cross Roads*, New Delhi: Palgrave Macmillan.
——(2011) 'Government–LTTE Peace Negotiations in 2002–2005 and the Clash of State Formation Projects', in: Jonathan Goodhand *et al.* (eds) *Conflict and Peacebuilding in Sri Lanka*, London and New York: Routledge.
Vahed, Goolam (1997) 'The Making of "Indianness": Indian Politics in South Africa during the 1930s and 1940s', *Journal of Natal and Zulu History*, 17(1): 1–36.
Vaid, Angeli, Merrill, Derek and Bage, Grant (eds) (1995) *Victorian India: Tea Garden of the World*, London: The British Library Publishing Division.
Vaidya, Tulsi Ram (1993) *Prithvi Narayan Shah: The Founder of Modern Nepal*, New Delhi: Anmol Publications.
Vaikuntham, Yallampalli (2002) *State, Economy and Social Transformation. Hyderabad State (1724–1948)*, Delhi: Manohar Publishers.
——(2010) *Water Resource Management. Riparian Conflicts, Feudal Chiefs and Hyderabad State (1901–1956)*, New Delhi: Manohar.
Vandal, Pervaiz and Vandal, Sajida (2006) *The Raj, Lahore, and Bhai Ram Singh*, Lahore: National College of Arts.
Vanina, Eugenia (2002) 'Reforms and Modernization in the Eighteenth Century Deccan States', in: Muhammad A. Nayeem, Aniruddha Ray and Kuzippalli S. Mathew (eds) *Studies in the History of the Deccan: Medieval and Modern*, Delhi: Pragati Publications.
Varma, Nitin (2006) 'Kuli Strikes Back: Collective Protest and Action in the Colonial Tea Plantations of Assam, 1880–1920', *Indian Historical Review*, 33(1): 259–87.
Veer, Peter van der (1994, 2nd edn 2000) *Religious Nationalism: Hindus and Muslims in India*, New Delhi: Oxford University Press.
——(1995) 'Introduction: The Diasporic Imagination', in: Peter van der Veer (ed.) *Nation and Migration: The Politics of Space in the South Asian Diaspora*, Philadelphia: University of Philadelphia Press.
Verma, Archanna B. (2002) *The Making of Little Punjab in Canada: Patterns of Immigration*, New Delhi: Sage Publications.
Vertovec, Steven (1992) *Hindu Trinidad: Religion, Ethnicity and Socio-Economic Change*, London: Macmillan Caribbean.
——(2000) *The Hindu Diaspora: Comparative Patterns*, London: Routledge.
——(ed.) (1991) *Aspects of South Asian Diaspora*, Delhi: Oxford University Press.
Vicziany, Marika (1986) 'Imperialism, Botany and Statistics in early Nineteenth Century India: The Survey of Francis Buchanan (1762–1829)', *Modern Asian Studies*, 20(4): 625–60.
Visaria, Leela and Visaria, Pravin (1982) 'Population (1757–1947)', in: Dharma Kumar (ed.) *The Cambridge Economic History of India. Vol. 2: c. 1757–1970*, Cambridge: Cambridge University Press.
Voigt, Johannes H. (1987) *India in the Second World War*, New Delhi: Arnold Heinemann.
Wagner, Kim A. (2007) *Thuggee: Banditry and the British in the Early Nineteenth-Century India*, Basingstoke, UK: Palgrave Macmillan.

—— (2010) *The Great Fear of 1857: Rumours, Conspiracies and the Making of the Indian Uprising*, Oxford: Peter Lang.

—— (ed.) (2009) *Stranglers and Bandits: A Historical Anthology of Thuggee*, New Delhi: Oxford University Press.

Walker, James (2003) 'The Canadian Connection: Canadian Identity, Immigration Policy and the Indian Diaspora in Historical Perspective', in: Sarva D. Singh and Mahavir Singh (eds) *Indians Abroad*, Kolkata: Hope India Publications.

Walton, Henry G. (1903) *A Monograph on Tanning and Working in Leather in the United Provinces of Agra and Oudh*, Allahabad: Govt. Press.

Washbrook, David A. (1988) 'Progress and Problems: South Asian Economic and Social History, c. 1720–1860', *Modern Asian Studies* 22(1): 57–96.

Watson, Ian B. (1980) *Foundation for Empire: English Private Trade in India, 1659–1760*, Delhi: Vikas Publishing House.

Watt, Carey A. and Mann, Michael (eds) (2011) *Civilizing Mission in Colonial and Postcolonial South Asia: From Improvement to Development*, London: Anthem Press.

Webb, James L.A. (2002) *Tropical Pioneers: Human Agency and Ecological Change in the Highlands of Sri Lanka, 1800–1900*, Athens: Ohio University Press.

Weber, Thomas (1994) 'Historiography and the Dandi March: The other myths of Gandhi's salt march', in: Subrata Mukherjee and Sushila Ramaswamy (eds) *Facets of Mahatma Gandhi. Vol. 1*, New Delhi: Deep and Deep Publications.

Wenzelhuemer, Roland (2007) 'Indian Labour Immigration and British Labour Policy in Nineteenth-Century Ceylon', *Modern Asian Studies*, 41(2): 575–602.

—— (2013) *Connecting the Nineteenth-Century World: The Telegraph and Globalization*, Cambridge: Cambridge University Press.

Werbner, Pnina (1990) 'Manchester Pakistanis: Division and Unity', in: Colin Clarke, Ceri Peach and Steven Vertovec (eds) *South Asians Overseas: Migration and Ethnicity*, Cambridge: Cambridge University Press.

—— (1995) 'From Commodities to Gifts: Pakistani Migrant Workers in Manchester', in: Alisdair Rogers and Steven Vertovec (eds) *The Urban Context: Ethnicity, Social Networks and Situation Analysis*, Oxford: Berg Publishers.

Werner, Hanna (2013) Arguing with Dams: Developmental Perspectives and Social Critique in 20th Century India. Dissertation Philosophical Faculty III, Humboldt-Universität zu Berlin (unpublished).

Whelpton, John (2005; 4th edn 2008) *A History of Nepal*, Cambridge: Cambridge University Press.

Whitcombe, Elizabeth (1971) *Agrarian Conditions in Northern India. Volume One: The United Provinces under British Rule, 1860–1900*, Berkeley: University of California Press.

—— (1982) 'Irrigation', in: Dharma Kumar (ed.) *The Cambridge Economic History of India, Vol. 2, c. 1757–1970*, Cambridge: Cambridge University Press.

—— (1996) 'The Environmental Costs of Irrigation in British India: Waterlogging, Salinity and Malaria', in: David Arnold and Ramachandra Guha (eds) *Nature, Culture, Imperialism: Essays on the Environmetal History of South Asia*, New Delhi: Oxford University Press.

Whyte, Timothy (1998) 'The Legacy of Slavery in Nepal', *Studies in Nepali History and Society*, 2(3): 311–39.

Wickramasinghe, Nira (1995) *Ethnic Politics in Colonial Sri Lanka, 1927–1947*, New Delhi: Vikas.

—— (2006) *Sri Lanka in the Modern Age: A History of Contested Identities*, Colombo: Vijitha Yapa Publications.

Wickremeratne, L. A. (1975) 'Kandyans and Nationalism in Sri Lanka: some Reflections', *Ceylon Journal of Historical and Social Sciences*, 5: 49–67.

Wickremesekera, Channa (2004) *Kandy at War: Indigenous Military Resistance to European Expansion in Sri Lanka, 1594–1818*, New Delhi: Manohar 2004.

Wink, André (1986) *Land and Sovereignty in India: Agrarian Society and Politics under the Eighteenth-Century Maratha Swarajya*, Cambridge: Cambridge University Press.

——(1990) *Al-Hind: The Making of the Indo-Islamic World, Vol. 1, Early Medieval India and the Expansion of Islam*, Leiden: Brill.

Winseck, Dwayne R. and Pike, Robert M. (2007) *Communication and Empire: Media, Markets, and Globalization, 1860–1930*, Durham: Duke University Press.

Withers, Charles W.J. (1993) 'Geography in its Time: Geography and Historical Geography in Diderot's and d'Alambert's Encyclopédie', *Journal of Historical Geography*, 19(3): 255–64.

Wittfogel, Karl A. (1957) *Oriental Despotism: A Comparative Study of Total Power*, New Haven: Yale University Press.

Wolpert, Stanley (1977; 8th edn 2009) *A New History of India*, Oxford: Oxford University Press.

——(2010) *India and Pakistan: Continued Conflict or Cooperation?* Berkeley: University of California Press.

Worster, Donald (1985) *Rivers of Empire: Water, Aridity and the Growth of the American West*, New York: Pantheon Books.

Wujastyk, Dominik, Cerulli, Anthony M. and Preisendanz, Karin (eds) (2013) *Medical Texts and Manuscripts in Indian Cultural History*, New Delhi: Manohar.

Yalland, Zoë (1987) *Traders and Nabobs: The British in Cawnpore, 1765–1857*, Wilton: Michael Russell.

Yang, Anand A. (1989) *The Limited Raj: Agrarian Relations in Colonial India, Saran District, 1793–1920*, Delhi: Oxford University Press.

——(1998) *Bazaar India: Markets, Society, and the Colonial State in Bihar*, Berkeley: University of California Press.

Yapa, Lakshman (1993) 'What are Improved Seeds? An Epistemology of the Green Revolution', *Professional Geographer*, 31(4): 254–73.

Yelling, James A. (1986) *Slums and Slum Clearance in Victorian London*, London: Allen & Unwin.

Yong, Tan Tai (2005) *The Garrison State: The Military, Government and Society in Colonial Punjab, 1849–1947*, New Delhi: Sage Publications.

Yunus, Mohammad (2011) *Bhutto and the Breakup of Pakistan*, Karachi: Oxford University Press.

Zachariah, Benjamin (2005) *Developing India: An Intellectual and Social History*, New Delhi: Oxford University Press.

Zakaria, Fareed (2006) 'India Rising', *Network* (6 March 2006).

Zaman, Naiz (1999) *A Divided Legend: The Partition in Selected Novels of India, Pakistan, and Bangladesh*, Dhaka: The University Press Limited.

Zastoupil, Lynn (2010) *Rammohun Roy and the Making of Victorian Britain*, New York: Palgrave Macmillan.

Zastoupil, Lynn and Moir, Martin (eds) (1999) *The Great Indian Education Debate: Documents Relating to the Orientalist-Anglicist Controversity, 1781–1843*, Richmond: Curzon.

Zavos, John (2000) *Emergence of Hindu Nationalism in India*, New Delhi: Oxford University Press.

Zimmermann, Clemens (1996) *Die Zeit der Metropolen: Urbanisierung und Großstadtentwicklung*, Frankfurt am Main: Fischer Verlag.

Zoysa, Arjuna de and Palitharatna, C.D. (1992) 'Models of European Scientific Expansion: A Comparative Description of "Classical" Medical Science at the Time of Introduction of European Medical Science to Sri Lanka, and Subsequent Development to Present', in: Patrick Petitjean *et al.* (eds) *Science and Empires. Historical Studies about Scientific Development and European Expansion*, Dordrecht: Springer.

Zutshi, Chitralekha (2011) 'Landscapes of the Past: *Rajatarangiri* and Historical Knowledge Production in Late Nineteenth-Century Kashmir', in: Indra Sengupta and Usman Ali (eds) *Knowledge Production, Pedagogy and Institutions in Colonial India*, New York: Palgrave Macmillan.

Index

Abdali, Ahmad Shah 22–23
Abdul Hamid, Sultan 40
adivasi population 195–96, 202–4, 207–8, 225–26
Advani, Lal Krishna 109
Afghan invasions 22
agrarian policy 172–74
agriculture in South Asia 5–6, 16–17, 137–80; in the eighteenth century 138–42; under colonial rule 142–72
Ahmedabad 306
Akbar 20, 321
Alam II, Shah 23, 34
Alivardi Khan 31–32
Allahabad 299; Treaty (1765) 46–48
All-India State People's Conference (AISPC) 102–3
Amin, Idi 240
Amritsar Golden Temple, storming of (1984) 108, 248
Anglicists 317, 322
apartheid 238
Arya Samaj 66–68, 73
Asaf ud Daulah 47, 49
Ashoka, Emperor 2, 20, 187
Asian Games 358
Assam 197–203
assimilation 258
Attlee, Clement 80
Auckland, Lord 121
August Revolution (1942) 77
Aurangzeb 20, 28
Awadh 38, 45–46, 150, 152
Awami League 111, 118
Ayub Khan 111
Ayurveda 332

Babur 20
Bahadur Shah (of Gorkha/Nepal) 120
Bahadur Shah II (Mughal) 61
Baksar, Battle of (1764) 23, 34
Balfour Declaration (1917) 77
Ball, Charles 58
Banaras/Varanasi 7, 35–36, 45, 268, 303
Banaras, Treaty of (1773) 46
Bandaranaike, S.W.R.D. 131
Bandaranaike, Sirimavo 131
Banerji, Surendranath 65
Bangalore/Bengaluru 8, 264, 280, 306–9
Bangladesh 112, 116–20, 248–49
Banks, Sir Joseph 327–28
Bansilal Abirchand (trading company) 279
Barani, Zia du Din 321
Barnes, Edward 331, 352
Baroda 281
Bates, Crispin 11–12
Bayly, Christopher 10
Bazin, Adolphe 353
Begam, Sadr un-nisa 47
Bengal 31–34, 143–49
Bentinck, William C. 317, 329, 335, 348
Besant, Annie 69
Bharatiya Janata Party (BJP) 106–9, 178, 207, 258–59
Bhutto, Benazir 113, 115
Bhutto, Zulfikar Ali 111–14
Birendra, King of Nepal 123–24
Bobbili, Battle of (1757) 39
Bombay 160–61, 292–97, 303
Bose, Subhas Chandra 73, 76, 241
Bose, Sugata 13
botanical gardens 327–28
brahmans 54, 67, 122, 185, 230, 256
Brandis, Dietrich 192–93

British Empire 35, 217
British India up to 1856 34–38
British Raj 2, 54–55, 90, 97, 142, 162, 318
broadcasting 358–59
Brown, Judith M. 11
Buchanan, Francis 326
Burke, S.M. 14
Burma 244–46

"Cabinet Mission" to India (1946) 78–80
Calcutta 293–97, 303
Canada, South Asian community in 249–50
canal system of India 339–41
cartography, scientific 329
caste system 169
Cautley, Sir Proby 339
Ceded and Conquered Provinces 150–51
censorship 65
Census of India 169, 224, 338
Central Doab 154–55
Ceylon 90, 124–28, 171, 179, 242–44, 331–32, 352; independence granted (1948) 130; renamed Sri Lanka 131
Chamber of Princes 92
Chandra Shamsher Rana 123
Chatterjee, Bankimchandra 323
Chatterton, Alfred 280
Chaudhary, Iftikhar 115
Chennai 306
Chettiyars 217–19, 245
Chipko Movement 202
cholera 336–37, 351
Churchill, Winston 76
circulation of people, information, goods and capital 213–14, 221–22, 257, 285, 290, 364
cities: development of 265–67, 296–301; small and medium-sized 268–69; *see also* megacities
civil disobedience 74–75, 95, 103, 287
"civilising mission" in India 9, 95, 296
Clive, Robert 321, 328
Colebrooke-Cameron Commission (1831) 127
colonial policy 36–37
Commonwealth Games 298, 309
Communist Party 72, 286–88
"Company State" 35, 54
Congress Party 89, 107, 109, 287–88
conversion, religious 234
Coolitude concept 231 *see also* kulis

Cornwallis, Lord 35
Cotton, Sir Arthur 339–40
Criminal Tribes Act (1871) 162–63, 288
Cripps, Stafford 76
Curzon, Lord 35, 68, 92

"dacoits" 57
Dalhousie, Lord 51, 192, 348, 353–54
dam projects 342–45
deforestation 185–86, 192, 199, 202–3
de-industrialisation 272
Delhi Darbars 91–92
deregulation 282–83
"desiccation theory" of forestry 196–97, 202
De Silva, Kingsley M. 14
Dev Shamsher Rana 123
Devonshire Declaration (1923) 240
Dhaka 299–301
Dharavi 306
Dharmapala, Anagarika 128
diaspora 17, 214–16, 219, 248, 258–59
Dirks, Nicholas 24
Donoughmore Commission (1927) 130
Doordarshan (DD) 358
dual labour markets 213
Dundas, Henry 34–35
Dutt, Romesh Chandra 93
Dyer, Rex 95

East Africa, South Asian community in 239–40
East India Company (EIC) 22–23, 26, 30, 33–38, 46–51, 54, 63, 89–90, 317, 322, 326–28
education system, Indian 316–20
emergency regulations 95
emigration from South Asia 221
Empress and Emperors of India 28, 91
environmental impact assessment 208
Ershad, General 117–18
Everest, George 329
expatriate Indians 246

Faraizi Movement 149
"fertile crescent" 265–66
First World War 69–70, 355
forest management 184–209; until 1820 187–92; 1860–1920 192–97; 1920–90 197–207; since 2000 207–9
forestry, scientific 185–86, 190, 192–97
French Mascarene, South Asian community in 235–36

Gandhi, Indira 10, 89, 107–9, 112, 248, 289, 358
Gandhi, Mohandas K. ("Mahatma") 14, 69–78, 84–85, 95, 107, 163, 237, 287–88, 319, 344
Gandhi, Rajiv 109, 132, 178, 282, 344, 356
Ganges Canal 339–41
Geddes, Patrick 267
Gene Revolution 176–80
geological investigations 329–31
Ghazi al Din 49
Ghose, Aurobindo 69
global financial crisis (2008) 283
globalisation 214, 217, 248, 264–65, 365
Godse, Nathuram 85
Gokhale, Gopal Krishna 69
Golwalkar, Madhav S. 73
Gorakhpur rebellion 36
Gorka kingdom 120–23
Government of India Act (1935) 96, 105–6
Governor-General's powers 94, 96–97
Great Britain, migration to 246–49
Great Depression (1929–39) 75, 173, 241, 245, 276, 278, 285, 342
Great Rebellion (Ceylon/Lanka, 1817–18) 171
Great Rebellion (British-India, 1857–59) 22, 54–63, 89, 151, 323–24, 335, 354
Great Trigonometrical Survey 328–29
Green Revolution 174–80, 205, 310
Gulf States, South Asian community in 253–57
Gupta Empire 2, 20
Gurgin Khan 33
Gurukul Kangri 318–19
Gyanendra, King of Nepal 124

Haider Ali 38–40
Haiderabad/Hyderabad State 100–105, 281, 343
Hannay, Alexander 36
Harischandra, Bharatendu 364
Hasina, Sheikh 118
Hastings, Warren 35–36, 46–47
Haussmann, Baron 297
Hedgewar, Kashav B. 72–73
Hermann, Paul 326
Hinduism and Hindu nationalism 64–69, 85, 108, 323
Hindutva concept 323–24
Hirachand, Walchand 280
historic regions of South Asia 7

Holwell, J.Z. 333
Home Charges 301
Hooker, Joseph D. 192

Ilbert Bill (1883–84) 65
improvement trusts 297–98
Inam Commission (1858–69) 167
indentured labour 220–32, 246, 255
India, Republic of 105–9; constitution 105–6
India Office 90
Indian Civil Service (ICS) 92–93
Indian Diaspora 17
Indian independence 80, 89
Indian Medical Service (IMS) 334
Indian National Congress (INC) 64–66, 71, 75, 79–81, 85, 103, 174, 196, 230, 237, 246, 281, 322, 343, 355
Indian Ocean 10, 215–18
Indian Princes 90–92, 98–99, 105
Indian River Inter-Link Project 345–46
"Indianness" 258–59, 358
industrialisation 265–67, 270–73, 279–83, 289
International Monetary Fund 283
Iqbal, Mohammad 77
iron and steel industry 277–78, 282
irrigation systems 138, 153, 156–58, 164, 167, 170–71, 174, 179, 205, 338–46
Irvin, Lord 75
Islam, Sirajul 14
"Islamic cities" 265–66
Islamisation 89, 113, 256, 324–25
Ismail, Mirza 280–81

Jaffrelot, Christophe 14
Jalal, Ayesha 13, 325
Jang Bahadur Kunwar 121–22
Jawaharlal Nehru Urban Renewal Mission (JNURM) 307
Jayewardene, J.R. 131–32
Jaykar, Ram Balkrishna 64
Jenner, Edward 333
Jinnah, Muhammad Ali 77–80, 84–85, 103, 111, 324
Jones, William 327, 335

Kalale family 38
Kandy 124–29
kangany system 229, 241–45
Kanpur 292
Karachi 116, 224, 264
Kartars 38–39

Kaye, J.W. 58
Kenyan Asians 240
Khilafat Movement 71
Khoti Settlement Act (1880) 160
Kipling, Rudyard 351
"knowledge corridors" 309–10
Koenig, Johann Gerhard 327
Koirala, B.P. 123
Kota 42–45
kulis 215, 220–23, 226–38, 241, 244–46
Kulke, Hermann 11, 24–25
Kyd, Robert 327

labour market sectors, "formal" and "informal" 213
Lakhnau 49, 51, 61, 84, 271, 292, 298
Lambdon, William 328
lascars 217
leather industry 270–71
legal system, Indian 93
legitimacy, generation of 29
Liaq Ali 104
Linlithgow, Marquess of 76
Linné, Carl von 325–26
literacy in South Asia 320
literature of South Asia 321
"little kings" 24, 35–36, 57, 92
logging industry 186, 192
Ludden, David 13
Lytton, Lord 65

Macaulay, Thomas B. 316–17
Mackenzie, Colin 326, 328
Madhav Rao 30
Mahanadi Valley 341–42
Maharao Bhim Singh 44–45
Maharao Umed Singh 42
Mahendra, King of Nepal 123
maistry system 245
Maisur 38–42, 279–81
Malaya, South Asian community in 240–42
Malleson, G.B. 58
managing agencies 275–76
mapping of India 326–32
Marathas 20–23, 28–31
Markovits, Claude 12
Marx, Karl 347–48
mass migration 214
Mauritius 226–27, 234–35
Maurya Empire 2, 20
medical science 332–38

Meerut conspiracy case (1929–31) 287
megacities 305, 310
Mehta, Pherozshah 69
Metcalf, Barbara and Thomas 13
middle-sized towns 309–10
migrant labour 283–85
migration 17, 212–59; in the agricultural sector 224; *internal* and *external* 225; and settlement 231–35; theories of 212–14; twice-migrants 247–48, 254
Mill, James 322
mining operations 207–8
Minto, Earl of 330
Mir, Titu 149
Mir Qasim 32–34
Mirat 58–59
Mohammad Ali Shah 49
monsoon conditions 5–6, 138, 170
Montague-Chelmsford reforms (1919) 94–95
Morley-Minto reforms (1909) 94, 303
Morse, Samuel 353
Mountbatten, Lord Louis 80–83
Mughal Empire 2, 7–8, 16, 20–23, 26–31, 34, 38, 54–56, 62–63, 97, 158, 185, 265, 321, 324, 333, 353
Muhammad Reza Khan 32
Mujibur Rahman 111–12, 116–17
Multi-Fibre Arrangement (1974) 248
municipal boards 302–3
Munn, Leonard 196–97
Murshid Quli Khan 31–32
Musharraf, Pervez 114–15
Muslim League 64, 68–69, 77–81, 84–85, 111, 114, 324

Nana Saheb 30
National Democratic Alliance (NDA) 109, 178, 259, 345
national parks 204–5
nationalism 110
Nāyakkar dynasty 124, 126
Nehru, Jawaharlal (and Nehruvian policies) 14, 74, 78–80, 84, 103–7, 123, 176, 179, 203, 246, 282, 287–89, 306, 320, 342, 344
Nepal 90, 120–24
New Delhi 298–300, 356
New Farmers' Movement 178
New York 251–52
Nightingale, Florence 335
North-Western Provinces (NWP) 151–52

oil crisis (1973) 246
Oldham, Thomas 330
Orientalism 249, 264–65, 317, 321–22
Orme, Robert 321
Orta, Garcia de 325
O'Shaughnessy, William 353–54
Osman Ali Khan 100, 103–4
overseas communities of South Asian extraction 234–46

Paigah family 101
Pakistan, Islamic Republic of 110–16; constitutions 111–12, 116; historical roots of 110, 324; Muslim identity of 110
Pal, Bipin Chandra 69
Panipat, Battle of (1761) 22–23, 30, 39
Panjab 153–58
"paramountcy" doctrine 28–31, 37, 90, 92, 104
partition of British India 80–84, 304
patriotism 56
Pax Britannica 37, 219
Permanent Settlement Act (1793) 32, 35, 79, 143–44
pilgrimage centres 364
Pitroda, Satyanarayan Gangaram ("Sam") 356
Pitt, William the Younger 34–35
planning: economic 282; urban 267–68, 294–96, 306–7
plantations 219, 225–26, 231–32
poetry 49–51
population growth 291–92
Premadasa, Ramasinghe 131–32
Presidency Towns 294, 296
President's Rule in India 106
Prithvi Narayan Shah 120, 122
prostitution 233
Puranas 320–21

"Quit India" Resolution (1942) 76
Quraishi, Salim Al-Din 14

Radcliffe, Sir Cyril (and Radcliffe Award, 1947) 81–83
Rahmad Ali 77
Rai, Lala Lajpat 69, 74
railway construction and railway networks 107, 273–74, 346–52, 364
Rajapaksa, Mahinda 132
Rajendra Bikram, King of Nepal 121
Ram Mohan Roy 63, 93

Ram Singh 45
Raman, Chandrasekhara Venkata 319
Ranade, Mahadev Govind 65–66
Ranchod Vira 162
Rao, Narasimha 283
rape 231
Rashtriya Swayamsevak Sangh (RSS) 72–73, 109
rebellions 36–37, 150, 160, 162; see also Great Rebellion
recruitment agencies 227–29, 245, 255
reforestation 190–91, 205
reform movements 63–65
remittances 223, 257–58, 273
Rennell, James 328
repatriation 243–44
residency system 48–49, 98–100
Réunion 235–36
Ribbentrop, Berthold 193
Ripon, Lord 302
Risley, Herbert H. 338
road network of India 347
Robb, Peter 12
Rothermund, Dietmar 11
Round Table Conferences (1930–32) 96
Rowlatt Act (1919) 95
Roxburgh, William 327
Roy, Arundhati 344
Roy, M.N. 72, 286
Royle, John Forbes 327
rulers, requirements of 27
"rurbanity" 268

Saadat Khan 45–51
Safdar Jang 45–46, 49
Salbai, Treaty of (1782) 30
Sangathan Movement 68–69
sanitation and hygiene 295–99, 335–36
Saraswati, Dayanand 65, 323
SarDesai, D.R. 15
Sarkar, Jadunath 323
Sarkar, Sumit 11
satyagraha 71, 74–75, 103
Savarkar, Vinayak D. 55–56, 108, 323
Schlich, William 193
science: modern idea of 315; natural 325–32; South Asian development of 315–16, 319–20; see also cartography, scientific; forestry, scientific; medical science
seasonal workers 284–85

Second World War 75–76, 243, 277
"segmentary state" concept 24
Senanayake, D.S. 130, 179
Shaha, Rishikesh 15
Sharif, Nawaz 114–15
Shepstone, Sir Theophilus 236
shipbuilding 190–91
Shivaji, King of the Marathas 28–29, 323
Shuja Khan 31
Shuja ud Daulah 46–47
Sikhs and Sikhism 81, 247–48, 250
silviculture 184–89, 194–95, 205; *see also* forest management
Simon Commission (1928) 73
Sinclair, Sir John 326
Singh, Manmohan 109
slavery and slave trade 17, 219, 227
slum clearance 305
small businesses 285–86
smallpox vaccination 333
Social Forestry policy 205–9
"social spaces" 364–65
Soulbury Commission (1944) 130
South Africa, South Asian community in 236–39
South Asia: "bottom-up" transformation in 366; climate 5–7; definitions of 1–2; historiography of 8–18, 23, 85, 320–25; regions and sub-regions within 2–8; thematic study of 15–18; use of the term 1; *see also* agriculture in South Asia
South Korea 254
sovereignty 96, 98, 103; *divided* and *undivided* 27
Sri Lanka/Lanka 14, 90, 132–33, 138, 217, 242–44, 256–57; *see also* Ceylon
Sriramalu, Potti 106–7
state formation process 26–51
Stein, Burton 13–14, 24–25
storytelling 51
Subaltern School of scholarship 325
subsistence economy 138–39
Suhrawardy, Husseyn 80
Surendra Bikra Shah 121
Swadeshi Movement 71, 106, 277–78, 285, 318

Tagore, Dwarkanath 272
Tagore, Rabindranath 319
Talbot, Ian 14
Tamils 129–33, 185, 241–44

Tarachand Ghanshymdas (trading company) 279
Tata, J.N. (and Tata Iron and Steel Company) 277–78, 280
telecommunications 352–59
television 358–59
Tennessee Valley Authority 342
textile industry 268–77, 280–89
Textile Labour Association 288
"thags" 57
Tilak, Bal Gangadhar 69, 323
Tipu Sultan 39–42, 166–67, 192
trade unions 286–89
trading networks 217–18
Tribhuvan, King of Nepal 123

United Progressive Alliance (UPA) 109
United States, South Asian community in 251–53
universities, Indian 317–19
urbanisation 264–67, 290–310; after 1947 304–10; double meaning of 290

Vajpayee, A.B. 109
van Rheede tot Draakestein, Hendrik Adriaan 325
van Schendel, Willem 14
Vedic texts 320, 323
venereal disease 335–36
Vernacular Press Act (1878) 65
Victoria, Queen 91
Vijayanagara Empire 158
Virkrama Rajasimha, King of Kandy 126
Vishvanath, Balaji 29
Vishwa Hindu Parishad (VHP) 108–9
Visvesvaraya, M. 280–81
Vohra, Bhagwati 74

Wallich, Nathaniel 327
Wandiwash, Battle of (1760) 39
"war on terrorism" 115–16, 253
waterlogging 158, 341–42, 351
Wavell, Archibald 78–80
Wellesley, Richard 30–31, 42, 48, 126, 293, 326
Western values 11–12
Whelpton, John 14–15
wild animals, protection of 204–5
Wilson, Woodrow 70, 322
Wink, André 25
Wolpert, Stanley 10

women, role and status of 232–33, 248, 256–57, 285
World Bank 344

Yahya Khan 111–12

Zakaria, Fareed 365
Zalim Singh 42–45
Zamindari Settlement (1789) 143, 166
zamindars 32–33, 37, 57, 140–44, 150, 156, 167–68, 270, 294
Zardari, Asif Ali 115–16
Zia, Khaleda 118
Zia ul Haq 113–14, 324
Ziaur Rahman 117–18